Canadian Sixth Edition

The Whole Child

Developmental Education for the Early Years

JOANNE HENDRICK
University of Oklahoma

KAREN CHANDLER
George Brown College

Prentice Hall Canada Inc.
Scarborough, Ontario

Canadian Cataloguing in Publication Data

Hendrick, Joanne, 1928-
    The Whole Child

6th Canadian ed.
Includes index.

ISBN 0-13-456559-2

1. Education, Preschool - Canada. 2. Early childhood education - Canada.
3. Preschool teachers - Training of - Canada. I. Chandler, Karen (Karen A. M.). II. Title.

LB1140.25.C2H46 1996   372.21   C95-932479-8

Prentice-Hall, Inc., Englewood Cliffs, New Jersey
Prentice-HISBN 0-13-456559-2
all International (UK) Limited, London
Prentice-Hall of Australia, Pty. Limited, Sydney
Prentice-Hall Hispanoamericana, S.A., Mexico City
Prentice-Hall of India Private Limited, New Delhi
Prentice-Hall of Japan, Inc., Tokyo
Simon & Schuster Asia Private Limited, Singapore
Editora Prentice-Hall do Brasil, Ltda., Rio de Janeiro

ISBN 0-13-456559-2

Acquisitions Editor: Marjorie Munroe
Developmental Editor: Karen Sacks
Copy Editor: Gilda Mekler
Production Editor: Lisa Berland
Production Coordinator: Sharon Houston
Permissions/Photo Research: Marijke Leupen
Cover Design: Monica Kompter
Cover Image: Sylvia Borda
Page Layout: Joan Morrison

Original U.S. edition published by Prentice-Hall Inc.
© 1996 Prentice-Hall Inc., Englewood Cliffs, New Jersey
18 19 20 DPC 07 06 05

Printed and bound in Canada

We welcome readers' comments, which can be sent by e-mail to
    collegeinfo_pubcanada@prenhall.com

ॐ Preface

Overview

The Whole Child is a practical methods book that explains how to go about teaching young children in ways that foster healthy development. It shifts the attention of the teacher away from "art" or "science" to what the child *is* and what he needs from the learning environment in order to thrive. For that reason it focuses on the child and pictures him as composed of a number of selves: the physical self, the emotional self, the social self, the creative self, and the cognitive self.

The physical self includes not only large and fine muscle development but also the handling of routines, since such things as eating, resting, and toileting contribute much to physical comfort and well-being. For the emotional self the book considers ways to increase and sustain mental health, to cope with crises, to use discipline to foster self-control, to cope with aggression, and to foster self-esteem. Under the heading of the social self are ways to build social concern and kindliness, learning to enjoy work, and learning to value the cultures of other people. The creative self covers the areas of self-expression through the use of art materials and creativity as expressed in play and applied in thought. Finally, the cognitive, or intellectual, self is considered in terms of language development and the development of specific reasoning abilities.

The Whole Child is based on the premises that physical and emotional health are fundamental to the well-being of children, that education must be developmentally appropriate if that well-being is to prosper, and that children need time to be children—time to be themselves—to do nothing, to

stand and watch, to repeat again what they did before—in short, they need time to live *in* their childhood rather than *through* it. If we offer the young children we teach rich and appropriate learning opportunities combined with enough time for them to enjoy and experience those opportunities to the fullest, we will enhance childhood, not violate it.

Inviting Features of This Textbook

New to This Edition

- A new chapter (Chapter 21) has been added on using the emergent approach to foster thinking and reasoning skills.

- This is the first edition adapted to the Canadian context throughout, rather than merely having chapters appended on Canadian issues.

- Material reflecting the philosophy of the schools of Reggio Emilia appears where it is relevant.

- A research study is highlighted in the majority of the chapters. The studies reinforce important points in the text and also illustrate different ways to conduct research studies.

- Relevant Canadian research, references, statistics, and legislation are cited throughout the text.

- New material has been added to assure currency of information, particularly in the areas of emergent curricula, violence, literacy, and integrating children with disabilities into the life of the school.

- A series of videotapes based on the U.S. Edition of *The Whole Child* is currently in production and will soon be available for broadcast U.S. on public educational TV stations—An Annenberg/CPB project).

Continuing Features

- Entire chapters are included on Multicultural, Nonsexist Education (Chapter 14) and on Welcoming Children Who May Have Special Educational Requirements Into the Life of the School (Chapter 9).

- An expanded teacher's manual is available at no charge to instructors, includes transparency masters describing "problem" for class discussion, suggested assignments, and a variety of test questions. ·

- The warm, practical approach is based on more than thirty years of teaching adult students and young children.

- The emphasis is on teaching methods that focus on children and their developmental needs rather than on science or art per se.

- Extensively updated annotated bibliographies follow every chapter (there are more than 400 new citations in this edition).

Acknowledgements

I owe so much to so many people that it is a well nigh impossible task to mention them all. The contributions of students and parents to my knowledge and point of view have been considerable, as have the contributions of the members of my staff. In addition, I am forever in the debt of my mother, Alma Berg Green, who not only began some of the first parent education classes in Los Angeles, but also taught me a great deal about young children and their families.

I am also indebted to Sarah Foot and her wonderful Starr King Parent/Child Workshop, which convinced me that my future lay in early childhood education, and to my own children, who bore with me with such goodwill while I was learning the real truth about bringing up young people.

The sixth edition has moved with the times and includes much new material. For their many suggestions in this regard, I wish to thank my reviewers: Sally Beach, University of Oklahoma, for her suggestions on revising the literacy chapter; Janie H. Humphries, Louisiana Tech University; Linda C. Sluder, Texas Woman's University; Jeri A. Carroll, Wichita State University; Kay Springate, Eastern Kentucky University; and Jane Billman, University of Illinois at Urbana-Champaign.

As far as the book itself is concerned, I would like to thank Murray Thomas for teaching me, among other things, how to write, and John Wilson for convincing me that some things remained to be said and changed in early education. To Chester and Peggy Harris I am forever indebted for a certain realistic attitude toward research, particularly in the area of cognitive development.

The people at Merrill/Prentice Hall have, as always, been of great assistance. In particular I want to thank Ann Davis and Carol Sykes for their encouragement. The contributions of Genevieve D'Arcy, freelance copyeditor, and Sheryl Langner, production editor, also deserve grateful notice. Without their careful help, the book would not exist.

Nor would my photographs be nearly as attractive without the advice and services provided by Color Chrome Photographic Laboratories. Along this same line I am indebted to the staff and children from several centres for making their schools and lives available for me to portray. These schools are The Children's Place at Baptist Medical Center, Oklahoma City; The Institute of Child Development, University of Oklahoma; The Oaks Parent/Child Workshop, San Marcos Parent/Child Workshop, Starr/King Parent/Child Workshop (all of Santa Barbara, California); and Tinker Air Force Base Child Development Center, Midwest City, Oklahoma.

It is a pleasure to welcome Canadian readers to this new edition of *The Whole Child: Developmen-*

tal Education for the Early Years because it has been so carefully edited by Karen Chandler a Canadian Profesor. In addition to including numerous charts and tables based upon Canadian information, Professor Chandler has also provided a wealth of additional information that makes this new edition of *The Whole Child* truly relevant to Canadian readers.

Revising this book about early childhood education is always stimulating—it has been an interesting task for me to set down what I know about this area and then to witness then changing needs that the past few years have brought to the fore. If it is also helpful to beginning teachers and to the children they serve, I will be pleased indeed.

Joanne Hendrick, 1995

Preface to Canadian Edition

In this Canadian edition of *The Whole Child* I have tried to indicate those aspects of history and culture that are unique to the Canadian experience. It has been my/our intention to adapt the American text to provide information that is important to learning and working in Canada. Terminology has been altered to reflect Canadian usage. Statistics, data, research, and charts of Canadian origin have been used wherever possible. Because of the differences between Canada and the United States with regard to legislation that governs services available to children, references to American programs where they do not apply have been eliminated.

Acknowledgements

I would like first of all to thank Joanne Hendrick for writing a book rich with theory and personal insights. The students I have taught at George Brown College have helped me formulate my ideas about the field and taught me a great deal about teaching. They also drew my attention to their need for Canadian materials. The many children, families, and staff I have worked with, over many years and in a variety of settings, continue to challenge my thinking and broaden my understanding.

My family—Rod McCormack and my children, Danielle and Brent (who are responsible for my interest in early childhood in the first place)—were almost always tolerant of my endless discussions about child care. Rod saw me at the computer or on the phone for many months and supported me in meeting each successive deadline.

One of the most rewarding aspects of this field has been the wonderful people I have met and become great friends with. For the past twenty-plus years I have learned an enormous amount from other early childhood educators, particularly those I met through my work with the Canadian Child Care Federation: Sandy Griffen, Joanne Morris, Cathy McCormack, Dorothy Dudek, Guida Chud, Elaine Ferguson, Sylvia Fanjoy, Diane Bascombe, Diana Smith, and many others.

I have had the opportunity to endlessly discuss new ideas and strategies with the people I work with daily in the Early Childhood Education program at George Brown College. My co-authors on the earlier editions—Donna McKenna, Carolyn Warberg, and Marilynn Yeates—also shared some meaningful times of frendship during team writing.

It has been my great pleasure to work with the people at Prentice Hall Canada, who were commited to making this wholly adapted Canadian edition a reality. I would like to acknowledge Marjorie Munroe and Karen Sacks for their efforts and encouragement, the contributions of Gilda Mekler, freelance copy editor, who helped me express what I had intended, and Lisa Berland, production editor.

Karen Chandler, 1995

Contents

✑ I

Beginning to Teach

1

How to Survive While Teaching: Suggestions and Guidelines for the First Few Weeks

2

What Makes a Good Day for Children?

1

How to Survive While Teaching: Suggestions and guidelines for the first few weeks

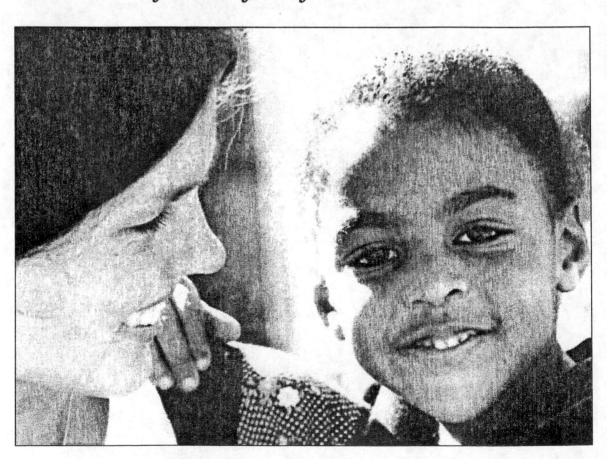

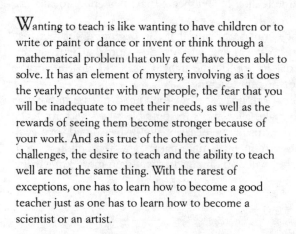

Have you ever wondered . . .

Whether you'll ever get used to teaching?

What to do about feeling helpless and incompetent?

Whether anyone else ever disliked a child in his class?

Why you feel terribly tired?

. . . If you have, the material in the following pages will help you.

Wanting to teach is like wanting to have children or to write or paint or dance or invent or think through a mathematical problem that only a few have been able to solve. It has an element of mystery, involving as it does the yearly encounter with new people, the fear that you will be inadequate to meet their needs, as well as the rewards of seeing them become stronger because of your work. And as is true of the other creative challenges, the desire to teach and the ability to teach well are not the same thing. With the rarest of exceptions, one has to learn how to become a good teacher just as one has to learn how to become a scientist or an artist.

Herbert Kohl

At the core of all education that makes a difference in children's lives—beneath all the methods, materials, and curricula—is a teacher who cares about each child, who teaches from the heart.

Mimi Brodsky Chenfeld

*T*eaching preschool children can be one of the best, most deeply satisfying experiences in the world. Young children ages two to five go through fascinating, swiftly accomplished stages of development. They are possessed of vigorous personalities, rich enthusiasms, an astonishing amount of physical energy, and strong wills. With the exception of infancy there is no other time in human life when so much is learned in so brief a period (Bloom, 1964).

This phenomenal vigour and burgeoning growth present a challenge to the beginning teacher that is at once exhilarating and frightening. The task is a large one: the teacher must attempt to build an educational climate that enhances the children's development and whets their appetites for further learning. The milieu must also nourish and sustain emotional health, encourage physical growth and muscular prowess, foster satisfying social interactions, enhance creativity, develop language skills, and promote the development of mental ability. Moreover, this must all be garbed in an aura of happiness and affection in order to establish that basic feeling of well-being that is essential to successful learning.

With such a large task at hand, it is not surprising that the beginning teacher may wonder somewhat desperately where to begin and what to do—and that is what this chapter is all about. It is intended to start you on the right track and help you survive those first perilous but exciting days of student teaching.

Granted, the first weeks of teaching are not easy, but they need not be impossible either. However, it is wise for you to make allowances for possible stress and not to be disappointed if you feel more tired than usual, or occasionally disheartened, or bewildered. These feelings will become less frequent as time passes and the children, staff, and routine become more familiar. They will also diminish as you gain more knowledge, skill and confidence.

❧ Some Thoughts About Getting Started

Think of Yourself As Providing a Life-Affirming Environment and Use That as a Yardstick when Working with Children

Life-affirming teachers see children and themselves as being involved in a positive series of encounters, intended to facilitate growth and happiness. They have faith that children want to do the right thing—that they can grow and change for the better—and they have confidence that teachers and parents can assist them in that task.

Such teachers accept their own humanness and that of other people, and they know it takes strength, determination, and knowledge to sustain these life-affirming policies in situations in which children are just learning the rudiments of socially acceptable behaviour, in a time when many families are disorganized and unhappy.

They realize that sometimes a child can seem lost in a morass of angry feelings and strike out at others, but they also have confidence that she knows deep inside that this behaviour is not working well. They know it is possible for a life-affirming teacher to lead

An early childhood professional:
- supports the uniqueness of each child through recognition of patterns of development, as well as family and cultural influences;
- establishes and maintains supportive relationships with children that promote positive self concept;
- provides and maintains a safe environment that promotes physical and social/emotional well-being;
- plans, implements and evaluates developmentally appropriate experiences that advance all areas of children's learning.

National Guidelines for Training in Child Care and Education. Canadian Child Care Federation, May, 1994. *Interaction.* Vol. 8, No. 2, p. 7, Summer, 1994.

that child onto the firmer ground of being socially acceptable if she is patient, positive, and consistent.

Increase Your Self-Esteem by Realizing You Are Part of a Noble, Though Young, Tradition

Interest in the study of children and awareness of the value of educating their parents in wholesome child-rearing practices began to grow around the turn of the century. That this interest continues today is shown by the continued popularity of child-rearing books and the growing awareness that what parents and teachers do during the early years of childhood can make a significant contribution to the future well-being of the child.

Along with the burgeoning interest in child development came a companion interest in early childhood education and child care. This began abroad, where such leaders as Maria Montessori and the McMillan sisters pioneered child care as a means of improving the well-being of children of the poor.

❧   *Sometimes a child can be lost in a morass of angry feelings.*

In 1907 Maria Montessori, an ardent young reformer-physician, began her *Casa dei Bambini* (Children's House). That child care centre was originally founded as part of an experiment in refurbishing slum housing in an economically distressed quarter of Rome (Loeffler, 1992). Supporters of that cooperative housing venture found that young children left unattended during the day while their parents were away at work were getting into trouble and destroying the property that people had worked so hard to restore. They therefore wanted to work out some way for the children to be cared for. Under Montessori's guidance, Children's House emphasized health, cleanliness, sensory training, individual learning, and the actual manipulation of materials (Montessori, 1912). Since Montessori felt that individual experience with self-correcting materials must come before other learning could take place, language experience, the use of imagination, and dramatic play were not recognized as being of much importance (Braun & Edwards, 1972). Montessori stressed that the teacher should be a cultivated woman and that she should live in the community wherein she taught.

In England, too, the deplorable condition of young slum children was being recognized. In 1911 two English sisters, Margaret and Rachel McMillan, founded their open-air nursery school. The McMillans had been interested in socialism and the women's movement and through these concerns came to know the condition of the London poor. They were horrified to discover that there were many children running around shoeless in the London slums suffering from lice, malnutrition, and scabies. Like Children's House, their school stressed good health, nourishing food, and adequate medical care. Unlike Children's House, it emphasized the value of outdoor play, sunshine, sandboxes, and regular baths. (The school featured deep tubs wherein the children were regularly bathed.) The McMillans advocated teaching children together in small groups. They stressed building independence and self-esteem. They also believed that young girls had natural gifts for working with children, so they gave them paid, on-the-job training as they worked with the children (Bradburn, 1989; McMillan, 1929).

The Development of Child Care in Canada

Industrialization, increased immigration, more urbanization, and the economic need for low-income women to enter the workforce led to the beginning of the child care movement in Canada. Initially the emphasis was on custodial care for young children, with centres operated by charities, churches, and settlement houses. The existence of organized child care before the twentieth century is well documented in Ontario and Quebec.

In Quebec, early childhood programs were primarily provided by the Roman Catholic church. As early as 1858, the Grey Nuns in Montreal operated the salle d'asile Saint Joseph, providing care for several hundred children aged three to seven. In Ontario, the earliest recorded child care program was established in 1890: the Crèche, which still operates today as Victoria Day Care Services. An educator in the Toronto public school system, Dr. Hughes, founded the first kindergarten programs to care for children so their older siblings would not have to bring them along to class while their mothers worked.

A few child care programs were developed in other parts of Canada shortly after the turn of the century. Organized early childhood programs are recorded in Ottawa, Halifax, Vancouver, Winnipeg, Regina, and St. John's.

With the establishment of the Institute of Child Study in 1924 at the University of Toronto and the McGill Day Nursery and Child Laboratory in Montreal, the emphasis shifted from custodial care to education and development. These university-affiliated bodies provided model programs to study child development scientifically and to educate early childhood teachers. The programs stimulated the development of many nursery schools with a child development focus. Nursery schools were operated primarily as educational centres and were quick to distinguish themselves from day nurseries that were recognized primarily for their custodial function for working mothers.

With the onset of World War II, single and married women, including women with children, were recruited to work in war-related industries. Canada's first federal government entry into funding child care was the Dominion-Provincial Wartime Agreement, passed by a federal Order-in-Council in 1942. This agreement enabled the federal government to cost-share child care with the provinces. Only the Ontario and Quebec provincial governments participated.

The postwar era has seen dramatic demographic, economic, and social changes that have created new challenges for families, communities, and governments. Many of Canada's social programs were designed in the 1950s and 1960s when a typical family consisted of three children and two parents, with the father in the labour force and the mother at home. In 1966, the Canada Assistance Plan was enacted, making child care a welfare services. It allowed federal funds to be used to share the costs of child care for low-income families. The terms of the plan encouraged provinces to initiate legislation to regulate child care. By the 1980s, all provinces and territories had legislated standards and limited funding arrangements.

The Gap in Child Care

Child care became a national issue in the 1980s. Women had returned to the workplace in steadily increasing numbers. Two paycheques had become a necessity. Child care was perceived as the responsibility of the family. Government's role was to inspect and license services. Only low-income, needy, or high-risk families were given financial assistance with child care costs. Labour groups, women's organizations, and child care advocates worked to influence government policy. Common themes of quality, availability, affordability, and accountability were part of the vision of child care.

Canadian families are more varied in their composition, work patterns, and needs than ever before. Economic and labour force changes over the past twenty years have resulted in economic insecurity for families: greater risk of unemployment, less job security, and more nonstandard jobs (part time, often with no benefits.) By 1990, in 70% of couples with school-age children, both parents were in the labour force, up from just 30% in 1950.

For many families today, two incomes are essential to maintain a secure and adequate standard of living. In 1993, 63.4% of all women were in the paid labour force, up from 35.5% in 1976. In 1991, 16% of families are single-parent families; 92% of these are headed by women. Single-parent families are likely to lack the social and economic resources of two-parent families, including the potential to share caregiving responsibilities and to distribute the cost of care across two incomes.

Table 1.1 Milestones in the Canadian history of child care

1850	Earliest child care centres established in Montreal.
1873	Dr. J.L. Hughes (Toronto) instigates the establishment of kindergartens on an optional basis in the public school system.
1889	Hester How (Toronto) allows students to bring younger siblings to school to reduce student absenteeism.
1890	The first recorded day care opens in Ontario with the encouragement of Dr. J.L. Hughes: the Crêche, now known as Victoria Day Care Services.
1910	Infants' Hospital in Vancouver opens an infant and preschool centre for working mothers.
1911	Ottawa Day Nursery (Andrew Fleck Child Centre) founded.
1914	Jost Mission Day Care Centre founded in Halifax during World War I.
1916	The Crêche (1910), organized jointly by the Associated Charities and the City of Vancouver, is placed under the jurisdiction of the provincial health department. Vancouver Crêche, under the jurisdiction of the Health Department, puts British Columbia ahead of the other provinces in terms of government intervention and support for day care centres.
1920	Mothers' Allowance Act of Ontario passes. Benefits alleviate extreme poverty, mainly to single-parent families.
1924	Dr. Clare M. Hincks, a leading figure in the early mental health movement, and Dr. E.A. Bott, head of the psychiatry department of the University of Toronto, with the help of the Laura Spelman Rockefeller Fund, establish the St. Georges' School for Child Study.
1925	Dr. William Blatz, the founder of Canada's Early Childhood Education Movement, becomes director of St. Georges' School. McGill University Nursery School established in Montreal.
1930	Mothers' Allowance is given to two-parent families on relief.
1939	World War II.
1940	Single working parents are compelled to place their children in orphanages (seeing them only on weekends) because no alternative exists.
1942	Federal government passes an Order-in-Council authorizing the Minister of Labour to enter into a cost-sharing agreement (Dominion-Provincial Wartime Day Nurseries Agreement) with any provincial government interested in establishing day care facilities. Ontario and Quebec are the only provinces to take advantage of this scheme and sign agreements within two weeks. The other provinces maintain they have no need for day care.
1945	Institute of Child Study (Toronto) develops the Day Nurseries Act, then administered by the Welfare Ministry. Quebec decides to close wartime centres. Federal, provincial, and municipal governments in Ontario try to close the wartime centres or shift the responsibility for their operation and funding; however, a substantial public campaign keeps the centres open.
1946	Federal government plans to end funding April 1, 1946. Ontario provincial government requests (and receives) federal support to June 30, 1946. Day Nurseries Act moves rapidly through the Ontario Provincial Legislature.

Table 1.1 continued

1966	Federal government makes day care a cost-sharing welfare service under the terms of the Canada Assistance Plan (CAP). Under legislation the federal government agrees to share the cost on a 50/50 basis with the provinces.
1967	Women make up 20 percent of the workforce.
1970	Royal Commission on the Status of Women first to recognize nationally the issue of child care as a societal rather than solely parental responsibility. It states that women will not achieve equality unless government becomes involved in child care.
1973	Canada has 28 000 regulated day care spaces available.
1977	All provinces have legislation enabling their governments to take advantage of federal funding (CAP).
1981	Women make up 42 percent of the workforce.
1982	Canada has 125 000 regulated day care spaces available.
1984	The Abella Report (Commission on Equality in Employment) states "for women who are mothers, a major barrier to equality in the workplace is the absence of affordable childcare of adequate quality."
1986	Report of the Task Force on Child Care (Cooke Report) is regarded as the definitive study of the child care situation to date in Canada.
1987	The National Strategy on Child Care presented as the federal government's response to the Martin Report. The government promises a financial commitment of $5.4 billion over seven years to expand and improve child care in Canada.
1988	The Child Care Initiatives Fund (CCIF) begins (April) a seven-year mandate to "encourage and evaluate innovations and to enhance the development of approaches and services" in child care in Canada.
	Child Care Expense Deduction and Child Care Tax Credit supplement are amended. Canada Child Care Act (C–144) is introduced.
	Canada Child Care Act (C–144) dies on the Senate Order Paper in October 1988 when a federal election is called.
	Approximately 1 814 000 children under the age of thirteen, representing almost 68% of the total number of children in care, are left in unregulated care. This figure compares with 578 000 children in kindergarten or nursery school; 202 000 in day care centres; and 83 000 in before-and/or after-school programs.
1990	Federal government places a "cap" on the Canada Assistance Plan (CAP). Cost sharing in Ontario, British Columbia, and Alberta is held to 5%.
	Health and Welfare reports 321 000 spaces are available in licensed facilities.
	Federal government makes changes to the Unemployment Insurance Act that allow for extended provisions for parental leave and improve maternity leave.
1991	Government Expenditures Restraint Act becomes law and includes the controversial "capping of CAP," which began in 1990 to limit cost sharing with Alberta, British Columbia, and Ontario.

Table 1.1 *continued*

1992	Brighter Futures, Canada's action plan for children, is released. It includes the ratification of the Convention on the Rights of the Child (the United Nations' Agreement), the Proposed Child Benefit, Canada's Plan for Children, and the Child Development Initiative.
1992	Donna Lero et al. direct Canadian Families and Their Child Care Arrangements, the 1988 National Child Care Survey. It involves detailed interviews with more than 24 000 Canadian families.
	A joint study is produced by the Canadian Child Care Federation and the Canadian Day Care Advocacy Association: "Caring for a Living—A National Study on the Wages and Working Conditions in Canadian Child Care."
	The Conservative government announces they will not pursue a National Day Care Act; therefore, the act dies. They then begin to target funding to address the poverty issue.
	Sixty percent of women with children under age three are in the work force. The proposed Child Benefit is issued by the federal government.
1993	The Child Benefit goes into effect.
1994	Liberals conduct social security review.
1995	Martin's budget proposes chopping $23 billion from 1996 spending. Proposed block transfer grant gives provinces the right to determine social spending.

Sources: Rosalie Silberman Abella, *Report of the Commission on Equality in Employment,* Ottawa: Supply and Services Canada, 1984; Florence Bird, *Report of the Royal Commission on the Status of Women,* Ottawa: Supply and Services Canada, 1991; *Brighter Futures: Backgrounder for Canada's Action Plan for Children,* Ottawa: Minister of Supply and Services, 1992; *Canada's Children: Investing In Our Future,* Report of the Standing Committee on Health and Welfare, Social Affairs, Seniors and the Status of Women, Sub-Committee on Poverty, Barbara Green, M.P., Chair, Sub-Committee on Poverty; Canada Assistance Plan Act, R.S.C. 1985, c. C–1; Canada Assistance Plan Regulations, Ottawa: Queen's Printer for Canada, 1978; Canada, House of Commons, Bill C–144: Canada Child Care Act, Ottawa: Supply and Services Canada, 1988; Canada, *Sharing the Responsibility: Federal Response to the Report of the Special Committee on Child Care,* Ottawa: Queen's Printer, 1992; Canadian Child Day Care Federation, *Caring for a Living,* press release of April 1992; Canadian Day Care Advocacy Association, "History of the Canadian Day Care Advocacy System," (draft), unpublished document, Ottawa: 1990; and *Bulletin,* Summer 1992; Katie Cooke, et al., Report of the Task Force on Child Care, Ottawa: Status of Women Canada, 1986; Susan Crampton, "Who's Looking After the Kids?— Child Care Arrangements of Working Mothers," in *Perspectives on Labour and Income,* Statistics Canada, Catalogue 75–001, Summer 1991, p. 12; Health and Welfare Canada, *Criteria for Child Care Initiatives.* Ottawa: Health and Welfare Canada, 1988, National Child Care Information Centre, Child Care Programs; Lynda Hurst, "A Death Blow for Day Care," *Toronto Star,* March 15, 1992; and several titles, all by Anne Maxwell; "Towards a National Child Care Policy," *Interaction,* Vol. 5 No. 3, Fall 1991, Ottawa: Canadian Child Day Care Federation; "Towards a National Child Care Policy," 1966–1991, Ottawa: Canadian Child Day Care Federation, October 1991; *Background Paper: Child Care in Alberta,* Ottawa: Canadian Child Day Care Federation, May 1992; *Background Paper: Child Care in British Columbia,* Ottawa: Canadian Child Day Care Federation, March 1992; *Background Paper: Child Care in Manitoba,* Ottawa: Canadian Child Day Care Federation, March 1992. Also used as source material were, National Council of Welfare, *The Canada Assistance Plan: No Time for Cuts,* Ottawa: Supply and Services Canada, 1991; Ontario Coalition for Better Child Care, *Childcare Challenge: Organizing in Ontario,* Toronto: Ontario Coalition for Better Child Care, 1990; Carol Page-Hayding, "A Death Blow for Day Care," *The ECE Link,* Toronto: Association for Early Childhood Education, Spring 1992; Portia Priegert, "Family Leave," *The Ottawa Citizen,* March 14, 1992.

A Patchwork of Systems

Canada does not have a national child care system. Over the past twenty to twenty-five years, child care has evolved in Canada through the efforts of voluntary initiative and governments, sometimes in experimental ways and sometimes in incremental ways.

Canada has a set of systems, each reflecting a unique history of local needs, preferences, and opportunities. The development of services has been ad hoc because of lack of funding and coordination.

Many areas and populations are underserviced; many needed programs are nonexistent or have inadequate resources. In some provinces, recent government cutbacks have resulted in child care programs struggling for viability. In 1994, during consultations with the Standing Committee on Human Resources Development, many child care organizations called upon the federal government to take leadership.

However, policymakers will move only within the limits of perceived public opinion. The only hope for major funding for child care is to shift public opinion towards full support for quality and corresponding staff compensation in early childhood programs. Regrettably, today's political climate seems more hostile than ever to such a shift. The mounting federal debt presents an argument to decrease, not increase, the role of the federal government.

A 1994 paper from Minister of Human Resources Lloyd Axworthy, "Improve Social Security in Canada: Child Care & Development", endeavoured to pair this concern with a focus on investing in people—a theme that logically includes greater support for quality child care (Human Resources Development Canada, 1994). However, the voices of angry taxpayers are urging a move to the right. In the budget of 1995, the federal government proposed replacing the Canada Assistance Plan with the Block Transfer Payment as of 1996. Under this arrangement, provinces would have $23 billion less to pay for education, health, and child care services.

In finding hope, child care advocates need to find common ground with social conservatives who oppose child care funding. Although the groups differ on whether child care funding is inevitable in Canada today, there should be agreement that the child care that does exist should be of the quality necessary to contribute to, rather than harm, children's development.

Choosing a Place to Teach

The manner by which students are assigned to their practice-teaching settings varies considerably among colleges. Sometimes students are allowed to select their placement from a list of satisfactory programs; sometimes the practice-teaching experience takes place in a demonstration school; and sometimes the student is assigned at the discretion of the supervising teacher.

Regardless of the method of assignment, you should know there are many kinds of situations in which to receive training in the field of early childhood education. These can be divided in the following categories: group care, school age care, home child care, aboriginal care, inclusive and exceptional care, and demonstration or laboratory schools.

Group Care

Group care refers to centre-based care for children ranging from newborn to twelve years of age. Many parents choose group care because of increased opportunities for socialization with children of a similar age, the child-centred environment, and the reliability that comes from having back-up care when a staff member is away.

❦ RESEARCH STUDY ❦
Who Is Caring for Canada's Young Children?

Research Question: The investigators who conducted the National Child Care Study wanted to determine who, besides parents, is caring for and educating our young children.

Research Method: The information was gathered in the fall of 1988 by means of interviews either by telephone or in person. This comprehensive national study, surveying more than 24 000 families, was designed by the principal investigators in collaboration with Statistics Canada. The researchers investigated many areas, but a portion of the study that is of interest to early childhood educators deals with child care arrangements. Respondents were asked about their employment and child care arrangements for their children under thirteen years of age in the week preceding the interview. Parents were asked how they found the care, which factors affected their decision making and how satisfied parents were with the child care arrangements they were using.

Highlights: The study found that the majority (57%) of Canadian children under the age of thirteen participate in at least one nonparental child care arrangement in a given week. The children spend an average of 18.3 hours in nonparental care. The largest proportion of infants were cared for by a relative in their home (17.7%) or an unlicensed home (15.9%), with the smallest number in a licensed centre (3.2%).

Informal arrangements with family members or relatives were used most frequently for toddlers (34.6%); 19.4% were with unlicensed family day providers and 17.4% in licensed care, primarily group care.

Preschool-age children were the group best served by licensed programs (49.4%), with the others cared for by family members, relatives, or unlicensed home care. School-age children were poorly served by the licensed group care sector. The predominant family form among children under three is the dual-earner family (46%). Balancing work and family roles is an experience shared by many families with young children. Close to 52% of all families with preschool-age children were either dual-earner couples or sole-support parents. Most parents (including about 67% of dual-earner families with children under age three) were employed full time. Employed parents in one-parent families most often worked full time; 80% of those with preschool children worked full time. Only 55% of parents, however, worked a standard work week, with working hours primarily falling between 8 a.m. and 6 p.m.

Implications: Canadian families rely on a variety of child care arrangements to enable parents to work or participate in education or training and to provide opportunities for their children's development. Most of these child care arrangements are unlicensed, the most common being care in a home that is not a relative's. Approximately 15% of all child care is provided by services licensed by the provinces and territories. There is a demand for more flexible care as well as child care centres. Parents' child care preferences and choices vary, depending on the age and number of children, family income, work and school schedules, and locations. For most families, quality, cost, stability, and convenience are ongoing concerns. Child care is more than an employment measure; it also contributes to early childhood development. A growing body of research confirms that the early development of children is strongly influenced by the quality of care they receive. The 1988 Canadian

National Child Care Study found that the greatest gap between child care preference and use is that parents would prefer licensed care, particularly centre-based care. Less than 45% of the parents who preferred licensed care actually received it. The fact that in 1988 an estimated 2.7 million children needed child care while their parents were employed reminds us of how seriously we must take our role as caregivers. As early childhood educators, we must be the best we can be when parents entrust such an important portion of the child's life to our care. Good child care is an investment in healthy children. It contributes to reducing child poverty; it supports parents; and it contributes to economic growth. We need to advocate the strengthening of partnerships between the federal government and the provinces and the redesign of funding to make child care more available and affordable.

Source: "The Canadian National Child Care Study" (1992). Statistics Canada, Health and Welfare Canada.

All of the provinces and territories offer group care. In some provinces, full- and part-time programs are regulated and children requiring either full- or part-day care are located in the same centre. Newfoundland does not provide group care for children younger than two years.

Nursery schools are part-time developmental programs for preschoolers. They are not designed as child care programs, since they do not correspond to parents' work hours. However, many working parents use these programs in combination with other child care arrangements. Centre-based programs may be operated by a nonprofit corporation, a for-profit operation (either individually owned or part of a chain or franchise operation) or a municipal government (in Ontario and Alberta).

Many centres have an arrangement whereby fees to low-income families are subsidized by the government. The caregivers in group programs are more likely to have some education in early childhood and child development. The required qualifications generally apply only to the lead caregiver. The options include nursery schools, preschools, Montessori programs, playgroups, and kindergartens.

School-Age Care

All provinces and territories have regulated programs for school-age children (usually ages six to twelve), typically located in or near elementary schools. In some provinces, there is a separate definition and set of regulations for this age group. Although local boards of education may provide some form of support, these programs are not generally operated under the jurisdiction of provincial departments of education. In Quebec, however, school-age child care is offered through the elementary school system.

There is a need for coordination among the different parties: the child, parents, school, and child care provider. Combinations of child care arrangements are often shaped to meet parents' overall needs, and often involve complicated scheduling around the school calendar. Some parents rely on "self care," in which children are on their own before and after school.

Home Child Care

Home child care of a small group of children is typically provided by a caregiver, who is not a relative, in her or his own home. Family child care can be licensed or informal, although it is usually unregulated. There are two main ways in which regulated family day care is organized in Canada. One approach has the province license individual homes. The other allows an agency, which is licensed by the province or territory, to supervise individual homes. Agencies are responsible for recruiting, screening, training, and monitoring the caregivers. Generally the caregivers are not required to have formal education in child development. In Prince Edward Island, a thirty-hour course is required. Informal arrangements are the norm for the majority of Canadian children. This care can be provided in the child's or a caregiver's home, by a relative, nanny, neighbour, friend, or babysitter. Nonmarket care typically includes care by a family member or spouse (for example, when two parents stagger their work hours so one can provide care while the other parent is working). Nonmarket care is frequently provided at no monetary cost to the family.

Inclusive and Exceptional Care

All programs should welcome cultural, racial, and linguistic diversity. Children require caring adults who not only meet their physical needs but are also concerned with their intellectual, social, and emotional growth. Children should be welcomed as individuals regardless of ability or disability, cultural background, family income, or parents' occupation. It is essential that early childhood educators who work with children of diverse backgrounds foster appreciation of different child rearing and nurturing styles, and of attitudes and values from other cultures.

In most regions of Canada, integration in mainstream early childhood programs is the preferred option for children with special needs. Children with special needs usually benefit from attending an integrated quality early childhood program. Integration with peers provides such children with opportunities to develop and enhance their social and adaptive behaviours. A program requires additional resources to accommodate the needs of these children. Most provinces, except British Columbia and Ontario, do not require specialized training for teachers working with children with special needs. The framework for the development of child care options should include the fundamental principles of access, equity, opportunity, and inclusion. Parents and support groups report that mainstream child care is in short supply, and children with special needs are relatively underserved.

Aboriginal Children

Aboriginal families, both on and off reserves, have few appropriate services available to them. First Nations see child care as a means of restoring aboriginal communities. Recent trends in aboriginal child care have focused on developing culturally appropriate models of services and related supports such as training programs for teachers. The emphasis has been on holistic models of service, which link preschool education, healthy child development, and language/cultural survival goals with those of enabling parents to participate in training, education, or employment. Aboriginal children living off reserve communities have access to provincially regulated and subsidized care. However, there is a shortage of care that is subsidized and affirms aboriginal languages and cultures.

Demonstration or Laboratory Schools

Demonstration or laboratory schools are typically connected with teacher training institutions or with research programs (Barbour & Bersani, 1991). They can be wonderful places for young students to begin their teaching, since they are the most likely of all the kinds of schools to be child- and *student*-centred. Ideally students should have teaching opportunities in both laboratory and real-life schools so that they receive a balance of ideal and realistic teaching experiences.

❧ Some Comforting Thoughts

Do Teachers Matter?

Two of the outstanding characteristics of beginning teachers are the caring and involvement that they bring with them to their work, and it is heartening to remember that these characteristics are important factors in achieving success. Weikart and Lambie (1970), for example, found that no matter what kind of curricular model was followed (that of Piaget or Bereiter, or a more traditional model), the involvement of the teacher and his or her implementation of the curriculum were fundamental to the success of the outcome. Another researcher (Katz, 1969) attributed the failure of a program she studied to the fact that the teachers gave lip service to the curriculum and failed to carry it through in practice.

In summing up a number of studies about the impact of teachers' behaviour on children, Phyfe-Perkins (1981) reports that successful teachers encouraged independent activity, planned a variety of activities, and used criticism and negative commands "sparingly." Such teachers were aware of several activities at the same time and could do more than one thing at a time. Their transitions between activities were smooth, and they were *involved with the children* but did not constantly try to direct their behaviour.

What teachers have learned makes a difference, too. In her analysis of what research tells us constitutes quality child care, Phillips (1987) cites numerous studies that support the finding that specialized training in child care is associated with better quality care. This is true for both family day care homes and centre-based care. In general, more training appears to produce more positive interactions with children.

So on days when things may not have gone just right, it may be a comfort to remember that involvement, caring, and child-care-related training are valuable qualities already possessed by the student. It is, of course, an ancient truth that the more one puts into any experience, the more one gets out of it—and teaching is no exception.

The Supervising Teacher Is Probably Ill at Ease, Too

Sometimes students are so wrapped up in their own shyness that they fail to realize that the teachers they are working with are shy of them. They attribute all the awkwardness of

ᵍ   *The ability to enjoy children is one of the basic elements of good teaching.*

the first days on the job to their own insecurities and inexperience. Actually the supervising teacher is willing to help but may also be a little uncomfortable, particularly if she has not had many students before. It will help her help the student if she knows that the student likes her.

One Poor Experience with a Student Will Not Ruin a Child's Life

Some conscientious new teachers are almost too sensitive to the effect their actions will have on the children. It is true that young children are more vulnerable to influences than older children are, and for this reason everyone attempts to do his or her very best. But the significance of the single traumatic experience has been overrated. It is usually the continuing approach or climate that moulds the child (Sorensen, 1993; Werner, 1984). Therefore, the student need not agonize over one mishandled situation on the grounds that it may have scarred the child for life; this is a most unlikely result.

Evaluating Activities Can Turn a Student into a Better Teacher

Analysing an activity after presenting it by noting its strengths as well as its weaknesses is one of the quickest ways to improve one's teaching. When things have not gone exactly right, it's easy to dwell on the negative aspects and forget the positive ones. Even when things could have gone better, rather than investing a lot of energy in regretting the errors, it is more healthy and productive to figure out what went wrong and decide how to be more effective next time. It is also helpful to repeat the experience as soon as possible (rather like getting back on a horse and riding again right after you've fallen off) so that bad memories are supplanted by better ones.

The excerpt on pages 18 to 19 illustrates how one student analysed an activity and improved the situation as the week progressed. Note, in particular, how sensitive she was to building on the interests of the children.

Remember There Is a Wide Variety of Places to Use Your Training in Addition to Conventional School Situations

Sometimes students become baffled and discouraged when after giving it a fair chance they just do not like teaching a group of children in a half- or full-day setting of any kind, yet they know in their hearts they wish to continue working with young children. In recent years students from my program, in addition to teaching in conventional school situations, have pursued the following careers: child life specialist in a children's hospital, resource referral adviser about children's services, motherhood, home visitor, teacher of special needs children, nanny, child care licensing agent, child abuse counsellor, staff in the national office of the Canadian Child Care Federation, college professor, toy store owner, director of a children's centre, and family child care provider. The possibilities are growing all the time.

Remember That Age Need Not Be a Negative Factor When Learning to Teach Young Children

One of the most interesting trends in recent years has been the return to school by women who have decided to reenter the working world outside the home. Sometimes it can be a bit daunting to women in their middle years to take classes surrounded by people newly graduated from high school. A number of such women have confided to me that it is frightening to return and have to compete with those they perceive as brighter or at least younger than they are.

The truth is that every age brings with it some special assets. It may well be the case that younger students are more accustomed to managing the routines of studying and college life. However, it can be a comforting thought to more mature learners to remember that they, in turn, bring special skills and benefits to the college experience. These usually include more experience with children (there's nothing like having a couple of children of your own to breed humility and compassion for other parents) and also a wider perspective on life that can serve reentry students well as they work to increase their teaching skills.

ॐ *Basic Professional Ethics*

Now that the student is becoming a member of a profession, it will be helpful to know from the beginning some ethical guidelines that are observed by most teachers. Appendix A gives the Code of Ethics prepared by the Early Childhood Educators of British Columbia.

A LET'S-FIND-OUT PROJECT: WHAT MIXES WITH WHAT!

I set up my Let's-Find-Out project at the science table. I had three large plastic containers with water in them mixed with salt, sand, and dirt so the children could shake them and see what happened. Plastic tubs of soap powder, sand, salt, flour, sugar, oil, baking soda, cornstarch, and dirt were placed out on a food tray with spoons. I had ten small plastic jars with water in them for mixing these things with. I placed out towels, paper towels, and a large metal bowl of water for cleanup. The questions and information sheets were taped onto the board in that area with a blue background of construction paper to make it look more attractive.

How I Changed It During the Week
Because this was such a messy project and because it required constant replenishing for every group, I found myself having to be at the Institute before every class. My schedule did not allow me to reset the project up on Tuesday afternoon or on Thursday morning. Some of the other teachers did that for me on Tuesday afternoon, but from what I understand the activity was not there for the three-year-olds on Thursday morning.

  I had some ideas of how to change the activity during the week by providing new things to mix, such as paint or food colouring, but after seeing and hearing how the children reacted to the project, I dumped my own ideas. The children were really using the activity as a trial-and-error cooking project so I went with their ideas. I deleted the sand and dirt from the plastic containers on Thursday afternoon and carried the stove over to the area to promote cooking experiments. Friday, I noticed that the class of four-year-olds had decided to have the teacher write down what they were making or make their own recipes. It would have been a good idea for me to include a pencil and pad of paper to encourage this.

Evaluation of Activity
The most noticeable aspect of this project was how messy it was. It really made me uncomfortable that I had planned an activity that made such a mess and required a teacher's assistance at all times when I wasn't present. But in the same light I took this positively because this meant that the activity was really being used. For any activity to be as meaningful as possible, it does require the teacher's

---

Some of the most fundamental ethical principles teachers should observe include the following items.

When in Doubt About the Value of a Decision, Put the Child's Welfare First

Granted, what is "best" may not always be easy to determine. There will always remain special circumstances in which we cannot be certain what is best for the child's welfare. For example, is it better for a three-year-old to stay with a loving but emotionally disturbed and disoriented single parent, or to place her with a less disturbed but apparently cold and emotionally remote grandmother? But it is also true that much of the time, if teachers honestly try to do what is best for the child rather than what is merely convenient or "the rule," they will be on the right ethical track.

presence to expand and explain. I think, and other teachers told me, that the children really enjoyed the activity. No matter how messy and inconvenient it was for the teachers, it was beneficial for the children and that's what counts! The children got a good idea of how different things mix or don't mix with water. They also got to see what happened when you mix things with water simultaneously. Since I have been at the Institute, I have never seen a Let's-Find-Out activity be used and enjoyed as much as this one. I think this is because the children could actually do so much instead of watching or looking. I also think it went over well because there were so many different possible combinations to test.

Suggestions for Improvement

This activity brought to my attention how important it is to have a teacher involved in Let's-Find-Out projects. There's no telling how many wonderful learning opportunities have been passed by because there was no teacher on the spot in this area to draw out ideas and extend the learning. It would be very beneficial to assign one teacher each week for each age group to get the full benefit. At first I thought that this would have been better as a one-day activity; but as I saw it being used by the same children day after day, I decided that I was wrong. The children that were using it were the same ones that had used it the day before. This discovery brought to my attention how important it is to repeat activities so that children are able to enjoy and learn as much as they wish to.

Another suggestion is to remind the teachers to use the information and questions posted to help extend the learning experience. Many more avenues could have been explored by using that information.

I toyed with the idea of using an evaporation project with this, and I'm glad I didn't. I think that would have been too overwhelming, and the educational value of it would have been lost. What was provided was enough to keep their minds full, especially when the teachers used their imagination and the children's, too.

Next time it would be nice to have some things to mix that have some colour; but then again, I think the all white and cream colours are what promoted the cooking play. I think if I could have been around more, I would have switched off to food colouring and paint towards the end of the week to extend the children's learning in another direction.

Source: Courtesy Melissa Kyle, Fundamentals of Instruction I student paper. Institute of Child Development, University of Oklahoma, Norman.

Strive to Be Fair to All Children

Another important guideline to observe is that all children deserve a fair chance and a reasonable amount of concern from each teacher. Perhaps the student will recall situations in his or her own school life in which a teacher made a scapegoat of some child and picked on her continually, or another teacher never seemed to notice some of the youngsters. Although nobody intends to have this kind of thing happen, sometimes it does, and teachers should be warned against behaving this way. Every child is important and is entitled to be valued by the teacher.

Keep Personal Problems Private During the Day

Teachers should not discuss their personal problems or emotional difficulties with the parents, nor should they discuss them with other teachers while school is in session.

Teachers need to leave personal problems at the door as they begin the day, since the time at school rightfully belongs to the children. The discussion of personal matters should take place after the children have gone home. Many a teacher has discovered that shutting such troubles out during the teaching day can provide interludes of relief and happiness that can make otherwise intolerable situations bearable.

Show Respect for the Child

One important way teachers of young children demonstrate basic respect for others is by refraining from discussing a child in her presence unless she is included directly in the conversation. Sometimes teachers thoughtlessly talk over the children's heads, assuming that the youngsters are unaware of what is being said. But students who have had the experience of eavesdropping while people were discussing them will no doubt remember the special potency of that overheard comment. Anything said about a child in her presence needs to be said with her included. Thus it is more desirable to say, "Peg, I can see you're feeling pretty tired and hungry" than to cock an eyebrow in her direction and remark to another teacher, "Oh, brother! We are in a nasty temper today!"

An even more fundamental aspect of respect between teacher and child can best be described as a valuing of the person: the teacher who truly respects and values the child pauses to listen to her with full attention whenever this is possible, remembering that each child is a unique person, relishing her for her differences from her companions, and allowing her to generate ideas of her own rather than subtly teaching her that it is better to accept unquestioningly the teacher's ideas as being best.

This kind of respect is, of course, a two-way street. Teachers who hold the child in such respectful regard set a model for the youngster, who will in time reflect this same fundamental consideration back to them. This process can be accelerated and strengthened if the teacher quietly makes a point of protecting her own rights, as well as the children's. She may say something as simple as, "Now, Margaret, I've listened to you; take just a minute and hear what I want to say," or she may make this same point with another child by saying, "You know, my desk is just like your cubby. I don't take your things out of that, and you must never take anything from my desk, either."

Observe Professional Discretion

Still another aspect of respect for people is respect for the family's privacy. Family affairs and children's behaviour should not be discussed with people outside the school who have no need to know about them. Even amusing events should never be told unless the names of the children either are not mentioned or are changed. Most communities are smaller worlds than a beginning teacher may realize, and news can travel with astonishing rapidity.

In general, student teachers should be wary of being drawn into discussions with parents about their own or other families' children. This kind of discussion is the teacher's prerogative, and it is a wise student who passes off questions about youngsters by making some pleasant remark and referring the parent to the teacher. Nobody is ever antagonized by a student who does this in a tactful way, but disasters can result from well-meant comments by ill-informed or tactless beginners.

In addition, students should not discuss situations they disapprove of at the school where they work or say anything critical about another teacher to outsiders. These remarks have an unpleasant way of returning to the source, and the results can be awkward, to say the least. The principle "If you don't say it, they can't repeat it" is a sound one here. It is better, instead, to talk the problem over in confidence with the college supervisor.

Observe the Chain of Command

In just about every organization there is a chain of command. It is always wise to avoid going over anyone's head when making a comment or request. Understandably, teachers hate being put in a bad light by a student's talking a problem over with the school director or principal before talking it over with the teacher first.

A related aspect of this authority structure is being sure to get permission before planning a special event such as a field trip or getting out the hoses after a videotape on water play. Answers to such requests are generally yes, but it is always best to check before embarking on a major venture.

❧ Some Recommendations for Starting Out

Although not always possible, it helps to find some things out before beginning the first student teaching day. For example, it is helpful to talk with the teacher and determine the expected arrival time and the recommended style of clothing. Most schools are reasonable and will recommend sensible but professional-looking clothes. Many teachers, both men and women, wear some sort of apron since the pockets and protection it provides are real assets. When clothing is protected, it is much more likely that teachers will gather a painty or messy child onto their laps for a hug than when they are dressed for classes later that day.

Some schools have written guidelines they can give the student to read. Time schedules and lists of rules are also very helpful to review. (For a typical schedule, see chapter 3.) If the school does not have these items written down, ask the teacher how basic routines such as eating and taking children to the toilet are handled, and ask about crucial safety rules and for a brief review of the schedule. If the student can come for a visit when the children are not there, the teacher will have a better opportunity to chat. During this visit make a special point of finding out where the children's cubbies are, where sponges and clean-up materials are kept, and where various supplies are stored. Don't hesitate to ask questions; just do your best to remember the answers!

❧ Practical Things to Do to Increase Competence

Gain Confidence in Your Ability to Control the Group

Almost invariably the first thing students want to discuss is discipline. Since this is the point everyone seems most concerned about, it is recommended that the reader begin preparation for work by reading the chapters on discipline and aggression in order to build skills in this area. While those reviews will help, observation, practice, and seeing situations all the way through are the best ways to gain competence in guiding children.

Get to Know the Children as Soon as Possible

One way to become familiar with each child is to make a list of names from the sign-in sheet and then jot down a few adjectives or facts to remember about each one. Calling the children by name at every opportunity will help, too. It will not take more than a day or two to become well acquainted, and it will help you belong to the group more quickly.

Develop the Proverbial "Eyes in the Back of the Head"

One of the most common failings of inexperienced teachers is their tendency to focus on only one child at a time. It is pleasant and much "safer" to sit down and read a favourite book with one or two lovable children and ignore the chaos going on in the block corner, but good teachers form the habit of total awareness. They develop a sense of what is happening in the entire area. This is true outdoors as well as inside. But to say that the teacher should never plan to settle down with any group would be an exaggeration. Of course, teachers have to centre their attention on specific children from time to time or there is little satisfaction in the experience for teacher or child, but teachers must keep tuned in to the whole room as well. Sometimes such a simple technique as learning to look up frequently will help build skills in this area. Another technique is sitting so that the whole room or whole playground can be seen. Many beginning students sit with their backs to half the room—this is simply courting trouble.

Take Action in Unsafe Situations Immediately

Since students are sometimes afraid of appearing too restrictive in a liberal atmosphere, they allow dangerous things to happen because they do not know the rule or school policy about it. The general rule of thumb is that when one is unsure whether the activity is dangerous, it is better to stop it and then check to see what the teacher thinks. Stopping a few activities that are safe is better than letting two children wrestle each other off the top of the slide while the student debates indecisively below. Things generally look less dangerous to students as they gain experience and feel less anxious, *but it is always better to be safe than sorry.*

Encourage the Growth of Independence and Competence; Avoid Overteaching, Overhelping, and Overtalking

As a general principle, we encourage children at the preprimary level to do everything they can for themselves. This is different from the behaviour of the teacher who sees the role of the teacher as doing *to* and doing *for* children. It takes self-control to wait while Katy fumbles for the zipper, insight to see how to assist her without taking over, and self-discipline not to talk too much while she is learning. But building competencies in the children by letting them do things for themselves increases their self-esteem so much that practising restraint is worth the effort.

Encourage Originality of Self-Expression

One of the most frowned-on things students can do is to make models of something for the children to copy when they are working with creative materials. It is easy to be trapped into making one child a snake or drawing a man for another youngster, but early childhood teachers dislike providing such models because they limit children's expression of their own feelings and ideas. It is better to relish the materials with the children and help them use them for their own purposes.

Keep Contacts with the Children as Quiet and Meaningful as Possible

Except in a real emergency, walk over to the child to talk with her rather than calling across the room. Use a low voice, and bend down so she can see your face and be less overwhelmed by your size. (An excellent way to find out how big an adult is from a child's point of view is to ask a friend to stand up and teach you something while you remain sitting on the floor. It's enlightening.)

Expect to Do Menial Tasks

No other profession requires the full range of abilities and effort that preschool teaching does. These extend from inspiring children and counselling parents to doing the most menial types of cleanup. Sometimes students do not realize this, so they feel imposed upon when they are asked to change a pair of pants or mop the floor or clean the guinea pig. This kind of work is expected of almost all early childhood teachers as just being part of school life. Not only is cleaning up to be expected, but also continual straightening up is necessary as the day progresses. Blocks should be arranged on shelves and dress-up clothes rehung several times to keep the room looking attractive. (Unfortunately there is no good fairy who will come along and do this.)

Learn from the Start to Be Ingenious about Creating Equipment and Scrounging Materials

Early childhood programs almost always operate on lean budgets, and every program develops a number of ingenious ways to stretch money and invent equipment. Students can learn from each place they work by picking up these economical ideas from the staff, and they can contribute much by sharing their own ideas about the creative use of materials and new sources of free supplies. Be on the lookout for so-called waste materials that other businesses throw away. The carpet company's colourful scraps can make handsome additions to the collage box, for example, and rubber tires can be used in fascinating ways to make sturdy play equipment.

♋   *Allowing children to do things "on their own" helps them build sound feelings of self-esteem.*

Organize Yourself Before Beginning to Teach

It is very helpful to arrive early on each teaching day so there is time to get everything together in advance for the morning or afternoon. Nothing beats the feeling of security this preparation breeds. Life is also easier if before going home the student asks what will be happening during the next teaching session. It is important to check in advance and make certain that needed supplies are on hand. Asking in advance also makes reading up on activities ahead of time possible—a real security enhancer!

It increases confidence when you know the schedule well enough to tell what is going to happen next, as well as what time it is likely to happen. This allows time for cleanup and also helps to avoid the disappointment of moving into a new activity just as the group is expected to wash up for lunch. For these reasons, it is advisable to always wear a watch.

When You Need Help, Ask for It

People usually are not critical when beginners admit they do not know something and have the courage to ask, but they are inclined to resent students who protect themselves by appearing to know everything already or who defend themselves by making constant excuses. When one is unsure of a policy at the school, it never does any harm to say to the child, "I don't know if it's all right to climb on the fence. Let's ask Melodie and then we'll both know."

The chance to chat with the teacher while cleaning up at the end of the morning, or at some other convenient time of day, is an invaluable time to raise problems and ask questions. During the day itself, students often have to muddle through—learning by observation and using their own common sense. Nothing disastrous is likely to take place, and teachers are usually too busy to be corralled for more than a sentence or two of explanation while school is in progress.

⁊ Recognize Stress and Deal with It as Effectively as Possible

It is inevitable to feel stress when dealing with a new situation such as beginning to teach, and it is valuable to recognize this fact so that you can deal with it effectively rather than just feeling anxious, overwhelmed, or disappointed because sometimes you are exhausted at the end of the day. So much about the experience is new. There are so many personalities to deal with and so much to learn, so much uncertainty and excitement, and such a great desire to please without knowing exactly what is expected. This situation is clearly a lot to handle. These stresses do not mean that teaching is bad or unpleasant. Many novel situations such as getting married or receiving a promotion are delightful; but nonetheless they are stressful because they represent change, and change requires learning and adaptation.

Symptoms of stress vary with the individual. Some people lose their appetites, while others try to comfort themselves by eating too much. Still others suffer from loss of sleep or find that they get angry at the slightest provocation.

Wise teachers acknowledge the possibility of stress and make practical plans for coping so they can avoid coming down with various ailments or experiencing the excessive fatigue that prevents them from functioning effectively. Unfortunately such plans require a certain amount of self-discipline. Deciding to get plenty of rest, for example, is rarely a favourite prescription for the young, and yet it really does reduce stress, as does adequate nutrition and provision for having fun off the job (Borysenko, 1987).

Truthful analysis of what is causing the most intense stress also helps. It might be apprehension about a child's threat to bite you, or it might be worry over how to keep the group attentive during story time, or it might be concern about whether other teachers or parents like you. Whatever it is, identifying the source is the first step toward reducing worry and strain. Solutions beyond that point vary according to case, but after identification, successful reduction of stress depends on making some kind of plan for coping with it and then having the fortitude to carry through with the plan. Selye (1981) was certainly correct when he commented that "action absorbs anxiety." For example, rather than just worrying over the coming group time, it is better to take action by acquainting yourself with the materials in advance, planning for variety, choosing activities the children are interested in, and having them actively participate.

Making realistic estimates about how long it will take you to accomplish something takes the strain and worry out of trying to get it done at the last minute. It is better to allow yourself too much time for planning than to come up short. Prioritizing helps, too. Choosing things that must be done and doing those first is a great stress reducer. Concentrating on just one thing at a time also blocks out worry and helps you appreciate the present experience to its fullest. After all, all anyone really has is the present moment of existence. Why not seek to be aware of it fully while it is here?

Deliberately creating opportunities for relaxation is still another effective way of handling stress (Lehrer & Woolfolk, 1993). Finding a quiet place and letting go from the toes all the way to the forehead and ears can be quieting and refreshing. Such strategies need not take long, but it is necessary to make a point of remembering to use them from time to time.

The final thing that can help reduce stress is having a safety valve available. Everyone should be aware of things they can do for themselves that take the pressure off for awhile when life is too demanding. These solutions vary a lot. I have had people tell me they do everything from going shopping, taking a swim, or reading a detective story, to telling another person how they feel. The important thing about such strategies is that they should not be used as ways of permanently avoiding the stressful situation, because ultimately they can increase anxiety. At best they are stopgap measures that provide temporary relief and refreshment so that the person can pick up and go on in a reasonable period of time. When they are resorted to, I believe they should be used deliberately, purposefully, and without guilt. When used in that manner, such indulgence provides maximum refreshment and benefit.

❦ Some Special Problems

The following problems have come up often enough with students that they deserve discussion. Of course, because each situation is different, recommendations are risky. Nevertheless the following suggestions may provide solutions that may not have occurred to the student.

What to Do If You Hate the School to Which You Are Assigned

We have already mentioned that there are several different types of preschool, child care, and kindergarten situations, and that even the same type varies a good deal from school to school. Some schools seem to suit some early childhood education students, and others fit other students better. Therefore, do not conclude that teaching is not for you just because one placement is less than satisfactory. Maybe a change to another school is the answer to the problem; maybe it is not. At any rate, the way to begin solving the difficulty is by talking over the reason for the unhappiness with the supervising teacher from the college. This is a more productive, as well as a more ethical, solution than complaining to a friend.

It is also wise to refrain from making snap judgements about a teacher or placement. The first two or three weeks in any program will be some of the most stressful weeks of the student's career, and it is essential to realize that some people react to stress by attacking what is frightening them and by criticizing it; others shrink up and feel paralysed or disillusioned. As time passes, the strain will probably lessen, and the school may seem more attractive, a little the way hospital food mysteriously improves as the patient recovers.

What to Do If You Don't Like a Child

It's no sin to dislike a child, but it *is* a sin not to admit your dislike, come to terms with it, and try to do something about it. Sometimes what will help most is getting to know him or her better, since insight often breeds compassion. Sometimes making progress of some sort with the child helps. Sometimes figuring out why you dislike the youngster will ease the feeling. With beginning students this can often be traced to the fact that some children challenge adults or put them on the spot. Students who already feel insecure find this behaviour particularly trying. Whatever the reason, it is more healthy to risk admitting your dislike to yourself and perhaps to your supervising teacher, if you feel safe with that person, and then to work toward resolving the problem. Although the suggested remedies may not overcome the dislike completely, they should help. At the very least, it is always possible to be fair and decent to all the children. Probably the liking will come in time.

❧ The Way to Your Supervising Teacher's Heart

We have already talked about the fact that it takes time to feel at home and to build a friendship with the supervising teacher. There are five more specific practices the student can follow that will help generate friendliness. The first is to be prepared to make the small, extra contribution of time and energy *beyond* what is expected. The student who stays the extra ten minutes on potluck night to dry the coffee pot is well on the way to becoming a popular member of the staff.

The second thing sounds simple but is often overlooked because new teachers tend to be nervous. It is to *listen* to what the teacher tells you, and do your best to remember it!

The third thing is to offer help *before* being asked to lend a hand. Some students are so afraid of being pushy or of making mistakes that they never volunteer. But always having to request help gets tiresome for the teacher, even if the student is willing when asked. It is better to develop an eye for all the little things that must be done and then to do them quietly. Such students are treasured by their supervising teachers.

Teachers also appreciate the student who contributes ideas for projects and activities. After all, it is not the supervising teacher's responsibility to provide all the ideas for your teaching days. Come prepared with a variety of suggestions so that, if one or two turn out to be impractical, you can be flexible and propose alternative possibilities.

Finally, the student should let enthusiasm show through. The vast majority of teachers follow their profession because they love it; the rigours of the job and the relatively low pay weed the others out very quickly. The teachers are, therefore, enthusiastic themselves. They are often "born" teachers, and they love teaching students as well as young children. Expressing thanks by being enthusiastic yourself will encourage them to keep on making the extra effort entailed in guiding student teachers.

ॐ *Summary*

The student should grasp three basic principles before beginning to teach: Supervising teachers are human, too; one poor experience won't ruin a child's life; and mistakes can be turned into valuable learning opportunities.

Even beginning students need to observe professional ethics when they are teaching. It is particularly important to respect each child and to preserve the privacy of the families whose children attend the school.

Gaining knowledge of the school's basic routines, schedules, and policies will make the early days of teaching a more comfortable experience for the young teacher. Some practical things to do that will increase the student's competence include gaining confidence in handling discipline situations, getting to know the children, being alert to the whole environment, taking swift action in situations that are dangerous, encouraging the growth of independence and originality of self-expression, making contact with the children as quietly and meaningfully as possible, being organized, realizing that age need not be a negative factor when learning to teach, and asking for help when it is needed.

Probably no other time in the life of the teacher is so exciting, unsettling, and challenging as the first days of student teaching. Teachers are fortunate who manage to retain at least some of this flutter of anticipation throughout their teaching lives.

Questions and Activities

1. Getting started in the first days of student teaching can be a special challenge, and it is helpful to know yourself and your own reactions well enough to be able to control them. How do you anticipate you will cope with the strangeness and unfamiliarity of the student teaching experience when you are just beginning? Close your eyes and think back to the last two or three occasions when you entered a new group and got acquainted. What was your personal mode of adapting? Did you talk a lot? Clam up? Act extremely helpful?

2. If you were guiding a young, new teacher, what advice would you give him or her that might help that person through the first days of teaching?

3. Do you believe that supervising teachers and professors are ever nervous or frightened when dealing with students, or do they seem invulnerable to such difficulties?

4. If you have ever had the good fortune to exist in a "life-affirming environment," identify the qualities you feel helped create that kind of emotional climate.

5. List some effective *do's* and *don'ts* for getting acquainted with young children. What are some effective ways of establishing friendly yet respectful relationships with them?

6. Do you know of some remedies that seem to help other people deal effectively with stress but do not seem to help you? What might these be, and why do you think they work for some people and not for others?

Self-Check Questions for Review
Content-Related Questions

1. Briefly outline the general history of the child care movement in Canada.

2. The text discusses the educational philosophies of two English women and an Italian woman who helped begin the child care movement in their coun-

tries. What are their names and what are some facts about the schools they founded?

3. Name several different kinds of child care situations and describe each of them in a general way.
4. Give some examples of ethical principles that teachers of young children should follow.
5. Name some practical things beginning teachers can do that will help them become competent as quickly as possible.

Integrative Questions

1. This book begins with a poem by Walt Whitman. What does the poem really mean, and how is it related to teaching young children?
2. The text lists some basic tenets of the Montessori and McMillan nursery schools. Compare the two schools. What do they have in common and how do they differ?
3. At this point in your experience, which kind of program (group care, home child care, school age, etc.) do you feel would best meet your needs as a student teacher? Discuss what might be the strong points and drawbacks of making that particular choice.
4. This chapter offers a number of suggestions for coping successfully with stress. Which of these suggestions do you feel would be the most helpful ones for you to use?

References for Further Reading

Overview

Dickinson, P. (1990). The early childhood professional. In I.M. Doxey (Ed.), *Child care and education: Canadian dimensions.* Scarborough, ON: Nelson. Dickinson reviews the history of programs and categories of early childhood professionals and discusses the philosophical disputes about education and care in Canada.

Maintaining Good Relationships with Children

Ayers, W. (1989). *The good preschool teacher: Six teachers reflect on their lives.* New York: Teachers College Press. This book is a collection of interviews given by six very different teachers of preschool children combined with descriptions of events in their child care situations. It provides insights into a variety of viewpoints about what good teachers of young chil-

dren think about and how they put their philosophies into action.

Read, K., Gardner, P., & Mahler, B. C. (1993). *Early childhood programs: Human relationships and learning* (9th ed.). New York: Holt, Rinehart & Winston. This is the all-time classic of nursery school education. As the title implies, it concentrates on the value of human relationships in the preschool. A must for beginning teachers.

Maintaining Good Relationships with Other Adults

Blanchard, K. (1992). *The one minute manager.* New York: Berkley. What this book has to say about communicating with people is valuable for all of us, not just managers!

Information About Approaches to Teaching Young Children

Chattin-McNichols, J. (1992). *The Montessori controversy.* Albany, NY: Delmar. The author carefully describes the philosophy and content of the Montessori Method. This book is particularly useful for readers who desire detailed information on the actual method.

Montessori, M. (1967). *The discovery of the child.* (M. J. Costelloe, Trans.) Notre Dame, IN: Fides. There are many books about and by Dr. Montessori that expound her theories. This one gives an overview and so is probably most useful for the beginning teacher.

Pratt, C. (1948). *I learn from children.* New York: Harper & Row. (Reprinted 1990). It is wonderful having this classic of early childhood literature available once again. *Highly recommended.*

Regan, I. M., Mayfield, M. I., & Stange, B. L. (1988). Canadian alternatives in early childhood programs. *International Journal of Early Childhood Education, 20*(1), 3-11. This article reviews the alternatives of ethnically oriented, employer- supported, and parent-child centres.

Stevenson, J. H. (1990). The cooperative preschool model in Canada. In I. M. Doxey (Ed.), *Child care and education: Canadian dimensions.* Scarborough, ON: Nelson. Stevenson reviews the history and philosophy of the cooperative movement in Canada and also provides practical suggestions for operating that kind of school.

Histories of Early Childhood Education

Friendly, M. (1994). *Child care policy in Canada: Putting the pieces together.* Don Mills, ON: Addison-Wesley. Friendly traces the development of child care as a social policy issue, reviewing the evolution of child care in Canada and possibilities for the future.

Pence, A. (principal author) (1992). *Canadian child care in context: Perspectives from the provinces and territories.* Ottawa: Statistics Canada, Health and Welfare, Canada. Individual histories of the development of child care in each province and territory.

Yeates, M., McKenna, D., Warberg, C., & Chandler, K. (1994). *Administering early childhood settings: The Canadian perspective* (2nd ed). Don Mills, ON: Maxwell Macmillan Canada. The authors review milestones in social policy development in Canada along with the roles of the various levels of government.

Dealing Effectively with Stress

Borysenko, J., with Rothstein, L. (1987). *Minding the body, mending the mind.* New York: Bantam Books. This book is filled with practical techniques for reducing tension and regaining a sense of stability and peace. Highly recommended.

Early Childhood Directors' Association. (1983). Survival kit for directors. St. Paul, MN: Toys 'n Things Press (distributor). The Survival Kit singles out specific problems, and then explains step by step how the difficulty was solved. Highly recommended for its positive approach to problem solving and stress reduction.

Jorde, P. (1982). *Avoiding burnout: Strategies for managing time, space, and people in early childhood education.* Washington, DC: Acropolis Books. This is a wonderful, relevant book stuffed with ideas for managing one's life as a teacher and as a human being. *Highly recommended.*

Miller, L. H., & Smith, A. D. (1993). *The stress solution: An action plan to manage the stress in your life.* New York: Pocket Books. A personal audit is included along with down-to-earth suggestions for reducing harmful tension.

Shafer, M. (1982). *Life after stress.* New York: Plenum Press. This sensible, very good book provides matter-of-fact advice about how to deal with stress—identifying it, resisting it, and coping with it when it happens. *Highly recommended.*

For the Advanced Student

Bradburn, E. (1989). *Margaret McMillan: Portrait of a pioneer.* London: Routledge. If you want to be inspired by an example of an amazing woman, track this book down. *Highly recommended.*

Cochran, M. (Ed.). (1993). *International handbook of child care policies and programs.* Westport, CT: Greenwood Press. This book provides quick overviews of early childhood education in 29 countries, including Canada, the United States, and various African and Latino countries. It often takes so long to compile this kind of information that it is out of date before it goes to press, but this volume is satisfyingly up-to-date.

Doherty-Derkowski, G. (1995). *Quality matters: Excellence in early childhood programs.* Don Mills, ON: Addison-Wesley. This book provides a comprehensive definition of quality backed up with major research findings regarding the relationship between the child's well-being and the overall quality of the program.

Lehrer, P. M., & Woolfolk, R. L. (Eds.). (1993). *Principles and practice of stress management* (2nd ed.). New York: Guilford Press. This book presents numerous, effective methods for alleviating stress that are described by authorities in their fields. *Highly recommended.*

Spodek, B., & Brown, P. C. (1993). Curriculum alternatives in early childhood education: A historical perspective. In B. Spodek (Ed.), *Handbook of research on the education of young children.* New York: Macmillan. Spodek reviews the history of early childhood education by identifying various educational models as they have waxed and waned.

Relevant Journals

Child Care Information Exchange. P.O. Box 2891, Redmond, Washington 98073. Filled with timely, practical articles, CCIE has bridged a gap in the literature on how to work in and operate child care centres successfully.

❧2 *What Makes a Good Day for Children?*

Have you ever wondered . . .

What to reply when a friend says your job is really just baby-sitting?

Whether early education makes any difference?

What a good program should include?

Why people are so excited about something called *Reggio Emilia*?

. . . If you have, the material in the following pages will help you.

In the evaluation of the dominant moods of any historical period it is important to hold fast to the fact that there are always islands of self-sufficient order—on farms and in castles, in homes, studies, and cloisters—where sensible people manage to live relatively lusty and decent lives: as moral as they must be, as free as they may be, and as masterful as they can be. If we but knew it, this elusive arrangement is happiness.

Erik Erikson

No doubt the reader is anxious to press on to discussions of discipline or eating problems or teaching children to share—these are valid concerns of all teachers of young children. However, it seems wise to take time first for an overview of whether early education is effective and what should go into a good day for young children. What elements should be included when planning the overall curriculum? Once these elements are clearly in mind, we can turn to a consideration of more specific problems and recommendations.

❧ Can Early Education Make A Difference?

For more than two decades, research on approaches to early childhood education has sought to investigate the effectiveness of various kinds of programs in changing the behaviour and enhancing the development of young children. The results of these investigations have been at times discouraging and at times heartening. On one hand the Westinghouse Report (Cicerelli, Evans, & Schiller, 1969), the Hawkridge study (Hawkridge, Chalupsky, & Roberts, 1968), and a report by Abt Associates (Stebbins et al., 1977) found little evidence of persistent, across-program change on measures of intellectual ability.

If IQ tests are to be accepted as the sole indicator of valuable changes that can result from early education, then these investigators are quite correct. Early childhood programs have not been shown to produce measurable, long-term (continuing beyond the fourth grade) changes in the intelligence quotients of children attending such programs.

However, if some additional measures of school and life success are taken into account, research now indicates that early education intervention can and *does* make a significant difference. For example, it has turned out that the young adults who participated in some experimental programs carried out in the 1960s repeated fewer grades while in school, and fewer of them spent time in classes for the educable mentally retarded.

It is important to know about the results of such studies because most members of the general public, including parents and legislators, are still uninformed about the potential value of early education and persist in seeing it as "just babysitting." If we are tired of this misguided point of view, we need to have the results of these studies on the tips of our tongues so that we can explain the value of our work with young children to those who need to be better informed about it.

The first of these retrospective studies was published by Irving Lazar (Lazar & Darlington, 1978, 1982; Lazar, Hubbell, Murray, Rosche, & Royce, 1977). Additional studies of the Perry Preschool Project detailed by Schweinhart, Barnes, and Weikart in *Significant Benefits: The High/Scope Perry Preschool Study Through Age 27* (1993), by Gray, Ramsey, and Klaus, in *From 3 to 20* (1982), and by McKey and colleagues (1985), who reviewed 210 Head Start studies, have supported and enriched these findings. More recently, the work of Doherty-Derkowski (1995) has emphasized the positive contribution *quality* group day care can make to the child's well-being and development. Moreover, in a study of high-risk premature babies, the benefits of intensive early education were also confirmed (Infant Health and Development Program, 1990).

Lazar's Consortium Study (Lazar et al., 1982) followed up on a number of infant and preschool programs (including work by Gray and Weikart) that took place in the 1960s. These were special, high-quality programs that used both experimental and control groups and drew their subjects from families of the poor. Members of each experimental group participated in a preschool program while their similar control companions did not have that advantage.

At the time of the follow-up, the questions Lazar and his coworkers (1977, 1978, 1982) wanted to answer about both groups were "Now that these children are either in their teens or early twenties, what has become of them?" "How have they turned out?" "Did early intervention make a difference in their lives?" To answer these questions, each project traced as many of the experimental and control children as possible, retested them on the Wechsler Intelligence Test, and, among many questions, asked whether they had ever repeated a grade in school or been placed in a class for educable mentally retarded children (an EMR classroom).*

An analysis of the intelligence test material (both current and prior tests) led the investigators to conclude that "although evidence showed that early education can produce significant increases in IQ (over a control group) which last for up to three years after the child leaves the program . . . it appears that the effect . . . is probably not permanent" (1977, pp. 19, 20).

The information related to grade retention and placement in EMR classrooms was much more encouraging, in part because of its implications for saving public moneys (Barnett & Escobar, 1990; Schweinhart, Barnes, & Weikart, 1993), but also because of what the findings mean in terms of human happiness.

Even though these data (shown in Figures 2.1 and 2.2) vary considerably between programs (probably because different school districts have different policies on having children repeat grades), they clearly indicate that early education can reduce the rate of repeating grades for low-income children, thereby preventing much humiliation and loss of self-esteem. And if repetition of a grade is humiliating to a youngster, one can only surmise how bad it feels to be placed in a classroom for cognitively delayed children. Here, once again, the Lazar data provide convincing evidence that early education is worthwhile, since substantially fewer project children were found to have been placed in such classes.

The research on children in the Perry Preschool Project carried these studies even further. Begun in 1962, that research is still continuing, and the data have been consistent over more than three decades of investigation. Table 2.1 illustrates the substantial differences between the experimental group of children who had experienced the benefits of a good preschool program combined with home visiting and a similar group of children who had not had those experiences (Weikart, 1990). Note that fewer of the Perry Preschool children had been in trouble with the law, more of them had graduated from high school, and more of them had jobs after graduation. The most recent data, published in 1993 (Schweinhart & Weikart), indicates that this trend toward self-sufficiency

---

*For a more complete interpretation and explanation of this study, the reader should refer to the original reports, which are well worth reading.

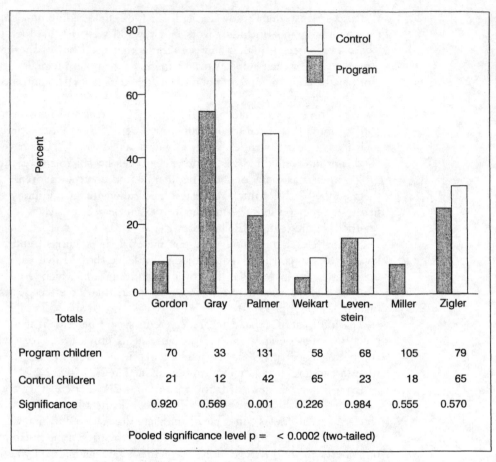

Figure 2.1   Percent of program and control children held back a grade
Source: From I. Lazar, V. R. Hubbell, H. Murray, M. Rosche, and J. Royce, *Summary Report: The Persistence of Preschool Effects* (Washington, DC: U.S. Department of Health, Education, and Welfare, 1977), OHDS 78-30129.

was continuing as the group neared age 27. They continued to have fewer arrests and significantly higher incomes than did those in the control group, and many more of them owned homes. When these results are translated into taxpayer dollars saved, it amounts to about $76,077 (1992 U.S. dollars) per participant—a return of $7.16 for every dollar originally invested in the preschool program.

The two studies discussed were selected because they are the most widely publicized pieces of research on this subject, but the reader should realize that they are but two of many studies that now support the value of well-planned early education for children who come from families of low income.*

---

*For additional information, the reader should refer to Howes (1986) or Cotton and Conklin (1989).

Table 2.1   Summary of the results of the Perry Preschool Project[*]

	Experimental Group (%)	Control Group (%)
In Education		
Classified as mentally retarded	15	35
Completed high school	67	49
Attended college or job-training programs	38	21
In Employment		
Hold jobs	50	32
Support themselves or are supported by spouse	45	25
Satisfied with work	42	26
In the Community		
Arrested for criminal acts	31	51
Birth rate[†]	64*	117*
Public assistance	18	32

*Age of subjects was 19 years.
†Birth rates are per 100 women.

Source: From Weikart, D. (1990). *Quality Preschool Programs: A Long-term Social Investment*. New York: Ford Foundation (p. 7). Used by permission.

❧ Underlying Philosophy of This Book

Despite these encouraging results, there remains a tantalizing question the research did not answer. It has not told us exactly which ingredients in these programs have what effects on children, since examination reveals that equally successful programs differ in many respects in their philosophy, teaching techniques, and program content (Berrueta-Clement et al., 1984; Chattin-McNichols, 1981; Schweinhart, Weikart, & Larner, 1986). Apparently, as long as the teachers have made a commitment to the program (Weikart, 1971) and the educational intention of the program is clearly defined, a variety of instructional approaches can be successful in producing a good day for children.

The Whole Child uses an eclectic approach that makes use of several theoretical bases: the application of behaviour modification strategies when appropriate, the application of Piagetian principles as expressed by the *constructivist, developmental interactionist approach,* and the application of the philosophical approach exemplified by the schools of Reggio Emilia. All of these approaches offer material of great value in relation to understanding and teaching young children.

Uses and Values of Behaviour Modification

The term *behaviour modification* tends to bring scowls to the faces of many teachers who object to the potential for manipulation inherent in that approach. However, it is impor-

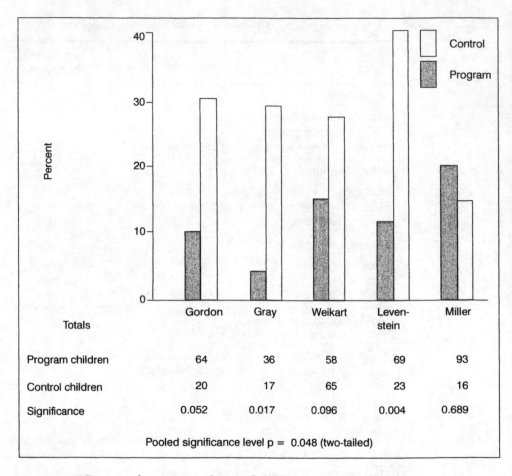

Figure 2.2   Percent of program and control children in special education
Source: From I. Lazar, V. R. Hubbell, H. Murray, M. Rosche, and J. Royce, *Summary Report: The Persistence of Preschool Effects* (Washington, DC: U.S. Department of Health, Education, and Welfare, 1977), OHDS 78-30129.

tant to understand its positive value as well. Learning theorists who practise behaviour modification have accumulated a great deal of carefully documented research that substantiates their claims that this approach, which rewards desirable behaviour and discourages undesirable actions, can be a powerful avenue for teaching (Thomas, 1992; Witt, Elliott, & Gresham, 1988). It has proven its usefulness particularly in work with children with a variety of disabilities (Bailey & Wolery, 1992; Berkson, 1993).

Behaviour modification theorists stress the importance of the influence of environment on behaviour. They maintain that children learn various behaviours as a result of experiencing pleasant or unpleasant outcomes or reinforcements. Pleasant outcomes or rewards such as teacher attention, praise, or candy tend to cause the behaviour to persist,

❧ *No matter what philosophy is involved, warm, caring relationships are the cornerstones of all good early childhood programs.*

while unpleasant negative consequences such as scolding or writing the child's name on the blackboard discourage it. If the child receives neither positive nor negative reinforcement, then he will gradually abandon the behaviour. Critics complain that this approach to human development emphasizes the role of external rewards and sees the child as a passive recipient of stimuli that regulate behaviour rather than as a human being capable of initiating novel ideas and behaviour.

It is true that the cut-and-dried, deliberately orchestrated manipulation of behaviour that might be possible if such a program were carried out in its purest form is repugnant, but it is also true that all teachers use this technique constantly and extensively whether they realize it or not. Every smile, every frown, every positive or negative bit of attention the child receives either encourages or discourages future behaviour. Therefore, rather than blindly condemning such theory, why not become aware of how often we employ such strategies on an informal basis and acknowledge their power? To use behaviour modification effectively it is not necessary to agree with Skinner (1974) that positive or negative reinforcement is the only activator of behaviour. Indeed, it seems impossible to use learning theory satisfactorily to explain how people generate original ideas or how they formulate language patterns they have not heard before. In the author's opinion, learning theory is simply a useful tool that explains a great deal, but not all, of why human beings behave as they do. As such, it cannot be ignored.

Uses and Values of Piagetian, Constructivist Theory

The reader will find that the work of the great theorist and investigator Jean Piaget is referred to again and again throughout this volume. His more than half-century of research into the developmental stages and characteristics of children's cognitive processes is invaluable, as are both his emphasis on the importance of dynamic interaction between the child and the environment as the child *constructs* what he knows for himself, and his emphasis on the significance of play as a medium for learning (DeVries & Kohlberg, 1990).

However, many scholars and teachers, including the author, are not satisfied with restricting themselves solely to Piagetian constructivist theory because they feel that Piaget did not say enough about social relationships, creativity, or emotional health. Piaget's primary interest was the investigation of children's thought processes. Although we must incorporate his work, we cannot limit ourselves to only his theory in a text of this scope.

A point of view that is closely related to Piagetian constructivism but is more comprehensive is the developmental-interactionist approach of the Bank Street program described by Biber (1981, 1984). It sees children as developing human beings in whom knowing about things (the intellectual self) combines with feeling about them (the emotional self). In this point of view, the impetus for growth lies in part within the maturing individual but also occurs in part as a result of the interaction between the child and the environment and people to whom the child relates.

This interaction is important because the child is regarded as being an active participant in his own growth. He learns by constructing and reconstructing what he knows as he encounters a variety of experiences and people that widen and enrich his knowledge. The teacher's role is one of guiding, questioning, and enabling—not just stuffing the child with an assortment of facts and rewards for good behaviour.

Because the child is a complex, interacting being composed of many attributes and aspects, we must see teaching as stimulating and enhancing the development of all these aspects, not just the cognitive one. That is why this book concentrates on the five selves of the child rather than on specific topics such as art or science. It is an attempt to shift the attention of the teacher to what the child *is,* and what he needs from the learning environment in order to realize his tremendous potential. Only when this is done can it be truly said that we are educating the whole child.

New Contributions from Reggio Emilia

In addition to drawing on the behaviour modification and constructivist points of view, the current edition of this book recognizes that a newer approach to early childhood education is gaining prominence. Ever since 1987, when the *100 Languages of Children* exhibit began its still-continuing tour of the United States, interest has been growing in some remarkable Italian schools situated in the city of Reggio Emilia. These schools enable very young children to explore and express their ideas through an astonishing array of media. Their productions, while lovely, are not only aesthetically pleasing, but they also represent a level of creative thought and problem-solving ability that goes far beyond North American expectations of what young children can do. These results are causing many North American teachers to reassess our current approaches to early education.*

The teachers of Reggio Emilia are confident about the preschool child's abilities (Gandini, 1993; Rinaldi, 1993). They see him as strong, competent, capable of constructing his own thoughts, and having great potential to offer to the world. In this approach the teacher becomes a compass that may point the child in a particular direction, and education is seen as an ever-developing process that cannot be predetermined because it emerges bit by bit.

The children's centres at Reggio Emilia are places where children and teachers interact—listening and talking with each other—to explore subjects in depth by exchanging ideas and trying those ideas out. Teachers select an aspect of the children's interests to develop further—an aspect that presents problems for them to consider and solve (or, as Reggian teachers put it, "provokes" the children into thought). A particular interest may be pursued in depth over a number of months, depending on how intrigued the children become with the topic.

The results of these joint investigations are then transformed by the children into visible products that communicate what they have found out to other people. As the staff members often say, "You don't know it until you can express it." Because the children are too young to write, the staff encourages them to express what they know by using all sorts of other languages. It might be the language of paint, or clay, or cardboard structures, or concoctions of bent wire bedecked with tissue paper, or shadow plays.

Canadian early childhood programs already espouse many ideas basic to the Reggian philosophy: parent involvement, fostering creativity, learning by doing, enquiry-based, child-centred, hands-on, cooperative learning, and so forth. But we are also tantalized by the evidence of the exceptional abilities demonstrated by these young Italian children, particularly because observers report that it is really the children themselves who are doing the work and accomplishing it without strain. It is my hope that inclusion of the Reggio approach in *The Whole Child* will encourage the application of many of its principles in our own work with children in this country.

❧ *Basic Premises of This Book*

Besides advocating that a curriculum be provided for every self, there are a number of additional basic premises on which this book is based. The first is that the purpose of education is to increase competence and mastery in all aspects of the developing self. It is much more important to teach children to cope by equipping them with skills than to stuff them full of facts. Confidence in their coping ability is what underlies children's sense of self-worth. Skills empower children.

The second premise is that physical and emotional health are absolutely fundamental to the well-being of children. Any program that ignores that fact is building its curriculum on a foundation of sand.

---

*Space permits only a brief overview of the Reggio approach in this chapter. Additional information is provided at appropriate points throughout the book.

The third is that children learn most easily by means of actual, involving experiences with people and activities. This is best accomplished in an open, carefully planned environment where children must take responsibility and make decisions for themselves and where they have ample opportunity to learn through play.

The fourth premise is that children pass through various stages as they develop. Piaget has, of course, thoroughly demonstrated this in regard to intellectual development, but it has been heavily documented for the other selves as well (Allen & Marotz, 1990; Brittain, 1979; Gesell, Halverson, Thompson, & Ilg, 1940; Shotwell, Wolf, & Gardner, 1979; Wickstrom, 1983).

It is important to realize that having a general sense of these landmark stages in mind can be both an asset and a liability for the teacher. Such knowledge is an asset if it fosters the development of activities and expectations that are known to be generally appropriate for a particular age. On the other hand, knowledge of developmental stages can be a liability if that information is used to blindly restrict what is offered to the children to encourage their development. The most sensible approach is to remain aware of the developmental level of the children we teach and then provide education that fits that level while encouraging children to reach a little beyond it (Vygotsky, 1978).

The fifth premise is that children do not exist in isolation as they develop. As Bronfenbrenner (1979) and Vygotsky (1978) remind us, we are all surrounded by ever-widening worlds of family, community, and the wider world—all of which influence the direction and degree of our growth.

The final premise is that children need time to be children. The purpose of preprimary education and child care should not be to pressure and urge youngsters on to the next step in a hurried way. The current term, *hothousing,* well describes the effect of such forced learning on the unfortunate children who experience it. Recent research now provides evidence that placing academic pressure on preschool children is a precursor to negative attitudes toward school and decreased creativity in kindergarten and academic accomplishments in later grades (Hyson & Hirsh-Pasek, 1990; Marcon, 1992, 1994a, 1994b).

Children need time and personal space in which to grow. They need time to be themselves—to do nothing, to stand and watch, to repeat again what they did before; in short, they need time to live *in* their childhood rather than *through* it. If we offer the young children we teach rich and appropriate learning opportunities combined with enough time for them to enjoy and experience those opportunities to the fullest, we will be enhancing that era of childhood, not violating it.

❧ Putting Premises into Practice: Planning a Good Day for Children

Good Human Relationships Are a Fundamental Ingredient of a Good Day

All good programs are built on the foundation of sound human relationships. Warmth and empathic understanding have been shown to be effective means of influencing young children's positive adjustment to school (Truax & Tatum, 1966). It is apparent that genuine caring about the children and about other adults in the program is fundamental to success.

For warmth and personal contact to flourish, the day must be planned and paced so there are numerous opportunities for person-to-person, one-to-one encounters. In practical terms this means that groups must be kept small and that the ratio of adults to children must be as high as possible. Many occasions must also be provided where the children move freely about, making personal choices and generating individual contacts. Such arrangements permit numerous interludes in which informal learning experiences can be enjoyed and human caring can be expressed. The moments may be as fleeting as a quick hug when the teacher ties a pair of trailing shoelaces or as extended as a serious discussion of where babies come from. It is the *quality* of individualized, personal caring and the chance to talk together that are significant (Stipek, Daniels, Galluzzo, & Milburn, 1992).

Parents Must Be Included as Part of the Life of the School

The day is past when parents were expected to pay their bill but leave their children at the centre's door. Of course, cooperative schools have long demonstrated the feasibility of including the family in the school experience, but today we can also point to mounting research that confirms that inclusion of the parent in the educational process, whether in home tutoring programs or the school itself, results in longer-lasting educational gains for the child (Garber & Heber, 1981; Gray et al., 1982; Levenstein, 1988; Mallory, 1993; Powell & Sigal, 1991; Swick, 1989). Parent inclusion is also a fundamental cornerstone of the Reggio approach, in which parents participate in day-to-day interactions, discussions of relevant issues, excursions, and celebrations (Gandini, 1993).

Nowadays, parent involvement goes far beyond attending parent education meetings and open houses. Parents serve as indispensable volunteers in the classroom, where they do everything from tutoring to sharing their cultural backgrounds with the youngsters. They serve on powerful advisory boards, raise money, and provide ideas and criticism about the curriculum.

Rather than feeling threatened by this vigorous interest, wise teachers do all they can to get to know the children's parents well in order to use their talents most effectively. There is no more valuable way to widen everyone's horizons than by strengthening the link between home and school. Chapters 7, 8, and 14 provide more detailed suggestions of practical ways to welcome parents into the life of the school.

A Good Program Must Be Developmentally Appropriate

Developmentally appropriate means that the learning activities planned for the children are placed at the correct level for their age and are also suited to individual children's tastes and abilities. This fact is important, because if the material is at the right developmental level, the children will be drawn to it and want to learn about it (Bredekamp, 1987).

On the other hand, when children are pushed too far ahead of their levels and the curriculum is unsuited to their abilities, it's like pushing them into deep water before they can swim—they're likely to dread the water and avoid it when they can.

At this early stage of schooling it is crucial for children to decide that learning is something to be pursued with verve, not that it is difficult and anxiety-provoking. For this reason

❧   *Part of the art of teaching (and the challenge!) is being able to meet many different needs at the same time (and it's only ten o'clock in the morning!).*

it is vital that teachers have a good grasp of the developmental characteristics of children at various ages, understand how they are likely to progress as they grow, and plan the curriculum to stimulate that growth without making it so difficult that children give up in despair.

A Good Program Is Individualized

The teacher must see every youngster not only in terms of what she knows in general about child development but also in terms of what that particular child is like developmentally and culturally. This is the real art of teaching—being able to clothe overall bare-bones educational goals in the raiment of individual children's abilities, needs, interests, and pleasures. Fortunately the small size and intimacy of preschool groups make it possible for teachers to know each youngster well and to plan with particular individuals in mind.

A Simple Test to Determine Whether the Curriculum Is Individualized

There are four questions the teacher can use to determine whether the curriculum is individualized:

1. Are there some recent instances in which the curriculum was based on a child's specific interests?
2. Can examples be cited in which curriculum plans were changed because a child revealed an unanticipated interest or enthusiasm during the day?

3. Can examples be identified in which a child was deliberately provided with opportunities to learn what evaluations had indicated that he or she especially needed to know?

4. Are there recent examples in which the children had opportunities to perceive and *value* the cultural and physical diversity of other youngsters in the group?

A Good Program Honours Diversity in Its Many Forms

Ever since its original publication in 1973, *The Whole Child* has included an entire chapter advocating cross-cultural education and another on inclusion of children who have special needs into the preschool group. Since this is the case I will content myself here with reminding the reader that everyone's experience is enriched when children from a variety of backgrounds are included in the school.

A Good Program Uses Reasonable and Authentic Methods of Assessment to Find out More about the Children

Although space does not permit an extensive discussion of assessment methods in a beginning text, even teachers who are just starting out need to know that assessing young children is a risky and problematic business (Meisels, Steele, & Quinn-Leering, 1993). At best, assessments can identify skills, needs, and promising potentials of such young children—at worst they can utilize totally inappropriate methods of evaluation (Hills, 1992).

Perhaps the most desirable way to think of assessment for the majority of young children is as an opportunity to record growth and deepen teachers' and parents' insights about particular children. There are a variety of ways that teachers can generate such records. These include information contributed by families, simple checklists based on developmental charts, snapshots or even videotapes of children's special accomplishments such as block structures or other creations, an occasional painting, and weekly anecdotal records citing events or interactions related to the child that the teacher feels are significant (Hendrick, 1994; McAfee & Leong, 1994). Remember, records are most helpful when they are begun early in the year so that progress is noted as it occurs.

When more comprehensive assessments are needed it is best to refer the family to someone who specializes in that area. See chapter 9 for a discussion about how to make effective referrals.

There Should Be a Balance Between Self-Selection and Teacher Direction—Both Approaches Are Valuable

Value of Self-Selection

The idea that young children can be trusted to choose educational experiences for themselves that will benefit them goes all the way back in educational theory to Jean Jacques Rousseau and John Dewey. At present this concept is being used at Reggio Emilia, as well as continuing its tenure in the majority of Canadian child care centres.

Philosophical support for the value of self-selection of activities comes from such disparate sources as the self-selection feeding experiments of Clara Davis (1939) and the psychoanalytic theory of Erikson, who speaks of the preschool child's "sudden, violent wish to have a choice" (1950, p. 252). The virtue of self-selection is that it fosters independence and builds within the child responsibility for making his own decisions. It also provides an excellent way to individualize the curriculum because each child is free to pursue his own interests and to suit himself when he is free to choose.

But self-selection needs to be balanced with opportunities for group experiences, too. Some of those experiences are small, casual, and informal, as when a group of interested children gather around the teacher to talk about where the snow went. Some, such as large group times (chapter 18) and mealtimes (chapter 3) require more management by the teacher. These more formal situations are essential ingredients in the early childhood program because they provide opportunities to make certain all the children are included in thinking and reasoning activities every day. Without these planned participation times, occasional children might graduate from preschool with a degree in trike riding coupled with a deadly inability to put five words together into a coherent sentence.

The self-selection parts of the program also require careful planning. This point is sometimes overlooked by visitors and beginning student teachers who are most aware of the children circulating freely from one activity to another as their interests dictate. But this appearance of openness and freedom can be deceptive. In actuality, the available choices have been carefully thought through in advance by the teacher, and every activity in the room is there because it provides educational experiences for one or another of the child's selves.

Of course, one would not want the use of a plan to be interpreted so rigorously that there is no room for spontaneity. There are times when the marvellous welling up of an idea or activity occurs, and these teachable moments are to be sought after and treasured—but this does not happen all the time. Nor does reliance on such events assure that every important area will be covered, that necessary goals will be achieved, or that the needs of individual children will be considered. *Only planning coupled with consistent evaluation can accomplish these objectives.*

A Good Program Should Be Comprehensive

An aspect of planning that deserves special consideration is that the curriculum should be comprehensive in coverage. As mentioned earlier, a valuable way to think about this is to picture the child as being composed of a number of selves: the physical self, the emotional self, the social self, the creative self, and the cognitive self. This book is based on this division of the child into selves, because experience has shown that various aspects of the curriculum fall rather neatly under these headings and that the five selves succeed in covering the personality of the child. ·

The physical self includes not only large and fine muscle development but also the handling of routines, since such things as eating, resting, and toileting contribute much to physical comfort and well-being. For the emotional self we consider ways to increase and sustain mental health, to use discipline to foster self-control, to cope with aggression, and to foster self-esteem. Included for the social self are ways to build social concern and kindliness, learning to enjoy work, and learning to value the cultures and abilities of other people. The creative self covers the areas of self-expression through the use of art materials and creativity as expressed in play and applied in thought. Finally, the cognitive, or intellectual, self is considered in terms of language development and the development of generalized and specific reasoning abilities. This last self is the newest one to receive intensive consideration and analysis in early childhood education, and much remains to be learned in this area.

Formulating an Effective Daily Plan

One way of assuring that the curriculum is both comprehensive and purposeful is to discipline oneself by filling out the Curriculum Analysis and Planning Chart each week (shown in Figure 2.3) to make certain there is something deliberately planned for each self of the child every day to purposely enhance his growth.

In the space where Activity is specified, the name of the activity, for example, "clay," should be written in. The specific purpose that day for offering clay might be "to relieve aggressive feelings." If so, clay would best fit the Emotional category. Or, if the primary purpose is to provide the materials as an opportunity for creative self-expression, then the clay activity would be listed in the Creative space.

Another more in-depth way of planning the curriculum involves the use of a daily plan wherein the provision of more detail is possible. An example of part of such a plan is included in Figure 2.4. The theme was selected to combine learning about the spring season with the needs of a hospitalized classmate.

While I would not advocate such detailed planning as a usual thing, the Institute staff has found it helpful for beginning teachers to use because it requires them to think through the purposes of their curriculum carefully. The bonus is that once teachers learn to think this clearly, they not only stop offering educational trash to children but also have no difficulty justifying the educational purposes of the activities to enquiring parents.

Formulating a Longer-Term Plan

Of course, planning needs to extend beyond the day and even the week. There is, however, a difficulty associated with a longer-term approach: formulating a detailed plan far in advance is likely to push teacher and children into a lock-step of unchangeable direction and activity. Sometimes this goes so far as a teacher using a plan from the year or even years before! Convenient as this may be, it destroys the possibility of truly moving with the children's interests as these develop.

A better way of doing extended planning is to anticipate several different directions the children's interest might take. I call these possibilities *pathways,* down which the teacher and children can adventure together. Thinking of several of these keeps the teacher's mind open to possibilities. Indeed, I have heard Amelia Gambetti (1993) say that the advantage of doing so is that when children think of yet another direction to go in, the teacher is better able to respond to the change and accept it more readily.

There are some alternative terms for this kind of topic development, such as *chaining, webbing,* and *project work.* I prefer *pathways* because a pathway has direction to it, but at

Plans for week of:

Children's Interests

Part of self being developed	Physical: Large motor	Physical: Fine motor	Emotional: Understanding feelings	Social	Multi-cultural	Nonsexist	Creative	Cognitive: Mental ability	Cognitive: Language
MON Activity									
Purpose									
TUE Activity									
Purpose									
WED Activity									
Purpose									
THU Activity									
Purpose									
FRI Activity									
Purpose									

Figure 2.3 Curriculum analysis and planning chart

Long-Term Interest: How Animals Live

Date: 5/11/94　　　　　　　　　　　　　　　　　　　　**Age of Children: 4½-5**

Self	Physical: Large Muscle	Physical: Fine Muscle	Emotional: Understanding feelings	Social	Multicultural	Nonsexist	Creative	Cognitive: Mental ability	Cognitive: Language
Activity	Trike ride to family's pond	Catching fish; Setting up aquarium	Hospital play; Discussions of hospital during group time	Make aquarium and get-well notes; Visit child's family	Lunch	Discuss who cares for fish pond	Collaged get-well soon cards; Arrange aquarium	Finding out about goldfish and aquarium	Dictate get-well messages; Listen to books about fish or giving presents
Educational Purpose	Bilateral coordination of legs and arms. Increase fitness and endurance.	Use nets to catch elusive baby goldfish—eye/hand coordination. Embed plants in rocks—dig, hold, press plants down under water.	Play out feelings about hospitals. Cope with worries about friend. Think about how to comfort someone else.	Do something kind for someone else. Do meaningful work. Consider what someone, *not yourself*, would really like for a present. Negotiate who will go to hospital to deliver aquarium. Help bond shy child and her family closer to school.	Food from another culture tastes good (tacos, fruit salad, milk).	Everyone in family takes turns maintaining pond, feeding and caring for fish and plants.	Fosters sense of balance, colour, and design. Use of own ideas and inspirations.	Opportunities for problem solving: What kind of present is practical in a hospital? How can we catch the fish? What can we use to transport them? How can we keep the plants from floating up in the aquarium? Specific Mental Abilities: *Cause/Effect:* What happens to fish out of water? *Common Relations:* Pair real fish and water plants to pictures in fish book. *Facts about goldfish:* They require cool, non-salty water. They can live a long time. There are many kinds: fantails, pop-eyes, etc.	Writing is a useful way to send a message. Reading helps us find out things we want to know. New vocabulary—such as "fins," "scales," "aquarium," etc. Group discussions of putting ideas and plans into words. *Fish stories* Swimmy (Lionni, 1987). *Stories about presents* Ask Mr. Bear (Flack, 1932). No Roses for Harry (Zion, 1958).

W E D N E S D A Y

Note: On this particular day the teacher had several primary educational purposes in mind: She wanted the children to deal with their feelings about hospitals and about their friend's injury; the previous day the children had proposed sending a little fish company and a child volunteered fish from her family's pond—hence the trike ride. The teacher hoped that visiting that particular family would also strengthen home/school bonds for one of the shyer children. She was pleased, also, with the possibilities the children's idea about giving the aquarium presented for being kind to someone else and for figuring out how to solve some interesting problems as well.

Figure 2.4 Daily analysis and planning chart

❥   *Having animals visit is a delightful way to add variety to the program.*

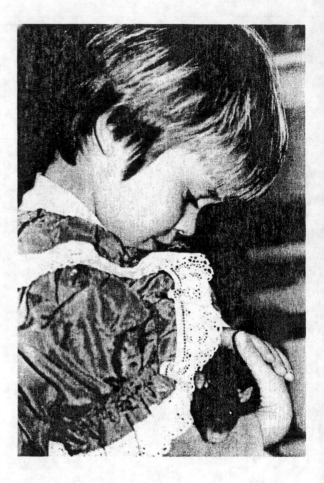

the same time, a pathway can lead to adventure—walkers don't always know at the beginning of the path exactly where they'll end up. The teacher who is truly sensitive to helping children advance down pathways of their true interests cannot predict at the beginning of an investigation where they will end up, either. However, she *can* make certain that along the way there is direction and focus to what the children are doing and that they are provided with opportunities to practise some basic mental ability skills, solve problems, and use a variety of graphic materials to express what they have learned. (For a more in-depth discussion of how to develop enquiry pathways, please refer to chapter 21.)

A Good Program Has Stability and Regularity Combined with Flexibility

Young children need to know what is likely to happen next during the day. This means that the order of events should be generally predictable. Predictability enables the child to prepare mentally for the next event; it makes compliance with routines more likely and helps children feel secure.

At the same time, time schedules and routines should not be allowed to dominate the school. Sometimes this happens because of a strong-minded custodian or cook. I once knew a school where it was necessary for the children to use only half the space from 10:30 until nap time because of the custodian's routine. Sometimes overconformance to time schedules happens because teachers are creatures of habit and simply do not realize that juice and raisins do not have to be served at exactly 9:15. Rather than sticking right to the clock, it is better to maintain an orderly but elastic schedule, where play periods can be extended when those moments occur when the majority of the children are involved in activities that interest them intensely.

A Good Program Has Variety

Children Need Many Different Kinds of Experiences as Well as Changes in Basic Experiences

Research on the effects of stimulus deprivation (Dennis, 1960; Walk, 1981) and early stimulation (White, 1979) has highlighted the value of supplying a variety of experiences even for babies, and variety should certainly be incorporated into a program for young children.

Many teachers think of variety of experience in terms of field trips or covering different topics, such as families or baby animals. But another kind of variety that should also be considered is variety in everyday basic learning experiences. What a difference there is between the school that has the same pet rat and bowl of goldfish all year and the school that first raises a rabbit, then borrows a brood hen, and next has two snakes as visitors. Lack of variety is also apparent in schools that offer the omnipresent easel as their major "art" experience or others that set out all the blocks at the beginning of the year and leave it at that.

Children Should Be Offered Various Levels of Difficulty in Activity Materials

If the children's centre combines age levels during the day so that three-, four-, and five-year-olds play together, it is important to provide materials that are challenging for all the ages within the group. Teachers need to be especially careful to offer materials that are genuinely interesting to the older four-year-olds and young five-year-olds. A dearth of stimulating, fresh curricular activities is the most common cause of a posse of children galloping through block areas and housekeeping corners, spreading destruction as they go.

Even when the group is composed of predominantly one-age children, the teacher will still need to provide a variety of activities for different developmental levels because there is so much difference, for example, between what younger and older four-year-olds can achieve.

The curriculum not only should offer a variety of levels of difficulty every day but also *should become more challenging and move from simple to more complex activities as the year progresses* and as the children mature and gain competence. The curriculum should not look the same in May as it did in September.

❧   *A dearth of stimulating things to do is the most common cause of posses of children galloping through the school, spreading destruction as they go.*

Children Need Changes of Pace During the Day to Avoid Monotony and Fatigue and to Maintain a Balance of Kinds of Experiences

The most obvious way to incorporate variation of pace is to plan for it in the overall schedule. For example, a quiet snack can be followed by a dance period.

Additional opportunities to meet individual temperamental requirements of children must be allowed for. The quieter, less gregarious child needs to have places available where he can retreat from the herd, and the more active youngster needs the escape hatch of moving about when the group has sat beyond his limit of endurance.

Some kinds of programs appear to have special problems associated with pacing. For example, some programs attempt to cram so much into such a short time (playtime, story time, snack, lunch, special activity time, not to mention visits from the psychologist, field trips, and special visitors) that the day goes by in a headlong rush of children being hurried from one thing to the next without the opportunity to savour any experience richly and fully. At the other extreme, some day care programs offer a variety of activities and changes of pace during the morning but turn the children loose in the play yard for three interminable hours in the afternoon. Such consistent conditions of hurried stress or unalleviated boredom, unless analysed thoughtfully and modified, can ultimately have only a deleterious effect on children.

Learning Must Be Based on Actual Experience and Participation

Anyone who has ever taken a young child to the market knows how strong his impulse is to touch and smell and taste everything he encounters. Although occasionally inconvenient, the child's behaviour illustrates a fundamental fact of early childhood learning: children learn best when they are allowed to use all their senses as avenues of learning. Participatory experience is an essential ingredient in preschool education. This means that the curriculum of the preschool must be based on real experiences with real things rather than limited to the verbal discussions and pictures commonly (though not necessarily ideally) used when teaching older children.

Because educators ranging from Piaget to Vygotsky and Reggio Emilia have emphasized the value of real experience as being fundamental to successful education since the turn of the century, one might think that this principle need not be reiterated. However, the persistent influx of word-oriented rather than action-oriented teaching materials on display in the commercial exhibits of most conferences on early childhood and the fact that these materials continue to sell make it evident that this point must be stated very clearly: Young children learn best when they can manipulate material, experiment, try things out, and talk about what is happening as it takes place. Talking without doing is largely meaningless for a child of tender years.

Play Is an Indispensable Avenue for Learning

Another long-held value in early childhood education is an appreciation of play as a facilitator of learning. Although research is still lacking in this area, evidence is beginning to accumulate (Bergen, 1988; Pellegrini & Boyd, 1993) that lends support to something generations of teachers of young children have learned through experience. Teachers who have watched young children at play know the intent, purposeful seriousness they bring to this activity. Play is the medium used by children to translate experience into something internally meaningful to them. Piaget (1962) agrees with teachers and maintains that children use play as an important symbolic activity, but it serves many purposes beyond this function. Play clarifies concepts, provides emotional relief, facilitates social development, and creates periods of clearly satisfying delight. Sometimes teachers see its value only as a teacher-controlled, structured experience used to achieve a specific educational end (role playing after visiting the fire station, for example), but it is crucial that there be ample time in the curriculum for self-initiated play.

The Program Should Be Evaluated Daily

Once a curriculum is planned and put into action, it is also necessary to evaluate the results, and these evaluations need to go beyond such statements as "My gosh! What a terrible day!" or "Things went well!"

Instead, teachers should ask themselves:

How did the day go? Were there any hitches and glitches?

If so, how can I rearrange things so they move more smoothly for the children next time?

What did the children learn today?

How are the children with special problems getting along?

What special interests emerged that I can respond to when planning the curriculum?

And finally, the most valuable question of all:

How can I help each child experience success tomorrow?

Thoughtful answers to questions like these will go a long way toward helping build a more effective curriculum for the children as the year moves on.

The Day Should Be Pleasurable

Probably the most significant value a teacher can convey to children is the conviction that school is satisfying, fun, and that they want to return the next day. This point has been deliberately left until last to give it special emphasis, in case the reader, having waded through the other elements of a good program, has begun to feel bogged down with the sobersided responsibilities of running a good program for young children.

The experience not only should be pleasurable for the children, but it also should be a joy for the adults. Young children have their trying moments, but they are also delightful. They see the world in a clear-sighted way that can lend fresh perspective to the eyes of their teacher, and their tendency to live for the present moment is a lesson to us all. Pleasure, enjoyment, humour, and laughter should be very much a part of each preschool day.

♋ Putting the Elements Together

What Does a Day Look Like That Combines These Basic Elements into a Coherent Whole?

The setting is established with children in mind: furniture is scaled to the right size, the building has easy access to the yard, and there is a general air of orderly, yet easygoing comfort and beauty that does not put people off because of its newness or perfection. This kind of atmosphere goes a long way toward making parents feel at home and part of the school family.

When it is necessary to form groups, the children are formed into small gatherings. Story hours and snack tables of four or five children and a grown-up, for example, should be the rule in order to facilitate conversation and participation. (My staff refers to this as Hendrick's law: "The larger the group, the smaller the learning.") The daily pace is easy enough and the staff unharrassed enough that there are many intimate little opportunities for teachers to talk with the children individually.

There is a reasonably repetitious scheduling of basic experiences planned to provide alternate periods of quiet and active experience. These periods include a morning welcome for each child as she arrives, a snack in the morning and afternoon, and lunch and rest in the middle of the day.

In between these landmark times many interesting events take place. These are developed with individual and group goals in mind, and they should include, every day, some activity that is creative, another that is messy, something that is new, something that requires the children to think, some carefully varied activities that foster motor development, some opportunity for the children to engage in meaningful work, and many chances to use books, pictures, poetry, and to listen and be listened to. Intertwined among these activities lie all the situations that the teacher must seize and use as they arise to develop social learning and emotional strength in the children.

For at least one generous block of time during the morning and afternoon, materials and possibilities are set out, and the child is expected to take the responsibility of selecting for himself what he wants to pursue. During this time the teacher moves from one place to another as the occasion demands, talking first with one child, helping another group settle a fight, and getting out a piece of equipment for a third. Another part of the day involves more focused participation but should not be cast in the mould of fifteen children doing the same thing in one large group at the same time.

If staffing and weather permit, children have access to inside and outdoors as they prefer. Failing this, large muscle activities are available indoors, and small muscle and more cognitive and creative materials are available outdoors to avoid the "recess" concept so common in elementary school.

This, then, is the overall framework of a sound preschool day. It provides opportunities for children to learn all kinds of things and to enjoy both the process and the satisfaction of the results. It includes many diverse things and many diverse people. The miracle of a good school is that, somehow, these all go together to produce a good day for both children and staff.

❧ Summary

After more than two decades of research, the accumulation of evidence indicates that early intervention in the form of quality education for young children and their families can make a difference.

The Whole Child advocates the use of three theoretical bases as the philosophical foundation for teaching young children: behaviour modification, Piagetian constructivism, and the pedagogical theory exemplified by the schools of Reggio Emilia.

Certain elements are emerging that appear to be common to the majority of effective early childhood programs. These include good human relationships, parent inclusion, and a curriculum that is developmentally, individually, and culturally appropriate. A good program uses reasonable and authentic methods of assessment, incorporates a balance of self-selection and teacher direction, educates all of the child's five selves, and is based on both daily and longer-term planning.

A good program for young children is basically orderly but also flexible; it provides for variety in experience, levels of difficulty, and pacing; and it is based on the principles that learning should be the result of actual experience, that play is a significant mode of learning, and, above all, that the centre should be a place of joy for both children and staff.

Questions and Activities

1. *Problem:* Suppose a parent said to you after touring the school, "My heavens, your fees are high. Why, my babysitter charges less than you do, and she comes to the house and does the ironing while she takes care of little Carolyn. I don't see what costs so much about just taking care of little children!" What should you reply?

2. What are some situations in your own educational background in which the learning was primarily by means of language and others in which there was an emphasis on experience and participation? Which method did you prefer? What were the advantages and disadvantages of each of these approaches?

3. What guidelines would you suggest to help a teacher determine whether there are enough free choices or whether there is too much structure in the children's day?

4. As a beginning teacher, how do you feel about the prospect of having parents at school? If a mother is helping at school on the day her youngster has a temper tantrum and refuses to come in to lunch, would it be easier to handle this situation if the mother were not there? Do you agree completely that parents should be welcomed at school? Why or why not?

5. Select a basic activity, such as using tricycles or easel painting, that tends to stay the same throughout the year in many schools, and suggest some variations that would add interest and learning to the activity.

Self-Check Questions for Review

Content-Related Questions

1. What are the names of two important research studies having to do with the effectiveness of preschool education? List three or four important findings from these studies.

2. *The Whole Child* uses both behaviour modification and Piagetian theory as a partial theoretical base. According to the author, what are the strengths and weaknesses of these two theories?

3. Describe several ways in which the preschools of Reggio Emilia appear to differ from those of Canada.

4. List several ways in which teachers can generate records that will help them and the parents assess how much a child has learned and what he is like.

5. What is the chief difficulty or problem associated with planning a curriculum far in advance of what the children are currently doing? Does this mean that long-term planning should be avoided?

6. Name the five selves discussed in this chapter and tell what aspects of the child each self includes.

7. List and discuss the ingredients that should go into a good day for young children.

Integrative Questions

1. Suppose a friend says to you, "What I don't understand is why you have to go to school so long to learn to take care of little kids—after all, it's just glorified babysitting." Explain what you might produce in the way of evidence to educate that person.

2. Compare the findings for the experimental and control groups from the Perry Preschool Project (Table 2.1). In which categories did the greatest differences between the groups show up? Imagine that you are explaining these differences to a politician. What basic points would you stress from the results as being most likely to influence her or him to vote for more money to finance preschool programs?

3. Give an example of a situation with a three-year-old in which it would be appropriate to use a behaviour modification technique.

4. Compare the developmental-interactionist philosophy of teaching to a behaviour modification approach. What do they have in common and where do they differ?

5. Describe some of the benefits children receive from the self-select parts of an early childhood program,

and contrast these to the benefits they gain from activities they participate in together as a group. Be sure to include consideration of social and emotional benefits as well as cognitive ones.

6. During the past year the following topics were proposed as possible educational themes to be used with three-year-old children: kittens, shapes, space travel, Quebec, air, and snow. Which of these would you select as being most appropriate and which as being least appropriate? Explain the reasoning behind your answer.

7. This chapter describes several concepts that are common to both Canadian and Reggian teaching philosophy. These include learning by doing, enquiry-based learning, and child-centred learning. Explain what you think each of these terms means, and provide a specific example that illustrates how you might implement each of these practices in your classroom of four-year-olds.

References for Further Reading

Overviews

Beardsley, L. (1990). *Good day, bad day: The child's experience of child care.* New York: Teachers College Press. This book contrasts fictitious good and mediocre schools by describing imaginary situations and how the schools handle them. These are followed by knowledgeable comments. *Highly recommended.*

Bredekamp, S. (Ed.). (1987). *Developmentally appropriate practice in early childhood programs serving children from birth through age 8: Expanded edition.* Washington, DC: National Association for the Education of Young Children. This indispensable resource spells out both good and undesirable teaching practices. It remains the most influential publication on this subject in the field.

Doherty-Derkowski, G. (1995). *Quality matters: Excellence in early childhood programs.* Don Mills, ON: Addison-Wesley. This book summarized over 100 recent Canadian and international research studies. It documents a common core of caregiver behaviours and program characteristics associated with positive outcomes for children.

Koralek, D. G., Colker, L. J., & Dodge, D. T. (1993). *The what, why, and how of high-quality early childhood education: A guide for on-site supervision.* Washington, DC: National Association for the Education of Young Children. This wonderful book discusses programs divided according to age and also includes a helpful chapter on family child care. It approaches the curriculum by describing what one should see and why, and it also identifies warning signs, suggests the cause of trouble, and recommends what might be done to correct the difficulty. *Exceptionally helpful.*

Information About Specific Curricula

Gandini, L. (1993). Fundamentals of the Reggio Emilia approach to early childhood education. *Young Children, 49*(1), 4–8. Gandini presents the best summary of Reggian philosophy in this concise article—an excellent place to begin.

King, M. A., Oberlin, A., & Swank, T. (1993). *Creating a child-centred day care environment for two-year-olds.* Springfield, IL: Charles C Thomas. The authors provide practical suggestions for working with this particular age group—one that is frequently overlooked in discussions of curricula.

Miller, K. (1985). *Ages and stages: Developmental descriptions & activities, birth through eight years.* Marshfield, MA: Telshare. This concise book does a good job of linking developmental characteristics to recommendations for curricula. Quick, easy reading.

Schweinhart, L. J., & Weikart, D. P. (1993). Public policy report: Success by empowerment: The High/Scope Perry Preschool Study through age 27. *Young Children, 49*(1), 54–58. A brief, excellent summary of the findings and cost benefits of the study are provided here.

Developing Good Human Relationships

Griffin, E. F. (1982). *Island of childhood: Education in the special world of the nursery school.* New York: Teachers College Press. Griffin conveys a sense of the atmosphere that should surround children and teachers during these early years. *Highly recommended.*

Conducting Authentic Assessments

Hendrick, J. (1994). *Total Learning: Developmental curriculum for the young child* (4th ed.). Englewood Cliffs, NJ: Merrill/Prentice Hall. Chapter 7, "Practical Methods of Recording and Evaluating Behaviour" suggests many ways to generate effective assessments.

Hills, T. W. (1992). Reaching potentials through appropriate assessment. In S. Bredekamp & T. Rosegrant

(Eds.). *Reaching potentials: Appropriate curriculum and assessment for young children.* Washington, DC: National Association for the Education of Young Children. This is a good, practical discussion that provides many examples of appropriate how-to's teachers can utilize when assessing young children.

McAfee, O., & Leong, D. (1994). *Assessing and guiding young children's development and learning.* Boston: Allyn & Bacon. A very thorough treatment of this subject is provided by two authors who know their children *and* the subject, too. *Highly recommended.*

Importance of Play

Guddemi, M., & Jambor, T. (Eds.). (1993). *A right to play: Proceedings of the American Affiliates of the International Association for the Child's Right to Play, September 17–20, 1992, Denton, TX.* Little Rock, AR: Southern Early Childhood Association. The value of play for young children is thoroughly documented by this collection of papers. *Highly recommended.*

For the Advanced Student

DeVries, R., & Kohlberg, L. (1990). *Constructivist early education: Overview and comparison with other programs.* Washington, DC: National Association for the Education of Young Children. DeVries and Kohlberg contrast the Piagetian constructivist point of view with the Montessori and Bank Street approaches. They make a good case for fostering autonomy in children through independent enquiry.

Edwards, C., Gandini, L., & Forman, G. (Eds.). (1993). *The hundred languages of children: The Reggio Emilia approach to early childhood education.* Norwood, NJ: Ablex. This collection of chapters by Reggio staff members and Americans presents the most useful, comprehensive explanation of the Reggio approach presently available. *Highly recommended.*

Goffin, S. G. (1994). *Curriculum models and early childhood education: Appraising the relationship.* Englewood Cliffs, NJ: Merrill/Prentice Hall. Goffin provides in-depth appraisals of several early childhood education models: Montessori, developmental-interaction, direct instruction, High/Scope and Kamii/DeVries constructionist. She includes excellent appraisals as well as a thoughtful discussion of implications for future investigations. *Highly recommended.*

Katz, L. G., & Cesarone, B. (Eds.). (1994). *Reflections on the Reggio Emilia approach.* Urbana, IL: ERIC Clearinghouse on Elementary & Early Childhood Education. This is a collection of papers presented during the summer seminar at Reggio in 1994. It is interesting work, most suitable for readers already familiar with the basic Reggian concepts.

Lazar, I., Darlington, R., Murray, H., Royce, J., & Snipper, A. (1982). Lasting effects of early education: A report from the Consortium for Longitudinal Studies. *Monographs of the Society for Research in Child Development, 47*(2–3, No. 195). The discussion presents the results and in-depth descriptions of that carefully constructed research investigation.

Meisels, S.J., & Shonkoff, J. P. (1990). *Handbook of early childhood intervention.* New York: Cambridge University Press. This intensive, thorough review of difficulties and results of strategies of early intervention is an outstanding reference.

Meisels, S. J., Steele, D. M., & Quinn-Leering, K. (1993). Testing, tracking, and retaining young children: An analysis of research and social policy. In B. Spodek (Ed.), *Handbook of research on the education of young children.* Englewood Cliffs, NJ: Prentice Hall. Meisels et al. present a sound overview of the difficulties associated with assessing very young children.

National Association for the Education of Young Children. (1991). *Accreditation criteria & procedures of the National Academy of Early Childhood Programs.* Washington, DC: The Association. The accreditation guide provides a list of standards that explicitly spell out the ingredients of a sound child care program—an indispensable resource.

Nuttall, E. V., Romero, I., & Kalesnik, J. (Eds.). (1992). *Assessing and screening preschoolers: Psychological and educational dimensions.* Boston: Allyn & Bacon. Readers who require information on particular commercial tests and the administration of standardized tests will find this to be the most appropriate reference.

Schweinhart, L. J., Barnes, H. V., & Weikart, D. P. with Barnett, W. S., & Epstein, A. S. (1993). *Significant benefits: The High/Scope Perry Preschool Study through age 27.* (High/Scope Educational Research Foundation, Monograph No. 10). Ypsilanti, MI: High/Scope Press. For readers who desire more thorough information on the currently determined benefits of this particular intervention program, this is the best resource.

❧ II
Fostering Physical Well-Being

3 Handling Daily Routines

How to stop nagging the children through transition times?

What children from differing cultures like to eat?

How to get that youngster off the climbing gym when it's time for lunch?

. . . If you have, the material in the following pages will help you.

The lunch period should be an occasion for the enjoyment of good food in a social situation. I can remember my first experience as an assistant teacher in an all-day program. Lunch was rolled into the classroom on a wagon. Children (already bibbed) were lying on cots for a pre-lunch rest. Teachers served the plates and summoned the children to the tables. Everything on the plate had to be eaten before melba toast chunks were distributed (these were great favorites!) and finally dessert and milk. There was one particularly dismal meal which appeared weekly: a barely poached egg (the white still transparent) sitting on top of some dreary spinach. No one liked it, and one little girl finally refused to eat it. She sat stolidly before the offensive plate, quietly but firmly asserting, "I won't eat it. I hate it. It's not even cooked." The teacher finally removed the plate to the kitchen with the comment that it would be waiting for her after her nap.

After nap, Jill was escorted to the kitchen to be confronted with the cool mess of uncooked egg and spinach. She was told that she could return to the playroom after she had eaten it.

When she returned to the playroom, the teacher asked her if she had eaten her lunch. Jill answered, "Yes, and then I threwed it up." And she had!

Evelyn Beyer

*R*outines, those omnipresent recurring sequences of behaviour, constitute the backbone of full- and half-day programs and serve as landmarks that divide the day into different sections. They typically include the activities of arriving, departing, eating, toileting, resting, and the transitions between them and the other daily activities of preschool life.

Adequate handling of routines can foster both emotional and physical health, but in recent years teachers have tended to be more aware of the significance of routines in relation to emotional health than of the physical significance of good nutrition and adequate rest. However, the pasty faces, vulnerability to illness, and low energy levels of children in some programs now serve to remind us that physical health is vital to well-being and that our young children need these routines to help them build strong bodies as well as stable personalities.

It is surprising to discover that although routines involve a good portion of the day and although strong feelings and convictions of what is "right" abound, little research has been carried out in these areas. What research there is deals with nutrition and the emotional process of attachment and separation rather than with the investigation of alternative ways to handle routines in school. Therefore, readers should understand that the following discussion is based on a consensus of generally followed practice and that the recommendations rest on experience and opinion and are not validated by research.

One other note of caution about routines: If the teacher is unwise enough to go to war with a child on the subject of routines, the child, if she is so inclined, can always win. Thus a child who absolutely will not eat, will not use the toilet, or refuses to go to sleep can win any time she wants to; there is little the teacher can do about it. Fortunately teachers and children rarely reach this kind of impasse, but it is important to understand that such power struggles *can* happen and *have* happened and that the most common way to bring about such a disaster is to reduce oneself to attempting to force a child to comply with any routine absolutely against her will. It just does not work.

The best way to prevent conflicts from developing is to realize that children usually find comfort in reasonable routines that contribute to their physical well-being. It also helps if the teacher determines what the most important learnings are to be derived from each routine and then works toward achieving those goals rather than becoming caught up in "winning" for its own sake. For example, it is more important that a child enjoy food and take pleasure in mealtimes than it is that she clear her plate, wait until everyone is served, or not rap her glass on the table. Bearing this primary goal in mind will reduce the amount of criticism and control that may otherwise mar snack and lunch times.

◌ Schedules and Transitions Into Routines

Schedules

Routines and transitions are best understood when seen in the perspective of the overall schedule, so a sample full-day schedule is provided (Figure 3.1).

Remember that a schedule should be regarded as a guide, not as dogma. Allowance should always be made for deviations when these are desirable. Perhaps it took longer for

7:00–7:30	Some teachers arrive, set out materials, and ready the environment for children.
7:30	Children begin to arrive. One teacher or the director is specially assigned to greet children and parents, chat, and carry out the health check. If possible, another staff member provides a cosy time reading books with those who desire it. Self-select materials are also available.
8:30–9:15	Breakfast available for children who want it. Breakfast area set up near schoolroom sink to facilitate hand washing before and after eating. Self-selected activity continues until 9:15 for those who are not hungry.
9:15–9:45	Small- or large-group time: this often continues quite a while for four-year-olds, less time for younger children. Its length should vary each day in order to adapt to the changing needs of the group.
9:45–10:00	Transition to activities.
10:00–11:40/11:45	Mingled indoor-outdoor experience or outdoor followed by indoor activity, depending on staffing and weather. Small-group experiences and field trips occur during this time. Self-selected activities, changed from the ones available in the early arrival period, are also provided.
11:40/11:45–12:00	Children help put things away, prepare gradually for lunch. Children go to toilet; children *and teachers* wash hands.
12:00–12:35/12:45	Family-style lunchtime; children are seated with adults in groups as small as possible.
12:35/12:45–1:00	Children prepare for nap: toilet, wash hands, brush teeth, snuggle down.
1:00–2:30/3:00	Nap time; children get up as they wake up, toilet, dress, and move out of nap area. Snack ready as they arrive and desire it.
By 3:30	All snacks completed. Indoor-outdoor self-select continues, again with special activities planned and provided for.
4:40	Children begin to put things away, freshen up (wash hands and faces, etc.), and have quiet opportunities to use manipulatives or sit with teacher for songs, stories, and general quiet, relaxing time as parents call for them.
5:30	Children picked up (except for the inevitable emergencies of course!)

Note: For a sample plan, see chapter 20, Developing Thinking and Reasoning Skills (The Conventional Approach).

Figure 3.1   Daily schedule for a full-day centre: three- and four-year-olds

the bread to rise than anticipated, or perhaps dramatic play is involving most of the group in an intensely satisfying way. There needs to be give and stretch in schedules to accommodate these kinds of possibilities. This is why overlap times and approximate times are listed in the sample. Even a modest amount of latitude allows children to proceed gradually from one activity to the next without being hassled by the teachers.

On the other hand, it can also happen that some schedules do not match what actually takes place in the classroom. The research study in this chapter describes the work

♋ **RESEARCH STUDY** ♋
Intentions Versus Reality

Research Question: Ostrosky and her associates asked how good a match there was between the activities scheduled by teachers in preschool special education classes and the activities in which the children were actually involved.

Research Method: The researchers observed children in twenty-four preschool classrooms for children with disabilities during the morning periods. Three to five children were randomly selected in each class, with the total sample of ninety-four children ranging in chronological age from thirty-eight to eighty-nine months.

Time samples were taken of the children's behaviour using the Ecobehavioral System for the Complex Assessment of Preschool Environments (Carta, Greenwood, & Atwater, 1986). This system uses twelve activity categories such as stories, fine motor activities, music, language programming, play, self-care, and so forth. The children's behaviour was classified according to these categories.

Detailed schedules of their class day were provided by the teachers, and the planned activities were classified according to the same system used to classify the children's behaviour.

Results: When the intended activities were compared with how the children actually spent their time, the researchers found that there was a close match between the amount of time planned for some activities—namely, preacademics and gross and fine motor activities—and the amount of time the children actually spent doing them. On the other hand, there were significant discrepancies in other areas. In common with teachers in many preschool classrooms serving typical children, the teachers underestimated or did not even include the time required for transitions. They also underscheduled the amount of time children spent in independent storybook perusal. From an early childhood point of view, the most serious discrepancy of all was the difference between the amount

done by Ostrosky and associates (1994), in classrooms for preschool-aged children with disabilities. Their observations reveal how in those classrooms some scheduled times were consistently shortchanged.

Note that the schedule in Figure 3.1 allows for breakfast to be served only to those children who desire it. For years our centre was plagued with the problem of having some children arrive at 8:30 or 9:00 stuffed to the gills while others were clearly famished. If we waited for snack until 10:00, when everyone had at least a little appetite, then they were not hungry for lunch! We finally decided to solve this problem by offering breakfast on a self-select basis with food kept appetizing on warming trays, and with a friendly member of the staff sitting in the breakfast corner at all times to assist the children and welcome them for a quiet personal chat as they ate. This solution, though unconventional, has done a much better job of meeting all the children's needs by freeing more of the staff to work with the youngsters who are not hungry and providing a homey, comfortable, slow-paced beginning of the day for children who are just waking up and do want breakfast. It also helps settle down children who may have been rushed off to school in too much of a hurry to have had more than a bite before departure.

of time the teachers planned for free play compared with the amount of time the children were actually involved in that activity. The researchers comment that "play may be perceived by early childhood special educators as the activity most easily given up." (page 31).

Implications: This study illustrates a condition common to many teachers—a condition especially challenging for teachers who work with young children with special needs: Teachers are experiencing tension between doing what they *have* to do versus doing what they *want* to do. Many teachers recognize the contribution play can make to children's development and yet when push comes to shove it is the first thing jettisoned from the schedule.

The value of this research to such teachers is that it may make them aware that it is the play period that is suffering most consistently from attrition. Once they realize that this is the case, it will be up to them to decide whether to reschedule the day to make certain that children are no longer denied this important avenue of growth.

The basic implication to be drawn by teachers in more typical preschool playrooms is that they, too, should take a careful look at how realistic their schedules really are. Is enough time being allotted for transitions or are the children constantly pushed to get ready for the next activity? Is there truly sufficient time included for the children to become deeply involved in their play or do they just get started and then have to put everything away? Might it be more satisfactory to rearrange the schedule into fewer, longer time blocks so that the number of transitions is reduced? These and other problems related to scheduling deserve consideration and *reconsideration,* as the year progresses.

Source: From *Teacher's Schedules and Actual Time Spent in Activities in Preschool Special Education Classes* by M. M. Ostrosky, A. C. Skellenger, S. L. Odom, S. R. McConnell, & C. Peterson. 1994. *Journal of Early Intervention, 18*(1), 25–33.

The same policy of eating by choice is followed after rest time since children drift out of the rest area a few at a time. Almost all of them at that point, of course, are ready for something good to eat, but it is still made a matter of self-decision for them. This not only prevents wasted food but also is part of our effort to encourage children to be aware of what their bodies are saying to them. Are they eating just because it is the thing to do, or are their bodies telling them that they are really hungry?

The primary rule that applies to both breakfast and snack time is that, once seated, the child stays until she is finished eating. No one walks around with food in her hands, and a staff member is always seated at the table to keep the children company.

Transition Times

A study of several different kinds of early childhood settings (Berk, 1976) makes the point that transitions (the time spent in moving from one activity to the next) occupy from 20 to 35% of activity time in programs depending on the centre, the particular day, and the skill and planning contributed by the teacher. This surprising statistic certainly emphasizes that transitions are worth thinking about and managing well so that children can move as smoothly as possible from one activity to the next. It also reminds us how necessary it is to plan for enough time when shifting, for instance, from music to lunch, or from lunch to rest, so that children are not unnecessarily harried in the process.

If you find yourself continually nagging and urging the children to hurry through their paces, here are some suggestions you may want to try in order to make transitions easier for you and them. In addition to allowing a realistic amount of time for transitions to take place, it always helps to warn *once* in advance when a change is in the offing, saying, "It's almost story time" or "You can have a little more time with the beads, but then we'll have to put them away." This gives the children a chance to finish what they are doing and makes their compliance more likely. It also helps to remember that transitions do not usually present an opportunity for a real choice (the child is supposed to come, not linger in the yard), so it is best not to ask, "Would you like to come?" or "It's time to come in, okay?" but to say more definitely, "In just a minute it's going to be time for lunch, and we will go indoors. What do you suppose we're having to eat today?" Occasionally singing a simple song such as "Here We Go A' Marching" will also help get children moving in the desired direction. Avoiding situations in which all the children have to do something at once is the best help of all because this avoids the noisy, crowded situations that seem to happen with particular frequency in the toilet room.

ᛓ Routines of Arrival and Departure

It is natural for young children to feel anxious when their mothers or fathers leave them at school. This feeling, called *separation anxiety,* appears to be strongest in children between the ages of ten and twenty-four months (Bailey, 1992). Even beyond this age, however, separation requires time and tactful handling by the staff in order that the child and the parent come to feel comfortable about parting.

This seems to be particularly true for three-year-olds (Cox & Campbell, 1968), two-year-olds (Bailey, 1992), and children who are developmentally delayed (Kessler, Gridth, & Smith, 1968). Although some research (Schwartz & Wynn, 1971) indicates that by the time children are four years old many can adjust rapidly to a school situation without their parents having to linger, it is not safe to make a blanket rule about this, since there are always individual cases in which a child becomes panicky when left at school.

Introduce the Child to School Gradually

It is common practice and good sense to recommend a visit by parent and child for the first day, then another short stay while the parent leaves for a brief period, followed by a gradual extension of time as the child's ability to endure separation increases.

Another way of helping children become comfortable is by having an open house during which families can come and go at their convenience. Still other schools begin the term with half the children coming on one day, and the other half, the next. At our centre we send each child a personal letter with a name tag, an invitation to the open house, and a short description of what we will be doing at school. The children love these let-

♋   *Waiting can seem an eternity to a young child.*

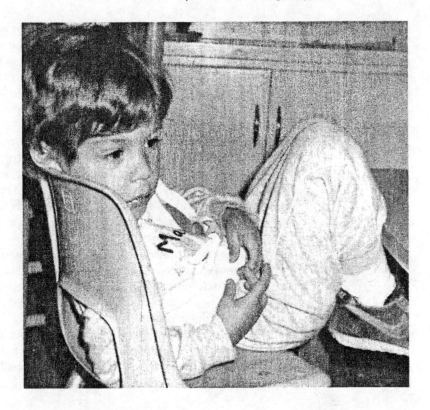

ters, and this preliminary contact does seem to overcome some of their initial apprehension.

These suggestions about gradual adaptation to the new environment are fine for many families whose schedules can be somewhat flexible, but they do not work for parents whose jobs demand that they appear promptly at 8:00 a.m. no matter what the teacher recommends or how hard the child is crying. If at all possible, special arrangements should be made for such families when their children begin attending. A grandfather or aunt might be pressed into service and stay while the child makes friends. Sometimes the parent can bring the child by for a visit around lunchtime, the teacher can make a Saturday visit to the home, or the child can come to school with a friend. Any of these arrangements, while not ideal, is preferable to allowing the child to walk in and simply be left in a strange place with strange people for nine hours on her first day.

Handling Outbursts of Emotion

It helps to recognize that a child must often deal with three feelings when her mother leaves her: grief (the emotion that seems most obvious and logical), fear (also not very surprising), and anger (the emotion that the teacher is least likely to recognize in these circumstances) (Bowlby, 1973; 1982). It is often necessary not only to comfort and reassure the child but also to recognize with her that she feels angry with her mother because she left her at school. I recall one forthright three-year-old who took real pleasure in biting the mama doll with our toothy rubber hippopotamus as soon as her mother departed. The teacher may also see this angry reaction at being left behind come out at the end of the day when the child insists (with just a touch of malice) that she wants to stay at school "for ever and ever" and does not want to go home. If the teacher interprets this reaction to her mother as being a way of relieving angry feelings, it will help maintain friendly relations all around.

Actually it is the children who make a forthright fuss as their mothers leave who seem to work through their feelings of loss with the greatest expedition, whereas the child who apparently makes an easy adjustment by becoming instantly involved in activities often becomes downcast a few weeks later as she lowers her defences. If this happens three to four weeks after entry to school, the parent is likely to assume something has happened there that makes her want to stay home. The best protection against this conclusion is to explain casually to her parent *before her facade crumbles* that the child may show her grief at a later time and that most children feel some sadness and loneliness when left at school.

It is also wise to prepare parents for the fact that children may go through a milder attack of separation anxiety again when they return from vacation. Otherwise this repeated behaviour can discourage parents who underwent a difficult separation experience at the beginning of school.

Other unexpected circumstances can also trigger anxiety. One spring the children in our centre walked to the college cafeteria and met their parents there for lunch. All went well until it came time to part, and suddenly we had several very unhappy children on

❧   *Parting isn't always easy.*

our hands. The unusual circumstances had made parting difficult once again for our small charges.

But learning to let go is part of becoming mature. A nice balance of comfort combined with a matter-of-fact expectation that she will feel better soon usually gets the child started on the day. Having something at hand that she especially enjoys will help, too. The teacher must take care to permit the child to form a relationship with him as a bridge to the other children yet at the same times not encourage this so much that the youngster droops around longer than necessary or becomes a careerist handholder.

❧ *Routines That Centre Around Eating*

Importance of Adequate Nutrition

In these days of imitation foods and casual eating habits it is important to emphasize the value of good food for young children. Too many schools depend on artificial juices and a cracker for snack, supposedly on the grounds that the children are well fed at home. But the underlying reason for serving this kind of food is that it is convenient and cheap. Yet studies continue to accumulate that indicate that good nutrition combined with other environmental factors is associated with the ability to pay attention and learn (Pimento & Kernstead, 1995; Pollitt, 1990; Ricciuti, 1991).

Family incomes and the parents' awareness of nutrition tend to have a direct effect on the quality of the family's dietary intake. Higher levels of family incomes and parents with knowledge of cooking contribute to better dietary intake, since parents are better able to afford and prepare a wider variety of wholesome foods. Careful planning of nutritious meals is so important that considerable attention will be paid to it in the following pages. As an overall guide for adults as well as children, it is helpful to bear in mind Canada's Food Guide to Healthy Eating, by Health Canada. Note the emphasis on grain products, vegetables and fruit, and meat and alternatives.

Planning Appealing and Nutritious Meals

One of the fortunate things about teaching at the preprimary level is that teachers and directors usually have opportunities to participate in planning what the children will eat. Therefore, it is helpful to have some basic principles of menu planning clearly in mind.

A useful way to begin such planning is to become acquainted with Canada's Food Guide (Figures 3.2a and 3.2b), and the adaptations for young children suggested in Figure 3.2c. These standards can serve as the basic guidelines, but there are some additional points to consider as well.

Variety, particularly as the year progresses and the children feel at ease, should be a keynote of the food program. Snacks should be different every day and can be based on seasonal fruits and vegetables to help keep budgets within reason.

Dessert should be unsugared fruit and should be regarded as a nutritional component of the meal, not a reward to be bargained for (Rogers & Morris, 1986).

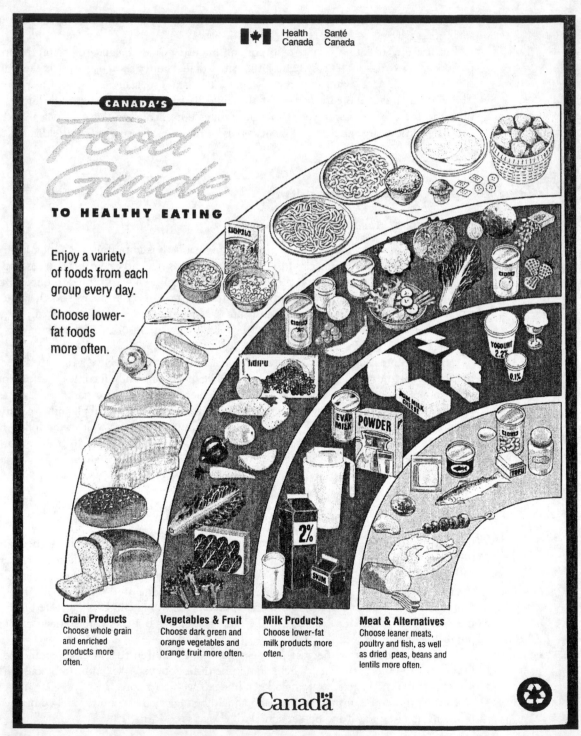

Figure 3.2a

Different People Need Different Amounts of Food

The amount of food you need every day from the 4 food groups and other foods depends on your age, body size, activity level, whether you are male or female and if you are pregnant or breast-feeding. That's why the Food Guide gives a lower and higher number of servings for each food group. For example, young children can choose the lower number of servings, while male teenagers can go to the higher number. Most other people can choose servings somewhere in between.

Grain Products
5-12
SERVINGS PER DAY

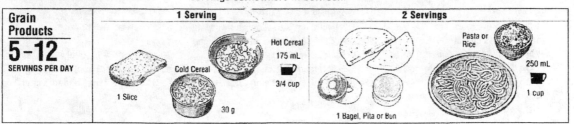

Vegetables & Fruit
5-10
SERVINGS PER DAY

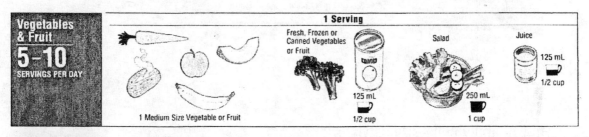

Milk Products
SERVINGS PER DAY
Children 4-9 years 2-3
Youth 10-16 years 3-4
Adults 2-4
Pregnant & Breast-feeding
Women 3-4

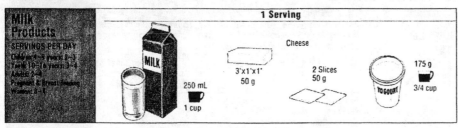

Other Foods

Taste and enjoyment can also come from other foods and beverages that are not part of the 4 food groups. Some of these foods are higher in fat or Calories, so use these foods in moderation.

Meat & Alternatives
2-3
SERVINGS PER DAY

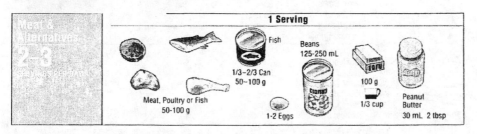

Figure 3.2b

What is a child-size serving?

There is a wide variation in portions of foods consumed by preschoolers. *That's why a child-size serving is anywhere from one-half to the full size for foods in each food group, as indicated in Canada's Food Guide to Healthy Eating.* Generally the size of portion increases with age. For example, a two-year-old may eat a half slice of bread, whereas a four-year-old is more likely to eat a whole slice. Both of these can be counted as one child-size serving of Grain Products.

Examples of one child-size serving

Grain Products

1/2-1 slice of bread

15-30 g cold cereal*

75-175 mL (1/3-3/4 cup) hot cereal

1/4-1/2 bagel, pita or bun

1/2-1 muffin

50-125 mL (1/4-1/2 cup) pasta or rice

4-8 soda crackers

* Approximate volumes for one serving:
flaked cereal 125-250 mL (1/2-1 cup);
puffed cereal 250-500 mL (1-2 cups);
granola or dense-type cereal 30-75 mL
(2 Tablespoons-1/3 cup)

Vegetables and Fruit

1/2-1 medium-size vegetable or fruit

50-125 mL (1/4-1/2 cup) fresh, frozen or canned vegetables or fruit

125-250 mL (1/2-1 cup) salad

50-125 mL (1/4-1/2 cup) juice

Milk Products

25-50 g cheese

75-175 g (1/3-3/4 cup) yogourt

Preschoolers should consume a total of 500 mL (2 cups) of milk every day.

Meat and Alternatives

25-50 g meat, fish or poultry

1 egg

50-125 mL (1/4-1/2 cup) beans

50-100 g (1/4-1/3 cup) tofu

15-30 mL (1-2 Tbsp) peanut butter

How to apply child-size servings

AN EXAMPLE WITH JENNY AND TOMMY

Jenny is five years old and her brother, Tommy, has just turned three. As shown by this example of yesterday's dinner, Tommy tends to eat the same foods as Jenny but in smaller portions.

Dinner	Serving Size	Number of Servings			
		Grain Products	Vegetables and Fruit	Milk Products	Meat and Alternatives
Jenny					
Noodles	125 mL	1			
Braised Beef	50 g				1
Carrot Coins	75 mL		1		
Fruit Salad	125 mL		1		
with Yogourt	100 mL			1	
Oatmeal Cookie	1 cookie	1			
Tommy					
Noodles	50 mL	1			
Braised Beef	25 g				1
Carrot Coins	50 mL		1		
Fruit Salad	50 mL		1		
with Yogourt	50 mL			1/2	
Oatmeal Cookie	1 cookie	1			

Both Jenny and Tommy drank 125 mL of milk with dinner, as part of the 500 mL of milk they have each day.

Figure 3.2c

❧   *When food is plain and tasty children eat it with relish.*

If the food is plain and familiar and a lot of it can be eaten with the fingers, children will eat more. As a general rule, young children are deeply suspicious of casseroles and food soaked in sauces and gravies. They prefer things they can recognize, such as carrot sticks, hamburger, and plain fruit.

Table 3.1 provides some sample lunch menus that show how appealing plain, relatively inexpensive food can be. Even if all the children are from one particular ethnic group, it is desirable to vary the suggestions in Table 3.1 by incorporating food from many cultures, bit by bit. For example, menus might include black-eyed peas with ham or pinto beans with melted cheese. Introduction of such foods at this time of the child's life is particularly desirable for two reasons. Good-tasting food that is identified as coming from a particular culture helps children feel friendly toward that culture. Secondly, research indicates that learning plays a big part in developing food preferences and that the preschool years may be a particularly sensitive period in the formation of such preferences (Birch, 1980b; Johnson & Fisher, 1995). If we wish to extend the range of children's food preferences, this is a good time to begin.

Table 3.1   Sample lunch menus

Monday	Tuesday	Wednesday	Thursday	Friday
Week I				
Oven-baked fish	Beef balls	Stewed chicken	Simmered steak	Jerk pork
Green beans	Lima beans	Buttered noodles	Scalloped	Stewed okra and
Carrot sticks	Tomato wedges	Grated carrot-	potatoes	tomatoes
Cheese biscuits	Whole wheat	raisin salad	English peas	Black-eyed peas
Milk	toast strips	Whole wheat	Whole wheat	Corn bread
Fresh pear halves	Milk	bread with	muffins	Strawberries
	Stewed prunes	apricot spread	Milk	Milk
		Milk	Fresh fruit cup	
		Orange slices		
Week II				
Meat loaf	Creamed chicken	Oven-baked fish	Toasted cheese	Stir-fried beef
Buttered carrots	Buttered rice	Buttered mixed	sandwich	with assorted
and peas	French green	vegetables	Tomato soup	leafy green
Whole wheat	beans	Whole wheat	Chopped	vegetables
bread and butter	Cornbread sticks	toast strips	broccoli	Rice
Milk	Milk	Milk	Milk	Pineapple slices
Oatmeal muffins	Seedless grapes	Apple wedges	Cantaloupe slices	Lichees (seeded)
				or raisins
				Milk
Week III				
Tostada with beef	Meat balls with	Cheese cubes	Beef stew with	Chicken
and cheese	tomato sauce	Twice-baked	peas, carrots,	casserole
Lettuce and	Green beans	potatoes	and potatoes	Buttered broccoli
tomato	Enriched bread	Buttered beets	French bread	Bran muffins
Platano or	and butter	Cooked spinach	pieces	Milk
spinach	Milk	with egg slices	Milk	Fresh pineapple
Orange slices	Banana bread	Milk	Cottage cheese	and banana
Milk		Vanilla ice cream	and peach slices	slices
Week IV				
Hard-boiled eggs	Braised calves	Tuna fish	Creamed chicken	Beef patty and
Green beans with	liver	sandwiches	Buttered spinach	gravy
bacon	English peas	Lettuce pieces	Grated carrot-	Peas and
Drop biscuits	Perfection salad	Buttered summer	raisin salad	potatoes
Milk	Whole wheat	squash	Whole wheat	Tomato wedges
Orange slices in	toast strips	Milk	bread	Milk
gelatin	Milk	Fresh fruit cup	Milk	Sliced bananas in
	Baked apple		Applesauce	orange juice

Source: Adapted, by permission, from "Ideas for Administrators," *The Idea Box*, by the Austin Association for the Education of Young Children, © 1973, National Association for the Education of Young Children, 1834 Connecticut Ave., NW, Washington, DC 20009.

Table 3.2   Foods common to most ethnic food patterns

Meat and Alternates	Milk and Milk Products	Grain Products	Vegetables	Fruits	Others
Pork*	Milk, fluid	Rice	Carrots	Apples	Fruit juices
Beef	Ice cream	White bread	Cabbage	Bananas	
Chicken		Noodles,	Green beans	Oranges	
Eggs		macaroni,	Greens	Peaches	
		spaghetti	(especially	Pears	
		Dry cereal	spinach)	Tangerines	
			Sweet potatoes		
			or yams		
			Tomatoes		

*May be restricted due to religious customs.

Source: From *Food, Nutrition, and the Young Child* (4th ed., p. 230) by J. B. Endres and R. E. Rockwell, 1993. Englewood Cliffs, NJ: Merrill/Prentice Hall. ©1993 by Prentice Hall Publishing Co. Reprinted by permission.

When there are children at the centre of various ethnic and cultural backgrounds, it is even more crucial to include foods that they like and are familiar to them. Teachers need to remember that some foods they have eaten all their lives can be dishearteningly unfamiliar to the Chinese youngster who is accustomed to rice and vegetables, or the Mexican child whose diet staple is the tortilla. Since many of us are unfamiliar with food preferences of various groups, it may be convenient to refer to Tables 3.2 and 3.3 for suggestions about the kinds of food to serve. Of course, not everyone from a particular cultural group necessarily likes all or any of the foods listed, but at least the table points the way to some probable food preferences that it would be desirable to include for the children at meal time. Additional resources for culturally familiar food are ethnic cookbooks and family recipes. A cook who comes from a background similar to that of the children can be a treasured asset. The references at the end of this chapter include a number of readily available ethnic cookbooks.

Some Basic Principles Having to Do with Eating

There is perhaps no area in our social life (except sex) that has as many restrictions and regulations attached to it as eating does. A class of mine once counted up the rules enforced by their families about mealtimes. We thought of forty-three rules within ten minutes. They ranged from "no dessert until you clear your plate" to "wait until the men are fed before you sit down." We will content ourselves here with enumerating only the principles that the majority of preprimary teachers have come to feel are important as they work with young children.

Table 3.3 Characteristic food choices for seven groups

	Vegetables	Fruits	Meats and Alternatives	Grain Products	Others
West Indian	Akee, potato, rice, pumpkin, okra, peas, peppers, corn, collards, plantain, squash	Guava, mango, banana, papaya, lime, coconut, pineapple, jackfruit	Goat, chicken, pork (in some groups), salt cod, sardines, shrimp, lentils, black-eyed peas, chick peas, kidney beans, eggs	Roti and other flat breads, pancakes, spice cake, bulla	Curry seasoning, jerk seasoning
Hispanic	Avocado, chilies, corn, lettuce, onions, peas, potatoes, prickly pear (cactus leaf, called *nopales*), zucchini	Guava, lemons, mangoes, melons, prickly pear (cactus fruit called *tuna*), zapote (or sapote)	Lamb, tripe, sausage (*chorizo*), bologna, bacon, pinto beans, pink beans, garbanzo beans, lentils, peanuts, and peanut butter	Tortillas, corn flour, oatmeal, sweet bread (*pan dulce*)	Salsa (tomato, pepper, onion relish), chili sauce, guacamole, lard (*manteca*), pork cracklings
Japanese	Bamboo shoots, broccoli, burdock root, cauliflower, celery, cucumbers, eggplant, gourd (*kampyo*), mushrooms, napa cabbage, peas, peppers, radishes (daikon or pickles called *takuwan*), snow peas, squash, sweet potatoes, turnips, water chestnuts, yamaimo	Apricots, cherries, grapefruit, grapes, lemons, limes, melons, persimmons, pineapple, pomegranates, plums (dried pickled *umeboshi*), strawberries	Turkey, raw tuna or sea bass (*sashimi*), mackerel, sardines (*mezashi*), shrimp, abalone, squid, octopus, soybean curd (*tofu*), soybean paste (*miso*), soybeans, red beans (*azuki*), lima beans, peanuts, almonds, cashews	Rice crackers, noodles (whole-wheat noodle called *soba* or *udon*), oatmeal, rice	Soy sauce, Nori paste (used to season rice), bean thread (*komyaku*), ginger (*shoga*; dried form called *denishoga*)
Chinese	Bamboo shoots, bean sprouts, bok choy, broccoli, celery, Chinese cabbage, corn, cucumbers, eggplant, greens (collard, Chinese broccoli, mustard, kale), leeks, lettuce, mushrooms, peppers, scallions, snow peas, taro, water chestnuts, white turnips, white radishes, winter melon	Figs, grapes, kumquats, loquats, mangoes, melons, persimmons, pineapple, plums, pomegranates	Organ meats, duck, white fish, shrimp, lobster, oysters, sardines, soybeans, soybean curd (*tofu*), black beans, chestnuts (*kuri*)	Barley, millet, rice, wheat	Soy sauce, sweet and sour sauce, mustard sauce, ginger root, plum sauce, red bean paste

	Vegetables	Fruits	Meats and Alternatives	Grain Products	Others
Vietnamese*	Bamboo shoots, bean sprouts, cabbage, carrots, cucumbers, greens, lettuce, mushrooms, onions, peas, spinach, yams	Apples, bananas, eggfruit (*o-ma*), grapefruit, jackfruit, lychees, mandarins, mangoes, oranges, papaya, pineapple, tangerines, watermelon	Beef, blood, brains, chicken, duck, eggs, fish, goat, kidney, lamb, liver, pork, shellfish, soybeans	French bread, rice, rice noodles, wheat noodles	Fish sauce, fresh herbs, garlic, ginger, lard, MSG, peanut oil, sesame seeds, sesame seed oil, vegetable oil
South Asian	Cauliflower, carrots, cucumbers, corn-gourds, leeks, eggplant, beets, radishes, hot peppers, bell peppers, peas, French beans, okra, pumpkin, red and white cabbage, mung sprouts, bean sprouts, potatoes, tapioca root, sweet potatoes	Oranges, limes, grapes, watermelon, mangoes, guava, honeydew, chiku, cantaloupe, pineapple, green, yellow, and red bananas, berries, custard apples	Lamb, beef, duck, chicken, shrimp, catfish, buffalo, sunfish, sardines, fresh crab, lobster, peanuts, cashews, almonds, chickpeas, split peas, black-eyed peas, dry mung beans	Rice pancakes, wheat chapati, puri, mixed-grain flour bread	Fresh coconut juice, curries, tomato sauce, tamarind sauce, dried grain curries (*pulses*), yogurt-curry garnished with coriander (fresh leaves)
Aboriginal†	Wild celery, onions, potatoes, fiddleheads, seaweed, mushrooms, carrots, wild asparagus	Thimbleberries, elderberries, currants, apples, rosehips, wild rhubarb, salmonberries, wild crabapples	Salmon, cod, char, clams, beaver, moose, duck, rabbit	Rice, bannock, oatmeal, corn mush	Sap, Indian tea, cedar bark, inner bark, oolichan grease, bear grease, deer grease, moose fat, seal grease, fish tails, shellfish

*Information supplied by Hanh-Trang Tran-Viet, Carbondale, IL.

†*Source: Interior B.C. Native Food Guide* (Health & Welfare Canada). Reprinted in G. Chud and R. Fahlman (1995). *Honouring diversity within child care and early education: An instructor's guide.* Victoria: Province of British Columbia, Ministry of Skills, Training and Labour.

Source: From Food, Nutrition, and the Young Child (2nd ed., pp. 182–183) by J.B. Endres and R.E. Rockwell, 1985, Englewood Cliffs, NJ: Merrill/Prentice Hall. © 1985 by Prentice Hall. Reprinted by permission. Please note that foods common to most ethnic groups have been omitted and presented in Table 3.2.

Some Children Eat More than Others Do

The quantity a child consumes is related to her physiological make-up as well as to her growth rate. Also, emotional states and needs can affect her appetite. All these factors must be considered when deciding whether a child's nutrition patterns are adequate. As long as the youngster remains healthy and her colour is good, there is little need to worry about whether she is eating a lot or a little.

Eating Should Be a Pleasure but Food Should NOT Be Used as a Reward

Most of us are shocked when we hear of parents punishing their children by sending them to bed with no dinner, but how many of us would feel equally concerned about the adult who habitually rewards a child with a cookie or other desired food for being good? And yet this tying food together with behaviour is one of the links in developing eating disorders in later years. Certainly eating should be (and is!) a satisfying pleasure, but that pleasure needs to be kept within bounds—it should not become the primary source of gratification in life. Food should not be used to punish or to bribe or to reward.

Eating Together Should Convey a Sense of Happy Family Life to the Children

There should be time both to eat and to chat. Discipline situations should be avoided whenever possible. Mealtime can also be a time to enjoy each other and to help the group by going for seconds, passing food to each other, and group clean-up.

Eating Should Help a Child Be Independent

When I think of the reason we encourage children to serve themselves, I remember the little girl who commented that when teachers are cold they make children put on their sweaters. The same thing is true of eating. When teachers are hungry, they serve the children too much; but if food is passed around the table, each child can take what she desires. It is up to her to choose. She knows how hungry she is, and she knows her preferences far better than her teacher does. Then, too, by serving herself she has the opportunity to learn to observe the social rule "Take some and leave some."

Having sponges close at hand also helps children become independent because they can mop up their own spills. Advertisements that stress the joys of carpeting to the contrary, it is much easier to clean up food from uncarpeted floors, so it is best to eat over a linoleum floor or even outdoors when possible.

Another way to help children retain independence is to make sure that they do not have to wait to be fed. When children are hungry and their blood glucose level is low, they are in poor control of themselves, so food should be ready to be served as the children sit down. If it is placed on a low table or nearby shelf, the teacher can start passing it out as soon as everyone has arrived.

Eating Should Be a Positive Experience

Although the quickest way to teach a child to hate a new food is to make her eat it all, it is desirable to encourage (but not force) everyone to take a taste of everything

Helping prepare snack provides a golden opportunity to contribute to the well-being of the group.

served. Generally the teacher can count on the combination of good appetites and enthusiasm to foster venturesomeness, but sometimes a child will refuse to try something new. One teacher of my acquaintance handles these outright refusals by simply remarking, "Well, when you're older, I expect you'll want to try it," and then he changes the subject.

Some interesting and carefully controlled research by Birch (1980a) indicates that children can also be influenced toward food in a positive way by the reactions of their peers. After determining who liked which vegetable, Birch studied a number of groups of children who were seated so that a child who preferred one kind of vegetable was placed with a group who most preferred a second kind. After several days, during which the first child witnessed the others choosing her unpreferred vegetable as their first choice, Birch found that the child changed to selecting the second vegetable first, also. This change in preference remained constant over a number of weeks.

Unfortunately, negative comments can be just as influential as positive examples. Remarks such as, "It looks like dog pooh-pooh!" should be discouraged. A wave of this kind of talk can sweep through a group of four-year-olds and actually spoil a meal if it is not controlled. The policy of "You don't have to eat it, but I won't let you spoil it for other people" is a sound one to enforce.

Perhaps one of the best ways to encourage children to try a new food is to allow them to prepare it. Cooking is a fine learning experience as well as a pleasure for preschoolers. Making vegetable soup, devilling eggs, or baking wholewheat muffins can introduce them to a whole range of taste experiences they might otherwise shun.

Eating Can Be a Learning Experience

Although the most important goal of the eating situation is to furnish nourishment and pleasure, this experience can provide many opportunities for intellectual learning, too (Berman & Fromer, 1991a; Endres & Rockwell, 1993). The lunch table is a fine place for conversation and the development of verbal fluency. Children can be encouraged to talk about their pets, what they did on the weekend, what they like best to eat, and what was fun at school during the morning. The opportunity can also be taken to talk about food, textures, colours, and more factual kinds of information, but some teachers seem to do this to excess and forget to emphasize the more valuable goal of fluency. No matter what kinds of learning experiences go along with the meal, the teacher should always remember that eating should, first and foremost, be pleasurable and satisfying.

Children with Special Eating Problems

Allergies and Other Food Restrictions

Children who have allergies can have a difficult time at the lunch table and so deserve special mention. The allergy that comes up most frequently is one that requires a restriction on milk and milk products. When this is the case, the parent should be asked to supply whatever the child requires instead. A simple explanation to the other children that the child's doctor has said she should not drink milk has always been sufficient at our centre. It is wise to be as matter-of-fact as possible in order to avoid making the child feel regretful or persecuted about the restriction.

Sometimes there are other reasons for dietary restrictions. For example, we have had several Muslim children and children from vegetarian families in our school, and we always do our best to honour their prohibitions. However, it can be very hard to see a little vegetarian hungrily eyeing the hamburger her neighbour is consuming with gusto. If the problem becomes too difficult, perhaps the teacher will want to invite the parent to a lunch and ask what to do about it.

The Child Who Won't Eat

Refusing to eat and obesity are luxuries that very few countries in the world can afford, so I suppose we should count our blessings. For most children, taking the pressure off eating at mealtimes and allowing a child to skip a meal if she so chooses will gradually solve the problem of not eating. Although it may seem hardhearted, I feel it is a mistake to allow a recalcitrant child to suddenly repent when she realizes that the food is going back to the kitchen. Good food should be set forth, a pleasant opportunity to eat should transpire, and when that time is past, it is past for everyone until it is time for snack. This policy should be carried out without vacillation or guilt on the teacher's part. It is up to the child to choose to eat or not eat; it is not the teacher's role to coax, bargain, or wheedle. No one ever starved to death because she missed her lunch.

❧   *Learning social skills is an important part of the lunch experience.*

There are rare occasions when the teacher will come across a youngster who either compulsively insists on eating only a narrowly circumscribed number of foods or refuses to eat altogether. This behaviour is almost always duplicated at home as well. Taking the pressure off and handling mealtimes in a casual manner may not be enough in these special cases, and the condition can be difficult to ameliorate. Under these circumstances *it is important to suggest counselling promptly* for the family in order to relieve the situation.

The Child Who Grabs Everything

Whereas the noneater is likely to make teachers anxious, the grabber is likely to make them angry. Some grabbing is due to lack of social experience and consideration of others, some is due to enthusiasm or hunger, but some is due to feelings of emotional deprivation.

The teacher may need to remind the child many times to take some and leave some, as well as recognize her feelings by commenting, "It looks so good to you that you just feel like taking it all, don't you?" It is also sound strategy to make sure the hungry one gets a second helping and that she is delegated to go to the kitchen for refills. When she remembers to leave enough for the other children, her thoughtfulness should be commended.

When the grabbiness seems to be a symptom of emotional deprivation, particularly when children cram their mouths so full they cannot swallow, a more indirect approach is required that emphasizes meeting the youngster's emotional needs rather than stressing consideration of others. Here, again, extreme cases may require psychological counselling.

❧ The Process of Toileting

Taking Children to the Toilet

In general, early childhood programs use the same toilet rooms for boys and girls. However, there are always exceptions to this rule where families may feel strongly that open toileting violates the modesty of the little girls.

One benefit of toileting together is that children learn to treat sexual differences quite casually. They will ask or comment about differences from time to time, and this provides golden opportunities to give straightforward, simple explanations. (Please refer to chapter 14 for a more detailed discussion about sex education.) Open toileting has the advantage of reducing the peeking and furtive inspections that may go on otherwise. It promotes a healthier attitude toward sexual differences and therefore should be encouraged.

The majority of children of preschool age can be expected to go to the toilet when they feel the need, but an occasional child will have to be reminded. Rather than lining everyone up at once and insisting that they use the toilet, it is better to remind children while washing up for lunch or before rest that they will be more comfortable if they use the toilet first.

It will encourage children to take this responsibility for themselves if their parents dress them in pants with elastic tops or other easily managed clothing. It is also sound to remark to children that it certainly feels good to go to the toilet, a point of view with which most of them will concur.

Handwashing should be a consistent part of the toilet routine as well as the food-handling routine. Children generally enjoy it and will gladly slick their hands with soap when they are reminded. *Teachers should always take time to wash their hands, too, and use soap as well.* Although this takes a little extra time, the reduction in colds and diarrhea that results for everyone is well worth the effort (Aronson, 1991; Kendall & Moukaddem, 1992).

Thoughts About Flushing

Some children, most commonly between the ages of two and three, are really afraid of sitting on a toilet while it is being flushed (perhaps they fear vanishing down the hole with their product). Therefore, as a general practice it is wise to wait until the child gets off before asking her to flush the toilet. We have achieved good cooperation at our centre by suggesting to children that it is thoughtful to flush the toilet so that it is fresh for the next person, rather than constantly reminding, "Don't forget to flush it; go back and flush it."

Handling Mishaps

When children wet themselves or have a bowel movement in their pants, they should be changed without shaming or disgust, but without an air of cosy approval, either. Such loss of control often happens when children are new to the school, are overly fatigued, or are coming down with something, as well as when children have not yet acquired the rudiments of control. Many children are humiliated by wet or soiled underwear, and the teacher should be sensitive to this and help them change in a quiet place. The inexperienced student may find it helpful to know that it is easier to clean a child who has had a bowel movement if the child helps by bending over during the process.

Theoretically, the children should always have a dry pair of pants stowed in their cubby, but actually these are often not there when needed; so it is necessary to have some extras on hand, with the name of the school written prominently across the seat. It is helpful to have these changes of clothing available in a bureau in the toilet room itself.

Children with Special Problems

Once in a while a parent will worry aloud to the teacher that her child "never" has a bowel movement. By this she usually means that the child does not have a bowel movement every day. This may be her natural pattern of defecation, or it may be true constipation. If the child is constipated, it is best to refer the parent to his/her paediatrician for help.

The same thing goes for a three- or four-year-old who leaks a little bowel movement in her pants from time to time and refuses to use the toilet. The child is often "clean" at school but messes her pants frequently at home. The name of this condition is *encopresis*, and it often becomes such a touchy issue between parent and child and can be so hard to treat that it requires help from a paediatrician or, more likely, from a competent psychologist (Schaefer, 1979).

❦ Handling Rest Times

If eating in a strange place with unknown people is disturbing to young children, going to sleep under such circumstances can be even more so. Releasing oneself into sleep is, among other things, an act of trust, and it is not surprising that this can be difficult for a young child to allow during her first days at school. Fortunately there are some things that the teacher can do to make this task easier for her.

Regularize the Routine

Keep daily expectations and the order of events the same when approaching the rest period. That is, try to do things the same quiet, steady way every day. One pattern that works well is to send the children one by one as they finish lunch to use the toilet, wash their hands, and brush their teeth. Then they are expected to settle down on their cots or mats with a book to look at quietly until all the children are ready to begin resting. Next the room is darkened, and the teacher moves quietly about, helping children take off their shoes; find their blankets, stuffed rabbits, and so forth; and set their books aside. This process should be accomplished with quiet affection combined with the clearly projected expectation that the youngster is going to settle down.

When the children are all snuggled in their blankets, some teachers prefer to read a story, while others sing softly or play a quiet record. It helps to have the children spread

❧   *Releasing oneself into sleep is an act of trust.*

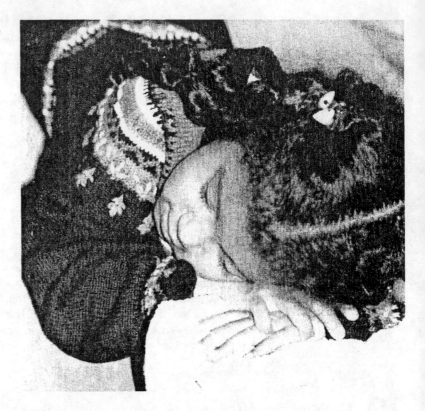

out as far from each other as possible and to have them lie head to toe; this reduces stimulation and also keeps them from breathing in each other's faces. Teachers need to be quiet and not talk among themselves, and other people must not be allowed to tiptoe in and out.

It takes at least two teachers to settle a roomful of children, and it may take as long as half an hour or 45 minutes. Some children like their backs rubbed to soothe them into slumber.

Allow Children to Get Up As They Wake Up

Usually after about an hour some of the children will wake up by themselves and begin to stir about. This gradual awakening is convenient because it means that each child can be greeted and helped to dress one by one, and it presents a nice opportunity for friendly, quiet chats with the teacher. Children are more likely to wake up in a good mood if they are wakened gradually by the activity around them rather than by having the teacher wake them up. They need time to collect themselves and to regain awareness before they begin their afternoon activities. It often works well to have a few staff members getting children up; the rest of the adults are in the play area, with snack being available as the children desire it and some quiet, attractive activity also available that the children may select when they feel ready for it.

How Long Should Children Sleep?

It is unfair to the parent to allow a child to sleep all afternoon, unless, of course, she does not feel well. A sleep of an hour or so is about right for most youngsters, but this does not include the time it takes for them to settle down.

Should All Children Nap?

All children of preschool age should be expected to lie down and relax for a while in the middle of the day. The need for sleep itself varies considerably among different children, and this difference needs to be taken into consideration. There will be some youngsters, particularly older children who are approaching kindergarten age, who never go to sleep during the daytime. They should not be expected to lie stiffly on their mats for two hours. Instead, following a reasonable rest period, they should be permitted to go outside or to another room and play under the supervision of a staff member. These more mature children often greatly enjoy helping to prepare the afternoon snack. It makes them feel important and pays tribute to their own grown-up status.

Occasionally there will be a child who needs to rest but who is so high-strung and active that she disturbs everyone at nap time. Our staff has concluded that it is more satisfactory to take these youngsters out of the nap room and give them something quiet to do in the director's office than to become involved in angry, usually noisy confrontations, which upset all the children as well as frighten the restless one.

A Practical Note About Cots

Storage of cots can be a real problem in some schools. In some provinces licensing standards permit the use of folding mats instead of cots if the floor is not too drafty. These work well except for children who wet their beds. Saran-covered cots are better to use with these youngsters so that the urine drips through and does not collect in a puddle on the mat. Tiled floors are, of course, indispensable to use in areas where children wet their beds.

❦ Summary

Routines, which consist of arriving and departing, eating, toileting, and resting, are an important part of the child's day. If they are handled well, they can contribute to both the physical health and emotional well-being of young children.

Teachers will experience greatest success in handling routines if they avoid trying to win for the sake of winning, but work instead toward the more worthwhile goals of helping the children become competent, independent people who have healthy attitudes towards their bodily needs and who look forward to eating, toileting, and resting because of the comfort and pleasure associated with these activities.

Questions and Activities

1. What foods do you particularly dislike? Can you remember the reason for your original dislike? Do you feel you learned anything from that situation that could be transferred to the way you handle eating situations with young children?
2. List all the rules you can think of that applied to eating, sleeping, or toileting in your own family as you grew up. After recalling the stated rules, think of some of the deeper, unspoken ones that were also observed.
3. *Problem:* You are the staff teacher who is delegated to greet children at the door every morning, and there is one little boy who always begins to whimper as he arrives. At that point the father jollies him along and finally gives him a smack on the bottom, telling him firmly, "Little boys don't cry!" You have learned in your student teaching days that it is important for children to express their feelings. How would you handle this situation?
4. Try an experiment wherein you just tell the children for three or four days that it is time to come in for snack, and then for the next few days try warning them ahead of time that it will soon be time to come in. Is there any difference in the way they respond?
5. *Problem:* Although you never meant to have things arrive at such an impasse, you have inadvertently made such an issue of a child's going to the toilet that he has become so balky about it he will not use the toilet any more but wets his pants instead. At this point, what approach would you try next to solve this difficulty?

Self-Check Questions for Review

Content-Related Questions

1. Why is it wise to avoid "going to war" with a child about conforming to a particular routine?
2. Name two things teachers can do to help children move easily through transitions.
3. Describe some sound procedures for helping children adjust to the new situation during their first days at the children's centre.
4. What basic principles can you think of regarding the management of routines such as eating, resting, and toileting?

Integrative Questions

1. Identify two different transition times that take place at the centre where you teach. Which one of the two goes most smoothly? Analyse why that is the case. Can procedures that are effective in managing that transition be applied to the less effective one?
2. Using Table 3.3, "Characteristic Food Choices for Seven Groups," select one particular cultural group and plan a week's lunch menus using its preferred foods that also meet the requirements of Canada's Food Guide to Healthy Eating in Figure 3.2b.

References for Further Reading

Handling Routines

Cherry, C. (1981). *Think of something quiet: A guide for achieving serenity in early childhood classrooms.* Belmont, CA: Pitman Learning. Chapter 5, "Getting the Most from Rest Times," is filled with practical suggestions about naptime and alternative approaches to rest times that are helpful for "difficult" nappers.

Read, K., Gardner, P., & Mahler, B.C. (1993). *Early childhood programs: Human relationships and learning* (9th ed.). New York: Holt, Rinehart & Winston. The chapter entitled "Helping Children in Routine Situations" contains a detailed discussion of toileting that will be of particular interest to students devoted to the psychoanalytic point of view.

Schedules

Maxim, G. (1989). *The very young* (3rd ed.). Englewood Cliffs, NJ: Merrill/Prentice Hall. Maxim provides interesting examples showing how schedules can reflect the educational values of the school.

Separation

Balaban, N. (1985). *Starting school: From separation to independence.* New York: Teachers College Press. Every teacher of young children should read this practical, insightful book.

Godwin, L. J., Groves, M. M., & Horm-Wingerd, D. M. (1994). "Don't leave me": Separation distress in infants, toddlers, and parents. In K. M. Paciorek & J. H. Munro (Eds.), *Early childhood education, 94–95* (15th ed.). Guilford, CT: Dushkin Publishing.

The authors discuss separation problems encountered at different developmental stages and include practical advice about easing this sometimes difficult transition from home to school.

Gottschall, S. (1989). Understanding and accepting separation feelings. *Young Children, 44*(6), 11–16. Sensitive, practical strategies for helping young children bridge the gulf between home and school are included here.

Nutrition

Berman, C., & Fromer, J. (1991a). *Meals without squeals.* Palo Alto, CA: Bull. A user-friendly book that should not be missed, it includes recipes, information on nutrition, cleanliness, recycling, feeding practices, and more! *Highly recommended.*

Endres, J. B., & Rockwell, R. E. (1993). *Food, nutrition and the young child* (4th ed.). Englewood Cliffs, NJ: Merrill/Prentice Hall. This book is full of practical, extensive information covering everything from menu planning to nutrition education to preparing baby formula.

Garland, A. W., with Mothers & Others for a Livable Planet. (1993). *The way we grow: Good-sense solutions for protecting our families from pesticides in food.* New York: Berkley Books. These people outline the potential dangers resulting from the overuse of pesticides and also present effective ways of advocating pesticide-free food.

Menu Planning

Edelstein, S. (1992). *Nutrition and meal planning in child-care programs: A practical guide.* Chicago: American Dietetic Association. (Available from the Association, 216 West Jackson Boulevard, Suite 800, Chicago 60606-6995.This book highlights important basic nutrition information and endears itself to me because the menus take into account diverse cultural food preferences ranging from Hispanic to lacto-ovo-vegetarian to Jewish menus. *Highly recommended.*

Minister of National Health and Welfare. (1995). *Canada Food Guide to Healthy Eating: Focus on Preschoolers.* Ottawa: Minister of Supply and Services Canada. This resource discusses how early childhood educators can promote healthy eating among children aged two to five years. There is information on essential nutrients they need to grow,

developing their enjoyment of different foods, and practices that form the basis of lifelong health-promoting eating and activity patterns.

Cooking with Children

Berman, C., & Fromer, J. (1991b). *Teaching children about food: A teaching guide and activities guide.* Palo Alto, CA: Bull. This excellent book takes a world-view approach and offers many suggestions for teaching about food as well as how to cook it. *Highly recommended.*

Jacobson, M., & Hill, L. (1991). *Kitchen fun for kids.* Washington, DC: Centre for Science in the Public Interest. Although this book is designed for older children, many recipes are included that are appropriate for young children to make. Excellent nutritional values—low fat, low salt, low cholesterol, and high fibre—are stressed. Recipes are child tested. *Highly recommended.*

Katzen, M., & Henderson, A. (1994). *Pretend soup and other real recipes: A cookbook for preschoolers & up.* Berkeley, CA: Tricycle Press. Mollie Katzen of *Moosewood Cookbook* fame has produced a delightfully illustrated, child-tested cookbook. Each recipe is pictured so that very young cooks can "read" what to do. Sensible advice is also included.

Lakeshore Learning Materials. (n.d.). *Multicultural cooking with kids.* Carson, CA: Lakeshore Equipment Company. This spiral-bound, plastic-coated book offers two to three recipes from each of several diverse cultures—Mexican, Japanese, and German, for instance—plus a cultural fact about each recipe.

Taking Cultural Food Preferences into Account

Copage, E. V. (1991). *Kwanzaa: An African-American celebration of culture and cooking.* New York: Morrow. Copage's book is rich with discussions of celebrating various aspects of Kwanzaa, as well as providing delicious recipes.

Crocker, B. (1993). *Betty Crocker's Mexican made easy.* Englewood Cliffs, NJ: Prentice Hall. Reasonably authentic Mexican recipes are featured that use readily obtainable ingredients.

Health and Welfare Canada. *Interior B.C. Native Food Guide.* In G. Chud & R. Fahlman, (1995). *Honour-*

ing diversity within child care and early education: An instructor's guide. Victoria: Province of British Columbia, Ministry of Skills, Training and Labour. An adaptation of Canada's Food Guide to a traditional First Nations diet, which provides an example of how a framework of sound nutrition can be applied cross-culturally.

Wilson, M. (1989). *The good-for-your-health all-Asian cookbook.* Washington, DC: Centre for Science in the Public Interest. Two hundred and twenty recipes are drawn from Korea, Indonesia, Malaysia, Pakistan, India, the Philippines, Singapore, Thailand, Vietnam, Japan, and China. Emphasis is on good nutrition as well as ethnic background.

Behaviour Problems Related to Routines

Ferber, R. (1985). *Solve your child's sleep problems.* New York: Simon & Schuster. Ferber, who is director of the Centre for Pediatric Sleep Disorders at Boston Children's Hospital, offers practical advice about this sometimes difficult problem.

Satter, E. (1987). *How to get your kid to eat . . . but not too much.* Palo Alto, CA: Bull. Satter provides sensible, expert advice on establishing normal feeding patterns for children together with suggestions about what to do when the pattern is not normal. Helpful for teachers and indispensable to parents.

Schaefer, C. E. (1979). *Childhood encopresis and enuresis: Causes and therapy.* New York: Van Nostrand Reinhold. Schaefer reviews prominent theories about bowel movement retention and wetting, and concludes with lists of practical recommendations.

For the Advanced Student

Bowlby, J. (1982). Attachment and loss: Retrospect and prospect. *American Journal of Orthopsychiatry, 52*(4), 664–678. This article summarizes how Bowlby, who has done important work on the effect of long-term separation of child from parent, developed his theory and supported it with research.

Pollitt, E. (1990). *Malnutrition and infection in the classroom.* Paris: UNESCO. Anyone who needs to be reminded how fortunate the majority of Canadian children are has only to read this UNESCO review of the prevalence of serious malnutrition and its impact on the physical and mental development of young children in many other countries.

Powell, G. J. (1983). *The psychosocial development of minority group children.* New York: Brunner Mazel. Powell offers information on specific nutrition problems of black, Hispanic, and Indian children.

Journals and Organizations of Particular Interest

Centre for Science in the Public Interest, 1875 Connecticut Avenue, NW, Washington DC 20009-5728. CSPI publishes a first-rate bulletin entitled *Nutrition Action* plus various attractive charts and books about nutrition. The Jacobson & Hill book and the Wilson book previously listed are some of their publications.

Development of the Physical Self

4

How can you double the space of your classroom without remodeling your facility? By opening your curriculum to the great outdoors! Ingenious and motivated teachers use the outdoor play yard DAILY to extend and enrich children's learning. Open air activities do more than educate, they rejuvenate the spirit—verified by children's frequent squeals of delight and exuberance. Mental health as well as physical health is enhanced from outdoor play. And nothing sparks children's intellect and curiosity as much as the good earth herself! Your outdoor play area offers a boundless array of hands-on learning activities for overall development.

Karen Stephens

The habit of exercise is one of the important gifts adults can give to their children. Exercise can not only be beneficial, but also fun, when it becomes part of a child's playtime, building strength, coordination, balance and confidence. In a loving and secure atmosphere, a child can play and prepare to master each physical development stage successfully. . . . A deliberate effort to develop a child's physical and mental capabilities should be made before s/he enters the school system. This responsibility lies with the parent and/or caregiver.

Canadian Child Day Care Federation

Have you ever wondered . . .

How to send a sick child home without hurting his feelings?

Whether it's really all right to admit a child to school whose parents are "going to get his booster shots just as soon as they can"?

What in the world you can do to provide some variety and range to large muscle play?

. . . If you have, the material in the following pages will help you.

Good food, reasonable toileting procedures, and adequate rest are important factors in maintaining the physical and emotional well-being of young children. Additional factors that affect the physical development of children include health and safety and the provision of maximum opportunities for their bodies to grow and develop in the healthiest way.

Promotion of Health and Safety in the Children's Centre

Providing Safe Transportation to School Is a Must!

As information continues to indicate that safety seats and seat belts help save lives, it becomes clear that teachers *must* encourage their consistent use (Kendrick et al., 1988). Preprimary teachers have a unique opportunity to foster automobile safety because they meet parents as they deliver their youngsters to school.

Many schools now insist that any child delivered to their premises be transported there "buckled up," and it is a policy that *every* centre must institute. Since some children don't like seat belts, teachers should also support the parents' efforts by discussing the value of safety restraints during large group times, explaining in a matter-of-fact, non-alarmist way how lucky we are that we have this practical way to keep us safe.

Basic Ways to Protect and Foster the Physical Health of Children

Beginning teachers sometimes do not realize how necessary it is for early childhood centres to take the lead in making sure young children have adequate health care. In 1966 the federal government instituted a national health care system for all Canadians. Services provided specifically for children included immunization at the request of the parents. Every family is entitled to receive medical assistance and care. Families may need to be encouraged to make sure their children have health check-ups and immunizations.

Since the first edition of this book was published in 1975, some encouraging progress has taken place in the area of immunization. For example, polio (infantile paralysis) has been virtually eliminated in Canada and smallpox throughout the world. In 1993, 95% of all children two years of age had completed immunization for measles, 85% for polio, and 83% for pertussis. (Canadian Institute of Child Health, 1994). This is a high rate compared with the United States, where in 1992 only 55% of two-year-olds had had all required immunizations (Children's Defense Fund, 1994).

Most provincial/territorial child care regulations require that children have a medical examination and up-to-date immunization upon enrolment; others require one or the other, and others require neither. Parents are encouraged to have their children seen by a physician regularly and to keep immunization up-to-date. A centre director can provide support and may be able to refer the family to a local public health nurse or to a physician to provide information about immunization.

There is concern that immunization is not a requirement in all parts of Canada. For this reason, *half- and full-day child care programs serving young children should be particularly adamant about requiring up-to-date immunization records from parents.* Such certifica-

❧   *But I don't want to put on my jacket . . .*

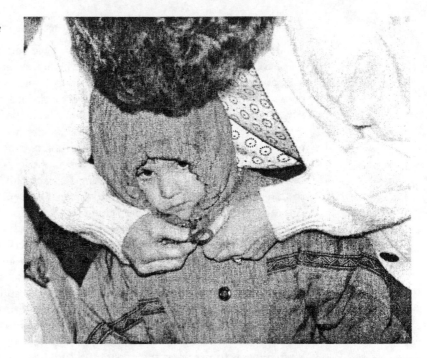

tion protects not only the child in question but also all the other children and adults in the school. Anything short of full enforcement of this policy is inexcusable.

Physical Examinations Should Be Required Before the Child Enrols

Because the child care program is often the first institution that comes into contact with families of young children in a formal way, it is particularly valuable for each school to require pre-entry physical examinations as well as inoculations. Careful evaluation of potential vision and hearing problems should be a part of this process. Some provinces/territories already make this part of their licensing regulations for child care centres and nursery schools; those that do not should be encouraged to add this requirement to their regulations promptly.

The Teacher Should Be Prepared to Help Parents Find Health Care During the Year Whenever Possible

There are a variety of health services and examinations available in many communities, and teachers need to make it their business to become acquainted with each one so that they can refer families who need their help. A good way to locate information about such services is to contact the public health nurses in your community. These people are usually gold-mines of practical information about sources of assistance.

The Teacher Should Act as a Health Screener

An alert teacher can often spot problems that have been overlooked by families and even by paediatricians, who, though expert, lack the teacher's opportunity to see the child over an extended period of time. The teacher should particularly watch for children who do not seem to see or hear well, who are very awkward, who seldom talk, who are unusually apathetic, or who are excessively active. The behaviour may be only an idiosyncrasy, or it may require professional help, and the sooner help is sought the better. (See chapters 9 and 17 for further details on identification of special problems.)

The teacher should conduct a health check of every child as he arrives at the program each day. This assures a personal greeting for each child and provides a quick once-over so that a child who is not feeling up to par may be sent home before his parent departs. Although there are some standard things to check for, such as faces that are flushed or too pale, rashes, and marked lethargy, the most important symptom to be aware of is any significant change in the child's appearance. Teachers who see the same children every day get to know how they usually look and behave and can often spot such variations promptly, and thus avoid exposing other children in school to the condition. (See Appendix B for a list of common diseases, their symptoms, and incubation periods.)

Providing care for sick children is a particularly difficult problem for families in which both parents work outside the home. Since there are very few services for the mildly ill child, parents should also be encouraged to develop a safety net of alternative care arrangements to use when their youngster is too sick to go to school and they must go to work anyway.

The Teacher Must Know What to Do When a Child Becomes Ill at School

No matter how careful the teacher and how conscientious the parent, an occasional child is going to come down with something during the day. Ideally the child should be sent home immediately, but in practice this can be very difficult to do (Aronson, 1991). Even when parents have been asked to make alternative arrangements for emergency care, these arrangements sometimes fall through, and the school and youngster have to make the best of it. Programs should try to keep children who are ill apart from the rest; usually the office serves this purpose fairly well. The child should have a place to lie down located as close to a bathroom as possible, and he will need to be comforted and reassured so that he does not feel bereft and lonely.

Because sending a child home from school often embarrasses and angers the parent and hurts the child's feelings as well, it is desirable to be firm but gentle when doing this. Sending something home along with the youngster, such as a book, will help him feel less rejected and make his return to school easier when he is feeling better.

General Health Precautions Should Be Observed Consistently by Children and Staff

Blowing noses on disposable tissue, washing hands before handling food and after toileting, and not allowing children to share food, cups, or utensils they have had in their

❧   *Washing hands before eating is an absolute must for children— and teachers.*

mouths are basic precautions that must always be observed. If teachers form the habit of washing their hands whenever they have children participate in that routine, it not only sets a good example but also helps to maintain the teachers' good health (Kendall & Moukaddem, 1992). Another routine that should be maintained is regular tooth brushing.

Sometimes when a youngster is well enough to return to school he must still continue taking medicine during school hours. A word of warning is in order here: Most schools make it a practice *never to administer any kind of medication (including aspirin)* without the express written request of the physician and parent (Aronson & Smith, 1993). This is part of the regulations in some provinces. See the publication *Well Beings* (1993) for helpful strategies recommended by the Canadian Pediatric Society for administering medication. Children recovering from illnesses need to be watched carefully to make certain they do not become overtired and suffer a relapse of their illness.

It is also important to be aware of the temperature of the day, to take jackets off indoors, and to dress the children warmly enough outdoors, but not too warmly. Particularly in the fall, some parents tend to weigh their children down with too much clothing, and the children may be so absorbed in their play that they can be dripping with sweat and not realize it. The teacher needs to remind them about staying comfortable and help them adjust their clothing to suit the temperature when necessary.

Maintaining the Physical Safety of Children

Teachers must never forget that the children in their care are not their own and that supervising them carries with it a special responsibility.

❦   *All schools should carry insurance.*

Even though insurance costs are high, it is very important for all schools to carry it both to protect them against being sued and also to provide accident coverage for the children.

In addition, the entire school needs to be checked continually to make sure it is maintained in a safe condition (Consumer Products Safety Commission, 1991). Broken equipment such as tricycles without pedals and wobbly jungle gyms *must be removed or repaired promptly*. Sticks, particularly those with nails in them, should be discarded. Safety precautions such as using swings with canvas seats should be observed. The danger area around swings must be clearly marked, and children should be taught to wait on the bottom step of the slide (which can be painted red to make it easier to identify).

Disinfectants, ant poisons, scouring powders, bleaches, and antiseptics, which are all commonly found in centres and schools, should be kept on high shelves in the kitchen, where children are not permitted or, better yet, in locked cabinets.

In chapter 1 it was suggested that inexperienced teachers stop an activity if it looks dangerous to them rather than permit an accident to happen. One other safety rule has proved to be generally helpful: The teacher should never lift a child onto a piece of play equipment if he cannot manage to get on it by himself (swings are an exception to this rule). Of course, youngsters sometimes climb up on something, feel marooned, and must be helped down; but that is different from lifting them onto the top of the jungle gym or boosting them onto a tippy gangplank before they are really able to cope with these situations.

One study of child care centres found that accidents occurred most frequently at 11 a.m. and 4 p.m., that the accident rate was highest for two-year-olds, and that the peak days for accidents were Mondays and Fridays (Sacks et al., 1989). It appears that these are times when teachers should be especially careful while supervising children.

It is particularly important to remember that high places such as slides and monkey bars are dangerous for young children. For this reason it is vital to maintain soft, deep surfaces such as sand, rubber, or bark mulch beneath such equipment. *Grass is not suitable* (Consumer Product Safety Commission 1991; Moore, Goltsman, & Iacofano, 1993).

Injury is the leading cause of death for children and youth in Canada. For children aged one to four years of age, 40% of deaths are caused by injuries (see Figure 4.1). Through public awareness, education, and technological and regulatory solutions, injury rates have gradually decreased. They remain, however, high. In a five-year period, 1212 Canadian preschoolers died from injury-related causes. Moreover, for every child that died, there were seventy-five admissions to hospital for injuries and it is estimated that a further one thousand children needed medical attention (Canadian Institute of Child Health, 1994). The territories and the prairie provinces have rates much higher than the national average. Groups are working to initiate community-based injury prevention programs that alter the environments in which children play. Caregivers can also help children learn traffic safety rules so that children can be responsible when crossing the street or wearing helmets when riding their bikes.

The concern for safety has to be moderated by the teacher's good sense and self-control. Children must be protected, but they also need the chance to venture and try things out. This venturesomeness is a hallmark of four-year-olds in particular. Occasional small catastrophes are to be expected, and teachers should not become so overly protective that they hover over the children and remonstrate with them constantly to be careful.

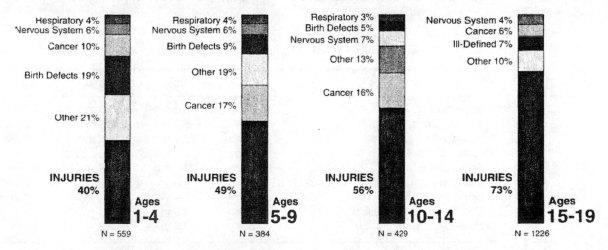

Figure 4.1 — Leading causes of death by age.

Source: Health Canada, 1995

Instead, they should try to maintain a generally high level of safety combined with the opportunity for the children to experiment with the mild risks that build feelings of competence as they are met and mastered.

✺ Basic Principles of Physical Development

Before reading about specific ways to foster psychomotor development, the student needs to understand some developmental principles that have important implications for education.

Development Occurs in Predictable Patterns and Sequences

Although some investigators have questioned the concept that chronological age should determine when children are taught various skills (Bruner, 1964; Gagné, 1968), it is still generally agreed that children progress through a predictable sequence of developmental stages (Schickedanz, Hansen, & Forsyth, 1990). The examples provided in Table 4.1 illustrate this clearly. (Appendix C provides a chart of normal development from infancy to six years of age, organized according to the various selves.) This is as true of physical development as it is true of intellectual development (Piaget & Inhelder, 1967). Children usually sit before they stand, stand before they walk, and walk before they run (Curtis, 1982). In addition, specific skills such as running, jumping, and throwing progress through a number of substages of competency before they emerge as mature physical abilities (Cratty, 1986; Thelen, Ulrich, & Jensen, 1989).

Teachers need to be able to recognize these stages of development so they can adjust their curriculum offerings to provide a good balance between opportunities for practice

Table 4.1   Age at which a given percentage of children perform locomotor skills

	25%	50%	75%	90%
Rolls over	2.3 mo	2.8 mo	3.8 mo	4.7 mo
Sits without support	4.8 mo	5.5 mo	6.5 mo	7.8 mo
Walks well	11.3 mo	12.1 mo	13.5 mo	14.3 mo
Kicks ball forward	15 mo	20 mo	22.3 mo	2 yr
Pedals trike	21 mo	23 mo	2.8 yr	3 yr
Balances on one foot 10 seconds	3 yr	4.5 yr	5 yr	5.9 yr
Hops on one foot	3 yr	3.4 yr	4 yr	4.9 yr
Catches bounced ball	3.5 yr	3.9 yr	4.9 yr	5.5 yr
Heel-to-toe walk	3.3 yr	3.6 yr	4.2 yr	5 yr

Source: From *Developing Motor Behavior in Children: A Balanced Approach to Elementary Physical Education* by D. D. Arnheim and R. A. Pestolesi, 1973, St. Louis: C. V. Mosby. Selected items from the Denver Developmental Screening Test by permission of William K. Frankenburg, MD, and Josiah B. Dodds, PhD, University of Colorado Medical Centre.

in order to consolidate the skill and opportunities for accepting the challenge of a slightly more difficult activity to go on to.

The Course of Development Moves from Head to Tail

This *cephalocaudal* principle means that children are able to control the region around their head and shoulders before they can control their hands and feet. This is an easy principle to remember if one recalls that babies can sit up and manipulate playthings long before they are able to stand on their feet and walk. Quite simply, children are able to reach, grasp, and use their hands with considerable skill before they are able to master the art of skipping or kicking accurately. The curriculum of the preschool should be planned accordingly.

The Course of Development Moves from Large to Fine Muscle Control

Large muscle activities have been identified by Guilford (1958), who factor-analysed activities from motor proficiency tests, as including activities involving static balance, dynamic precision, gross body coordination, and flexibility. *Fine muscle* activities include such things as finger speed, arm steadiness, arm and hand precision, and finger and hand dexterity. Development from large to fine muscle control means that children gain control over their larger muscles first and then gradually attain control over the finer muscle groups. Thus a child is able to walk long before he is able to construct a tabletop house of tiny plastic bricks.

The educational implication of this developmental principle for early childhood teachers is that young children need ample opportunities to use their large muscles in vigorous, energetic, physical play. It can be torment for young children to remain confined too long at chairs and tables. However, since the finer muscle, eye-hand skills are also beginning to develop during this period, activities that stimulate children to practise these skills should also be offered—but not overdone to the point that excessive demands are made on the children's self-control.

☙ Fostering Large Muscle Development in Young Children

Use of Apparatus to Promote Large Muscle Skills

In general, the school should furnish a large assortment of big, sturdy, durable equipment that provides many opportunities for all kinds of physical activity. It should also provide a teacher who values vigorous large muscle play and encourages children to participate freely in this pleasure.

Equipment good for crawling through, climbing up, balancing on, and hanging from should be included. Children need things they can lift, haul, and shove around to test their strength and use to make discoveries about physical properties that the equipment possesses. They need things they can use for construction, and they need equipment that provides opportunities for rhythmic activities, such as bouncing and jumping and swinging. In addition, there must be places of generous size for them to carry out the wonderful sensory experiences that involve mud, sand, and water. Finally, they need plenty of space in which to simply move about.

I have been deliberately nonspecific about suggesting particular pieces of large muscle equipment in the hope that talking about children's activity requirements will encourage the teacher to consider afresh what might be used to meet these needs. However, for those who wish to pursue this question in detail, an excellent publication provides detailed lists of indoor and outdoor equipment and firms that manufacture it: *Selecting Educational Equipment and Materials for School and Home* (Moyer, 1986).

There is also a continuing and heartening trend toward designing play equipment that is novel, often beautiful, and occasionally cheaper than our more mundane playground furnishings (Eriksen, 1985; Greenman, 1988, 1993; Talbot & Frost, (1989).

Equipment need not be expensive to provide sound play value. Several references that give suggestions about how to combine economy with beauty and ingenuity are included at the end of this chapter (Werner & Simmons, 1990). It is wise to remember, though, that poorly constructed, cheap equipment can be the poorest kind of economy in the long run. Children are hard on things, and it does not pay to buy or make playthings that are flimsy—better to have a bake sale and raise money for better quality equipment than be stuck with buying two cheap swing sets two years in a row.

In general, the more movable and versatile the equipment is, the more stimulating and interesting it will remain for the children. Observation of many schools has convinced me that movable outdoor equipment is one of the things in shortest supply in the play yard; yet it is vital to have plenty of boards, sawhorses, large hollow blocks, ropes, rubber tires, and barrels lest the children feel starved when they cannot complete their more ambitious projects. Centres should budget for more of this kind of equipment every year; there is no such thing as owning too much of it.

Before buying outdoor equipment, however, every teacher should read the discussion by Kritchevsky and Prescott (1977) about how to plan and develop play centres that will have maximum attractiveness and play value for young children. Material explaining the English concept of adventure playgrounds should also be investigated (Allen, 1968; Brett, Moore, & Provenzo, 1993). These wonderfully messy, casual-looking playgrounds place great emphasis on freedom to try out and explore.

Once the equipment has been acquired, it is important to maintain it carefully. Hollow blocks, which are very costly, should be used on grass or outdoor, grass-type carpeting, not on cement or asphalt, where they will splinter badly when knocked down. Most wood equipment has to be sanded and varnished every year to keep it smooth, and over a period of time this treatment can make it beautiful as well. Wooden items must be stored under cover at night. Metal items should be stored under cover when possible to avoid rust.

Of course, children's vigorous activities do not need to be restricted to the playground. Children will be delighted with the chance to visit parks with large open spaces where they can run freely and roll down hills. Many communities have wading pools for preschoolers or special play areas set aside for younger children. Even a trike expedition around the block with a pause at an interesting long set of steps can offer challenges that should not be overlooked, particularly in a full-day program.

ᴄᴈ   *It is particularly important to remember that high places can be dangerous for young children. Clearly, this youngster is having second thoughts!*

The Role of the Teacher in Fostering Large Muscle Play

In addition to providing equipment to enhance large muscle play, teachers can do much to encourage this kind of activity. Probably the most important thing they can do is provide enough uninterrupted time for satisfying play to transpire. Children need time to develop their ideas and carry them through, and if they build something, they need time to use it after they build it.

Outdoor playtime at the early childhood level is not treated in the same way that teachers often handle recess in the elementary school. Playtime at this level requires active involvement of the teacher with the children. She does not do this by participating as a companion in their play, but by observing and being alert to ways to make the play richer by offering additional equipment or tactfully teaching an intrusive child how to make himself more welcome to the group. Because her function is to encourage the continuation of play, she tries to be as facilitative yet unobtrusive as possible. The research study for this chapter illustrates what a valuable contribution teacher planning and participation can make to the physical development of children.

It is especially important for teachers to be aware of children with special needs during outdoor play time. According to Merle Karnes (1994), some ways in which teachers

❧ **RESEARCH STUDY** ❧

Can a Little Instruction Make a Big Difference?

Research Question: Can instruction in large muscle skills really make a significant difference in the way young children develop physical motor abilities?

Research Method: In this two-part study, fourteen college students majoring in physical education worked with fifty-three children. After all the children were assessed on a competency-based test of motor skills, half of them (Group A) worked with the physical education majors for an hour once a week, and half (Group B) did not. At the end of ten weeks the children in both Group A and Group B were retested. During the second half of the study Group B received physical training and Group A did not.

Research Results: The retest results clearly demonstrated that training in motor skills significantly improved the children's abilities. Statistical analysis revealed that "for Group A, scores for tests 2 and 3 were significantly higher than test 1 (p=.0001). For Group B the test 3 score was sig-

nificantly higher than tests 1 and 2 (p=.0001)" (page 81). Boys and girls showed similar gains in their skills.

Implications for Teaching: This study provides evidence that as *little as one hour a week of instruction in physical skills can make a real difference in what children are able to do.* When we consider the contributions to improved self-esteem and the foundations these skills lay for the development of more complex motor activities as the children grow, the value of providing carefully planned outdoor play opportunities becomes clear. Of course, this finding does not imply that every minute of outdoor play should be devoted to planned activities. It does, however, make a good case for the value of providing a range of large motor activities that help children gain command and satisfaction over what their bodies can do.

Source: From "Physical Education for Head Start Children: A Field-based Study" by A. A. Ignico, 1991, *Early Child Development and Care, 77,* 77–82.

can help children with disabilities enjoy playtime include letting these children become familiar with the play area without having other children around to overwhelm them, making certain such youngsters understand outdoor safety rules, encouraging them to take part in large motor activities, encouraging them to play with or at least near other children, and encouraging them to try out things that are within their abilities while keeping a sensible balance between overprotection and poorly judged risk taking.

If the teacher keeps her eyes and mind open to possibilities, there are many ways to adapt outdoor equipment to make it accessible to everyone. For example, wide pathways paved with a relatively solid material such as crushed brick makes the use of wheelchairs simpler. Slides that have handrails for protection and are within reach of the teacher make slides safer, more enjoyable, and accessible to all the children. Straps or extra-thick pedals on tricycles allow more children to ride. If a portion of the sandbox is built waist-high, children with crutches or in wheelchairs can reach the sand more easily. The same is true for water tables. If a child with limited vision is attending the school, it may be necessary to add physical barriers around such areas as swings. Large muscle play also offers excellent opportunities for children with disabilities to play with the other children if equipment is included that requires two or more youngsters to make it work: Rocking boats, trikes with wagons, and round tire swings can all help meet this need.

While the teacher needs to keep the environment safe, at the same time she should keep an open mind about the uses to which equipment can be put. If they are encouraged, children often come up with original or unconventional uses of materials that are not dangerous and that should be welcomed by the teacher because they are so creative and satisfying to the child. For example, one of our centre children recently got together all the beanbags to use as a pillow in the playhouse, and another youngster used the hose to make a worm tunnel in the sandbox. These harmless, innovative activities are all too easily squelched if the teacher is insensitive to their value or too conventional in her thinking.

Finally, the teacher should keep on the lookout for children who are at loose ends and involve them in activities before they begin to run wildly and aimlessly about. Teachers need to be comfortable with a good deal of noise and to welcome the vigorous activity so characteristic of four-year-olds, because they need this opportunity for vigorous assertion and movement in order to develop fully.

❧ Use of Perceptual-Motor Activities to Enhance Physical Development

Reports concerning the general level of physical fitness in young children are not encouraging. A recent study that assessed activity patterns and fitness levels of children aged six to nine years reported that schools do not offer enough scheduled physical education time and that recess times also provide inadequate physical education experience (Ross & Pate, 1987).

Early childhood educators, too, are inclined to turn the children loose during outdoor play and just supply an assortment of equipment such as swings and slides, hoping that the children will seek out the experiences they need by using this apparatus in a variety of ways (Poest, Williams, Witt, & Atwood, 1989). But we now know that perceptual-motor activities can go beyond this sort of thing without requiring children to be regimented and drilled. We really should offer them a broader selection of physically developmental activities than we formerly did if we wish to enhance the full range of their skills. Moreover, children should be encouraged to play vigorously and to sustain their efforts while avoiding overfatigue so that they increase the level of their physical fitness while playing. Just as wholesome eating habits contribute to better lifelong health, so, too, does the establishment of healthy habits of exercise in early childhood (Aronson, 1991).

There are two ways to approach the area of planned perceptual-motor activities: The first provides opportunities for practice in specific skills, and the second uses physical activity to promote creative thought and self-expression. Both approaches have merit.

Planning for Specific Perceptual-Motor Activities

After considerable review of the literature I have concluded that a moderate program offering the clearest language combined with a structure easily understood by teachers and applicable to preschool children is the one first utilized by Arnheim and Sinclair in

❦   *Rocks provide interesting challenges to practise dynamic balance.*

their book *The Clumsy Child* (1979). They divide motor tasks into the following categories: locomotion, balance, body and space perception, rhythm and temporal awareness, rebound and airborne activities, projectile management, management of daily motor activities (including many fine muscle tasks), and tension releasers.

It is relatively simple to think of motor activities in relation to these headings once they have been identified and to make certain that opportunities for repeated practice in each of the categories are included in curriculum plans. The trick lies in concocting ways of presenting them that appeal to children. Obstacle courses, simple want-to-try-this kinds of noncompetitive games (Orlick, 1982), and movement activities can all be used effectively if only the teacher will keep in mind the diversity of action that should be incorporated. Fortunately the mere challenge of having such possibilities available often provides attraction enough since youngsters are almost irresistibly drawn to physical activities that are just challenging enough without being too difficult. As a matter of fact, if children are encouraged to experiment, they will often develop the next hardest task for themselves following mastery of its simpler elements.

Fostering Fine Muscle Development (Daily Motor Activities)

Table 4.2 primarily stresses large muscle involvement; but the reader should remember that fine muscle (eye-hand) skills are just as important. These skills include sewing and working with pegboards, puzzles, beads, and put-together materials (often termed *manipulatives*). Block building (which taps stacking and balancing skills), pouring and spooning in their many forms, and manipulating art materials (most particularly pencils, brushes, scissors, and crayons), also require careful coordination of eye and hand, as does woodworking—it takes a good deal of skill to hit a nail with something as small as a hammerhead.

❧   *Fine-muscle skills are absorbing but tiring for young children to pursue.*

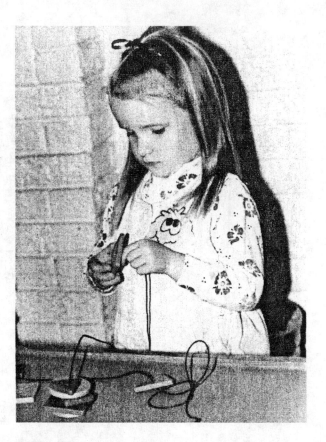

Things to Remember When Presenting Fine Muscle Activities

Offering a range of challenge in levels of difficulty is particularly important in a group of mixed ages, but even in a relatively homogeneous group of three-year-olds, provision must be made for the fact that the level of fine muscle skill—not to mention the amount of emotional control and ability to concentrate—will vary considerably from child to child. Rather than setting out three or four puzzles of sixteen pieces each, the children's range of abilities will be better met if one or two inset puzzles, and perhaps seven-, fif-teen-, and twenty-two-piece puzzles, are set out and changed as they become boring.

Sometimes it adds interest to offer two levels of otherwise identical material. Large and small wooden beads make an interesting contrast, or occasionally puzzles that have the same picture but vary in the number of cut pieces can be purchased and made available for use. Children enjoy having access to both levels and like to put into words what it is that makes the materials similar and what it is that makes them different.

Fine muscle activities should be of reasonably short duration. It is difficult for young children to hold still for very long, much less sit and concentrate on a fine muscle task that requires considerable self-control. For this reason, several activities should be available at the same time, and children should always be free to get up, move around, and shift to more or less taxing experiences as they feel the need. Quiet periods such as story

Table 4.2 Categories of physical activities and some suggestions for providing practice of these skills at the preschool level

Category	Illustrative Activities	Comments
Locomotion		
Rolling	Roll over and over, sideways, both directions. Forward roll (somersault).	Nice to have tumbling mats, but not essential—rug, grass, or clean floor also works.
Crawling, creeping	Move by placing weight on elbows only, dragging feet. Crawl using arm and leg in unison, on same side of body, or use alternating arm/leg crawl.	Works well to give these movements animal names such as "bear walk," "duck waddle."
Climbing	Apparatus valuable here—good to incorporate stretching, hanging, and reaching in this activity.	Necessary to be careful of safety.
Walking	Can vary with big, little steps, fast or slow. Encourage movement in different directions.	Good to do walking activities barefoot on contrasting surfaces for sensory input.
Stair climbing	Nice to use this during an excursion unless the school has a five- to six-step stairway.	This is an interesting indicator of developmental level: Younger children take steps one at a time, drawing second foot up to meet leading foot. Older children alternate feet in this task.
Jumping, hopping, and skipping	Children can jump over lines or very low obstacles, as well as jump down from blocks of various heights. Hopping is difficult for young children; it is a prelude to skipping. Encourage learning to hop on either foot and alternating feet. Skipping is often too difficult for nursery school youngsters. Valuable skill to ultimately acquire, since it involves crossing midline in a rhythmical alternating pattern.	Can use animal names here, also. Don't encourage running backward—young children often catch feet and trip themselves.
Running and leaping	Nice to find a large, grassy area for these kinds of activities; makes a nice field trip.	Often provides emotional relief, too. Gives marvelous feeling of freedom, power, and satisfaction.

Balance		
Static (balance while still)	Balance lying on side. Balance standing on tiptoes. Balance on one foot, then the other, for short periods of time.	
Dynamic (balance while moving)	Use balance beam many ways, or use large hollow blocks as stepping stones, or walk on lines. Build a beam that tapers from wide to narrow for children to use.	A swinging clatter bridge of loosely joined boards to step on, if available, is a particularly challenging task; may overwhelm some children.
Balance using an object	Balance beanbags on hands, or back, or head. Work with unbalanced objects—pole with weight on one end, for example, or an umbrella.	
Body and space perception	Movement education techniques apply to this category particularly well. How big can you be? How little? Can you make a sad face? Can you fit inside this circle? Can you fill up this circle (a very big one)? How much of you can you get in the air at once? Use shadow dancing for effective awareness building.	Helps to refer to other people's bodies, too; for example, "Where is Henry's elbow?" Listening, imitative actions such as "Simon says" are fun if not carried on too long. Can stress position in space—"over," "under," and so on; tedious if overdone.
Rhythm and temporal awareness	Any moving in time to music or to a rhythmic beat. Can be varied in many ways—fast, slow, or with different rhythmic patterns. Important to keep patterns simple and clear with preschoolers. Remember that many nursery school activities such as swinging and using rocking horses, also fit this category; fun to add music to these for a change.	Creative dance is the usual medium—"rhythm band" is a typical kindergarten-level activity, which is essentially conforming rather than creative. (See also material on dancing in chapter 15.)

Category	Illustrative Activities	Comments
Rebound and airborne activities	At preschool age these are generally thought of as "bouncing" activities; mattresses, bouncing boards, and large inner tubes offer various levels of difficulty.	Do not use a trampoline; it requires extraordinarily careful supervision. Many insurance companies absolutely refuse to provide insurance for this piece of equipment.
	Swings and hand-over-hand bars are also, in a sense, airborne.	
Projectile management Throwing and catching	Throwing and catching usually require teacher participation. Children throw best using relatively small objects but catch best using large ones!	Use objects that move slowly and are harmless; Nerf balls, beanbags, large rubber balls, whiffle balls, and fleece balls meet this requirement.
	Can throw objects at a target such as a wall, or into a large box.	
	For catching, older children can use a pitchback net; useful for understanding effect of force in relation to throwing.	Need lots of beanbags; not much fun to have to run and pick them up every two or three throws.
Kicking	Begin with kicking a still ball, then go to a gently rolling one.	Children whose families are interested in soccer are particularly fond of this activity.
Striking	Hit balloons with hands and then with paddle.	Many teachers are nervous about striking activities, but these activities are challenging to children and worth the careful supervision and rule setting they require.
	Can hit a ball balanced on traffic cone with light plastic bat (whiffle ball good for this).	
Bouncing	Best with a large rubber ball; use two hands then go to one hand; bounce to other children.	
Daily motor activities (fine muscle activities)	Includes many self-help skills such as buttoning and even tooth brushing! Also includes use of almost all self-expressive materials and use of tools in carpentry and cooking.	Be careful of overfatigue.
	See discussion on fine muscle activities in text.	
Tension releasers and relaxation techniques	Refer to material in text.	

Source: Based on *The Clumsy Child* (2nd ed.) by D. D. Arnheim and W. A. Sinclair, 1979, St. Louis: C. V. Mosby. These activities are only a handful of a great many possibilities. For more extensive

hours or snack times should not be followed by additional quiet, fine muscle play but by more vigorous large muscle activity.

When children are using fine muscle materials, the teacher should watch out for signs of unusual frustration. I once had a little boy in my nursery school who participated with enthusiasm and happiness in almost everything we did, with one notable exception. Whenever he played with floor blocks, he would work for a while and then in a rage send them flying. Yet he was drawn to them as a moth to a flame. His mother and I were baffled; he seemed well adjusted and easygoing, with only this exception. The staff tried building his skills, investigated whether he was happy at home, and watched to see whether other children interfered with his work and made him angry, but we could find no satisfactory answer. Finally one day his mother arrived beaming at school with the following tale. Alan and his father had been looking out the window the week before, and he had said, "Oh, look Papa, see those two kitties!" But his father had looked and asked, "What two kitties?" since he could see only one. "Why, those two little black kitties right over there," said Al. Shortly thereafter, when his eyes were examined, the answer to his block problem became clear—he was slightly cross-eyed, just enough so that stacking small blocks was a particularly irritating problem for him to solve, and it was this condition that caused him to send them tumbling down when his self-control was exceeded by the difficulty of the task.

❧   *Providing large pieces of equipment that can be moved around by the children challenges them to test their strength.*

This story may help other teachers remember to be alert to activities that seem to provoke consistent frustrations in some children. Such a reaction can often be a symptom of a physical problem that warrants further investigation, since early remediation makes correction more likely.

Relaxation and Tension-Relieving Activities

Sometimes we do not think of relaxation as being a motor skill but rather the absence of one, since "all the child has to do is hold still!" However, the ability to relax and let go can be learned (Humphrey, 1993; Jacobson, 1976), and the ever increasing stress of life as people mature in our culture (Selye, 1981) makes acquiring these techniques invaluable. Moreover, since full-day programs invariably include naps as part of their routine, knowledge of relaxation techniques is doubly valuable there. Tension, of course, is intimately tied to emotional states as well as to activity level. We all know that children who are emotionally overwrought find it more difficult to relax. It is worth taking extra time and pains with such youngsters to teach them relaxation skills because of the relief they experience when they can let down even a little.

When one is encouraging children to relax, reducing stimulation from the outside is a good principle to bear in mind. This is often done by darkening the room, playing quiet music, and providing regular, monotonous sensory experience such as rocking or gently rubbing backs.

Yawning, breathing slowly, shutting eyes, and lying somewhat apart from other children will make relaxation easier. The attitude of the teacher moving slowly about and talking quietly is a significant influence as well. Sometimes young children are able to use imagery and picture a quiet place they would like to be. For very young children it is usually necessary to suggest such places—perhaps rocking in their mothers' laps, or lying on a water bed, or resting on the grass on a warm, sleepy day.

During movement and dance activities, children should alternate between quiet and active activities. They can be encouraged to sense their own bodies and purposefully relax themselves by being floppy dolls or boiled noodles or melting ice cream. Relaxation should be contrasted with its opposite state of intense contraction. Even young children can learn to make their bodies stiff and hard and then become limp and soft, thereby applying Jacobson's techniques of progressive relaxation (1976). Stretching, holding the stretch, and then relaxing are also easily understood by young children, and it does feel wonderful. As we come to understand more about meditation, it becomes evident that some of these techniques can be used with children, also. An interesting example of such an application is *The Centering Book,* which lists many kinds of awareness and relaxation activities, some of which can be adapted for preschool children (Hendricks & Wills, 1975). Cherry's book *Think of Something Quiet* (1981) also provides many practical ideas of ways to help even very young children learn to attain at least a modicum of inner peace by using various relaxation and meditative techniques.

Even more fundamental than relaxation techniques, however, should be the goal of alleviating whatever is generating tension in the first place. There are numberless reasons why children or adults feel tense, ranging from suppressed anger to shyness or that general feeling of apprehension commonly termed anxiety. Since methods of fostering emotional health and reducing anger are discussed in considerable detail later on, suffice it to say here that perhaps the most basic way to help people become less tense is to enable them to become more competent in as many areas of their lives as possible. This feeling of competency—being in command of oneself and one's life—is a highly effective, long-term antidote for tension.

Using Physical Activity to Promote Creative Thought and Self-Expression

Using Movement Exploration

One of the newer aspects of creative physical education is termed *movement education* (Benzwie, 1987; Bresson, 1990; Hemmett, 1992). It is a nice blend of physical activity and problem solving that can be considerable fun for children. The teacher may ask a youngster, "Is there some way you could get across the rug without using your feet?"and then, "Is there another way you could do that?" Or she might question, "What could you do with a ball with different parts of your feet?" or "Can you hold a ball without using your hands?"

It is obvious how this kind of teaching fosters the development of fluency in ideas, and some research by Torrance (1970) indicates that when this approach was used with first and second graders in a dance class, they placed significantly higher on tests of creativity than did untrained third graders.

A nice example of how this kind of material can be presented is provided by Mimi Chenfeld (1993):

> We stay very still. Now move just one part. Move another part. And another. The miracle of the moving parts. Now move two parts of you. Another two. Now three—four—five!
>
> We make Thumbelinas with our thumbs and watch them dance. We dance all the toys in the toy store: windup toys that spurt to action, then slow down; cars, trucks, trains, planes; limp rag dolls that leap into limp rag doll dances; fluffy soft toys that make everyone feel wonderful.
>
> We imagine the sounds our bodies would make as they move. We make the sounds of a finger wiggling, a head shaking, feet kicking, a back bending, arms waving.
>
> We wear a "Happy face" button and wonder how we would move if we were "Happy faces." How would a happy face move shoulders? Feet? How would a happy face dance? (p. 38).

Using Creative Dance as a Means of Self-Expression

Dancing can be the freest and most joyful of all large motor activities. For young children, dancing usually means moving rhythmically to music in a variety of relatively unstructured ways. The quandary beginning teachers often feel is just how unstructured this should be. It is rarely effective to just put on a record, no matter how appealing, and expect the children to "dance." On the other hand, the teacher who sets out to teach specific patterns, often in the guise of folk dances, surely limits the creative aspects of this experience. Besides that limitation, patterned dances are usually too complicated for young children to learn unless these are stripped to very simple levels.

What works best is to have an array of records or tapes on hand with which the teacher is very familiar and that provide a selection of moods and tempi. It is important also to have several activities thought out in advance to fall back on if something does not go over well and to plan on participating with the children. Finally, as the session moves along, more and more ideas and movements can be drawn from the children themselves—an approach that makes the activity truly creative and satisfying for them.*

ᔥ Fostering Sensory Experience

It has been maintained that 80% of everything we learn comes to us through our eyes, but it seems to me that our society encourages use of this one sense far more than is necessary. One has only to watch the deodorant and disinfectant advertisements on television to become aware of the tremendous emphasis on the desirability of smelling only a few choice fragrances. Children are continually admonished not to touch things, and as they mature, they are also taught not to touch other people except under carefully restricted circumstances. As for tasting, how many times have you heard a mother warn, "Don't put that in your mouth; it's dirty." The latest victim of the war against the senses appears to be hearing. In self-defence, people seem to be learning to tune out the continual piped-in music of the supermarket and the constant noise of the television set.

Teachers need to contend with this narrowing and restricting of the use of the senses by deliberately continuing to use *all* of them as avenues of learning. Children should be encouraged to make comparisons of substances by feeling them and smelling them, as well as by looking at them. Science displays should be explored by handling and manipulation rather than by looking at bulletin board pictures or observing demonstrations carried out by the teacher. Stress should be placed on developing auditory discrimination skills (telling sounds apart) as well as on paying attention to what is said by the teacher. Learning through physical, sensory participation should be an important part of every preschool day.

The Sensory Experience of Close Physical Contact Is Important to Children

The recent handful of sensational court cases concerning sexual abuse in children's centres has made some teachers of young children uneasy about touching or cuddling youngsters lest they, too, be accused (Mazur & Pekor, 1985). They feel torn between the desire to protect themselves and the knowledge, well substantiated by practical experience, that young children require the reassurance and comfort of being patted, rocked, held, and hugged from time to time.

Research as well as experience supports the value of close physical contact. Montagu (1986) has reviewed numerous studies illustrating the beneficial effect of being touched and the relationship of tactile experience to healthy physical and emotional development. Investigations documenting the link between touching and the development of attachment confirm those findings (Brown, 1984).

Yet staff members must realize that parents are understandably concerned about the possibility of sexual abuse. Centres need to do everything in their power to reassure them. No one, teachers included, wants children to be molested, and parents worry

---

*Please refer to chapter 15 for more detailed suggestions.

❧   *There's just no substitute for cuddling.*

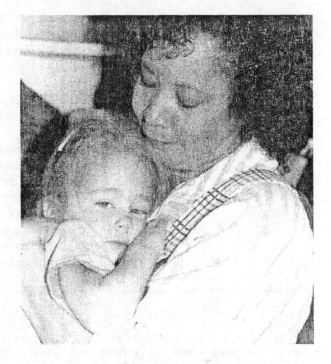

about this particularly when children are away from home. To allay these fears, centres should have clearly stated policies encouraging parents to drop in for unannounced visits, and they should create opportunities for families and teachers to become well acquainted so a climate of trust develops between them. If the centre is staffed so that more than one person is with the children at all times, so much the better.

When such openness is the case, parents are reassured, and children and staff are more comfortable, too. In these circumstances the children will grow and thrive, and Cornelia Goldsmith's statement will prove as true today as when she said it forty years ago—"The teacher's most important piece of equipment is her lap!"

❧ Summary

The promotion of health and safety is vital to the physical well-being of young children. During the hours when children are at school, it is the teacher's responsibility to see that they follow good health practices and to keep the children as safe as possible without nagging them or being overprotective.

In addition, it is desirable to offer equipment and activities that foster large and fine muscle development. Attaining competence in these physical areas enhances children's self-esteem and provides opportunities for them to gain social expertise as they develop wholesome feelings of vigour and good health.

Equipment for large muscle activities should be versatile, sturdy, safe, and well maintained. The teacher can encourage active play by tuning in on what is happening and being alert to ways to add to its richness rather than by regarding large muscle play time as a recess period when she can sit down and relax.

Fine muscle activity is also valuable to offer, but it is important to provide an assortment of levels of difficulty and to be sure that such activities do not continue for too long a time without relief.

Increasing knowledge of perceptual-motor development has made it necessary for preprimary teachers to broaden the range of activities offered to young children in order to provide opportunities for practice in specific motor skills: locomotion, balance, body and space perception, rhythm and temporal awareness, rebound and airborne activities, projectile management, fine muscle activities, and relaxation techniques. Movement activities that encourage creative thinking and self-expression should also be included.

Use of all the senses is important in education. Encourage children to touch, taste, and listen as well as look in order to make the fullest use of these potential pathways for learning.

By using this comprehensive approach involving large and fine muscle skills and various sensory abilities, teachers can assure themselves that the physical development of the child is brought to its fullest potential.

Questions and Activities

1. *Problem:* A little girl has just fallen out of the swing and is brought into the office bleeding heavily from the mouth. Examination reveals that her front tooth is still whole but has cut entirely through her lower lip. As the teacher in charge, how would you handle this emergency? Remember to think about both short- and long-term aspects of the situation.

2. Are there any conditions in the centre where you are teaching that are particularly well handled in terms of safety precautions? Are there some possible hazards that warrant attention?

3. Suppose you were beginning a new program and had a budget of $3000 for large muscle equipment. In your opinion, what would be the most satisfactory way to invest this money? What would you buy and why?

4. Could there be advantages to putting children through a planned series of physical exercises on a regular basis? This might not be calisthenics as such; it might be tumbling or learning ball skills. What might be the disadvantages of this approach to physical education?

5. Some preprimary teachers, particularly male ones, appear to avoid physical contact with children. What do you think might be the reasons for this restraint? Is it always fear of being accused of sexual abuse, or could there be other reasons for this behaviour?

6. What are some examples from your own experience in which you are aware that the use of every sense except vision is restricted or curtailed?

Self-Check Questions for Review

Content-Related Questions

1. Explain why it is so important for children's centres to insist that children be immunized and that they have a physical examination before attending school.

2. List some general health precautions teachers should follow when caring for children.

3. List three principles of physical development.

4. Name the categories of large muscle behaviours discussed in the text and give an example of an activity that would fit each category.

5. Describe some possible adjustments that could be made to an outdoor yard that would enable children with various kinds of special needs to participate more fully.

6. What are some typical fine muscle activities offered to young children in preprimary schools? Why is it important not to keep children doing these for overly long periods of time?

7. Discuss some effective ways to help children learn to relax.

8. What are some effective policies that schools might follow to reassure parents their children are safe from sexual abuse?

Integrative Questions

1. You are now the director of a child care centre, and the annual visit by the licensing inspector is due very soon. When you check the immunization records of the children in preparation for that visit, to your surprise you find that about a third of the children's immunizations are not up-to-date. You send out a notice requesting parents to take their children to the doctor to have the necessary shots. Three weeks later, only two parents have turned in updated reports. What steps would you take next to ensure compliance with the regulations?

2. The teacher in the room next door is very interested in promoting physical fitness, so she usually organizes her four-year-olds into teams and has them compete to see which team can get through the obstacle course fastest. Explain whether you would include that kind of activity in your plans for the children in your room. Be sure to include reasons why you would or would not do this.

3. An obstacle course that includes crawling through a cement pipe, swinging across the grass holding onto a rope with both hands, and walking along a narrow line drawn on the sidewalk has been planned for outdoor play. Which of the eight categories described in this chapter are included in this activity? What categories are *not* included? Suggest activities to add to the obstacle course that would provide practice for two more categories.

4. You have a child with limited vision in your three-year-old group. She can tell light from dark and see coarse details of objects that are held close to her eyes, but her distance vision is almost nil. Explain what changes you are going to make in your playground to keep her safe and enable her to participate happily in many outdoor activities.

References for Further Reading

Overview

Gabbard, C. C. (1991). Early childhood physical education: The essential elements. In K. M. Paciorek & J. H. Munro (Eds.), *Early childhood education, 91/92.* Guilford, CT: Dushkin. Gabbard provides a good, brief overview of and justification for the value of physical education activities for young children.

Health and Safety

Canadian Pediatric Society (1992). Well Beings: A guide to promote the physical health, safety and emotional well-being of children in child care centres. Toronto: Creative Premises Ltd. This comprehensive two-volume publication details everything an early childhood educator needs to know about good health care practices for young children in Canada.

Kendall, E. C., & Moukaddem, V. E. (1992). Who's vulnerable in infant child care centres? *Young Children, 47*(5), 72–78. The answer to that question is that both infants and adults are vulnerable, and adults should take consistent sanitary precautions to reduce the risk of infection.

Kendrick, A. S., Kaufmann, R., & Messenger, K. P. (Eds.), (1991). *Healthy young children: A manual for programs* (2nd ed.). Washington, DC: National Association for the Education of Young Children. The authors cover everything from nutrition to child abuse to infectious diseases. The writing style is simple and practical.

Pimento, B., & Kernstead, D. (1995). *Healthy foundations in child care.* Don Mills, ON: Nelson. This book represents the holistic nature of health and incorporates the essential aspects in Canadian child care centres. There is a comprehensive chapter on promoting physical well-being with information on fostering a healthy lifestyle as well as a chapter on safety promotion.

Information about Physical Development

Gallahue, D. L. (1993). *Developmental physical education for today's children.* Madison, WI: Brown and Benchmark. The author provides many suggestions for exploratory activities that provide practice in basic physical skills. He lists developmental acquisition stages for skills and includes a full spectrum from early childhood to adulthood. The book includes a chapter on disabilities.

Payne, V. G., & Isaacs, L. D. (1987). *Human motor development: A lifespan approach.* Mountain View, CA: Mayfield. This comprehensive text treats the subject of motor development in depth. Useful for the serious student of this subject.

Poest, C. A., Williams, J. R., Witt, D. D., & Atwood, M. E. (1990). Challenge me to move: Large muscle development in young children. *Young Children, 45*(5), 4–10. The authors present a well-reasoned case for improving the quality of large muscle experiences for young children.

Including Children with Disabilities in Large Muscle Activities

Block, M. (1994). *A teacher's guide to including students with disabilities in regular physical education.* Baltimore, MD: Paul H. Brookes. There are two chapters in this book that are particularly valuable for preschool teachers. One provides suggestions for adapting activities to specific disabilities. The other discusses how to draw preschool children who have disabilities into active physical participation—and shows how to translate an individual education program (IEP) into actual activities. *Very practical.*

Activities and Playgrounds That Foster Balanced Physical Development

Frost, J. L. (1992). *Play and playscapes.* Albany, NY: Delmar. This is the outstanding reference in the field—well written and informative.

Greenman, J. (1988). *Caring spaces, learning places: Children's environments that work.* Redmond, WA: Exchange Press. Greenman provides wonderful ideas for anyone redesigning or designing space for children. The book is delightful to read—written with humour and experienced insight.

Hammet, C. T. (1992). *Movement activities for early childhood.* Champaign, IL: Human Kinetics. Written by an obviously experienced teacher of preschool children, this book presents many activities for developing movement skills.

Hôpital Maisonneuve-Rosemont, (1994). *Guide on the safety of children's playspaces and equipment.* Montreal, QC: Direction de la santé publique. This guide is designed for organizations involved in the design, purchase, and maintenance of play equipment and play spaces.

Kruger, H., & Kruger, J. (1989). *The preschool teacher's guide to movement education.* Baltimore, MD: Gerstung. Carefully divided according to developmental stages, this book is rich with ideas and practical suggestions for fostering movement exploration.

Miller, K. (1989). *The outside play and learning book: Activities for young children.* Mount Rainier, MD: Gryphon House. Many age-appropriate, attractive, fresh suggestions for outdoor activities are included here. Topics range from ideas for riding toy play to snow and woodworking activities.

Pica, R. (1990). *Toddlers moving and learning.* Champaign, IL: Human Kinetics. I include this book of activities because it is so difficult to locate material simple enough for these very young children. The book comes complete with three audiotapes of appropriate music.

Sanders, S. W. (1992). *Designing preschool movement programs.* Champaign, IL: Human Kinetics. Readers of *The whole child* will find Sander's book especially helpful because it follows the same outline of physical skills used in chapter 4. It offers lots of ideas about activities that are appropriate and stimulating for practice in large muscle skills. *Highly recommended.*

Stephens, K. (1993). Making the most of outdoor play: A bounty of ideas to motivate the hesitant teacher. *Child Care Information Exchange, 91,* 49–54. Stephens presents a wealth of suggestions for snowy, rainy, and windy days, open-air art, shadows, wheel toys, and so forth.

Teaching Children to Relax

Humphrey, J. H. (1988). *Teaching children to relax.* Springfield, IL: Charles C. Thomas. After discussing the causes of tension, Humphrey provides instructions for progressive relaxation, meditation, and other techniques. Many of the suggestions could be used successfully with preschool children.

For the Advanced Student

Allen, Lady of Hurtwood. (1968). *Planning for play.* Cambridge, MA: The MIT Press. Lady Allen, a progressive thinker, was among the first to advocate the development of adventure playgrounds. She describes the purpose of this book as being "to explore some of the ways of keeping alive and sustaining the innate curiosity and natural gaiety of children." It does that. A classic.

Aronson, S., & Smith, H. (1993). *Model child care health policies.* Washington, DC: National Association for the Education of Young Children/American Academy of Pediatrics, Pennsylvania Chapter. A concise summary of health and safety checklists and standards is included, plus health charts conveniently listed two ways—by symptoms and by the condition's name. *Highly recommended.*

Brett, A., Moore, R. C., & Provenzo, E. B. (1993). *The complete playground book.* Syracuse, NY: Syracuse University. For a useful overview of playgrounds past and present, this is an excellent resource. Particular attention is paid to European playgrounds, and plentiful illustrations enrich the text.

Canadian Institute of Child Health (1994). *The health of Canada's children: A CICH profile* (2nd ed.) Ottawa: CICH. This document gives an overview of trends and statistics in the broad area of health and illness, including childhood injuries.

Consumer Product Safety Commission. (1991). *Handbook for public playground safety.* Washington, DC: Consumer Product Safety Commission.. This is the basic reference in the field—it includes standards for preschool play yards. Indispensable.

.Stinson, W. J. (Ed.). (1990). *Moving and learning for the young child.* Reston, VA: American Alliance for Health, Physical Education, Recreation, and Dance. A collection of papers from a conference about preschool children and physical education, this book has a touch of everything in it.

Publications and Associations Having Related Interests

Canadian Bike Helmet Coalition, c/o Canadian Institute of Child Health, 885 Meadowlands Dr. E., Ste. 512, Ottawa, ON, K2C 3N2. The Coalition offers resources to help initiate community bike helmet promotion campaigns.

Canadian Children's Safety Network, c/o Canadian Injury Prevention Foundation, 20 Queen St. W., Ste. 200, Toronto, ON M4H 3V7. The group has a national online computer communication system for injury prevention advocates to maintain and enhance prevention efforts.

Canadian Institute of Child Health, 885 Meadowlands Dr. E., Ste. 512, Ottawa, ON K2C 3N2. The institute offers many publications and resource materials committed to improving the overall health and well-being of children in Canada.

KidsCare National Program, Product Safety Bureau, Health Protection Branch, Health Canada, Place du Portage, Phase I, 17th floor, 50 Victoria St., Hull, QC K1A 0C9. Concerned with product safety awareness for children, parents, and anyone interested in child safety.

III

Nourishing and Maintaining Emotional Health

5

Fostering Mental Health in Young Children

6

Developing Self-Esteem in Young Children

7

What Parents Need

8

Tender Topics: Helping Children Master Emotional Crises

9

Welcoming Children Who Have Special Educational Requirements into the Life of the Program

Fostering Mental Health in Young Children

Have you ever wondered . . .

How to get a child to say what she's feeling instead of hitting somebody?

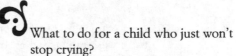What to do for a child who just won't stop crying?

How to tell whether a child is mentally healthy?

If you have, the material in the following pages will help you.

Children of all ages need an atmosphere of warmth in which to thrive, the warmth of close, honest human contacts. They need the feeling that adults, teachers, and parents like them, are interested in them, enjoy them, and feel ready to be responsible for them, to protect them even from themselves when occasion demands.

Barbara Biber

*T*he valuable contribution early childhood programs can make to fostering mental health was emphasized as long ago as 1970, when the Joint Commission on the Mental Health of Children repeatedly pointed out that day care centres and early childhood programs present outstanding opportunities for carrying out preventive and remedial work in this area. The potential value of these programs to children's mental health continues to be recognized today (Mrazek & Haggerty, 1994).

Emotionally, preschoolers have great needs for security and nurturing. During this time, they are learning a sense of who they are and developing self-esteem. They rely heavily on support, encouragement, and positive feedback from the adults in their lives. We do not have emotional and mental health indicators that are population-based for this age. We do know that the basis for forming a trusting relationship and developing a positive sense of self takes place during these years. We also know that the majority of children are in inadequate child care facilities. We know that there is solid evidence that quality early childhood education benefits children, particularly children from disadvantaged settings. We need to ensure that children are provided with environments that support their emotional and mental health. There are many practical things an early childhood educator can do to foster mental health in children.

For this reason, several chapters of this book are devoted to establishing general policies that enhance emotional well-being, dealing with crisis situations, handling discipline and aggression, and building self-esteem, because these are all important aspects of developing emotional health. Additional aspects of mental health, covered under the development of the social self, include learning to care for other people, valuing cross-cultural education, and taking pleasure in meaningful work. An ounce of prevention is worth thousands of dollars worth of remedial care.

ℭ Importance of Developing Basic Attitudes of Trust, Autonomy, and Initiative in Young Children

The most fundamental thing the teacher can do to foster mental health in young children is to provide many opportunities for basic, healthy emotional attitudes to develop. Erikson (1959, 1963, 1982) has made a significant contribution to our understanding of what these basic attitudes are. He hypothesizes that during the life span, an individual passes through a series of stages of emotional development wherein basic attitudes are formed. Early childhood encompasses three of these stages: trust versus mistrust, autonomy versus shame and doubt, and initiative versus guilt. Although children at the preprimary level are likely to be working on the second and third sets of attitudes, it is important to understand the implications of the first set, also, since Erikson theorizes that the resolution of each stage depends in part on the successful accomplishment of the previous one.

In the stage of *trust versus mistrust* the baby learns (or fails to learn) that other people can be depended on and also that she can depend on herself to elicit needed responses from them. This development of trust is deeply related to the quality of care that the mother provides and is often reflected in feeding practices, which, if handled in a manner that meets her needs, help assure the infant that she is valued and important. Although by the time she enters child care the balance between trust and mistrust will have been tipped in favour of one attitude or the other, the need to experience trust and to have it reaffirmed remains with people throughout their lives. This is also true for the other attitudes as they develop.

Therefore, it is vital that the basic climate of the centre encourage the establishment of trust between everyone who is part of that community. If the teacher thinks of establishing trust in terms of letting the children know they can depend on him, it will be fairly easy for him to implement this goal. For example, consistent policies and regularity of events in the program obviously contribute to establishing a trustful climate. Being reasonable also makes it clear to the children that they can depend on the teacher. In addition, if he is sensitive to the individual needs of the children and meets these as they arise, the teacher can once again confirm the message that they are worthy of love and thus further strengthen trust and self-esteem.

In our society the attitudes of *autonomy versus shame and doubt* are formed during the same period in which toilet training takes place. During this time the child is acquiring the skills of holding on and letting go. This fundamental exercise in self-assertion and control is associated with her drive to become independent and to express this indepen-

∿ *What would this child have done if he couldn't have turned to his teacher for help? A friend in need is a friend indeed!*

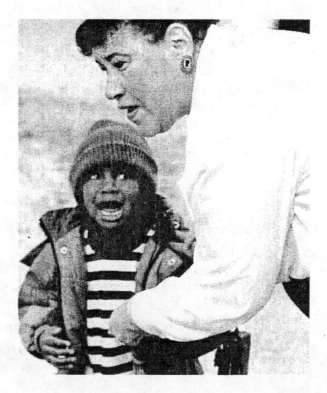

dence by making choices and decisions so often couched in the classic imperatives of the two-year-old: No! Mine! and Me do it! Erikson maintains that children who are overregulated and deprived of the opportunity to establish independence and autonomy may become oppressed with feelings of shame and self-doubt, which result in losing self-esteem, being defiant, trying to get away with things, and in later life developing various forms of compulsive behaviour.

The desirable way to handle this strong need for choice and self-assertion is to provide an environment at home and school that makes many opportunities available for the child to do for herself and to make decisions. This is the fundamental reason why self-selection is an important principle in curriculum design. At the same time, the teacher must be able to establish decisive control when necessary, since young children often show poor judgement and can be tyrannized by their own wilfulness unless the teacher is willing to intervene.

Gradually, as the child develops the ability to act independently, she embarks on building the next set of basic attitudes. Around the age of four or five she becomes more interested in reaching out to the world around her, in doing things, and in being part of the group. At this stage she wants to think things up and try them out; she is interested in the effect her actions have on other people (witness her experimentation with profanity and "bad" language); she formulates concepts of appropriate sex roles; she enjoys imaginative play; and she becomes an avid seeker of information about the world around her. This is the stage Erikson has so aptly named *initiative versus guilt.*

To feel emotionally satisfied, a child of this age must be allowed to explore, to act, and to do. Early childhood programs are generally strong about meeting children's need to explore and create, but they often underestimate the ability of older four- and five-year-olds to participate in making plans and decisions for their group or to attempt challenging projects. Of course, the teacher must make allowance for the fact that four- and five-year-olds are better planners and starters than they are finishers. Satisfaction in completing projects is more likely to be part of the developmental stage that follows this one: the stage of *industry versus inferiority,* which is characteristic of the child during early years in primary school. But encouraging the ability to initiate plans and take action will enhance the child's feeling of self-worth and creativity as well as her ability to be a self-starter—all highly desirable outcomes necessary for future development and happiness.

ॐ Hallmarks of an Emotionally Healthy Young Child

To determine whether the child is in good emotional health, the teacher should ask the following questions about her. If the majority of them can be answered affirmatively, chances are good that she is emotionally healthy.

Is the Child Working on Emotional Tasks That Are Appropriate for Her Age?

We have already talked about the fundamental need for planning a curriculum that provides many opportunities for children to exercise their autonomy and initiative. When looking at individual children, the teacher should consider whether they are taking advantage of these opportunities. He will find that the majority of them are achieving independence, choosing what they want to do, and generating their own ideas with zest and enthusiasm; but there will be a handful of youngsters who need sensitive help to venture forth. This usually involves taking time to build a strong foundation of trust between the child and teacher and then helping her advance to increased independence as her confidence grows (Balaban, 1989).

Is the Child Learning to Separate from Her Family without Undue Stress and to Form an Attachment with at Least One Other Adult at School?

In chapter 3 considerable space was devoted to handling separation anxiety in a constructive way, because the ability to separate from significant others and form additional relationships is an important skill. The teacher should realize that most children, particularly shy ones and those who are younger, make friends with a teacher at school before they branch out to make friends with other children. This link between teacher and child is, of course, not so strong as the bond between parent and child (Godwin, Groves, & Horm-Wingerd, 1994). However, it seems reasonable to propose that in a milder way a wholesome attachment between teacher and child encourages the youngster to explore and venture out in the centre setting, just as it has been demonstrated by Ainsworth and her colleagues (1978) that toddlers who are well attached to their mothers are more likely to venture and explore new experiences when that parent is present. The teacher who is aware that this is a typical and valuable pattern can relax and enjoy this process without fretting about the child's dependency because he has confidence that in time most children will leave his side in favour of being with other youngsters. This bond between teacher and child may not be so evident with socially able four-year-olds as it is with younger children, but it should exist all the same. If the child has not formed a relationship with some adult after she has been at school for a while, she should be encouraged to do so. Being attached to the teacher makes it more probable that she will use the teacher as a model or come to him for help when it is needed. Affection between teacher and child is also important because it is a fundamental ingredient of good discipline— but more about that later.

At the same time, the teacher has to be sensitive to the quality of the attachment. Oversolicitude for the child's feelings of loneliness or the teacher's own unmet needs for affection can occasionally create a form of dependency that is undesirable because it restricts the child's venturing out and making friends with her peers. This situation should, of course, be avoided. The teacher must learn to tell the difference between a youngster who genuinely needs the emotional support of a close relationship at first and the one who is using her as an emotional crutch.

Is the Child Learning to Conform to Routines at School without Undue Fuss?

Of course, conforming to routines varies with the age of the child and her temperament, and teachers anticipate some balkiness and noncompliance as being not only inevitable but healthy. Two-year-olds are particularly likely to be balky and at the same time insist that things should be done the same way every time. Self-assertiveness appears again rather prominently between the ages of four and five. The quality of the behaviour seems different though: The assertiveness of age two comes across as being more dogmatic and less logical, whereas the assertiveness of age four seems to be more of a deliberate challenge and trying out of the other person. However, consistent refusal to conform differs from these healthy behaviours because it goes beyond these norms. When this is the case, it should be regarded as a warning sign that the child needs help working through the behaviour.

Is the Child Able to Involve Herself Deeply in Play?

A characteristic of severely disturbed children in residential settings is that they cannot give themselves up to the experience of satisfying play. Indeed, when they become able to do so, it is encouraging evidence that they are getting ready to be released. Being able to play is also important for more typical children. The child's ability to enjoy participating in play by herself or with other children as she grows older not only is a hallmark of emotional health, but also contributes to maintaining mental health.

Is the Child Developing the Ability to Settle Down and Concentrate?

Children may be distractible or restless for a variety of reasons, and no child is able to pay attention under all circumstances. Excitement, boredom, the need to go to the toilet, fatigue, interesting distractions, or not feeling well can all interfere from time to time with any child's ability to concentrate. But occasionally the teacher will come across a child who never seems to settle down: She flits continually from place to place and seems to give only surface attention to what she is doing. There are a multitude of reasons for this behaviour, ranging from poor habits to birth injuries, but a common cause of distractibility is tension or anxiety.

One study that followed children who were particularly restless at age three to age eight found that restlessness predicted an antisocial outcome at age eight (Richman, Stevenson, & Graham, 1982), so teachers need to be aware of this behaviour and make efforts to encourage such youngsters to settle down to an activity as often as possible. (For further discussion of restless behaviour possibly due to attention deficit disorder, please refer to chapter 9). Since maternal depression appears to be linked to children's restlessness, a possible referral for counselling for the mother and child may be desirable.

Is the Child Unusually Withdrawn or Aggressive for Her Age?

One of the great advantages teachers have is that by becoming acquainted with hundreds of children over a period of time, they are able to develop some norms for behaviour that make it relatively easy to identify youngsters who behave in extreme ways. Very withdrawn behaviour is more likely to be overlooked than aggressive behaviour because it is much less troublesome to the teacher. He should be aware, however, that either response

ઈ   *The ability to lose oneself in play is an indicator of emotional health.*

is a signal from the child that she is emotionally out of balance and needs some extra thought and plans devoted to helping her resolve whatever is causing her to cope in that manner.

Does the Child Have Access to the Full Range of Her Feelings, and Is She Learning to Deal with Them in an Age-Appropriate Way?

Some children have already learned by the age of three or four years to conceal or deny the existence of their feelings rather than to accept and express them in a tolerable way. Early childhood teachers can help children stay in touch with the full repertoire of their emotions by showing them that they, too, have all sorts of feelings and that they understand that children have feelings as well, whether these be anger, sadness, or affection (Locke & Ciechalski, 1985). Healthy children should also begin to learn during their early years to express their feelings to the people who have actually caused them and to do this in a way that does not harm themselves or others. Learning to do this successfully takes a long time but has its roots in early childhood.

𝄃 *Personal Qualities That Will Help the Teacher Establish a Healthy Climate in the Early Childhood Program**

Early childhood teachers should use their personal qualities as well as what are commonly referred to as "teaching techniques" to foster an emotionally healthy, growth-enhancing climate for young children. Such a climate consistently favours the active development and maintenance of an atmosphere conducive to mental health. It frees people to develop to their fullest potential as balanced, happy individuals, and the personal qualities of a "sensitive" teacher have a lot to do with establishing this desirable climate. For this reason they are discussed next.

Consistency

One way to build a sense of trust between teachers and children is to behave in ways children can predict and to be consistent about maintaining guidelines and schedules—a very basic form of being "trustworthy" and dependable. Thus, the children know what to expect and do not live in fear of erratic or temperamental responses to what they do. For this reason, emotional stability is a highly desirable trait for teachers of young children to possess. Of course, consistency does not mean that rules must be inflexible, but their enforcement should not depend on the whim of the teacher or the manipulative power of various children.

Reasonableness

Coupled with the steadiness of consistency should go the trait of reasonableness, which I define as "expecting neither too much nor too little from children." One practical way to increase reasonableness is to learn the characteristics of the developmental stages when these are discussed in child development courses. The brief developmental summaries presented in this book are intended to remind the student of general developmental characteristics. Knowledge of these characteristics prevents inexperienced teachers from setting their standards too high or too low. They do not expect a two-year-old to have the self-control of a four-year-old. On the other hand, when a four-year-old starts making demands more typical of a two-year-old, they know that she is regressing and that they must search for and alleviate the stresses causing her retreat.

Another excellent way to help children (and other adults also) see that the teacher is reasonable is to really listen when people try to tell you something. Walter Hodges (1987) describes this kind of active listening to perfection:

> Active listening requires giving undivided attention to children and accepting what they say without blame, shock, or solving their problems for them. Giving undivided attention is signalled by positioning squarely in front of a child, getting close to the child's eye level, and lean-

---

*The work in this section owes much to the humanistic philosophy of Carl Rogers and his client-centred approach to psychotherapy.

ing forward without crowding. Active listening enables us to reflect the feelings of the child, respond appropriately, and to check to see if we understand. Active listening communicates respect, warmth, and empathy. Children know that they are important and that they belong when they are heard. (p. 13)

I am indebted to one of my students for the following example of what can happen when one shuts out such information.

> We were in the playhouse corner and Heidi was wearing a coat while doing all her kitchen duties. Jennifer came in and stood beside me and said, "I want that coat!" I was about to see if maybe Heidi was wearing Jennifer's coat when a nearby student teacher said it was Heidi's and that Jennifer had a sweater in her cubby.
>
>   "Jennifer, why don't you get your sweater from your cubby?" I suggested.
>
>   "But I want that coat!" she said, on the verge of tears.
>
>   "I can see you want that coat very much, but I can't take it away from Heidi," I said.
>
>   "But it's mine; I don't want a sweater."
>
>   "Do you have a coat at home that looks like that? Is that why you think it's yours?" I asked.
>
>   "Uh-huh. Give it to me!" she demanded (tears still there in the eyes).
>
>   "I'm sorry, Jenny, I can see that you're very unhappy not to have your coat, but I can't take Heidi's," I said.
>
>   "My mommy said I could have it!"
>
>   By now I was finally suspicious, so I checked the coat Heidi was wearing. There, written across the collar, was the name *Jennifer!*
>
>   Heidi gave up the coat without a fuss, Jenny put it on, I apologized to her, and she went out to play!

The student concludes by commenting, "All I can say is that I would make sure next time of what I was talking about. It taught me, 'Look before you leap!' to which I would add the advice, 'Take time to listen—you may learn something important.'"

Courage and Strength of Character

Particularly when dealing with outbursts of anger, the student will find that courage and the strength of character commonly called "fortitude" are required to see such outbursts through. Understandably the embarrassment and insecurity of fearing that the scene may not turn out all right may make it easy to placate an angry child or, more usually, to allow her to run off or have her way. But the trouble with allowing this to happen is that the child will repeat the behaviour and feel contemptuous of the adult who permits it. Therefore, being courageous and seeing a problem through are worth the struggle when coping with the strong emotional reactions so common at this age. (Please refer to chapters 8, 11, and 12 and for more detailed discussions of how to do this.)

Trustful Confidence

Trustful confidence is the teacher's faith that the child wants to grow and develop in a healthy way. Interestingly enough, psychoanalysts maintain that this ability to have trust or confidence in the good intentions of other people goes back to the individual's own experiences as an infant when she found she could or could not generally depend on her environment to be a nurturing one. Be that as it may, research bears out what many teachers and parents have determined empirically: Children respond to what is genuinely expected of them by the people who matter to them (Rosenthal & Jacobson, 1968). The teacher who optimistically trusts children to act in their own best behalf is likely to obtain this response from most of the children most of the time.

Congruence

The teacher also promotes trustful confidence between himself and the child by being honest with himself and with the youngster about his own feelings. This is what Rogers and Dymond (1954) call "congruence" and Patterson (1977) terms "genuineness." A congruent person attempts to recognize and accept his own feelings and be truthful about them to other people. Thus, a teacher might level with one child by saying, "I don't want you to kick me again; I feel really angry with you when you do that to me" or with another by saying, "I'm glad to see you today. I've been looking forward to hearing about your new kittens."

However, a note of caution is in order. Rogers advocates revealing such feelings *when it is appropriate to do so.* Children should not be subjected to outbursts of temper or angry attacks by adults in the name of congruence. Uncontrolled outbursts are too disturbing to children, since they know they are relatively helpless and at the mercy of the teacher.

Empathy

Empathy is the ability to feel as other people feel, to feel *with* them rather than *for* them. Empathy is valuable not only because it allows teachers to put themselves in the child's place, but also because it helps them identify and clarify for the child how she is feeling. Research supports the value of this quality. A study by Truax and Tatum (1966) has shown that the teacher's empathic ability combined with the ability to express warmth is effective in fostering positive adjustments to the preschool setting and to peers.

Warmth

Warmth is so important and deserves special emphasis because its presence has been linked to the development of positive self-concepts in children (Rohner, 1986). The warm teacher lets the children and staff know that he likes them and thinks well of them. Both children and adults flourish in this climate of sincere approval and acceptance. But being warm and accepting does not mean that the teacher just sits around and smiles at the children no matter what they do. There is a difference between expressing warmth and being indulgently permissive, and there are times when the teacher must exert control because a child is unable to. But when a teacher does this for a child, he must make it plain that he is taking control because he truly cares for her and not because he wants to obtain power for its own sake or have the satisfaction of winning.

Interestingly enough, a new study by Stipek et al. (1992) indicates that the quality of teacher warmth is typically linked to the style of instruction provided by the teacher.

They found that classrooms in which teachers used a "didactic," teacher-directed approach stressing academic skills ranked low on subscales evaluating teacher warmth, child initiative, and positive control. On the other hand, teachers who used a more child-centred approach scored high on those same subscales, thereby making the presence of a positive social climate more probable.

Appreciation

Teaching must be unbearable, or at least much less satisfying, for those who fail to take time to relish and enjoy the children in their care. What a shame it would be to overlook the comment, "Oh see! That little cat is licking her sweater!" or not sense the impact for a two-year-old who bids her mother adieu and then says stoutly, "I'm my own Mommy, now!" Such precious moments can be a major reward of teaching if only teachers take the time to savour and appreciate the children and their reactions.

I hope "appreciation" is not interpreted by the reader to mean "be amused by the children." Appreciation is not the same thing as amusement. Appreciation is composed of perceptive understanding and empathy—with a dash of delight thrown in! When children sense this attitude, they blossom because they feel the approval it also implies. I suspect it feels to them as if a generous sun were shining in the room.

༄ *Being warm and close with children is an important part of teaching.*

Good Health

The longer I teach and observe students teaching, the more firmly I become convinced it is necessary to emphasize the significance of valuing and taking care of oneself if one wishes to facilitate health in others.

We all have times when there seems to be no other choice than to operate on the ragged edge of energy. Some teachers, however, appear to accept this as being a continuing, necessary style of life. Teachers who wish to do their best with children, as well as with their other personal relationships, need to recognize what their bodies and spirits need and honour these needs to remain physically and emotionally healthy. The prescription includes adequate rest, exercise, wholesome food, and someone to care about who cares in return. Providing oneself with these requisites should be viewed as being part of one's own basic self-respect as well as being plain good sense.

Attaining These Qualities

Some of the aforementioned qualities, such as consistency, fortitude, and reasonableness, can be acquired through practice and experience. The others—empathy, trustful confidence, congruence, warmth, and the ability to appreciate others—can often be enhanced by participation in well-run encounter groups or through psychological counselling if they do not seem to come naturally. Many teachers have found that such experiences have improved both their teaching abilities and their personal relationships.

⌒ꓽ Practical Things the Teacher Can Do to Help Young Children Achieve Healthy Emotional Development

Before turning to a discussion of more concrete things the teacher can do to contribute to a supportive milieu, the student should remember two principles. The first principle is that young children respond with encouraging quickness to a change in atmosphere or approach. It is possible to quickly bring about positive changes in their feelings and behaviour by using appropriate methods.

The other principle has been mentioned before: Children are resilient (Wang & Gordon, 1994; Werner, 1984). They bounce back from their own and others' mistakes, and it is unlikely that one imperfect handling of a situation will inflict permanent damage on a child (Yarrow, 1980). This is not said to sanction irresponsible actions by teachers but to reassure beginners that when dealing with difficult situations they should not be unduly hesitant on the grounds they may injure the child. It is the repetition of procedures and the overall quality of the milieu, rather than the single episode, that are likely to enhance or damage.

Develop Friendly, Close Relationships with Each Family

Entrance to the children's centre usually marks the occasion in the child's and parents' lives when she leaves their protection for the first time on a regular basis. If the school and family establish a feeling of closeness and a shared interest in the child's welfare, it is easier for her to make this transition, since her world is thereby widened rather than split into two pieces.

Teachers are quick to see the advantage that a friendly, comfortable atmosphere means the family is more likely to seek advice from the school. But another advantage should not be overlooked: The teacher is also in a better position to accept advice and suggestions from the parents when a caring, sharing atmosphere is established. This two-way respect fosters genuine mutuality and lays the basic foundation for emotional health at school.

Reduce Frustration for the Child when Possible

Children should not have to spend time waiting for things to happen when this can be prevented. Children's needs are *immediate, intense,* and *personal,* and the longer they are kept waiting the more irritable they become. Snacks should be available as the children sit down, and someone should be outside for supervision as the children are dressed and ready to go out and play. Duplicates of equipment mean that there is generally enough to go around; two or three toy trucks are much more satisfactory than just one. A good assortment of developmentally appropriate activities must be available so that three-year-olds are not expected to stack tiny plastic blocks and five-year-olds do not have to make do with eight-piece puzzles. The day should be planned so that few and moderate demands are made on children at points when they are likely to be tired and hungry.

Of course, the teacher cannot and should not seek to eliminate all frustrating circumstances. Comparative animal studies indicate that a moderate amount of adversity may foster socialization (Elliot & King, 1960; Hess, 1960). But so many interruptions and frustrations happen even in well-run nursery schools (Jackson & Wolfson, 1968) that the elimination of unnecessary sources of frustration makes sense.

Learn to Identify and Describe Children's Feelings to Them and Help Them Express These Feelings to the Relevant People in an Acceptable Way

In our society we seem to have reached the conclusion that it is dangerous to allow some emotions to be expressed, the assumption being that if they are expressed they will become stronger or the person will act the feeling out, but if we ignore them or deny their presence they will vanish. Actually, the opposite of this premise is psychologically true. The following stanza from William Blake's "A Poison Tree" puts this neatly:

I was angry with my friend,
I told my wrath, my wrath did end.
I was angry with my foe,
I told it not, my wrath did grow.

Negative emotions that are recognized, accepted, and expressed usually fade, but if they are not expressed they seem to generate pressure that ultimately causes the person to relieve them in a more explosive or veiled, yet hostile way. Also, if children are *not* provided with ways of telling others how they feel, they are almost inevitably driven to show them how they feel by acting the feelings out.

❧   *Nobody wants a child to feel the way Aimee does, but it's better to share the feeling with her than deny it by just trying to cheer her up.*

The advantage of helping the child know how she feels is not only that she avoids these overwhelming explosions or complicated emotional displacements but also that she learns that all emotions are acceptable and that, therefore, an important part of herself is acceptable. As she matures, this self-knowledge forms a foundation for learning to express feelings in a way that harms neither herself nor other people.

It takes practice and sensitivity to acquire the skills of describing the child's feelings to her and helping her express them, but research shows that teachers can learn these skills (Kane, Wiszinckas, & Fourquer, 1981). There is more to it than just saying to an angry child, "You're feeling really mad at him, aren't you?" Some examples will help illustrate the technique.

Evelyn says goodbye to her mother and then hangs by the gate, looking after her sadly as she drives away. Her teacher bends down, picks her up, and says, "You look like you wish she'd stay this morning, Evelyn." "I do, I do, I want her to stay—[emphatically] I hate her, that mean old mommy of mine, I hate her, and I wish she'd stay!" "Yeah, I know how it is—you feel sad she's left you, and it makes you mad because you wanted her to stay." "Yes! And I'm never, never going to speak to her again." (They move toward the nursery school room and go inside.) "And I'm just going to feed her turnips and beans for dinner—turnips and beans, turnips and beans, turnip and beans!" But this is said with decreasing venom and increasing humour as she trails off toward the housekeeping corner to embark on her busy day.

Sometimes it helps to look at the other side of the coin. A student submitted the following example and analysis when asked to submit an insensitive response that did *not* take the child's feelings into account.*

One evening I was staying with Vickie, age three, while her father visited her mother in the hospital. Grandmother had dropped by with a covered dish for supper and some sweet rolls for breakfast. Vickie hadn't eaten a very big dinner. She went over to the counter and tried to reach the rolls.

"Can I have a roll?"

"No, Vickie, those are for breakfast."

"But I need just one."

"You can have one for breakfast."

A few minutes later she said, "How about a roll?"

"No, Vickie." Later as I was cleaning the kitchen, Vickie was colouring at the table while Stephen, age one-and-a-half, watched. He snatched a crayon.

"No, Stevie, no!"

"Vickie, maybe we could let Stevie use a crayon."

"Well, I think maybe a roll would help."

"How about some cheese? Are you hungry? Would you like some cheese and bread?"

"Yes!"

Rather than giving Vickie reasons, next time I would try to look at the real problem first. I would have liked the scene to have gone more like this:

"Can I have a roll?"

"Those rolls look awfully good to you, don't they?"

"Yes! I want one—my tummy says so!"

"You really want one because you feel kind of empty inside! But there are just enough for breakfast. I can't give you a roll now."

"Oh!"" (Vickie looks pensive.)

"How about some cheese?—you like that?"

"Okay!"

(Then I'd pick her up and rock her while she ate it and talk about feeling empty because she was missing her mommy—and that her mother would be coming home on Sunday—I also realize, now, I should have put those rolls out of sight!)

In the following example the teacher, working with an older child, encourages him not only to express his feelings but also to deal with the person who is causing the unhappiness.

Jonathan arrives at the woodworking bench very excited by the box of new wood he has spied from across the play yard. He reaches for Henry's hammer as it is laid down and is really surprised when Henry snatches it back. The teacher tells Jonathan that all the hammers are in use and he will have to wait. Jonathan stands on one foot and then the other—his hand obviously itching to snatch Henry's hammer. At this point, rather than trying to redirect him to the swings, the teacher says to him, "It's hard to wait, isn't it? I can see how much you want that hammer." "Yes, it is. I wish old Henry'd hurry." "Well, tell him so. Tell him what you want." "Henry, you son of a bitch, I want that hammer when you're done." (The boys grin at each other.) The teacher suggests, "Why don't you saw some wood while you're waiting?" "Don't mind if I do," says Jonathan.

---

*Courtesy Paige Gregory, University of Oklahoma, Norman.

In these examples the teacher did not content herself with the simple statement "You feel angry" or "You're hungry" or "You feel impatient." Instead she tried to describe to the child what he felt like doing and to name the feeling for him since she was fairly sure she could identify it. Describing feelings or intended actions is particularly helpful when working with young children because they understand the statement "You want her to stay" or "It's hard to wait," better than they grasp the label "angry" or "impatient." In addition, description has the advantage that it stands a better chance of being correct and that it is always better to talk about what a person does rather than what he is.

With a younger or less controlled child the teacher may need to go further and reassure him by saying, "It's okay to want to grab it as long as you don't really do it." Sometimes she will need to go even further than that and actually restrain him, saying, "I can see you want to hit Henry, but I won't let you hurt him. Tell him you feel like taking his hammer." It takes many experiences for a young child to reach the level of the children in our examples, but it can be done. The moral is: Feel what you want, but control what you do.

Teach Children the Difference Between Verbal Attack and Self-Report

Note that in the examples presented the teacher neither moralized, "Of course you really love your mother" nor said, "If you'd eaten your dinner you wouldn't be hungry now!" nor offered an involved interpretation to the children of the reasons behind their behaviour. Instead she concentrated on letting the children know that she understood what they felt, that it was all right to talk about it, and that she would help them draw the line between feeling and acting if they needed that help.

When teaching children to express their feelings, we must teach them gradually to understand the difference between saying how one feels about something (self-report) and telling another person what they are (verbal attack). There's a big difference between allowing a child to attack by shouting, "You selfish pooh-pooh pants! You nerd! Gimme that shovel right now or you can't come to my birthday party!" and teaching her to tell the same child, "I need that shovel—I'm dying for it! I can't wait another minute!"

Admittedly this is a sophisticated concept for little children to grasp. Sad to say, even some adults seem unable to make this distinction. Nevertheless it is such an extraordinarily valuable emotional and social skill to acquire that teachers should begin to model and teach the rudiments of self-report very early to children. Acquisition of this skill will benefit them all their lives.

There are many additional ways to express feelings through play and through the use of sublimative and expressive materials, (which are discussed later on), but the ability to acknowledge feelings openly is the soundest and most fundamental skill to use to foster mental health.

Learn to Recognize Signs of Stress and Emotional Upset in Children

Children give many signals besides crying or fussing that indicate emotional stress. Reverting (regressing) to less mature behaviour is a common signal. We are all familiar with the independent four-year-old who suddenly wants to be babied while recovering from the flu or the child who wets her bed after the baby arrives.

❧   *Never underestimate the comfort a well-placed thumb can deliver in times of stress.*

Various nervous habits, such as hair twisting, deep sighing, nail biting, or thumb sucking, also reveal that the child is under stress. Increased irritability, sometimes to the point of tantrums, is another indicator, as are lethargy and withdrawing from activities. Sometimes children suddenly begin to challenge rules and routines; sometimes they cry a lot; sometimes expressions of tension or stress are more subtle and are conveyed only by a strained look about the eyes or a tightened mouth; and sometimes stress is expressed in the more obvious form of excessive activity and running about (Barton & Zeanah, 1990).

In addition to this knowledge of common symptoms, as the year progresses and the teacher gets to know the children well, he will have the additional advantage of knowing how each child usually behaves. This makes it easier for him to spot changes and identify children who are signalling for special help.

Know What to Do for Children Who Are Emotionally Upset

Emotional upsets have to be handled on a short-term basis and sometimes on a long-term basis as well. (See also chapter 9.)

Short-Term, Emergency Treatment

The first thing to do for a child who is upset to the point of tears is to comfort her. But the manner of comfort will vary from child to child: Some youngsters need to be held and rocked, whereas others do best when they are allowed to reduce themselves to hic-cupping silence while the teacher putters about nearby. Children who are using emo-tional outbursts as a means of controlling the adult's behaviour require still a third response—mildly ignoring them until they subside. When in doubt, it is better to err on the side of comfort than to ignore unhappiness.

No matter why a child is crying hard, it is a waste of energy to try to reason with her until she has calmed down. However, it can help soothe her to repeat something in a qui-eter and quieter tone of voice so that she gradually quiets herself to hear what is being said. This may be as simple a sentence as, "When you've stopped crying, we'll talk things over" or "I'm waiting to help you when you've stopped crying." Occasionally it can also be helpful to remark matter-of-factly if the occasion warrants, "You know, I will keep on holding you, even when you've stopped crying."

As the child calms down, getting a drink of water or wiping her eyes may also soothe her. It is often effective at this point to talk over the difficulty, but sometimes it is better to wait and discuss it in a casual way later in the day to clarify how she felt or why she broke down. Each situation has to be judged in its own context.

Finally, the teacher should either help the child return and resolve the problem in the group, or, if he deems it wiser, he should help her get started on another satisfying activ-ity. Activities that are particularly helpful at such times include swinging, water play, and messy activities such as finger painting or working with clay. Water play generally seems to be the best choice.

Long-Term Treatment

It is always wise before deciding that an emotional upset represents a serious long-term difficulty to wait and see if the child is coming down with something; incipient illness is a frequent source of loss of emotional control. It is also wise to consider whether an approaching holiday could be causing the disturbance. Christmas and Halloween are notorious tension increasers, and we have found in our campus children's centre that the weeks before and during college examinations are likely to be edgy ones also. Many episodes of fighting, crying, and other exaggerated responses to minor crises will disap-pear after such times have passed.

If the symptoms of stress do not subside, it is necessary to find out more about what is causing tension in the child. The behaviour may be due to something going on at home or to something going on at school, or to a combination of these things.

One helpful way to locate the cause is to think back to the point when the signs of stress appeared and then to confer with the parent about what else changed in the child's life at about the same time. Perhaps the youngster was moved to another room at school, or her close friend was absent because of chicken pox; perhaps her grandfather died, or her father was away, or house guests were visiting. Once the cause has been discovered, steps can be taken to help the youngster feel more at ease. Sometimes just recognizing the source helps a lot, without doing anything more.

Other signals of disturbance can be traced to continuing environmental situations. Perhaps discipline policies are erratic at home, or affection is lacking, or the child is excessively fatigued because she watches the late show on television. These are more difficult situations to deal with, but even they can often be successfully resolved by working together with the family.

If the situation is too complicated or difficult to be quickly eased by the teacher's intervention, he must encourage the family to seek counselling from a psychologist or a psychiatrist. The area of guidance and referral is such an extensive one that it cannot be treated in detail here. The reader is invited to pursue the subject further in chapters 7, 8, and 9.

❧ Summary

Growth-enhancing child care seeks to create as many opportunities as possible for young children to develop their sense of autonomy and initiative in a setting that is reasonable, consistent, trustful, empathic, warm, and appreciative. Children who are mentally healthy are working on emotional tasks appropriate for their age. They are learning to separate from their families and to conform to school routines without undue stress. They can involve themselves deeply in play, and they are developing the ability to settle down and concentrate. Emotionally healthy children are not excessively withdrawn or aggressive; they have access to the full range of their feelings and are beginning to learn to deal with these feelings in appropriate ways.

Early childhood teachers can help the children in their care develop in emotionally healthy ways by forming good relationships with their families, reducing frustration for them when possible, identifying and describing the children's feelings for them and helping them express these to the relevant people, recognizing the signs of stress that signal that help is needed, and handling emotional problems on a short-term and long-term basis, as necessary.

Questions and Activities

1. What are some matter-of-fact ways to express warmth and liking to young children?

2. Looking back on your own education, give an example of a teacher who had unreasonably high expectations of you as a pupil. What was the effect on your learning?

3. With other members of the class, set up some role playing situations that provide opportunities for "children" to express their feelings and "teachers" to practise phrasing responses that would help the child identify how she feels and show that the teacher understands her. Practise this a lot!

4. Do you believe it is always wise to be forthright about your own feelings? What limitations might be helpful to remember? On the other hand, can you think of times when it would have been better to take the risk and be more open and frank in your response? What did you do instead of being direct? Do you think that it was a satisfactory solution?

5. What are some examples in which you have seen adults ignore, suppress, or mislabel a child's feelings? Could you see how the child was immediately affected by this kind of response? What would you predict might be the long-term effects of a child's experiencing many such responses to his feelings?

Self-Check Questions for Review

Content-Related Questions

1. Name the first three stages of emotional development identified by Erikson, and list some things early childhood teachers can do to foster the successful mastering of each stage.

2. Identify the hallmarks of an emotionally healthy child.

3 Select four personal qualities of teachers that would help foster emotional health in the children, and explain why each is important.

4. What are some common behaviours of children that might alert you to the fact that they are experiencing stress?

Integrative Questions

1. What is the difference between feeling sympathy for someone and feeling empathy for her? Provide an example of some emotional situation with a child and explain what you would say if you were expressing sympathy and what you would say to show you were experiencing empathy.

2. Analyse the following gem contributed by a student and suggest what the adult might have said, instead, that would have described the children's feelings to them.*

   I was babysitting two children in their backyard late in the afternoon. Robby is about five years old and Joel is about three.

   Robby: "Hey, look at this rock I found!"

   Me: "Make sure you don't throw it at somebody."

   Joel: "I'm gonna throw that rock at Jimmy's mean cat!"

   Me: "You'd better not, young man."

   Robby: "I wanna throw rocks!"

   Me: "Not now Robby, it's time to go in and eat dinner, okay?"

   Both boys: "No!"

   Me: "Why don't you want to eat dinner?"

   Robby: "I'm not hungry. I wanna stay out here and play."

   Me: "You've played long enough; now you need to get your vitamins."

   Robby: "Mom said I already have enough vitamins."

   Me: "You'll really like what we're having; meat loaf and baked potatoes, and spinach."

   Joel: "I hate spinach!"

   Me: "You should eat it, it's good for you!"

3. Analyse the following statements and categorize them according to whether they are examples of "self-report" or "verbal attack."

   "I feel pretty worried when you climb that high."

   "Let Suzanne have some crackers too. Don't be so selfish!"

   "You're always so quick to criticize others!"

   Then change each statement into the opposite form. For example, if the original statement was "You're always making me do things I don't want to do," you might change it into "I just feel too shy to do that—please don't press me to try it."

References for Further Reading

Overviews

Allen, E., Paasche, C., Cornell, A. & Engel, M. (1994). *Exceptional children: Inclusion in early childhood programs* (1st Can. ed.). Scarborough, ON: Nelson Canada. This book provides early childhood educators with the information and skills necessary to effectively integrate children with special needs into existing programs. Included is a chapter to facilitate positive behaviours.

Brazelton, B. (1992). *Touchpoints: The essential reference.* New York: Addison-Wesley. Brazelton's book is filled with understanding comments about children that are sensible, reassuring, and practical. It is a useful book both to recommend to parents and for use by the teacher herself. *Highly recommended.*

Curry, N. (Ed.). (1986). *The feeling child: Affective development reconsidered.* New York: Haworth Press. These articles will help the reader understand the significance and role that emotions play in the lives of developing children.

Keubli, J. (1994). Young children's understanding of everyday emotions. *Young Children, 49*(3), 36–47. This first-rate article summarizes recent research concerning what young children understand about emotions. It includes practical applications and a list of children's books about feelings.

Developmental Stages and Emotional Needs of Children

Curry, N., & Bergen, D. (1987). The relationship of play to emotional, social, and gender/sex role development. In D. Bergen (Ed.), *Play as a medium for learning and development: A handbook of theory and practice.* Portsmouth, NH: Heinemann. This chapter provides a comprehensive review of how the emotional self develops.

---

*Courtesy Sarah Strain, University of Oklahoma, Norman.

Erikson, E. H. (1963). *Childhood and society* (2nd ed.). New York: W. W. Norton.

Erikson, E. H. (1971). A healthy personality for every child. In R. H. Anderson & H. G. Shane (Eds.), *As the twig is bent: Readings in early childhood education.* New York: Houghton Mifflin.

Erikson, E. H. (1982). *The life cycle completed: A review.* New York: W. W. Norton. These publications contain original source material that explains in detail Erikson's concepts of the eight stages of man and the emotional attitudes of paramount importance at various stages of development.

Greenspan, S. I., & Greenspan, N. T. (1985). *First feelings: Milestones in the emotional development of your baby and child.* New York: Viking Press. Greenspan proposes six steps in emotional development occurring in the very early years. Interesting reading that also provides practical recommendations.

Building Sound Emotional Relationships with Children

Balaban, N. (1989). Trust: Just a matter of time. In J. S. McKee & K. M. Paciorek (Eds.), *Early childhood: 89/90.* Guilford, CT: Dushkin. The author presents a number of practical examples of ways teachers can build trust with children.

Faber, A., & Mazlish, E. (1980). *How to talk so kids will listen, & listen so kids will talk.* New York: Avon Books. Numerous examples of describing and sharing feelings make this book a treasure trove of helpfulness.

Hyson, M. C. (1994). *The emotional development of young children: Building an emotion-centered curriculum.* New York: Teachers College Press. Hyson presents a good review of recent research on emotional development. The second half of the book provides sound advice on ways to honour and support the role of emotions in the classroom.

Roemer, J. (1989). *Two to four from 9 to 5: The adventures of a daycare provider.* New York: Harper & Row. Insightful, sensitive encounters with children are a hallmark of this delightful reading. Highly recommended.

Rogers, C. R. (1961). *On becoming a person.* Boston: Houghton Mifflin. Rogers sets forth his philosophy that desirable emotional relationships between people are facilitated by the presence of warmth, congruence, and empathy.

Samalin, N., & Jablow, M. M. (1987). *Loving your child is not enough.* New York: Viking Press. The chapter on acknowledging feelings provides many examples of how to reflect and describe feelings to children. Helpful reading.

For the Advanced Student

Cicchetti, D., & White, J. (1989). Emotional development and the affective disorders. In W. Damon (Ed.), *Child development today and tomorrow.* San Francisco: Jossey-Bass. The relative lack of research on emotions and their development is cited here, and many promising areas for future research are identified.

Izard, C. (1991). *The psychology of emotions.* New York: Plenum Press. For a first-rate, comprehensive review of a wide variety of emotions (including happy ones), this is an authoritative resource.

Mash, E. J., & Barkley, R. Q. (Eds.). (1989). *Treatment of childhood disorders.* New York: Guilford Press. Another first-rate book, this one provides a thorough discussion of history, causes, and recommended treatments of children with a wide variety of serious emotional disorders such as extreme fears, obesity, encopresis, autism, and so forth.

Powell, G. J. (1983). *The psychosocial development of minority group children.* New York: Brunner/Mazel. Powell's excellent book devotes over 200 pages to the emotional development and mental health of children from a wide variety of ethnic groups.

Strayhorn, J. M. (1988). *The competent child: An approach to psychotherapy and preventive mental health.* New York: Guilford Press. Strayhorn includes a valuable list of psychological skills children need in order to function successfully in the social world and then proposes practical ways of increasing these.

Weil, J. L. (1992). *Early deprivation of empathic care.* Madison, CT: International Universities Press. Weil discusses the long-term implications of the deprivation of such care and outlines why teachers need to be sensitive, tender, and responsive. Chilling examples of how deprived individuals develop in later life are included.

Wenar, C. (1990). *Developmental psychopathology: From infancy to adolescence* (2nd ed.). New York: McGraw-Hill. The author offers a detailed overview of developmentally related emotionally-based problems. The book includes a chapter on working with children from minority groups.

Zeanah, C. (Ed.). (1993). *Handbook of infant mental health*. New York: Guilford Press. Foundations for sound emotional health are established well before teachers meet these children in preschool. For this reason it behooves interested adults to acquaint themselves with the rapid growth of information about practices that foster or hinder the growth of emotional health in infancy. *Highly recommended.*

Journals of Continuing Interest

American Journal of Orthopsychiatry. American Orthopsychiatric Association, 49 Sheridan Ave., Albany, NY 12210. The journal describes itself as being dedicated to providing information "relating to mental health and human development from a multidisciplinary and interprofessional perspective."

Harvard Mental Health Letter. 74 Fenwood Rd., Boston, MA 02115. This publication describes its goal as being "to interpret timely mental health information, but . . . not to provide advice for individual problems."

IDEAS: The Journal of Emotional Well-Being in Child Care. IDEAS Alliance and George Brown College, Nightingale Campus, P.O. Box 1015, Stn. B., Toronto, ON M5T 2T9. This vehicle discusses new research and strategies on emotional well-being in child care. It intends to provide a forum in which program issues can be developed and debated.

Pediatric Mental Health. PO Box 1880, Santa Monica, CA 90406-1880. A bimonthly newsletter, this publication covers research and practice on such topics as supporting parenting, play, and preparation for hospitalization.

Developing Self-Esteem in Young Children

6

The deepest urge in human nature is the desire to be important.

John Dewey

*Have you ever wondered
what to do about . . .*

The child who habitually protests, "I can't—I know I can't—don't make me!"

Or the one who always wants to know, "Did I do it right?"

Or the youngster who says sadly, "Nobody likes me—nobody!"

. . . If you have, the material in the following pages will help you.

*P*erceiving oneself as a person who has something worthwhile to contribute to the life around one is such an important aspect of being emotionally healthy that it is necessary to devote an entire chapter to this concept. It is this feeling of internal worth that I have in mind when describing individuals who possess positive self-esteem. People who feel like this are able to venture out into the world, work toward attaining what they hope for, and welcome life with pleasurable anticipation (Curry & Johnson, 1990). As the research study in this chapter indicates, such people are also likely to get along more cooperatively with others.

On the other hand, individuals who suffer from low self-esteem fit, to varying degrees, the following description.

> The child with low self-worth focuses on failure instead of success, problems instead of challenges, difficulties instead of possibilities. A child with low self-esteem experiences the world as a dark and gloomy place, filled with danger and threat (Smith, 1988, p. 5).

Moreover, an English study of young adolescents found that "individuals who were anxious, depressed, neurotic or *have poor self-esteem* [italics mine] do tend to be more prejudiced than others. They have to a greater extent chosen the cultural symbols of racism as a means of protecting their identity, or enhancing their view of themselves" (Bagley, Verma, Mallick, & Young, 1979, p. 194).

More recently Mecca, Smelser, and Vasconcellos (1989) have published an extensive analysis of the interrelationships between low self-esteem and child abuse, poor school achievement, teenage pregnancy, crime, and drug and alcohol overuse.

It is clear from a perusal of these findings and others like them that a good self-concept and adequate self-esteem are highly desirable qualities to foster in young children, since no one wants children to suffer from the feelings and experiences just described. What teachers and parents need to understand more clearly is how to help children generate good feelings about themselves that are based on reality. It is these good feelings that form the basis for healthy self-esteem.

ℰ Relationship of Self-Esteem to Self-Concept

Self-esteem and self-concept are closely related. Self-concept refers to an individual's idea of who he is, and self-esteem is a part of this because his feelings of self-esteem result from his reaction to what he judges himself to be and to his anticipation of being accepted or rejected (Kosnik, 1993; Marshall, 1989). Thus a youngster who is well coordinated, who is sought after by his playmates, and who gets along well with his teacher will probably see himself as adequate and will possess good feelings of self-esteem, whereas an overweight high school girl suffering from a poor complexion and few friends may come to think of herself as being unattractive and unlovable and as a result will hold herself in low esteem.

ℰ Sources of Self-Esteem

Although individuals should ultimately develop internal resources for generating self-esteem, in the early stages of growth the child's feelings of self-esteem come from the

⌘ *R E S E A R C H   S T U D Y* ⌘

Is Positive Self-Esteem Related to Positive Social Behaviour Towards Other People?

Research Question: Cauley and Tyler wanted to find out whether a child's positive self-concept was related to the prosocial behaviours of sharing, helping, and cooperation.

Research Method: To investigate this relationship, they studied thirty-two boys and twenty girls who were four and five years old. The majority of the children came from white, middle-class families.

The researchers used a combination of measures to find out about the children. They asked the children to assess themselves using the Purdue Self-Concept Scale for Preschool Children. This scale offers paired pictures showing a child being successful (for example, running fast) or not being successful (not running fast) and asks the child to point to the picture that he feels best describes himself. They also used teacher evaluations of each youngster that ranked the frequency of helping, sharing, and cooperating behaviour with other children and the teacher's perceptions of the child's self-concept.

In addition to the paper evaluations, trained observers recorded twenty minutes of observations of each child over several days' time. The observers recorded only instances of the prosocial behaviours included in the study: sharing, helping, and cooperating.

Results: Careful statistical analysis revealed there were some factors such as gender, age, family size, and number of years in day care that were not related to the prosocial behaviours selected for study.

When the researchers looked at the relationship between the presence of positive self-esteem and the three prosocial behaviours, only one of the three was found to be significantly related ($p < .01$) to self-concept. This was the amount of cooperative behaviour that various children demonstrated during the observation periods. As the authors put it, "a child with a positive self-concept has less need to engage in competitive interactions with other children and is more willing to engage in cooperative behaviour" (p. 57). They found that when cooperative prosocial behaviours were initiated *by the child,* the result was likely to be more effective than when the behaviour was urged upon him from without. Finally, the study revealed that teachers' assessments of the child's self-concept and the child's self-assessment matched closely.

Implications for Teaching: In these days when so much of the world seems involved in tooth-and-nail competition, it is heartening to find information that suggests a practical way to foster cooperation rather than competition among children. Evidently, when children think well of themselves, this frees them to relate more generously and less selfishly with their peers, particularly when the impulse to cooperate comes from within themselves rather than being teacher suggested.

The other finding of note is the correlation between teachers' knowledge of children's feelings about themselves and the feelings actually reported by the children. Apparently, teachers should trust their judgement when assessing how children feel about themselves. That evaluation could alert teachers to the necessity of helping some children increase their self-esteem by applying the recommendations included in this chapter.

Source: From "The Relationship of Self-Concept to Prosocial Behavior in Children" by Kate Cauley and Bonnie Tyler, 1989, *Early Childhood Research Quarterly,* 4(1), p. 51–60.

❦   *A nice example of prosocial behaviour.*

people around him. Parents are very significant influences (Coopersmith, 1967; Powell 1989). As children move out into the larger world, the opinions of other adults, such as teachers, become important, too, as do the opinions of their peers. That society also has an impact is evident from studies indicating that a higher percentage of people of minority groups possess low self-esteem than people of nonminorities do (Nieto, 1992; Powell, 1983a). Because the unhappy effects of persistent prejudice on the self-image and self-esteem of minority children cannot be overestimated, an entire chapter is devoted to a discussion of ways to sustain or improve the self-image of such youngsters (chapter 14).

Since there are so many powerful factors that influence the development of self-esteem, teachers should not believe they can completely alter the way a child sees himself. However, the numerous research studies cited by Curry and Johnson (1990) and Geraty (1983) support the idea that teachers can establish policies in their classrooms that will help build a child's self-esteem, and they can meticulously avoid employing practices that are likely to have destructive side effects.

❦ *Common School Practices Likely to Reduce Self-Esteem*

One way to think of self-esteem is to picture it as a balloon—a balloon that just a little prick of criticism will puncture and wither. Unfortunately, there are many ways teachers prick these balloons every day, often when they do not intend to.

Using Comparison and Competition to Motivate Good Behaviour

Although younger children seem unaffected (Stipek, Recchia, & McClintic, 1992), competitiveness reaches a peak in children around the age of four to five years (Stott & Ball, 1957). It is all too easy for the teacher to use this fact to obtain quick results by asking, "I wonder who can get his coat on quickest today?" or by commenting, "See how carefully Shirley is putting her blocks away? Why can't you do it like that?" The trouble with motivating behaviour by drawing such comparisons and setting up competitive situations is that only a few children "win" under this system. Even the child who turns out to be "best" and whose self-esteem has presumably been enhanced pays an unfortunate price, since he has obtained his self-esteem at the expense of the other children's well-being and may have earned their dislike in the process.

A more desirable way to use comparison is by invoking it in relation to the child's own past performance (Katz, 1994). This can be a true source of satisfaction for him when the teacher says, "My goodness, John, you're learning to pump better and better every time you try!" or "Remember the way you used to bite people? You haven't done that in a long time now. I'm proud of you!"

Overhelping and Overprotecting Children

Teachers may unintentionally lower a child's self-esteem by doing too much for him. Thus they rush in to carry the bucket of water so that it will not slop or without thinking put all the shoes and socks on the children following nap time. Helping in these ways has the virtues of saving time and assuring that the job will be done properly, as well as keeping the teacher busy. But it is much more desirable to wait and let children do things for themselves, since this allows them to experience the triumph of independence that such achievements bring.

Judging Children Within Their Hearing

Children often develop ideas of who they are from hearing what other people say about them. Sometimes this happens in direct form, as when the teacher says impatiently, "Come along now; you're always so slow," or asks, "How can you be so selfish?" Other children are also prone to deliver pronouncements such as "You pig! You never share anything" or "Hazel is a pooh-pooh pants, Hazel is a pooh-pooh pants!" Labels such as these tend to stick; enough of them plastered on a child can convince him that he is neither liked nor worth much, so he might as well not try. This is one of the reasons why teaching children to use self-report rather than verbal attack is so important. Verbal attacks are destructive to other people's self-esteem.

Consider the difference in effect between the child who shouts, "I'm so mad I'd like to sock you! You gotta let me play!" and the one who sneers, "Aw, I don't like you anyway—you stink!"

Sometimes negative evaluations are not delivered directly to the child, but are said over his head to someone else instead: "My, aren't we in a terrible temper today!" "I see he's having a hard day again!" "There's no point in asking him—he always holds on like grim death" (Kostelnik, Stein, & Whirin, 1988). Somehow, overheard comments have a special, painful power to compel belief. Teachers should avoid making them not only for this reason, but also because they may hurt a child's feelings and can strengthen a negative self-image. On a more subtle level, talking over children's heads implies that they are not important enough to be included directly in the conversation.

ॐ Positive Methods of Enhancing Self-Esteem

Unconditional Positive Regard

The most effective way to help a child build a basic feeling of self-esteem is, unfortunately, also the most elusive for some teachers to achieve: It is the ability to feel and project what Rogers terms *unconditional positive regard.* This kind of fundamental acceptance and approval of each child is not contingent on his meeting the teacher's expectations of what he should be; it simply depends on his being alive, being a child, and being in the group. A good test of being accepting or not is to become aware of what one is usually thinking about when looking at the children. Ask yourself, "Am I taking time to enjoy the children, or am I looking at each one with a critical eye—noting mainly what behaviour should be improved?" If you catch yourself habitually noting only what should be changed, this is a sign you are losing sight of half the pleasure of teaching, which is to

ॐ   *Sharing a child's satisfaction is a fine way to increase her self-esteem.*

appreciate the children and enjoy who they are right now, at this particular moment in time—no strings attached.

This ability to be uncritical implies a kind of faith in the way the child will turn out, an attitude that subtly makes him aware that the teacher has confidence he will grow in sound directions. There is no substitute for these underlying feelings of trust and confidence in the child. Some teachers are fortunate enough to have developed optimism about people as a result of their own trust-building childhood experiences, some gain it from long experience with children themselves, and some acquire it by means of psychotherapeutic treatment, which helps restore their own confidence as well as their faith in others.

Acceptance of the child as he is also includes accepting his right to be different from the teacher and from other children. Here again, ethnic and cultural differences come particularly to mind. Teachers can make a significant contribution to increasing the self-esteem of the minority child by unconditionally valuing him and by using themselves as models to influence the attitude of the other children and their families.

Honest Recognition and Praise

Rewarding a child with praise is usually the first way teachers think of to build self-esteem. Unfortunately, sometimes praise is the *only* method they think of. Actually it is only one of several and perhaps not one of the better ways to enhance a child's feelings of self-worth.

Morgan (1984) lists more than 80 research projects that have been carried out on the effects such external rewards as praise or prizes have on motivating repeated behaviour. These studies have asked the question "Do children work harder when they receive a reward?" (praise is one kind of reward) and the answer, generally, has been "No!"

Even the effects of praise vary quite a bit (Cannella, 1986; Kohn, 1993). To be an effective esteem raiser and motivator, praise should include information about something specific a child has achieved; that is, praise should be based on performance. Used in that context it can heighten the inner *intrinsic* satisfaction of the child. For example, it is better to say to a four-year-old, "Thanks for letting Mary Lou play—it cheered her up" than to say, "You sure are a nice little boy!" Erikson is right when he says, "Children cannot be fooled by empty praise and condescending encouragement" (1963).

We must be wary of teachers who use praise continually as a means of reinforcing behaviour and who often dole it out in such a mechanical way that it comes to have almost no meaning at all. On the other hand, some teachers hardly ever take time to comment favourably on what a child has done. They seem to feel that praise weakens character and that individuals should do things simply because it is right to do them. But praise that is merited should surely be given; everyone who has experienced it knows that honest recognition is sweet indeed.

Using encouragement rather than praise is another effective way of building self-esteem while recognizing what a child is accomplishing (Poresky & Hoover, 1991). Such comments as "I bet you can do it if you try," or "Look how much work you've done," or "Atta girl!" encourage children without passing judgement on what they've done.

Children need to learn that failing at something is not the end of the world. For this reason it is also important to appreciate the effort of children when they have not been successful. They particularly need encouragement at this point, since the reward inherent in successful accomplishment has not been realized. The teacher can say "I see how hard you've worked on that," or "I'm proud of you; you really tried," or "It takes a while to learn to do that. You've really stuck with it; it's *hard* to learn things sometimes, isn't it?"

Respect

Respecting the child is such a high-minded phrase that examples of behaviour must be provided in order to see how respect can be implemented when working with young children. One basic way to show respect is to abide by the child's decision when he has been given a valid choice (see also chapter 11). When a teacher does this, she is really saying, "What you want is important. I have confidence that you know yourself better than I do, and I count on you to choose what will enhance your existence most." Children also feel respect when the teacher asks their opinion and listens carefully to their replies. Even young children can answer "Do you think we should . . ." kinds of questions.

Another way to show respect, and thus sustain the child's self-esteem, is to avoid humiliating a child in front of other people. It is best to carry out discipline measures as unobtrusively as possible. Belittling a child's behaviour at any time is, of course, fundamentally disrespectful as well as destructive of self-esteem.

A third valuable way to show respect is to pay the child the compliment of explaining the reason behind the rule. Coopersmith (1967), who carried out an extensive study of children possessing high self-esteem, found that parents of such youngsters were firm in their control of them but also took time to explain the reason for their actions. Such reasoning confers respect because it assumes that the child is important enough to be entitled to an explanation and intelligent enough to comprehend it.

Finally, we must never lose sight of the fact that children are intensely aware of how teachers feel about their families. Teachers who truly respect and value the child's family show this each day in the way they welcome them to the classroom, by the way they avoid making derogatory remarks about them, and by the way they really listen to a family member who has something to say.

❦ *Helping the Child Achieve Competence*

Positive regard, respect, and merited praise are sound in that they help build positive self-pictures for children, but they have one weakness in common: *They all depend on the goodwill of another person for implementation.* Yet the ultimate goal should be the internalization of esteem so that the individual will not remain permanently dependent on others to supply his feelings of self-worth.

But how can children be helped to shift from relying on external praise or other supports to experiencing *intrinsic* satisfaction from within themselves? The most effective answer is that helping children achieve competence is the surest way to instil internal feelings of self-worth. Every time a youngster does something that works out well,

ભ   *Please, Mom—I'd rather do it myself! Sometimes waiting patiently offers the best support for learning a new skill.*

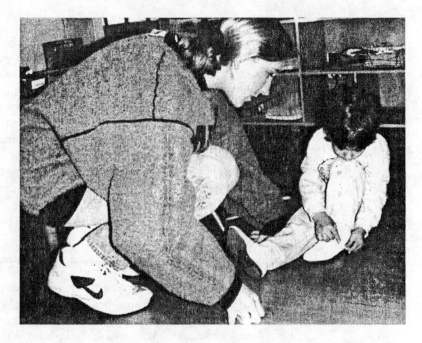

whether it be standing up for his rights in the trike area or pumping himself on the swing, the reward of success is inherent in the act, and the child feels competent because of what he *did,* not because of what someone said (Messer, 1993; Strayhorn, 1988). This knowledge of capability makes children (and adults, too, for that matter) feel good about themselves, feel that they are worth something—*and in that knowledge lies the foundation of inner self-esteem.*

White (1968, 1976) summed this up when he pointed out that people have a continuing drive toward competence, which is a powerful motivating agent in their lives. He defined competence as "effectiveness in dealing with the environment." It is this sense of being effective that builds the child's self-esteem internally. No one can take it away from him, and no one, as White comments, "can confer this experience. No one can give another person a sense of competence" (1976, p. 9). What teachers *can* do is provide many opportunities for children to *become* competent. A good place to begin is by asking oneself, at the start of every morning, "How can I help each child experience success today?" Once a child is able to do something well, whether it is practising diplomacy in the housekeeping corner or using the brace and bit, he has gained a small portion of confidence in himself that does not require the plaudits of others to sustain it.

Allow Children to Experience Mastery by Making Their Own Choices and by Being as Independent as Possible

Making choices and being independent are two ways to encourage competence that have already been discussed. Maccoby (1980) speaks of this as keeping the *locus of control* as much within the hands of the child as possible. She cites a number of studies that support the value of encouraging children to feel they are in control of their environment at least part of the time. Of course, this should not be interpreted as meaning that the teacher or parent should submit unquestioningly to every passing whim. Rather, it does mean that encouraging children to make choices and decisions and to do things for themselves is worth doing whenever reasonable and possible, because granting them such "power" reduces their feelings of helplessness and increases their feelings of mastery by placing the locus of control within rather than outside themselves.

Along with allowing children to do things for themselves and have choices about what they choose to do goes the establishment of reasonable standards of achievement. For instance, a teacher who wishes to build self-esteem in a newly generous little boy appreciates his helpfulness when he volunteers to pass the snack and overlooks the fact that he has served himself the largest portion first, just as she thanks the child who has stuffed his boots away in his cubby and refrains from telling him to fix them so the toes point out.

Provide Many Different Ways for Children to Experience Success

Sheer variety of activities is important here, since one child may excel at assembling puzzles, whereas another's forte may be hanging by her heels on the jungle gym. It is important, also, not to be too hidebound when selecting curriculum activities, since a youngster may possess a special skill not usually thought of as being age appropriate but one that, when well used, can confer distinction on her and enrich the lives of the other children. Our centre, for example, had a child attending who loved to embroider. She knew several stitches, and two or three of the older children relished learning them from her, even though "everyone knows" that embroidery is too difficult for preschool children to carry out successfully.

Provide Opportunities That Are Challenging but Not Excessively Difficult to Give Children the Chance to Test Themselves Against Difficulties

The derring-do of four-year-olds is a prime example of this desire to make things a little bit harder every time they attempt them. (The reader may recall learning the game of jacks and its steady progression from *Rolling Down Broadway* to the more difficult game *Around the World,* and finally on to *Eggs in a Basket* and *Shooting Star.*) In general, children should always be allowed to attempt more difficult feats as they think of them unless it is evident that they have not anticipated any serious dangers that may be involved.

Something else students sometimes forget is that it takes practice to acquire a new skill. I have seen students offer an activity once and assume that would be sufficient opportunity for the children to learn how to do it. Whether it be using the scooter or cutting around a circle or playing lotto, other things being equal, repeated practice increases competence, so it is important to provide chances for children to do something more than once if you want them to become skilful.

Emphasize the Value of Building Cross-Sex Competencies of Various Kinds

It is still the case that girls often grow up unable to use power saws or drills or lacking even rudimentary understanding of the combustion engine, and boys are sometimes described as limited in their ability to express emotion. Most women (and many men) have only to recall the last time they dealt with a garage mechanic to realize the sense of inferiority such incompetence produces. Methods of remedying these deficiencies are discussed at greater length in chapter 14, so it will only be noted here that broader and more various educational experiences for both sexes should be encouraged.

Offer Creative Activities, Since They Provide Excellent Opportunities for Experiencing Competence

There is so much latitude for individual abilities and differences to be expressed in creative activity areas that they must be singled out as avenues for building self-esteem. Indeed, as the work from Reggio Emilia demonstrates, the very essence of a child's ideas and being can be revealed through paint or clay or collages. What adult has not experienced the satisfaction and boost in self-esteem that came from attempting a new art or craft? Children feel the same way. It feels good to make something attractive generated by oneself. Therefore, the value of creative self-expression is an avenue to building self-esteem that must not be overlooked.

In Addition to Competence in Activities and Motor Skills, Interpersonal Competence Is of Great Importance

The final vital source of positive self-esteem stems from the child's perception of how adequate he is in dealing with other people. The youngster who feels that he can get along with others, that he is liked by them, and that he generally manages to have his needs met is likely to feel socially competent and able to take care of himself. Chapters 10, 11, and 12 present more detailed discussions of how to help children gain these all-important skills and competencies in interpersonal relationships.

❧ Summary

Early childhood teachers who wish to increase feelings of self-esteem in the children in their care have at their disposal many ways of accomplishing this. However, practices such as using comparison and competition, being overprotective, and judging children within their hearing should be avoided since these tend to lower self-esteem.

Esteem-building practices that should be part of the child's life include the expression of unconditional positive regard, the provision of recognition and praise when warranted, and the expression of genuine respect.

Finally, the attainment of competence should be valued highly. The more opportunities children have to acquire instrumental and interpersonal skills, the more likely they are to acquire an inner conviction of their own ability to cope. This inner conviction of basic competence is, in the long run, the most satisfactory builder of self-esteem. .

Questions and Activities

1. Pick a school or family life situation (perhaps a trip to the grocery store) for role playing and include in it as many possible ways as you can think of to deflate and lower the self-esteem of the "children" who are involved.
2. Select a youngster in your school who seems to suffer from low self-esteem. As far as you can tell, what are some principal reasons for this self-image? What could you do to modify it in a more positive direction?
3. Many activities, even for community college students, centre on externalized sources of self-esteem. Grades are a prime example of external input. What college-related policies appear likely to produce internalized sources of positive self-esteem?
4. This chapter questions the value of competition to motivate behaviour, since competition often reduces feelings of self-esteem. Is this necessarily true in all cases? Are there times when competition is both satisfying and desirable?
5. Listen to yourself for several days while you are working with the children. Every day put ten pennies in your pocket, and whenever you hear yourself talking about a child in front of him, transfer a penny to your other pocket. Can you go an entire day without shifting any pennies?
6. Go down your roster and try to identify opportunities during the past week in which each child had the chance to gain competence in some activity. Did each youngster have a chance to accomplish this in some manner?

Self-Check Questions for Review

Content-Related Questions

1. Explain how low self-esteem and being prejudiced against other people are related.
2. Describe what methods Cauley and Tyler used to find out whether there was a relationship between positive self-esteem and the prosocial behaviours of helping, sharing, and cooperating with others. What

would be the weakness of using only one of these approaches to study this subject?
3. What are three common things teachers might do that tend to lower the self-esteem of the children in their care?
4. Is praise the most effective way of increasing the self-esteem of a young child? Explain the reasoning behind your answer.
5. Why is competence such an effective builder of self-esteem?
6. What is the difference between extrinsic and intrinsic methods of increasing self-esteem? Which do the authors feel is more desirable, and why?

Integrative Questions

1. Suggest some reasons why having a strong sense of positive self-esteem might make a child more likely to be cooperative with other children than he would be if he had a poor self-concept.
2. Imagine that a new rule has been passed at your child care centre: You may not praise a child for anything during the day, and yet you must increase his self-esteem substantially. How would you go about doing this?
3. Give an example other than praise of something that could be an extrinsic source of self-esteem for an adult, and then give an example of something that could be an intrinsic source of self-esteem for an adult.
4. Briefly describe three children whom you know well and propose something you could do that would help them gain a new skill.
5. How does nonsexist education contribute to girls' sense of self-esteem? How does it contribute to boys' sense of self-esteem? Might it detract from boys' self-esteem? Explain your conclusions about that answer.

References for Further Reading

Overviews

Briggs, D. C. (1970). *Your child's self-esteem: The key to his life.* Garden City, NY: Doubleday. Brigg's book deals with building self-esteem in children and its influence on the entire life of the child. Still in print.

Curry, N. E., & Johnson, C. N. (1990). *Beyond self-esteem: Developing a genuine sense of human value.* Washington, DC: National Association for the Education of Young Children. Curry and Johnson provide a good balance of reviews of research coupled with much practical information about how to foster the growth of self-esteem.

Greenberg, P. (1991). *Character development: Encouraging self-esteem & self-discipline in infants, toddlers, & two-year-olds.* Washington, DC: National Association for the Education of Young Children. The chapter entitled "How Does Good Character Develop? Self? Self-Esteem: Self-Discipline? Do We Have Anything to Do With It?" is particularly worthwhile. *Highly recommended.*

Harter, S. (1985). Competence as a dimension of self-evaluation: Toward a comprehensive model of self-worth. In R. L. Leahy (Ed.), *The development of the self.* New York: Academic Press. This chapter explores the relationship between competence and feelings of self-esteem.

Kosnik, B. (1993). Everyone is a V.I.P. in this class. *Young Children, 49*(1), 32–37. The development of self-esteem is reviewed here together with practical suggestions of ways to foster its development in children and adults.

Saderman Hall, N., & Rhomberg, V. (1995). *The affective curriculum: Teaching the anti-bias approach to young children.* Scarborough, ON: Nelson Canada. This book examines the link between the anti-bias approach and the affective development of children from infancy through the school age years.

Practical Ways to Increase Self-Esteem

Harris, J. M. (1989). *You and your child's self-esteem: Building for the future.* New York: Carroll & Graf. This book is filled with practical recommendations that are useful for parents and teachers, too.

Kostelnik, M. J., Stein, L. C., & Whiren, A. P. (1988). Children's self-esteem: The verbal environment. *Childhood Education, 65*(1), 28–32. The authors provide many examples of positive and negative ways that teachers use the verbal environment to construct self-concepts in children. *Highly recommended.*

Marshall, H. H. (1989). The development of self-concept. *Young Children, 44*(5), 44–51. Marshall traces

developmental stages and includes practical suggestions for positively influencing self-concept.

Factors That Reveal or Contribute to Poor Self-Esteem

Chud, G. & Fahlman, R. (1985). *Early childhood education for a multicultural society.* Victoria: Pacific Educational Press, University of British Columbia. This book offers an introduction to the principles and practices of an early childhood program for a multicultural society.

Kohn, A. (1993). *Punished by rewards: The trouble with gold stars, incentive plans, A's, praise, and other bribes.* Boston: Houghton Mifflin. Kohn makes a well-documented, impassioned plea against extrinsic rewards and urges the substitution of intrinsic rewards in their place.

Nieto, S. (1992). *Affirming diversity: The sociopolitical context of multicultural education.* New York: Longman. Nieto combines case studies of children with discussions intended to deepen the reader's understanding. The book is replete with examples and research. *Highly recommended.*

Peplau, L. A., Miceli, M., & Morasch, B. (1982). Loneliness and self-evaluation. In L. A. Peplau & D. Perlman (Eds.), *Loneliness: A sourcebook of current theory, research and therapy.* New York: John Wiley & Sons. There is good material here on loneliness as a cause of low self-esteem. Readers should realize that loneliness may occur even in the lives of very young children as the result of loss of parental attachment through death, divorce, or extended separation.

Zimbardo, P. G. (1977). *Shyness.* Menlo Park, CA: Addison-Wesley. Many children and adults react to stress with undue shyness. This readable book provides insight and practical advice on how to deal with this agonizing emotion so closely related to poor self-esteem.

For the Advanced Student

Bednar, R. L., Wells, M. G., & Peterson, S. R. (1989). *Self-esteem: Paradoxes and innovations in clinical theory and practice.* Washington, DC: American Psychological Association.

Cannella, G. S. (1986). Praise and concrete rewards: Concerns for childhood education. *Childhood Education, 62*(4), 297–301. This is a first-rate summary of recent research on the effect of extrinsic rewards.

Coopersmith, S. (1967). *The antecedents of self-esteem.* San Francisco: W. H. Freeman. Coopersmith recounts a classic study that sought to identify the factors within the family that influence self-esteem either positively or negatively.

Katz, L. G. (1993). *Distinctions between self-esteem and narcissism: Implications for practice.* Urbana, IL: ERIC Clearinghouse on Elementary and Early Childhood Education. Katz delivers well-taken comments on ways to foster true self-esteem in children. Also included is an annotated list of ERIC references on the same subject.

Maccoby, E. E. (1980). *Social development: Psychological growth and the parent-child relationship.* New York: Harcourt Brace Jovanovich. This excellent book has an entire chapter, "The Sense of Self," that reviews Coopersmith's work and also discusses locus of control in clear detail.

Mecca, A. M., Smelser, N. J., & Vasconcellos, J. (1989). *The social importance of self-esteem.* Berkeley: University of California Press. This book provides extensive documentation about the value of promoting good self-esteem as a prevention against a wide variety of social ills. *Highly recommended.*

Messer, D. (1993). *Mastery motivation in early childhood.* London: Routledge. A variety of well-known authorities explore the links between mastery and self-concept. *Highly recommended.*

Stipek, D., Recchia, S. A., & McClintic, S. (1992). Self-evaluation in young children. *Monographs of the Society for Research in Child Development 57* (1, Serial No. 226). The results of these studies, which have to do with the expression of feelings and competitiveness, are well worth reviewing. The material is also valuable as an example of how to investigate interesting questions in age- and child-appropriate ways.

Thomas, A. (1989). Ability and achievement expectations: Implications of research for classroom practice. *Childhood Education, 65*(4), 235–238. The chilling effects of "learned helplessness" are detailed by Thomas together with an analysis of how children come to see themselves as unworthy and incapable.

White, R. W. (1976). *The enterprise of living: A view of personal growth* (2nd ed.). New York: Holt, Rinehart & Winston. The chapter on competence, which discusses its importance in relation to development, traces its growth through various stages, and talks about why the concept is significant, is excellent. The entire book is superlative reading.

What Parents Need[*]

7

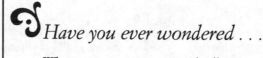

Have you ever wondered . . .

Why a parent seems to avoid talking with you?

How to open a discussion with parents about a problem their child is having?

How to deal with your disappointment when parents refused your advice?

If you have, the material in the following pages will help you.

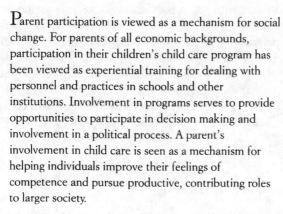

Parent participation is viewed as a mechanism for social change. For parents of all economic backgrounds, participation in their children's child care program has been viewed as experiential training for dealing with personnel and practices in schools and other institutions. Involvement in programs serves to provide opportunities to participate in decision making and involvement in a political process. A parent's involvement in child care is seen as a mechanism for helping individuals improve their feelings of competence and pursue productive, contributing roles to larger society.

Karen Chandler

*Adapted from "What Mothers Need" by J. B. Hendrick, 1970, *Young Children, 25*, pp. 109–114.

No matter how dedicated and meticulous we are about establishing a good life for the child in an early childhood program, teachers must never forget that the most significant part of the young child's environment lies outside the school. Quite wholesomely and rightly, there is a much more profound influence in the child's life: her home and the members of her family. Thus it makes good sense, if we hope to establish the best total environment for the child, to include her family as an important part of the preprimary experience (Doherty-Derkowski, 1995; Powell, 1989; Swick, 1991).*

There are a number of formal and informal ways to build these links between home and school. The current interest at the elementary and secondary levels in developing parent advisory boards and encouraging parent participation in the classroom (Snider, 1990) offers interesting confirmation of principles that early childhood teachers have championed for many years (Greenberg, 1989; Taylor, 1981). Such involvement ranges from making home visits (Powell, 1990) to inviting parents to volunteer in the classroom or asking them to serve on the parent board. All these avenues encourage interchange and communication between families and teachers if they are well done. One teacher-parent skill lies at the heart of them all—the ability to talk together in a sincere, nonthreatening way.

❧ Problems that Interfere with Good Communication

Despite the important advantages of keeping communication open, many parents and teachers do not get along comfortably together. The teacher may dread the parents' criticisms ("Why does Joe have paint on his shirt again?") or feel financially at their mercy because displeased parents may take their child out of the centre. Moreover, the teacher may blame the parents for the child's shortcomings; this is bound to interfere with a good relationship between them.

In these times when 63.4% of all mothers with children under the age of six work outside the home (Human Resources Development Canada), the additional burdens of fatigue and guilt that such added responsibilities may entail take an additional toll on parent energies. The results can be that, although the parents remain as loving and concerned as ever, the time for contact between school and home is diminished. Indeed, one survey found that one-third of the parents didn't enter the day care centre at all when delivering their children for care (Powell, 1978).

When parents *do* have contact, they, like the teachers, feel vulnerable to criticism. After all, their child, who is an extension of themselves, is on view. First-time parents particularly can be quite frightened of the teacher's opinion, and all parents yearn to know that the teacher likes their child and that she is doing well. The relationship is doubly touchy because a parent, particularly the mother, may be seeking validation of her own worth as a person by ascertaining that the teacher approves of her offspring. She is all too ready to believe the teacher (and also to feel threatened and angry) if blame is implied.

---

*For additional material on parents' participation in the school, please refer to chapter 14, "Providing Cross-Cultural, Nonsexist Education."

Parents may also fear that if they speak frankly and mention something they do not like about the program or about what their child is doing there, they will antagonize the teacher. They may worry about the possibility of reprisals against the child when they are not there. This is comparable to the parent who fears complaining to hospital personnel lest they discriminate against the child. The fact that most professional people are more mature than this may not affect the parent's innate caution in this matter.

Besides being vulnerable to criticism and wishing to protect her child, the mother may dread being displaced by the teacher in the child's affections. Separation involves mixed feelings for her. On one hand, she deeply wants to wean her child: She is tired of changing his pants and tying his shoes and never going anywhere alone. But, at the same time, something inside her resents having the teacher take over. To add to her confusion, the mother may also be struggling with guilty feelings over the relief she feels at being able to parcel her child out for a few days a week. Surely, if she were a "good mother," she wouldn't feel so elated at the thought of going shopping by herself! So she worries about what the teacher would think of her if the teacher only knew.

For both parents and teacher there remain all the past experiences and previous relationships with other teachers and parents that set the tone of what each expects of the other. In addition to pleasant memories, there are the emotionally powerful ones of the principal's office, having to stay after school, authoritarian teachers, and militant, unreasonable parents that lie at the back of consciousness and plague parents and teachers during their initial contacts. It is no wonder then, with all these things conspiring to build walls between families and teachers, that we must invest some effort and understanding if we wish to establish a more rewarding relationship between the adults who are so important in the life of the young child.

🝆 Suggestions for Establishing a Good Relationship between Parent and Teacher

Surely there must be some way to establish a bond that leads to problem solving rather than to defence building. The question is, how can the teacher go about doing this?

Probably the most essential ingredient in a more satisfactory relationship between teacher and parent is that the teacher have the child's welfare truly at heart and that she be genuinely concerned about her. My experience has been that when parents believe this to be true—which means, of course, that it has to *be* true and not just something the teacher *wishes* were true—when parents really sense the teacher's goodwill, they will forgive teachers their inadvertent transgressions, and the relationship will warm up as trust develops.

Genuine concern and caring can be expressed in a variety of ways. Faithful caretaking is one way. The teacher takes pains to see that everything the child has made is valued by being put in her cubby for her to take home, her belongings are kept track of, her nose is wiped when it needs it, and, although she may not be the pristinely clean youngster at the end of the day that she was upon arrival, she is tidied up and has had her face washed before her parent picks her up. The teacher also shows that she cares by carefully enforcing the health and safety regulations and by planning a curriculum that is interesting, varied, and suited to the needs of individual children.

Another way for the teacher to show concern is by expressing genuine interest in each child to her parent. For example, it is always sound practice to comment on something the youngster has enjoyed that day. It may be the friendly statement "Helen really loves our new bunny; she fed him and watched him half the morning," or it might be "I think Jerry is making friends with our new boy, Todd; they spent a lot of time with the trains in the block corner today." These comments assure the parent that the child has had attention from the teacher and that she is aware of her as an individual rather than as just one of the troop.

Teachers can also demonstrate that they truly care about the children and their families by taking special pains to learn about differing points of view concerning children that families have who come from cultures other than the teacher's. Several resources on this subject are included at the end of this chapter as well as in chapter 14, Providing Cross-Cultural, Nonsexist Education.

Still another kind of caring can be indicated on a more subtle level by letting the parent know that the teacher is on the child's side *but not on the child's side as opposed to the family's.* Occasionally teachers fall into the fantasy of thinking, "If only I could take that child home with me for a week and give her a steady, loving environment." Or sometimes a child will say in a rush of affection, "Oh, I wish *you* were my mother!" To avoid an emotionally confusing and difficult situation for the child, it is important that the teacher clarify her role. She can handle this by gently replying, "We *are* having fun, and I like you, too; but, of course, you already have a mother—I'm not your mother, I'm your *teacher.* I take care of you at school, and your mother takes care of you at home." This avoids rivalry and makes a friendly alliance between mother and teacher more likely.

It is difficult to be on the family's side if the teacher blames the parent for all the child's problems. Such disapproval, even if unspoken, cannot help being sensed by parents. In any situation where I feel critical of a parent, I have found it helpful to remember what Leonhard (1963) recommends: "Ask yourself, if *I* were that mother, with that set of problems and that background, could I do any better with that child?"

Another thing to remember, as any parent of more than one child knows, is that children are born with different temperaments. No matter what fathers and mothers do, children are different to start with and remain so, no matter what their environment. It is therefore ridiculous to hold the parent accountable for all the child's shortcomings.

Thus we see that the teacher can put parents at ease by letting them know that she is concerned about the child, that she is on both the child's and parents' sides, and that she does not feel that everything the child does is the family's fault. After all, parents, like teachers, also want what is best for their children. A sense of common, shared concern is worth working for, because once parents feel its existence, they are freer to work with the teacher on the child's behalf.

Of course, sometimes, despite our best intentions, a relationship with a parent may not be so harmonious. When this is the case, it can be helpful to know how to handle such encounters.

❧ What If the Relationship Is Not Good?

It is inevitable that, from time to time, there will be parents who make teachers so angry it is almost impossible to resist the temptation to lose one's temper in return—a response that usually just makes things worse. Fortunately, there are alternative ways of coping with angry feelings that can help teachers (and other people) retain control of themselves and the situation—an important skill for a professional person to acquire (Samalin, 1992).

The Preamble: What to Do Before the Situation Arises

A good way to begin is to know one's own points of vulnerability. I picture these points as being a series of red buttons people can push—red buttons that, when pushed, make me see red, too! Different things make different people angry. For some teachers it's the bossy, domineering parent, while for others it is the parent who is always late or who sends her child to school with a deep cough and runny nose.

Whatever the buttons are, it is helpful to identify them in advance, because once they are identified it is possible to summon up the extra reserves of self-control that are needed when someone begins to push one.

Coping with the Initial Encounter: What to Do When That Button Is Pressed

Surviving an encounter with an angry parent is really a three-part process. It includes the immediate first encounter, what happens afterward, and the final resolution of the situation.

For the sake of example, let's take an angry complainer, because teachers do have to deal with such people from time to time. The usual response to complaints is to give in to the impulse to defend and explain. However, this is not what complainers want. They want to complain and have the teacher apologize and do what they wish. Now, sometimes an apology is justified, but sometimes it is not! Either way, the teacher is likely to feel angry in return.

Rather than jumping right in with a defensive reply, the more effective approach is to wait a minute before responding and actually *listen* to what the parent is saying (Studer, 1993). These precious seconds provide valuable lead time that allows an opportunity to recognize the anger inside oneself and to consider the reply.

Next, instead of defending or explaining, take time to rephrase what the complainer is saying, adding a description of her feelings. This is exactly the same strategy that was advocated in the chapter on emotional health and will be emphasized again in the one on discipline. *There is no more effective way of dealing with strong feelings than using this response.* (Fenwick, 1993).

Admittedly, it can be even harder to remember to do this with a grown-up than with a child because grown-ups are so much more threatening than children are, but it does work like magic. For example, you might say, "You don't want me to . . ." or "You're upset because I . . ."

After the person has calmed down, it may be appropriate to explain your side of the situation or it may not. Many times, when a matter of policy is in question ("You mean you lost his mittens again?" or "If you let that kid bite Ann once more, I'm calling licensing"), the wisest thing to do is refer it to the director, or at least say you'll need to discuss it with the person in charge.* This is called "referring it to a committee," and it serves the

---

*Student teachers should *always* follow this procedure.

♋   *Unfortunately, not all parents are as delighted with their preschool as this mother is.*

invaluable purpose of spreading the responsibility for the decision around as well as providing a cooling-off period.

For the bravest and most secure teachers there is another way to cope with the initial encounter. After listening and rephrasing an attack, some people are comfortable enough to put their own honest feelings into words. "I'm feeling pretty upset (angry, frightened, worried) right now about what you've said. I don't know what to say. Let me think it over, and I'll get back to you." This kind of self-disclosure is too risky for some people to attempt, but it is an effective way of dealing with feelings for those who feel able to try it.

What to Do After the Complainer Departs

The problem with controlling anger as I have suggested is that it doesn't always melt away after the attacker has left. A common but undesirable way teachers deal with this residue is to justify themselves to other people, describe the situation (perhaps slanted a trifle in their favour!), and explain why they were right, thereby getting other people to take their side of the argument. Or they take revenge by undercutting the attacker, saying bad things about her so that the staff or director is turned against the parent.

A third, equally undesirable way of unloading anger is to pick on some hapless victim who cannot defend herself. This is called *displacement*. For example, parents may yell at children when they fear confronting a spouse, or teachers may pick on children when they're afraid of antagonizing another adult.

But is there a better way—one that doesn't require us to swallow our anger and that does no harm to other people? There is. And it is simple and available to everyone. All it requires is a good friend with a listening, uncritical ear.

Everyone needs someone to talk with—someone who has confidence enough in us that they can listen while we express our feelings without arguing with us or telling us we shouldn't feel that way, someone who knows we can draw the line between talking about what we would like to do for revenge and actually doing it. This opportunity to ventilate feelings in a safe place is a wonderful luxury that eventually can lead to forming constructive solutions to whatever problem exists.

It is also helpful to think through the best and worst case scenarios during that discussion. Facing up to the worst thing that could happen when you speak with the parent again and the best thing that might happen will reduce anxiety a great deal and increase confidence when the meeting actually takes place.

The Return Engagement

A benefit of waiting and then returning to discuss an emotion-laden problem is that the other person has had time to calm down, too. They may even be a little ashamed about how they behaved, so it may be necessary to help them save face.

It can also be helpful to include a third person in the discussion, particularly if the problem has been "referred to a committee." Many times this person is the director or someone else who can support both teacher and parent.

This is the point at which various alternatives for solving the problem can be proposed, so it is a good idea to have several such possibilities in mind that are acceptable to the school and that allow the parent the opportunity to participate in the final solution, also.

Whatever that solution turns out to be, if the teacher has listened, rephrased, dealt with her own anger in safe surroundings, and offered explanations or solutions, it is probable that the parent will see the teacher as a reasonable person. The teacher will have the comfort of knowing she has done nothing that she need be ashamed of at a later date.

🎜 Maintaining Good Relationships: Keeping the Lines of Communication Open

Fortunately, most relationships with parents do not involve such difficult encounters. For these parents, too, it is important to keep communication lines open. Thus it is necessary for the teacher to be accessible in two senses of the word. First, she must be approachable because she cares about the child; second, she must be physically available when the parent is around the school. In some schools, availability can be hard to come by. The teacher may be occupied with setting up as the children arrive and able to give the parent only a passing word, or at the end of the day she may be so harassed that she has no time or energy to talk.

❧   *Informal contacts as families come and go build comfortable relations between teachers and parents.*

It is possible and even desirable to arrange the schedule so that one teacher is free to greet parents the first and last fifteen minutes of the day or during peak arrival and departure times. If she is free from other responsibilities at that time, she can see each parent for countless casual meetings and can build relationships of friendliness and trust more easily. The sheer informality of this encounter robs it of a good deal of threat. Chatting right by the gate, the parents know that they can hasten away if the conversation takes too threatening a turn. In addition, they are likely to see the teacher in a variety of moods and predicaments, which increases the teacher's humanity.

This repeated, consistent contact is far superior to relying solely on the more formal and frightening "conference" that may occur once or twice a year. After a comfortable, everyday relationship is well established, an occasional conference with a longer uninterrupted opportunity to talk can be used to better advantage.

A helpful way to broaden teacher-parent communication skills is to think over past encounters with a parent to see who is doing most of the talking. If this analysis reveals that the teacher is talking most of the time it probably means either that the chats are too hurried or that the teacher needs to monitor herself to make certain she is truly listening to what the parent has to say. The research study in this chapter, which is about the quality and frequency of teacher-parent communication in child care situations, can help teachers become more aware of another potential problem.

❧ Counselling with Parents

Once lines of communication are open, the question remains, "What do we do then?"

When people talk together, many levels of relating can exist between them. During the year all these levels can be used by the teacher, depending on the situation.

The simplest level is a verbal or written message in which the teacher may say to the parent, "This is what we did in school today" or "Samantha learned to ride the scooter today." On this level, at least the parents know that the teacher wants them to know what is happening at school. Most new relationships have to start about here.

On another level the teacher acts as the supportive information provider and general comforter. In this guise she interprets the child's behaviour to the parent on the basis of her extensive experience with other children. For example, the simple information that many four-year-olds relish "disgraceful" language can be a great relief to a family secretly tormented by the worry that they suddenly have a pervert on their hands.

At yet another level the parent-teacher relationship has more of a counselling flavour to it. This is guidance, but not guidance in the sense that the teacher tells the parents what to do. Guidance means that the teacher works with the parents in terms of conscious motivation and behaviour to help them discover what may be causing various behaviour problems in the child and to help them figure out how to cope with them.

My impression is that teachers who have had special training are more likely to have the aplomb to attempt this third level. However, all teachers could increase their skills and do no harm and probably considerable good by offering themselves in a guidance role to parents in need of help, especially if they concentrate on listening rather than prescribing. The truth is that even when parents ask for help, they usually know the answer already. They are simply having difficulty applying it.

Excluding the occasional special situation in which more professional help is required, what parents need in order to work out a difficulty is the chance to talk out how they feel and evaluate whether a tentative solution is right for them and their unique child. Tremendous comfort comes to a distressed family when they are given the opportunity to air a problem with someone who can listen attentively and who is not too shaken by the confession that Jennifer and Mary have been sitting behind the back fence doing you know what! Allowing them to express their feelings of shame, or occasionally even anguish, over their child's behaviour is a positive benefit to offer parents in a counselling situation.

It is also true that teachers who have known literally hundreds of youngsters do have a broader background of experience than most parents do. It seems only right to pool this knowledge with the family's, as long as the teacher's alternatives are offered in such a way that parents feel free to accept or reject them. Parents will be able to use the teacher's range of knowledge most easily if the teacher points out to them that no matter how much she knows in general about children, she will *never* know as much about the individual child as the parent does.

Instead of providing instant answers to all problems posed by parents, the teacher will find it more useful to ask questions, such as "Why don't you tell me what you've tried already"" or "What are your thoughts about what to do next?" When a mother

❦ **RESEARCH STUDY** ❦

Which Kinds of Children's Centres Are Likely to Do the Best Job Communicating with Parents?

Research Question: Ghazvini and Readdick wanted to find out whether the frequency of various kinds of communication between parents and children's centre teachers was related to the overall quality of the child care centre.

Research Method: The investigators surveyed the parents, teachers, and directors of twelve centres. Four centres were completely government subsidized, four were a combination of profit and nonprofit settings providing a mix of private pay and subsidized child care, and four were completely nonsubsidized, private, for-profit programs. The investigators studied three kinds of communication: one-way (teacher to parent), two-way (teacher to parent and parent to teacher) and three-way (parent to teacher to community resource). (For the pur-

poses of simplicity only one- and two-way exchanges are considered in this review.)

Ghazvini and Readdick had the parents and teachers complete questionnaires about parental perceptions of communication and caregiver perceptions of communication. The questionnaires asked about the frequency and kind of communication that took place. Some examples of what the researchers considered to be one-way communication were parents reading the bulletin board, getting a newsletter, and seeing a calendar of daily activities planned for the children. Examples of two-way communication included teachers talking with parents during arrival or departure times, parent-teacher conferences, and parents attending field trips or special events. Two hundred and one parents returned the questionnaires, as did forty-nine caregivers.

comes to say that her child has begun "misbehaving" in some new way (perhaps she is fighting a great deal with her sister or has begun having nightmares), the best question to ask is "I wonder if you could tell me what else happened at about the same time." The typical response is "Well, nothing much. Let me see, now, I guess that was about the time my in-laws came to visit, and, oh yes, her little dog was run over, and . . ." By this means the mother gains useful insight into what has upset her child and usually can formulate a plan about what she might do to help her get on an even keel again (Koulouras, Porter, & Senter, 1986).

Another cornerstone of good counselling is patience. It seems to be human nature that we want instant results, but change often takes a long time. I used to despair when I made a suggestion that the parent ignored. I was most concerned on the occasions when I referred the family to a specialist, and the parent declined to act on the referral. My implicit assumption was that if the family did not do it then, they never would. Happily, I have found this to be a false assumption. To be sure, parents may not be ready this year to face the problem of Jeffrey's temper tantrums and hyperactivity, but they have at least heard that the possibility of a problem exists, and the next professional person who approaches them may have greater success because the ground has been prepared.

The investigators also rated the quality of the twelve centre environments by using The Early Childhood Environment Rating Scale (Harms & Clifford, 1980).

Research Results: The subsidized or partially subsidized centres were judged to be of higher quality than the nonsubsidized, private, for-profit centres were. In those higher quality centres, both parents and caregivers reported greater frequency of both one- and two-way communication than did parents and caregivers in private settings. However, in those same higher quality centres, the teachers rated all forms of parent communication as occurring more often and being more important than did the parents.

Implications for Teaching: For one thing, teachers and directors should note that private, for-profit centres evidently tend to be weak in the area of talking with parents. Thus everyone who works in those settings should make more of an effort to communicate with parents.

The question of why teachers in the higher quality centres felt that they did more communicating with parents than the parents felt they did is an interesting one. The researchers suggest that it may *seem* to the teacher that more communication is taking place because she is talking to fifteen or twenty parents each day, whereas individual parents do not have that experience. The result is that these teachers may think they are doing a better job of talking with parents than they really are. Whatever the reason for insufficient contact, it seems reasonable to conclude that *all* teachers in *all* settings should make more of an effort to talk with every parent as often as possible. Doing so is absolutely the most effective way to build wholesome bonds between home and school.

Source: From "Parent-Caregiver Communication and Quality of Care in Diverse Child Care Settings" by A. S. Ghazvini & C. A. Readdick, 1994, *Early Childhood Research Quarterly, 9*(2), 207–222.

Nowadays I am more wary of the person who agrees completely and instantly with my suggestions. Usually there is not very much movement in these cases. The chance to think out, backtrack, consider various solutions, and take time to get used to an idea is indispensable in a guidance situation.

❧ *Practical Pointers about Conducting a Parent Conference*

Getting ready for the conference is as important as the conference itself, since neither teachers nor parents want to waste time just chatting. Preparation may involve accumulating a series of quick observations or developmental checklists if these are used by the school. Some teachers also take pictures of significant events or activities the youngster has participated in and find that sharing these at the beginning of the conference starts conversation off on a friendly note. When these as well as other materials are assembled in a portfolio, it provides a useful, consistent record of how and what the child is doing during her time at the centre.

In addition to these tangible documents, it helps focus the conference to think through the points to be covered before beginning, but, at the same time, it is important to remember that a conference is just that: It is an opportunity to *confer*. So, while making plans on what to cover, it is also essential to allow plenty of time and opportunity for parents to talk and to raise concerns of their own. Always bear in mind that even more important than exchanging information is building and maintaining the bond of warmth and trust between teacher and family.

As obvious as it may sound, a conference consists of three parts: a beginning, a middle, and an end. It is a good idea during the conference to convey a sense of this structure as things move along.

In particular, it is helpful to *set a clear time limit at the beginning* so you and the parent can pace yourselves. This avoids a sense of rejection when the teacher suddenly jumps up like the white rabbit in *Alice in Wonderland* and says she must hurry away! Perhaps you might say, "I'm so glad we have this half-hour to talk together; I've been looking forward to it," or "It's wonderful you're so prompt—that gives us our whole 45 minutes for discussion," or (over the phone) "That'll be fine if you come at two; that should allow us to finish by the time the children are due to go home."

Avoid Interruptions

Of course, avoiding interruptions is easier said than done sometimes, but most parents resent the teacher's or director's taking a phone call during a conference. Doing so not only interrupts the flow of talk but also infringes on the parents' rightful time, and parents of young children are often paying a babysitter for the privilege of attending. So it is best to find a place to talk that cuts intrusions to the minimum. It might be outside in an undisturbed corner of the play yard during nap, or it might be in the teacher's office, or even the parent's car will do in a pinch. The essentials are privacy and quiet. The child, of course, should not be present (Bjorklund & Burger, 1987).

Some Ways to Begin

In addition to the common pleasantries about weather and being busy, there are ways of opening a conference that can get things off to a businesslike and not too threatening start. For example, one of the best therapists I ever knew often began conferences with the friendly question, "Well, what's new?" Some additional friendly ways to get the ball rolling suggested by Rue Watkins (1993) include asking parents what they're most proud of about their child, where her favourite place to play is, what the child has recently learned to do, or what the family enjoys doing together. Watkins suggests things the teacher might make a point of sharing with the parents could include what the teacher likes about the child, whom their child plays with and what they enjoy doing together at school, and new things their youngster is interested in or learning.

Sometimes it works well to begin with a quick explanation of what you want to talk about. "Dave tells me you're moving soon, and I thought, if you like, we might do a little talking about how to help him adjust to the change." Or you might mention a concern

❧   *Sharing pictures of the child at school can provide a warm and informal opening to a conference.*

expressed by the parent at a previous meeting. "I remember last time we were talking about Janie's stuttering. How's that coming along now at home?"

An even *better* way to begin is to encourage parents to express their concerns first. "Have you special things in mind you want to talk over about Brian?" Even though their initial response may be, "Well, no, not really," this kind of early opening question often enables parents to bring something up later in the conference they were too shy to mention at first. More frequently, however, the parent will leap at this chance and start right in with a genuine concern, often phrased as a return question. "Well, I was wondering how he's . . . ?" It is gratifying how often this concern is related to that of the teacher.

During the Conference, Stay as Relaxed as Possible

Take time to really listen to what the parent says. (A good way to monitor yourself about this is to check whether during conversations you are usually busy formulating a reply in your own mind. If you find yourself doing this habitually, it is probably an indication that you should focus your attention more completely on the speaker and be less concerned about your response.) If you think of the conference as being a time for the parent to do most of the talking, it will help you at least to share the time more equally.

It is all right to admit to a parent that you are not sure about something. A parent asked me last week whether her youngster was acting "mopy" at snack time. I had no idea since I am never with that child at that time, but it was easy to promise to find out and get back to her, and then to ask, "Are you wondering about that for some special reason?" This led to a helpful talk about this four-year-old's sulkiness and belligerence at home because her grandfather, who had recently moved in with the family, was insisting she eat everything on her plate. (Ultimately I anticipate offering some appropriate referrals or activities that will facilitate the grandfather's making friends in his new community and, perhaps, recommending a little family therapy to help them get their shifting roles straight under these new circumstances.)

Drawing the Conference to a Close

As the time to close draws near, there are a number of ways to signal this. (Remember, the wise teacher has mentioned the potential limit in the beginning in some tactful fashion.) These ending signals range from shifting a little in your chair to (in desperate circumstances in which past experience has indicated that a parent is insensitive to time limits) having someone primed to interrupt in a casual way.

It is always worthwhile to sum up what has been said as part of the closing process. "I am really glad we had a chance to talk. Even though William is getting along so well, it never hurts to touch base, does it? I'll remember what you said about the allergy tests.

❧   *It's this one, Daddy—*
No-o-o—I think it's this one!

We'll make sure he gets water instead of milk and that the other children understand and don't tease him about it." Or "I'm sure sorry to hear your family's going through that. We're here when there's something we can do to help. Give me a ring any time, and meanwhile, we'll do those special things with Jennifer we worked out today and let you know how they turn out."

What to Do After the Conference

For one thing, it is vital to follow up on any promises or plans you and the parents have made together. For the teacher who has spoken with fifteen families, it can be all too easy to forget something or to defer doing it because she is so busy; but for the parents who have only that one particular conference to recall, it is much easier to remember! If you wish to maintain a condition of trust between you and the families you serve, it is necessary that *you* remember, too. This is one reason why it is valuable to make notes immediately following the conference. They can serve as a reminder of promises and plans that should be carried out.

Notes also provide useful takeoff points for the next conference. I have even known them to be valuable in court, when the teacher was asked to document that a parent had demonstrated a faithful interest in the well-being of her child by attending a series of conferences during the year.

Finally, Remember That Information Shared by Parents During a Conference Is Confidential

It is unethical as well as unwise to repeat what was said in private to anyone else unless that person (the director, perhaps, or another teacher who works with the child) has a genuine need to know that information. Indeed, if you foresee the need to share such material with another person, it is a good idea to ask the parents first. That way you do not risk violating their trust.

❧ Limits to Guidance Work

When planning and carrying out conferences, we must also recognize that some behaviour and developmental problems are beyond the teacher's ability, training, and time to handle. It is vital to be clear about where to draw the line and how far to go in guidance work. My rule of thumb is "When in doubt, refer." If the situation looks serious or does not respond to matter-of-fact remedies, it is time to suggest a specialist. In general, it is too risky and takes more advanced training than a typical preschool teacher possesses to draw implications and offer interpretations to parents about deep, complex reasons for behaviour. Fortunately there are highly trained, skilled specialists on whom we can rely to solve serious problems, so let's leave Oedipus and his troublesome kin to our psychiatric cohorts.

❦ *Summary*

Sensible caution and referral to an expert are advisable under some circumstances, but teachers can offer a lot of help and work with parents in many ways to bring about a happier life for their children. To do this, it is first necessary to overcome various problems that make communication between parents and teachers difficult. One of the most effective things teachers can do is make it plain to the parent that they have the welfare of the child at heart and that they want to join with the family to help the child. Teachers can also take care to be available when the parent wants to talk, and they can provide the opportunity for many easygoing, casual contacts.

Once the lines of communication are open, teachers can offer help by serving as friendly listeners who assist the parent in assessing the nature of the difficulty and in proposing alternatives until they find the one best suited for parent and child. Teachers who assume this guidance function offer parents what they need the most: an accepting attitude, an open ear, and a warm heart.

Question and Activities

1. Have the class split into pairs. One person in each pair should select a problem or difficulty to discuss while the other person listens. The only restriction on the listener is that, before making any other reply, she must first restate in her own words what she hears the speaker saying; that is, her primary task is to be open to the feelings and import of the communication. Then shift roles and have the speaker practise this sort of listening and responding.

2. Select children in your group who appear to require special diagnostic help of some kind. List the reasons for your conclusion that they need help. With another student, practise how you might broach the subject of referral with the family. It is helpful to practice this with a "parent" who is resistant, one who is overly agreeable, and one who is obviously upset about your suggestion.

3. If you have children of your own, have you ever been summoned to school to discuss a problem? Share with the class how you felt about being asked to come in and do this.

4. *Problem:* You are now head teacher in a class of three-year-olds. One afternoon a father is half an hour late picking up his child. When you ask why he is late he snarls, "None of your damn business" and yanks his child out the door. How would you handle this situation?

Self-Check Questions for Review
Content-Related Questions

1. What are some reasons parents and teachers sometimes feel ill at ease with one other?
2. Give some practical examples of ways a teacher can show parents that she really cares about their child.
3. List and describe the three-part process involved in dealing with an angry parent.
4. What do parents really need in a parent conference?
5. List some practical pointers for conducting a successful conference.
6. Give two examples of one-way communication between teachers and parents. Then give two examples of two-way communication between teachers and parents.

Integrative Questions

1. How might the feelings of mothers who work outside the home and mothers who do not be similar when placing their three-year-old in child care?
2. Teddy, a four-year-old boy in your group, has taken to pinching children when they sit next to him, tearing pages out of books when you aren't looking, and doing other destructive things. You are quite concerned and ask his mother if she could come to a conference with you. Give three examples of things

you would say to this parent during the conference that would blame her for her son's behaviour. Be sure to use actual quotations.

3. Now that she's really mad at you, suggest an angry sentence or two she would say in reply. Then, for each of her sentences, phrase a response that would describe her feelings to her.

4. Now, suggest some approaches you could use instead that would *not* blame Teddy's mother for his behaviour.

5. Is it accurate to say that the research by Ghazini and Readdick revealed that parents thought teachers in higher quality children's centres talked as much with them as the teachers themselves thought they did?

References for Further Reading

Overview

Berger, E. H. (1991). *Parents as partners in education: The school and home working together* (3rd ed.). Columbus, OH: Merrill. A solid, comprehensive coverage of the subject is offered by this textbook. *Highly recommended.*

Talking with Parents

Fenwick, K. (1993). Diffusing conflict with parents: A model for communication. *Child Care Information Exchange, 93*, 59–60. Fenwick provides a clear, brief discussion of how to respond to an angry parent by reflecting, reframing, and reviewing what the parent has said.

Lawler, S. B. (1991). *Teacher-parent conferencing in early childhood education.* Washington, DC: National Education Association. Down-to-earth, humane approaches to conferencing with parents are suggested. The list of do's and don'ts about conflict resolution is particularly helpful. *Highly recommended.*

Morgan, E. (1989). Talking with parents when concerns come up. *Young Children, 44*(2), 52–56. Morgan contributes some practical ideas of ways to foster communication with parents.

Rotter, J. C., Robinson, E. H., & Fey, M. A. (1987). *Parent-teacher conferencing* (2nd ed.). Washington, DC: National Education Association. This pamphlet includes many sample questions, tips related to conferencing, and sensible advice. *Highly recommended.*

Studer, J. R. (1993). Listen so that parents will speak. *Childhood Education, 70*(2), 74–76. The author provides very practical advice on how to become a truly active listener. *Highly recommended.*

Beyond the Conference

Coner-Edwards, A. F., & Spurlock, J. (1988). *Black families in crisis: The middle-class.* New York: Brunner Mazel. The chapter by Benoit on child advocacy in the schools is particularly relevant. There are also helpful chapters on counselling.

Corbett, W. (1993). A complicated bias. *Young Children, 48*(3), 29–31. Corbett offers helpful discussions of ways to build sensitivity to and welcome the children of lesbian and gay families into the group.

Gonzalez-Mena, J. (1992). Taking a culturally sensitive approach in infant-toddler programs. *Young Children, 47*(2), 4–9. Gonzalez-Mena's recommendations apply equally well to older children and their families. *Highly recommended.*

Haycock, K., & Duany, L. (1991). Developing the potential of Latino students. *Principal, 70*(3), 25–27. This article includes practical suggestions for working with Latino parents as well as children.

Leister, C. (1993). Working with parents of different cultures. *Dimensions of Early Childhood, 21*(2), 13–15. Leister provides good, general advice on this subject.

Morrow, R. D. (1991). The challenge of Southeast Asian parental involvement. *Principal 70*(3), 20–22. The title is self-explanatory—the article includes a useful list of resources.

Swick, K. J. (1989). Understanding and relating to transformed families. *Dimensions, 17*(4), 8–11. Special situations related to single, foster, teen, and stepparent families and some ways teachers can assist them are reviewed here.

Wickens, E. (1993). Penny's questions: "I will have a child in my class with two moms: What do you know about this?" *Young Children, 48*(3), 25–28. This is another helpful article about welcoming children from gay and lesbian families.

Anger

Samalin, N. (1992) *Love and anger: The parental dilemma.* New York: Viking. Samalin provides practical advice for parents *and for teachers* on coping successfully with anger.

For the Advanced Student

Bronstein, P., & Cowan, C. P. (Eds.). (1988). *Fatherhood today: Men's changing role in the family.* New York: Wiley. This book uses extensive research citations as bases for discussing everything from gay fatherhood to Latino and African American fathers to fathers with toddlers.

Hill, R. B. (Ed.). (1993). *Research on the African-American family: A holistic perspective.* Westport, CT: Auburn House. This book provides a wealth of statistical and other documentation on the current circumstances of black families. It concludes with a series of sensible recommendations.

Mallory, B. L., & New, R. S. (Eds.). (1993). *Diversity & developmentally appropriate practices: Challenges for early childhood education.* New York: Teachers College Press. Not only does this book raise interesting questions about the suitability for all children of what is currently defined as being developmentally appropriate education, but it also points out the differing values about education that parents who come from a variety of cultures may hold. Thought-provoking reading.

Powell, D. R. (1989). *Families and early childhood programs.* Washington, DC: National Association for the Education of Young Children. Powell presents a research-based discussion of these relationships from children's, parents', and teachers' points of view.

Other Resources of Special Interest

Child Care Information Exchange, PO Box 2890, Redmond, Washington 98073-9977. CCIE invariably contains a wealth of useful information on child care practices and management. It is listed here because it often includes practical information about working with parents.

Tender Topics

Helping Children Master Emotional Crises[*]

I, a stranger and afraid
In a world I never made.

A. E. Housman

Have you ever wondered . . .

What to advise a parent who asks if he should tell his son his grandfather is dying?

How to help a three-year-old get ready to have her tonsils removed?

What you should do when you are helping a child undress for nap and find something that looks like a cigarette burn under his arm?

. . . If you have, the material in the following pages will help you.

*I am indebted to Donna Dempster (McClain) of Cornell University for suggesting that a chapter on "tender topics" be included in the revised edition of *The Whole Child*.

Young children are as subject to stress and strain when a crisis strikes their families as adults are, but this may be difficult for the family to recognize. They often hope that if nothing is said, the child will be unaware of the problem, or they may be so overwhelmed by the crisis that they have little emotional reserve available to help their children through their troubles at the same time. But children are keen sensors of emotional climates, and they are aware of telephone conversations, comments by neighbours, and so forth. As Furman says,

> Children are so observant of and sensitive to their parents' moods and nuances of behavior that, in our experience, it is impossible to spare them from knowing or to deceive them about the true nature of events. (1974, p. 18).

Indeed the secrecy and avoidance often practised by families when crises occur may serve only to deepen the child's anxiety (Schaefer, 1984). It is far better, then, to reduce this misery when we can by facing facts squarely and providing as much stability as possible than to worsen the problem by failing to deal with it.

Moreover, the experience of crisis is not always undesirable in itself. It is important to realize that adverse circumstances do not always weaken children. In their book *Overcoming the Odds: High Risk Children from Birth to Adulthood,* Werner and Smith (1992) trace the development of Hawaiian children living under the stressful conditions of chronic poverty from birth to adulthood. They found that even in the harshest circumstances, many children succeeded despite such adversity. In a comparison of these resilient children with their less successful peers, three clusters of protective factors were found to be significant. These were that the child had at least average intelligence and personality attributes that drew forth positive responses from other people (robustness, vigour, and a sociable temperament), ties of affection with parent substitutes such as grandparents or siblings, and an external support system such as a youth group, church, or school.

Wang and Gordon (1994) also present evidence that some children can find purpose and hope in some of the most apparently hopeless situations. So, as we approach this discussion of the perils and problems that will confront many of the children we teach, we should remember what Werner and Smith (1982) say so well:

> The terrors of our nature and the world remind us forever how vulnerable we are. Hence biological and behavioral scientists have spent a great deal of time, energy, and resources exploring the roots of our aggression, alienation, disease, and unease. What is often overlooked, but seems more awesome and miraculous, is our resilience as a species. (p. 152)

Crisis *can* constitute "a dangerous opportunity" for growth if it is handled well. Needless to say, this is not always the case. Young children seem particularly vulnerable to potential disaster, in part because they lack experience and in part because they are relatively powerless and helpless. If they are lucky, they have adults who can help them through these difficult times. Because preprimary teachers occasionally have such opportunities, the following material is included.

❧ What Constitutes a Crisis?

We usually think of a crisis as being something sudden, and surely death and illness or a trip to the emergency room all fall in this category. Other crises are of longer duration:

✎   *When a child has waited all day for the parent's return, a late pickup can constitute a genuine crisis for that youngster.*

the mental illness of a parent, a divorce, a new baby, physical abuse, moving to a new neighbourhood, and even adjusting to child care outside the home.

Some crises are unhappy events—loss of a job, for example—and some are happier occasions—a marriage, perhaps, or the adoption of a child. The one thing all crises have in common, whether sudden or chronic, unhappy or joyful, is that they all involve change. These changes occur far more commonly than one would wish.

It is difficult to determine the exact number of children affected by divorces in Canada because there is no official information about out-of-court custody decisions. In 1990, approximately 34 000 children were involved in divorce cases in which courts made custody decisions.

Fortunately some of the effects of crises can be mitigated if families and teachers know where to turn and what to do. It is my hope that the following material will be useful in this regard. *However, because of the nature and gravity of the crises presented, the reader should understand that this chapter represents only the barest minimum of information and that it is intended only as a starting point, not as a comprehensive guide.*

✎ *Some General Principles for Helping Families Deal with Crises*

There is no other time in life when the parent is more important to the child than during a time of crisis (Wallerstein & Blakeslee, 1989). Teachers, psychologists, social workers, and caregivers may also offer meaningful aid, but the family is the most significant influence; for this reason the fundamental goal of the teacher should be to support the family as well as possible. There are a number of ways to accomplish this.

Make Certain the Parents Understand That It Is Better to Include the Child in the Situation Than to Exclude Him

Particularly in matters of death, serious parental illness, or job loss, adults may attempt to shield children from what is happening, but as mentioned before, children always know when something is wrong. Parents may not realize how frightened this can make youngsters when they are left to fantasize about the nature of the trouble or the reason for it. It is the primaeval fear of the unknown. To remedy this, the teacher should encourage the family to explain in simple terms the nature of the emergency.

The same recommendation applies to expressing feelings: Children should be allowed to participate in feelings of concern or grief rather than be excluded. I would caution that this principle should be followed within reason. The point to get across to the family is that it is all right for children to understand that grown-ups sometimes feel sad or frightened or upset—as long as this is mingled with steady assurances from family members that the child will be taken care of and that life will continue.

Try Not to Overreact, No Matter What the Parent Tells You

Teachers can be of little help if they allow themselves to become as upset as the parents are over a crisis, though I cannot deny that crises such as suicide or the rape of a child are deeply shocking to everyone. However, if teachers can present a model of relative calm as well as concern, they can influence the parent to behave in the same manner. By providing information on what will help the child, they can encourage the institution of rational steps in dealing with the situation.

Teachers should also guard themselves against being overcome with pity for a youngster or the parents, because pity is not beneficial for the family, either. I recall one situation in which a little boy, returning to school after his mother died, was greeted by a teacher who threw her arms around him and burst into tears, saying, "Oh, you poor child! Whatever will you and your poor papa do now?" This unfortunate response overwhelmed the boy and froze him into an inexpressive state from which it was very difficult to retrieve him. One would think an adult would have more sense, but crises do strange things to people.

Of course, pity is not always so obvious. It may manifest itself in the more subtle forms of overindulgence or spoiling, and this is equally undesirable. Pity is a weakening experience for the person who is its object. It encourages feelings of despair, self-pity, and helplessness (Peterson, Maier, & Seligman, 1993)—the exact opposites of competence. It is far better to substitute compassionate understanding and to express quiet confidence that, although the family and child feel bad right now, you are certain they are ultimately going to come through the experience all right and that you are there to do whatever you can to help them.

Do Not Violate the Privacy of the Family

Particularly when something sensational has happened, whether it be a car accident or a home burning to the ground, it can be tempting to participate in the tragedy by gossiping about it with other parents. It is impossible to avoid discussion of such events entirely when they are common knowledge in the community, but care should be taken to keep private details private. For one thing, any parents who hear the teacher repeat such personal details are bound to conclude that the teacher will gossip about their personal affairs also. For another, behaving this way is a breach of professional ethics.

Offer Yourself as a Resource

As chapter 7 emphasized, being a good listener is one way to do this, as long as parents do not come to feel that you are mainly interested in the sensational aspects of the crisis or that you cannot wait for them to stop talking so you can offer advice. Remember, also, that sometimes families do not want any help, and this desire must be respected, too.

Sometimes, after the emergency aspect has subsided, parents find it helpful when the teacher has a good reference book to lend them. If the centre has a reserve of at least a few such basic books on hand, they can be instantly available when needed.

Finally, the teacher can also be a resource for referral to other supporting agencies. This ticklish matter is discussed in greater detail in chapter 9, so I will only comment here that it is necessary to be careful of offering referral resources too hastily lest the family interpret this as your wanting to get rid of them and their uncomfortable problem. On the other hand, crises that result from a sudden deep shock or trauma, such as being in a severe automobile accident, experiencing rape, or witnessing a murder or suicide, require immediate psychiatric attention.

☙ Some General Principles for Helping the Child Deal with Crises

Don't Ignore the Situation by Pretending It Hasn't Happened*

It takes a sensitive teacher to face a crisis with a child in a matter-of-fact way without overdoing it or rubbing it in. This is not to say that the teacher should imply that everything is fine and dandy and that getting over the disaster will be easy or that everything will be just like it was before. It is better to admit that it is not a happy time while making the point that it is not the end of the world, either.

It helps to be alert to clues that the child wants to talk about his feelings or that he has the problem on his mind. Sometimes this occurs long after the event in question. For example, one of the children in our centre suffered a serious burn on her arm that caused her a good deal of misery. Although she seemed fully recovered, later events proved she had not come to terms with it completely at that time. Several months after-

---

*For further discussion of coping with emotional disturbance in children please refer to chapter 9. Indications of disturbance are discussed in chapter 5.

ward, she happened to be part of a group of youngsters who went on a field trip to inspect the skeleton in the biology department. She was very quiet while she surveyed the bones, and slipping her hand into the teacher's on the way home, she whispered to her, "But what happened to the skin?" To which the teacher responded, "Are you wondering if it got burned off?"—and all of Amy's concerns about skin and injuries came tumbling forth.

But it is best if the situation can be dealt with while it is happening. If the child is unable to bring the problem up, the teacher can provide play experiences for working through the event, or include a book on the subject at story time, or mention the problem casually himself when the opportunity for a quiet private interlude presents itself. Sometimes this can be done tactfully by saying, "I remember when I was little and had my tonsils out—I didn't know what was going to happen in the hospital. I wondered if my mother would stay, and if . . . [include a shrewd guess about what is troubling the particular child]. I wonder if you are wondering about that, too."

The focus of such discussions should be on what the child thinks and what he is worried about. Reassurance and explanation have their place in talking problems over with young children, but they are not nearly so helpful as listening and encouraging youngsters to express their worries through talk and, most valuably, through play (McCormick, 1994).

Remember, It Is All Right for Children (and Adults) to Cry and to Feel Bad

We early childhood teachers do better than most people at accepting children's right to cry about everyday matters, but sometimes we find ourselves feeling very uncomfortable when children sob over more serious situations, such as the death of someone they love or a parent's going to jail. Perhaps this is because we know these griefs represent more serious situations, and so we feel more concerned and sorry that the child must go though those experiences. It is natural, when you care about someone, not to want them to feel bad.

But it is important to remember that crying brings relief in serious situations just as it does in more mundane ones, and this relief is valuable and helpful to the child. Therefore it is important for us not to cut off such a response because of our own discomfort and consequent need to comfort the child. Unfortunately, feeling bad is a part of life, just as feeling joyful is. Teachers who realize this learn to endure and accept children's expressions of grief rather than blocking them by providing too swift reassurance, hastily distracting them, or telling them, "Don't feel bad . . . it's all right!"

This does not mean, of course, that one stands coldly by while a youngster sobs forlornly in a corner; supportive warmth and cuddling are appropriate comforts to provide for grieving children. It *does* mean that children should be encouraged to cry as well as talk about their feelings if they feel the need to do so.

Provide Play Opportunities to Express and Clarify Feelings About the Crisis, and Try to Be on Hand to Help the Child Interpret Them

Imaginative play is a very satisfactory way for children to resolve their feelings about crises. Some kinds of play, such as hospital play, benefit children most if special equipment is provided. This might include a set of crutches, something that can stand in for shot needles (we use turkey basters for this purpose), aprons, surgical gowns, and masks.

Hand puppets, little rubber dolls, dollhouse furniture, and a housekeeping corner well equipped with dolls and other paraphernalia of family life are props that can be used to express concerns related to the family situation.

An alert teacher can be aware of the turn the play is taking and help a troubled child ease his feelings. She might, for example, remain close enough to a housekeeping group to comment quietly to a three-year-old pounding on a baby doll. "Gosh! You really want to show that baby she makes you mad! You want her to stop bothering you and crying so much. That's okay—it's okay to feel that way. You can pretend anything you want. Of course we can't do that to the real baby even when we feel that way, but we can *pretend* anything we want. We can *feel* what we wish, but we must control what we do."

Play opportunities that permit the sublimated expression of feelings are also valuable (see chapter 12). Some materials are especially good as aggression relievers—dough and finger paint that can be pounded and squished, and simple hammering come to mind— and some are more relaxing and tension relieving—water play and swinging, for example. In general, unstructured materials that make few demands for performance are the most effective ones to use for such purposes.

Absolve the Child from Guilt

Young children are not good reasoners about cause and effect. Piaget has provided us with many examples in which children have reasoned that effect was the cause. (For instance, a child may see trees bending in the wind and conclude that trees bending make the wind blow!) Piaget also teaches us that young children are self-centred and see things mainly in relation to themselves. And, finally, we know that children are prone to magical thinking, tending to believe that the wish has the same power as the act.

If we think about the implications of these developmental facts, it becomes easier to understand why children often conclude that they are the cause of the family's disaster— something usually so far from the actual truth it may not even occur to adults that the child is blaming himself for the trouble and feeling guilty and unhappy as a result (Essa & Murray, 1994). Warren (1977), in her excellent pamphlet *Caring*, suggests that the teacher can offer comfort in this kind of situation by helping the child separate adult from child business. For example, she suggests that the teacher might say:

> When your parents fight, that is very hard for you and sometimes makes you cry. But grown-ups' fighting is really grown-up business. Even if they are fighting about you, it is because they are mad at each other and not because of you or anything you did. (p. 22)

Maintain as Stable and Dependable an Atmosphere as Possible for Her While She Is in Your Care

This means that the child is expected to adhere to regular routines and that, in general, the same rules are applied to his conduct as are usually applied. It does not mean that allowances are not made—they must be. The teacher needs to be extra understanding and tolerant if the youngster cannot eat or is particularly irritable or has trouble falling asleep or cries a lot. However, keeping the routines and rules as steady as possible means that at least part of the child's world has not changed, and this offers substantial comfort to a child whose home world is in turmoil (McCormick, 1994).

Help the Child Know What to Expect

Sometimes families know in advance that a crisis is approaching, since they can generally anticipate such events as having a new baby, undergoing routine surgery, or moving to a new town. In such cases it is important not to build up unrealistic ideas of what such a change entails. The new baby will *not* be a wonderful little playmate for the preschooler as soon as she arrives, and ice cream is *not* going to taste wonderful after a tonsillectomy.

It is not necessary to be negative about changes and build undue apprehension. It just helps to talk over what will happen in advance to reduce the element of the unexpected. This is particularly true if the teacher and family talk to the youngster in terms of the plans being made for him—how his pet dog will get to the new house and where the family will have dinner on the day of the move. It is this kind of simple detail that children find reassuring and that adults sometimes forget to tell them, since they already know the answers or consider them unimportant.

🙐   *Advance preparation helps reduce anxiety.*

ও *Help the Child Retain a Sense of Being in Control*

During stormy times of crisis when children are upset, they often revert to less mature, more uncontrolled behaviour. It may seem paradoxical to recommend they be given as many opportunities to control their lives as possible during such difficult periods, but there is a sound reason for urging this strategy. It is that feeling "in charge" combats the sense of helplessness and panic the youngster must also contend with.

Fortunately, there are some age-appropriate, commonsense ways of helping even young children retain at least some confidence that they can control what is happening to them.

For example, I have already alluded to the value of providing, when possible, appropriate information about what is going to happen. This frankness not only relieves the child of the burden of free-floating anxiety but also provides opportunities for him to make simple plans about how to cope with the change. "I hear you're going to your grandma's while Mommy's in the hospital. What will you do when you get there?"

Opportunities to make simple choices and decisions also contribute to the child's sense of being in command. "Would you like to paint a picture to take to her, or is there something else you'd rather make?"

Knowing what to do beforehand helps, too. For this reason, earthquake, fire, and tornado drills have value that goes beyond the commonsense one of improving safety. By helping children know how to protect themselves, such drills also increase their confidence and sense of control. This is an important alleviator of panic (Saylor, 1993).

Finally, it can restore a child's feelings of being in control if he is encouraged to do something for someone else—even such simple things as helping the teacher set out the cups or hammering in a nail can help a youngster retain his sense of being an able, effective person.

ও *Helping Children Cope with Specific Crises*

Adjusting to School and Dealing with the Parent Who Picks the Child up Late

Ways of helping the child adjust to the centre were already discussed in chapter 3, but it should be pointed out here also that coming to school can represent such a change in the child's life that it may be a real crisis from his point of view. Particularly if the adjustment is a difficult one, we should not underestimate the anguish he is experiencing when separated from his mother, and we should do all we can to alleviate it.

Moving from preschool to kindergarten is such a big change from the child's point of view that it, too, may constitute a crisis. Although there are many sensible ways to alleviate the child's concern about this change, studies continue to reveal a disheartening gulf between the two situations (Love & Logue, 1992). For example, only 10% of primary schools reported systematic communication between kindergarten teachers and preschool teachers, and less than half of them had formal programs for visits by parents prior to enrolment. Worse yet, only 12% of the primary schools utilized a curriculum designed to build on what the children had learned in preschool.

In addition to deliberately increasing communication and coordination between the two situations—a process fraught with difficulties in many cases—there are a number of sensible, immediate things everyone can easily do to ease the transition. Among those suggested by Lombardi (n. d.) that directly help children are scheduling a visit to the new school, talking over what will be expected of the child in the new setting without making him apprehensive, inviting parents to a back-to-school night in late summer, and generally following the procedures recommended in chapter 3 such as sending each child a special welcome letter.

Another part of attending school that can be a crisis to a child is a late pick-up by his parent. I have known children to fly into a panic over this if it is not handled well by the teacher, so a few suggestions are in order. First of all, be careful to reassure the child that his parent *will* come and that you will stay with him until she does. It also is reassuring to say that you know there are some good reasons why she is delayed (but avoid speculating within the child's hearing about what various disasters may have befallen the parent along the way). Second, locate an alternative person to come as soon as possible. The entry record for each child should include a list of the telephone numbers of people to be contacted in case the child becomes ill during the day or the parent is late. However, do not let the child stand beside you as you dial number after number, getting no response! Remember, too, that *no child should ever be released to any adult who is not on the parent's list.*

Third, hold your temper and do not make the child pay for the parent's sins. It is really hard at the end of a long day to wait and maybe miss the bus, but it is not the child's fault her parent is tardy. In some schools in which parents are consistently inconsiderate, policies are established of charging extra for overtime care, or asking the parent to drive the teacher home if he missed the bus. These penalties should be avoided if possible because they breed ill will. It is usually sufficient to explain, when tempers have cooled, why the teacher prefers to leave on time and to ask the parent to be more considerate in the future.

Arrival of a New Baby

Parents who often go out of their way to prepare a youngster for a new baby during the nine-month wait somehow assume once the infant arrives that the preschooler will be delighted and certainly not jealous! But the reality of the mother's going to the hospital, possibly having someone unfamiliar take over meanwhile, and then seeing his world changed by the homecoming of the baby with all the demands on the parents' time and energy can turn out to be an unpleasant surprise to a preschooler.

These demands on parents' time that common sense and experience tell us are likely to take place have also been measured in a study of firstborn children (Dunn & Kendrick, 1981). They found that the arrival of the second child really *did* change the mother-firstborn relationship since the mother no longer spent as much time playing with the child or beginning conversations with him. This was coupled (not surprisingly) with a significant rise in the number of negative confrontations that took place between them. No wonder the arrival of a baby constitutes a crisis in the lives of some youngsters!

Some simple remedies that the teacher can apply to help alleviate these feelings of intrusion and jealousy are to not dwell on how wonderful it is to have a new baby in the family and to provide plenty of opportunities for the preschooler to act like a baby if he wants to. I recall one youngster who derived deep satisfaction from sitting in the privacy of my office being rocked.

It also helps to be realistic about the situation: point out the things the baby *can't* do, as well as all the obvious privileges and attention accruing to the preschooler. Help the older child find satisfaction in his own abilities and competencies that are related to being more mature, and make it clear that he will retain this advantage for a long time to come. After all, he will always be the older child.

Finally, if jealousy is interpreted to the parents as *the fear of being left out,* it may enable them to stop deploring or denying it and make plans that show the child he is definitely included. These can be as simple as reading to him by himself for a little while before bedtime, or making a special time of going to the store while the baby remains at home. When the baby begins to crawl, it is only fair to provide a safe place for the older child's belongings. Sometimes older children appreciate having a barrier that they can hook across their doors to keep the baby out. It is an interesting fact of human nature that the more protection of the child's rights the parent provides, the less protective the child will feel driven to be.

Hospitalization of the Child

Preparation in Advance

When surgery or other inpatient treatment for the child can be anticipated in advance, there is time for home and school to help the child grasp what will happen, and he is entitled to this information (Hughes, 1991; Trawick-Smith & Thompson, 1986). After all, it is his body that will, in a sense, be violated. There are several good books for children about doctors and hospitals, and a couple of bibliographies are included in the References for Further Reading at the end of this chapter. Hospital play and discussion of the forthcoming hospitalization will also help—not only to reassure the child himself but also to comfort his playmates. In these discussions I have found that using the word "fix" is often helpful. Saying the doctor is going to fix a bad leg or the infected tonsils seems to be a concept that children can grasp and that they find comforting. Haller (1967) comments that using hospital masks in dramatic play is of special value, since such masks are often one of the more frightening aspects of hospitalization (remember how upsetting masks are to some children at Halloween?).

Some hospitals permit children to visit before their stay. This possibility should be suggested to the parents, even if it means they must ask the doctor to make special arrangements. (I will never forget the relief of one of my own children, aged six, when she went for such a visit and discovered there would be a television set in her room, something it had not occurred to me to mention. Since she was not allowed to watch TV during the day at home, this was indeed a selling point for the hospital!).

Another encouraging trend is the policy of admitting children for minor surgery on a day basis only. Under these circumstances the youngster is admitted early in the morning before surgery and released to go home as soon as the effects of the anaesthesia have worn off. This sensible procedure not only cuts hospital costs but also reduces the potential for misery and fright caused by parental separation.

When day surgery is out of the question, a longer stay is often mitigated by providing opportunities for play experiences for the child during his stay in the hospital. Such

ॐ   *Hospital play helps children work through fears and misunderstandings.*

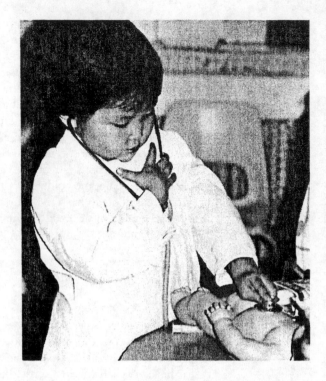

opportunities help the child understand what is being done to him to get him well, puts him in temporary control of the situation, and allows him to express his concerns and anxieties (Hughes, 1991; Kampe, 1990).*

While the child is recovering and out of school, it is important to consider the feelings of his playmates as well as the youngster himself and to provide something they can do for their friend. Children often have very good ideas about this, such as baking something special or making a card with all their handprints on it.

Once again, upon the child's return, more hospital play is definitely of value. This enables the child to work out his feelings and clarify them and helps inform the other children of what went on as well. Incidentally, the mastery role of being doctor or nurse as well as that of victim is particularly satisfying to children who are struggling to overcome their feelings of angry helplessness often generated while under treatment. Many children find that giving shots to someone else feels best of all.

Information for Parents

Parents should be encouraged to stay with their child as much of the time as possible while their youngster is hospitalized. Many hospitals today maintain open visiting privileges with

---

*The professional people who offer these experiences are called *Child Life Specialists.* Training in early childhood education offers an excellent foundation for such a career.

no time limits for parents, but a few still do not. It is worthwhile becoming acquainted with the policies of various hospitals in your area so you can inform parents about these in advance. Older four- and five-year-olds can also maintain contact with their families, particularly siblings, by talking with them on the phone, and this should be encouraged.

Some parents are cowed by hospitals and apprehensive of antagonizing staff. They may not know their rights, and they are also likely to be upset and worried. A chat beforehand can alleviate some of their concerns and enable them to insist on what is best for their particular child. Moreover, they should be reassured that it is desirable for children to express their feelings. Indeed it is the quiet, passive child conforming unquestioningly to hospital routine who arouses the greatest concern among psychological consultants (Bowlby, 1973; Robertson & Robertson, 1989). Children should not be admonished ("Don't cry") or lied to ("This will just sting a little") or threatened ("You do it, or I'm going to go home!"). It is truly surprising that parents sometimes expect more of their children in these difficult and especially trying situations than they normally would dream of expecting at home.

Parents may also need to be prepared for the fact that children sometimes reject their mothers when they finally return home. This can come as a painful shock to families unless they have been prepared by an explanation of the reasons for the hostility. This reaction is thought to really be an expression of the child's anger at being separated from her parents, particularly the mother, so in a way the hostility expressed by the child is a compliment to the family for the strength of their emotional bonds. But it can be a confusing compliment if it is misunderstood (Robertson & Robertson, 1989).

The Emergency Room

One of the most trying crises for young children to experience is a visit to the emergency room. This is because no advance preparation is possible, the parents are very upset, time is short, and the reason for being there is generally serious and painful. The prevalence of such emergencies is staggering—more than 185 000 Canadian children sought emergency care in Canada in 1990 (Canadian Institute of Child Health, 1994). It probably comes as no news to readers of these pages who are experienced parents to learn that accidents are most likely to occur between 3 and 11 p.m. and that twice as many boys as girls require emergency care (Resnick & Hergenroeder, 1975).

One can make a very good parents' night out of offering a discussion of what to do in the emergency room to buffer the child from the worst shocks. Recommendations for parents include staying with the child as much as possible, staying as calm as possible, explaining very simply to the child what is going to happen next so he is not taken completely by surprise when a doctor suddenly materializes with a shot needle, and modelling fortitude by explaining, with assurance, that it may not feel good, but the doctor has to do whatever she is doing because it will help the child get well.

Hospitalization of Parents

A rare series of three studies reported by Rice, Ekdahl, and Miller (1971) reveals that emotional problems are likely to result for children whenever a parent is hospitalized for any length of time, whether it be for physical or mental illness. The impact of mental illness, particularly illness of the mother, causes the most marked difficulties. At least half the children studied gave evidence of such disturbance. This is due to several factors. There is the unhappiness and disorganization that typically precede confinement in a mental institution as well as the fact that families usually have no time to prepare children for the hospitalization. Child abuse or neglect may have taken place before hospitalization, and confinement of the parent makes it more probable that the child will have to be cared for outside his home—often thereby losing the security of his familiar surroundings and friends as well.

Of course, the centre plays only one part in solving the overall problems of families involved in such difficulties, but it can be a significant one if the provision of child care means the child can stay within the home and that he is provided with a stable, understanding environment while at school. The general recommendations given at the beginning of this chapter capsulize what will help these children; here are three additional suggestions:

1. In such circumstances the children's centre should make a special effort to coordinate its services with those of other agencies and be prepared to report undue distress to the social worker or psychologist along with a request for help.

2. Young children are often particularly distressed over the unpredictability of the disturbed parent's behaviour (Sameroff & Seifer, 1983). Because of the possibility that angry encounters took place between parent and child or that a depressed parent may have been unreachable by the child, it is of great importance to explain in simple terms to the youngster that he was not the reason his mommy went to the hospital.

3. Despite the prehospitalization difficulties that may have troubled the child, remember he is also feeling pain over separation from his parent. This produces deep feelings of loneliness, confusion, and anger.

4. Finally, it is still true that many—perhaps the majority of—people regard mental illness as a shameful stigma, and being near former mental patients fills them with unease. The preschool teacher who can master this apprehension by behaving naturally with recovered patients offers a gift of acceptance much appreciated by the family.

Helping Children Through Divorce

Some useful facts to have in mind about divorce are that children's reactions to divorce vary widely in relation to their age, gender, emotional resources, subsequent life experience, and interpersonal relationships. In general, boys have more difficulty adjusting than girls do, younger children seem to cope more easily with the situation than older ones do, and children from divorced families are allowed more responsibility, independence, and decision-making opportunities than children of nondivorced families are. Blended families—married or common-law couples with at least one stepchild—become increasingly common as divorce and remarriage rates go up. In 1990 there were 343 000 blended families, representing about 7% of families raising children in Canada (Vanier, 1994). So it is probable that children will need to make a further adjustment by joining a mingled family as part of that long-term divorce experience (Hetherington, 1992).

Occasionally teachers are aware in advance that families are having marital difficulties, but the announcement of an impending divorce often takes them as much by surprise as it does the child. Here are a few points to remember when this happens.

For one thing, try not to take sides. This is difficult to avoid, in part because blame assigning by friends and acquaintances seems to be part of the cultural pattern of divorce, and in part because the parent who confides in the teacher tends, understandably, to present the other parent in a bad light. Something else the teacher should remember is to invite each parent to make an appointment with her when it is time for parent-child conferences (Frieman, 1993). All too often, the noncustodial parent is ignored by the school following a divorce, and yet these parents remain deeply concerned for their children and greatly appreciate being included. Third, be prepared for the fact that the child himself is likely to exhibit irritability, regression, confusion, and anxiety during and after the divorce.

Still another difficulty that may be encountered by the centre is related to custody. Occasionally members of the school staff are subpoenaed to testify in custody altercations. This is usually the case when one parent wishes to prove neglect by the other one. Here, written records of attendance, written reports of parent conferences, and observational records of the child are valuable to have available for citation.

Potential custody problems constitute an additional reason for requiring written, signed lists of individuals to whom a child may be released when the parent is not picking the youngster up from school. Refusing release can create temporary inconvenience and bad feeling, but the school is legally responsible for the child while not in his parent's care. This explanation will usually appease irritated would-be helpers, and enforcement of the rule may protect the child from "parentnapping."

All parents, should, of course, be welcome visitors at school—although once or twice I have found it necessary to make it clear they are welcome just as long as the occasion remains a happy one for the youngster and is not used by parents to generate an upsetting scene.

When a parent remarries, it is equally important for the school to welcome the stepparent and additional siblings into the life of the school. Children in newly blended families often experience bewildering mixtures of feelings ranging from delight and relief to jealousy and insecurity about who is in charge. The teacher who is able to accept the child's positive and negative comments about the remarriage in a matter-of-fact, nonjudgemental way can hasten the child's adjustment to the changed situation.

Explaining the Divorce to the Child

Although most children ultimately adjust to this profound change in their family life (Emery & Forehand, 1994), the effects of divorce on children have been found to be long-lasting and painful (Hetherington, 1992). Wallerstein and Blakeslee (1989) maintain that it is one of the most severe stressors children can experience—even more severe than the death of a well-loved person—since divorce carries with it an additional burden of uncertainty because it may not seem as final to the child as death does. The possibility of continuing and repeated tension between parents also complicates the situation.

Children are also confused because many parents give their children no explanation at all about the divorce, leaving them to sad fantasies about the reasons and their own possible role in the break-up. For these reasons, then, it is of *great* importance that parents be encouraged to provide children with truthful, clear information so that various misapprehensions and possible guilt may be allayed.

Kalter (1990) recommends that parents give simple explanations about the divorce, for example, "We aren't getting along anymore. When grown-ups who are married can't get along and don't love each other anymore, they need to stop being married and live in different homes" (p. 134). In addition to such clear, simple explanations, children need repeated reassurance that parents will keep right on loving *them* and that the divorce is not the result of something the child has done.

Commonly seen behaviour changes include fear of separation in routine situations such as coming to the centre or going to bed at night, sleep disturbances, being more tearful, irritable, and aggressive, and being more likely to be inhibited in play (Kalter, 1990).

But parents should also know that divorce is not always perceived as being unfortunate, even by young children. Youngsters are often well aware that their parents are unhappy and may experience real relief when the final separation takes place. Indeed, a few studies indicate that children from frankly split homes generally do better than those from intact but unhappy households (Hetherington, Stanley-Hagen, & Anderson, 1989).

If parents are advised to avoid degrading the other parent within the child's hearing, the youngster will be less distressed. Children are usually feeling pain enough over divided loyalties anyway, and being party to the denigration of the other parent only complicates their emotional problems further. It is also of great value to explain to the child which parent he will be living with and reassure him that he will (ideally) have many regular opportunities to be with the other parent as well.

Divorce frequently means a move, often from a house to an apartment. For the child this may mean the loss of a beloved pet, a change of friends, and sometimes even a change of schools. It almost always includes financial hardship as well. His mother may be leaving him for a full-time job for the first time, too. No wonder Mitchell (1985) likens the experience of divorce to death for young children, since so many, often painful adjustments must transpire.

Building Sensitivity to Single-Parent Families within the School

The teacher needs to be especially sensitive to single-parent children at school, not only because they may be unhappy or exhibit various kinds of emotional distress, but also because so many activities in a children's centre typically revolve around family life. Contemporary teachers need to broaden their cultural awareness to include the many patterns of single parenting that now exist and must divest themselves of the tacit assumption that most of the children in the school undoubtedly belong to two-parent families. At least in day care this is not likely to be true.

Teachers may also need to divest themselves of ingrained prejudices against divorce and divorced people. There is not necessarily anything "wrong" with people who are no longer married or perhaps never have been (Ball, Newman, & Scheuren, 1984). Indeed many single parents, men and women, should be admired for the extraordinary manner in which they have held their families together and continued to care for them. As Herzog and Sudia (1975) put it in their review of research on fatherless homes, "To focus only on problems and weaknesses [of fatherless homes] is to distort the picture and obscure some clues to ways of building on strengths" (p. 202). It is kinder also if the teacher learns to speak of "single-parent families" rather than "broken homes."

In terms of the curriculum, Mother's Day and Father's Day can take on a peculiar significance for single-parent children, as can vacations. Unless the teacher is careful, some children will be routinely expected to make gifts for parents they rarely or never see. Rather than have this happen it is better to be well acquainted with the youngster's living arrangements. It may be that he would prefer to make something for a grandparent or his babysitter or his parent's friend.

The teacher also should take care in selecting books, so that all kinds of family structures are represented. It is as unfortunate for some children to be continually confronted with the stories of the happy, two-parent family going on a picnic as it was for minority children of the last generation to be exposed only to "Dick and Jane."

Research on the relation of father absence to the establishment of adequate male and female role concepts remains inconclusive, but it is probably an especially good idea to employ male teachers in centres that serve single parents because divorce makes it more likely that children will be deprived of male companionship outside the school. Surely it is more desirable for children of both sexes to have some regular opportunities to relate to men rather than to be raised during their preschool years entirely by women (Weugebauer, 1994).

Helping Children Understand Death

Although death remains a taboo subject for many people, the increasing frequency of publications and discussion about it provides evidence that at least a few people are no longer pretending that death does not exist. And, even though we might prefer to deny it, we must face the fact that death is a part of life for young children as well as for their elders. Five percent of children in the United States will lose a parent through death before they reach age eighteen (Wessel, 1983). Children are also exposed to the deaths of grandparents, other family members, friends, and beloved animals, not to mention the continual accounts of death and murder reported endlessly on television. For these reasons it is necessary to learn how to help children cope with this subject, even though we may be barely learning to talk about it ourselves.

What Can the Teacher Do?

It is heartening to learn that in the area of death education there *is* something the early childhood teacher can do that can be of real assistance to young children. Kliman (1968) terms this *psychological immunization* and describes it as helping children acquire at least a modicum of "mastery in advance." By this he means that it is helpful if the subject of death is included matter-of-factly as part of the curriculum of the centre in order to desensitize children by providing both information and mild experiences with it before a more emotionally laden death occurs. This can be accomplished in many ways.* Perhaps the most effective of them is based on the death of animals at school. This should

---

*For a more complete discussion of teaching about death in the curriculum, please refer to Hendrick, 1994, *Total Learning: Curriculum for the Young Child* (4th ed.), Columbus, OH: Merrill, chapter 9, "Teaching Children to Understand and Value Life."

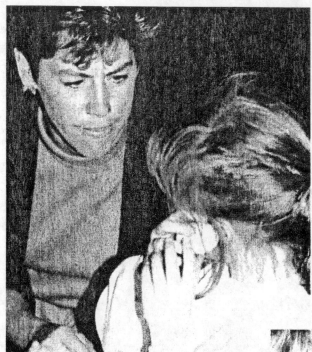

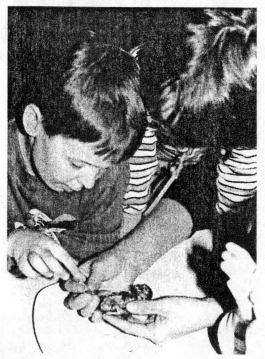

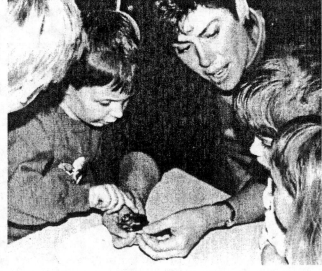

❧ Although adults are often squeamish about dead animals, children find them deeply interesting. Here Deb Parkinson helps our four-year-olds understand what being dead means, while also helping them appreciate the delicacy and wonder of the little chicken's feet.

include talking about how the animals have changed and what will become of them, as well as helping children carry out the simple burials that are of such intense interest to them. Books and discussions are also helpful, and some schools even advocate visiting cemeteries, which are, after all, quite beautiful places (Riley, 1989).

❧   *Helping the Child and the Family When Death Occurs*

Kliman also points out that teachers and other nonmedical personnel, such as clergy, are more likely to be asked for help when a death occurs than doctors are, probably because the families feel less hostile toward such people than they do toward the medical profession following bereavement. For this reason the teacher should be well prepared with some down-to-earth suggestions for helping the children by supplying resources for further information and providing knowledge of possible referral sources should these be requested.

Once again I must repeat that the fact of a death should not be avoided by telling a child that her father has gone away on a long trip or that Grandma will come back in the spring or that Snowball is just asleep. This principle must be reiterated because studies reveal such statements are *particularly prevalent* when families with preschool children deal with death (Johnson, 1987). Children need to be allowed to participate in the family's grief because it strengthens their feelings of belonging instead of feelings of isolation, and it helps them express their own sadness, too.

As time passes, a child should be encouraged to reminisce about the absent parent. All too often once the initial crisis has passed, families and teachers hesitate to reawaken memories, but recall actually helps ventilate feelings so that the emotional wound can heal cleanly. It also helps the child retain his identification with and feelings of affection for his parent. Family stories about "Do you remember when . . . ," photographs, and even movies and tapes have been found to be helpful.

Reliving old memories is also the second of three stages of mourning. The first one is the acceptance of loss, the second is remembering the past, and the third is substitution of a new relationship.

Parents can do a better job if they also understand that the emotion of grief for children (and for adults as well) is not composed only of sadness. There is also a component of anger (Bowlby, 1980; Shuchter & Zisook, 1993). Just as children feel a mixture of grief and anger when they are left at the centre, so too do they experience, to a much stronger degree, these same feelings when a parent abandons them in death. It is doubly important to understand this, because young children often connect this anger back to some angry interlude before death and conclude they have caused the parent to die (just as they may believe this about divorce). They then may reason that the death is a punishment for their misbehaviour—truly a terrible burden of guilt for a child to bear.

To counteract this, simple reasons for the death must be given ("Your father didn't want to leave us, but he was so sick the medicine couldn't help any more"), combined with reassurances that the surviving parent and child are not likely to die for a long time yet (Furman, 1984). A child should also be told that the surviving parent is going to go right on taking care of him and be reminded that there is also Grandma, Grandpa, and Aunty Margaret, all of whom love him and care for him. The presence of siblings can provide an additional source of strength and family feeling, particularly among children who are older. The anger should be acknowledged by mentioning its presence and its naturalness. Statements such as "I guess you feel mad your dad died and left us. . . . I see you feel like socking things a lot. . . . We know he couldn't help dying, but it's hard to take sometimes, isn't it?" usually relieve some of the hostile impulses.

Adults must also be cautioned against likening death to sleep. We surely do not want anxious children to guard themselves against sleep because they fear death may come while they are sleeping. A second, less obvious reason for this recommendation has to do with the way some researchers believe that preschool children perceive death. They maintain that inexperienced young children view it as being a temporary condition, one from which the person can be revived (Grollman, 1990). However, with experience comes understanding. Even though young children may experience initial difficulties grasping the finality of death, experts also agree they can learn to accept its permanency if the event is handled truthfully (Bowlby, 1980; Essa & Murray, 1994). On the other hand, when adults speak of death as "being asleep" it perpetuates serious misunderstandings and promotes false hopes. Even more fundamentally, equating it with sleep is untruthful. Why speak euphemistically of "sleep" and "slumber rooms" when what we mean is "death" and "a visiting room where people can view the body"? Why not face facts?

Finally, student teachers often ask me about religious beliefs and children in relation to death. In general, writers on this subject maintain that talking about religion tends to be confusing to young children and should not be stressed when death occurs (Furman, 1982). Surely it is not the teacher's place to do this, anyway, although she may find it helpful to be conversant with the points of view of the major religions.

The question really raised by students, however, is what to do about statements by children with which they personally cannot agree. For example, a child may say, "My mommy says my puppy went to heaven, and now the angels are singing over him. Someday I'll see him up there" or, "You know what? My grandmother has it all fixed so she'll be froze solid when she dies—then she can come alive again when she wants to."

Actually it is not necessary to agree or disagree with such statements. All one has to do is show that one respects the family's teaching by listening, and then either ask the child what he thinks or say something that responds to the child's feelings, such as "I can see you really miss him" or "You'd like to see your puppy again, wouldn't you?" or at least say something noncommittal, such as, "So that's what your grandma is planning."

AIDS: A Serious New Crisis in the Lives of Children

The issue of AIDS (acquired immunodeficiency syndrome) and young children is a terribly troublesome one. For one thing, there is the question of what if anything to tell children of preschool age about the condition, and, for another, what to do about admitting children with AIDS (also spoken of as "HIV"—human immunodeficiency virus) to the preschool.

What Is Appropriate AIDS Education for Preschoolers?

Very little has been written on this subject to date, and yet, with the media constantly bombarding us with the word and precautionary recommendations, it seems impossible that it has entirely escaped young children's awareness.

Once again, a matter-of-fact explanation is the best approach to take. When a young-ster appears to be concerned, these explanations could include the information that AIDS can make people very sick, so sick they often die; that it is very hard "to get"; that it is a grown-up sickness that doesn't usually afflict children; and that people can take care of themselves and protect themselves from becoming infected. Because of the emphasis on needles that is so prevalent in some commercials, one or two mothers have reported that their five-year-olds objected more strenuously than usual when they had injections. For this reason, it may also be helpful to realize that occasionally children may require additional reassurance that the needles the doctors are using are brand-new ones, so nobody has to worry about getting sick from them.

For the more anxious child it may also be necessary to add, just as one does when dis-cussing death, that there will always be particular people who will take care of him—even if something did happen to Mother or Daddy—and reiterate, if he is worried, that there is almost no chance the child could become infected.

Of course, it is true that all these statements are only "mostly true," and tragic excep-tions to them do occur. However, for most young children they are still accurate.

Admitting HIV-Positive Children to the Preschool

No one knows how many people in Canada are infected with HIV. Although all provinces and territories require physicians and laboratories to report a diagnosis of AIDS to a public health authority, not all provinces require them to report new HIV infections. In addition, many people do not realize that they are infected and don't seek testing. Health Canada estimates that approximately 30 000 to 35 000 Canadians are liv-ing with HIV. The proportion that are women has risen in recent years. Because most women are of child-rearing age, and because the virus can be transmitted during preg-nancy and delivery, many people are concerned that we will see larger numbers of chil-dren infected with HIV. (The good news is that only one-third of babies born to such infected women become infected themselves.)

In 1993, the parents and staff at a Montreal child care centre learned that a two-year-old girl was infected with HIV and voted to exclude her. The action was incompatible with Quebec and Canadian human rights laws.

Although it may be against the law to refuse admission to HIV-positive children, the fact remains that there is a great deal of uncertainty and negativity expressed by both caregivers and parents about such admissions. The research study included in this chap-ter investigated just how widespread these feelings are.

A child with HIV has the same right as any child to quality child care. Human rights commissions in most provinces have stated that they consider HIV a disability; and by law, discrimination on the basis of disability is no more allowed than is discrimination on the basis of race or religion. Child care plays an important role in the lives of children infected with HIV, providing them with peers and an opportunity to a stimulating envi-ronment that facilitates the development of new skills. Early childhood educators are in an ideal position to give emotional support. This support is vital to families with HIV, providing them with a sense of continuity.

⁊ **RESEARCH STUDY** ⁊
Would You Do It?

Research Question: The investigators wanted to know how much children's centre staff and parents know about the way AIDS is transmitted, and how the staff really feel about having HIV-positive children in their day care centre.

Research Method: Questionnaires were distributed to day care providers working in twelve centres and to parents of children attending four centres. The questionnaires included questions assessing, first, knowledge of how HIV is transmitted, and second, attitudes about potential inclusion of infected children. There was an exceptionally high rate of questionnaires returned. A total of 161 day care staff and 203 parents replied.

Extent of Knowledge about HIV Infections: Ninety-eight percent of the adults knew that sexual intercourse and sharing needles could transmit HIV, and 84% knew that contact with blood from a cut could transmit it. However, when it came to knowing about other possible ways HIV could be transmitted, there was a wide range of uncertainty. Almost half of both groups incorrectly thought that tears, sharing food or utensils, changing diapers, vomit, and kissing could spread the disease. One in five of the adults thought toilet seats could spread the infection and one in four thought coughing and sneezing were a cause.

Attitudes about Child Inclusion: The questionnaires revealed that almost two-thirds of the parents surveyed would be either unwilling or unsure about whether they would keep their child in a classroom with a child infected with AIDS. Eighty-six percent of child care staff responded that they would be either unwilling or at least uncertain about whether they would care for a child infected with AIDS in their classrooms.

Another important finding of this study was that both staff and parents agreed they wanted to know if an infected child was enrolled in the classroom.

Implications for Teaching: If we assume that this careful study accurately reflects the opinions of parents and staff in typical child care centres, it becomes obvious that inclusion of HIV-infected children will require very careful and compassionate handling in order to be successful.

One part of bringing this success about must be the provision of increased education and understanding about what constitutes safe contact between infected and noninfected people. Another aspect must be a continuing emphasis on consistent use of such universal health precautions as handwashing and wearing gloves when coming in contact with anyone's blood. Still another is the immediate implementation of increased education and precautions so they are in place *before* admission of a particular child is contemplated.

There is such a high degree of agreement between parents and staff about wanting to know if an infected child is attending their centre that it calls into serious question whether the recommendations concerning confidentiality set forth by the Canadian Pediatric Society can possibly be followed. It is likely some sort of compromise will need to be worked out in this regard.

Source: From "Knowledge and Attitudes of Day Care Centre Parents and Care Providers Regarding Children Infected with Human Immunodeficiency Virus" by A. L. Morrow, M. Benton, R. R. Reves, & L. K. Pickering, 1991, *Pediatrics, 87*(6), 876–883.

❧   *Using a blanket is a common way children comfort themselves when feeling upset—and such comfort should not be denied to them.*

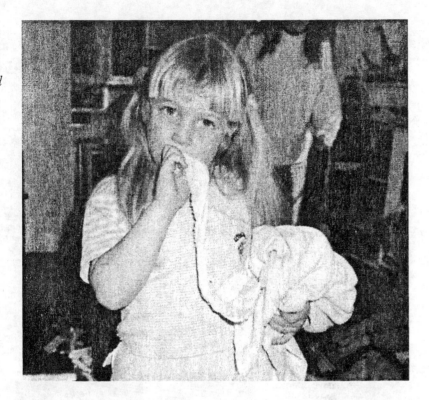

Working as a team, a child's parents, doctor, and public health official will decide whether to place a child infected with HIV. They will carefully consider the child's health as well as any potential risk to other children. They are unlikely to suggest enrolling a child with oozing wounds, with a bleeding problem, or with an aggressive biting behaviour. If a child becomes too ill to benefit from child care, they will arrange a more appropriate setting.

It is important for the centre and parents to work together to develop policies dealing with HIV. Centres need to practise good hygiene and universal precautions for managing exposure to blood-borne disease; to develop exclusion criteria for ill children; to establish procedures for informing parents about contagious diseases; and to arrange access to a health consultant. A policy of screening all children for the HIV antibody is considered unnecessary. The Canadian Pediatric Society believes that parents of the other children in the program do *not* have the right to know if a child is infected. Caregivers *do* need to know the child has an immunodeficiency but not that it is the result of HIV infection. (However, it seems highly probable to this author that any caregiver so informed would very likely reach a diagnosis of the problem on his own.) In any case, strict rules governing confidentiality and the need to know should be followed. Precautions to avoid the transmission of blood-borne diseases are outlined in Figure 8.1. There are also a number of useful documents listed in the References for Further Reading.

UNIVERSAL PRECAUTIONS
TO PREVENT TRANSMISSION OF BLOOD-BORNE DISEASES
Adapted for Child Care Settings

Cover cuts or scratches with a bandage until healed.

Use disposable absorbent material like paper towels to stop bleeding.

Wash your hands for 30 seconds after contact with blood and other body fluids contaminated with blood.

Wear disposable latex gloves when you encounter large amounts of blood, especially if you have open cuts or chapped skin. Wash your hands as soon as you remove your gloves.

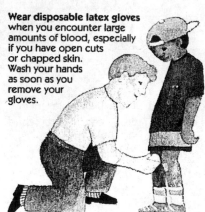

Immediately clean up blood-soiled surfaces **and disinfect** with a fresh solution of one part bleach and nine parts water.

Put blood-stained laundry in sealed plastic bags. Machine-wash separately in hot soapy water.

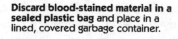

Discard blood-stained material in a sealed plastic bag and place in a lined, covered garbage container.

A project of the Canadian Child Care Federation in partnership with Health Canada

This project was funded by the AIDS Education and Prevention Unit under the National AIDS Contribution Program of the National AIDS Strategy, Health Canada. The views expressed herein are solely those of the authors and do not necessarily reflect the official policy of the Minister of National Health and Welfare.

NEVER DELAY EMERGENCY ACTION BECAUSE YOU CAN'T APPLY UNIVERSAL PRECAUTIONS. THE RISK OF TRANSMISSION OF BLOOD-BORNE DISEASES IS TOO SMALL TO JUSTIFY ENDANGERING A CHILD.

❧ RESEARCH STUDY ❧
HIV/AIDS and Child Care

HIV (Human Immunodeficiency Virus), the virus that leads to AIDS (Acquired Immune Deficiency Syndrome), is not transmitted through everyday contact. HIV is a fragile virus, and no cases of transmission through casual contact have been reported in a child care setting anywhere in the world.
HIV is not transmitted by:

- touching, hugging, or kissing;
- sharing food, dishes, drinking glasses, or cutlery;
- being coughed, sneezed, or cried on;
- sharing toys, even those that have been mouthed;
- diapers or toilet seats;
- urine, stool, vomit, saliva, mucus, or sweat (as long as it is untainted by blood).

HIV is transmitted from one person to another by sperm, vaginal secretions, breast milk, blood, and body fluids containing blood, usually through unprotected sexual intercourse or the sharing of contaminated needles. It is also transmitted from mother to child during pregnancy or delivery or by breastfeeding.

Simple contact between blood and intact skin is not enough to transmit HIV. Three conditions are necessary for transmission:

- The blood must be fresh.
- There must be a sufficient quantity.
- It must have a route of entry into the bloodstream of the uninfected person.

Biting often concerns parents, but there has never been a confirmed case of transmission by biting. To risk transmission, a child infected with HIV would have to have fresh blood in his mouth and break the skin of an uninfected child. An uninfected biter would have a theoretical risk of exposure only if he broke the skin of a child infected with HIV and drew blood into his mouth. Such events are very unlikely. Parents also worry about accidents and fights, but fresh blood-to-blood contact among children is extremely unusual.

Children infected with HIV have the same right to attend child care as other children. HIV is considered a disability, and by law discrimination on the basis of disability is not allowed. Staff also cannot be discriminated against, fired, or non-renewed because of their HIV status.

Child care plays an important role in the lives of children infected with HIV, offering them peers, stimulation, stability, and the chance to learn new skills. A child's parents, physician and social worker will decide whether child care is suitable and monitor the child's progress.

Child care staff probably will not know if a child is infected with HIV. Many children have no symptoms, and if no one in the family has been diagnosed as HIV-positive, the family may not even suspect that the child has the virus.

If the parents know, they have no obligation to tell the centre. Because they may fear discrimination, they may keep the information to themselves. If they decide to tell an educator, he or she has an ethical obligation to keep the information confidential. There is no need for the parents of other children to know since a child with HIV poses no danger.

It is important for child care centres to develop a health policy that respects the rights of all children and staff to privacy and confidentiality. For everyone's protection, the policy should include the use of universal precautions and proper hygiene, procedures for informing parents about contagious diseases, and procedures for excluding sick children and children with serious behaviour problems.

Source: Adapted from *HIV/AIDS and Child Care: Fact Book* by Barbara Kaiser and Judy Sklar Rasminsky. A project of the Canadian Child Care Federation, funded by Health Canada through the National AIDS Strategy.

Violence Against Children

It is a source of great sadness to me that this section of *The Whole Child* gets longer every time I revise the book. Now, in addition to discussing abuse and molestation, it is necessary to include a new aspect of that problem—violence in the community and its effects on children.

Coping with the Crisis of Community Violence

There is no doubt the problem of community violence is worsening. Countless more youngsters are witnesses to violent events on their way to and from school, while playing, or within their own home. The truth is that no one is exempt—even children who are fortunate to live in more sheltered circumstances are subject to endless examples of violence portrayed on television.

The question that must be answered is, "Can anything be done to stem this potentially overwhelming tide?" The answer is that *there are a lot of things that can be done and are being done.* Among them are the following:

Begin with the individual child in your preschool group. Teach children to reduce conflicts by controlling their aggressive impulses and also teach them many practical nonviolent ways to get what they want without hurting other people. Chapter 11, "Helping Young Children Establish Self-Discipline and Self-Control," and chapter 12, "Aggression: What to Do About It," offer considerable advice about how to accomplish this.

Be sensitive and alert to what is happening in the community and to the children's responses to what is going on. Make certain the mental health principles advocated earlier in this chapter and in chapter 5 are put into practice. Remember, even very young children will benefit from talking about how they feel as well as from playing out their feelings. Provide many opportunities for them to express their concerns by using self-expressive art materials, too.

Become active in your community. Take a stand against the portrayal of violent acts on television, at least during peak viewing hours for children. Remember that only 10% of children's viewing time is spent watching children's television—on which the cartoons are bad enough—while 90% of their viewing time is spent watching programs designed for adults (NAEYC, 1990). Sensitize parents to the content of such programs. If you personally don't like what you're seeing, protest to your local television stations—many of them are surprisingly sensitive to such criticism—and remember to commend them when they improve.

Become aware of positive steps being taken in your own community to make the neighbourhood a safer place for everyone. Support churches, community leaders, and elected officials who are working hard to make that happen.

Child Abuse, Neglect, and Sexual Molestation

Abuse of many kinds takes place in a great many Canadian families. This reality has received increasing attention in recent years, mainly because women started speaking out against the violence. It is hard to gauge the extent of violence and abuse within Canadian families. Child abuse, like other kinds of abuse within families, is vastly underreported. There are more reports of abuse among lower-income families, which may be partly due to higher levels of stress, frustration, isolation, and despair experienced by poor or vulnerable families.

Reports of child sexual abuse are on the increase. A federal government study in Calgary, Edmonton, Regina, Saskatoon, and Hamilton determined that there was an increase in the number of cases reported to the police between 1988 and 1992. Seventy-eight percent of the victims were female; most were under the age of twelve, and 15 to 22% were under the age of five (Vanier, 1994).

Neglect is also a serious problem. Studies of severe neglect are coming into the literature under such headings as *failure to thrive* and *prenatal exposure to drugs* (Gaudin, 1993). But these discussions centre on extreme cases of neglect, and data remain thin on the results of less flagrant cases of neglect and on the results of psychological abuse, although the effects of such adverse experiences are undoubtedly serious for children.

Much activity continues to centre on problems resulting from physical attack, but there is growing awareness and concern about sexual abuse as well. Perhaps this is because physical and sexual abuse are particularly horrifying, since they may result in the death of the child; and perhaps it is also because, though still difficult to prove in court, such abuse is easier to substantiate than is psychological abuse or neglect.

Whereas the average age of children involved in abuse/neglect cases is seven years, the average age of children experiencing major physical abuse is five and the average age of children who are fatally injured is about two-and-a-half. (Tzeng & Hanner, 1988). This may be because very young children are unable to retaliate or tell others of their peril, or it may be due in part to other reasons discussed later in this chapter. Although many of these cases occur in infancy and toddlerhood, children of preschool and early elementary school age are not immune. Teachers of young children must learn to identify possible cases of abuse and understand what to do and *what not to do* when our suspicions are aroused, not only for moral reasons but also because we must report abuse (Koralek, 1992). In fact, in recent times a number of lawsuits have been brought against educators who did not do this (Rothman, 1990). Children's centre teachers need special advice about how to handle such problems, not only because they are more likely than most teachers to note evidence since they undress children for naps and toileting, but also because most centres operate autonomously without benefit of advice from school nurses, principals, social workers, and so on.

What to Do When Abuse Is Suspected

Teachers who discover evidence of abuse are very upset about it. They may find it hard to believe that such a "nice" family could do a thing like that and thus they deny it, or they may be so frightened for the child's safety that they do not think clearly and therefore act impulsively. For this reason, before going any further with this discussion, *I want to emphasize that handling such cases requires skill and delicacy.* The first approach made to the parents is thought to be crucial in successful management of the case (Helfer & Kempe, 1987). The consequences of unsuccessful management may be so serious that we cannot risk jeopardizing such chances by acting in an ill-considered way. *Therefore, teachers must not suddenly plunge into the problem by accusing the parents or even reveal suspicions by questioning them or the child too closely.* Instead, if they suspect a case of abuse, they should contact whatever agency or individual in their community has the responsibility for handling such cases and report it. *They should ask these people for advice and do what they tell them, to the best of their ability.*

How to Find Help

The agency the teacher should seek out is whatever agency in the community is responsible for children's protective services, such as the Children's Aid Society or the provincial or territorial ministry responsible for health, social, or community services. Still another way to locate protective services is to ask the public health nurse whom to call.

Action Should Be Prompt

Because abusers often repeat their behaviour, prompt action is advisable; yet teachers sometimes hesitate to get involved. The teacher should realize that all provinces and territories now have mandatory reporting laws and that many of these specifically identify teachers as being among those people *required* to report cases in which abuse is suspected (Canadian Pediatric Society, 1992). Even when teachers are not specifically mentioned, the law is generally on the side of anyone reporting such a case "in good faith." Besides the necessity of conforming to the law, *reporting such cases is an ethical and moral responsibility that the teacher must not overlook.*

What to Look for

Many of us are so inexperienced in identifying the results of abuse that it is necessary to include the following information, which has been extrapolated primarily from the work of Helfer & Kempe (1987), as well as from my own experience.

The teacher should be alert for evidence of bruises, particularly a combination of old and fresh ones, or ones on soft parts of the body, or of burns such as cigarette burns. These are likely to occur in relatively concealed places, often on the small of the back or the buttocks. Red weals or strap marks should also arouse suspicion, as most certainly should a black eye (although children also suffer black eyes for a multitude of other reasons) or swollen ears. Bite marks are another fairly frequent sign of abuse. One author cautions that the soles of the feet should be checked also since this is a "popular location" (Weston, 1980). If a child arrives at school smelling of alcohol or under the influence of drugs, this is also evidence of abuse—and this does happen.

A more general reason for concern exists when the parent's voluntary account of the accident does not match the kind or extent of the injury. The usual excuse for bruises is falling down stairs or out of a crib or bed (Weston, 1980), but common sense often tells the teacher that such an event could not possibly have caused the series of diagonal welts across the child's bottom. Still another cause for suspicion of abuse, or at least neglect, occurs when the child is subject to repeated injuries. The laughing comment by a parent who "guesses the child is just accident prone" should not be repeatedly accepted by the teacher, particularly when the level of the child's physical coordination at school does not support this parental conclusion.

Literature on the emotional symptomatology of these children describes their behaviour as generally either very passive or very aggressive (Koralek, 1992; Mirandy, 1976). Mirandy, reporting on the first nineteen preschoolers admitted to Circle House Playschool (a centre for abused young children), comments that most of them were very passive and inhibited, and she describes their behaviour during their first months in school as being

> overly compliant, anxious to please, seeking out permission before initiating any new action. They were quite hypervigilant to the total environment of the preschool. None of the children demonstrated any separation anxiety in leaving mother, and they were indiscriminately and often physically affectionate with adult strangers. They were oblivious to peer interaction. There was often a hollow smile on a child's face and a complete void of emotions. . . . All lacked true joy. The children rarely expressed anger or pain, they had a poor sense of safety, frequently injuring themselves. Crying was either *highly* infrequent or continual. . . . Most abused children appeared compulsively neat. . . . Play was often noncreative and use of materials highly repetitive, the majority of such children appear to be lacking basic play skills. . . . Most have poor expressive language skills.
>
> It is crucial to stress that most of these traits, such as neatness, perseverance, quietness, compliance and politeness, are valued in the "normal" child and that if the teacher is not aware of the abused child's special needs, these traits may be further reinforced. An abused child has the ability to initially blend in too well and slip by unnoticed.*

Finally, there are some commonsense indications of possible abuse to which the teacher should be sensitive. Children who startle easily and cringe or duck if the teacher moves suddenly may be revealing that they are often struck at home. Then, too, it is sometimes evident in conversations with parents that they expect too much or are too dependent on their children, or that they themselves know they get too angry and "do things they shouldn't" or "wish they hadn't." Such statements are really cries for help and should not be brushed aside on the grounds that everyone feels like that sometimes. These people often benefit from referrals to Parents Anonymous or to local child abuse hot lines.

Evidence of Sexual Molestation

Based on recent findings, it appears that sexual abuse typically begins when the child is between four and twelve years old. At the younger ages this is attributed to children's naïveté and sexual curiosity and at older ages to their loyalty, desire to please, and trust of the adult (Wolfe, Wolfe, & Best, 1988). This finding reminds us that we must be alert to the possibility of such abuse when young children complain they "hurt down there," when they complain it hurts to walk, when genitals are inflamed, or when underclothes or odours reveal the presence of pus or infection. Although venereal disease may seem

---

*From "Preschool for Abused Children" by J. Mirandy, in *The Abused Child: A Multidisciplinary Approach to Developmental Issues and Treatment* (pp. 217–218) by H. P. Martin (Ed.), 1976, Cambridge, MA: Ballinger. Copyright 1976 by Ballinger. Reprinted by permission.

an unthinkable condition in children so young, we cannot afford to blot this possibility entirely from our minds because instances of this have also been reported. When venereal disease is present, it is almost always an indication of sexual abuse (Hibbard, 1988).

Some sexual attacks are perpetrated by strangers, and these are deeply upsetting to families who, nevertheless, often prefer not to report them rather than risk notoriety for the child and endless rehashing of the event with authorities. Of course, if such attacks go unreported, the attacker is immune from arrest, but this can be a difficult and touchy situation to deal with. Actually such an attack is likely to be more extraordinarily upsetting to the parent than to the child until the child picks up his parent's anxiety about it (Layman, 1985). *Referral for psychological help for both parent and child is strongly recommended in such cases.*

However, the majority of sexual molestations are *not* perpetrated by strangers. Eighty-five to ninety percent of them are carried out by people the child knows, and almost half of that total are family members (Conte & Berlinger, 1981; Metro Toronto Special Committee on Child Abuse, 1993).

Children need to be empowered to protect themselves, too. They should be taught never to take anything (typically candy) from any stranger and never to get in a car with strangers (even if a stranger knows the child's name). They need to understand the difference between "good touching," such as snuggling and hugging, and "bad touching" that doesn't feel right (i.e., behaviour that is inappropriate). They should be assured that their bodies belong to themselves, that it's okay to say "No!" and that, no matter what the threat, they should tell their parents right away if anyone makes that kind of advance to them. In recent years a number of educational programs have become available that offer guidelines in such preventive kinds of instruction. In general they stress, "If an older, more powerful person touches you on any part of the body covered by a bathing suit, except for health reasons, say NO and tell someone" (Kraizer, Witte, & Fryer, 1989).

It can certainly be difficult to teach all this without frightening children too much, so it is important to be definite but matter-of-fact in order to avoid arousing too much anxiety during such discussions.

Helping the Child's Family After the Referral Has Been Made

Even when teachers have taken the expert's advice, have handled the referral successfully, and the family is receiving help, they must still deal with their feelings about the child and the parent or parents if they believe it is important to retain the child in the centre. The relief to parents that such a respite provides, as well as the protection and education of the child it affords, means that continuing at school is usually *very* important. Here we are confronted with a paradox. Teachers are more than likely experiencing feelings of revulsion and outrage over what the parents have done, and their impulse may be to judge and punish them. Yet experts tell us that what the parents need, among many other things, is understanding and acceptance—something they may have been woefully short on in their own childhoods. This is because a characteristic of abusers is that many of them are social isolates. The question is, how can teachers possibly behave in a nurturing fashion toward people they regard with aversion?

One thing that may help teachers master their feelings, or at least control them, is to understand the causes of child abuse as far as they are understood at the present time. It has become commonplace to assert that abusing adults were abused as children, and it is true that there may be generational links in some instances. However, research now documents the fact that the great majority of abused children do *not* grow up to physically abuse their own youngsters (Kaufman & Zigler, 1990).

Recent studies (Belsky & Vondra, 1990; DePanfilis & Salus, 1992) emphasize that the causes of child abuse stem from a complex combination of factors rather than from a single circumstance. These include such psychological factors as unreal parental expectations of the child's abilities, poor impulse control, low self-esteem and feelings of helplessness, inadequate knowledge of how to control children without using violence, and a past history of being abused themselves, combined with a terrible insensitivity to the child's needs and feelings. Social factors such as poverty (although child abuse occurs at all economic levels), being out of work, social isolation, and inadequate education also increase the likelihood of abuse. Several researchers have pointed out that some children particularly appear to elicit abuse, whereas others in the same family do not (Crosse, Kaye, & Ratnofsky, 1992; Freidrich & Einbender, 1983; Kadushin & Martin, 1981). But the fact that the child is irritating can in no way be permitted to justify the behaviour of an abusing parent. Frequently an immediate precipitating factor such as alcohol, drugs, or a persistently colicky baby is also involved and becomes the last straw for the parent.

The basic generalization that can be safely drawn at this point is that the causes of child abuse are rooted in a complex mixture of personality traits of parents and children combined with various malign environmental influences. Disentangling this complicated web in order to reduce parental violence remains a serious challenge to everyone involved in working with young children.

What we *can* do is be aware of signs indicating there is a high risk that abuse or neglect *may* take place. Research reveals that the people at highest risk "include parents who abuse drugs and alcohol, young parents who are ill-prepared for the parenting role, families experiencing great stress who have poor coping skills and have no one to turn to for support, and parents who have difficulty with or who have not developed an emotional bond with their infant. We need to be alert to these and other high-risk indicators and offer assistance, support, counselling, and/or parent education to these families before their children are harmed" (National Centre on Child Abuse and Neglect, 1992, p. 11). Teachers, who know so many of these families well, are in a particularly advantageous position to help them in time.

When teachers are feeling upset about an abusive situation, it may also help them moderate their reactions to the parents if they realize that only a few of these people are estimated to suffer from serious psychotic disorders (Emery, 1989). It is more realistic to think of the majority of child abusers not as "crazy people" but as people who are often deeply ashamed of their behaviour, who have been unable to control it, and who are the products of their own childhoods and environments as perhaps their parents were before them. Many of them lack even rudimentary knowledge of practical, wholesome child-rearing techniques. The statement that "abusive parents care much for their children but do not care well" sums it up.

Finally, teachers will benefit by doing some thinking about the reasons why they themselves are so angry over what these parents have done. Certainly part of the reaction stems from the ugly painfulness of seeing a child suffer and from the teacher's commitment to helping children, but it seems to me that there is more to the anger than that. Perhaps some of the reaction comes also because, more than most people, teachers have had to learn to control their own angry impulses toward children. Teachers who are honest with themselves must admit there have been times when they too have felt rage toward a child surge within them. Their anger toward the abusive parent may turn to compassion if they realize that the difference between themselves and those parents at that instant was that they were able to stop in time!

Helping the Child While His Family Is in Treatment

As Starr (1988) correctly points out, most of the material having to do with the treatment of child abuse deals with the treatment of the adults or amelioration of the family's environment, but the child needs help, too—help that must go beyond the simple level of physical rescue. In addition to whatever may be prescribed in the way of special therapies, nursery school and children's centres are frequently recommended, and Starr places considerable faith in what can be accomplished in that environment to help the child. The points he makes as being desirable ones in caring for abused children are those generally stressed throughout *The Whole Child* as being important in the care of all children.

In particular, it is important with such youngsters to emphasize the building of trust and warmth between them and their teachers; steadiness and consistency are invaluable elements of such trust building. The enhancement of self-esteem is also important to stress. Since developmental delays of various kinds appear to be characteristic of these children, a careful analysis of these deficits should be made and attention paid to remediating them when this can be done without undue pressure. (Both Martin [1976] and Mirandy [1976] comment particularly on apparent deficits in perceptual-motor development skills and expressive language ability.)

Above all, every effort should be made to retain the child in school; to maintain consistent, regular contact with the other people who are working with the family; and to be as patient and caring with both the child and his family as possible.

Protecting the Centre from False Accusations of Abuse

As the McMartin and other cases have demonstrated, child care centres need to protect themselves as well as the children against abuse (Wakefield & Underwager, 1988). Some of the recommendations offered by Koralek (1992) and Strickland and Reynolds (1989) that will reduce the possibility of false accusations include the following:

1. Conduct careful, thorough interviews of potential employees, complete with whatever background checks and references are legally permitted by the particular jurisdiction.

2. Work to keep stress at a reasonable level for centre staff—including adequate breaks, decent pay, and fair arrangements for special problems and circumstances.

3. Provide ongoing staff training, particularly in regard to working through discipline situations.

4. Have two adults present with the children whenever possible.

5. Never allow new or volunteer people to be alone with the children.

6. Establish a well-publicized open-door visiting policy for parents.

7. Welcome each child as he arrives, take a careful look for obvious signs of injury before admitting him, and mention these to the parent.

8. Encourage the director to tour centre rooms on a consistent but irregular basis.

9. Make certain the centre insurance policies cover court cases related to abuse.

❦ *Summary*

Practically all young children experience some form of crisis during their preschool years, and there are many things parents and teachers can do to help them come through these experiences in good condition and perhaps with added strengths. Teachers should encourage parents to *include* rather than exclude the child at such times. They should try not to overreact to the problem or violate the family's privacy and should offer themselves as a resource of information when the family needs such assistance.

The teacher can help the child and his family by facing the reality of the crisis with him, making certain he does not blame himself for situations he has not caused, keeping his life at school steady and calm, providing play opportunities for him that help him work through and understand his feelings, and helping him anticipate what will happen next.

A discussion of various specific crises of particular concern to children concludes the chapter. Problems related to sending the child to the children's centre, the arrival of a new baby, and hospitalization of either the child or one of his parents are some of these important crises. Additional ones discussed specifically include problems related to divorce, death, AIDS, and child abuse and molestation. Information and recommendations are provided to help teachers and families cope with each of these situations.

Questions and Activities

1. One of the youngsters at your school has been scratching his head a lot, and upon inspection, you discover that he has lice. How would you handle this minor but important crisis with the child and his family?

2. The guinea pig at your preschool has been getting fatter and fatter, and it is obvious he has a tumour. The veterinarian pronounces it inoperable—what to do? How would you approach this matter with the children?

3. Keep a list for a month noting all the crises that happen to children and staff during this time. How many were there? How were they handled?

4. Are there some crises children should *not* know about? What might these be, and how would you protect children from them?

5. Can you recall being jealous of a brother or sister? What did it feel like? Would you handle it as your parents did if you had a child in a similar situation?

6. *Problem:* A child comes to school acting listless and looking pale and washed out. At nap time, when he undresses, you find he has several bruises on his chest and around his arms, and he complains that his neck hurts. There has been a previous occasion on which he arrived with a bump on his head and a black eye, which his mother said were due to his falling down a flight of steps. Under these circumstances do you think it wisest to approach the parent

with your concern, or are there alternative solutions that should be explored? If the parent, in your judgement, should not be approached, what agencies in your own community would be the most appropriate and effective ones to contact?

7. How do you think you *ought* to feel and how would you really feel if your director came to you and told you she has admitted a child who is HIV positive and he will be in your class? What would you do about your feelings?

Self-Check Questions for Review

Content-Related Questions

1. Are crises always events that happen very suddenly?
2. Name four ways the teacher might help a family that was experiencing a crisis.
3. Explain why it's important to tell children the truth when a crisis occurs.
4. What are the basic principles teachers should remember when helping children work through a crisis?
5. Review the specific crises discussed in the chapter and explain, for each, what a teacher could do to help.
6. Does the author recommend that the teacher confront the parents immediately if she suspects the child has been abused in some manner?

Integrative Questions

1. I've stated that crises *can* strengthen people. Select from your personal experience or from history an individual who experienced a crisis and explain how it strengthened that person.
2. Granted that marrying and starting on a first job both represent a change in life, analyse other aspects of the two experiences that are similar.
3. A child arrives at school and tells you that his father was in a car accident the night before. Give two examples of what you might say that would tend to deny his concerns about his father. What might you say that would reflect his concern?
4. The talk about the accident continues. The child tells you that his brother socked him and he yelled, and that's what made his father run into the bridge. Predict how you think the child is feeling about his behaviour, and then give an example of what you would reply and explain why you chose that particular reply.

5. One of the four-year-olds caught her foot in a railroad tie, and it was crushed by a switching engine and later amputated. She is due back at school in a week. Basing your plans on recommendations from this chapter, explain how you would handle this situation with the other children in the group.
6. What are some ways the crises of death and divorce are similar, and how might the experiences differ?
7. Do you think that preschool-aged children with HIV infections should be admitted to child care? Why or why not? In your opinion should other parents be informed of that child's condition?

References for Further Reading

Overviews

Garbarino, J., & Stott, F. M. (1989). *What children can tell us: Eliciting, interpreting, and evaluating information from children.* San Francisco: Jossey-Bass. This book reviews many ways adults can be sensitive and perceptive about what children have to tell about themselves and their lives. *Highly recommended.*

Kersey, K. (1986). *Helping your child handle stress: The parent's guide to recognizing and solving childhood problems.* Washington, DC: Acropolis Books. Kersey offers helpful advice on problems and crises ranging from jealousy to alcoholism.

Saylor, C. F. (Ed.). (1993). *Children and disasters.* New York: Plenum Press. Ideally, none of us will ever need more than a passing acquaintance with the information provided here—but it can be extremely helpful to have this book handy as a reference if it is needed. *Highly recommended.*

Stress and Resiliency in Childhood

Anthony, E. J., & Cohler, B. J. (Eds.). (1987). *The invulnerable child.* New York: Guilford Press. A refreshing change in emphasis is provided by these authors because they recount several studies in which the wholesome emotional process of coping and adapting successfully have been studied.

Furman, R. A. (1995). Helping children cope with stress and deal with feelings. *Young Children, 50*(2), 33–41. Defining stress as "anything that imposes an extra demand on children," Furman points out that stress also creates opportunities for learning. Good advice and examples of how to put feelings into words are included.

Humphrey, J. H. (1993). *Stress management for elementary schools.* Springfield, IL: Charles C. Thomas. Although this book is written with slightly older children in mind, many suggestions of ways to relieve stress that are appropriate for preschoolers are included—a rare and useful book.

Wang, M. C., & Gordon, E. W. (Eds.) (1994). *Educational resilience in inner-city America: Challenges and prospects.* Hillsdale, NJ: Erlbaum. The editors provide a sound overview of children's potential for positive development despite seemingly overwhelming difficulties. Chapters on recommendations are included. *Highly recommended.*

Transitions

Jalongo, M. R. (1994/1995). Helping children to cope with relocation. *Childhood Education, 71*(2), 80–85. This is a thoughtful discussion of what it means in many ways to children when families move. An outstanding list of preschool/primary books about moving is included.

Lombardi, J. (n. d.). *Easing the transition from preschool to kindergarten: A guide for early childhood teachers and administrators.* Washington, DC: United States Department of Health and Human Services, Administration on Children, Youth and Families, Head Start Bureau. This extremely useful pamphlet is based on recommendations stemming from the National Transition Study. In the space of twenty-three pages it sums up similarities and differences between preschool and kindergarten and recommends procedures for staff, children, and parents to follow to make the transition more comfortable. *Highly recommended.*

Hospitalization

Kampe, E. (1990). Children in health care: When the prescription is play. In E. Klugman & S. Smilansky (Eds.), *Children's play and learning: Perspectives and policy implications.* New York: Teachers College Press. The value of play in the stressful situation of hospitalization is assessed, together with many examples of the way it is used there.

Trawick-Smith, J., & Thompson, R. H. (1986). Preparing young children for hospitalization. In J. B. McCracken (Ed.), *Reducing stress in young children's lives.* Washington, DC: National Association for the Education of Young Children. Helpful advice is provided for helping children adjust to this crisis.

Divorce

Frieman, B. B. (1993). Separation and divorce: Children want their teachers to know—meeting the emotional needs of preschool and primary school children. *Young Children, 48*(6), 58–63. A good case is made here for the value of listening to and recognizing children's feelings during this stressful experience.

Kalter, N. (1990). *Growing up with divorce: Helping your child avoid immediate and later emotional problems.* New York: Free Press. In this helpful book, Kalter offers two chapters relevant to preschoolers—one on the experience of divorce and the other on how to help children cope with the experience.

Wallerstein, J. S., & Blakeslee, S. (1989). *Second chances: Men, women, and children a decade after divorce.* New York: Ticknor & Fields. As the title implies, this is, in part, a follow-up of case studies. Teachers will find it particularly interesting because of the down-to-earth analysis of the psychological tasks resulting from a divorce that must be mastered by adults and children.

Death and Dying

Essa, E. L., & Murray, C. I. (1994). Research in review: Young children's understanding and experience with death. *Young Children, 49*(4), 74–81. This article includes a summary of research as well as practical recommendations for helping children come to terms with death.

Fox, S. S. (1985). Good grief: Helping groups of children when a friend dies. Boston: New England Association for the Education of Young Children (Edward Klugman, 5 Pilgrim Rd., Boston, MA 02215). In this sound, practical book, Fox covers just about every aspect of death and young children that the teacher needs to know. *Highly recommended.*

Grollman, E. A. (1990). *Talking about death: A dialogue between parent and child* (3rd ed.). Boston: Beacon Press. This book contains many examples of what to say to children when death occurs, as well as chapters on honesty, denial, anger, guilt, funerals, suicides, and special deaths such as by AIDS. *Highly recommended.*

Johnson, S. E. (1987). *After a child dies: Counseling bereaved families.* New York: Springer. This book has a wider scope than the title implies. It includes much helpful information on helping children cope with death. *Highly recommended.*

Knowles, D., & Reeves, N. (1983). *But won't Granny need her socks? Dealing effectively with children's concerns about death and dying.* Dubuque, IA: Kendall/-Hunt. This is a first-rate primer on how the subject of death can be approached with children of various ages, as well as on helping adults come to terms with their feelings about it. *Highly recommended.*

National Institute of Health. *(1993). Talking to children about death.* Washington, DC: United States Department of Health and Human Services. In nineteen pages this inexpensive pamphlet sums up just about everything adults need to know when talking about death to children. *Highly recommended.*

Seibert, D., Drolet, J. C., & Fetro, J. V. (1993). *Are you sad too? Helping children deal with loss and death.* Santa Cruz, CA: ETR Associates. The advice in this book focuses on children from preschool age to age ten. Both helpful and practical, it includes an annotated bibliography.

AIDS/HIV Infections

Canadian Child Care Federation (1995). *HIV/AIDS and child care: Resource kit.* Ottawa: CCCF. This fact book and facilitators' guide are intended to increase the awareness of early childhood practitioners working with children and families who may be infected with HIV, as well as providing universal precautionary strategies.

Canadian Pediatric Society (1992). *Well beings: A guide to promote the health, safety, and emotional well being of children in child care centres.* Ottawa: Creative Premises. This reference book provides strategies and resources to help diagnose child abuse; it identifies treatment and resources for abusive parents. Information on AIDS and HIV is also detailed.

Jessee, P. O., Nagy, C., & Poteet-Johnson, D. (1993). Children with AIDS. *Childhood Education, 70*(1), 10–14. This excellent, concise article touches on all the most important aspects of this problem.

LeRoy, C. H., Powell, T. H., & Kelker, P. H. (1994). Meeting our responsibilities in special education: HIV and AIDS: A review. *Teaching Exceptional Chil-*

dren, 26(4), 37–44. This is another sound article about children with AIDS that outlines the responsibilities of educators for the care of such youngsters.

National Pediatric HIV Resource Centre (n. d.). Parent information booklets. Newark, NJ: Children's Hospital of New Jersey (United Hospitals Medical Centre, 15 S. Ninth St., Newark, NJ 07107). This is a series of 10 booklets about children with AIDS. Simple, direct, and very practical. *Highly recommended.*

Pressma, D., & Emery, L. J. (1991). *Serving children with HIV infection in child day care: A guide for center-based and family day care providers.* Washington, DC: Child Welfare League of America. If you require only one reference about children and AIDS in your library, this is the one to get. It covers inclusion of infected staff, precautions, and recommended care of afflicted children—outstanding.

Children and Violence in the Community

Garbarino, J., Dubrow, N., Kostelny, K., and Pardo, C. (1992). *Children in danger: Coping with the consequences of community violence.* San Francisco: Jossey-Bass. This helpful book shows how professional people, including teachers, can work together for the benefit of the children.

Horton, J., & Zimmer, J. (1990). *Media violence and children: A guide for parents.* Washington, DC: National Association for the Education of Young Children. This brief pamphlet would be a helpful way to alert parents to TV-related problems and what they can do about them.

National Association for the Education of Young Children. (1993). NAEYC position statement on violence in the lives of children. *Young Children, 48*(6), 80–84. Violence is not something endemic that cannot be alleviated. The position paper outlines the problem and presents many practical ways everyone can begin to prevent it and counteract its evil effects. *Highly recommended.*

Osofsky, J. D., & Fenichel, E. (1994). *Caring for infants and toddlers in violent environments: Hurt, healing, and hope.* 2000 14th St. N, Suite 380, Arlington, VA 22201-2500: Zero to Three: National Centre for Clinical Infant Programs. The effect of various forms of violence together with recommendations about prevention and treatment are provided here. *Highly recommended.*

Reiss, D., Richters, J. E., Radke-Yarrow, M., & Scharff, D. (1993). *Children and violence.* New York: Guilford Press. This is a useful reference for readers who require in-depth information about sources of violence and its effect on children.

Wallach, L. B. (1993). Helping children cope with violence. *Young Children, 48*(6), 4–11. Wallach singles out four practical ways teachers can help children who have witnessed or been subject to violence. *Highly recommended.*

Child Abuse and Neglect

Association for Early Childhood Educators, Ontario (1990). *Child abuse: A handbook for early childhood educators.* Toronto: AECE. This booklet is intended as a guide for those who have received training in the prevention of child abuse. It details legal and professional responsibilities as well as possible indicators of abuse.

Emery, R. E. (1989). Family violence. *American Psychologist, 44*(2), 321–328. Emery provides an excellent, brief overview of research about violence toward children and women.

Helfer, R. E., & Kempe, R. S. (Eds.). (1987). *The battered child* (5th ed.). Chicago: University of Chicago Press. This is *the* classic handbook for individuals interested in reading more about child abuse.

Koralek, D. (1992). *Caregivers of young children: Preventing and responding to child maltreatment.* Washington, DC: United States Department of Health and Human Services, Administration on Children, Youth and Families, National Centre on Child Abuse and Neglect. For a brief yet comprehensive discussion of child abuse as it affects abused children in children's centres, this publication is the most helpful one I've found. It may be obtained by calling the Clearinghouse on Child Abuse and Neglect and should be in every centre library. It discusses recognizing and reporting child abuse, protecting the centre from accusations of abuse, and working with abused children and their parents. *Highly recommended.*

MacFarlane, K., Waterman, J., Conerly, S., Damon, L., Durfee, M., & Long, S. (1986). *Sexual abuse of young children: Evaluation & treatment.* New York: Guilford Press. This is a comprehensive reference that deals with the molestation of preschool children.

Recommended Bibliographies

Bernstein, J. E., & Rudman, R. R. (1989). *Books to help children cope with separation and loss* (Vol. 3). New York: R. R. Bowker. This useful reference includes annotated bibliographies of books for children aged three to sixteen years covering every kind of separation—the first days at school, divorce, death, AIDS, suicide, homelessness, and so forth.

Cuddigan, M., and Hanson, M. B. (1988). *Growing pains.* New York: American Library Association. This bibliography focuses on children aged two to eight and singles out books that help children deal with problems and crises such as divorce, the death of a pet, child abuse, and so forth.

For the Advanced Student

Arnold, L. E. (Ed.). (1990). *Childhood stress.* New York: John Wiley. This book covers just about every kind of crisis one can think of. It is research based and focuses on causes and outcomes, with less time devoted to prevention and treatment.

Crocker, A. C., Cohen, H. J., & Kastner, T. A. (Eds.). (1992). *HIV infection and developmental disabilities: A resource for service providers.* Baltimore: Paul Brookes. This entire book is devoted to the subject of children and AIDS and presents the most thorough treatment of the subject readily available to the lay public.

Emery, R. E., & Forehand, R. (1994). Parental divorce and children's well-being: A focus on resilience. In R. J. Haggerty, L. R. Sherrod, N. Garmezy, & M. Rutter (Eds.), *Stress, risk, and resilience in children and adolescents: Processes, mechanisms, and interventions.* New York: Cambridge University Press. The authors present a thoughtful, up-to-date assessment of the effects of divorce and what can be done to help children adjust to it as well as possible.

Hetherington, E. M. (1992). Coping with marital transitions: A family systems perspective. In E. M. Hetherington and W. G. Clinempeel, (Eds.), Coping with marital transitions. *Monographs of the Society for Research in Child Development, 57*(2–3, Serial No. 227). Hetherington provides a valuable review of research concerning divorce and children.

Masters, W. H., Johnson, V. E., & Kolodny, R. C. (1994). *Heterosexuality.* New York: HarperCollins. For a complete, current overview of the status of AIDS in the United States and around the world, the chapter on this subject in *Heterosexuality* is highly recommended.

Papadatou, D., & Papadatos, C. (Eds.). (1991). *Children and death*. New York: Hemisphere. This book includes material on children's understanding of death, the dying child, and effective ways of helping children, parents, and health professionals cope with death—good but saddening.

Van Hesselt, V. B., Morrison, R. L., Bellack, A. S., & Hersen, M. (Eds.). (1988). *Handbook of family violence*. New York: Plenum Press. This extensive overview of violence covers all kinds of family-related abuse.

Wass, H., & Corr, C. A. (Eds.). (1984). *Childhood and death*. Washington, DC: Hemisphere. This book covers just about every aspect of death and young children—valuable for the serious reader.

Yawkey, T. D., & Cornelius, G. M. (1990). *The single parent family: For helping professionals and parents*. Lancaster, PA: Techtonic. The authors provide useful reviews of research concerning both male and female single parents, stress, and the learning needs of children—a good research source.

Resources of Special Interest

The National Clearinghouse on Family Violence, Family Violence Prevention Division, Social Services Program Branch, Health Canada, Ottawa, ON K1A 1B5, toll free 1-800-267-0454. The Clearinghouse is a wonderful resource for information on this subject.

Coalition for Quality Children's Videos, 535 Cordova Rd., Suite 456, Santa Fe, NM 87501. The Coalition provides a good list of quality children's videos.

Compassionate Friends, PO Box 3696, Oak Brook, IL 60522-3696. The Friends offer a number of helpful newsletters, pamphlets, and publications as well as providing group meetings in many communities.

Concerned Educators Allied for a Safe Environment (CEASE), 17 Gerry St., Cambridge, MA 02138. This organization continues to advocate peaceful, healthy solutions to various kinds of conflicts. A subscription to their newsletter costs $10 a year.

Kids Help Phone, Box 513, 2 Bloor St. W., Suite 100, Toronto, ON M4W 3E2, toll free 1-800-668-6868.

National Centre for the Prevention and Treatment of Child Abuse and Neglect, 1205 Oneida St., Denver, CO 80220.

Parents Anonymous. An organization for parents who wish to stop abusing their children.

Resource: A Newsletter for Providers Who Serve Children, Youth, and Families with HIV. Newark, NJ: National Pediatric HIV Resource Centre, 15 South Ninth St., Newark, NJ 07107. The title is largely self-explanatory—the Newsletter always lists the most up-to-date publications, which are generally excellent and practical.

Welcoming Children Who Have Special Educational Requirements into the Life of the Program

Inclusion is a philosophical stance and an approach to practice that assumes that all individuals have equal worth and rights. In early childhood education settings, this means that all children will be accepted and served within a program, with the implication that "special" or minority needs will not be stigmatized or marginalized. Inclusion means to bring people in rather than exclude them—in thought, word, or deed.

Guida Chud & Ruth Fahlman

Whether they're handicapped or healthy, homeless or affluent, safe or at-risk, children need each other to grow. Children need to be together, in a safe, warm and caring environment—to play together, learn together. The rooted and the displaced, the graceful runner and the child who'll never walk, the sure-of-himself, easy smiler, and the child who's afraid to risk loving again all become part, each of the other.

Gretchen Buchenholz

Have you ever wondered . . .

About a child who might need special help but were unsure what to say to the parent about it?

How to tell if a child really needed help from a psychologist?

What to do with that exceptionally bright little girl who acts so bored when she comes to school?

If you knew enough about a particular disability to admit a child with that condition to your class?

. . . If you have, the material in the following pages will help you.

Although most children have special educational needs at one point or another in their lives, some children require specialized attention more consistently. This group includes a wide assortment of youngsters, ranging from those with physical challenges to those who are emotionally disturbed to those who are experiencing intellectual development that either lags behind or is markedly ahead of their peers. In short, the category of exceptionality covers children who deviate in at least one respect far enough from the typical that they are noticeable in the group because of this deviation.

In 1991, it was estimated that over half a million children and youth under nineteen years of age residing in households had at least one disability—7.2% of all children in Canada. The rate of disability was higher among boys (7.9%) than girls (6.3%) (Canadian Institute of Child Health, 1994).

In Canada, policies related to the rights of individuals with exceptionalities are formulated at the federal, provincial, and local levels of government. Except for the Declaration of Human Rights, there is no federal law to outline or guarantee the rights of exceptional children; the right of every child to education is not entrenched by any constitutional provision. In the absence of constitutional provisions, the responsibility for education rests with provincial legislation. Only two provincial human rights codes (Saskatchewan and Quebec) list education as a right (Winzer, 1993).

Law and public policy have had a profound effect on the type and quality of education offered to exceptional children and youth. In some cases, they decide whether students with special needs are educated at all; in others, they determine how these children are educated. In recent years, all the provinces and territories have adopted the ideology of equal access. However, how each province or territory enacts this principle ranges from making access to education for all mandatory, as it is in Ontario and Newfoundland, to a more permissive approach, as in Alberta and British Columbia. The United States has a powerful piece of national legislation, passed in 1975, to guarantee special education to all children who need it.

Perhaps the reader is thinking "Well, it's nice these laws exist, but what do they mean to me?" The answer is threefold. First, passage of these laws means that help for young children with disabilities is more readily available than it was in the past. This is a wonderful comfort to teachers who still come across children who need help but have escaped the notice of other professionals before entering school. Second, it means that, because of certain requirements in the laws, many more children who have disabilities will be attending our "regular" public or private early childhood centres. Finally, it means that we teachers are expected to become part of the treatment teams engaged in working with such children.

These circumstances make it increasingly important for teachers to have a practical, working knowledge of the commoner ways children deviate from the typical and also to understand how to work with such youngsters and the specialists who help them. Examples and resources are provided throughout *The Whole Child* in relevant chapters, but experience has taught me it is also helpful for students to have a concise source of information presented all together. That is the reason this chapter is included in the text. It is important to realize, however, that the subject of exceptionality is *huge,* and so only an introduction can be offered here. I hope it will pave the way to further reading and education in this important area.

❧ Identifying Children with Special Needs and Finding Help for Them: The Early Childhood Teacher as a Screening Agent

One of the advantages teachers have that physicians do not is that they see the same children for extended periods of time, and this makes it possible to be aware of physical, emotional, and cognitive behaviour that may indicate a serious underlying difficulty. It is a mistaken notion that such difficulties are always first noticed in the physician's office or by parents. Doctors see children for brief periods of time, often under conditions quite stressful to the child. In addition, they can be hampered by parents who either raise questions about insignificant symptoms or who resist being told anything about their youngsters that may be upsetting. When physicians are caught in this kind of situation, it is only to be expected that occasional difficulties slip past without notice. These comments are not intended to imply that a highly trained medical specialist knows less than early childhood teachers do. Rather, teachers should keep their eyes open because they have the advantage of seeing the child in a natural setting for extended periods of time, and they have seen many youngsters of similar age and background. Thus it is possible that they may become aware of difficulties that should be drawn to the attention of the physician or psychologist.

The sooner such potential handicaps are identified, the sooner they may be ameliorated and further formation of undesirable habit patterns and emotional reactions reduced. Sometimes early diagnosis means that a condition can be cleared up entirely (as when a child's hearing is restored following a tonsillectomy-adenoidectomy), and sometimes the effect of the condition can only be mitigated (as is often the case with youngsters who have cognitive delays) (Accardo & Capute, 1991). But *nothing* can be done until the child is identified as needing assistance and a referral has been successfully carried out. These are points at which the teacher's help is crucial since he is the person most likely to provide day-by-day linkage between the family and the services that can help them.

Referring Children for Special Help: Calling the Difficulty to the Parents' Attention

Calling a parent's attention to a special problem requires delicacy and tact on the part of the teacher, since it is all too easy for the parents to feel that they are being attacked or criticized and that they have failed to be good parents. This is particularly true if the teacher must raise the issue of a pronounced behaviour problem. However, the teacher can do several things to reduce the strength of this understandable defensive reaction.

If Teachers Listen Carefully While Conversing with the Parents, They May Find That the Parents Themselves Are Raising the Problem Very Tentatively

For example, the mother may ask nervously, "How did she do today?" or comment, "He's just like his older brother. Doesn't he ever sit still?" Many a teacher responds to such questions by just as nervously reassuring the parent, saying brightly, "Oh, he did just fine!" (while thinking wryly to himself, "Just fine, that is, if you don't count biting John, destroying Emily's block tower, and refusing to come to story time.") Rather than being falsely reassuring, the teacher could use the opening the parent has provided by responding, "I'm glad you asked. She *is* having some difficulties at school. I'm beginning to think it's time to put our heads together and come up with some special ways to help her."

It Takes Time to Bring About a Referral

It is best to raise problems gradually with parents over a period of time because it takes a while for families to accustom themselves to the fact that their child may need special help. Even such an apparently simple thing as having an eye examination may be hard for some families to arrange or to face, and teachers should not expect acceptance and compliance with their recommendations just because they have finally worked their courage up to the point of mentioning a difficulty.

The Teacher Should Have the Reasons Why the Child Needs Special Help Clearly in Mind Before Raising the Issue with the Parent

This recommendation is not intended to mean that teachers should confront parents with a long, unhappy list of grievances against the child, but that they should be prepared to provide examples of the problem while explaining gently and clearly to the family the reason for their concern.

For example, while examining photographs I had taken for this book, the staff and I were surprised to notice that one of the children was looking at a seriation game with her eyes consistently close to the material. It was helpful to use these snapshots with the family when suggesting that they have her eyes examined.

Usually, of course, one does not have something as concrete as a picture to share, but episodes or examples of the problem can be described almost as well and are essential to have in mind when discussing such difficulties with parents.

It Is Not the Teacher's Place to Diagnose

A particular behaviour can have many different causes. For example, failure to pay attention in story hour may be the consequence of a hearing loss, inappropriate reading material, borderline intelligence, fatigue, poor eyesight, or simply needing to go to the toilet. The teacher's role is to recognize that a difficulty exists, do all he can to mitigate it in the group, inform the parent, and suggest a referral to an expert professional person for diagnosis and treatment when necessary.

Therefore, when he confers with the parent, the teacher should discuss the symptoms and express his concern but avoid giving the impression that he knows for certain what the real cause of the problem may be. Instead, he should ally himself with the parent in a joint quest to find the answer together.

Finding the Appropriate Referral Source

Teachers need to acquaint themselves with a variety of referral sources available in their community, since it is both senseless and cruel to raise a problem with parents and have no suggestions about where they can go for help. When a problem appears to need further attention, it is important to be aware of community agencies, hospital assessment departments, and associations that can offer help.

Other resources include directories of community services, public health nurses, paediatricians, local children's hospitals, county medical societies, and mental health clinics. The same resource and referral agency that provides lists of child care sources for parents and employers often knows of appropriate referrals. Whenever possible, it is always desirable to list more than one referral possibility so that the family has the opportunity to select the one they feel suits them best. For more advice on how to make a referral, see Kaiser & Sklar Rasminsky, 1993.

Observing Professional Ethics

I have already pointed out that the teacher should not assume the role of diagnostician. However, he often possesses information that is of value to the specialist to whom the child is referred. It can be a temptation to pick up the telephone and call this person without pausing to ask the parent's permission, but this is a violation of professional ethics. The teacher must obtain the parent's consent before he talks to the specialist. Professional people often require that this permission be in writing before any information is exchanged. After permission is obtained, exchanges of information and suggestions from the specialist can be extraordinarily helpful and should be used whenever the opportunity presents itself.

Also, when dealing with a special case, the teacher may be tempted to discuss it with people who are not entitled to know about it, because it is so interesting and perhaps makes the teacher feel important. This gossiping is an unforgivable violation of the family's privacy, and a teacher must never indulge in the desire to do this.

❦ Including Children Who Have Disabilities

In most regions of Canada, integration in mainstream child care programs is the preferred option for children with disabilities. There is general agreement among groups representing persons with disabilities that this provides the best developmental opportunities for children with additional needs. Some provinces are phasing out segregated child care for these children, and many are providing some enriched funding for integrated programs. There are no figures available on the number of programs that can accommodate children with exceptionalities. However, parents and advocacy groups report that appropriate mainstream child care is still in short supply and children with disabilities are relatively underserved.

The Individualized Program Plan (IPP) is the usual approach to providing services to children with special needs. The written IPP includes the process of designing, implementing, and evaluating that plan. The written plan provides the structure and direction of the services and activities to be provided to the child and family by the early childhood program. Teachers are essential throughout the IPP process, both in their observations of the child's behaviour and in their evaluation.

Does Inclusion Benefit Children?

There is general consensus that the primary benefits of integrating children with special needs into ordinary early childhood settings are that doing this helps all the children accept each others' differences and that integration provides more normalized experiences and chances to socialize for children with disabilities (Wolery, Holcombe, Venn, et al., 1993).

Research supports this consensus (Diamond, Hestenes, & O'Connor, 1994). For example, when groups of mildly delayed preschool children were compared, one study found that the children in the integrated settings participated in twice as much social interaction and displayed higher levels of play than did the children who were in the segregated groups (Guralnick & Groom, 1987).

However, just integrating children with special needs into typical preschool environments is not enough. In addition to needing to be with typical children, they also need to have their special educational needs met. This is where the IPP comes in.

When Planning the IPP It Is Essential to Have a Careful Assessment of the Child's Accomplishments and Abilities Available

This assessment is usually carried out by a team of professional people versed in the areas of development in which the child's difficulties lie. Working with the parents, the team does its best to identify the youngster's strengths and problem areas. Then it recommends things to do to help her develop as well as possible. As discussed in chapter 2, these assessments should involve a range of measures including naturalistic observations, parent reports, various standardized tests, a physical examination if it is warranted, and whatever special measures are appropriate to gain further insight into the individual youngster's disability (Bailey & Wolery, 1992; Hendrick, 1994).

Once the assessment has been accomplished, the information is pooled. A team may be composed of whoever will be working with the child, at least one of her parents, and, if it is a first meeting, a member of the assessment team. During this conference, the IPP is developed, outlining the most important learning goals and objectives for the child.

For example, one child's IPP might include developing muscular dexterity and social independence by pushing the bar handle of the water tap while washing her hands, while for another, it might be paying attention to hand gestures when the teacher uses sign language.* Follow-up meetings are scheduled to revise and update the IPP as needed.

Although this may sound like a good deal of paperwork (and it is!), the clear intention of the process is to benefit children who have special needs and to protect their rights to a free, public education—a right sorely abused in prior times. It also has the virtue of protecting the family's right to privacy and their right to participate actively in planning what is best for their child's well-being and future.

---

*For a detailed description of this process see Cook, Tessier, & Klein, 1992.

❧ *Providing an extra set of crutches helped Jennifer understand John's problem when he was admitted to the school.*

❧ Learning to Work as a Member of the Team

Currently, the trend is to incorporate special services into the setting right along with the child, and to encourage the teacher and other specialists to combine their skills. This is called the *transdisciplinary approach* (Gallivan-Fenlon, 1994). It is a desirable change from former days when the speech therapist, for example, would arrive and take the child away to a quiet place where she drilled her on building language skills in isolation from ongoing classroom life. In addition to disrupting whatever the child was doing, the problem with this approach was getting the training to carry over into real-life situations.

Nowadays, physical therapists, speech pathologists, and other specialists are more likely to integrate their work into the ongoing school program—seizing opportunities for the child to practise desired skills as they arise during her play (Bricker & Cripe, 1992). This is particularly easy to do at the preschool and kindergarten level because the self-select, open-choice periods provide golden opportunities for practice to take place in a natural life setting.

The advantages of this activity-oriented approach are obvious, but it is up to the teacher and specialist to make it work, and this is not always easy! For example, the educational philosophies of the two people may differ considerably. Just as preschool teachers are well aware that some elementary school teachers do not understand or appreciate early childhood methods of instruction, so too are they aware that neither do many special education teachers—some of whom unfortunately have no background in early childhood. To these uninitiated people, self-select time may appear to be more like bedlam than the carefully planned array of educational opportunities the early childhood teacher perceives it as being.

Then, too, many special education specialists are devoted to the behaviour modification approach to learning. In my opinion, there's no denying that approach has merit, particularly when one is working with certain kinds of severe disabilities. However, the early childhood teacher often finds the charts and reward systems this approach typically depends on to be repugnant.

Clearly, both teacher and specialist will need to develop generous amounts of appreciation for each other's points of view and the unique strengths they bring to the children if the team effort is to succeed. Without that mutual appreciation, the specialist may feel so unwelcome and the teacher so irritated and threatened that the old, isolated approach to instruction will be reinstated. Unfortunately, it is the child who pays the price in this ego-fraught situation (Rose & Smith, 1993).

The best way to overcome prejudices and build respect is to make certain there are *regular* times scheduled for team members to talk together—*hurried conferences at the door when the children are present are not sufficient*. Sometimes these chats can fit in during the lunch break or they can even take place over the phone. They present invaluable opportunities for teacher and specialist to exchange concerns and ideas and to coordinate strategies. This mutual approach to problem solving, *particularly when families are included,* maximizes the child's opportunities to thrive.

❧ Getting Started

It Is Important to Make It Clear to the Family
That the Staff Has Great Goodwill but also Has Certain Limitations
and Will Not Be Able to Work Miracles

Few early childhood teachers have much training in working with exceptional children. In addition, it is unlikely that during the year they will be able to devote a large amount of extra time to studying this subject. On the other hand, they do know a great deal about working with children in general and will bring to this particular child the benefit of these insights and practical, matter-of-fact treatment that emphasizes the normal rather than the exceptional.

The Staff Will Have to Come to Terms with How Much Extra Effort the Child Will Require Them to Expend Every Day

It is one thing to accept a child with developmental delays in a flush of helpfulness and sympathy, but it may turn out to be quite another when her pants have to be changed three or four times each morning. Some children who are emotionally disturbed may also require an inordinate amount of time and attention. The difficulty is that the staff has obligations to all the children, and the time required to work with an exceptional child may eventually deprive the other youngsters of their due share of energy and concern.

Fortunately, the examples given above are the exception rather than the rule, but the possibility of overtaxing the staff must be taken into consideration when discussing an admission. However, experience has taught me that most exceptional children can and should be gathered in. Usually the amount of special care is considerable during the first few weeks but gradually declines as the child and staff make the adjustment.

It Will Be Necessary for the Staff to Examine Their Feelings About Why They Wish to Accept the Child

It is all too easy to succumb to a rescue fantasy and decide that what the youngster really needs is plenty of love and she will be all right. This is, of course, untrue. Children, whether exceptional or ordinary, require a great many other talents from their teachers besides the ability to express affection, and teachers should not delude themselves that affection can overcome all problems. If they intend to work with the child effectively, they must plan on learning the best ways to help her in addition to loving her.

Information garnered from the various specialists serving the child is, of course, invaluable, but never forget that the most valuable resource the teacher can call on is *the parents.*

Many Seemingly Insurmountable Problems Can Be Solved During the Trial Period if the Staff and Family Are Creative Minded

For example, a child who cannot negotiate a flight of stairs and who is too heavy to be lifted can come to the centre if her father builds a ramp over the stairs. A child who requires a good deal of extra physical care may be able to attend if she is accompanied in the beginning by her mother or, if the parent needs relief, by an aide who tends to the extra chores until the child becomes more self-sufficient (Safford, 1989).

There Are Several Ways to Ease Entry Pangs

The regular practice of asking the parent to stay with the child until she has made friends should be followed when welcoming children with special needs into the group. Research has shown that this policy is of special importance for young children who are cognitively delayed (Kessler et al., 1968).

A chat with the child's physician or other team members may also reassure the teacher and provide special guidelines that may be necessary for handling the youngster. Children with heart conditions, for instance, occasionally require special treatment but sometimes arrive with firm instructions to let the child alone so she can pace herself.

Sometimes it also helps to begin with a short day and gradually extend the time the child attends as her skills and toleration of the group increase. The shorter day means that she can go home while she is still experiencing success and has not been overwhelmed with fatigue. It may be easiest if the child arrives in the middle of the morning and leaves when the other children do, since this means she does not have to depart when everyone else is still having a good time.

Many Disabilities Will Pass Unnoticed by the Other Children in the Group, but Some Will Require Explanation

As the research study in this chapter reveals, the other children will conjure up their own explanations for the child's disability unless they are provided with the correct one. The explanations need not be elaborate. They should avoid the condescension of pity and should stress matter-of-fact suggestions about how to get along with the child about whom they are asking (Derman-Sparks et al., 1989). It may be necessary, for example, to help the children understand that a particular child uses her ears and hands in place of her eyes since she cannot see, to coach them to stand in front of a child who is hard of hearing and catch her attention before speaking to her, or to explain that another youngster has to use the table sandbox to keep the grit out of her leg braces.

When our school recently included a child who had severe emotional problems, we found it helped the children and us a lot to discuss together what we could do to help him. It was heartening to see how our four-year-olds, who were at first nonplussed by Stewart's behaviour, came to ignore it in time and to brush off his panicky attacks. This was followed by a gradual shift to telling him he should "Stop it!" (which he often did, with staff assistance), and finally a gentle kind of pushing back and dogpiling took place while the children coached him about what to say. I recall one child saying, "Tell me to stop—*tell* me to stop and I will!" There is no denying the therapy the child was undergoing concurrently had a very significant effect on his growth and development, but some of the credit must also go to the staff and children who worked together to understand, accept, and help Stewart.

ᔕ General Recommendations for Working with Children Who Have Disabilities

See through the Exceptional to the Typical in Every Child

It can be easy to become so caught up in the differences of an exceptional child that the teacher loses sight of the fact that she is largely like the other children in the group and should be treated as much like them as possible. Feeling sorry for a child weakens her character and ultimately does her a terrible disservice. Many exceptional children have too many allowances made for them out of pity, misguided good intentions, and inexperience—and sometimes, where parents are concerned, as a consequence of guilt. The

❧ RESEARCH STUDY ❧
Do Preschool Children Recognize Disabilities in Their Peers?

Research Question: Diamond wanted to know if four-year-old children without disabilities recognize the presence of a disability in their peers, and, if they do, how they explain the reasons for such a disability.

Research Method: Diamond questioned 28 four-year-old children without disabilities who participated with fourteen preschool children who had disabilities. These youngsters had played together during the free play period every day at their nursery school during the school year. The disabilities included mild to severe developmental delays including cerebral palsy, Down's syndrome, severe language delays, moderate to severe hearing loss, and developmental delay.

At the end of the school year she asked the children who did not have disabilities a series of questions. After a few get-acquainted questions she showed them photographs of each child in the class, and asked them to tell her their names. Next she said, "Show me if there's anyone who (1) doesn't walk or run the way the other kids do, (2) doesn't talk as well, . . . (3) doesn't behave the way the other kids do—you know, they're silly or goofy." When a child was identified as fitting any one of these categories, she followed up by asking such questions as "Why do you think he (or she) can't talk so well?" All the children's replies were then sorted into various categories.

Research Results: In all but three out of 196 opportunities the children who were questioned knew all the other children's names. Twenty-seven of the twenty-eight youngsters identified at least one child with a disability. The disabilities that were particularly noticed were obvious physical disabilities and mental retardation. On the other hand, children with mild to moderate speech and language delays were not selected as having a disability. Only eight children mentioned a child who

had unusual behaviour—and, interestingly enough, all of those behaviour nominations singled out boys who actually did not have disabilities.

Two-thirds of the children gave reasons why the child was disabled according to a variety of causes. Most typically they explained why a peer couldn't walk or talk as being due to the child's age ("He's small," "She's a baby," "When she gets bigger she can walk like everybody else," and so forth.) Other explanations referred to the equipment the child used ("He's got a walker") or used a label (She's handicapped"). The third kind of explanation was based on reasons such as accidents or trauma ("He broke his leg," or "He can't talk because he got hit in the mouth").

Implications for Teaching: Even though Diamond describes this as a preliminary study, it leaves no doubt that children as young as age four are aware of the more obvious forms of disability.

Since this is true, the policy followed by some teachers of just ignoring a disability so the children will assume everyone is "the same" simply isn't effective. Just as we shall see in the chapter on multicultural education, children are well aware of many kinds of differences, and these differences must be acknowledged and dealt with if they are to acquire positive attitudes about them. Ignorance is the handmaiden of prejudice.

Since the explanations offered by the children indicate that many of them were not only aware of the differences but also had speculated about the reasons for them, the study also emphasizes the value of providing simple but correct explanations of causes in order to deepen the children's understanding of the disability.

Source: From "Preschool Children's Concepts of Disability in Their Peers" by K. E. Diamond, 1993, *Early Education and Development, 4*(2), pp. 123–129.

❧   *Even temporary handicaps like this eye patch can make children self-conscious.*

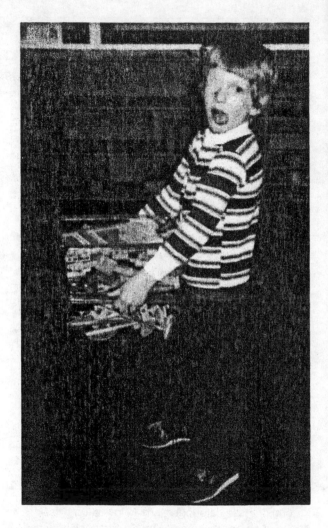

outcome is that the child may become a demanding and rather unpleasant person to have around. In other words, she becomes just plain spoiled.

Consistency, reasonable expectations, and sound policies are, if anything, *more important* to employ when dealing with exceptional children than when dealing with typical children. Teachers should feel comfortable about drawing on their common sense and considerable experience, but they should also be able to turn freely to experts for consultation when they feel puzzled and uncertain about how to proceed.

Try to Steer a Middle Course, Neither Overprotecting nor Overexpecting

The most common pitfall in working with an exceptional child is becoming so concerned for her safety and well-being that the child is stifled and deprived of the opportunity to be as normal as she might be were she not overprotected. In general, the teacher should proceed on the assumption that the child should be encouraged to participate in every activity, with modifications provided only when necessary to ensure success. Thus a child who is behind her peers in intellectual development should be expected to participate in story hour but may enjoy it most if she sits with the youngest group.

On the other hand, some parents and teachers set their expectations unreasonably high and are unwilling to make any exceptions for the child with a handicap. This causes unnecessary strain and even despair for the youngster. Teachers can be helpful here by pointing out what is reasonable to expect of three- or four-year-old children in general and helping the parents understand what a reasonable expectation would be for their particular youngster. It is often helpful with such families to note each step as the child attains it and discuss what the next stage of development will be so that the parent can see progress coming bit by bit. This may reduce the feeling of desperately driving toward a difficult distant goal.

Be Realistic

It is important to see the child as she is and to avoid false promises and unrealistic reassurances when talking with parents or the child herself. Everyone yearns for an exceptional child to "make it," and sometimes this yearning leads to unwitting self-deceptions, which can do the family and child a disservice by delaying acceptance of the disability or by encouraging them to make inadequate future plans. I once watched as a preschooler who was blind said to her teacher, "I can tell by feeling things with my hands what they are like; but when I grow up, then I will be able to see the colours, too, won't I?" The teacher replied, with tears in his eyes, "Yes, then everything will be all right."

Acceptance of the child's limitations as well as capitalization on her strengths is the balance to strive for and to model for the family. Some children will in time overcome a disability entirely, but others will not be able to do this. Helping the parents and the child accept this fact, as well as accepting it oneself, is difficult to do but valuable.

Keep Regular Records of the Child's Development

Since progress with all children, including exceptional ones, occurs a little at a time, it is easy to feel discouraged from time to time and to lose sight of how far the youngster has come. If teachers keep regular written records, however brief, an occasional review of that material can be encouraging.

It is particularly important to keep records on an exceptional youngster so that they may be summarized and referred to at the next IPP meeting or passed on to her next teacher to acquaint him with her interests and progress. The records should cover whatever incidents seem particularly important to the child, indications of growth or slipping backward, special interests and tastes, effective educational approaches, and significant information contributed by the parents, physician, and other support personnel.

Occasionally the teacher may be asked to participate in an in-depth study of an emotionally disturbed youngster and may want to make more detailed written observations to be used in discussion and consultation. Although time-consuming, this kind of study can be helpful and revealing. The teacher can refer to references at the end of the chapter for models and suggestions about how to carry out such observations successfully.

Remain in Constant Contact with the Family

All parents are concerned about their children and need consistent contact with teachers, but parents of children who have special problems require this even more, and so do the teachers who have welcomed such youngsters to their group (McWilliams & Strain, 1993).

Parents can help the teacher with many details about child management. It may be as simple as explaining the easiest way to slip the arm of a cerebral palsied child into her snowsuit or an offer of special equipment for pedals for a spina bifida child who is dying to ride the tricycle. Moreover, parents are often the go-between between specialist and teacher, relaying information from one to the other.

Parents often hang on the teacher's words about how their exceptional child is getting along at school. For this reason teachers should choose their words with care while remaining sincere and truthful. As many opportunities as possible should be created for quick, friendly chats. Even notes sent home can help, but chatting is really to be preferred because of the direct person-to-person encounter it provides.

Do not limit your ideas of how families can help by thinking of them as only supplying physical labour. Always remember that parents are the foremost authorities on their child. They know that youngster in ways the specialists never can, and they can contribute an endless amount of advice and information if only the teacher will ask for it.

Moreover, including the parents in discussions and plans makes it more probable there will be consistency in expectations and handling at both home and school. This consistency of approach is very valuable.

✑ Identifying and Helping Children Who Have Physical Handicaps

Some Physical Conditions and Symptoms of Which the Teacher Should Be Aware

Speech and Hearing Problems

Various speech difficulties and symptoms of possible hearing impairment will be reviewed in the chapter on language, so it will only be noted here that speech and hearing problems are among the physical disorders that occur most frequently in childhood (Tureen & Tureen, 1986). Speech difficulties are likely to be noticed, but hearing loss may be overlooked as a possible cause of misbehaviour, inattention, or lack of responsiveness. However, once hearing loss is suspected, it is a relatively simple matter to refer the child to an otolaryngologist for examination. Since such losses may be due to infection, they can and should be treated promptly.

Difficulties of Vision

Another physical disability that may pass unnoticed but that occurs frequently is an inability to see clearly. The incidence of visual defects may run as high as one in four or five children of elementary school age (Reynolds & Birch, 1988). Although actual statistics on the incidence of vision defects in preschoolers could not be located, it seems probable that the incidence would be about the same. This means that in a group of fifteen preprimary children there may be as many as three or four youngsters who have some kind of difficulty with their eyes.

The presence of the following symptoms should alert the teacher to the possibility that the child needs to have her eyes examined (Kirk, 1972):

1. Strabismus (crossed eyes); nystagmus (involuntary, rapid movement of the eyeball)
2. How the child uses her eyes; tilting her head, holding objects close to her eyes, rubbing her eyes, squinting, displaying sensitivity to bright lights, and rolling her eyes
3. Inattention to visual objects or visual tasks such as looking at pictures or reading
4. Awkwardness in games requiring eye-hand coordination
5. Avoidance of tasks that require close eye work
6. Affinity for tasks that require distance vision
7. Any complaints about inability to see
8. Lack of normal curiosity in regard to visually appealing objects

In addition to such symptoms, physiological ones include reddened or crusty eyelids, watery eyes, eyes that are discharging, excessive rubbing of eyes, shutting or covering one eye, squinting, blinking, frowning, and distorted facial expressions while doing close work (Cook, Tessier, & Klein, 1992).

❧   *This youngster is suffering from the condition called lazy eye or amblyopia. He usually wears glasses to help correct the condition.*

One defect of vision in particular requires treatment during early childhood, since later attempts at correction are not so effective (Batshaw & Perret, 1992). This is *amblyopia,* sometimes called *lazy eye,* a condition in which one eye is weaker than the other because of a muscle imbalance (Batshaw & Perret, 1992). Common signs of this condition include squinting with one eye or tilting the head to one side in order to see better. Since early treatment of this condition is important, *if there is any possible way to incorporate visual screening tests into the school program it should be done.* Sometimes local ophthalmological or optometric societies will sponsor this service; sometimes a public health nurse can be prevailed upon, or an interested civic group will employ a trained nurse to visit centres and nursery schools and conduct such tests.

Screening is best done at school rather than at a central clinic because coverage of children attending the school is likely to be more complete and the environment in which testing takes place is familiar to the children, so they will be more at ease. Giving the children practice before the actual examination day in holding the E according to instructions will facilitate testing and help save the examiner's sanity. Central clinics should also be offered as a service to children who do not attend school.

It is important to remember that a screening test does only that—it screens for some of the more obvious vision disabilities. For this reason, even though a youngster may have passed the screening test with flying colours, if she continues to have difficulties she should be referred for further testing. Of course, when the screening test *does* pick up a possible problem, that youngster should be referred to an ophthalmologist or qualified optometrist for diagnosis and follow-up also.

Attention Deficit Disorder (Hyperactivity)

Attention deficit disorder (ADD) is the term used by experts to describe a neurobiological disorder that the general public labels *hyperactivity* (McBurnett, Lahey, & Pfiffner, 1993). Because the hallmarks of this condition include impulsiveness, inattention, and, in some cases, overactivity, there is a tendency on the part of some school personnel and inexperienced parents to misuse the term to describe every active, vigorous child. In the past this has occasionally led to overprescription of medication to control behaviour that was actually within normal bounds.

As the following list makes clear, there is a tremendous difference between normal behaviour and the behaviour of youngsters who fit into this category.

1. Restlessness—the child appears to be a bundle of energy. The mother may come to feel that she can't take her eyes off him for a minute without his climbing on the refrigerator or running into the street. At nursery school, the child may be incessantly in motion except that he seems able to settle down when given one-to-one attention.

2. The child is easily distracted and has a short attention span. In nursery school he may rush from activity to activity and then seem at a loss for what to do. He may do as the teacher asks but forget quickly and revert to his former behaviour.

3. The child demands attention insatiably—monopolizes conversations, teases, badgers, repeats annoying activities. May be emotionally unresponsive or undemonstrative.

4. Shows a weaker-than-average ability to control his impulses. Hard for him to wait, he may become upset rapidly, has many temper tantrums, acts on the spur of the moment—often with poor judgment. Parents may complain that the child is incontinent.

5. About half of these children exhibit difficulties in the coordination of fine muscle activities such as using scissors, colouring and so forth, or with problems of balance.

6. The child may have various kinds of interpersonal problems including resistance to social demands from parents and teachers, excessive independence, and a troublesome tendency to dominate the children he plays with, which makes him unlikable.

7. He may have various emotional problems including swings of mood, becoming excessively excited over pleasant activities, sometimes appearing to be insensitive to pain, demonstrating a low tolerance to frustration and overreaction to it when frustrated, and low self-esteem.

8. Some of these children have real difficulty tolerating change.*

Of course, most young children exhibit these kinds of behaviours from time to time. What sets the truly hyperactive child apart is the *intensity and consistency of the behaviour.* Some, though not all, of these behaviours may appear to subside by adolescence, but the years of stress and the unhappy side effects of this condition have usually taken a painful toll by then (Silver & Hagin, 1990).

The most adequate referral is one made to a child psychiatrist or a paediatrician conversant with this disorder, since medication often contributes to the successful management of this condition (Fadely & Hosler, 1992). A child psychologist or social worker can also provide valuable assistance because behaviour modification techniques may be helpful to use with some of these youngsters (Fiore, Becker, & Nero, 1993).

Convulsive Seizures

A condition that responds particularly well to medication is epilepsy. Indeed, *generalized tonic clonic seizures* (formerly termed *grand mal* seizures) in which the individual loses consciousness are now rarely witnessed in children's centres. Unless a major convulsive seizure occurs for the first time at school, teachers usually need not worry about referring such children, since it is almost certain that they are already under treatment by their physician. They should, however, report seizures to the family. If an attack occurs at school, the following procedure should be carried out:

1. Remain calm. Students will assume the same emotional reaction as their teacher. The seizure itself is painless to the child.

2. Do not try to restrain the child. Nothing can be done to stop a seizure once it has begun; it must run its course.

3. Clear the area around the student so that he does not injure himself on hard objects. Try not to interfere with his movements in any way.

4. Do not force anything between his teeth. If his mouth is already open, a soft object like a handkerchief may be placed between his side teeth.

5. It generally is not necessary to call a doctor unless the attack is immediately followed by another major seizure or if the seizure lasts more than 10 minutes.

---

*From *The Hyperactive Child: A Handbook for Parents* by Paul H. Wender, MD. © 1973 by Paul H. Wender. Used by permission of Crown Publishers, Inc.

6. When the seizure is over, let the child rest if he needs to.*

The teacher will also need to explain to the other children, who may be either curious or distressed, what happened. The explanation should be simple and matter-of-fact to make it as easy as possible for the child to return to the group with little comment.

Epilepsy is not contagious, and people who have this condition are not mentally ill or mentally retarded (Kirk & Gallagher, 1989). The seizures are the result of disturbances to the nervous system due to inappropriate electrical activity within the brain, but the causes of such activity are largely unknown at this time. Stress and fatigue may increase the probability of a seizure, but erratic use of prescribed medication is the most common cause of difficulty (Lectenberg, 1984). When medication is taken consistently, about 85% of all patients afflicted with convulsive seizures experience good control (Thurman & Widerstrom, 1990).

The teacher needs to be more alert to the much milder form of convulsion, formerly called *petit mal* but now called *generalized absence* (pronounced to rhyme with *Alphonse*). It is important to pay particular attention to this kind of lighter seizure because it sometimes escapes the notice of the family, to whom it may seem to be a case of daydreaming or inattention.

According to Batshaw and Perret (1992), these brief episodes are characterized by the child having a glazed look, blinking, and being unaware of her surroundings. She may interrupt what she is saying and then pick up where she left off. Although this condition is uncommon, these seizures may occur hundreds of times a day and yet be undetected because they usually last less than ten seconds. It is worthwhile to identify this behaviour and refer the child for treatment to a paediatrician or neurologist because the probability of successful control by means of medication is high.

Excessive Awkwardness

The teacher should also notice children who are exceptionally clumsy. These are youngsters who, even though allowance has been made for their youthful age, are much more poorly coordinated than their peers. They may fall over their feet, run into things, knock things over, have trouble with climbing and balancing (and are often apprehensive about engaging in these activities), run consistently on their toes, or be unable to accomplish ordinary fine muscle tasks. This kind of behaviour should not be "laughed off." Instead it should be drawn to the attention of the parent and referral to the paediatrician suggested. There are numerous causes for such symptoms and many are amenable to treatment, but only if they are identified.

Sickle-Cell Anaemia

I have included a discussion of sickle-cell anemia because it is both painful and serious for some children, and most teachers don't know much about it. It is a serious, chronic, inherited condition that occurs mainly among blacks (Shirah & Brennan, 1990). It also

---

*From "Epilepsy," published by the Epilepsy Foundation of America, 4351 Garden City Dr., Landover, MD 20785.

occurs in some other populations; for example, some Turkish and Greek youngsters and those of Italian (primarily Sicilian) stock can also be afflicted (Gaston, 1990).

Because it confers immunity for certain types of malaria, possession of this condition has been a biological advantage for some African peoples, but in North America, where malaria is not prevalent, the advantages are far outweighed by the disadvantages.

Teachers should understand there is a difference between having the sickle-cell trait and being afflicted with sickle-cell anaemia. Those who carry the trait as part of their genetic heritage do not necessarily experience this condition. Possession of the trait is harmless. It is only when a child inherits the trait from both parents that it becomes dominant and that the anaemia develops. In the United States it is estimated that 1 in 400 black children is born with sickle-cell anaemia (Gaston, 1990).

This serious disorder is not infectious and cannot be "caught." It is incurable at present and causes much pain and misery, but it *can* be treated. As in other anaemias, the child may lack energy and tire easily. When people have this condition, their red blood cells become sickle-shaped rather than round (hence the name), and painful episodes occur when these red cells stiffen because of lack of oxygen and stack up in small blood vessels. The plugging up of capillaries then deprives surrounding cellular tissues of oxygen. This is termed a *vaso-occlusive crisis,* and it may occur in various parts of the body. Depending on where it happens, the individual may have severe abdominal pain or an enlarged spleen, or the brain, liver, kidneys, lungs, or eyes may be affected. Children under age three are particularly likely to experience swollen hands and feet. Young children suffering from this condition are often characterized by a barrel-shaped chest, an enlarged, protruding abdomen, and thin arms and legs (Lin-Fu, 1978). They have little ability to resist infections. Sometimes, for unknown reasons, production of red blood cells stops altogether (aplastic crisis). Symptoms of this include increased lethargy, rapid heart rate, weakness, fainting, and paleness of the lining of the eyelids (Leavitt, 1981). *(If this occurs at school, the family and the doctor should be notified because this condition requires immediate medical attention.)*

Children who have been diagnosed as suffering from sickle-cell anaemia must be under regular care by their physician. The teacher can help by encouraging families to keep medical appointments and by carefully carrying out the doctor's recommendations at school. These may include prohibiting vigorous exercise, since lowered oxygen levels increase the likelihood of a vaso-occlusive attack. Such youngsters tend to drink more water than most children do and so may need to urinate more frequently. Careful, early attention should also be paid to cold symptoms because these youngsters are very vulnerable to pneumonia and influenza (Shirah & Brennan, 1990).

Because the condition is inherited, parents sometimes ask advice on whether they should have more children. This question is a ticklish one to answer and is best referred to their physician for discussion.

Other Physical Problems

In general, the teacher should watch for pronounced changes in the physical appearance of every child and, in particular, should take notice of children who are excessively pale or who convey a general air of exhaustion or lassitude. These conditions often develop so gradually that parents are unaware of the change. It is especially important to watch a child with care during the week or two after she has returned from a serious illness, such as measles, chicken pox, scarlet fever, or meningitis, since occasional potentially serious problems develop following such infections.

Guidelines for Working with Physically Challenged Children

Since physical disabilities range from blindness to cerebral palsy, it is, of course, impossible to discuss each condition in detail here. The references at the end of the chapter provide further information on particular problems.

The suggestions already included apply to these children. A physically challenged youngster should be treated as typically as possible, and she should be neither overprotected nor underprotected. Conferences with her physician, physical therapist, or other specialist can help the staff ascertain the degree of protection and motivation that is necessary.

The teacher who bears these guidelines in mind and approaches each situation pragmatically will find it relatively simple to deal with children who have physical handicaps. Also, parents are often gold-mines of practical advice about how to help the child effectively, and their information, combined with the fresh point of view provided by the centre staff, can usually solve problems if they arise.

೨ Identifying and Helping Children Who Have Emotional Difficulties

Signs of Emotional Disturbance That Indicate a Referral Is Needed

Deciding when referral for emotional disturbance is warranted and when it is unnecessary can be a difficult problem, because symptoms of emotional upset are common during early childhood (Bower, 1981). One study, for example, found that the average child of nursery school age manifested between four and six "behaviour" problems and that they seemed to appear and disappear over a period of time (Macfarlane, 1943). A good child care centre environment can accomplish wonders with children who are emotionally upset, and many physicians routinely refer children who are having emotional difficulties to nursery schools or centres because they have witnessed many happy results from such referrals.

There may come a time, however, when the staff begins to question whether the centre environment, no matter how supportive, can offer sufficient help to a particular youngster. Perhaps after a reasonable period for adjustment and learning, she persists in "blowing her stack" over relatively inconsequential matters, or perhaps she insists on spending most of each morning hidden within the housekeeping corner or even crouched beneath a table. These behaviours, to name only two of a much wider list of possibilities, should arouse feelings of concern in the staff, since they are examples of behaviour that is too extreme, happens too often, and persists too long.

The teacher should also apply a fourth criterion when considering the necessity of a referral: whether the number and variety of symptoms manifested by the child at any one period are excessive. We have seen that signs of upset are common and often disappear either spontaneously or as a result of adequate handling by parents and teachers. Occasionally, though, a child will exhibit several reactions at the same time. She may begin to wet her bed again, be unable to fall asleep easily, insist on always having her blanket with her, cry a great deal, and refuse to play. When a cluster of these behaviours occur together, it is time for the staff to admit their limitations of time and training and to encourage the family to seek the advice of a qualified psychologist or psychiatrist.

Early Infantile Autism: A Special Case

From time to time the preschool teacher is still likely to come across children who seem truly out of the ordinary. A family may enrol a youngster who can generally be described in the following terms: She pays scant attention to other children or adults and seems emotionally distant and uninvolved; it is difficult or impossible to get her to look the person speaking to her in the eye; she may become very distressed when asked to change from one activity to another (for example, she may fly into a panic when asked to stop swinging and go inside for snack); her speech may be minimal or nonexistent; she may repeat phrases in a meaningless way; and she may show a marked interest in things that spin or twirl, such as a tricycle wheel, which she may sit by and spin absorbedly, or a spoon, which she will twirl with great skill (Howlin, 1986; Kanner, 1944). When several of these symptoms occur together, the youngster may be suffering from infantile autism. This condition is rare, occurring in approximately two to four people per 10 000 (Silver & Hagin, 1990).

With such unusual symptoms, it may be surprising that the teacher may be the first person who realizes how unusual this combination of behaviours is. (In my thirty years of working with children, I have come across eight such youngsters—none previously identified as unusual except by their concerned parents, and sometimes not even by them.) Treatment is difficult, and *these youngsters need highly professional help as soon as they can get it.* Therefore, the family should be urged to seek help from a child psychiatrist or psychologist promptly.

Parents and teachers wonder a good deal about the causes of this condition because the behaviour can be so unusual. Although included here in the category of emotional disturbance, research now indicates that the underlying cause of infantile autism is a disruption in the development of the brain. This has been traced to a variety of factors. Among these are rubella or other viral infections during pregnancy, phenylketonuria (PKU), genetically regulated disturbances, and many additional, yet-to-be-ascertained physiological insults or developmental anomalies (Farber, 1991). This is valuable information to remember because it takes away a lot of the mystery and the possible tendency to blame parents. However, much more remains to be learned about this unusual condition, and working with autistic children continues to be an exceedingly difficult challenge for their parents and teachers (Silver & Hagin, 1990).

Guidelines for Working with Emotionally Disturbed Children

Even though teachers may not have a youngster who is chronically disturbed in their school, it is certain they will have to deal with children who are at least temporarily upset from time to time. These upsets may be as minor as occasional emotional outbursts or as major as a child who weeps frantically when she comes to school, refuses to eat anything, and is unable to lose herself in play.

Adults often discount the effect of important family crises on young children, either assuming that the children do not understand or that they simply are not aware of what is going on; but this is far from the truth. Children are sensitive to the emotional climate of the home, and although they may draw incorrect conclusions about the reasons for the unhappiness, they are almost always aware that something is going on and are likely to respond with a variety of coping mechanisms.

There are many causes of such disturbances, including hospitalization of the child or of a family member, desertion by one of the parents, a death in the family, divorce, the birth of a sibling, moving from one home to another, a mother going to work, a father losing his job, or chronic alcoholism or involvement with drugs by a family member. Even something as relatively innocuous as a long visit from a grandparent can be upsetting to the child if it becomes an occasion for disturbances in routine or for dissension.*

The teacher should watch for any pronounced change in children's behaviour, as well as signs of withdrawal, inability to give or receive affection, reduced ability to play either by themselves or with other children, reduced interest in conversation, aggressive acting out, marked preoccupation with a particular activity or topic, and extreme emotional responses, such as bursting into tears or temper tantrums. He should also notice the usual signs of tension commonly seen in young children who are upset: whining, bed wetting, increased fretfulness and irritability, hair twisting, thumb sucking, stuttering, an increased dependence on security symbols such as blankets or toy animals, and so forth.

Teachers should realize that these behaviours are not reprehensible and that it is not desirable for them to concentrate their energy on removing them from the child's repertoire. They *are* signals that the child is suffering from some kind of stress either at home or school and that this should be looked into and mitigated.

Short-Term Techniques

First, a note of caution is in order. When a child who has been getting along well at school suddenly falls apart, it is always best to consider whether the upset could be due to physical illness. Many an inexperienced teacher has spent a sleepless night over such a child only to have her mother call and report chicken pox the next morning.

Make a special point of offering tension-relieving activities to the youngster who is upset. The best of these is water play in a relaxed atmosphere in which the child can have her clothing well protected or can change afterward into something dry. Mud, dough, and soft clay can also be helpful, as are the sublimated activities listed in the chapter on aggression.

Relax standards somewhat in order to take stress off the child. This does not mean that anything goes; it does mean that the teacher should ease the child's way through the day with only the more important demands enforced. In other words, he should take the pressure off when he can without creating additional insecurity by letting the child get away with murder.

---

*For a more detailed discussion of handling specific crisis situations, the reader is referred to chapter 8, "Tender Topics: Helping Children Master Emotional Crises."

Talk things over with the family and work with them to identify what may be generating the upset in the child. Discussing a child's emotional problems requires a delicate touch to avoid the impression the teacher is prying into personal matters that are none of his business, but the insight gained from such discussions can provide valuable information that enable the teacher to draw the child out and express in play or words what is troubling her. Increased understanding of the cause will help the teacher be more tolerant of the child's behaviour. He may also be able to offer some helpful counselling resources for the family to explore or may sometimes offer help himself by listening and assisting the parents in clarifying alternative ways to solve the difficulty.

Help the child work through her feelings by furnishing opportunities to use dolls, puppets, and dramatic play to express her concern. For example, a child who has been through a term of hospitalization may delight in using a doctor's kit and administering shots to dolls or other children with spirited malevolence. When such play is combined with the teacher's perceptive comments that recognize how frightened and angry the child is, this activity can do a world of good.

✑ *The opportunity to play out feelings harmlessly is worthwhile for children. Believe it or not, this is not real rage—just an intense game of "monster."*

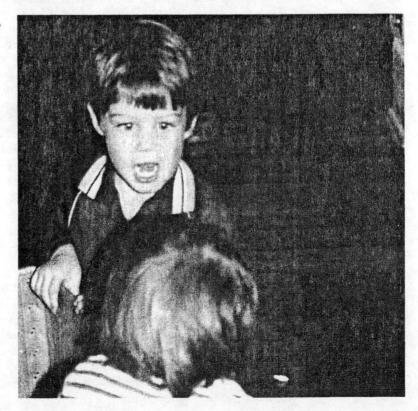

Long-Term Techniques with Youngsters Who Are Severely Disturbed

There are a few fortunate communities that offer special preschool experiences for children categorized as chronically disturbed. However, because such opportunities are still rare and because these children profit from inclusion in at least half-day school, it is desirable for preprimary teachers to offer this special service whenever they feel they can manage it. Apart from treating psychotic children, who generally require a specialized environment that allows more one-to-one contact combined with special expertise, there is nothing particularly mysterious about providing care for more severely disturbed youngsters. What it really takes to make such a placement turn out successfully is common sense, patience, a steady temperament, determination, faith in oneself, and faith that the child and her family will be able to change.

Treat the chronically disturbed child as much like the other children as possible, and use her strengths to bring her into the life of the group. In my school one boy who was unable to talk with either children or adults loved using the large pushbroom and spent many hours sweeping sand off the tricycle track. The first words he ever used at school grew out of this participation when, after weeks of sweeping, he yelled at one of the children who had bumped into his broom, "You just stay outta my way or I'll pop you one!" Once the sound barrier was broken, this youngster became increasingly verbal and was able to move on to kindergarten with reasonable success.

Anticipate that progress will be uneven. Children who are chronically disturbed may move ahead in an encouraging way and then suddenly backslide. This should not be cause for despair. If she progressed once, she will do it again, and probably faster the second time. It is, of course, desirable to identify and ameliorate the reason for the regression if this can be discerned.

Provide support for those who are working with the child. The staff members who make the decision to include a severely disturbed child will also require many opportunities to meet together and discuss the child's behaviour. This is important so that consistency can be maintained in the way she is handled, so that everyone's insights and information can be pooled together, and so that group decisions on what should be done next can be made.

Working with such youngsters requires stamina and the ability to take a long-term perspective. It also requires enough staff so that someone can be spared as needed when the child flies off the handle. At the end of an exhausting day a touch of humour—but never in the sense of ridicule or denigration of the child—can help staff maintain perspective and provide the sense of camaraderie needed when people are under stress.

Draw on the advice of specialists and encourage the family to continue to do this. A child who is disturbed often comes to the program because she has been referred by a specialist. A regular arrangement for calling and reporting progress to the expert, invitations to him or her to come and visit the program, and perhaps some written reports during the year should be part of the teacher's professional obligation when he agrees to enrol a youngster who is chronically disturbed. Needless to say, the specialists who make such referrals should be willing to discharge their responsibilities by guiding the teacher when he requires their help.

❧ *Identifying and Helping Children Who Have Delayed or Advanced Mental Ability*

Children with Developmental Lags

All teachers of young children need to know enough about developmental sequences and the ages at which behavioural milestones can be anticipated that they can tell when a child is developing normally or when she is lagging markedly behind her peers or is quite advanced for her age. Lists of developmental standards have been included in many chapters in this book, not with the intention of urging developmental conformity, but in the hope that they will help the teacher be tolerant of behaviours characteristic of various ages and also alert to children who are developing so far out of phase that they require special help. Appendix C also provides a chart of developmental guidelines.

Many preprimary teachers do not recognize cognitive delay when they see it. Being unaware of the exceptionality can be an advantage in a way, since it means that a child is not stuck with a stereotyped reaction to her condition or burdened with an undesirable label. On the other hand, it may also mean that an undiagnosed, slow-learning four-year-old who is actually operating at a two-and-a-half-year-old level may be expected to sit with the other four-year-olds for long stories she does not comprehend or may be criticized and disciplined for refusing to share equipment when actually she is behaving in a way typical of her developmental but not chronological age. An adequate diagnosis would enable the teacher to match his expectations to the child's real level of ability.

Behaviour that should be cause for concern includes a widespread pattern of delayed development that is a year or more behind the typical in physical, social, and intellectual areas. Such lags are usually accompanied by speech that is obviously immature for the child's chronological age.

Causes of slow development are numerous, ranging from chromosomal disorders to pseudoretardation induced by an insufficiently stimulating environment, and it is often impossible even for specialists to determine why the child is developing slowly. For example, Weiss and Weisz (1986) state that "at present there are several hundred known causes of mental retardation; many professionals, however, believe this to be only a fraction of the total number of actual causes" (p. 357).

The simplicity and adaptability of the preschool curriculum mean that many mildly or moderately delayed children can fit comfortably into that environment. Some, of course, require more specialized educational services. Since children who are truly retarded do not outgrow their condition or ultimately catch up with their more fortunate peers, it is necessary for teachers and parents to come to a realistic understanding of what can be expected of them. Knowledgeable specialists can provide many helpful suggestions about how to maximize learning for these youngsters.

Guidelines for Working with Children Who Are Cognitively Delayed

Cognitive delay, sometimes termed *mental retardation*, is defined as "significantly subaverage intellectual functioning resulting in or associated with concurrent impairments in adaptive behaviour and manifested during the developmental period" (Grossman, 1983, p. 11).

The severity of the condition varies widely; children who are mildly or moderately affected are the best prospects for inclusion in children's centres. The child who is mildly delayed will probably fit so easily into a program serving a heterogeneous age group that no special recommendations are necessary other than reminding the teacher to see the child in terms of her actual developmental level rather than her chronological age.

The moderately affected child will also often fit comfortably into the heterogeneous centre, but many teachers find it helpful to have a clear understanding of the most worthwhile educational goals for these children and also to understand some simple principles for teaching them most effectively.

Basic learning goals for a moderately delayed preschool youngster should centre on helping her to be as independent as possible, which includes learning simple self-help skills as well as learning to help other people by doing simple tasks; helping the child develop language skills; and helping her learn to get along with other children in an acceptable way.

These goals are really no different from those that are part of the regular curriculum. The only differences are that the child who is developing more slowly will be farther behind other children of her age and that she will need a simpler manner of instruction. Children who learn slowly should not be confused with a lot of talk and shadings of meaning. *They need concrete examples, definite rules, and consistent reinforcement of desired behaviour.* In general, the bywords with these children are keep it concrete, keep it simple, keep it fun, and be patient.

Some specific suggestions may also help the teacher:

1. As much as possible, treat the child as you would treat all children in the group, but exercise common sense so that you expect neither too much nor too little.

2. Know the developmental steps so that you understand what she should learn next as she progresses.

3. Remember that children with cognitive delays learn best what they repeat frequently. Be prepared to go over a simple rule or task many times until the child has it firmly in mind. (This need for patient repetition is one of the things inexperienced teachers may find most irritating, particularly when the child has appeared to grasp the idea just the day before. Don't give up hope; if the teaching is simple and concrete enough, she will eventually learn.)

4. Pick out behaviour to teach that the child can use all her life; that is, try to teach ways of behaving that will be appropriate for an older as well as a younger child to use. For example, don't let her run and kiss everyone she meets, since this will not be acceptable when she is just a little older. She has enough to do without having to unlearn old behaviour (Odom, McConnell, McEvoy, 1992).

5. Take it easy. Give short directions, one point at a time.

6. Allow sufficient time for her to accomplish a selected task. Complex things take longer; simpler things take less time.

7. Encourage the child to be persistent by keeping tasks simple and satisfying. This will encourage her to finish what she starts.

8. Remember that independence is an important goal. Make sure the child is not being overprotected.

9. Teach one thing at a time. For instance, teach her to feed herself, then to use a napkin, then to pour her milk.

10. Provide lots of concrete experience that uses as many of the senses as possible.

11. Don't rely on talking as the primary means of instruction. Show the child what you mean whenever possible by modelling it.

12. Encourage the development of speech. Wait for at least some form of verbal reply whenever possible. Gently increase the demand for a "quality" response as her skills increase.

13. *Remember that these children are just as sensitive to the emotional climate around them as ordinary children are.* Therefore, never talk about a child in front of her. It is likely that she will at least pick up the sense of what you are saying, and this may hurt her feelings badly.

14. Show the child you are pleased with her and that you like her.

15. After a fair trial at learning something new, if she cannot seem to learn it, drop the activity without recrimination. Try it again in a few months; she may be ready to learn it by then.

There is much to be said for the value of step-by-step, prescriptive teaching for children with cognitive delays in particular. This requires careful identification of the present level of the child's skills as well as knowledge of the appropriate next step. Knowledge and application of behaviour modification techniques can be very helpful when working with some of these youngsters (Rojahn, Hammer, & Marshburn, 1993).

Intellectually Gifted Children

Although the child who is slow to learn has received special attention for several decades, it is only during the past few years that intellectually gifted preschoolers have received any attention at all. Why this should be the case is hard to understand. Surely such promising children deserve the interest and support of their teachers. Perhaps they are overlooked because many of them fit smoothly into the centre curriculum (although it may present insufficient challenges for them), or perhaps most preschool teachers are uncertain about what kinds of behaviour indicate outstanding mental ability and thus fail to identify the children.

A child with exceptional mental ability usually exhibits a general pattern of advanced skills, but not always. Sometimes the pattern is quite spotty or its manifestations may vary from day to day (Lewis & Louis, 1991).

In general, a gifted child may exhibit some or all of the following skills: She learns quickly and easily; her language is more elaborate and extended than that of other children of the same age and her vocabulary is likely to be large; her attention span may be longer if her interest is aroused; she grasps ideas easily; she probably possesses an exceptional amount of general information, which is characterized not only by more variety but also by greater detail. Gifted preschoolers like to pursue reasons for things, talk about cause-and-effect relationships, and compare and draw conclusions. They are particularly sensitive to social values and the behaviour of those around them. They are often almost insatiably interested in special subjects that appeal to them. Some of them already know how to read. They may prefer the company of older children or adults.

Children who have disabilities and those who come from minority groups tend to be overlooked to an even greater extent than others as possibly being gifted children (Karnes & Johnson, 1991; Barclay & Benelli, 1994; Maker, 1989).

Teachers who do not build their curriculum and increase its complexity sufficiently during the year may find that gifted children become increasingly restless and gradually get into difficulties because they have lost interest in what is happening at school. Teachers who meet this challenge and deal with it satisfactorily modify the curriculum so that it meets the needs of these youngsters by adding more difficult and interesting learning activities. Some suggestions for accomplishing this are offered next.

Teaching Preschool Children Who Are Mentally Gifted

Although there have been many interesting investigations of intellectual giftedness and education, ranging from Terman and coauthors (1925) to Marland (1972), these have focused on older children and adults, and the possibility of educating intellectually gifted preschool children is just beginning to receive the attention it deserves (Karnes & Johnson, 1989; Reis, 1989; Stile et al., 1993). Yet it is obvious that children of exceptional mental ability must be present in this portion of the population since they exist at an older age. However, it is still the case that when I raise the question of making special provision for such youngsters at the preschool level, many of my students and teaching colleagues appear bewildered at this possibility.*

Perhaps this is because we have fought a battle against undue intellectual pressure on young children for so long that we forget that gifted children thrive when provided with additional stimulation and that we may be cheating them when we deprive them of it. Of course, gifted children should not be treated as precocious little adults or worshipped because of their special talents, but they should be provided with stimulating things to learn while at the same time keeping their social and emotional life as natural and easy as possible.

The provision of an enriched curriculum does not necessarily mean that the teacher must teach the child to read, although about 25% of children who are gifted already know how to read before they enter kindergarten (Cassidy & Vukelich, 1980). I will never forget my surprise when one of the bright lights in my school wandered into my office, picked up a plain bound book from my desk and commented, "Hmmmmm, this looks interesting—*All About Dinosaurs.* Can I borrow this?" (I let him.)

What the teacher *can* do is make sure such children have plenty of opportunities to pursue subjects that interest them in as much depth as they desire. It is important to avoid the trap of thinking to oneself, "Oh, well, *they* wouldn't be able to do *that*." It is astonishing what such children can do if they are provided with encouragement and

---

*Giftedness, of course, is expressed in many different forms (Karnes & Johnson, 1989), such as in the self-expressive giftedness of creative artists or the physical giftedness of talented athletes. Because ways of fostering such aspects of the child's abilities are covered in other chapters, this discussion will be limited to the giftedness of the intellectually superior preschooler.

materials. For example, I once had two young students, a boy and a girl, who were interested in the weather. They went from this to an interest in temperature and how heat makes thermometers work. Of course, all the children were interested in this subject to an extent, but these two youngsters, who later proved to be gifted, were truly absorbed. Their investigations included breaking open a thermometer to discover what it was made of, collecting different kinds of thermometers to see if they all worked the same way and if they all measured the same kinds of things, and even working out a number scale with drawings to show the range of temperatures measured by different instruments.

Preschool children who are intellectually gifted often love discussion that focuses on "What would happen if . . . ?" or "How could we . . . ?" These questions require creative reasoning as well as transforming old information into new solutions. Asking them to evaluate the potential results of these ideas, if done sensitively so they do not feel crushed, will give them even wider scope for their talents.

These children will also relish the more difficult activities suggested in the chapters on mental development since these activities can be adjusted to their level of ability and thus sustain their interest. (For readers who wish to have more detailed information on how to teach gifted children, the book by Shore, Cornell, Robinson, and Ward (1991), entitled *Recommended Practices in Gifted Education,* is recommended.) Perhaps a few examples of some specific ways of enriching the curriculum for them will best illustrate how to accomplish this.*

Investigate how things work, either by close observation or by taking them apart and reassembling them. A music box, a vacuum cleaner and all its parts, a Christmas tree stand, a flashlight, an old bicycle, and so forth can be offered.

Build additional language skills. Make a time to read books to the child that are longer and have more detail in them than picture books do. After story time, have a special discussion with her. Encourage her to expound on the stories that were just read— were they true? Has she ever had a similar or opposite experience? What did she like or dislike about the story? What would she have done differently if it had been her? Encourage the child to do most of the talking, and try to introduce new vocabulary. Select several pictures from the picture file, and ask the child to link them together by telling you a story about them—or allow her to select the pictures.

Offer more complex materials or advanced information. A good example of this is the use of more difficult puzzles. Cube puzzles can be used to reproduce particular patterns, or jigsaw puzzles can be offered rather than only the framed wooden ones typical of nursery schools. On a library trip take the child to the older children's section and help her find books on a particular subject in which she is interested.

Offer an enriched curriculum in the area of science. Be prepared to allow for expanded scientific activities. For example, provide vinegar for testing for limestone in

*My thanks to former nursery school majors at Santa Barbara City College for these suggestions.

various materials such as tiles, building materials, and so forth. Or explore the concept of time. The child could learn to identify specific hours on the clock and take responsibility for telling the teacher when it is snack time. Talk about ways of keeping track of time— perhaps help the child make a simple sundial with a stick, letting her mark the spot where the shadow falls when it is group time or time to go home. See if that spot stays at the same place over several weeks. Encourage the child to seek out people who speak different languages to tell her the names of different times of day in their own tongue. Visit a clock shop and write down for her all the kinds of clocks she sees there.

Note that language activities are particularly dear to these preschoolers. They enjoy more advanced stories than average children do and also can put their superior ability to work by concocting tales of their own that are almost invariably complex, detailed, and advanced in vocabulary. An interesting example of this is the book *Barbara* (McCurdy, 1966), which begins with the writings of an intensely gifted four-year-old and continues through her young adulthood. Discussion and conversation should be employed at every opportunity to allow these children to put their ideas into words and to test them against the ideas of other people.

Above all, the use of instructional methods that foster problem solving and encourage development of creative ideas should be employed (Barclay & Benelli, 1994). How can everyday items be put to new uses? How can old problems be solved in new ways? Here, once again, the value of asking pertinent questions and providing rich opportunities for children to propose answers and test them out, to see if they are correct, must be emphasized. I refer the reader to chapter 21, "Using the Emergent Approach to Foster Creativity in Thought," for suggestions on how to go about doing this.

🕉 Summary

Teachers who work with an exceptional preschool child must seek all the information they can on her particular condition if they really want to be effective teachers. This chapter can do no more than scratch the surface.

There are increasing numbers of courses in exceptionality being offered by schools of education, as in-service training, and by university extension units as the general trend toward including exceptional children in regular public school classes gains ground. In addition to these courses, books are also available, and many are listed in the references at the end of this chapter.

Societal support for inclusion of children with special needs means that help for young children with disabilities is more readily available than it was in the past, that many more children who have disabilities will be attending "regular" early childhood centres, and that preschool teachers will become part of the treatment teams responsible for working with such children.

Early childhood teachers have two main responsibilities they owe to children who have special needs. First, they must serve as screening agents and help identify possible problems (physical, emotional, or mental) that have escaped the attention of the physician. Following identification of a difficulty, teachers should attempt to effect a referral to the appropriate specialist.

Second, they must do all they can to integrate children with special problems into their group. This requires careful assessment before admission and flexibility of adjustment following entrance to school. It is vital that they treat the exceptional child as typically as possible and encourage her independence without demanding skills that lie beyond her ability. Specific suggestions for working with physically handicapped, emotionally disturbed, cognitively delayed, and intellectually gifted preschool children conclude the chapter.

Questions and Activities

1. Do you feel it is generally wise to suggest medication as a means of controlling hyperactivity in children? Why or why not?

2. This chapter makes a strong case for the early identification of potentially handicapping disorders. What are the real disadvantages of labelling children as being *different*? What are some ways to obtain help for such youngsters without stigmatizing them at the same time?

3. What do you feel accounts for the fact that very intelligent children are often overlooked at the preschool level? Might the provision of a special curriculum for them result in precocity and overintellectualization, thereby spoiling their childhood?

4. *Problem:* You have a four-and-a-half-year-old girl attending your school who is cognitively delayed and functions at about the two-and-a-half-year-old level. She hangs around the housekeeping corner and the blocks a lot, but the children push her aside. One of them, in particular, makes a point of saying, "She can't play here. Her nose is snotty, and she talks dumb." (There is more than a modicum of truth in this.) What would you do?

5. *Problem:* You have a four-year-old boy in your group who has a heart condition. In addition to looking somewhat pale, he is not supposed to exert himself by climbing or other vigorous exercise, which, of course, he yearns to do. He is well liked by the other children, who invite him frequently to climb around and play with them. What would you do?

Self-Check Questions For Review
Content-Related Questions

1. What is one of the most important services preprimary teachers can provide for young children?

2. List some symptoms that should alert the teacher to the possibility that a child might need to have her eyes examined.

3. What is it, basically, that sets the hyperactive child apart from other young children?

4. If a child had a *generalized tonic clonic seizure* in your room, what would you do to help her? What about the other children?

5. What is sickle-cell anaemia? Is it contagious? What does the teacher need to know about when to call the physician? What symptoms should he be aware of?

6. What are the guidelines for deciding when to refer a child who seems to be emotionally disturbed for outside help? What behaviours might signal that the child has possible autistic tendencies? What are some guidelines teachers may use when working with emotionally disturbed children?

7. What kinds of behaviours might alert a teacher to the possibility that a child could be developing more slowly than normal? What are some practical things to remember when teaching such a child?

8. Describe some behaviours that might signal to a teacher that a four-year-old is intellectually gifted. Suggest some ways the teacher could adjust the curriculum to meet the needs of that youngster.

9. Explain some important steps in making a referral when a child has a special problem.

10. What are some general principles for working with exceptional children?

Integrative Questions

1. The book states that teachers should "see through the exceptional to the typical in every child." Explain how doing this could be an antidote for either expecting too much or too little from the youngster with a disability.

3. It is important for teachers and parents of all children to remain in close contact. Using the example of a special need, give an example of something a parent might share with the teacher that would be helpful. Now, give an example of something the teacher could share with the parent. Be as specific as possible.

4. *Problem:* Jody, a two-and-a-half-year-old, has been in the next-door teacher's classroom for three months and does not talk at all. At lunch the teacher tells you that she arranged a conference with the parents to tell them she thinks that Jody is mentally retarded. Analyse all the elements of this situation and explain why you would or would not agree that she has done the right thing.

5. Many people are confused about the difference between children who are termed *emotionally disturbed* and those termed *developmentally delayed*. Explain the similarities and differences between these conditions.

References for Further Reading

Introductions to the Field

Allen, E., Paasche, C., Cornell, A. & Engel, M. (1994). *Exceptional children: Inclusion in early childhood programs* (1st Can. ed.). Scarborough, ON: Nelson Canada. This book provides early childhood educators with the information and skills necessary to effectively integrate children with special needs into existing programs. Included is a chapter to facilitate positive behaviours.

Chandler, P. S. (1994). *A place for me: Including children with special needs in early care and education settings.* Washington, DC: National Association for the Education of Young Children. Chandler provides a simple introduction suitable for early childhood teachers anticipating their first encounters with children who have disabilities. She provides an outstanding list of support organizations.

Derman-Sparks, L., & the ABC Task Force. (1989). *Anti-bias curriculum: Tools for empowering young children.* Washington, DC: National Association for the Education of Young Children. Bias, of course, occurs against children with disabilities as well as in other situations. Derman-Sparks provides a practical approach to dealing with this problem at the preschool level.

Irwin, S. H. (1993). *The special book: On the road to mainstream child care.* Sydney, NS: Breton Books. This book identifies strategies for integration.

Katz, L. G. (1994). All about me. In K. M. Paciorek & J. H. Munro (Eds.), *Early childhood education, 93/94.* Guilford, CT: Dushkin. Katz makes clear the difference between encouraging narcissism in young children and building genuine self-confidence and self-esteem. A not-to-be-missed article.

Paasche, C., Gorrill, L., & Strom, B. (1990). *Children with special needs in early childhood settings: Identification, intervention, mainstreaming.* Don Mills, ON: Addison-Wesley Canada. This handbook of fundamental skills and knowledge is for educators concerned with early intervention. In contains strategies for behavioural, social, and emotional problems.

Trister Dodge, D. (1993). *Places for ALL children: Building environments for differing needs.* Child Care Information Exchange, 93, 40–44. Recommendations for practical overall approaches to working with children with differing needs are included here.

Winzer, M. (1993). *Children with exceptionalities: A Canadian perspective* (3rd ed.). Scarborough, ON: Prentice Hall Canada.

Advice on Particular Disabilities

Bailey, D. B., & Wolery, M. (1992). *Teaching infants and preschoolers with disabilities* (2nd ed.). Englewood Cliffs, NJ: Merrill/Prentice Hall. Preschool teachers will find the detailed suggestions on teaching children with various disabilities to be concrete, practical, and helpful. Of particular usefulness is the chapter on room arrangement, and the one stressing the value of careful assessment. *Highly recommended.*

Batshaw, M. L., & Perret, Y. M. (1992). *Children with disabilities: A medical primer* (3rd ed.). Baltimore: Paul Brookes. This first-rate book offers concise overviews of normal physiological functions as well as descriptions of associated problems. The emphasis on practicality makes this reference a must for every centre library.

Canadian Institute of Child Health (1994). *The health of Canada's children* (2nd ed.). Ottawa: CICH. This report provides a profile of Canadian children and youth with disabilities, with many charts and a discussion of strategies needed to improve the situation.

Cook. R. E., Tessier, A., & Klein, M. D. (1992). *Adapting early childhood curriculum for children with special needs* (3rd ed.). Englewood Cliffs, NJ: Merrill/Prentice Hall. This textbook provides a rich resource of references and carefully assembled tables of information. It presents a description of what is generally accepted as sound preschool teaching and combines that philosophy with general information about teaching children with special needs.

Kaiser, B., & Rasminsky, J. K. (1993). Telling parents their child needs help. *Interaction: Publication of the Canadian Child Care Federation, 6*(4), 13–14. This article is filled with sound advice about how to make a referral. *Highly recommended.*

Transdisciplinary Team Collaboration

Bricker, D., & Cripe, J. J. W. (1992). *An activity based approach to early intervention.* Baltimore, MD: Paul Brookes. Bricker's and Cripe's book is replete with examples of ways practice in various skills can be integrated into the typical preschool day. Long-term advocates of this method, they suggest using a combination of child-initiated, teacher-planned, and routine activities for such instruction. *Highly recommended.*

Raver, S. A. (1991). *Strategies for teaching at-risk and handicapped infants and toddlers: A trandisciplinary approach.* Englewood Cliffs, NJ: Merrill/Prentice Hall. Although Raver's book emphasizes educational aspects of working with very young children, she also includes general information on a wide range of disabilities together with practical recommendations that apply to the preschool level. The book provides rich examples of ways team members can work together to benefit the child and her family.

Especially for Parents

Trainer, M. (1991). *Differences in common: Straight talk on mental retardation, Down Syndrome, and life.* Rockville, MD: Woodbine House. This is a sensitive but unsentimental collection of essays about growing up with a child with Down syndrome. *Highly recommended.*

Winton, P. J., Turnbull, A. P., & Blacher, J. (1984). *Selecting a preschool: A guide for parents of handicapped children.* Baltimore: University Park Press. As the title indicates, this book is for parents. It provides sensible, in-depth discussions of all aspects of selecting a preschool that fits the individual needs of children with particular disabilities. *Highly recommended.*

For the Advanced Student

Atwater, J. B., Carta, J. J., Schwartz, I. K., & McConnell, S. R. (1994). Blending developmentally appropriate practice and early childhood special education: Redefining best practice to meet the needs of all children. In B. L. Mallory & R. S. New (Eds.), *Diversity and developmentally appropriate practice: Challenges for early childhood education.* New York: Teachers College Press. This sensible chapter builds bridges of understanding between the two disciplines by identifying points of agreement as well as possibly contradictory points of view.

Brown, R. T., & Reynolds, C. R. (1986). *Psychological perspectives on childhood exceptionality: A handbook.* New York: John Wiley & Sons. Information on general issues related to exceptionality and on specific handicaps is contained here. *Highly recommended.*

Capute, A. J., & Accardo, P. (Eds.). (n.d.). *Developmental disabilities in infancy and childhood.* Baltimore, MD: Paul Brookes. The first part of this book covers various issues and concerns related to working with children who have disabilities. The second portion provides valuable discussions of individual disabilities. *Highly recommended.*

Fuchs, D., & Fuchs, L. S. (1994). Inclusive schools movement and the radicalization of special education reform. *Exceptional Children, 6*(4), 294–309. The authors raise many problems and issues associated with merging special education with general education. They conclude by questioning the eventual success of that trend if it is taken to extremes.

Sexton, D., Snyder, P., Sharpton, W. R., & Stricklin, S. (1993). Infants and toddlers with special needs and their families. *Childhood Education, 69*(5), 278–286. This is the carefully documented position paper from the Association for Childhood Education International. It specifies what constitutes appropriate access, sound quality, and necessary preparation for personnel serving very young children who have special needs.

Task Force on Recommended Practices: Division for Early Childhood, Council for Exceptional Children. (1993). *DEC recommended practices: Indicators of quality in programs for infants and young children with special needs and their families.* Pittsburgh, PA: The Task Force. As the title implies, this publication specifies what constitutes best current practice when working with children who have disabilities. It is explicit and progressive in tone.

Wolery, M., Strain, P. S., & Bailey, D. B., Jr. (1992). Reaching potentials of children with special needs. In S. Bredekamp & T. Rosegrant (Eds.). *Reaching potentials: Appropriate curriculum and assessment for young children. Vol. I.* Washington, DC: National Association for the Education of Young Children. This chapter discusses integration from the other side of the fence—i.e., from the point of view of the early childhood teacher's philosophy.

Wolery, M., & Wilbers, J. S. (Eds.). (1994). *Including children with special needs in early childhood programs.* Washington, DC: National Association for the Education of Young Children. The monograph presents research stressing the need for teachers to collaborate with families and other support staff and provides a lot of very helpful, succinct advice. *Highly recommended.*

Other Resources of Particular Interest

Learning Disabilities Association of Canada (LDAC), 323 Chapel St., Ste. 200, Ottawa, ON K1N 7Z2. A national, nonprofit organization that seeks to advance the education, employment, social development, legal rights, and general well-being of people with learning disabilities.

SpeciaLink: The National Child Care Mainstream Network, 186 Prince St., Sydney, NS B1P 5K5. SpeciaLink is committed to an increase in the quality and quantity of child care mainstreaming in Canada, through research, advocacy, personal contact, and information. SpeciaLink has published a provincial and territorial Early Intervention Directory.

IV
Fostering Social Development

Developing Social Competence in Young Children

ॐ 10

This point was brought home to me by the comments of a distinguished Soviet psychologist, an expert on development during the preschool years. He had been observing in an American day-care center for children of working mothers. The center was conducted under university auspices and reflected modern outlooks and methods in early childhood education. It was therefore with some concern that I noted how upset my colleague was on his return.

"I wouldn't have believed it," he said, "if I hadn't seen it with my own eyes. There were four children sitting at a table, just as in our nurseries. But each was doing something different. What's more, I watched them for a whole ten minutes, and not once did any child help another one. They didn't even talk to each other. Each was busy in his own activity. You really are a nation of individualists."

Urie Bronfenbrenner

Peer relations contribute substantially to both social and cognitive development and to the effectiveness with which we function as adults. Indeed, the single best childhood predictor of adult adaptation is not school grades, and not classroom behavior, but rather, the adequacy with which the child gets along with other children.

Willard W. Hartup

*E*arly childhood is a time that can be rich in social learnings; it is a dynamic period characterized by many beginnings but few completely attained learnings in the development of social skills and interactions. Although the home is profoundly influential in this area, early childhood teachers can also make a valuable contribution to social development. Before pursuing important social goals for the young children in their care, however, teachers should review the developmental theories of social growth discussed here in order to help them understand what social behaviour to expect from the children.

৩ *Developmental Trends in Social Growth*

In the past, many people tended to view young children as generally self-centred human beings who were insensitive and uncaring about others. However, recent research now supports a more encouraging view of young children's nature. Prosocial behaviour—behaviour intended to help or benefit someone else—begins at an early age. For example, one study by Rheingold (1982) found that all the two-year-olds included in the research spontaneously helped their mothers complete at least one household chore within a twenty-five-minute period. Another study found that, although most helping behaviour in the nursery school happened because the teacher asked for it, during the observations two-thirds of the children also volunteered help of one sort or another (Eisenberg et al., 1987). Moreover, several longitudinal studies reveal that children who are prosocially inclined during the early years continue that behaviour as they become older and that children who are helpful in one situation are often (though not always) likely to be helpful in other situations (Eisenberg & Mussen, 1989).

Tables 10.1 and 10.2 summarize some of the many additional social behaviours characteristic of children at various ages.

How Do Children Become Socialized?

Although opinion remains divided about how children become socialized (Eisenberg & Mussen, 1989), social learning theory provides some matter-of-fact explanations of the way it comes about that are helpful for teachers to understand. That theory emphasizes that children learn to become like other people and to get along with them as a result of identifying with and imitating them and also by experiencing reinforcement for desirable social behaviours.

Considerable evidence indicates that children learn by observing grown-ups and other children and that, particularly if the person is nurturing and powerful, they will seek to be like the model and imitate his behaviour (Bandura, 1986). There is also evidence indicating that although children may be somewhat influenced by how people tell them they should behave, they are even more strongly influenced by actual modelling of desirable behaviour (Eisensen, 1992; Oliner, 1988). So it behooves teachers to model the behaviour they wish to encourage rather than just talking about it or, worse yet, preaching something they do not practise.

Research indicates that children also learn socially acceptable responses as a result of reinforcement either by adults or by peers (Grusek & Redler, 1980; Furman & Masters,

Table 10.1 Progress indicators of social development, first 3 years

Behaviour Item	Age Expected*
	Weeks
Responds to smiling and talking	6
Knows mother	12
Shows marked interest in father	14
Is sober with strangers	16
Withdraws from strangers	32
Responds to "bye-bye"	40
Responds to inhibitory words	52
Plays pat-a-cake	52
Waves "bye-bye"	52
	(Years, months)
Is no longer shy toward strangers	1, 3
Enjoys imitation of adult activities (smoking, etc.)	1, 3
Is interested in and treats another child like an object rather than a person	1, 6
Plays alone	1, 6
Brings things (slippers, etc.) to adult (father)	1, 6
Shows beginning of concept of private ownership	1, 9
Wishes to participate in household activities	1, 9
Has much interest in and watches other children	2
Begins parallel play	2
Is dependent and passive in relation to adults	2
Is shy toward strangers	2
Is not sociable; lacks social interest	2, 3
Is ritualistic in behaviour	2, 6
Is imperious, domineering	2, 6
Begins to resist adult influence; wants to be independent	2, 6
Is self-assertive; difficult to handle	2, 6
Is in conflict with children of own age	2, 6
Refuses to share toys; ignores requests	2, 6
Begins to accept suggestions	3
Has "we" feeling with mother	3
Likes to relive babyhood	3
Is independent of mother at nursery school	3
Tends to establish social contacts with adults	3
Shows imitative, "me too" tendency	3
Begins strong friendships with peer associates, with discrimination against others in group	3, 6

*As is true for all developmental charts, these ages should be regarded as approximate.

Source: Abridged from *The Longitudinal Study of Individual Development,* by L. H. Stott, 1955, Detroit: Merrill-Palmer Institute. © 1955 by the Merrill-Palmer Institute. Reprinted by permission.

Table 10.2 Progress indicators of social development, ages four through ten

Behaviour Item	Age Expected (Years)
Is assertive, boastful	4
Has definite preference for peer mates	4
Tries to gain attention; shows off	4
Tends to be obedient, cooperative; desires to please	5
Seeks approval; avoids disapproval of adults	5
Shows preference for children of his own age	5
Shows protective mothering attitude toward younger sibling	5
Is sensitive to parents' and others' moods, facial expressions	6
Has strong desire to be with father and do things together (especially true of boys)	6
Insists on being "first" in everything with peers	6
Bosses, teases younger siblings	6
Has rich capacity to "pretend" in social play	6
Shows compliance in family relations	7
Desires to be "good"	7
Begins to discriminate between sexes	7
Forms close friendships with one of the same sex; the age of "bosom pals"	8
Sex cleavage is definite; girls giggle, whisper; boys wrestle, "roughhouse"	9
The age of "clubs"	9
Sex differences are pronounced: girls show more poise, more folk wisdom, more interest in family, marriage, etc., and in their own personal appearance	10

Source: Abridged from *The Longitudinal Study of Individual Development,* by L. H. Stott, 1955, Detroit: Merrill-Palmer Institute. © 1955 by the Merrill-Palmer Institute. Reprinted by permission.

1980). This can be negative reinforcement in the form of punishment that may suppress behaviour (Parke, 1972), or positive reinforcement in the form of recognition, praise, approval, and admission to the group, or other positively reinforcing responses and satisfactions that come from without or within themselves. In addition, a study by Thompson (1944) shows that teachers can facilitate the development of some specific social behaviours by assuming an active, guiding role.

A differing point of view about how children become socialized has been contributed by the developmental interactionists typified by Piaget (1948), Kohlberg (1985), and Damon (1983). Supporters of this theory contend that, to exist successfully in the social world, the intricacies of learning require explanations that go far beyond the simplicities of reinforcement and modelling theory. They maintain that social development occurs as a result of interaction between people. The cognitive, intellectual learnings that result from the experience of that interaction coupled with maturation produce the widening range of social knowledge and skills necessary for social survival (Edwards & Ramsey, 1986).

It is not only interaction between adults and children, of course, that enhances such learning. Child-child interaction becomes of ever increasing importance during the early years as groups of children make it clear to their members that they favour positive, friendly behaviour and dislike aggression and selfishness (Hymel, Wagner, & Butler, 1990). Such groups rate socially competent children highly (Vaughn & Waters, 1980), and these attitudes, which are often frankly expressed, help shape the behaviour of the children in the group. Then, too, as children become four or five years old, they turn to their peers for help more frequently than to adults (Hartup, 1992). This aid seeking promotes additional opportunities for positive social interactions and learning to take place.

The quality of emotional attachment between mother and child is an additional important influence on socialization. Children who are closely attached to their mothers tend to be more compliant, that is, conform more readily to the wishes and instructions of their families (Honig 1985c) and are better liked and accepted by their peers (Sroufe, 1983). Securely attached children also tend to be more sensitive to other people's feelings (Ianotti, Zahn-Waxler, Cummings, & Milano, 1987).

Information about how socialization takes place continues to grow as new investigative techniques are employed to study this process. For example, an interesting addition to research strategies is being contributed by researchers taking the *ethnographic* approach. Rather than using questionnaires or doing experiments, ethnographers rely on observing and recording what is happening in a particular environment—a child care

❧   *Aram is yearning to join the fun but evidently needs to acquire the cultural passwords in order to be included.*

❧ RESEARCH STUDY ❧
Learning the Secret Passwords for Group Inclusion

Research Question: Kantor, Elgas, and Fernie used the ethnographic approach to find out why some children are welcomed into a group and others are rejected. They asked, "What is the difference between these youngsters?" and "What did the children have to understand about the culture of the group—i.e., what cultural passwords did the children need to know—in order to be admitted to membership?"

Research Method: The investigators chose to look at the culture of a particular friendship group of children operating in the context of a laboratory nursery school to investigate why two children were included in the group and a third youngster was not. The children within that group they selected to study were Bob, the leader of the group, Lisa, the only girl member, and William, who yearned to belong but did not.

For three-quarters of the year the investigators videotaped, took field notes, and used teachers' retrospective notes of free play episodes that involved the friendship group.

After all the information was collected, the next step in the analysis was *not* to look at how the three children were behaving. Instead, the play itself was analysed to find out what basic elements or ingredients were essential parts of that play. What elements did the children have to know about and participate in to be included? The researchers identified six ingredients: possession of certain objects (sticks and capes), use of objects in certain ways (pretend weapons), certain pretend roles (superhero, firefighter, etc.), certain kinds of language ("I'm a bad guy" etc.), exclusion of teachers, and mock intimidation of teachers.

After these essential cultural elements of the play were identified, participation by each of the three children was examined in relation to their incorporation of these elements in their play. This examination revealed that Bob, the leader, always used some of those elements. For example, he used object possession and use, role playing, and language appropriate for the play 100% of the time. Lisa's activity was similar to Bob's, particularly in regard to object possession and use, role playing, and appropriate language.

---

centre, for example (Rizzo, Corsaro, & Bates, 1992; Lubeck, 1985). Then they analyse the total context of what they have seen in order to construct meaningful interpretations of what is going on.

An example of this approach is provided in the research study in this chapter to show how ethnography can shed new light on individual and group social dynamics.

Implications for Teaching

As far as teachers of young children are concerned, both social learning theory and developmental interactionist theory have merit since both make it plain that teachers need to do more than sit idly by while the children grow and develop: Teachers should assume a role based on active teaching. Since one way children acquire social behaviours is by

On the other hand, William, the outsider, "rarely acted in tune with the group" (p. 139). He just did not seem able to figure out what the group's sociocultural expectations were. For example, although he realized that having a cape was an important aspect of the play, he would choose to play firefighter when the group was playing superhero, or use language that didn't fit the role. Moreover, rather than excluding the teachers, he tried to use them to help him enter the play. In other words, he was unable to crack the social password code.

Results and Conclusions: From an ethnographic point of view, the investigators concluded that, to be socially competent, William would have needed to understand not only that offering a prized object such as the sticks or wearing a cape was a way of obtaining admission to the group, but also how to use the sticks in play, how to act toward the teachers, and what to say while playing in order to be admitted.

Kantor, Elgas, and Fernie drew three more general conclusions from their research. In order to be socially competent a child must be able to read the entire ongoing cultural context of the group rather than relying on a single, partial strategy. The child's personality and behaviour influence his

ability to make those assessments. Ongoing interactions among the children form a pattern of expectations for the future—in this case, these ongoing interactions spelled continuing success for Bob and Lisa and failure for William.

Implications for Teaching: This approach to research reminds us that, as teachers, we need to look at the entire context of what is happening within a group rather than single-mindedly focusing only on individual children. Taking this wider view can be a source of refreshing and more perceptive insights.

It also emphasizes that social behaviour is a complex tapestry woven of many different threads. This means that even when we do look at individual children we should not be too quick to single out individual strands to work with—one simple remedy may not cure a social difficulty. Instead, we need to look at the whole cloth as well as the whole child if we are to truly understand what is happening in the groups of children with whom we work.

Source: From "Cultural Knowledge and Social Competence Within a Preschool Peer Culture Group" by R. Kantor, P. M. Elgas, and D. E. Fernie, (1993), *Early Childhood Research Quarterly, 8*(2), 125–147.

identifying with models and imitating their behaviour, obviously teachers should provide good examples (Wittmer & Honig, 1994). In addition, the relationship between themselves and the child should be based on mutual liking and warmth in order to encourage imitation of positive behaviour (Eisenberg, 1992). Because young boys may tend to imitate male models more readily than they do female ones, it is also desirable to include male teachers and volunteers in the centre whenever possible.

Since children learn as a result of positive reinforcement, teachers need to be sure that children receive satisfaction from acting in socially desirable ways. Sometimes this reinforcement will be in the form of a pleasant comment or expression of affection, but a more desirable approach is for the teacher to point out to the child that it feels good to help other people so that the pleasure stems from this inherent reward rather than from a calculated external one.

In addition to these teacher-child interactions, plentiful opportunities for the children to interact together must also be included during the day because so much social learning takes place during play. As Hartup (1977) puts it, "Children learn many things through rough-and-tumble activity that would not be possible in adult-child relations" (p. 5). This, then, furnishes us with yet another reason for including ample opportunities in the centre day for social learning to occur among children.

❧ *Suggestions for Teaching Appropriate Social Skills*

When young children want something, be it attention, assistance, or possession of an article, *their need is immediate, intense, and personal.* Their reactions, therefore, to having to wait or to consider the rights of others can be very strong, and it takes patient teaching backed by fortitude to help them develop the ability to wait a little, to control their feelings to a degree, and to consider the rights and desires of others when necessary. All these skills are central to the process of getting along in a social world. If teachers remember to take into account the strength of these immediate, intense, and personal needs as they read about more specific social learnings, they will gain an added appreciation for the magnitude of the child's task in learning to become a socialized human being.

There are, of course, many more social goals than the seven listed here, but these goals have been selected because they are frequently listed by teachers of young children in Canada as being important and as having real social value.

Goal 1: Help Children Develop Empathy

Being able to feel what another person is feeling is a valuable social skill for many reasons. It helps us anticipate how someone will react to what we do, it helps us understand possible motives for other people's behaviour, and it may encourage prosocial behaviour, i.e., acting to benefit someone else when we realize how they feel.

Little children are just beginning to learn to separate themselves and their feelings from the feelings of other people. Indeed, Piaget (1926, 1959) long maintained that young children are egocentric and are unable to put themselves in the place of another. But research, as well as the experience of many early childhood teachers, indicates that this egocentrism is not an all-or-nothing condition. As children grow from two to five, they become increasingly able to assume roles and to perceive complex feelings (Grusec & Arnason, 1982; Radke-Yarrow, Zahn-Waxler, & Chapman, 1983). With training they can also become more sensitive to other people's feelings and to the effect their actions have on these feelings.

As children become more sensitive to those feelings, they can begin to feel concern for the person who expresses them. In one study (Zahn-Waxler, Radke Yarrow, & King, 1979) a seventeen-month-old was reported comforting her mother when she began to cry. I recall my own twenty-one-month-old daughter hugging me and patting my back after I shut the door on my finger, consoling me with tears in her eyes as she murmured, "Tired and hungry! Tired and hungry! We fix! We fix."

❧   *"I just bet that little pig's thirsty," said Bill—a nice example of social concern and empathy.*

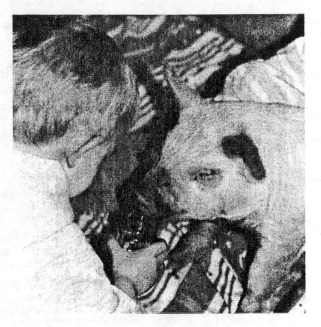

The interesting thing about Zahn-Waxler and colleagues' study was the consistency of the style of empathic response displayed by youngsters as they developed. For example, a little boy who pushed a child aside to protect another child at age two protected his grandmother when someone pushed ahead of her in line when he was seven years old.

Encourage Role Playing

There are several things the teacher can do to increase the awareness of how it feels to be someone else. One of the most obvious of these is to provide many opportunities for dramatic and imaginative play involving taking roles about what people do. Most early childhood settings maintain housekeeping corners, which facilitate the role playing of family life so dear to three- and four-year-olds. We have seen that as children reach four and five years of age, their interest in the world around them increases and extends beyond the family and the school. For these youngsters, enriched role opportunities can be offered with accessories for doctors and nurses, bus drivers, preschool teachers, or anyone else who is familiar to the children. The costumes need not be complete. Indeed, it seems wise to leave some things out to exercise the children's imaginations. Hats are particularly fun, and it is good to have a variety of them representing different characters. For example, children in rural areas often relish wearing the farm caps given away by seed and feed companies.

Help the Child Understand How the Other Person Feels

Teaching children how other people *feel* in addition to what they *do* is more difficult but not impossible. One virtue of encouraging children to tell each other what they want or how they feel is that in addition to relieving the speaker's feelings, it informs the other child about someone else's emotions and desires (Buzzelli, 1992). The other important reason for doing this, according to Piaget, is that children are freed of egocentrism by experiencing interactions with other people. He maintained that social conflict and discussion facilitate cognitive growth and the accompanying ability to put the self in another's place (Piaget, 1926; Smedslund, 1966).

Teachers can increase empathy for another's feelings by explaining how a child is feeling in terms that are personal to the observing child, relating the feeling to one they too have experienced. For example:

Henry, who has just caught his finger in the door, is crying bitterly as the teacher holds him and comforts him. Frankie comes in and stands watching silently, his thumb in his mouth. He looks interested and worried, and as the teacher pats Henry on his back, she explains to Frankie, "Henry hurt his finger in the door. Remember when I rocked on your toe with the rocking chair?" Frankie nods. "Well, his finger feels like that." "It hurt," says Frankie. "It hurt a lot. But we put cold water on it and that made it stop. Let's put his finger in cold water." The teacher says, "That's a great idea! Henry, Frankie is telling you something." Frankie says, "Come on, Hennie, we'll put your finger in water—that will help." And off they go.

Here, the teacher related Henry's feelings directly to what Frankie already knew from his own experience. This helped make the feeling real to him and also encouraged him to use this insight to provide practical comfort for his friend.

During group time, showing pictures of people expressing strong emotions is yet another way to build awareness and sensitivity. Children can often identify the feeling (remember, it can be a positive as well as a negative one) and talk over what might have made that person happy or sad and how they might offer help or comfort if that is deemed necessary.

Goal II: Help Children Learn to Be Generous, Altruistic, and Able to Share Equipment, Experiences, and People with Other Children

It is worthwhile to do what we can to develop the ability in children to feel empathy because it appears that this ability to sense someone else's feelings is related at least in younger children to a second prosocial skill as well (Eisenberg, McCreath, & Ahn, 1988): the development of altruistic behaviour—behaviour performed by a child with the unselfish intention of making another person feel good or happy.

Although much of the research on social development dates back to the 1930s, renewed interest has blossomed in the development of such altruistic behaviour (Damon, 1988; Eisenberg & Mussen, 1989). This research has indicated that when affection from the teacher is combined with verbal comments about what is happening, the greatest number of charitable responses is produced in children (Midlarsky & Bryan, 1967). Modelling generosity also increases this behaviour (Grusec & Arnason, 1982; Rosenhan, 1972), and paternal nurturing facilitates generosity in boys of preschool age (Rutherford & Mussen, 1968). Thus we again find support for the recommendation that *teaching a prosocial behaviour is accomplished most effectively by a teacher who sets a good example and expresses affection while at the same time clarifying what is happening by discussing it with the children.*

Help Children Learn to Share Equipment

Teaching a specific aspect of generosity such as sharing (a social skill of real concern in the centre) requires something more than nurturing and setting a good example. It requires following through with clear-cut policies directed toward building the generous impulse within the child rather than relying on externally enforced generosity supervised by the teacher. As one of my students put it, "I want her to share from her heart, not because I make her do it."

Many teachers try to teach sharing by regulating turn taking ("You can have it for two minutes, then she can have it for two minutes"). They seem to interpret sharing as meaning that the child has to hand over anything he is using almost as soon as another child says he wants it. Teachers who enforce taking turns on this basis find they are constantly required to monitor and referee the turn taking themselves. This is not only tiresome but also *puts the locus of control and decision making outside the child rather than within her.* It also means that a child may not be permitted to have enough of an experience to be filled up and truly satisfied by it. Such deprivation builds a kind of watchful hunger and avarice that should be avoided. It is still true that one doesn't cure hunger by snatching the bread away.

Rather than struggling to institute the policelike control of the previous procedure, the teacher can establish a climate of generosity by making sure the child has enough of

❧   *Lots of social cooperation makes this a successful tower.*

most experiences. Therefore, she does not limit him to two paintings or allow him to ride the trike around the course only three times because another child is waiting. Instead she follows the rule that the child may keep what he has or do what he is doing until he has had enough of it. This means that children do not have to be calculating and defensive about hanging on to things. It also makes settling arguments easier, because it is relatively simple to base decisions on who was using it first and then to state the rule, "Whoever had it first may keep it until he's done with it."

Once assured his own rights and desires will be protected, it becomes much easier for a child to share. When another child is waiting, the teacher can point this out, perhaps saying, "John, when you're done with the swing would you remember to tell Helen? She'd like a turn when you're through." The final step in this process is recognizing when he *does* remember to tell Helen that he is through by commending him and pointing out, "Look how pleased Helen is that you remembered. She's really smiling at you. I guess you're her friend."

It helps in such situations to have enough equipment available that children do not have to wait and wait. Several easels are better than one, and feeling free to improvise in order to meet peak demands will help, too. For example, if painting is suddenly very popular, setting out paint tables might help, or giving children cans of water and old brushes to paint the fence could satisfy their need and reduce waiting.

Help Children Learn to Share the Teacher

Children not only have to learn to share equipment, they also have to learn to share their teacher and her attention with other children. Again, the best model is the generous one, where each gets what he needs rather than each getting an identical, metered amount. This may mean that only one child is rocked while several others play nearby in the block corner rather than every child's being rocked a little. As long as each child receives comfort when he needs it, teachers do not have to worry about whether they are being "fair." They can explain to the children that different people get different special things according to what they need, and then, to remind them that this policy applies to everyone, they can cite examples of times when those children received special attention.

Sometimes individual satisfactions have to be put off, since it is not possible for one child to monopolize the teacher's attention throughout lunch or story time. To handle such demands the teacher might say, "You know, lunch is for everyone to talk together, but I can see you really want to talk just to me. I promise we'll have time for that while I'm getting you ready for nap."

Goal III: Help Children Learn That Being Kind to Other People Feels Good

Helping Other People is One Way of Expressing Kindness

I agree with the Soviet psychologist's implication at the beginning of this chapter that North American children are not encouraged to help their friends as much as they might be. Providing opportunities for children to experience the satisfaction and pleasure that come from helping someone else appears to be a sound way to generate willingness to take prosocial action because the resulting good feeling reinforces the behaviour (Bar-Tal

ᴓ   *Sometimes opportunities to help someone else come up unexpectedly.*

& Raviv, 1982). Sometimes helping others takes the form of comforting another child; sometimes it is as simple as passing the cups at snack; sometimes it is as sophisticated as thinking of an excursion everyone will enjoy.

Children should be encouraged and expected to help each other. The teacher should emphasize that helping other people is a worthwhile, important thing to do. Here are some simple examples furnished by student teachers* of how this can be clearly and consistently taught at the preschool level when teachers are sensitive to incorporating these values.

This episode took place in the hollow block area with some cardboard blocks that have foam packing glued to their insides. Janelle, Timothy, and Jenny were all climbing around on them.

Timothy: "What, I can climb out of here by myself." He proceeds to do so.

Me: "Boy, Timothy, you sure can. I wonder if it's just as easy to climb in?"

Timothy: "Yeah, I can. I got to put my leg over first." He climbs in the box, accidentally putting his foot on Janelle's shoulder.

Janelle: "Watch out, Timothy!"

Me: "Whoops! He accidentally hit your shoulder, huh?"

---

*My thanks to Mary Kashmar, Lauren Davis, Sandi Coe, and the children for the following episodes.

Janelle: "Yeah. Watch me hide in this corner." She does so, and almost gets stuck between the layers of foam. She finally gets herself out. "I almost got stuck!"

Me: "Yeah, you finally slipped your way out."

Jenny (who has crammed herself in more firmly, shrieks): "Help me, teacher. I can't get outta here!"

Me: "Uh oh! Now Jenny's stuck in there. (Jenny continues to twist and struggle.) Janelle, do you remember how you got out?"

Janelle: "Yeah! Here, Jenny, I'll help you." With Janelle pulling and Jenny pushing, Jenny manages to get out.

Me: "Good, you guys! She sure needed you, Janelle!"

Jenny: "Yeah, I was stuck! I woulda spent the night in there!" (She laughs.)

Or sometimes helping takes the form of one youngster's teaching another something.

Roe (aged four years, eight months) is washing and drying some toy animals when Yvonne (aged two years, three months) walks up, takes up the other towel, and wants to play. Roe takes the towel away from Yvonne and looks at me.
Roe: "Will *you* dry?"

Me: "Yvonne looks like she really wants to play. Why don't you ask her to dry them for you?"

Roe is agreeable to the suggestion.

Roe: "Yvonne, will you dry?" (Yvonne nods her head "Yes." She begins to dry but is having difficulty.)

Roe: (snatching the towel away impatiently) "She's too slow. You dry."

Me: "I think you should give Yvonne a chance. Maybe you can show her how to do it."

Roe: "Here, Yvonne, do it this way."

Yvonne catches on quickly and squeals with delight.

Roe: "Wow, now she's waiting for me. I better hurry up."

Me: "You girls work well together. Thanks, Roe."

Soon all the toys are washed and dried.

Or it takes the form of both comfort and help.

At the swings two children were playing and unhooked the seats from the chains. Anathea (playing in the cornmeal) looked over and saw this. "They broke it!" she cried. She seemed really upset by it.

Earon reached over and patted her on the back, saying, "It didn't break," and went on playing. Then he repeated this about three more times. "It didn't break, Anathea; it didn't break."

I said, "You're right, Earon, but can you tell Anathea what happened?"

"They didn't break it—they just took it off of there. See?" (He goes over and hooks them up.) Anathea smiled at him, and they both went back to playing in the cornmeal.

Note that it is necessary to handle these situations carefully in order to avoid the undesirable effect of comparing children with each other. For example, rather than saying, "Why don't you do it the way Alan does—he's a big boy," it is better to say, "Alan just learned how to zip his coat. Why don't you ask him to show you how it goes together?" Children are often generous about teaching such skills to each other as long as it does not take so much time that they lose patience.

The Presence of Children Who Have Special Needs Presents
Special Opportunities for Children to be Kind and Considerate

Although it is desirable to treat children who have special needs as much as possible like we treat all the other children, it is also true that sometimes these youngsters require special consideration. For example, a child who is hard of hearing benefits from having those around him know at least some sign language (Antia, Kriemeyer, & Eldredge, 1994), just as child with Down's syndrome benefits from frequent repetition and enforcement of simple social rules.

Experience has taught me that other children in the group can be quick to offer practical help in a kindly, matter-of-fact way if they are encouraged by the teacher to do so. The problem is helping them understand the difference between kindness and pity and the difference between offering help that empowers the child to do all he can for himself and overwhelming him by being too solicitous or babying him. While it is definitely worth encouraging such simple acts of thoughtfulness as moving the crayons within the reach of a child in a wheelchair, the best, kindest thing the children can do is include the child with the special need in their play. The teacher cannot force them to do this but she *can* encourage it by pointing out a practical way the youngster can participate and by subtly expressing approval when that takes place.

Not Doing Something Can Also Be a Way of Being Kind to Someone

Children also need to learn that kindness goes beyond doing something nice for somebody else. Sometimes it means *not* doing something you feel inclined to do. Although we cannot expect young children to always anticipate when their comments may be tactless or even hurtful, there are many times they know unequivocally that they are saying something with the intention of being mean. For example, the child who says with a sneer, "You can't come to my birthday party" or "You talk funny" or "Only guys with clean socks can come in" is saying those words with the deliberate intention of hurting the other youngster not only by excluding him but also by denigrating him.

The teacher should not tolerate this kind of deliberately hurtful behaviour any more than she would permit a child to hurt an animal. Instead, she should take the speaker aside and explain that what he said was unkind and made the other child feel bad. While acknowledging that nobody has to play with everybody, the teacher should tell the child that causing pain that way is not permitted in the group and he is not to do it again. Then, of course, she must also deal with the feelings of the child who has been hurt. Perhaps she might say, "I'm sorry he was feeling mean and wanted to hurt your feelings. Everybody has stuff to learn at school and he's just learning to be kind. Let's see what we can find you'd like to do in case it doesn't work out for you to play here right now."

Goal IV: Teach Children That Everyone Has Rights
and That These Rights Are Respected by All

I made the point earlier that children have individual needs and that teachers should not hesitate to meet these on an individual basis; that is, they should not interpret fairness as meaning that everyone gets exactly the same thing. But children do, in general, have to conform to the same rules. This impartiality of rule enforcement will help children gradually understand that everyone is respected as having equal rights.

Teach Children That Rules Apply to Everyone

A good example of this may be seen in handling sharing problems. At the beginning of the year there always seem to be one or two children who seize possession rather than asking and waiting for turns. Of course, the teacher often has to restrain such a youngster from doing this. It is particularly important with this kind of child that the teacher also watch carefully and almost ostentatiously protect the seizer's rights when someone tries to take his trike away, so that he sees that everyone, himself as well as others, has his rights of possession protected. This is an effective way to teach fairness and to help the child see what the rule is and that it applies to every child. The message is, "You may not intrude on their rights, and they may not intrude on yours, either." As the year progresses and the child learns to know and apply these rules himself, he will become increasingly able to enforce them without the teacher's help and thus be able to stand more securely on his own in social interaction situations.

Teach Respect for Others' Rights by Honouring Personal Privacy

Children enjoy bringing things from home; it is a cheerful link between their families and the school. Since these items are their personal possessions, it should be their choice whether to share them or not. Even the teacher should ask, "May I see it?" before she reaches out to handle a personal possession.

When he does not choose to share something, the child should put it in his cubby. Keeping his possessions there provides an opportunity to teach privacy and personal rights if the rule is enforced that a child may go only in his own cubby, never in anyone else's without permission. Of course, there will be many transgressions of this rule, but the children will learn to honour this policy over a year's time, just as they will learn to stay out of the teacher's desk and out of the staff rest room if these rules are enforced.

Goal V: Emphasize the Value of Cooperation and Compromise Rather Than Stressing Competition and Winning

Competition and winning are so much a part of Canadian life that it hardly seems necessary to emphasize them with such young children, and yet many teachers do so because appealing to children's competitive instincts is such an easy way to get them to do what teachers want. It is particularly easy to employ competition as a manipulative device with four- and five-year-olds because rivalry increases around that time (Stott & Ball, 1957). Examples include, "Oh, look how well Joan's picking up the blocks; I bet you can't pick up as many as she can!" or "It's time for lunch, children. Whoever gets to the bathroom first can sit by me. Now, remember, no running!" The trouble with these strategies is that they reward children for triumphing over other children and neglect the chance to teach them the pleasure of accomplishing things together.

In Place of Fostering Competition, Model Cooperation and Helping Behaviour Yourself

One effective way for the teacher to substitute cooperation for competition is to model it by helping the children herself. Thus when it is time to put away the blocks, the teacher warns in advance and then says, "It's time to put the blocks away. Come on, let's all pitch in. I guess I'll begin by picking up the biggest ones. Henry, would you like to drive the truck over here so we can load it up?" Henry may refuse, of course, but after a pause he will probably join in if the teacher continues to work with the group to complete the task, meanwhile thanking those who are helping.

Teach the Art of Compromise

Being able to compromise is another basic part of learning to cooperate. Four-year-olds love to strike bargains and are often able to appreciate the fact that everyone has gained some of what he wants when a fair bargain or agreement is reached. The following episode, which occurred at our children's centre, is a good example of this.

> Jimmy has been pulling some blocks around the play area in the wagon. Finally, tiring of this, he asks the teacher to pull him instead. Just at this moment Alan arrives and wants the wagon. This is too much for Jimmy who, dog-in-the-manger style, suddenly decides he wants to pull it after all. He says, "No, Alan! You can't have it! I'm using the wagon. I'm not done. I want to pull it! Get off!" "My gosh, Jimmy," says the teacher. "Weren't you just saying you wanted a ride? Here's your chance. Weren't you just asking for someone to pull you?" She pauses to let this sink in. "Maybe if you let Alan have a turn pulling the wagon, he would give you the ride you want." She turns to Alan. "Would you do that, Alan?" She turns to Jimmy, "Would that be okay with you, Jimmy?"

Thus the teacher helped the boys strike a bargain whereby both got what they wanted.

As children become more socially experienced, the teacher could encourage the boys to think the situation through for themselves rather than intervening so directly herself. Perhaps she might say at that point, "Jimmy, Alan is telling you he really wants to use the wagon, too. Isn't there some way you can both get something good out of this?" If the boys cannot conceive of any solution, then she can go on to the more obvious approach outlined above.

Teach Children to Work Together

The teacher should also be on the lookout for opportunities for which it takes two children (or more) to accomplish what they want. Perhaps one youngster has to pull on the handle while the other shoves the wagon of sand from behind, or one must steady the juicer while the other squeezes. When these circumstances arise, encourage the children to help each other, rather than hurrying too quickly to help them yourself (Adcock & Segal, 1983).

There are also a few pieces of play equipment that require cooperation for success, and a point should be made of acquiring these. Double rocking horses, for example, just will not work if the children do not cooperate and coordinate their efforts; neither will tire swings that are hung horizontally. Some kinds of jump ropes also need at least two people participating for success, as does playing catch.

✍   *Learning to compromise usually requires help from the teacher.*

Goal VI: Help Children Discover the Pleasures of Friendship

Children become more and more interested in having friends as they grow older. By age five they are likely to spend more than half their playtime with other children (Valentine, 1956), and friendship bonds between particular children are generally much stronger at this age than they are in younger children (Hartup, 1992). By second grade it is almost intolerable to be without a friend.

As early as the preschool years, friendships occur typically between children of the same sex (Hartup, 1989), and those friendships persist over longer periods of time than was previously thought. For example, some recent research by Howes (1988), which studied children in day care situations, reported that some friendships continued for as long as three years, although most of the children in the study also made new friends, separated from old friends, and ended friendships during that same time.

Ways of demonstrating friendship pass through a number of developmental stages (Youniss, 1975), moving from a young child's interpretation of showing friendship by means of sharing toys and material items, through the stage of playing together as a primary indication, and going on to showing friendship by offering psychological assistance, such as giving comfort when needed.

One list compiled by a group of four-year-olds at the Institute included the following ways of showing friends they liked them: hug them, kiss them, play with them, have a party, celebrate Valentine's Day, run to them, mail them a letter, sing a song to them, tell a secret, give them a present, and let them spend the night.

Friendship depends on many variables, including similarity of age and interests, proximity, gender, and sociability, as well as the less readily analysable qualities of personal attractiveness (Ramsey, 1991). There also appears to be considerable variation in the capacity and need for close friendships at the preschool age.

Rubin (1980) reports a study by Lee that was carried out in a day nursery and that found that some children were friendlier and better liked by other children even during the first six months of life (Lee, 1973). He reports another extensive study by Hartup et al. (1967) that found that the most popular, sought-after children in the program were the

> ones who most often paid attention to other children, praised them, showed affection, and willingly acceded to their requests. Children who frequently ignored others, refused to cooperate, ridiculed, blamed or threatened others were most likely to be disliked by their classmates. In short, for a child to be included and accepted, he must also include and accept. (p. 52)

It sometimes seems that the only friendships teachers are aware of are the ones they try to break up between older boys who egg each other on into trouble. Yet we must remember there are many desirable relationships, which should be noted and nurtured in the preschool. Having friends is important at every age.

♋ *Playing together is one of the most satisfying results of having adequate social skills.*

Facilitate Friendliness by Using Reinforcement to Reduce Isolated Behaviour

Social interaction between children can be increased by the judicious use of reinforcement. This is a particularly helpful technique to employ with shy, isolated children. Using this approach, the teacher provides some kind of social dividend whenever the child approaches a group or interacts with them but withholds such recognition when the child withdraws and plays by himself. (It is hoped that over a period of time the pleasure the youngster finds in being part of the group will replace this more calculated reward.) Note that this approach is just the opposite of the pattern that often occurs where the teacher tends to "try to draw the child out" when he retires from the group, thereby rewarding with attention the very behaviour it is desirable to extinguish.

Increase the Social Skills of Disliked Children

Another way to foster friendships among children is to teach less likable youngsters social skills that make them more acceptable to the other children.* For example, a child who has learned to ask for what he wants is generally more welcome than one who rushes in and grabs whatever appeals to him.

As the research study in this chapter indicates, identifying just which skills a child needs in order to fit in with a group can require careful observation and analysis if it is to be truly helpful. However, it is well worth the time and trouble it takes to do this. Research by Coie and Kupersmidt (1983) indicates that among the 20% of children who are typically rejected by their classmates, about half remain rejected from year to year. Such an experience can really dishearten and discourage a youngster as well as having an unfortunate effect on his self-esteem unless someone lends an effective hand (Hartup, 1992).

This kind of social instruction can sometimes be best accomplished on a one-to-one basis whereby children are coached by the teacher in more successful ways to behave. Sometimes, for example, it really clarifies things when the teacher simply points out, "You know, when you knock their blocks down, they don't like you. It makes Hank and Charley really mad, and then they won't let you play. Why don't you try building something near them next time? Then maybe they'll gradually let you join them and be your friends."

Particularly with four-year-olds, simple small-group discussions of what works and what doesn't also help children learn techniques that foster friendly relations. It is, of course, important not to single out specific personalities during these discussions as being either "good" or "bad" examples.

Asher, Oden, and Gottman (1977) report two fascinating studies on the effect of teaching social skills by means of modelling (Evers & Schwarz, 1973; O'Connor, 1972), in which a film demonstrating successful methods of entering a group was shown to young children. Observation of their behaviour following this film revealed marked and continued improvement in their use of these strategies.

Although such films are not readily available, other ways of presenting models can be developed easily. I recently observed two teachers acting out such situations in brief, simple skits for their four-year-olds at group time. The children were delighted and readily

---

*Please refer to the discussion of teaching children alternative ways of getting they want in the chapter on aggression (chapter 12).

talked over the skits afterward. When presenting such skits, remember that it is important to avoid the temptation to parody specific personalities in the group.

Pair Children Together

Pairing children sometimes helps them make friends. Coming to school in a car pool or going home from school to play together can cement a friendship, as can doing a number of jobs together or sharing an interest in common. In the long run, though, it is up to the child to form the friendship; all the teacher can do is make such possibilities available to him.

Help Children When a Friend Departs

Sometimes teachers underestimate what it means to a child when a friend moves away, or makes a new friend and rejects the former one, or is transferred to another room. Children often feel quite despondent and adrift when this occurs. Indeed, in her study of friendships among children in day care, Howes (1988) found that "children who lost a high proportion of friends because the friends moved, and children who moved to new peer groups without familiar peers were less socially skilled than were children who stayed with friends" (p. 66).

When someone is transferring rooms or leaving the program, everyone needs to be prepared for the change. This should include the child and his parents and the other children as well. When a child is transferring, we have often prepared everyone by inviting the child for a "visit" to the new room once or twice before making the total switch. And, if we have warning, we often serve a festive snack when a child is moving away. Allowing the departee to choose it adds to the fun.

As in working through any other kind of separation, the leaver's and the left-behinds' feelings of grief, apprehension, and, sometimes, anger need to be recognized and honoured. There is no shame in feeling saddened when a friend has departed, and children should be allowed to mourn this without being ridiculed. They should also be assisted, in an unpushy way, to strike up a new friendship at the right moment.

As Rubin (1980) points out, rejection by a former crony hurts, too. Teachers of young children need to be on the lookout for these happenings, which occur all too frequently, and ease the ache when they can. Sometimes the break is only temporary, but sometimes one of the pair is simply ready to move on. When this happens, about all the teacher can do is acknowledge the child's feelings and encourage a new beginning with another friend or group.

Goal VII: Help Children with Special Needs Fit into the Life of the Group

The primary advantage of including children with special needs into typical children's centre environments, often cited by proponents of inclusive early education, is that everyone derives great social benefits from that inclusion (Chandler, 1994).

This chapter has already pointed out that one of many social benefits typical children receive is learning matter-of-fact kindness from that experience, but there are other benefits as well. While learning to accept and adapt to those special needs, the group also learns that all children are more alike than different and, ideally, to feel comfortable rather than uneasy around such youngsters.

The other side of the coin is that the child with special needs has the opportunity to learn to fit in with a group of ordinary peers and get along with them (Odom, McConnell, & McEvoy, 1992). He sees typical behaviour modelled all around him, including various strategies the children employ for getting what they want and playing together. These can be emphasized quietly by the teacher, showing him how he, too, might use the same strategies.

Chapter 9, "Welcoming Children Who Have Special Educational Requirements into the Life of the Program," discusses many things the teacher can do to help all the children get along together, and many helpful resources are included at the end of that chapter. Therefore, I will restrict myself here to reminding the reader how important it is to remember the 5 P's when teaching social skills to children with special needs: *Don't* pity or overprotect these children. *Do* be patient, persistent, and practical.

❧ Summary

Social competence develops at a rapid rate during the years of early childhood. Children become socialized partly as a result of identifying with and emulating models they admire and partly as a consequence of reinforcement that encourages or suppresses various kinds of social behaviour.

Although children begin to attain many social skills during this period, seven of them were selected in this chapter as being particularly important: developing empathy, learning to be generous, learning that it feels good to be kind to other people, understanding that everyone has rights that must be respected, discovering the value of cooperation and compromise rather than stressing competition, discovering the pleasures of friendship, and helping children with special needs fit into the life of the group.

Questions and Activities

1. *Problem:* You are working as a teachr in a child care centre. One of the volunteers is supervising the trike area and is firmly telling each child that he can ride his trike around the track three times and then must give a turn to the next child who is standing in line (there are several children standing there already, making plaintive noises about wanting turns). What would you do to handle this situation on both a short- and long-term basis?

2. During the next week, watch for situations in which a child could be helped to understand another person's feelings or point of view. Using the situations you observed, discuss possible ways that genuine feeling for another person could have been developed from these situations.

3. How much do *you know* about effective ways of entering a group? Make a list in class of strategies adults and children can employ for successful entrée.

4. Have you witnessed examples at your school of children seeking to comfort each other? Share the situation with the class, and explain what the comforter did to help the other child.

5. *Problem:* You agree with the author that children should have a special place of their own to keep their personal belongings while at school. Your school provides hooks for the children's hats and coats and a shelf above that for storage. What would you suggest could be done to provide private places for each youngster?

Self-Check Questions for Review

Content-Related Questions

1. What are some typical social behaviours of two-year-olds? How does the social behaviour of three-year-olds differ from that of four-year-olds?
2. After reviewing the processes by which children become socialized, discuss what the implications are for teachers. Basing your comments on what is known about the process of socialization, explain how teachers can apply that knowledge to further socialize the young children in their care.
3. Review the seven social learning goals and then list some practical pointers you would give a new teacher about how each of those goals might be accomplished.

Integrative Questions

1. Review the equipment in the school where you are teaching or have taught and identify which things facilitate social interaction between children. Are there items, for example, that require two people using them at once to make them work effectively? Suggest additional activities you could offer that would be more successful if two or more children worked together to accomplish them.
2. The book discusses two theories about how children become socialized. What do the two theories have in common and how do they differ? Do these differences mean that only one of them is correct and the other wrong?
3. Propose two or three brief skits or episodes the staff might act out that demonstrate social situations and/or social problems for the children to discuss. For example, two people might act out a problem at the snack table where two children both want to get refills. Be sure to think of at least one situation that demonstrates positive social interaction.
4. The woodworking table is very popular this morning—everyone wants to hammer and saw. Carpentry is offered several times a week. Which of the following solutions to regulating participation would you favour? Be sure to explain the pros and cons for following each of the four policies. (a) Allow each child to make one item and then let the next child have a turn. (b) Have the teacher keep a list and have the children sign up in order for turns. (c) Tell requesters the table is full right now and to please come back later. (d) Suggest to children as they finish that they alert waiters there is space for them.

References for Further Reading

Overviews

Bos, B. (1990). *Together we're better: Establishing a coactive learning environment.* Roseville, CA: Turn the Page Press. This book burgeons with fresh ideas about things children can do that encourage being together. *Highly recommended.*

Eisenberg, N. (1992). *The caring child.* Cambridge, MA: Harvard University Press. This is a very readable yet research-based book on helping children becoming caring people. *Highly recommended.*

Katz, L., & McClellan, D. E. (1991). *The teacher's role in the social development of young children.* Urbana, IL: University of Illinois, ERIC Clearinghouse on Elementary and Early Childhood Education. The authors provide a good, research-based overview of factors that influence social development and what teachers can do to steer it in a positive direction.

Kohn, A. (1990). *The brighter side of human nature.* New York: Basic Books. Studies from a wide variety of academic disciplines are drawn on in this book to support the contention that humans are more caring and altruistic than pessimists assume.

Encouraging Friendships

Adcock, D., & Segal, M. (1983). *Making friends: Ways of encouraging social development in young children.* Englewood Cliffs, NJ: Prentice Hall. Although focusing on friendship, Adcock and Segal also provide sagacious comments about helping children with different social styles get along comfortably with other children and with the teacher. *Highly recommended.*

Bullock, J. (1993). Lonely children. *Young Children, 48*(6), 53–57. Bullock calls our attention to children who feel lonely for a variety of reasons and provides some suggestions about how to help them overcome that feeling.

Ramsey, P. G. (1991). *Making friends in school: Promoting peer relationships in early childhood.* New York: Teachers College Press. This is the best, most readable, all-round book dealing in detail with friendships of preschool children. There is a noteworthy chapter on how, when, and if the teacher should intervene. Also included are bibliographies of children's books on aspects of friendship. *Highly recommended.*

Wolf, D. P. (Ed.). (1986). *Connecting: Friendship in the lives of children.* Redmond, WA: Exchange Press.

Many practical suggestions are included for helping preschool children build friendship skills.

Fostering Cooperation in Play

Adcock, D., & Segal, M. (1983). *Play together, grow together.* Mount Rainier, MD: Gryphon House (Distributors). Interesting and unusual activities are proposed for many areas of the curriculum that have the potential for fostering cooperative play.

Sobel, J. (1983). *Everybody wins.* New York: Walker. This book is full of delightful ideas for cooperative, noncompetitive games suitable for nursery school or kindergarten. *Highly recommended.*

For the Advanced Student

Adler, P. A., & Adler, P. (1988). The carpool: A socializing adjunct to the educational experience. In G. Handel (Ed.), *Childhood socialization.* New York: Aldine De Gruyter. This delightful bit of research investigated the potential social learnings and contretemps available in the social life of the car pool. It deals with five-year-olds and older.

Eisenberg, N., & Mussen, P. (1989). *The roots of prosocial behavior in children.* New York: Cambridge University Press. This well-written, fairly brief book sums up what is known about the development of prosocial behavior from a variety of aspects. *Highly recommended.*

Grusec, J. E., & Lytton, H. (1988). *Social development. History, theory, and research.* New York: Springer-Verlag. This is a thorough, comprehensive review of social development useful for advanced students.

Hartup, W. (1992). Peer relations in early and middle childhood. In V. B. Van Hasselt & M. Hersen (Eds.), *Handbook of social development: A lifespan perspective.* New York: Plenum Press. In this well-written chapter, Hartup reviews what research has to tell us about children's friendships.

Odom, S. L., McConnell, S. R., & McEvoy, M. S. (1992). *Social competence of young children with disabilities: Issues and strategies for intervention.* Baltimore: Paul Brookes. Because the development of social skills is an area in which preschool teachers can make a particularly significant contribution, this book is included as a reference. It is research based, citing what is known and not known about effective current approaches. It discusses the development of social skills in relation to particular disabilities (vision, hearing, etc.) and also from the point of view of relationships with peers, siblings, and parents.

Pettit, G. S. (1992). Developmental theories. In V. B. Van Hasselt & M. Hersen (Eds.), *Handbook of social development: A lifespan perspective.* New York: Plenum Press. Pettit reviews current theories of social development under the major headings of psychoanalytic theory, cognitive-developmental theory, and social information-processing approaches.

Roopnarine, J. L., & Carter, D. B. (1992). *Parent-child socialization in diverse cultures: Annual advances in applied developmental psychology, Vol. 5.* Norwood, NJ: Ablex. Socialization in thirteen cultures is discussed, including the influence of parents and schools. Very interesting reading.

Zahn-Waxler, C., & Smith, K. D. (1992). The development of prosocial behavior. In V. B. Van Hasselt & M. Hesen (Eds.), *Handbook of social development: A lifespan perspective.* This is the best current review of research on this subject. *Highly recommended.*

Helping Young Children Establish Self-Discipline and Self-Control

But What if She Won't Do What I Say?

𝒮11

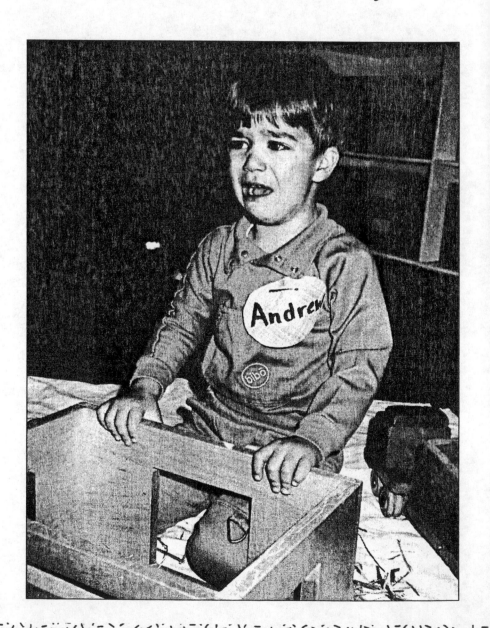

The goal of discipline is not to make the teacher's life easier. The goal of discipline is to guide the behavior of children in such a way that they will internalize our outward expectations and develop the inner controls they need to function as whole and happy individuals.

Marianne Modica

Have you ever wondered . . .

How to help children control themselves instead of depending on other people to control them?

How to make it easier for children to behave in acceptable ways?

What to do when a child won't stop doing something she shouldn't be doing?

. . . If you have, the material in the following pages will help you.

*B*ecause discipline worries beginning teachers the most, it is usually the subject they want to discuss first when they begin teaching. Sometimes this is because they fear physical aggression or that the children will not like them, but more frequently they fear losing control of the situation because they do not know what to do next. So when teachers say fervently that they want to discuss "discipline," what they usually have in mind is how to control the children, or, as one forthright young student put it, "how to get the kids to do what I want."

Two Basic Goals of Discipline

Although "getting the kids to do what I want" is undeniably part of the package, should it be all that is encompassed by the concept of discipline? The teacher should also have in mind the higher goal of instilling inner self-controls in the child in place of teacher-maintained external ones. Therefore, every discipline situation not only should achieve a workable solution to the current crisis (and this will be discussed in the second part of the chapter) but also should seek to interiorize self-control.

Establishing Inner Controls: Ego Strength and Moral Development

Why Does Self-Control Matter?

Self- rather than "other" control is desirable for a number of reasons. People who can control themselves are trustworthy and responsible. They can be counted on to do the right thing whether or not a police officer is standing on the corner watching to see if they run the red light. Because the control is internal, it is more consistent; and most valuably for mental health, the individual who is "inner-controlled" makes choices on her own behalf. This is the opposite of the neurotic personality who feels powerless, unable to control what happens to herself, and who sees herself as "done to" and in the power of others.

Granted that such internalization is desirable, the questions that remain for early childhood teachers to answer are "How can I begin to establish these inner controls in such young children?" "How can I teach them not only to *know* what is right but to *do* what is right?" Teachers must realize that this is a long process taking many years, and it rests on the gradual development of ego strength and moral judgement. A strong ego enables the child to control her impulses, and moral judgement (telling right from wrong) enables her to decide which impulses she must control.

Building Ego Strength

Fraiberg (1977) describes the ego as being the part of the personality that has to do with the executive and cognitive functions of the individual and that also regulates the drives and appetites. Obviously it is this part of the personality we want to strengthen in order to make it available to the child to help her control her impulses.

One way to do this is to *increase the child's feelings of mastery by giving her many opportunities for making decisions.* However, the choices offered must be appropriate and not too difficult. I recall a four-year-old who was asked by her divorcing parents to decide which parent she wished to live with—an intolerably difficult choice for a child of that age to make.

On the other hand, the preschool day abounds with opportunities for decisions well within the ability of most three- and four-year-olds to handle. The catch is that *the teacher must be prepared to honour the choice once the child has made the decision.* Such questions as "Do you want dessert?" "Would you rather finger-paint or play with the blocks?" or "Would you like to pass the napkins today?" are examples of valid choices because it is all right if the child chooses to refuse. Unfortunately, many teachers use "Would you like … ?" or "Would you please … ?" or "okay?" as a polite camouflage for conveying an order. Thus they inquire, "Let's get on the bus, okay?" or "Would you like to put on your sweater?" Young children are likely to retort "No!" when asked such questions, and then the teacher is really stuck. It is better not to ask, "Let's get on the bus, okay?" if the child has to get on the bus anyway, but to try saying, "The bus is here, and it's time to go home. Where do you want to sit?" or "It's cold today. If you want to go out, you will need to put on your sweater." In short, honour choices when given, *but give no choice when there is no valid opportunity to make one.*

It is also important to see to it that the child experiences the consequences of her decisions. Perhaps the reader will recall the example in the chapter on routines in which the child who elects to skip snack is not permitted to change her mind at the last minute. Abiding by decisions once they are made teaches youngsters to make responsible choices.

Increase the Child's Feelings of Being a Competent, Worthwhile Person

The feelings of self-esteem generated by competency also make the ego stronger. The child who thinks well of herself because she is competent is in a favourable position to assume command and control of herself, because she sees herself as being effective and strong (Faber & Mazlish, 1980).

Unfortunately some children are noticed only when they do something wrong. This continual negative relationship with the teacher does not enhance their feelings of self-worth. Even the "worst" child in school does not misbehave all the time. A considerable part of her day is spent in acceptable activities. If her self-esteem and self-mastery are to remain intact, it is vital that she receive credit for her good behaviour as well as control for her transgressions.

However, as we saw in the chapter on self-esteem, the most desirable source of self-worth stems not from the opinion of the teacher, but from the acquisition of competencies. These may range from being able to walk the balance beam to knowing effective strategies for worming one's way into a play group. It does not really matter what the competency is, as long as it contributes to the child's perception of herself as being an able person who is in command of herself.

Encouraging Moral Development: Fostering the Interiorization of Conscience

Another aspect of helping children establish inner controls has to do with the establishment of conscience and instilling a sense of what is right and wrong. Conscience (sometimes termed the *superego*) can be described as that inner voice that tells us what we should or should not do. Theoretical arguments continue over how this voice is instilled

(Kagan & Lamb, 1987), but Hoffman's comprehensive reviews of research on this subject (1970, 1975), which have been further supported by Edwards (1980), indicate that growth of conscience is facilitated most strongly by the presence of two factors, both of which can be easily used by parents and teachers. One of these is the presence of affection and a nurturing relationship between the adult and the child—a condition that should generally pertain in school as well as in the home. This factor was identified as being present in about half the studies reviewed by Hoffman. The second factor, which appears to be even more potent since it was more consistently present in the reported studies, is the use of what is termed "induction techniques" (Honig & Lansburgh, 1994). In simple language this just means giving a child a reason why she should or should not do something. For example, one might say, "I can't let you hit Ginny with the block—it hurts too much" or "We always flush the toilet so it's fresh for the next person." Another more advanced example might be "We have to put the candy back. We didn't pay for it. We always have to give the clerk money when we take something. That's how people who work here get money to buy what *they* want." Surely such an explanation is preferable to the "You're a bad, naughty girl for stealing that candy" that is so frequently heard.

The examples of reasons given in the preceding paragraph have another quality that also appears to help children grow toward moral maturity. Each example gives the child a particular kind of reason. It is what Bearison and Cassel (1975) term a "person-oriented" and Hoffman (1985) terms a "victim-oriented" reason for decent behaviour. "Victim" here refers to the other person involved in the situation. Saying "We flush the toilet because it leaves it fresh for the next person" rather than "Remember the rule, flush the toilet" encourages children to think of other people's well-being. In other words, it begins to teach them perspective taking—thinking of the other person and taking her point of view or perspective into consideration. Even though young children are not skilful at doing this, they can begin to learn such consideration. It is certainly a better approach than teaching blind obedience to a rule.

Teachers often try to use this person- or victim-oriented approach by saying to a child who has just tossed sand into another youngster's face, "Stop that! How would *you* like it if *you* were Maggie and someone threw sand into *your* eyes? How would *you* feel then?" This what-if-*you*-were-her approach may work with older children but is too complicated and involves too much role reversal for a three- or four-year-old to understand. It just leaves them bewildered.

The same lesson can be taught much more effectively by making a simple change in approach that is still person-oriented but is related more directly to the sand thrower's own experience. This teacher might begin by saying "Stop that—keep the sand down! Throwing sand hurts too much when it gets in Maggie's eyes. Remember when Jim threw sand in *your* eyes? Remember how that hurt? Well, that's how Maggie's eyes feel now." This remember-when approach may not sound like a major difference from the what-if-you-were-her approach, but it is *much easier* for young children to understand. It really does help children learn to think about how their actions affect other people's feelings.

Moral Development Occurs in a Number of Stages

There is one more fascinating thing about the growth of conscience that the teacher needs to understand. It is that children and adults have very different ways of thinking about what is right and wrong. The works of Damon (1988), Kohlberg (1985), Piaget (1932), and Rest (1983) reveal that there is a developmental sequence to moral development just as there is a sequence in the development of reasoning. Ideas of what is "right" or "wrong" vary from culture to culture too (Shweder, Mahapatra, & Miller, 1987).

Progression from one stage to the next is a result of interplay between cognitive maturation and social experience (Damon, 1988). Although some research indicates that children who are on the verge of passing on to the next stage may be influenced by teaching (Turiel, 1973; Vygotsky, 1973), in general such growth is thought to be the result of construction by the child rather than direct instruction by the teacher. Nor should it be assumed that everyone attains the final level. Some adults remain at stage 1 or 2, and many at stage 4 (Kohlberg, 1985).

The interesting thing about the stage theory of moral development is that as a result of her moral developmental level the conscience of a child may tell her something is wrong when an adult's conscience tells him the same action is right. Examples of this will be presented later in this chapter. This developmental difference can certainly confuse teachers if they do not understand how young children view right and wrong and do not make allowances for their differing points of view.

Stages of Moral Development*

A. Preconventional level

Stage 1: Unquestioning obedience based on external power and compulsion. Right or wrong is what is rewarded or punished. Right is "following the rule." Rules are accepted unquestioningly. Child has not "decentred, and self-interest is a strong motivator in his decision making." Moral judgements are based on observable, physical consequences rather than on intentions of person.

Stage 2: Instrumental-relativist orientation. Right or wrong is what instrumentally satisfies own needs and sometimes the needs of others. "Backscratching" kind of reciprocity is understood. One behaves well in order to get what one wants.

B. Conventional level

Stage 3: Right behaviour is what pleases others. Behaviour is often judged by the intention behind it ("She means well."). Good girl/bad girl idea of morals.

Stage 4: Law and order. Right behaviour is doing one's duty, showing respect for authority, following rules because they are "right."

C. Postconventional, autonomous, or principled level

Stage 5: Social-contract legalistic orientation. Right is a matter of personal values, which have been examined and agreed on by the whole society. Laws are not absolute but subject to modification. The Canadian Charter of Rights and Freedoms is an example of this level of moral development.

Stage 6: Universal ethical principle orientation. Right is defined by individual conscience in accord with self-chosen, ethical principles of justice, reciprocity and

---

*Based on Kohlberg (1976) and Turiel (1973).

equality of human rights, and respect for dignity of human beings as individual people (Golden Rule is an example of this).*

Stages 1 and 2: Implications for teaching. Young children define "right" as being what the rule says. A rule is right because a parent or teacher says it is right. This does not mean children necessarily obey the rule (Power & Reimer, 1978), but it does mean that they do not reason and question whether the rule itself is fair or just.

Nor do young children make allowances for what someone intended or meant to do (Maccoby, 1980). They render judgement only on the observable consequences. (This is similar to their reasoning in the realm of conservation of materials—seeing is believing.) As Piaget (1932) pointed out, children of preschool age conclude that the child who has broken more cups has done a greater wrong than the child who has broken only one, regardless of the reason for the breakage. That is, preschool children reason that the child who breaks several cups while helping her mother should be punished more than the child who breaks a single cup while stealing cookies. Older children would, of course, reach a quite different conclusion, based on the fact that stealing itself is "bad," whereas an adult who had advanced to a still higher moral level might decide that the fact the child was starving negated the "sin" of theft because preserving human life is a greater good.

Understanding that young children take results rather than intentions into account may help the teacher comprehend the continuing resentment expressed by a child toward someone who has knocked her down, even after the teacher has explained it was an accident. Despite the teacher's interpretation, it remains difficult for her to grasp the transgressor's harmless intention when she is experiencing the actual result.

Four-year-olds approaching stage 2 are beginning to understand a very simple form of reciprocity as justice—"I do something for you, and you do something for me." The implication for teaching (and it is borne out by experience) is that this is a practical time to introduce the concept of bargaining as an alternative to simply demanding what one wants. An obvious example of this that I heard recently was a child who bargained, "Well—I'll let you sit in the cradle, but you can't 'waa-waa' all the time!" (A less obvious example occurred when a five-year-old said to an importuning three-year-old, "Well, okay. I'll tell you what— you *can* be the leader, but in *this* gang, leaders always go at the end of the line!")

Additional Information about Moral Development

Besides understanding these stages of moral development, it is helpful for teachers of young children to know about some additional research concerning moral development that touches on how children develop more mature concepts about what constitutes moral behaviour. In a review of recent research, Buzzelli (1992) singles out two features as being important elements in developing that moral understanding. As children grow older they gradually acquire knowledge of social rules and standards and also gradually develop deeper understanding of how other people feel. When these two elements are combined, the result is the growth of moral understanding.

Standards and rules stem from a variety of sources—parents, teachers, and peers— and children become increasingly able to internalize them as they acquire linguistic and

---

*Kohlberg has stated he no longer differentiates clearly between stages 5 and 6 (1978).

cognitive sophistication. Their growing ability to feel empathy for others and their desire to become more like their parents and to attain feelings of mastery and competence also contribute to their understanding and desire to incorporate the social rules that govern reasonable behaviour into their repertoire.

Buzzelli concludes that parents and teachers can facilitate the growth of moral understanding by valuing the growth of cognitive and language skills that form the foundation for moral understanding, setting clear and appropriate standards for the children's behaviour so they know what the rules are, and consistently pointing out how certain actions by the children affect other people in a positive or negative way.

🙞 *Practical Things to Do to Make it Easier for Children to Behave in Acceptable Ways*

It is evident from the foregoing discussion that establishing ego strength and conscience in young children is a complex and lengthy task that can only be begun in the early years. While this is in process, the teacher must be willing to assume control when necessary, always bearing in mind the ultimate goal of helping children achieve responsibility for themselves. There are many practical ways to go about doing this, as well as some things teachers do that make discipline of any kind more difficult.

Ten Ways to Make Discipline Situations Worse!

No one intentionally makes trouble for themselves by creating a poor environment; yet so many of the situations in the following list happen in centres and nursery schools from time to time that it seems appropriate (as well as fun) to begin by pointing them out.

1. Make the children wait a lot and expect them to sit quietly while they wait, preferably like little ladies and gentlemen with their hands in their laps and their feet on the floor.

2. Be inconsistent: Let the children ride their trikes on the grass on days when you don't feel up to par, but take their trikes away when you're feeling better, because it's against the rules to ride on the grass.

3. Be unreasonable: Never make allowances for children who are tired, hungry, coming down with something, or getting over something. It will also help ruin the day to have a great many arbitrary rules that are never explained although they are rigidly enforced.

4. Decide that the way to let children learn for themselves is never to intervene; pay no attention to the possibility that the younger, smaller children are being bullied and that some older ones are actually learning that "might makes right."

5. Be consistent: Always punish the children by doing the same thing to them. For example, no matter what they do, make them sit in the office, or don't let them have dessert at lunch.

6. Give up halfway through a confrontation, and let the child run off. After all, you're not supposed to leave your work station.

7. Lose your temper and yell at the children. This will frighten them into behaving and will make you feel better.

8. Strike a child; pinch her, or jerk her arm when no one is looking. This will also frighten her badly, but maybe she'll behave after that.

9. Ignore the problem; just send the troublemaker off to play with the new teacher. It will help him gain experience.

10. Talk too much. Confuse the child: Moralize, shame, or embarrass her, or warn her that you're going to tell her mother! This will help her understand the consequences of her actions and set an example of verbal control for her.

When behaviours such as these are singled out, it is clear how undesirable such approaches are. Yet they are more common than one would wish them to be in many schools, probably because they reflect discipline practices many teachers experienced in their homes while growing up. However, if the following principles are put into practice, the need for these more unproductive methods will be reduced.

Positive Approaches to Discipline

Besides fostering ego strength and the development of conscience, there are two other fundamental things to do to help young children behave in acceptable ways and to improve the ease and quality of discipline and control in the group: Prevent discipline situations when it is possible to do so, and know what to do when a crisis occurs.

Some Practical Ways to Stop Discipline Situations Before They Start

Reward behaviour you want to see continued; don't reward behaviour you wish to discourage. Children (and adults) repeat behaviour from which they obtain satisfaction. This reward does not necessarily come in the form of payoffs of chocolate chips or gold stars. Whether teachers realize it or not, they use rewards every time they say "thank you" or "that's a good job" or even when they smile at a child. The value of this technique, which is one form of behaviour modification called *positive reinforcement,* has been well proven (Hilgard & Bower, 1966; Walker & Shea, 1991). There is no doubt that it is an effective way to deal with recurring discipline and behaviour problems. Therefore, when undesirable behaviour persists, it is a good idea to take a look at what the child is getting out of it. Preventing the payoff can help eliminate the behaviour. It is also effective to note positive actions on the part of the child and to respond to them with pleasure, since this positive reward, combined with the pleasure inherent in successful accomplishment, is a potent reinforcer.

It is not effective to "extinguish" aggressive behaviour in young children by simply ignoring it. In my experience such behaviour does not subside when ignored—apparently because children interpret this laissez-faire attitude as permission. Not only that, one cannot overlook the fact that there are inherent gratifications (payoffs) in attacking other children; these range from simply seizing what is desired to enjoying hitting someone—if you are angry, hitting somebody feels pretty good. For these reasons, *it is important to take more assertive action and stop undesirable behaviour* rather than let it slip past on the grounds that it will go away if no attention is paid to it.

Be persistent. When working with a child who repeats undesirable behaviour, remember that, in addition to analysing and preventing the payoff, it takes time to change behaviour. Sometimes teachers try something for a day, or even just once or twice during a day, and expect such a short-term change to work miracles. When it doesn't, they give up. Don't give up! Be consistent and persistent. It often takes repeated experience for learning to take place, but children can and *will* learn if you stick to your guns!

Consistently position yourself so that you are able to see a large area of the room or play yard at the same time. All too often beginning teachers focus on only a small group of children at a time. This is partly because it is less scary to do so and partly because many teaching lab situations unintentionally encourage this by assigning specific areas to students for supervision. But no matter what the underlying reason is for such behaviour, it is wise to teach oneself to avoid the kind of tunnel vision this promotes.

Learning to position yourself close to a wall or fence, for example, means that you have a clear view of a larger area, just as sitting at a table so that you face most of the room makes it easier to scan the larger space (providing you remember to look up occasionally from what you are doing). Such scanning has been shown to be one of the qualities that differentiates good classroom managers from ineffective ones (Anderson, Evertson, & Brophy, 1979).

Teachers who circulate within the supervision area instead of remaining planted in one place are also more likely to be aware of what is going on. This awareness can help children avoid many unnecessary confrontations and misunderstandings by providing opportunities for timely interventions and positive teaching to take place instead of tears and fights.

When trouble repeats itself, analyse the situation and try changing it rather than nagging the child. When something happens over and over, in addition to checking up on payoffs, the teacher should also think about changing the situation instead of the child. For example, instead of telling a restless youngster to be quiet all the time, it might be better to let her leave after hearing one story, to ask a volunteer to read to her alone, or even to let her play quietly nearby during story time until she becomes more interested and can be drawn gradually into the group.

Emphasize the positive rather than the negative; always tell the child the correct thing to do. This habit can be formed with a little practice. When using directions, rather than saying "Don't get your feet wet" or "Stay out of that puddle," say "Walk around the puddle." Or say "Put the sand in the dump truck" rather than "Don't throw the sand." This technique is desirable not only because it reduces negative criticism, but also because it directs the child toward something she can do that is acceptable.

Warn ahead of time to make transitions easier. The teacher should anticipate transitions with the children a few minutes before the activity is due to change. He might say, "It's going to be lunchtime pretty soon. I wonder what we're going to have?" Or he might warn, "There's just enough time for one more painting. Then you can help me wash the brushes, and we'll have a story." Warning ahead gives the children time to wind up what they are doing. Sometimes just walking around the yard and commenting here and there that soon it will be time to go in will serve this purpose. It takes the abruptness out of the situation and makes compliance with routines much easier for children.

Arrange the environment to promote positive interactions. Interest is continuing in studying the ecological relationship between children and their environments (Bronfenbrenner, 1979; Pence, 1988; Prescott, 1981; Smith & Connolly, 1980), and some of these findings about the interconnections are helpful to know about when planning ways to prevent discipline situations from occurring.

Rohe and Patterson (1974) found that a combination of many children in a small space (a high density of children) combined with few resources produced more aggression and more destructive and unoccupied behaviour. In another study, Smith and Connolly (1980) found that reducing square footage per child to fifteen square feet also produced more aggression, more parallel (rather than social) play, less rough-and-tumble play, and less running (and even walking) activity.

The conclusion from such studies seems obvious. If enough space is provided for the children to use, discipline problems will be reduced accordingly.*

The area illustrating this situation that comes most glaringly to my mind is the block area of many early childhood settings. Although interest can run high in this activity, all too often blocks are cramped into a corner where there is no possibility for play to expand as interest dictates. Moreover, unless they are encouraged to carry blocks a little distance away from the storage shelves, children tend to crowd as near the source of supply as possible. This combination of restricted space plus the crowding near the shelves at the beginning of a project promotes territorial struggles and consequent discipline situations.

On the other hand, if the block area is planned so there is room to spread out when enthusiasm mounts and if children are taught to start their projects two feet away from the shelves, the likelihood of positive interaction in play is enhanced.

Another matter-of-fact thing to do about room arrangement that decreases the necessity to restrain and discipline children is separating areas with high levels of activity from each other in order to provide protection. In one situation where I taught, only one large open area was available for block and large muscle activity. Noisy chaos was often the result in winter weather when children tried to use the same space for both activities at the same time. Students and staff dreaded working there.

With some rearranging, two widely separated areas were created. The result was that block play and the wonderful social-cognitive learnings that accompany it increased dramatically. The second area was then available for large muscle activities and for dance and group time. The entire tone of the group of four-year-old children became calmer and more pleasant.

Attention to traffic patterns can also increase constructive participation and reduce problem behaviour. When the large rooms frequently used in child care situations are broken up with dividers so that children are physically detoured around activity centres, the temptation to disrupt what other children are doing is reduced. Such dividers can be low bookcases, bulletin boards, or even a Japanese futon. Defining areas by using rugs for this purpose also helps guide children's feet away from trouble in a more subtle way.

---

*Note that these studies also have significant implications for licensing regulations: Adequate regulations can help promote desirable behaviour.

A final facet of environmental planning that will help reduce the need for discipline is the provision of quiet places to which children can retreat when they feel the need for such refreshment. We adults know that constantly being with large numbers of people is tiring, but we tend to forget that it is tiring for children, too. Cosy corners for books, a quiet retreat with some simple manipulative activity, or simply an area in which to stretch out and do nothing can meet this need and reduce the fatigue and irritability that so often lead to loss of self-control.

Have as few rules as possible, but make the ones you do have stick. Unless the teacher is watchful, rules will grow up like a thicket around each experience. But if situations are reviewed from time to time, unnecessary restrictions can be weeded out.

On the other hand, some rules are genuinely necessary, and their enforcement is desirable not only because research shows that establishing firm limits, coupled with warmth and a simple explanation of the reason behind the rule, enhances children's self-esteem (Coopersmith, 1967; Honig, 1985a, 1985b), but also (as we have seen earlier in the chapter) because it increases their ability to establish inner controls.

The problem is to decide, preferably in advance, which rules are really important. Students in particular seem to have trouble in this area—sometimes treating relatively minor infractions such as not saying "please" or "thank you" as though they were major transgressions, while dealing indecisively with more serious misbehaviour such as tearing up picture books or running out the front door without an adult. In general, the most serious infractions of rules are those related to hurting other people, hurting oneself, or destroying another person's property. If a reason for a rule is not easy to come up with, it may be a sign that the rule is not important and could be abandoned.

Although we adults regard following rules as being important, there is another interesting way to think about them—that is, from the point of view of the child. In an amusing and enlightening analysis of that point of view, Corsaro (1988) selected several rules enforced in a nursery school he observed: Running was okay outdoors but not inside; guns and shooting were not permitted; bad language was not permitted; and everyone had to participate in cleaning up. Terming the children's evasion of these rules "the underlife of the nursery school," Corsaro identified common ploys such as pretending not to hear the clean-up time signal and continuing to play, or developing indoor games such as Policeman that required using guns and running to catch the bad people. He maintains that these responses of the children serve more than one purpose. Obviously, they do provide ways of getting around rules, but they also foster the children's ability to function in the culture of their peers. Although this bonhomie is inconvenient for the teacher, it is important to realize that being able to function in their peer group becomes of ever increasing importance as the children grow older. Mildly "beating the system" is one of the ways they learn to do this.

When supervising children, plan ahead. Try to anticipate the point at which the children will lose interest or the play will fall apart and have alternatives ready to propose that will help the play continue to flourish. An insightful teacher might think, "Now, if I were she, what would I like to do next with those blocks and cars?" Perhaps it would be getting out the arches or the wood strips to make a garage, or maybe it would be constructing ramps for the cars to run down. Tactfully posing several possibilities to the children will serve to continue play and to lengthen concentration as well as keep the children happily occupied and out of trouble.

Keep the day interesting. To combat idleness, the centre day needs variety—not only variety of pace to avoid the fatigue that leads to misbehaviour, but also a variety of things to do to maintain interest and fun and to keep the children busy in productive ways. Accomplishing this requires planning and sensitivity, but it is well worth the investment of effort.

Some Things to Do When a Crisis Occurs

Of course, the ideal to work toward even in crisis situations is to teach the children to solve their own problems, since in their adult life they will not always have a teacher present to arbitrate differences. The situations discussed in the following sections, however, are ones in which it is evident that the child has to have help to control herself and to be able to take action that is socially acceptable. Even in these situations the focus should never be on the powers of the teacher to bring about justice, but on development of the child's ability to do this for herself.

Be decisive; know when to step in and control misbehaviour. Inexperienced teachers are often unsure of when they should interfere and when they should let children work the situation through between themselves. As I said earlier, the general rule of thumb is that children should not be allowed to hurt other people (either children or grown-ups), to hurt themselves, or to destroy property. This policy leaves considerable latitude for noninterference, but it also sets a clear line for intervention. An occasional teacher is particularly unsure about whether he should allow children to hit him or kick him as a means of "getting their feelings out." Children should not be allowed to attack adults any more than adults should attack children. Aside from the fact that it hurts and cannot help making the teacher angry, permitting such attacks makes the child feel guilty and uncomfortable. She really knows she should not be allowed to do it.

In the unusual emergency situation in which it is necessary to prevent physical attack, the most effective thing to do is hoist the child on your hip, with her head forward and her feet stuck out behind. This unglamorous pose, known as the *football carry,* works very well to stave off attack and permit the teacher to carry the child somewhere if he has to. Although it is rarely necessary to resort to such measures, it helps to know what to do in a real emergency.

When trouble brews, take action yourself before the child does. Over and over again I have seen teachers sit on the sidelines and let a situation go from bad to worse until it explodes, and then step in to pick up the pieces. If the situation is one that will have to be stopped at some point, *it is much more effective to step in before trouble starts* rather than a minute after blood has been shed (Oren-Wright, 1992).

Prompt intervention makes it more probable that the teacher can use a rational approach with the children; indeed, this is a better environment for teaching any skill. Intervening before the fight occurs also prevents either child from receiving gratification from the attack. For example, stepping in before one child bites another takes preternatural quickness but is vital to do because biting feels so good to the biter that no amount

❧ *Adding a second piece of equipment is just one of the many alternatives to use when teaching children how to get what they want without hurting someone else.*

❦ RESEARCH STUDY ❦
Who's to Blame? Teachers' Reactions to Children's Misbehaviour

Research Question: Scott-Little and Holloway wanted to find out what factors influence the way teachers respond to children's misbehaviour.

Research Method: To investigate some factors that might cause teachers to respond more severely or less severely to children's misbehaviour, the researchers observed the teachers and children together, noted episodes of misbehaviour and the teacher's response to those episodes, and then questioned them afterwards about the reasons they had responded that particular way.

Forty head teachers from thirty-four different centres working in classrooms of predominantly four-year-olds were selected. Their educational backgrounds ranged from high school to master's degrees. They were each observed working with the children during a two-hour period. The observers documented two examples of aggression or noncompliance by the children to which the teacher responded in some way; these were used as the data base for the interviews later on. The teacher responses were classified as belonging to

one of four types: *non-power-assertive* (the teacher might comfort the victim but do nothing about the aggressor), *mildly power-assertive* (the child is asked to think about her behaviour without the teacher making a direct attempt to exercise adult authority to correct it), *moderately power-assertive* (the teacher takes action to assert her authority and correct the behaviour), and *highly power-assertive* (the teacher attempts to force the child to correct the behaviour—perhaps by punishing the child).

At the interviews that followed, the teachers were asked to explain why they thought the child had misbehaved as she had—what did the teachers see as being the reasons (causes) for the misbehaviour? These reasons were then classified according to whether the causes were external or internal, whether the child could or could not control the causes, and how consistent the child's response was.

Statistical analysis revealed that when the proportion of internal, controllable, and stable reasons (attributions) for the misbehaviour were correlated

---

of punishment afterward detracts sufficiently from the satisfying reward of sinking teeth into unresisting flesh.

Accept the fact that physical restraint may be necessary. We have already discussed using the football carry as an emergency means of fending off an attack by a child; but even when children are not attacking the teacher directly, it is often necessary in a crisis situation to move swiftly and take hold of a child before she can strike someone else again.

When doing this, it is important to be as gentle as possible and yet be firm enough that the child cannot slip away. Usually just catching an arm is enough, though sometimes it is necessary to put both arms around the obstreperous one. Unfortunately this often makes the child struggle harder against the restraint, but at least it prevents her from having the satisfaction of landing another blow on her victim. As soon as the child is calm enough to hear what is being said to her, it will help bring things under control if the teacher says something on the order of "As soon as you calm down, I can let go of you, and we can talk."

with the power-assertion responses of the teachers, it turned out that the teachers who rated children's behaviour as being the result of their internal impulses and controllable by them used stronger power-assertion techniques in response to those behaviours than they did when they thought the reasons for the behaviour were externally caused and uncontrollable by the children. In other words, teachers used more authority and punishing techniques when they blamed the child for her behaviour than they did when they felt something or someone else was the cause of that behaviour.

An interesting additional finding was that the amount of education/training the teachers had was not related to how much and what kind of power-assertive techniques they used to control the children.

Implications for Teaching: The investigators conclude that "adults who respond to children with more power assertion, or by asserting their authority over the child, seem not to facilitate children's development" (p. 603).

Scott-Little and Holloway suggest that one remedy for using too-strong power-assertion strategies would be to train teachers to become more aware of external causes of misbehaviour that lie beyond the child's ability to control. They reason that such insight would encourage teachers to use milder approaches. Evidently, something needs to be changed about the way we educate teachers since the research indicates that at this point, the degree of power-assertion does not correlate with the amount of education to which teachers have been exposed. Better education would likely provide teachers with more effective, less aggressive methods of controlling children.

The other contribution this research can make to fostering teachers' insights is that once our consciousness has been raised about the general tendency to come down hard on children who seem to be wilfully misbehaving, we should be especially careful to put the responsibility for choosing more acceptable ways to behave squarely on the shoulders of the child instead of just punishing her. The six learning steps outlined in this chapter illustrate an effective way of stopping misbehaviour by being firm but not punitive when coping with it.

Source: From "Child Care Providers' Reasoning About Misbehaviors: Relation to Classroom Control Strategies and Professional Training" by M. C. Scott-Little and S. D. Holloway, 1992, pp. 595–606.

When a situation has deteriorated to the extent that physical restraint is needed, it is usually best to draw the child or children away from the group so that they do not continue to disrupt it. It is seldom necessary to take them out of the room, and it seems to me it is more desirable to remain where the other children can see that nothing too terrible happens to the offenders. Otherwise, anxious children fantasize too much about what was done to the fighters.

When dealing with misbehaviour, avoid using control strategies that are unnecessarily overwhelming. The way a teacher responds to a child's misbehaviour depends on a lot of circumstances. Among these are the teacher's mood and energy on that particular day, how many prior run-ins he has had with that youngster, how secure he feels when dealing with misbehaviour, and a myriad of other imponderables. The research by Scott-Little and Holloway described in the research study in this chapter provides an additional and often unrecognized reason for the way teachers react in discipline situations.

When immediate control is necessary, follow the six steps for teaching children self-control. Since children do not always stop throwing sand or grabbing tricycles simply because the teacher tells them to or redirects them to another activity, it is necessary to know what to do when a child occasionally continues to misbehave. I call the approach I use the six learning steps in discipline: (a) warning the child, (b) removing her, (c) discussing feelings and rules, (d) waiting for her to decide when she is ready to return, (e) helping her return and be more successful, and (f) following through with losing the privilege when this is necessary.

Warn the child and redirect her if she will accept such redirection. For example, you might warn a youngster that if she continues to throw sand, she will lose the privilege of staying in the sandbox; then suggest a couple of interesting things she could do with the sand instead of throwing it. It is important to make the child understand *that her behaviour is up to her.* It is *her* choice; but if she chooses to continue, you will see to it that you carry out your warning.

If necessary, remove child promptly and keep her with you. Warn only once. If she persists in doing what she has been told not to do, act calmly and promptly. Remove her and insist that she sit beside you, telling her she has lost the privilege of playing in the sand. This is much more valuable than just letting her run off. Having her sit beside you interrupts what she wants to do, is a mildly unpleasant consequence of her act, and prevents her from substituting another activity she would enjoy or taunting you by running away.

Instead of keeping the child right beside him, many teachers send the child off to sit in a "time-out" chair. Although this time-hallowed method is certainly an improvement over spanking or saying hurtful things, there are some drawbacks to its use that must be considered. Basically, what is happening when the time-out chair is used is that the child is sent to the corner—all that is lacking is the old-fashioned dunce cap. Sent off by herself, the child is emotionally abandoned. Besides that, teacher and child frequently become involved in secondary struggles when the child tries to sneak away and the teacher catches her. Finally, as Clewett (1988) points out, many time-out episodes go on way too long, either because it's such a relief to the teacher to have the child removed or because he forgets she's there. For all these reasons, despite its inconvenience, it is more desirable to keep the child nearby.

Discuss feelings and rules after a reasonable degree of calm has prevailed. This is a very important part of handling a discipline crisis. Even if the child is saying such things as "I hate you—you're mean! I'm going to tell my mother and I'm never coming back!" it is possible to recognize her feelings by replying, "You're really angry with me because I made you stop grabbing the trike. [Pause] But the rule here is that people can keep something till they're done with it." If more than one child is involved, it is vital to put each child's feelings into words for them as well as you can. The virtue of doing this is that when children know you understand what they feel, even though you don't agree, they don't have to keep *showing* you how they feel.

Once feelings have been aired and everyone is calmer, this is also a good time to state whatever rules apply and discuss alternative ways of solving the difficulty. If the child is mature enough, she should be able to contribute her own ideas as well as hearing what the teacher has to say.

Internalize responsibility; that is, have the child take the responsibility for herself of deciding when she is ready to return. At this step many teachers say something on the order of "Now you sit here with me until lunch is ready," thus shifting the responsibility for the child's behaviour to their own shoulders instead of putting the child in command of herself. But if the long-term goal of internalizing self-control is to be reached, it is much wiser to say, "Now, tell me when you can control yourself, and then we will go back" or, more specifically, "When you think you can remember to keep the sand down, tell me, and then you can go back and play." Some children can actually say they are ready, but others will need help from the teacher, who can ask them when they look ready, "Are you ready to go back now?" (Perhaps she nods or just looks ready.) "Good, your eyes tell me you are. What would you like to do for fun there?"

Finally, *it is important to go with the child and help her be successful* when she does go back so that she has the experience of substituting acceptable for unacceptable behaviour. It will probably be necessary to take a few minutes and get her really interested. Be sure to congratulate the child when she has settled down, perhaps saying, "Now, you're doing the right thing. I'm proud of you!"

Follow through with suspending the privilege if the child repeats the behaviour. Occasionally the teacher will come across a glibber customer who says hastily when removed from the sandbox, "I'll be good, I'll be good!" but then goes right back to throwing sand when she returns. At this point it is necessary to take firmer action. Have her sit beside you until she can think of something acceptable to do, but do not permit her to go back to the sandbox. You might say, "What you did [be explicit] shows me that you haven't decided to do the right thing; so you'll have to come and sit with me until you can think of somewhere else to play. You've lost the privilege of playing in the sandbox for now." Then when she decides, *go with her and take her to another teacher and tell him about her special need to get started on something productive.* Avoid sounding moralistic or "nasty-nice" while explaining the situation to the teacher, because this will just prolong bad feelings.

Keep your own emotions under control. One way children learn attitudes is by observing models (Bandura, 1986). Teachers need to control their own tempers, since by doing so they provide a model of self-control for the children to copy as well as because intense anger frightens children. Also, when discipline situations arise, it is not just one child and the teacher who are involved: Every child in the room is covertly watching what is happening and drawing conclusions from it. Therefore, it is often valuable for the teacher to talk over what happened with various children afterward to help them deal with how they felt about it and to clarify and consolidate what they learned from it. For example, he might explain to a worried-looking three-year-old, "Jacob was crying because he wanted that car, but Teddy had it first so Jacob had to let go. He was pretty upset, wasn't he? Did he scare you?"

Sometimes, of course, it is simpler to advocate self-control in the teacher than to achieve it (Samalin, 1992). Things that can help teachers retain control include remembering that one is dealing with a child, deliberately keeping control of oneself, and acknowledging the feeling and saying to the child, "Let's wait just a minute until we're both a little calmer. I feel pretty upset about what you did." The biggest help, though, comes from analysing scenes and upsets after they have occurred and planning how best to handle them the next time they happen. This experience and analysis builds skills and confidence, and confidence is the great strengthener of self-control. Children sense this assurance in the teacher just the way dogs know who loves or fears them, and children become less challenging and more at ease when they feel the teacher knows how to cope and has every intention of doing so.

Remember, you don't have to make an instantaneous decision. Not only does admitting to a child that you need time to control your feelings help you regain control of them, it also models self-control and provides time to think about what to do next. In the heat of the moment it is easy to make a decision about punishment that the adult regrets later because it is inappropriate or too severe. For example, a child who has tried the teacher's patience all morning may be shoved into a chair with the statement "You're gonna stay here 'til your mother comes, no matter what!" or a culprit who has smeared paint all over the sink will be told "Well, you just can't use any more paint this week!"

Once the physical action has been halted, it is not necessary to render instant justice in this manner. Waiting a minute and thinking before speaking gives the teacher time to remember that he is going to have to keep that child sitting in that chair for an entire hour or decide it would be more effective to have the youngster wash the paint off the sink rather than deny her the privilege of using paints for four long days.

❦   *Remember, when one child is disciplined, many other children are watching, too.*

Knowing where your flashpoints are is helpful, too. Different behaviours make different teachers (and parents) angry, and it is helpful to take time to analyse what your particular flashpoints are because this awareness can help you control your response to them.

Some examples of flashpoints students and staff provided to me recently included deliberate insolence, withdrawing and acting coy, intentionally hurting another child (particularly after the teacher has stopped the behaviour a moment before), outright defiance, use of "bad" language, calculated ignoring of the teacher, and pouting or sulking and refusing to tell why.

No doubt all these behaviours are irritating to all teachers sometimes, but each of them had a special power to evoke anger in some particular member of our discussion group. The reasons that lie behind these specific vulnerabilities range from the teacher's early upbringing to his lack of knowing how to respond effectively to a particular child's style. Sometimes, however, a teacher has no idea why he is sensitive to a particular behaviour. Although knowing the origin can be helpful, it is not essential to understand why you become especially angry when such behaviour occurs. Just *knowing* that you are vulnerable can be sufficient because the knowing can be linked to reminding yourself to make a special effort to keep your temper under control and be fair and reasonable when a child behaves in that particular way.

Settle fights by helping children to express their feelings. In the chapter on mental health, considerable time was spent in explaining how to help children express their feelings verbally. Although this is fairly easy to accomplish when the teacher is dealing with only one child, it is considerably more difficult *but just as important* when dealing with more than one. When two children are involved, it is a wonderful opportunity to help both of them develop this social skill, and the teacher should urge them to talk things over and to tell each other what they want and how they feel (Wichert, 1989). Telling each other how they feel and knowing these feelings have been heard often mean that children are no longer driven to act them out, and the way is opened for compromise.

It is also essential that teachers avoid being trapped into rendering judgements about situations they have not seen. Four-year-olds are particularly prone to tattle about the misdeeds of others. A polite name for this is *prosocial aggression;* it is a natural if unappealing stage in the development of conscience. Unless the reported activity is truly dangerous, the best course of action in the case of tattling is for the teacher to encourage the child to return with him and settle the matter. He should avoid taking sides or the word of one child. When it is a case of who had what first, it may be necessary, if a compromise cannot be reached, to take whatever it is away from both youngsters for a while until they calm down. Remember, it is often the child who is crying the loudest who began the fight, although she may appear to need comforting the most. The only thing to do in situations such as this is be fair and deal with both children in a firm but nonjudgemental way. Impartiality is the keynote.

When a fight develops, it can also be helpful to call a meeting of the children who are nearby to discuss ways of settling it. Some three-year-olds and the majority of four-year-olds are capable of offering practical remedies if the matter catches their interest. The point of such discussions is not to ask the witnesses who was to blame (remember, it takes two to make a fight) but to ask them for ideas and suggestions about how to arbitrate the

❧   *Keeping sand down can be
a problem.*

difficulty. The fighters can often be prevailed upon to listen to what their peers have to suggest, and children often come up with surprisingly practical solutions, although these tend to be severe (Kohlberg, 1976; Turiel, 1973). It is fine experience for them to think about how to get along together and work out solutions based on real-life situations.

When a child has gone so far that she has hurt another youngster, she should be allowed to help remedy the injury. Perhaps she can put on the bandage or hold a cold towel on the bump. This constructive action helps her see the consequences of her act, relieve her guilty feelings, and show concern by doing something tangible. I do not believe children should be asked to say they are sorry. Often they are not sorry, and even if they are, I fear teaching the lesson that glib apologies make everything all right. Moreover, a replicated study by Irwin and Moore (1971) supports the idea that young children grasp the concept of restitution (doing something to right a "wrong") before they understand the true significance of apology, so making restitution by righting the wrong is a more developmentally appropriate approach.

Whenever possible, let the punishment fit the crime. Preprimary teachers (and enlightened parents) avoid doling out punishment in its usual forms. Teachers do not spank children, shut them in closets, take away their television privileges, or deny them dessert because they have not been good. But they do *allow* another form of "punishment" to happen when it is appropriate. This is simply permitting the child to experience the natural consequences of her behaviour (Samalin, 1992). Thus the child who refuses to come in for snack is permitted to miss the meal; the child who rebelliously tears a page from a book is expected to mend it; and the youngster who pulls all the blocks off the shelf must stay to help put them away. Even young children can appreciate the justice of a consequence that stems logically from the action. It is not necessary to be unpleasant or moralistic when any of these results transpire; it is the teacher's responsibility only to make certain that the child experiences the logical outcome of her behaviour.

When the encounter is over, forgive and forget—don't hold a grudge. Inexperienced teachers sometimes dread confrontations because they fear that the child will be hostile afterward or actively dislike them for keeping their word and enforcing their authority. However, such confrontations almost invariably build a closer bond between the teacher and the child, who usually seeks him out and makes it evident that she likes him after such encounters. Teachers are often surprised by this commonplace result. What I want to suggest here is that, since children do not usually hold a grudge when disciplined fairly, teachers too should be willing to wipe the slate clean.

It is very important for a child's sense of self-esteem that she be seen in a generally positive light. If the teacher allows a couple of negative encounters to colour his perception of the youngster so that she is seen as a "bad girl," it is difficult for her to overcome this image and establish a more positive relationship. For this reason, particularly with "difficult" children, teachers need to call upon all their reserves of generosity and maturity and make every effort to concentrate on the youngster's positive qualities.

Most important, notice when children do the right thing, and comment favourably. This entire chapter has been spent talking about preventing or coping with misbehaviour. Fortunately most of the centre day does not revolve around such episodes; many days go smoothly and the children get along happily. When the day is a good one, when the children are obviously making progress, when they mostly talk instead of hit each other, when they share generously and enjoy the opportunities to help each other, let them know that you are pleased with their good behaviour. They will share your pleasure in their accomplishments, and this recognition will help perpetuate the growth and self-discipline they have displayed.

A Final Thought

There is no teacher (or parent, for that matter) in the world who handles every discipline situation perfectly! When one of those less than perfect situations happens between you and a child, it is all too easy to spend energy on feeling guilty or regretful about how things went. Rather than doing that, it is wiser to think over what happened and learn from it, because every discipline situation provides opportunities for *two* people to learn something. When things have not turned out well, think about what the child learned and what you learned, and consider possible alternatives. Then resolve to use a different approach the next time a similar situation comes up. Perhaps it will be rearranging the environment, or perhaps stepping in sooner, or perhaps firmly seeing a struggle all the way through. Taking positive steps to analyse difficulties and improve your skills is infinitely more desirable than exhausting yourself over past mistakes.

❦ *Summary*

Discipline should be more than just "getting the kids to do what I want." The real goal should be the development of self-control within the children. This is accomplished, in part, by strengthening the ego and by fostering the beginning of conscience. Two ego-strengthening experiences often used by early childhood teachers are offering appropriate choices to children to give them practice in decision making and helping children feel masterful through becoming competent.

The growth of conscience is facilitated by the presence of warm, nurturing relationships between child and adult, as well as by the use of person-oriented induction (reason-giving), techniques; but the moral judgements rendered by the conscience are profoundly influenced by the stage of moral reasoning the child has attained. Progress from one stage to the next depends on cognitive maturation combined with social experience. From this interaction the child constructs the next step in moral growth.

There are many undesirable ways to control children, but there are also more desirable approaches that can be subsumed under the general heading of preventing discipline situations when possible and knowing what to do when a crisis occurs. When all these strategies fail and a child continues to misbehave, it is important to take her through all six of the steps in learning self-control: (a) warning her, (b) removing her from the activity while keeping her with the teacher, (c) acknowledging feelings and stating rules, (d) waiting for her to make the decision to return to the activity, (e) helping her return and be more successful, and (f) following through with losing the privilege when that becomes necessary. Consistent use of this approach will be effective in helping children gain control of themselves, thus helping them become socially acceptable human beings.

Questions and Activities

1. Give three examples of choices you could encourage the children to make for themselves the next time you teach.

2. Have you ever had the experience of deciding, theoretically, how you intended to handle misbehaviour and then finding yourself doing something different when the occasion actually came up? How do you account for this discrepancy?

3. *Problem:* A child is throwing sand in the sandbox, and you want her to stop. What should you say to put your statement in positive form rather than telling her what not to do, that is, rather than saying, "Don't throw the sand"?

4. Select an activity, such as lunchtime, and list every rule, spoken and implicit, that you expect children to observe in this situation. Are there any that could be abandoned? Are there any that are really for the teacher's convenience rather than for the purpose of fostering the children's well-being?

5. Team up with another student and take fifteen-minute turns for an hour, keeping track of how many times you reinforced positive behaviour of the children. Then, keep track of how many opportunities for such reinforcement you overlooked.

6. *Problem:* Jamal, who is four-and-a-half, is playing at the puzzle table and keeps slipping little pieces of puzzle into his pocket. No one except you sees him doing this. You have already told him twice to keep the puzzles on the table so the pieces won't get lost, but he continues to challenge you by slipping them into his pocket. What should you do next to handle this situation?

7. *Problem:* As you enter the room you see Miyok and Ovid hanging on to a truck, both shouting "I had it first!" and "I can keep it until I'm done with it!" How would you cope with this crisis?

Self-Check Questions for Review

Content-Related Questions

1. What are the two basic goals of discipline? In the long run, which is of greatest value?
2. Is it true that someone who possesses ego strength is conceited? Please explain your answer.
3. According to Hoffman's review of research, what are the two most important factors involved in interiorizing conscience?
4. Why are four-year-olds likely to reason differently about a "crime" from the way twenty-year-olds do?
5. List and explain several principles teachers can follow that will help prevent discipline situations from developing.
6. There are six learning steps the child and teacher should go through when the child has done something she shouldn't have. Explain these six steps.
7. What two features did Buzzelli single out as being important elements in the development of moral understanding?
8. According to Scott-Little and Holloway, how do teachers tend to react when they feel a child is to blame for her misbehaviour?

Integrative Questions

1. The book discusses self- versus "other"-controlled behaviour. Using college-age students as examples, how might a student who is "other controlled" behave compared with one who has established inner controls? Give an example of potential behaviour in a group social situation and one involving taking a class.
2. Give two examples of choices that are developmentally appropriate for a four-year-old to make and two that would not be developmentally appropriate.
3. Review the list of ways *not* to reach the basic goals of good discipline and provide descriptions of actual situations that show how teachers sometimes enforce those undesirable policies.
4. *Problem:* Jerry and Austin are squabbling over a sprinkling can in the garden, each wanting to water the radishes with it. Finally Austin tips it over and pours water on Jerry's shoes, and Jerry begins to cry. He seizes a shovel and whacks Austin's hand with it. Using this situation as the example, explain how you would use the six learning steps to control the boys'

behaviour. Next, explain some longer-term actions you might take to make it less likely that behaviour would happen again.
5. Do you agree with the positive social values for nonconforming that Corsaro (1988) suggests in the discussion of the "underlife" of the early childhood setting? Explain your reasons for agreeing or disagreeing.
6. Is it necessarily a "bad" idea to use more power-assertive responses when a child has misbehaved by deliberately doing something that she knows she should not have done? Why do you think teachers come on stronger in that kind of situation than in one in which they feel the child was not at fault?
7. Using the Scott-Little and Holloway definition of degrees of power-assertive techniques, how would you rank the six steps for teaching children self-control?

References for Further Reading

Overviews

Allen, E., Paasche, C., Cornell, A., & Engel, M. (1994). *Exceptional children: Inclusion in early childhood programs* (1st Can. ed.) Scarborough: Nelson Canada. This book includes a very useful chapter designed to facilitate positive behaviours.

Betz, C. (1994). Beyond time-out: Tips from a teacher. *Young Children, 49* (3), 10–14. In this very good article, Betz makes a case for using alternatives to time-out except in the most trying circumstances.

Gartrell, D. (1994). *A guidance approach to discipline.* Albany, NY: Delmar. Basing his presentation on a consistent theoretical approach, Gartrell discusses various aspects of discipline as it relates to children in the early childhood classroom. *Highly recommended.*

Greenberg, P. (1992). Ideas that work with young children: How to institute some simple democratic practices pertaining to respect, rights, roots, and responsibilities in any classroom (without losing your leadership position). *Young Children, 47*(5): 10–17. This article summarizes the most important basics of discipline and control—particularly noteworthy is the page on preventive discipline. *Highly recommended.*

Honig, A., & Lansburgh, T. (1994). The tasks of early childhood: The development of self-control—Part II. In K. M. Paciorek & J. H. Munro (Eds.), *Early childhood education 94/95.* Guilford, CT: Dushkin. This is a helpful, practical discussion of positive ways to foster self-control in young children.

Marion, M. (1991). *Guidance of young children* (3rd ed.). Englewood Cliffs, NJ: Merrill/Prentice Hall. Marion's book is filled with a sound combination of research, theory, and practical advice on this subject.

Mitchell, G. (1982). *A very practical guide to discipline with young children.* Marshfield, MA: Telshare. Mitchell brings a world of experience to this useful book that discusses a general approach to discipline combined with discussions of typical problems.

Saifer, S. (1990). *Practical solutions to practically every problem: The early childhood teacher's manual.* St. Paul, MN: Toys 'n Things Press. My only problem with this book is where to place it in the references because it covers such a wide range of problems such as gifted children, death, and biting, to name just a few. This is a good, useful book.

Moral Development

Schulman, M., & Mekler, E. (1985). *Bringing up a moral child: A new approach for teaching your child to be kind, just, and responsible.* Reading, MA: Addison-Wesley. Writing in laymen's language, Schulman and Mekler base their recommendations on research mingled with common sense.

Settling Fights

Oken-Wright, P. (1992). From Tug of War to "Let's Make a Deal": The teacher's role. *Young Children, 48*(1): 15–20. The author provides practical examples of ways to substitute language for violence when settling fights.

Wichert, P. (1989). *Keeping the peace: Practicing cooperation and conflict resolution with preschoolers.* Philadelphia, PA: New Society Publishers. This not-to-be-missed book combines practical discussion with a number of specific activities intended to enhance the children's conflict resolution skills.

For the Advanced Student

Buzzelli, C. (1992). Young children's moral understanding: Learning about right and wrong. *Young Children, 47*(6: 47–83. Buzzelli discusses a variety of approaches currently being used to investigate how moral behaviour develops in young children.

Kagan, J., & Lamb, S. (1987). *The emergence of morality in young children.* Chicago: University of Chicago Press. The authors present several differing points of view about how morality develops.

Kohlberg, L. (1976). The development of children's orientations toward a moral order. Sequence in the development of moral thought. In P. B. Neubauer (Ed.), *The process of child development.* New York: Jason Aronson. Here is a lucid explanation of Kohlberg's six-stage theory of moral development, including good examples of the attitudes characterizing each stage.

Piaget, J. (1932). *The moral judgement of the child.* London: Routledge & Kegan Paul. A hallmark study of moral attitudes that forms the foundation for much of the later work in this area; easier reading than most works by this master.

Schickedanz, J. A. (1994). Helping children develop self-control. *Childhood Education, 70*(5): 274–278. Schickedanz discusses recent findings concerning the development of moral understanding in young children and concludes with some practical recommendations on using discipline techniques that encourage development of that understanding in young children. *Highly recommended.*

Shweder, R. A., Mahapatra, M., & Miller, J. G. (1987). Culture and moral development. In J. Kagan & S. Lamb (Eds.), *The emergence of morality in children.* Chicago: University of Chicago Press. This fascinating study contrasts Brahmin and Untouchable Indian ideas of morality with those of the American middle class.

Aggression
What to Do About It[*]

$\mathcal{G}$*12*

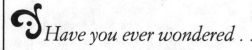

Punishing children does teach some lasting lessons, though. Take the use of violence to discipline children. Regardless of what we are trying to get across by spanking, paddling, or slapping them the messages that actually come through are these: "Violence is an acceptable way of expressing anger" and "If you are powerful enough you can get away with hurting someone."

Alfie Kohn

Have you ever wondered . . .

What to do about a child who is particularly aggressive?

What to teach a youngster that would help him enter a group peacefully instead of by starting a fight?

What you could substitute in place of direct aggression that might still relieve an angry child's pent-up feelings?

. . . If you have, the material in the following pages will help you.

*Adapted from "Aggression: What to Do About It" by J. B. Hendrick, 1968, *Young Children, 23*(5), pp. 298-305.

Now that the general subject of discipline has been discussed, it is time to talk about dealing with aggressive behaviour in particular. When we work with young children we must consider two kinds of aggression. The first, and by far the commonest, kind of aggression is *instrumental aggression*. This is aggression that occurs without basic hostile intent. For example, a child reaches over and takes away another child's felt-tip marker because he wants to draw, or a two-year-old pushes another child aside so he can reach a book. While these actions may require arbitration, explanation, and protection of the second child's rights by the teacher, they differ from the hostile types of aggression discussed in this chapter. *Hostile aggressive* behaviour refers to "actions that are intended to cause injury or anxiety to others, including hitting, kicking, destroying property, quarrelling, derogating others, attacking others verbally and resisting requests" (Mussen, Conger, & Kagan, 1969, p. 370)

Berkowitz, a well-known authority on this subject, concurs, saying "Whatever other goals highly aroused persons may have, we must remember that they also want to hurt their targets. They may be gratified if they can assert their power or control over their victim, or maintain their values, but deep down—and at times more than anything else—they are trying to hurt the persons they are attacking" (1993, p. 17). Tavris (1982) points out that aggression is the result of anger—anger being the feeling and aggression being the expression of that feeling.

At the preschool level we see examples of this kind of behaviour manifested when children barge through the room leaving a bedlam of smashed blocks or ravished housekeeping corners behind them, or when they spend most of their time whooping wildly about being tigers or monsters, or when they deliberately seek to injure other children by destroying what they are doing, teasing them, or physically hurting them. Such aggression differs from ordinary rough-and-tumble play because it is marked by angry frowns and unwillingness to stop until someone has been really hurt (Kostelnik, Whiren, & Stein, 1986).

ᔆ Undesirable Ways To Cope With Aggression

Teachers and parents deal with acting out behaviour in both useful and not so useful ways. Some of the more undesirable methods of responding to such behaviour follow.

The Authoritarian Teacher

At one extreme are teachers who are tightly controlling authoritarians. These teachers are similar to the authoritarian parents described by Baumrind (1989) in her studies of parenting styles. She describes authoritarian parents as intending to shape, control, and evaluate the way their children behave according to absolute standards of what is right. Such parents value obedience and favour taking punitive, forceful measures when children's behaviours conflict with those standards.

Authoritarian teachers also tend to respond to conflict between themselves and the children as if expressing their own aggressive tendencies, garbed in the disguise of authority and control, were the only way to cope with the problem. In forthright cases, schools dominated by such teachers are likely to be riddled with many rules generally determined by what is convenient for the teacher. Don't run! Don't make noise! Sit down! Line up! Be quiet! Don't easel paint with your fingers! Stay clean! Don't splash! Take turns! Tell him you're sorry!—and a thousand other tiresome injunctions are typical. Punishments used by such teachers are apt to be severe, occasionally to the point of being emotionally destructive or physically painful.

Sometimes beleaguered teachers feel that controls of this type are necessary because the classes are too large or too obstreperous for them to cope with any other way. Sometimes they believe that this kind of control is what the parents expect and that they had better conform to this expectation or the children will be withdrawn from school.

More than likely the real reason for their reaction runs deeper than this and has to do with strong patterns carrying over from their own childhood, when little tolerance and freedom were granted to them by the adults in their lives, and they were provided with

✑ *Not all aggression is hurtful.*

very authoritarian models. The frustration, resulting hostility, and covert aggression instilled by this treatment are particularly likely to be rearoused when they are confronted by the challenge of a belligerent four-year-old or a balky two-year-old. Transgressions are often dealt with by stringent punishments, and contests of will are highly probable if these teachers cross swords with a genuinely spirited child.

What of the aggressive child who exists in this tightly controlled environment? What is the effect of overcontrol on him? For a few youngsters the bright edge of creative expression is dulled. Some children cannot afford to risk nonconforming (which is the essence of creativity) under these circumstances, and so most of their energy is used up holding onto themselves and "doing the right thing." These children have had their spirits broken. They conform—but at what a price!

There are almost bound to be other defiant young souls who continue to challenge or sneak past such teachers. Common examples of such underground, continued aggression may range from quietly pulling the fur off the guinea pig to being unable to settle down for stories, or consistently destroying other children's accomplishments at the puzzle table or in the block corner. Other children internalize the angry feelings generated by authoritarian restrictions and become resistant and sullen; still others settle for becoming openly defiant.

In such schools a basic restlessness and tension seem to simmer in the air, and teachers work harder and harder to hold the line, an exhausting business for all concerned. They tend to operate on the assumption that stronger punishment will result in greater control of aggression, but this is not necessarily true. Overwhelming evidence from research studies indicates that strong punishment, particularly physical punishment, actually increases the amount of aggressive behaviour (Baron & Richardson, 1994; Dewolfe, Michels, Pianta, & Reeve, 1993; Eron & Huesmann, 1984; Hart & Burts, 1992). This finding holds particularly true for children who already show aggressive tendencies (Patterson, 1982). Such teachers also overlook the fact that there is a limit to how far they can go to enforce dicta. What will they do if matters persist in getting out of hand?

Unfortunately, the next step for some of these teachers is resorting to corporal punishment. Although hitting and otherwise physically terrorizing young children at school may seem unthinkable to many readers, the fact is that such treatment does occur.

The evil results of such an approach are well summed up by Moore (1982):

> Any parenting technique will work some of the time, but as a general rule, using harsh punishment to curb high levels of aggression does not work. Highly punitive parents [and we might equally well substitute the word *teachers* for *parents* here] not only provide their children with aggressive interpersonal models to emulate but they also risk undermining their child's sense of personal worth, frustrating and embittering the child, and orienting the child toward his own misery rather than to the plight of another. (p. 74)

The Overpermissive Teacher

At the other disciplinary extreme are teachers who feel that "anything goes." Such teachers are often confused about the difference between freedom and licence, and they fail to see that true freedom means the child may do as he wishes *only as long as he does not interfere with the rights and freedom of other people.* This extremely permissive teacher is fairly rare in children's centres because the pandemonium that occurs quickly makes parents uneasy. Apparently the results of this kind of mishandling are more obvious to the unprofessional eye than are the results of overcontrol.

In response to overpermissiveness the children may display behaviour similar to the response for overcontrol (Olweus, 1980). They may destroy other children's accomplishments or unconcernedly take whatever appeals to them. Sometimes they seem driven to tyrannical desperation trying to find out where the limits are and just how far they must go before the teacher at last overcomes her apathy and stirs herself to action. A common example of children's behaviour in these circumstances is defiant teasing and baiting of the teacher by being ostentatiously, provocatively "naughty."

What the children really learn in such overpermissive circumstances is that "might makes right." This is a vicious circle, since the aggressor is often rewarded by getting what he wants and so is more likely to behave just as aggressively next time. Indeed, research indicates that attendance at a permissive nursery school does increase aggressive behaviour (Patterson, Littman, & Bricker, 1967), and additional research by Bandura and Walters (1963) indicates that the presence of a permissive adult generally facilitates the expression of aggression. Appel (1942) also found that when adults did not intervene in an aggressive encounter, the child who began the fight was successful about two-thirds of the time; but when an adult stepped in, the aggressor's success rate fell to about one-fourth of the time. Clearly an overly permissive attitude by teachers can promote the expression of aggression by allowing such behaviour to be rewarded.

The Inconsistent Teacher

The third undesirable way to deal with aggressive behaviour is to be inconsistent. Teachers may be inconsistent because they are unsure that it is really all right to control children, or they may be uncertain about how to control them, or they may be unaware that consistency is important; hence, they deal erratically with out-of-hand behaviour, sometimes enforcing a rule when they think they can make it stick and other times sighing and letting the child run off or have his own way.

This approach creates deep unease in children and fosters attempts by them to manipulate, challenge, and bargain in order to gain special dispensations. Whining, nagging, wheedling, and implied threats by the youngsters are all likely to be prime ingredients in this environment. For example, a four-year-old may threaten, "If you don't give me that trike right now, I'll have to cry very, very hard, and then I'll prob'ly throw up, and you will have to tell my mother!"

Inconsistent handling may sound merely weak; however, it may actually be the most undesirable approach of all, since it has been found to increase aggressiveness in children (Hom & Hom, 1980; Parke & Slaby, 1983). The probable reason for this result is that the reward for aggressive behaviour is intermittent rather than continuous. It has been effectively demonstrated that an intermittent reinforcement schedule is a powerful means of causing behaviour to continue (Duer & Parke, 1970; Parke & Duer, 1972), particularly when there are additional payoffs involved such as having got what one wanted by grabbing it.

Conclusion

It is fairly easy to see that teachers who are overcontrolling (authoritarian) or undercontrolling (extremely permissive) or very inconsistent bring special difficulties upon themselves when dealing with aggressive behaviour. It is less easy to determine what constitutes a reasonable balance between aggression and control and to decide how to handle this problem in an effective and healthy way. We want to harness and direct this energy, not abolish it (Kostelnik et al., 1986). Teachers often feel confused about how and where to draw the line. They think it is important to relish the burgeoning vitality of young children, and so they want to provide vigorous, free, large muscle play, and plenty of it. But most teachers do not think that large muscle activity should be permitted to be expressed in preschool as endless, aimless, wild running about or terrorization of the quieter children.

Many teachers can go along with the idea that the child has the right to destroy anything he has made so long as it is his own and not someone else's. However, they also believe that direct aggression in the form of throwing things at people, biting, hitting others with objects in hand, outright insolence, and defiance of basic rules are generally unacceptable.

The problem is how to channel the expression of these feelings into acceptable ways at school and in society. The remainder of this chapter provides some basic approaches that will help the teacher solve this problem.

❦ Desirable Ways to Cope with Aggression

Assess the Underlying Causes of Aggression, and Ameliorate Them When Possible

First, it is helpful to remember that pronounced self-assertiveness is part of the developmental picture for four-year-old boys and girls. Many boys show evidence of this by attempting feats of daring, being physically aggressive, and swaggering about with an air of braggadocio. Girls are more likely to express it by being bossy or tattling in a busybody way on the wrongdoings of other children. It is important to realize that this rather out-of-hand phase serves a healthy purpose for these youngsters who are busy finding out who they are by asserting their individuality (it is somewhat like adolescence in this regard).

Additional evidence that aggression should not be regarded as "all bad" is furnished by Lord (1982), who cites studies showing that "preschool children who are more aggressive than average often are also more friendly, empathetic, and willing to share materials than other children" (p. 237). But she also stresses that this finding holds true only for preschoolers and not for aggressive children who are older.

Besides the influence of the developmental stage, native temperament may have a lot to do with the expression of aggression (Soderman, 1985). Some children can stand more frustration than others can without exploding (Block & Martin, 1955). Sex-linked characteristics also affect its expression (Eagley & Wood, 1991). Maccoby and Jacklin (1974) summarize many studies indicating that in our culture more direct physical aggression is expressed by boys than by girls, and Feshbach and Feshbach (1972) have

🕉   *An impasse like this presents rich opportunities for the teacher to help children work things through.*

reported that girls are more likely to employ indirect means of expressing aggressive feelings. However, how much of this behaviour is due to biological differences and how much to culturally instilled values has yet to be determined (Berkowitz, 1993; Lott & Maluso, 1993).

In extreme cases of aggression, particularly when it is combined with hyperactivity, the possibility of brain damage should be considered, since lack of impulse control may be indicative of such a condition. In these *unusual* circumstances medication can produce considerable improvement in such behaviour for some acting out youngsters.

Parental mishandling is the reason most frequently given by teachers as the cause of undue aggression in children; and it is true that rejection, particularly cold, permissive rejection by parents, is associated with aggressive behaviour in children (Glueck & Glueck, 1950; McCord, McCord, & Howard, 1961; Patterson, DeBaryshe, & Ramsey,

1989). If such rejection appears to be the case, the teacher should encourage the parents to seek counselling.

It is all too easy for teachers to slough off their responsibility for aggression in a child by raising their eyebrows and muttering, "He sure must have had a tough morning at home—what do you suppose she did to him this time?" But it is more practical to ask oneself how the school environment might also be contributing to the child's belligerent behaviour, since this is the only area over which the teacher has any real control. Instead of blaming the parents, teachers should ask themselves, Am I teaching him alternative ways of getting what he wants or am I just stopping his aggressive behaviour? How frustrating is the centre environment for this child? Take a look at him and assess how he is relating to the program. At what time of day does he misbehave? With whom? What circumstances bring on an outburst? Does he receive more criticism than positive recognition from the staff? Does he have to sit too long at story hour? Does he consistently arrive hungry and so need an early snack? Is the program geared to tastes of little girls and female teachers and lacking in areas that hold a boy's interests?

Use Direct Control When Necessary, Then Teach the Child to Find Alternative Ways to Get What He Desires

There is nothing quite like the agonizing dread some beginning teachers experience because they fear they will be unable to control one or more children in their group. There is no denying that the problem of gaining confidence in control situations is one of the major hurdles students have to get over in the early days of their teaching. Reading about handling aggression will help to a degree, of course, but the truth is that to learn to cope with aggressive children, you have to get in there and cope! It does not work to shrink away or to let your master teacher do it for you. Sooner or later, every teacher must be willing to confront children and exercise direct control over them because doing this is an essential method of coping with children's aggressive behaviour.

To recapitulate what was said in the previous chapter, a child must definitely be stopped from hurting himself or another person or destroying property. It is important that the teacher step in *before* the child has experienced the gratification of seizing what he wants or of hurting someone. This is particularly true if it is unlikely that the child he has attacked will retaliate. It is also important to intervene promptly because this allows teachers to act before they are angry themselves, and it is highly desirable to present a model of self-control for an aggressive child to imitate (Bandura, 1986; Berkowitz, 1993).

Once the teacher has stopped the aggressive action, I cannot emphasize too strongly how important it is to go through the six steps for learning self-control outlined in chapter 11. In particular, it is vital to emphasize recognizing and translating the child's feelings into words in place of actions, and placing responsibility on the child to decide when to try again. These are essential steps in establishing *self*-control rather than eternally maintaining control from outside the child. As a reminder, the six steps are (a) warning and redirecting, (b) removing the child and keeping him beside you, (c) putting his feelings into words and discussing rules, (d) having him wait with you with you until he takes the responsibility of deciding to return, (e) getting him started on something that is all right for him to do, and (f) following through with losing the privilege when this is necessary.

ᏬᏨ   *Teasing and two-against-one encounters are typical situations that make children angry (and frantic!).*

The encouraging thing to realize is how infrequently young children resort to the sort of aggression that requires use of these steps. The research study in this chapter reminds us that even very young children have many less-violent responses to aggression in their repertoire and that they use these much of the time.

Teach Children Alternative Ways of Getting What They Want

We cannot expect children to simply stop seizing what they want or to stop attacking other children when they are angry unless we teach them other effective ways of getting what they want in place of those behaviours. In previous chapters we have talked about helping children to substitute words and to talk about their own feelings in place of verbally or physically attacking other children.

The other important thing to teach is how to get what you want without hurting somebody else. The strategies teachers usually use are either trying to distract the "wanter" by redirecting him ("There's room at the easel—let's see what colours we have today."), offering him something else as a substitute ("Here's another truck, why don't you use it? See, it has a bell you can ring."), or telling him he has to wait for a turn ("Jerry's using it now—what's our rule?").

While all of these strategies work some of the time, it is a shame for teachers to limit themselves and the children to so few alternatives. This is particularly true because none of these three strategies provides ways for the wanter to learn beginning negotiation skills.

✑ RESEARCH STUDY ✑
What Kinds of Things Make Young Children Angry and What Do They Do in Response?

Research Questions: Fabes and Eisenberg asked, How do young children cope with their feelings when they are angry with other children or with teachers? What is the relationship between their degree of social competence and popularity and the kind of anger-related responses they use? Do boys and girls handle anger in different ways?

Research Method: Twelve research assistants observed seventy-nine children (thirty-three boys and thirty-six girls) who ranged in age from forty-two to seventy-one months. The children were from English-speaking, white, middle-class families and were attending a university day care centre. Aggressive situations in which they were involved were observed every school day for three months during the free play periods. Rather than observing individual children for a prescribed period of time, the observers rotated from one play area to the next on a regular basis, recording whatever angry episodes happened in that area during ten-minute periods.

Later on, each episode was classified according to what caused the angry reaction. The causes were *physical* (the child was hit, kicked, etc.), *verbal* (the child was teased or insulted), *rejection* (the child was ignored or not allowed to play), *material disputes* (property or space was taken or destroyed), *compliance* (being asked or forced to do something—such as teacher requests), and *other.*

Next, the way the angry child responded or coped was analysed and classified. These categories included *revenge* (physical or verbal retaliation), *active resistance* (physical or verbal defence in nonaggressive ways such as telling the aggressor to return an item), *venting* (expressing angry feelings without taking direct action—crying, sulking, tantrums) *avoidance* (leaving the area), *adult seeking* (tattling or seeking comfort), *expressing dislike* ("I don't like you" or "You can't play"), or *other.*

Research Results: The most common cause of anger turned out to be material disputes, i.e., fighting over possessions and territory, and the second most frequent cause was physical assault by another child.

Interestingly enough, the most common responses were not physical or verbal retaliation and revenge. Rather, the most common responses to these provocations were venting and actively resisting the provocateur, although these responses differed somewhat according to sex. Boys most frequently responded by venting their angry feelings—not taking direct aggressive action but expressing feelings in such ways as sulking or crying. Girls most frequently defended themselves by actively resisting the aggressor in nonaggressive ways such as holding on.

Revenge and retaliation were most likely to occur when the initial aggressor had physically

Additional approaches that *do* encourage negotiation and interaction include coaching the wanter to play beside the group and, if possible, to begin to contribute to what they are doing in some way. (I urge the reader to recall the research study in Chapter 10 on the importance of children learning to observe what is happening in the ongoing play and identifying the social passwords required to obtain entry.) Encouraging cooperation by pointing out to both children how doing something together can enhance the pleasure of the activity is yet another way to foster interaction ("If she holds the bowl while you whip

assaulted the youngster. But even when children were physically attacked, they only responded in kind 18% of the time.

Children who were identified by their teachers as socially competent and popular were not involved in angry conflicts as often as were children who were not well liked. The children's responses were also age-related. Older youngsters used fewer avoidant strategies and were more likely to defend themselves in nonaggressive ways rather than running off or going to the teacher for help.

Implications for Teaching: There is so little research available on the subject of anger and young children that it is particularly useful to review Fabes's and Eisenberg's pioneering study. Perhaps because physical and verbal vengefully aggressive responses attract so much attention when they do occur, it may surprise teachers to learn how relatively infrequent such responses actually are. It is indeed heartening to realize that nonviolent responses are used much of the time by even such young children.

One of the most useful features of this research for teachers is the categories it singles out for identification. For example, it is helpful when thinking about a child who always seems to be flying off the handle to keep track of which kinds of situations make him angry. Does he go to pieces when he's rejected or does it happen when somebody takes something he's using? Once the type of situation is identified, the teacher has a clue about what to work on with him—it might be

teaching him skills about how to accept rejection and work through it, for instance, or how to negotiate a mutually satisfactory cooperative sharing situation, or how to defend his rights without hitting back if it is conflicts over material things that cause him the most difficulty.

The same suggestion holds true when considering the responses the children make to others' demands. It can broaden teachers' perspectives to consider the kind of response the child has selected. For example, an occasional teacher may dislike sulking so much that she categorically insists children never sulk, thereby losing sight of the fact that, unattractive as such behaviour may be, it is certainly a more desirable response than biting or hitting someone else would be.

In closing, I want to comment that there is another, more esoteric implication to draw from Fabes's and Eisenberg's research. This particular study illustrates a practical way to sample and study a specific type of behaviour in context—i.e., in a natural setting. The result not only has been new insights about children's anger and how they respond to that feeling, but also has demonstrated a reasonably rigorous approach to collecting that information—an approach that can be used to deepen our understanding even further in coming years.

Source: From "Young Children's Coping with Interpersonal Anger" by R. A. Fabes and N. Eisenberg, 1992, *Child Development*, 63, 116–128.

the egg whites it won't slide around so much"). Or sometimes the wanter can figure out how to strike a bargain to facilitate getting what he wants ("I'll let you see my sore knee if you'll let me be the patient").

Whatever alternative is employed, the teacher should make certain the child clearly understands that hurting others is not allowed but that this need not mean he must swallow his anger and knuckle under; instead, there are a variety of both effective and acceptable alternative ways to get what he wants.

Permit Reasonable Deviations from the Rules

Despite the fact that consistency is important and should generally prevail as a policy, there are exceptions to this rule. We have all seen timid children at school and have rejoiced when they finally ventured to shove back and stand up for their rights. It is important for such children to express these aggressive feelings in some form and come out of their shell as a first step; learning control can come later. Teachers simply have to use their knowledge of the children and their good judgement in these matters.

Teachers must also make allowances for children when they are under special stress. For example, standards should not be unreasonably high at 11:00 in the morning, since lower blood sugar levels at that time usually mean less self-control. This is the time to practise adroit avoidance of confrontations, since children cannot be expected to control themselves very well under such circumstances. The same thing holds true for children who are recovering from illnesses or experiencing family problems. They may require that special allowances be made for them until they have regained their emotional balance.

Reduce Frustrating Circumstances When Possible

Although controversy continues over whether aggression is an inherent trait (Lorenz, 1966) or a learned behaviour (Bandura, 1986), there is considerable evidence that frustration makes the expression of aggression more likely (Baron & Richardson, 1994). Thus it makes sense to reduce aggression by reducing frustration when it is possible to do so.

Frustration usually occurs when a child is thwarted or prevented from getting what he wants, be it the teacher's attention, going outside to play, the new fire engine, or even the blue sponge at the snack table. It is not possible to remove all frustrating circumstances from the life of a child, and it would not be desirable to do so anyway, since this would mean that he never had a chance to learn to cope with these feelings. However, there are so many restrictions and frustrations in everyday life that we really do not have to be concerned over the possibility of living in an environment without frustration.

As previously described, the most effective way to reduce frustration is to empower the child by helping him learn a variety of acceptable ways of getting what he wants. Another way to reduce frustration is to have a plentiful amount of play equipment available. The value of having sufficient equipment is borne out by a study done in England by Smith and Connolly (1980). They reported that the provision of plentiful equipment had several effects: Although children tended to play by themselves more frequently or to play in small groups, there was also less aggression, less competition, and less chasing and running about.

This supports the idea that it is desirable to have several tricycles, three or four swings, and a number of toy trucks and cars, sandbox shovels, and hammers. Young children cannot endure waiting very long, and enough play materials will reduce the agony of anticipation, which if unassuaged can lead to frustration and acting out.

Still another way to reduce frustration is to keep rules to a minimum. The enforcement of the many petty rules cited in the discussion of the authoritarian teacher is one of the quickest ways to build anger in children. Such rules often go hand in hand with unreasonably high expectations of behaviour, such as insisting that young children stand in line, sit for extended periods while waiting for something to happen, or never raise their voices.

Finally, two other good frustration preventers, also previously mentioned, are following the policy of warning in advance so that children have the chance to prepare themselves for making a transition to a new activity and providing many opportunities for choices in order to reduce children's feelings of defiance by helping them feel they are masters of their environment.

Provide Substitute Opportunities for Socially Acceptable Expressions of Aggression

The cathartic (emotionally relieving) value of substituting socially acceptable but nonetheless aggressive activities has been questioned by some researchers who maintain that such activities do not drain off or relieve aggression but rather reinforce such behaviour. Their arguments are persuasive, and I can only comment that my own experience and that of other early childhood teachers continue to convince me that offering substitute ways of working off steam does have value, cathartic or not, when working with aggressive children and children who have strong needs for high levels of physical activity (Roskies, 1987). Such activities are obviously emotionally satisfying to children, they are safe for those around them, and they provide chances to be assertive in a harmless way for youngsters too immature to resist the need to express aggression in some physical form.

These activities are best offered, however, *before* the child reaches the boiling point. It is generally unsatisfactory to march a youngster over to a punching bag after he has hit someone and say, "It's all right to sock this!" By the time this happens, or by the time he gets the boxing gloves on and the mock fight set up, a lot of the flavour has gone out of the experience. It is better to offer acceptable aggressive activities as part of each day, as

✎   *It's difficult sometimes to decide when it's rough-and-tumble and when someone's likely to get hurt.*

well as to make sure they are available when the teacher anticipates that the day will be especially tense either for an individual child who is upset or for the entire group (on Halloween, for example). Fortunately there are a great many activities that will help. Remember, though, that these activities are substitutes for what the child would really prefer to do. When offering someone a substitute experience, be as free with it as possible, and supply plenty of material, plenty of time, and as few restrictions as you can tolerate.

In general, any kind of large muscle activity that does not have to be tightly controlled is valuable. Jumping on old mattresses spread out on the grass or jumping off jungle gyms or boxes onto mattresses works off energy harmlessly and satisfies a need to be daring as well.

Swinging is particularly effective because the rhythm is soothing and because it isolates the child from his companions and calms him at the same time. If the teacher has time to do some friendly pushing, the one-to-one relationship is easing, too.

Trike riding, climbing, and sliding, or, as a matter of fact, anything that works off energy harmlessly helps.

Some preschool teachers buy play equipment too small or flimsy to take the vigorous activity of four- and five-year-old children. It is always better to invest in sturdy, large equipment that will stand up to hard use rather than to continually nag the children, "Don't shake the jungle gym, you'll break it" or "Not too high now!"

Activities that provide for vigorous use of the hands in an aggressive yet acceptable manner should also be included. If the teacher joins in with gusto from time to time and uses the material herself, the child will often participate with more spirit.

Beanbags are fine to use for this purpose, but rules should be established about where they are to be thrown. A large wall with a target marked on it is best, and the more beanbags the better. It is no fun to have to stop and pick them up after every three throws. Thirty bags is about the right number.

Punching bags have some use, but it is hard for young children to coordinate really satisfying socks with the bag's tendency to rebound.

Inflatable clowns are somewhat useful, but there may be trouble with maintaining them in airtight condition.

Hammering and sawing and even smashing things, such as old egg cartons, orange crates, or piano cases, are appealing. Very young children can use knock-out peg benches for this same purpose.

Large quantities of dough (not tiny, unsatisfying dabs) are fine aggression expressers. We restrict the tools the children use with it (such as cookie cutters) and encourage the children to stand at the table so that they can work forcefully, using their hands to pound and squeeze and pinch and punish the dough to their heart's content.

In finger-painting and other types of smearing techniques such as soap painting, emphasis should be placed on richness of colour and lots of gooey paint base, be it liquid starch, wallpaper paste, or home-made, very thick, cooked starch.

Once in a while a particular child finds relief in tearing and crumpling paper or stomping on crumpled balls of it. Again, large amounts are better than small amounts.

Noise is an excellent outlet for expressing aggression. The aggression-expressing possibilities of sheer noise (at least on the days when the teacher does not have a headache) should not be overlooked. It is wise to remember that noise has an infectious effect on the entire group and may accelerate activity too much. However, on the many occasions when things are in good order, I am all in favour of noise! Drums are an all-time, satisfying "best" for noise, but pounding on the piano is good, too. Real music and dancing can be added for those who enjoy it. Sitting on top of the slide and kicking one's heels hard makes a wonderful, satisfying noise. Yelling, playing loudly, and crying (the louder the better) also serve to express feelings harmlessly.

Opportunities for dramatic play can also help the child come to terms with aggressive feelings. Direct participation by dressing up and playing house will let youngsters work through situations that may be troubling them. Anyone who has ever watched an irate young "mama" wallop her "naughty" baby doll will understand the merit of providing this kind of play material as an aggression reliever. Dollhouse furniture and little dolls are useful, but more so for four-year-olds than for three-year-olds.

Sets of fairly large rubber wild animals and hand puppets lend themselves admirably to controlled aggressive play. Interestingly enough, the animal that produces the greatest amount of this play is not the lion or tiger, but the hippopotamus. I have concluded that it is the open mouth and all those teeth that brings this out. It makes me think how angry adults with toothy open mouths must appear to children, particularly since youngsters tend to look up and in!

The best thing for out-of-hand children to play with is water. It is deeply relaxing in any form. Washing doll clothes or plastic cars, playing with soap bubbles, or playing with water in the housekeeping area is beneficial. Even when it is squirted it does no lasting harm.

Whenever weather permits, the best thing of all is a running hose and lots of sand and mud. This combination has led to some of the calmest, happiest days we have ever had in our school, but pouring and playing with water in tubs or basins can also be satisfying. At home a warm bath can work miracles.

Finally, encouraging very overactive youngsters to take time out to go to the toilet often simmers things down considerably.

Additional Techniques to Help Reduce the Amount of Aggressive Behaviour

So much for the specifics. There are also some general techniques that the teacher may find helpful for handling aggression.

Provide kindly, one-to-one attention for acting out children. A few minutes consistently invested every day with an aggressive child when he is doing positive things (that is, before he gets into difficulties) often works wonders.

Teach children to use words in place of teeth and fists. Once more I want to remind the reader of the value of teaching children to tell other youngsters what they want and what their feelings are, instead of physically showing them what they feel.* Even as simple a sentence as "I want that!" or "Give it here!" is a step up from snatching what is desired. Of course, the other child may well refuse, but the teacher can support the requester by saying, "I'm sure glad to hear you asking him instead of just grabbing it." Then she can go on to teach the next step. "Jennie says you can't have it now. Why don't you ask her if

---

*For a more in-depth discussion of this principle, please refer to chapter 5, "Fostering Mental Health in Young Children."

you can have it when she's done with it. Say, 'Jennie, can I have a turn when you're done?' I bet she'll let you have it then!"

A more mature child can be encouraged to ask, and then add, "I really want that trike!" or "Gosh, I wish you'd give it to me now!" Remember, these statements should *focus on what the child is feeling* and what he wants, not on calling the other child bad names or insulting him.

Stopping some activities before they start saves criticism and discipline later. I have learned, for example, to keep an eye out for "angry monster" games or Ninja Turtles or Power Rangers. When such a game gets too high pitched, the quickest way to bring it under control is to look for the ringleader and get him involved in something else that he particularly likes to do.

Our staff discourages toy gun play at our centre, because we believe that children should be encouraged to use more desirable play themes than killing each other. More-over, research by Watson and Peng (1992) has revealed that toy gun play was one of the two strongest predictors of real aggression observed in the children's centre. (The other predictor was the use of physical punishments by the parents.) Therefore, when guns are brought to school, our staff insists they be stored in the cubbies until it is time for the children to go home.

Be on the lookout for combinations of personalities that are currently poisonous, and do what you can to dilute them. Children who egg each other into trouble should not snack together or rest near each other, and other friendships for both children should be encouraged.

Finally, plan, plan, plan! Plan to provide interesting activities that children really like, and plan the daily program with specific children in mind. ("John is coming today; I'd better get out the hammers and saw.") The program must not make undue demands on their self-control and should include acceptable outlets for their energy. As a general

✑   *"He did it!" Tattling is a typical form of prosocial aggression in 4-year-olds.*

principle, consistent opportunities that allow children to achieve mastery and compe-tence in acceptable areas should be provided. Every time a youngster can do something well, whether it's building with blocks, doing meaningful work, creating a painting, or learning to pump on the swing, his aggression has been channelled into accomplishing something constructive.

❧ Summary

Aggressive behaviour is defined in this chapter as action intended to cause injury or anxi-ety to others. This kind of behaviour needs careful handling and guidance so that chil-dren are not forced to suppress such feelings completely but learn instead to channel these impulses into socially acceptable activities.

Three approaches to coping with aggression in young children are particularly undesir-able, since they are all likely to increase aggressive responses from them. These include authoritarian, overpermissive, and inconsistent methods of dealing with such behaviour.

On the more positive side, several approaches for working with acting out children are effective in reducing and channelling such behaviour. Among these are assessing the underlying causes of aggression and ameliorating them when possible, using direct con-trol when necessary, and teaching the child to find alternative ways to get what he wants. In addition, permitting reasonable deviations from the rules in special cases and reducing frustrating circumstances when possible are helpful. Finally, substituting socially accept-able opportunities for expressing aggression can relieve the child's feelings without jeop-ardizing the safety and happiness of those around him.

Teachers who apply these principles when handling aggressive behaviour will reduce tension within the child and themselves by preventing aggressive feelings from building up and will also help the child remain happier, more open, and more ready to welcome life with enthusiasm.

Questions and Activities

1. Everyone seems to have different "breaking points" in tolerating aggression. For example, one person sees red if a child is insolent, whereas another finds it more difficult to cope with a child who is cruel to animals or who deliberately hurts another child. Compare notes among the people in class about what they feel constitute acceptable ways to express aggression, where their breaking points are, and what they do to control themselves when they reach that point.

2. Keep an eye out during the coming week and observe and briefly record several situations in which children or staff members appeared to be angry. Note what each individual did about this feeling. If

the teacher was working with a child, what did she do to help the youngster recognize and express his feelings in an acceptable way?

3. Are there any "discipline" situations in your program that seem to recur? For example, are the children always being told not to run inside the building? Suggest several ways the situation could be changed instead of continuing to "teach the children to behave."

Self-Check Questions for Review

Content-Related Questions

1. Describe three styles of teaching that are likely to increase an aggressive response by some children.

2. Does aggression always stem from the same cause? If not, what are some things that tend to generate such behaviour?
3. List several alternative approaches children can be taught that will help them get what they want without hurting other people.
4. Suppose that you have a high-energy, aggressive child in your group. Suggest several ways he or she could work off this energy without hurting other people.
5. Does the research by Fabes and Eisenberg support the idea that children usually solve physical aggression by hitting back when someone hits them?

Integrative Questions

1. Some reasons why a teacher might be too authoritarian are suggested in this chapter. What are some reasons that might lie behind the behaviour of the teacher who is too permissive?
2. The book defines *instrumental* and *hostile aggression*. Give two examples of behaviour that fit each kind of aggression.
3. *Problem:* Four-year-old Sarah is reading a book, and Nancy tries to grab it. Sarah hits Nancy's hand, and when she tries again, Sarah pinches her very hard. Nancy begins to cry. You have worked through the first steps in the "Learning Self-Control" sequence with both Nancy and Sarah and now Nancy is ready to return to Sarah. Suggest at least two alternatives you could propose to her about how she might get a chance to look at the book she wants to see so badly. What alternatives might you suggest to Sarah about how to protect her rights without hitting or pinching?
5. *Problem:* You have a four-year-old child named Billy in your group who is angry a lot of the time. For example, when children are building in the block corner and he arrives at school, he barges into the block corner, picks up some blocks, and begins to build. At that point the other children yell at him, saying, "We were here first—you can't play—go away!" Billy begins to cry and as the other children hold firm, he starts to knock down what they are building as the teacher intervenes. If you were a researcher using the categories that Fabes and Eisenberg used in their study, what category or categories of behaviour would you use to describe the angry reaction by the children who found his intru-

sion to be unwelcome? What category or categories of behaviour would you use to describe Billy's response to *their response?*

References for Further Reading

Overview

Berkowitz, L. (1993). *Aggression: Its causes, consequences and control.* Philadelphia: Temple University Press. This is a very readable—almost chatty—yet very sound and comprehensive discussion of aggression. *Highly recommended.*

Reducing Aggressive Behaviour

A reminder: Many additional references of value on this subject are included in chapter 11, "Helping Young Children Establish Self-Discipline and Self-Control". Violence and aggression *against* children is discussed in chapter 8, "Tender Topics".

Dinwiddie, S. A. (1994). The saga of Sally, Sammy, and the red pen: Facilitating children's social problem solving. *Young Children, 49*(5), 13–19. The strategies needed to help children negotiate a conflict situation are illustrated by means of a practical example.
Samalin, N. (1991). *Love and anger: The parental dilemma.* New York: Viking. Samalin discusses reasons for adult anger and outlines eight steps for controlling it effectively.
Samalin, N., & Jablow, M. M. (1987). *Loving your child is not enough: Positive discipline that works.* New York: Viking. This is a good, practical book about getting along peacefully with children. It was written for parents but is helpful for teachers, too.
Solomon, H. C., & Elardo, R. (1989). Bite injuries at a day care centre. Early *Childhood Research Quarterly, 4*(1), 89–96. This article is noteworthy because biting is a recurring problem in many centres. The article not only contains information on its frequency but also includes some matter-of-fact recommendations of ways to reduce it.

Corporal Punishment

Hyman, I. A. (1990). *Reading, writing and the hickory stick: The appalling story of physical and psychological abuse in American schools.* Lexington, MA: Lexington Books. The title of this useful book is self-explanatory.

For the Advanced Student

Baron, R. A., & Richardson, D. R. (1994). *Human aggression* (2nd ed.). New York: Plenum Press. A comprehensive and chilling research review of this subject is presented here. It covers everything from theoretical causes to careful analyses of what may be effective techniques for controlling the expression of aggression.

Baumrind, D. (1989). Rearing competent children. In W. Damon (Ed.), *Child development today and tomorrow*. San Francisco; Jossey-Bass. In this valuable chapter, Baumrind reviews her decades of research concerning long-term effects on children of authoritative, authoritarian, permissive, and rejecting parental styles.

Patterson, G. R., Debaryshe, B. D., & Ramsey, E. (1989). A developmental perspective on antisocial behaviour. *American Psychologist, 44*(2), 329–335. The authors review research that traces the development of antisocial behaviour from infancy to adolescence.

The Pleasures of Meaningful Work*

13

H ow can children serve the group? Many four- and five-year-old children can answer the phone graciously. Most children can scrub the table for snack time or lunch, can serve themselves from serving bowls, and can pass the trash basket afterwards. Children love to pick flowers, bring them from home, and arrange them. . . . A small group of children could paint a mural for a wall; perhaps another group could create another mural the following month.

Polly Greenberg

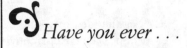

Have you ever . . .

Thought that young children were too young to do anything really helpful at school?

Wondered just what kinds of things children might do that would be real work but not too hard for them?

Wondered how to get children to want to pitch in on work projects?

. . . I f you have, the material in the following pages will help you.

*Adapted from "The Pleasures of Meaningful Work for Young Children" by J. B. Hendrick, 1967, *Young Children, 22*(6), pp. 373–380.

Does the idea of young children performing meaningful work sound ridiculous, or even impossible? Apparently it does to many preschool teachers because it is an area rarely considered in textbooks on early childhood education,* even though we know it is vitally important for adults to have good feelings about their work. In *Childhood and Society* (1963), Erikson quotes Freud, when asked the question, "What should a normal person be able to do well?" as replying, "To love and to work." Maslow also supports the value of work in his comment: "This business of self-actualization via a commitment to an important job and to worthwhile work could also be said, then, to be the path to human happiness" (1965, p. 5).

But is early childhood too soon to begin laying the foundation for enjoying work? Pleasure in work cannot be expected to suddenly appear full blown as the child attains adulthood; at some point in human development it must begin to be nurtured and encouraged. Since work is such a fundamental part of our culture, teachers should start with children as young as age three or four to establish a wholesome conviction that work is rewarding and that it can be a significant way of giving meaning and satisfaction to life (Wenning & Wortis, 1988).

ᓬ *Teaching Children to Dislike Work*

We all know of people who face the working day as though it were a deadening burden, an oppression to be struggled through; this is nothing short of tragic. What happened to these·people that caused them to feel like that? Some of our work-burdened adult friends must have been subjected to very negative training about work as they grew up. Let us picture what such a negative teaching model might be, bearing in mind that this model may exist at home as well as at school.

Suppose we begin by asking, "How do you teach a three- or four-year-old child that work is to be loathed, shirked, and put off as long as possible?" For people who have such an aim in mind, the following commandments should be followed faithfully to teach children to hate work—and what better time to begin than in the early, formative years?

1. Select the chores you dislike most yourself, such as picking up every one of the small blocks, and insist that each time a child uses such equipment she pick it all up immediately as soon as she has finished. Never offer to help her with such jobs, because this will make her too dependent on you. Bright children catch on to this quickly: "Oh, no! Let's not get those out, we'll just have to put them all away!"

2. Be sure that all work is tedious and long drawn out. Also insist that the child finish every task she begins on the grounds that this will teach her to be diligent.

3. Be sure that everyone always works at the same time because this is fair.

4. Provide no variety to the work; keep it dull. Expect each child to repeat the same portion to perfection, over and over, because repetition is valuable habit training and preparation for later life, when a lot of things will be boring anyway.

---

*Montessori is a rare, welcome exception to this statement.

❧ *Children love the opportunity to take on grown-up roles.*

5. Never allow enough time, and remind the child constantly that she should hurry. This will encourage her to stick to business.

6. Expect a great deal, and be very critical of any work a child attempts. This will teach her that high standards are important.

7. Tell the child exactly how to do the work; be rigid; be demanding; watch closely so that she doesn't make any mistakes, and be quick to call her attention to all errors so that she will learn to do it the "right" way. This will prevent her from forming bad habits.

8. Compare her achievements with the other children's; draw her attention to where she has failed and how she could do better by copying them. This will help her appreciate other children's strong points.

9. If a child does express interest in doing some helpful job, accept her help with condescending indulgence rather than with thanks and respect. After all, she's only a child.

10. Above all, act abused yourself. Talk to the other adults about how tired you are, how much work everything is, and grumble over the unfairness of it all. Be careful to do this in front of the children because it will teach them to appreciate you more and to look forward to becoming a grown-up working person.

ॐ *Teaching the Positive Values of Work*

What if we want the children in our care to relish work, to find deep rewards in accomplishment, and to anticipate each day with at least mild pleasure because of the interest their jobs hold for them? Then we must not fall into the trap of assuming that work should consist only of doing what we do not like or do not want to do. We must be wary of thinking that work for young children can never be more than helping out in routine tidying up, and we must stop assuming, even tacitly, that the only work children are capable of is the routine, lengthy, repetitive kind of chore usually disliked by both teachers and children.

In place of such negative attitudes we must substitute an appreciation of the potential that meaningful work holds for young children's development and understand the kinds of work they are likely to find satisfying.

Work Allows the Child to Experience the Pleasure of Accomplishment Linked with Helping Other People

One of the most important values of work is that it provides children with the opportunity to experience achievement, which possesses obvious social value, since doing a job often results in accomplishing a task and helping other people at the same time. Thus the four-year-old who has washed the dishes after making cookies or who has sawed off the sharp corners of the woodworking table experiences not only the glow of satisfaction that comes from honest labour but also feels good because she has contributed to the welfare of the group, particularly if the teacher points this out to her and remembers to say "thank you."

Work Increases the Reality of Role Playing

Another pleasure inherent in work grows out of young children's passion for imitating adults. When Joel repairs the seat of the rowboat "just the way my mom would," he gains insight into what it is like to be a grown-up. Perhaps he thinks, "This is the way grown-ups do things. I am just a little boy, but one day I, too, will be doing things like this all the time, and it's good to do them."

Role playing need not stop at the "family" level. In the past few years interest in career education has increased for children of all ages (Beach, 1986; Jalongo, 1989). Although information on career awareness and attitudes for children of preschool age remains very scanty, one trend is apparent. Leifer and Lesser (1976) cite two studies revealing that even as early as preschool, girls show a more restricted number of career choices than boys. Girls saw themselves as parents, teachers, and nurses, whereas boys chose a wider range of occupations including doctor, police officer, and firefighter. This finding was further supported by Beuf's study (1974), which showed that the vast majority of preschool children chose sex-stereotyped jobs for themselves. In addition, the study found that "all the girls could suggest occupations they might hold if they were boys, while many of the boys could not imagine what jobs they might hold if they were girls." The report of a conversation with one preschooler illustrates the boy's perplexity: He put his hands to his head and sighed, "A girl?" he asked. "A girl? Oh if I were a girl I'd have to grow up to be nothing" (Leifer & Lesser, 1976, p. 18).

That this attitude continues to persist is documented by a study of second-, fourth-, and sixth-grade girls who replied that they wished to be teachers and nurses, although the investigator also found that girls whose mothers worked outside the home had a more liberal attitude toward breaking such traditional role stereotypes than did those whose mothers did not (Nemerowicz, 1979).

Nor have these limited stereotypes changed in the past decade. Even though the realities of family life are changing and the majority of women now work outside the home, children continue to see the roles of mothers and fathers as being quite different. For example, a recent study of day-care- and kindergarten-age children reported that mothers were perceived as doing most of the domestic work and custodial child care, and fathers were much more likely than mothers to be perceived as working for pay, despite the fact that two-thirds of the mothers in the study were employed outside the home (Smith, Ballard, & Barham, 1989).

If the teacher wishes to conduct a nonsexist, nonracist classroom, the implications of these findings on career awareness are obvious. Even at the preschool level we should

๑ *Talk about the pleasure of accomplishment: Courtney worked and worked on washing these blocks prior to painting them.*

surely make a point of widening both boys' and girls' ideas of job possibilities that are becoming available for both men and women of all cultural backgrounds.

Using work as a means of experiencing many careers can be done successfully even with very young children. I am thinking of such possibilities as helping the visiting nurse unpack tongue depressors and assemble the examination light, or raking up leaves for the gardener, or helping the delivery person store the milk cartons in the refrigerator. This kind of education takes considerable cooperation, briefing, and patience by the adults involved but can be very effective from time to time.

In addition, various work roles can be investigated by taking the children on field trips, particularly to places where their parents work (Nachbar, 1992; Wenning & Wortis, 1988). Having visitors come to school to show children what they do is also helpful. A special effort should be made to include people in nontraditional occupations and to make certain that people from a variety of ethnic groups are included. Parents and grandparents are wonderful resources for occupations—not only because of the variety of jobs they do themselves, but also because of their acquaintance in the community with other people on whom they can prevail to visit the school. It is always a good idea to talk with these visitors in advance. Explain carefully the kinds of things the children will understand and encourage them to wear their work clothes and bring their tools. Otherwise, visitors tend to talk too long at too advanced a level.

Work Presents Many Opportunities to Achieve Something Together

Although some jobs can be done alone, many simply require more than one person's contribution to be successful. One child can hold the dustpan while another sweeps or dry the dishes another has washed. Working together in this fashion has special merit because it presents such fine opportunities for learning the benefits of cooperative endeavours.

Work Also Presents Many Opportunities for Doing Something That Benefits the Group

If we want children to develop a sense of family and togetherness at school, a fine way to do this can come from doing helpful work for the good of the group. This may be as simple as passing the napkins at snack, or it can be as long and drawn out as a complete block washing, painting, and storing experience. The point I wish to make here is that, while the activities are satisfying in themselves as work projects, they can be made even more satisfying if teachers point out that what the child or group of children is doing helps the group in some way. It is a good thing for children to feel they can contribute to everyone's welfare. It makes them socially aware and helps them feel personally valuable as well.

Work Is an Ego Strengthener

The experience of success in work can strengthen the ego and build self-esteem. Every time a child accomplishes something tangible and sees the results turn out reasonably well, her image of herself as being a capable person is strengthened. This is particularly valuable for very retiring or very aggressive children (Wenning & Wortis, 1984).

At school one year our staff had a boy who had been removed from kindergarten. At the age of five he was already convinced that he was helpless, worthless, and a menace, and he expressed this self-despair in the kindergarten room by throwing scissors, destroying other children's achievements, and refusing to try anything himself. When he joined us at nursery school, we all held our breath. Although the teachers worked on the problem from a number of angles, what appeared to do the most direct good for him was the staff's thinking of some specific, simple jobs he could do to help them. I recall that the first one of these was smashing, and I mean *smashing,* an old piano box we no longer needed. It was a real help to us and a genuine relief and achievement for him. His self-image was rebuilt largely through this avenue of productive work. We are still using a beautiful tree in our insect cage that he made for us.

There is something to be said, too, for the value of work in reducing guilt feelings. I would much rather help a child "fix" something she has broken, clean up after a spill, or apply a bandage to someone she has hurt than settle for "Say you're sorry!" It is valuable not only because a child should experience the actual consequence of her action through repairing the result, but also because it is a good way for her to learn that doing something "wrong" is not the end of the world and that one can often make amends.

❧ Incorporating Meaningful Work into the Life of the Program

Now that the reasons have been reviewed why work can be beneficial for young children, the question remains, "Just what kinds of jobs can they do?" The following list consti-

❧ *Any work involving water is the most fun.*

tutes some of the activities I have seen young children participate in that were both productive and pleasurable. Most teachers will be able to supply many more examples from their own programs.

Washing dishes after cooking with them

Loading sand in a small wheelbarrow, carting it to the swing area, and shovelling it under the swings after a rainy day

Planting and weeding the garden

Fertilizing and watering the garden

Spreading and digging in compost in the garden

Cutting flowers and arranging them

Cleaning the aquarium

Setting up the rabbit cage for a new baby rabbit

Feeding and cleaning the rabbit (which reminds me of one three-year-old who looked at the rabbit droppings and informed me, soberly, "Dem's not raisins!")

Mixing paint

Washing the finger-painting tables

Cutting up fruits and vegetables for snacks

Helping set up the snack baskets

Fetching juice for the snack table

Doing all kinds of cooking (making butter, wholewheat pizza, soup, vegetable dip, cranberry-orange relish; using a grinder is a special joy because children can carry out the work of assembling it as well as using it)

Carrying simple messages such as, "Mrs. Marquis needs some more clothespins"

Sanding and waxing blocks and then stapling different grades of sandpaper to them to make music blocks for our music corner

Sawing square corners off the tables to make them safer

Puttying up the holes in the much drilled on woodworking table

Filling the holes in the edges of a new shelf with putty

Dyeing eggshells and crushing them for collage material

Nailing the seat more firmly into the boat when it works loose

Hammering nails back into the benches so that clothing is no longer snagged on them

Taking down bulletin board displays and helping put up new ones

Hosing off the sandy sidewalk

Mopping the housekeeping corner when the water play runs deep

Oiling tricycles when they begin to squeak

Using the flatbed ride-'em truck to load up and deliver the baskets of sand toys to the sand pile

Washing easel brushes (a favourite)

Shovelling snow

Pumping up the big inner tube to bounce on

Washing the teacher's car

These chores, which adults regard as rather run-of-the-mill, were all performed with interest and enthusiasm by the children. Their pleasure did not come mainly from satisfaction with the finished job. Children are more fortunate than that in their approach to work. They love the process as much as the product and do not drive relentlessly toward the single-minded attainment of the goal; their satisfaction is spread throughout the experience. Wouldn't it be ideal if this were also true for more adults in their own working lives?

Not All Work Experiences Are Successful

It may also be illuminating to talk about some of our failures as well as our successes, because, of course, some work projects do not turn out well.

The second year of the garden was one of these occasions. We gave the children some excellent shovels and talked about seeds, flowers, and worms, and they started to dig with a will—and quit almost as promptly. We couldn't get any enthusiasm going for the garden: The earth was packed too hard. We had assumed that since it had been dug up the previous season, that would be sufficient, but it wasn't. The job was too difficult and took too much strength. However, after we spaded it up, the children returned with a gleam in their eyes and dug deeply and well until they pronounced the time ripe for planting.

On another occasion we needed the large hollow blocks sanded lightly before revarnishing them. "Aha!" thought the adults, "This isn't hard work, and it will be a real help." But the children tried it and wandered away. The job was too tedious and dull. We gave up on that one and did it ourselves. The adult goals of saving money and preserving the blocks motivated us, but the children couldn't have cared less.

We had only partial success with another task: The tricycles needed to be painted, and we had to remove the dirt and grease (from all the lubricating by the children) so that fresh paint would stick. The children enjoyed scrubbing with stiff brushes and soapy water, but our standards were pickier than theirs, so we teachers had to really scrub to finish the job to our satisfaction.

Once we tried to bake and decorate cookies all in one day (at least we had the sense not to attempt to roll and cut cookies). This was too extensive a task, and working under too much pressure made us all cranky. Now we buy wholesome cookies and content ourselves with decorating them at school, or we bake them and eat them plain.

These less successful experiences raise the problem of how to handle failure. In the cases above, in which the teachers failed, we admitted honestly to the children that things had not worked out as well as we had hoped and promised we would try to work out something better next time. Then we analysed what was wrong and changed what we could.

Sometimes, too, we ask children why they did not like a project. They will often go right to the heart of the matter and tell you, "It's no fun," "It's too hard," "I don't want to," or, from the more sophisticated four-year-olds, "My mother doesn't want me to do that today."

When a child tries and fails, there is no point and possibly real harm in pretending she has done something well when she has not. Maybe she cannot tie that shoelace or get the nail in straight. Honest recognition is still possible, and reassurance is also highly desirable in these situations. The teacher can say, "You're really trying, Nancy. One of these days you're going to get that knack," or "Thank you. I can see you really want to help, and I appreciate it," or "You're working hard. Can I help you?"

There Are Many Ways to Plan Work Opportunities So They Remain Appealing

One basic suggestion for keeping work attractive is that *jobs should be short* or capable of being broken down into short portions. When we made the sandpapered music blocks, some of the children enjoyed putting the wax on the blocks, but an older crowd was attracted by the use of the stapler and did that part of the job.

Except in the late spring when the group of children has grown older, and the teacher may deliberately plan projects that take two days to finish (such as painting and shellacking something), tasks should be finished in one day. Part of the pleasure of the music blocks was that we made and used them in the music corner the same morning. Young children need the immediate reward and satisfaction of seeing something through promptly.

In Many Cases the Child Should Have the Privilege of Selection and the Right of Rejection in Choosing Jobs

Research reveals that the way young children tell work and play apart is *not* based on whether or not they think it is fun. In one study, preschoolers defined work (no matter what) as being any activity that was teacher structured or dominated, and play as being whatever was not! (Romero, 1991). In another study the children defined work as something you have to do (i.e., you have no choice in the matter). Play, on the other hand, is what you want to do (King, 1979). In this respect, schools are luckier than families because, with so many children available, chances are good that almost every task will appeal to someone. Since some chores attract particular children and some draw others, a perceptive teacher should try to think of specific things likely to be attractive for each individual.

Reasonable Expectations by the Teacher Are Very Important

The goal should basically be pleasure in process and accomplishment, not perfection in performance. If a job is too hard or the child must be too meticulous, much of the joy in working that we hope to foster falls by the wayside. Work must be adjusted to the reality of the child's ability and to what she wants to do. A good way to find out what each child likes to do is to listen for the times children volunteer and take them up on their offers of help. Even if the tub of water is too heavy to carry by themselves, they can turn on the faucet and help carry the tub, with the teacher's hand on the handle, too.

Children Need Real Tools to Do Work

Real tools, not dime store imitations, are needed. Sometimes tools are best if they are scaled to size. For example, clamming shovels, which are strong but short-handled, are superior to the longer variety. Sometimes regular, adult-sized tools are necessary and sur-prisingly easy for the children to manipulate. Stout hammers and well-sharpened saws, real C-clamps, and a standard-sized vegetable grinder are all worthwhile investments. Dull, tinny tools build frustration and encourage children to give up in disgust.

In General, Three Kinds of Materials Attract All Children and Can Be Successfully Incorporated When Planning Work Experiences

These can be stated very simply by the following axioms:

Anything involving food is fun.

Anything involving earth is fun.

Anything involving water is the *most* fun!

Most Work Requires Supervision

Almost all jobs require some supervision by the teacher. This is perhaps one reason why children are not allowed to do more work at home as well as at school (until they are too old to want to do it, of course). Adults often feel it is easier on a short-term basis to do it themselves than to allow the time and exercise the patience it takes to let the child make the effort. The other common reason children are not allowed to help more is that adults underestimate their abilities. But think what such consistent underestimation does to the child's self-concept!

❧   *The opportunity to really fix the truck was deeply gratifying to this three-year-old.*

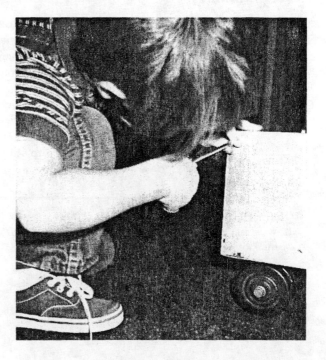

Take Time to Talk About How Hard the Children Are Working

Children love the sense of doing *real* work, and a fine way of sharing and deepening their pleasure is to talk about the fact that they are working when they are involved in that kind of task. Making such comments as, "This sure *is* a big job!" or "My gosh! You're *really* working hard on that" will not discourage them. Rather, it makes children feel grown-up and important to realize they are doing something really worthwhile.

The Teacher's Own Attitude Towards Work Is Significant

The teacher's attitude towards work can influence the way the child feels about it, since children acquire attitudes from models about whom they care. The teacher who willingly lends a hand if the job is onerous (picking up blocks again comes to mind) is setting a pattern for the future young mother who may one day offer her help with equal generosity to her own child. The teacher who enjoys his own job is helping convey the idea that work can be pleasurable as well as challenging. Finally, the teacher who expresses a genuine attitude of respect for the child's work helps her build good attitudes toward it even more directly. If the teacher reveres the child's power of concentration and refrains from interrupting her while she is working, if he values her suggestions about how to accomplish the task, and if he is quick to acknowledge her achievements, the child's pleasure in this kind of activity will be deepened, and she will be more likely to participate in working again when the opportunity arises.

❧ Summary

Although we would never wish to emphasize work in early childhood settings to the extent that it minimizes the significance of play, work is a valuable experience to offer young children. It allows them to enjoy the pleasure of accomplishment linked with helping other people, it builds reality into role playing, it promotes an expanded awareness of job opportunities, it strengthens the ego, and it enhances self-esteem.

Many different jobs, ranging from preparing the snack to making simple repairs, are both interesting and not too difficult for children to perform. Their pleasure in these tasks can be increased if teachers keep them reasonably short and easy, provide tools that are effective, allow children to select jobs they prefer to do, and maintain a healthy attitude toward work themselves.

Questions and Activities

1. What is it about work that causes many people to think of it as a difficult, tiresome activity to be avoided if possible?
2. If you happen to be someone who feels that work is enjoyable, can you account for how you came to feel this way about it?
3. Why do you think real work is an activity appealing to young children?
4. Do you feel children should be paid for doing chores around the house, or should they be expected to do them because they are contributing members of the family unit?
5. Watch during this coming week for opportunities for children to participate in new kinds of work experiences they have not tried before. Be prepared to assess what made these experiences successful or unsuccessful.

Self-Check Questions For Review

Content-Related Questions

1. What did Freud reply when asked what a normal person should be able to do well?
2. List at least five things you could do that would help a child learn to *dislike* doing work.
3. Explain what benefits might accrue to a child involved in doing meaningful work.
4. List several possibilities for meaningful work that might be available at the school where you are teaching.
5. Imagine you are explaining to a new teacher how to go about making shovelling snow off the school sidewalk appealing to the children. What suggestions would you give to him?

Integrative Questions

1. In your opinion, would it be practical to rely on children to volunteer to help with work spontaneously as the opportunities arise, or is it fairer to have a list of jobs that must be done each day and assign the children to different ones at different times? How might the research by King on defining work and play affect your policies about assigning work?
2. *Problem:* The three-year-olds in your group have played happily with the blocks all morning, but now it is time to put them away. Suggest three things you could do that would make participating in this work reasonably attractive to the children. Give two examples of what would be unreasonable expectations for accomplishing this work for three-year-olds.
3. The children see you working as a teacher every day. If you were to use that role for career education, suggest how you might involve the children to make it real for them.
4. The author makes quite a point of the stereotyped ideas about work roles held by young children. Why is it valuable for teachers to realize that these attitudes continue to persist?

References for Further Reading

Overview

Montessori, M. (1967). *The discovery of the child* (M. J. Costelloe, Trans.). Notre Dame, IN: Fides. The practical life activities recommended by Montessori (in this and other books describing her curriculum) remain one of the rare discussions of work that can be successfully performed by young children.

Nachbar, R. R. (1992). What do grown-ups do all day? The world of work. *Young Children, 47*(3), 6–12. This article illustrates an effective way to make learning about how adults work relevant and therefore interesting to young children. It includes a bibliography of children's books about working.

Wallinga, C. R., & Sweaney, A. L. (1985). A sense of real accomplishment: Young children as productive family members. *Young Children, 41*(1), 3–7. The authors describe a project centring on children doing work at home, but the list of suggestions for making work appealing apply equally well to work opportunities at school.

Wenning, J., & Wortis, S. (1984). *Made by human hands: A curriculum for teaching young children about work and working people.* Cambridge, MA: The Multicultural Project for Communication and Education. While mainly dwelling on understanding work done by others, *Made by Human Hands* does include a brief discussion of jobs children can do. Suggested teaching units and bibliographies are included.

Wenning, J., & Wortis, S. (1988). Work in the child care centre: A curriculum about working people. *Day Care and Early Education, 15*(4), 20–25. The authors suggest many ways children can learn about the jobs adults do at the centre and also suggest ways children themselves can participate in meaningful work.

For the Advanced Student

Jalongo, M. R. (1989). Career education: Review of research. *Childhood Education, 66*(2), 108–115. This review covers the subject of career education for children of all ages.

Lewko, J. H. (Ed.). (1987). How children and adolescents view the world of work. *New Directions for Child Development, 35* (Spring), 1–96. This issue of *New Directions* reports a number of research studies on how children above preschool age perceive work.

Providing Cross-Cultural, Nonsexist Education

14

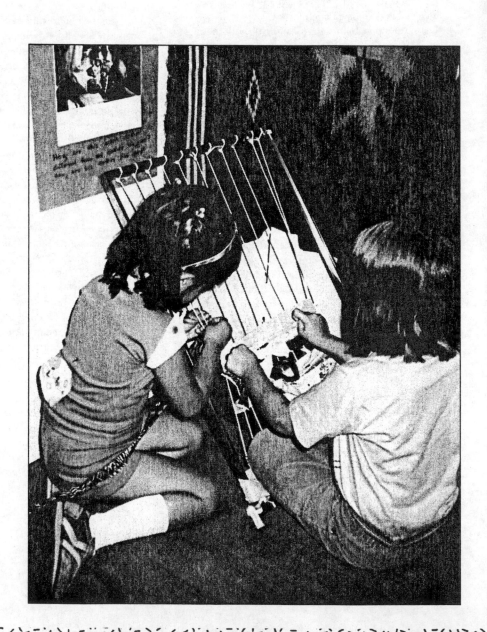

I hear the train a comin',
A comin' round the curve.
She's using all her steam and brakes
And straining every nerve.

Get on board, little children,
Get on board, little children,
Get on board, little children,
There's room for many-a-more.

The fare is cheap and all can go,
The rich and poor are there.
No second class aboard this train,
No difference in the fare!

Get on board, little children,
Get on board, little children—
Get on board, little children!
There's room for many-a-more!

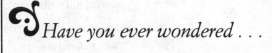

Have you ever wondered . . .

What to say when a youngster says to an Asian child, "I won't sit by you—your skin is dirty"?

What to tell a four-year-old who asks where babies come from?

What to do about name calling and racial insults?

How to help children value everyone, no matter what their race or colour or sex?

. . . If you have, the material in the following pages will help you.

*T*he wonderful lines of the old gospel tune,

No second class aboard this train,
No difference in the fare!

sum up what is meant by *equity in education,* because in a well-presented cross-cultural, nonsexist curriculum there are no second-class children and surely no difference in what children must do or be when on the train with the other youngsters.

Perhaps the reader is thinking indignantly, "What does she mean! Of course there are no second-class children," but the truth is that sometimes teachers *do* treat some children as being second-class people.

Examples of Teacher Prejudice

Many examples of the way teacher prejudice shows through in relations between teachers and students are presented by Leacock (1982), who reviewed studies of teacher attitudes toward low- and middle-income children who were black or white. She reported that teachers not only spoke less frequently about curriculum matters to the black children but also made many more critical and negative remarks to them, with poor black children receiving the brunt of the negative comments. This was true even when teachers were black themselves and when little difference in behaviour by the children could be noted.

More recently, Boutte, LaPoint, and Davis (1993) report several episodes in which teachers either did nothing to protest the expression of prejudice by children in their classrooms or revealed their own negative feelings about certain youngsters who came from ethnic backgrounds different from their own.

Prejudice shows through in the different ways some early childhood teachers treat boys and girls. For example, Serbin, Connor, and Citron (1978) report that in one study boys were more likely to be reprimanded for aggression than girls were, that they received much more detailed instruction on how to solve problems than girls did, and that little girls had to be closer to the teacher than little boys did to be noticed by her.

Prejudice can also be expressed in more subtle ways. For example, when Hendrick and Stange (1990) analysed the conversational behaviour of children and their teachers at the snack table, they found that not only did four-year-old boys interrupt the teacher more than the girls did, but also that teachers interrupted the girls far more often than they interrupted the boys.

Can we deny, with such evidence before us, that many of us, however inadvertently, are actually relegating some children to second-class status?

Can Such Attitudes Be Changed?

Fortunately, the answer to this question is yes—at least to some degree. Although we must realize that attitudes and responses to groups, or individual representatives of certain groups, stem from long ingrained habits and prejudices, research shows that teachers *can* change, and children can, too.

Changes in Teachers' Attitudes

In the follow-up study, Serbin and colleagues (1978) reported that after instruction and "consciousness raising," teachers were able to change their behaviour and notice children of both sexes whether they were nearby or across the room—one of the results being that the little girls stopped hovering around the teacher so much and began to make fuller use of the room's opportunities. In her journal, *White Teacher,* Paley (1979) gives an encouraging description of how she grew and changed as she came to appreciate the value of cultural pluralism as an approach to teaching.

Changes in Children's Attitudes

Although research indicates it is not easy to modify racial and gender stereotypes, it *can* be done. For example, in an English study of teachers who were concerned about prejudice against the children of West Indian and Pakistani immigrants, Milner (1981) reported that the use of multiethnic materials in kindergarten and first grade had a somewhat positive effect on the English children (results almost reached statistical significance) but had a pronounced effect on the immigrant children, who had been ambivalent about the value of their racial identity. By the program's end more than half of the immigrant youngsters "had thoroughly identified themselves with their own racial group" (p. 10).

❧ *Children are stimulated by having friends from many ethnic groups.*

Tozzo and Golub (1990) compared two groups of third-graders. They had men and women in traditional and nontraditional career roles visit and involve the children in a career-related activity. For example, for the group that had the nontraditional role models visit, the female police officer demonstrated fingerprinting. Pre- and post-tests revealed that, although both groups of children retained some stereotypical ideas such as that men are stronger, they did shift other ideas to be less gender specific. For example, post-test girls believed that both sexes could be "fussy, talkative, and complaining" (p. 126).

Suggestions for Controlling and Overcoming the Expression of Prejudice

Of course, none of us wants to be prejudiced, but studies such as the ones just described force us to examine our consciences. We must also realize that different people are preju-diced against different things. Some teachers who are not concerned about skin colour or ethnic background may find they have real difficulty accepting the lifestyles of some fam-ilies they serve. They may feel ill at ease with unmarried couples or with vegetarians, or they may disapprove of how welfare recipients spend their money.

The problem for the teacher is that it is difficult to see things from another's point of view and to accept rather than wish to change the attitudes of someone with different values. Most teachers either consciously or unconsciously intend that families and chil-dren will move over to the teacher's side of the value scale. Thus teachers are likely to use the term *culturally deprived* to describe children who, though deprived of middle-class Anglo culture, actually possess a rich culture of their own.

For example, many teachers deplore the high noise levels and large numbers of people often present in the home environment of black families, seeing it as being chaotic, but other researchers see it as producing a stimulating environment that produces greater "verve" in children (Hale, 1986).

A wonderful quotation from Tolstoy that comes to mind sums it all up. "Everyone thinks of changing the world, but no one thinks of changing himself." If we could only learn to accept some differences as being just that, *differences,* without condemning them, it could be the beginning of changing ourselves and accepting a wider, more tolerant view of the world.

Sometimes, of course, people either cannot or do not wish to change their points of view, and the rest of us need to accept that. The behaviours we demonstrate in the class-room are a reflection of our values. Early childhood educators must examine their own values and behaviour patterns. Cultural acceptance is not carried by genes: it is a learned behaviour. What teachers see and hear and what they choose to act on or ignore are strongly influenced by their own cultural beliefs, unexamined attitudes, and prejudice. We must come to terms with our own identities before we can understand others. Self-knowledge affects interactions between the teacher, the child, and the family. Preschool-ers are in the process of acquiring and constructing concepts of and attitudes towards themselves and others. Early childhood educators play a significant role in helping chil-dren develop positive attitudes. In practice this means examining their own attitudes.

- Consider your feelings about race, gender, culture and ethnicity, age, physical and mental ability, family compositions. Explore how and why you feel a certain way. Think about how your attitudes influence the children with whom you are working.

- Accept that we are all hurt by racism and sexism and make a commitment to always expressing appropriate attitudes and modelling appropriate behaviours.

- Increase your knowledge of particular groups and related issues so that you can give correct information to children.

- Practise sensitive and caring teaching.

- Believe that you can make a difference.

The scope of an adult's influence on how the children view the world is determined by what a teacher does and does not do.

Acquisition of knowledge about difference ethnic groups and cultures fosters understanding and acceptance and helps the teacher overcome her own cultural deprivation. For example, a teacher visiting the home of a Japanese family would not refuse a cup of tea offered as a welcome. Finally, learning the language of the families and actually using it form the best cultural bridge of all, since the use of their language says to the families, "I'm really trying to meet you halfway."

Ethnic studies programs offer a wealth of information on particular cultures, and teachers should take such courses whenever they can. It will not only broaden their horizons but may also teach them how to avoid offending those whom they really want to help. Even just reading about the characteristics of various ethnic groups can help build appreciation and sensitivity to variations in cultural style. Personal interviews, which are assigned in some courses, are particularly valuable in overcoming stereotypes and building relationships.

❧ *Do Young Children Notice Ethnic and Gender Differences?*

It is evident from the studies cited that what teachers and parents do in this area of cross-cultural and nonsexist education can really make a difference—a difference for good or bad. But the question remains, "Do young children really notice the ethnic or gender differences of other children?" If not, perhaps they are too young to require instruction. Might it not be better to ignore these issues and practise "colour blindness" rather than make children self-conscious about such differences when they are so young?

Although some teachers might still prefer to answer yes to these questions, research on the perception of differences in skin colour shows that children as young as age three respond to skin colour (Derman-Sparks, 1993; Katz, 1982; Parrillo, 1985). Moreover, the number of these differentiating responses increases markedly from age three to five. A study by Derman-Sparks, Higa, and Sparks (1980) of the questions and comments by preschool children provides continuing evidence of their concern with and awareness of racial and cultural differences. These ranged from "Is Mexican my colour?" to "I didn't know that babies came out black."

Awareness of ethnic differences precedes the development of prejudice, so we must also ask, "When do positive or negative *attitudes* toward ethnic differences begin to surface?" After an extensive review of the literature, Aboud (1988) concludes:

Ethnic attitudes are acquired by most children some time between the ages of 3 and 5 years. The age of 4 is probably a safe bet if one wanted to pick a single age at which children express negative reactions to certain ethnic members. Whether the negativity is directed toward their own or other ethnicities depends to a certain extent on the child's own ethnic membership. White children are consistently negative toward members of another group. Of the minority groups discussed here, only Native Indians were consistently more negative to their own group than to Whites. The other minority children—Blacks, Hispanics and Asians—were more heterogeneous in that some were initially more negative to their own ethnic members [than to Whites]. (p. 43)

Aboud goes on to say that as children approach ages 7 and 8, there is an increasing tendency for all groups to assign the most preferred rating to children who come from their own ethnic background.

Awareness of sexual differences also begins as early as the age of two, as any teacher of young children can attest, and children will comment freely on such differences unless they are suppressed (Lively & Lively, 1991). One has only to listen during any toilet period in a children's centre to hear such remarks as "Why don't she have a hole in her pants?" or "Don't you use that thing to wet on me!"

These kinds of comments and questions from children, as well as the more formal research already cited, make it clear that the children are indeed revealing a dawning awareness of ethnic and gender differences and developing feelings about these differences at a very early age. If we want them to learn at this same sensitive time that such differences are to be valued rather than scorned, that is, if we wish to combat the formation of bias and prejudice at the earliest possible moment, then we must conclude that early childhood is the time to begin.

❧ What Do Cross-Cultural and Nonsexist Education Have In Common?

Perhaps the reader has been startled to find cross-cultural and nonsexist topics linked together in one chapter, even though it is now clear that the common problem of bias ties them together. They are linked together also because there are two underlying educational principles that apply to both subjects. One principle is that we want children to value their *unique* identity in relation to both their ethnic background and their gender. The other is that we want children to learn that people of all races and both sexes have many *needs and abilities in common,* and we must recognize these held-in-common needs and abilities and encourage their satisfaction if we want to enable all children to make use of their potential.

In the following pages these principles will be applied first to cross-cultural and then to nonsexist education.

❧ Principles of Cross-Cultural Education

Encourage Equity by Recognizing and Honouring Cultural Differences

It is particularly important that the teacher seek to honour each child for his cultural and ethnic uniqueness because this positive valuing has a profound effect on increasing self-esteem, and positive self-esteem is vital in maintaining good mental health. Such acceptance and honouring of diversity, sometimes termed *teaching cultural pluralism,* helps children learn that different does not mean inferior. The emphasis in the following pages is placed primarily on this *cultural pluralistic education* because that appears to be the area in which teachers need the most help.

Importance of Sensitivity

The policy of recognizing cultural differences and honouring them used to be the exception rather than the rule in elementary schools. Readers may recall the books used in their own elementary school days wherein pink and white children visited Grandpa's farm and pulled their puppy around in a shiny new wagon. Now we are able to purchase books and learning materials that have true relevance to family life in a variety of cultures and family situations.

Although these materials are of value, the student should also realize that teaching about differences must be done with sensitivity. In their extensive study of children's views of people from other countries, Lambert and Klineberg (1972) question the desirability of teaching that emphasizes that these people are different or peculiar. The desirability of emphasizing differences should also be questioned when teaching about friends and neighbours. We do not want young children to deduce from our presentations of varying cultural strengths and values that a child should be set apart because of variation in custom or behaviour. It would defeat the entire purpose of cross-cultural education if we generated experiences in which people felt they were being used or as though they were being mounted on the head of a pin and examined.

Instead, the basic learning should be that everyone is worthwhile and that each child brings with him from his family special things that enrich the group and that are fun to share. In other words, we hope to teach that each child is special, not that each child is peculiar.*

Relate Cross-Cultural Learnings to the Here and Now

Just as other learnings are linked to reality, cross-cultural learnings should be linked to present experiences in which the children are actually involved. I don't know what leads otherwise sensible teachers to lose their heads and retreat to quaint pictures of little Dutch girls when they begin to talk about people of different cultures.

However, even when the people are real, there can still be limited benefit in exposing young children to the concept of people from other countries. An incident comes to mind that illustrates this point. The Institute was visited by a delegation of Russian women touring the country. Our families had, as usual, been informed of the impending

---

*Since it is impossible to discuss each ethnic or cultural group in detail in a single chapter, in the following discussion examples were used from as many individual cultures as possible. There is, of course, no one set of culture-based learning experiences universally appropriate to all early childhood programs, because each group of children has its own ethnically and socially unique composition (Mallory & New, 1993). Teachers who want to provide culturally responsive environments for the children in their particular group will find it helpful to peruse the references included at the end of this chapter for more detailed information on specific cultures. Fortunately there are also some general principles that can be applied in almost all circumstances.

visit, so on the following evening one of the fathers asked his little girl if she had enjoyed the visitors. "Oh, yes," she replied. "They were real nice grandmas!" "Ah," he said, "that's good, I'm glad you liked them. By the way, where did you say they came from?" "Oh," she replied, "they didn't say—" she paused, wrinkling her brow in thought, "but I think they were from some place out of town."

An interesting example of an effective way of helping children relate cross-cultural experiences to the here and now of their daily lives comes from some teachers at Pacific Oaks College who have been doing just that with considerable success. They are developing what is called "The Anti-Bias Curriculum" (Pacific Oaks College, 1989), and they define the purpose of that curriculum as being to "empower people to resist being oppressed or to resist oppressing others." The work includes dealing with concerns about bias against gender and handicaps as well as about racial prejudice.

Although space does not permit a review of all their ideas here, I want to provide a taste of what they suggest in the hope that interested readers will pursue the matter further on their own (Derman-Sparks, 1993; Derman-Sparks & the ABC Task Force, 1989). The curriculum, which emerges from day-to-day life experiences at the program, stresses the importance of fostering direct, open communication with children that helps them become aware of racially oppressive beliefs and learn that they can begin to counter these beliefs with positive action.

The teaching varies with the child's age, of course, in order for it to be developmentally appropriate. For example, they favour providing two-year-olds with direct information about race, such as the fact that the brown colour of skin does not wash off and is not dirty; whereas older five-year-olds are encouraged to participate in more activist possibilities. These have included helping the children recognize examples of unfair practices and take action to correct them. One instance involved the youngsters writing to an adhesive bandage company advocating the development of bandages not geared to pinkish-white skins, and another involved painting over a wall near their school that had been covered with racist graffiti.

How much more meaningful it is to children to offer such down-to-earth experiences that are closely related to their own lives and that include activities they can do and enjoy rather than exposing the youngsters momentarily to people "from out of town"! The satisfaction they experience while participating in such activities can build a foundation of positive attitudes toward other cultures on which we can build more advanced concepts at a later date.

Provide a Cross-Cultural Link Between Home and School

The past fifteen years have witnessed the publication of more authentic stories about Caribbean, First Nations, Central American, and Asian children. Tapes and pictures are also available, but it is not necessary to depend on only commercial sources. Children often know rhymes and songs from their families, and the teacher can learn these with the parents' coaching and then help youngsters teach them to the group. Most homes have popular audiotapes or CDs, but this is a resource frequently ignored by teachers. Many of the children's homes are saturated with reggae or rap music, and using such music in school can draw children into movement and dance who spurn less colourful songs about little duckies waddling around the fish pond.

ঌ   *The children are mixing cornstarch, water, and tempera to make "skin" gloves that match their skin color.*

Reaching the child by using his dominant language is even more important. Someone must be available in every preschool room who can understand what the child has to say and who can make friends with him in his own language. Even such simple courtesies as learning to pronounce the child's name as his family does rather than anglicizing it can make a difference. Teaching English as a second language is discussed more fully in chapter 17. I pause here only to emphasize that a bicultural or multicultural program is a farce if we deny the child the right to speak his native tongue or dialect. To be truly effective, cross-cultural programs must honour language as well as other traditions.

Serving familiar food is another excellent way to honour particular backgrounds and to help children feel at home. Sometimes a shy child who appears to be a poor eater is actually just overwhelmed by the strangeness of the food served to him. Food in some day care centres still seems to be planned with the best of nutritional intentions but with total disregard of local food patterns and customs. This situation can be remedied by asking parents for suggestions about appropriate food, by using recipes from ethnic cookbooks (see the references following chapter 3), and by employing a cook who comes from a culture similar to that of the majority of the children.* Children can also be encouraged to bring recipes from home that they can cook at school, or parents or grandparents may have time to come and participate in this way. As the children feel more at ease, it can also be fun to branch out and visit local markets and delicatessens that specialize in various ethnic foods. For example, even in a small community, there may be a Chinese market, a West Indian roti shop, and German and Greek delicatessens. (Delicatessens are particularly good to visit because the food is ready, and it smells good and looks attractive.)

The special customs of the children must be considered, too. For example, we discovered the reason one Saudi Arabian child was not eating much lunch was because he had been taught that it is good manners to refuse food the first time it is offered!

Holidays and other special occasions are also good times for children to share various customs. I recall one event in our group when a young boy lit Hanukkah candles and explained their purpose and the custom of gift giving very clearly. (It was especially fortunate that he was able to do this because he had recently experienced a severe burn, and the prestige of lighting the candles helped him overcome his fear of fire as well as add enrichment to the life of our group.)

A note of caution should be inserted here about the need to increase our sensitivity to the way some people feel about certain holidays. Consider the complexity involved in celebrating holidays when their observance may be counter, even offensive, to some families' beliefs or cultures. Although Christmas is celebrated as a national holiday, it reflects a specific religious belief system. For children who are not Christian—be they Jewish, Buddhist, Muslim, or atheist—Christmas can be a problem. Some centres integrate holidays from several cultural groups into their celebration, such as Hanukkah and the winter solstice. Thanksgiving as a holiday might be an occasion of loss rather than a celebration for Canadian aboriginal families. The celebration of holidays should not be avoided but should be considered carefully, taking into account the attitudes, needs, and feelings of the children, families, and staff. Holiday celebrations should focus on respect and understanding of cultural observations.

The background of each child may be savoured by the group in many additional ways. Dress-up clothes that reflect the occupations of various parents or national costumes, when they can be spared, contribute much to the life of the school. Stories brought from home, ethnically accurate and attractive dolls, and integrated pictures are also good choices. *Such cross-cultural materials should be available consistently rather than presented as isolated units.* Dolls, pictures, books, and music from many cultures should be deliberately, though apparently casually, woven into the fabric of every preschool day.

It is, of course, also necessary to take a continuing close look at the materials, particularly books, offered to the children to make certain they are not teaching undesirable attitudes. Just as we are making the effort to become sensitive to sexist books that perpetuate certain stereotypical role models for girls or boys, so must we also become more sensitive to racist themes and roles. Unfortunately such slanted books abound.

Teachers should be alerted to the continuing necessity of reviewing the books we read to the children with great care. Appendix D offers some helpful guidelines to follow

---

*Refer also to Table 3.3 for cultural food preferences of several ethnic groups.

when selecting books about minority children. We need also to be aware that the supply of these materials ebbs and flows as the market dictates. Publishers print what the public will buy. If we want to have a continuing supply of good quality books that represent the cultures of all the children we teach, we are going to have to write to publishers and make our desires known.

Suggestions That Foster Cross-Cultural Understanding

Going Beyond Foods, Books, and Holidays

What worries me about listing such ideas as the ones above is that so many teachers seem to think this is all there is to multicultural education, whereas it is actually only the beginning. We must realize that the basic purpose of providing multicultural experience is *not* to teach the children facts about India or Japan, or to prove to the community that the teacher is not prejudiced. *The purpose of a multicultural curriculum is to attach positive feelings to multicultural experiences so that each child will feel included and valued and will also feel friendly and respectful toward people from other ethnic and cultural groups.*

When you get right down to it, all the multiethnic pictures and recipes and books in the world will not make much difference if teachers, in their hearts, cannot appreciate the strong points of each child and his family and help the other children appreciate them also.

Dealing with Racial Comments and Slurs at the Preschool Level

Preprimary teachers often ask me how they should reply when a three- or four-year-old comments on the difference in skin colour of one of his classmates.

It seems to me there are two kinds of comments. The first is the kind of information-seeking question cited previously by Derman-Sparks and coworkers (1980): "Will it rub off?" or "How come her backs [of hands] are brown but her fronts are pink?"

Such comments should be welcomed (rather than brushed aside in an embarrassed way) because they provide opportunities to clear up confusions about skin colour. Our black head teacher has taught us all never to allow such opportunities to slip past. She is quick to explain and demonstrate that skin colour does not wash off and that it is not dirty. She also points out that people may be different colours on the outside, but we are all the same colour on the inside.

The second kind of comment, however, is more difficult to handle. When four-year-old Sue yells at Veejay, "That's my trike, you paki, get off!" it is easy for teachers to feel so upset and angry they lose sight of the probable reason such a young child resorts to such an ugly slur.

First of all it is necessary to remember that three- and four-year-olds do not comprehend the full extent of the insult. What they *do* know about such words is that they have a strong emotional power to hurt, and the children who are using these words use them because they *are* angry and they *do* intend to hurt. This means that the problem has to be dealt with in two parts.

Part one has to do with pointing out to *both* children the real reason Sue is angry. She is angry because she does not want Veejay taking her trike, not because he is South Asian. It is important for Veejay to understand this to protect his self-esteem. It is important for Sue to realize that it is not the colour of the person taking her trike that matters, it is the fact she does not want *anyone* taking it at all. *She needs to learn to attach anger to its real cause rather than displacing it by substituting innocent or incorrect reasons.* This not only helps prevent the formation of prejudice but also is a basic principle of mental health everyone needs to learn and practise: Always admit to yourself why you are really angry. Don't displace anger: face facts.

Following this clear labelling of the reason for the fight, coupled with a brief description of each child's feelings ("I can see you're angry, and I can see you don't want to wait"), the argument has to be settled just as any other fight would have to be. The second part of the problem must also be faced. No one likes having his feelings hurt, and name calling of any sort is intended to and does hurt feelings. Although the usual advice about such matters is that if "bad" language is ignored it will go away, experience in the real world of day care has taught me that sometimes ignoring such words works and sometimes it does not. It is also true that some name calling hurts worse than others, and when this is the case, it is essential for the teacher to be quite firm and clear with children about what is acceptable and stop what is not.

These standards of acceptability vary from program to program. My own level of tolerance is that although I can ignore many insults and bathroom words, I will not tolerate racial or sexist insults to myself or to anyone else. So, after dealing with the social contretemps just described, I would take Sue aside for a quiet, firm talk about hurt feelings, reiterating the rule, "We do not use the word paki because it hurts too much. When you're mad at Veejay, hold onto the trike and tell him 'You can't have the trike—I'm using it now. You have to wait till I'm done,' *but we do not use the word paki here."*

As the moment presents itself, I would also say again to Veejay that Sue was mad at him because he grabbed her trike, and she wanted to get even by calling him "paki." Next time he had better ask for the trike instead of just taking it. If she calls him "paki" again, pay no attention, she just does not know any better yet.

It is important to understand that the problem of helping minority children deal with such attacks is a difficult one and could fill a book by itself. Wilson (1980) suggests many ways families can help children defend themselves against such attacks. She states that it is important for children to be able to respond with dignity and keep control of themselves. They might respond by saying, "Call me by my name!" or say, "Don't call me that again." She stresses that youngsters need a range of strategies that include ignoring the taunt, walking away and then returning with a reply, getting help from someone else, combining a response with getting help, and sharing the sadness at home, where she cautions parents that children should be allowed to cry about it if they feel like doing so and they should be comforted. In addition, it should be pointed out once again that providing the continuing countermeasure of building pride in race, which was discussed earlier in the chapter, is probably the strongest defence of all.

Show Respect for People of Differing Ethnic Origins by Employing Them as Teachers

Cross-cultural learning in the children's centre should be based on real experiences with real people whenever possible. An effective way of teaching young children that people of all ethnic backgrounds are important is to employ them in positions of power. Many programs employ people from minority groups as aides. Programs need to ask themselves, "are staff from racial, cultural, linguistic, and other minority groups fairly represented at all levels of the organization?" Children are quick to sense the power structure of the program, and they need to see people of all ethnic backgrounds in respected positions as teachers and administrators.

Unfortunately, Asian and native teachers are still relatively rare. Many First Nations people would prefer to have their children cared for by native staff who understand the native family network, including elders, the nuclear, and the extended family. For example, elders participating in native child care act as a safeguard against the loss of culture. Ideally, there would be a separate early childhood training program designed to incorporate native cultural values (Chud & Fahlman, 1995). A non-native teacher working with native children should at least try to develop a knowledge and understanding of native traditions.

Programs need to adopt policies and practices that support and reflect diversity. For example, do personnel policies address diversity issues such as leave for religious holidays or observances as well as or instead of Christian statutory holidays? Administrators should undertake hiring, promotion, and personnel practices that encourage inclusion and support of people traditionally discriminated against in employment, including people of colour and cultural and linguistic minorities; people of differing religions, abilities, sexual orientations, ages, and socioeconomic classes (Early Childhood Multicultural Services, 1995).

Involve and Honour All Parents When They Visit the Centre

All families play a central role in the socialization of young children. Some immigrant families want their children to learn English quickly and adopt Canadian ways, while others worry that life in Canada will gradually result in the loss of their own language, culture, and traditions. These differing perspectives will be clearly transmitted to children within their family setting and may cause the families to question the educational experiences of the children.

I recommended earlier that teachers should seek to acquaint themselves with various cultures by reading, taking courses, learning the language, and so forth, but I want to emphasize here that the most vigorous and lively source of ethnic learning is right on the program's doorstep, namely, the families themselves. In the long run, cooperative sharing of themselves and their skills will teach the teacher and the children the most about the personal strengths of family members. As a matter of fact, I do not see how one could conduct a multiethnic classroom without drawing on these resources.

Successful communication is vital. The teacher who is unafraid of parents and who genuinely likes them will communicate this without saying anything at all; there is really no substitute for this underlying attitude of good will and concern for the children. All parents appreciate the teacher who has the child's welfare genuinely at heart, and this mutual interest in the child is the best base on which to build a solid teacher-parent relationship. Since listening is so much more important than talking, teachers should particularly cultivate that ability in themselves.

Other matter-of-fact things about communication can help when speaking with newcomers to Canada. If teachers determine that families are unable to communicate adequately in English, they can make use of bilingual support people. Assistance with translating and interpreting, volunteer and/or paid, may be forthcoming from other members of the family, other bilingual families currently using the program, friends and colleagues, members of cultural associations, church groups or community centres, immigrant settlement organizations, or social service agencies.

There are a number of ways in which teachers can make use of these resource people. They may request that posters, notices, letters, and other materials be translated into appropriate languages (see, for example, Figures 14.1a and 14.1b). Apart from the obvious benefits for parent-teacher communication, the use of this assistance conveys the teacher's commitment to accommodate culturally and linguistically diverse families. To immigrant families, it conveys a desire to welcome them into the program.

Welcome parent volunteers. The problem with making parents feel at ease and glad to participate in the early childhood program is that they may feel a little out of their element

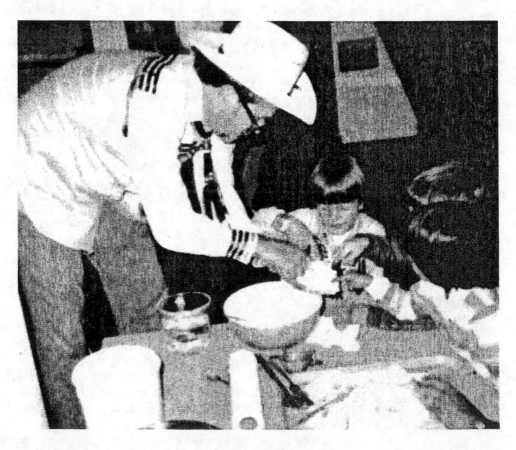

♋   *Mr. Duff is helping the children make fry bread. Contact with native people can help children understand them better.*

Figure 14.1a   An example of a simple multilingual notice.

WELCOME TO OUR CENTRE.
OUR STAFF MEMBERS ARE:

Cantonese 歡迎光臨， 我們中心的工作人員如下：

Farsi ۹ ـ به موّسسه ما خوش آمـــدید. ضمناً مسئولین مربوطه عبارتند از :

Polish WITAMY W NASZYM OŚRODKU. NASZYMI PRACOWNIKAMI SĄ:

Punjabi ਸਾਡੇ ਕੇਂਦਰ ਵਿੱਚ ਜੀ-ਆਇਆਂ ਨੂੰ । ਸਾਡੇ ਕਰਮਚਾਰੀ ਇਹ ਹਨ:

Spanish BIENVENIDO A NUESTRO CENTRO. EL PERSONAL DEL JARDIN/GUARDERIA ES:

Vietnamese Chào mừng quý vị đến trung tâm của chúng tôi. Nhân viên của chúng tôi gồm có:

Source: Multilingual Services Development Program, Westcoast Child Care Resource Centre.

Figure 14.1b   Another simple notice translated into several languages.

IF YOU ARE BRINGING MEDICATION FOR YOUR CHILD, PLEASE GIVE IT TO A STAFF MEMBER.

Cantonese   請交你孩子服食的藥物給予工作人員

Farsi   ۱۰ ــ اگر داروئی خاصی را میبایستی برای فرزندتان به این موسسه بیآورید لطفا به مسئولین‌تحویـل دهیـد.

Polish   W PRZYPADKU PRZYNIESIENIA LEKARSTWA DLA TWOJEGO DZIECKA PROSZĘ DAĆ JE KOMUŚ Z PERSONELU.

Punjabi   ਜੇ ਕਰ ਤੁਸੀਂ ਆਪਟੇ ਬੱਚੇ ਲਈ ਕੋਈ ਦਵਾਈ ਲੈ ਕੇ ਆ ਰਹੇ ਹੈ ਤਾਂ ਕਿਰਪਾ ਕਰਕੇ ਉਹ ਕਿਸੇ ਵੀ ਕਰਮਚਾਰੀ ਨੂੰ ਫੜਾ ਦੇਵੋਂ ।

Spanish   SI UD. TRAE MEDICAMENTOS PARA SU NIÑO, POR FAVOR, ENTREGUE UD. A UNA DE LAS SUPERVISORAS.

Vietnamese   Nếu quý vị muốn cho con em quý vị uống thuốc khi đang ở nhà trẻ, xin vui lòng trình những thuốc này cho nhân viên

Source: Multilingual Services Development Program, Westcoast Child Care Resource Centre.

in the beginning. I have often thought that it would be fair to require the teacher to visit and help out in the families' homes on a turnabout basis. If this were possible, it would certainly help teachers gain a better insight into how it feels to step into a strange situation.

I have witnessed teachers asking mothers to wipe off tables or help in the kitchen, or letting them simply stand around, smiling a lot, but knowing in their hearts their time is being wasted. Some visitors may prefer simple tasks in the beginning because these are familiar, not threatening, and because they do not want to make waves or antagonize the teacher. However, keeping them at such tasks is fundamentally denigrating, teaches the children that parents are not important at school, and deprives the children of the unique contribution such people can make when they are properly encouraged. For example, instead of setting up the tables for lunch, a mother might share with the children a book she has kept from her own childhood or bring pictures of her family's latest trip to India, or help the children make her child's favourite recipe or talk about her job. Last fall one of the fathers in our group helped the children make an authentic (and tasty) squash and cornmeal dessert. The children were delighted, and his son was ecstatic!

Remember that the fundamental purpose of providing these experiences is to create emotionally positive situations for the children and the adults who are involved. For this reason the teacher should concentrate on doing everything possible to help visitors feel comfortable and successful. It takes considerable planning, but the results are worth it.

Although it is not fair to put parents on the spot and ask them to control a group of children they do not know, it can be genuine fun and very helpful to have parent volunteers come along on field trips during which everyone can be together and everyone takes some responsibility. Families may enjoy such opportunities to get out and do things, and field trips can be a refreshing change

Families can often provide ideas for excursions, too. The children at our centre greatly enjoyed a visit to a communal organic garden one spring, and they also loved a trip to a pizza parlour owned by one of the families.

Make visitors welcome for meals. Breaking bread together binds people in basic friendliness. An open, welcoming attitude at mealtimes, with parents spontaneously invited to share meals with the children, can be very rewarding. When finances cannot support this drain, visiting parents can order lunch a day in advance and pay a nominal fee to defray the cost.

Trust and use parent expertise on the advisory board. Parent participation is viewed as a strategy for improving the service. Programs benefit when parents are involved in decision-making. A parent advisory committee can provide feedback and recommendations to the centre and advocate for parents and their involvement in the program. Parents can be effective fundraisers and powerful advocates for increased societal support for children's programs.

Some programs use committees as rubber stamps and present parents with programs and plans literally for approval rather than for consideration and modification—a policy that certainly does not make parents feel welcome or respected. A much better way to make plans is to trust the parents. It is unlikely they will suggest activities or policies detrimental to the children; and when differences arise, they can usually be settled by open discussion, which educates everyone.

In practice, it is not always easy for directors and staff to share responsibility when decisions must be made. Often conflicting views about what is good for children must be reconciled, potentially a challenging process. Staff must guard against dominating meetings with their training and experience in formal meetings and decision making.

Teachers who seek out parents' suggestions because they value their practical experience with their children will find that this approach reduces the parents' feelings of defensiveness when the teacher happens to be better educated. If meetings are held during times when child care is available, more committee members are likely to attend. Attendance also increases when parent suggestions are actually used and when parents are thanked sincerely for coming.

Emphasizing the Similarities As Well As Valuing the Uniqueness of People

Children and families not only need to have their cultural uniqueness welcomed and valued, they also need to learn that all people have many things in common and that they are alike in some fundamental ways.

Teach the Commonality of Biological and Psychological Needs

One way to teach the similarities of all people is to emphasize the commonality of biological and psychological needs. Thus, when talking about the children's favourite food or what they traditionally eat for various holidays, the teacher can remind them that no matter what we like to eat best, everyone gets hungry and everyone likes to eat some things or can point out at the right moment that it feels good to everyone to stretch and yawn or to snuggle down in something warm and cosy.

The same principle can be taught in relation to emotions: Everyone feels mad sometimes, everyone wants to belong to somebody, most people want to have friends, and most children feel a little lost when their mothers leave them at school.

In addition, the teacher can draw the children's attention to the fact that people often use individual, unique ways to reach a goal that most people enjoy. For example, Josie's father plays the guitar, while Heather's mother uses the zither; but they both use these different instruments for the pleasure of making music and singing together with the children.

Help Families Look Beyond Various Differences to Focus on Common Goals

Early childhood programs of various types can provide opportunities for friendships to form and thrive. Cooperatives are famous for doing this, of course, but it can also be accomplished in other groups. Advisory boards can draw families into projects that focus on the children and benefit everyone. This activity can take the form of a potluck dinner, with slides of what the children have been doing; it can be a series of discussions on topics chosen by the parents; it can be a workday combined with a picnic lunch for which everyone pitches in to clean and paint and tidy up. (There is nothing like scrubbing a kitchen floor together to generate a common bond.) It makes little difference what is chosen, as long as it results in the realization of a common goal and creates opportunities for everyone to be together in a meaningful, friendly way.

Keep Working Toward the Basic Goals of Socialization
That Teach Children to Consider the Rights and Needs of Everyone

Finally, the teacher should remember that working towards the goals of socialization discussed in chapter 10 will help children learn that everyone has the same basic rights and privileges and everyone is respected and treated fairly at school. The social goals most important to emphasize in relation to cross-cultural education are developing empathy for how other people feel, learning that everyone has rights that are respected by all, and gaining skill cooperating rather than achieving satisfaction by competing and winning over others. If these social skills are fostered, living in the group will be a good experience for all the children, and a healthy foundation will be laid for a more truly integrated society in the future.

🙦 Can Teaching about Cultural Uniqueness and Similarity of Needs Be Combined?

There is at least one way to teach preschool children both concepts—that is, that people are enjoyably unique and that they have many similar needs in common at the same time. The staff at our child care centre gradually evolved this approach after passing through two earlier stages.

During the first stage, in an effort to make experiences more real for the children, students and staff tended to bring in things from other cultures for the children to pass around and look at during group time, or the items were displayed on a table accompanied by books and pictures about the culture. This was, basically, a beginning attempt to honour cultural uniqueness. We now refer to this as "our museum period."

During the second stage we increased the here-and-now aspect by doing a lot of the sort of thing described in the first part of this chapter. We cooked ethnic foods together and enjoyed them, or we celebrated a holiday or made a piñata and talked about how there were many wonderful ways of satisfying hunger or having parties. We still continue to offer many of these stage-two experiences during the week, and the children continue to appreciate them.

However, the staff remained unsatisfied with these approaches. It just did not seem to us that we were helping the children grasp the reality and value of other cultures and appreciate the common humanity that binds us all. With such young children we felt we needed to link things together in more explicit and literal ways.

To accomplish *this* goal we developed a stage-three approach. In this current stage we are offering the children comparative experiences through which they can actually try out what it is like to sleep in a Czechoslovakian feather bed, a Guatemalan hammock, and a child-sized bed, and we make these comparative play experiences available for a week at a time.

In another example we set up a comparison between Japanese and Western eating styles. On the Japanese side the children took their shoes off upon entering, sat on low cushions, and used bowls and chopsticks as they partook of ramen noodles and Japanese cookies. (Our Japanese children were gratifyingly proficient with chopsticks!) On the Western side they wiped their shoes on a mat, sat on low chairs, used plates and bowls, and had noodle soup and wheat crackers. In the offing is an experience comparing the different methods by which mothers carry their babies around.

Experiences do not have to be this elaborate to get the point across. During a warm spring rain last year, one of the students brought a number of banana leaves (often used in Thailand when it rains), and the children delighted in using them and comparing them with their more familiar umbrellas. Another easy comparison to offer is a simple tasting experience. For example, it's interesting to compare French bread, tortillas, matzo, and pita bread, or various cheeses, or fruits that come from different countries such as mangoes, oranges, and guavas.

Once again, remember that families can make invaluable contributions of advice and resources if you decide to attempt stage-three activities, and it is most beneficial when these experiences are family related and based on the cultural backgrounds of children in the group.

Please understand that these more concentrated experiences do not constitute our entire approach to cross-cultural education. If they did, that would be too much like reverting to "Japanese Day" or "Cinco de Mayo." We continue to make certain that multiethnic materials such as books, pictures, puzzles, and other equipment are used throughout the school on a matter-of-fact, daily basis. The purpose of the stage-three activities is to accentuate the fact that there is more than one satisfactory way to meet a human need and, most important of all, that many of these ways are *fun*.

❧ Encouraging Equity by Providing a Nonsexist Education and Helping Children Value their Own Sexuality

Today, when educational emphasis tends to be placed on the value of nonsexist education, it may be necessary to remind the reader that it is also important to teach children about reproduction and gender differences and to help them value their maleness or femaleness.

Even though many of us want to enable children of both sexes to step beyond the narrowly restricted ideas of sex roles and stereotypes that presently exist, we must be careful to help them value their basic sexuality as well because that is an important and deeply elemental part of every individual's personality. If children grow up with the idea that sexuality is unimportant or not valued, or, worse yet, that reproduction and sex are smutty topics to be snickered about and investigated in secret, we may have unwittingly undone much of what we hoped to accomplish by adding a nonsexist emphasis to teaching.

Teaching Simple Physiological Facts

The more open and matter-of-fact teachers and parents can be about differences in the anatomy of boys and girls, the more likely it is that children will not need to resort to "doctor" play or hiding in corners to investigate such differences "on the q.t." Open toi-leting has long been the rule in most preschool settings because, when children use the same toilets, secrecy about sexual differences and toilet practices is avoided. This approach also generates opportunities for the teacher to supply answers to things young children wonder about, such as explaining why boys urinate standing up whereas girls sit down. The teacher makes simple statements about these matters: "Yes, boys and girls are made differently. Boys have penises, and so they stand up to urinate. Girls have vulvas, so they sit down." If little girls still want to know why they cannot stand up, the teacher can invite them to try it. There is no substitute for learning by experience! Casualness and answering the questions actually asked, rather than ones the teacher is nervously afraid the children will ask, should be the order of the day.

Sometimes it helps clarify matters if the adult replies to questions by asking the youngster what he thinks the answer is, since this can provide a clue to how complicated the adult explanation should be. Sometimes, though, such a return question embarrasses an older four-year-old who is sophisticated enough to suspect he should not be asking about such things anyway, and questioning in return can cause him to stop asking. So it takes a delicate perception of the child to know whether to respond with a question or just answer as simply and clearly as possible. Of course, if you want to keep the line open for more questions, it is deadly to betray amusement at some of the naïve answers you will receive.

Although the use of accurate words such as *penis* or *vagina* is more commonplace than it used to be, teachers and parents should note there is an interesting piece of research that points out that grown-ups are more likely to use explicit terms when referring to boys' genitalia than when talking about the genitalia of little girls. Koblinsky, Atkinson, and Davis (1980) surmise this is because boys' genitals are more visible. It seems that what we adults need to learn from this research is that we must make a special effort to remember to discuss the anatomy of little girls as well as that of little boys, even though that part of the anatomy is not as apparent.

Since every child's self-concept is intimately tied to her or his sense of sexual worth, we must be careful to teach that each sex has an important role to play in reproduction. When grown, girls have the opportunity to carry and bear children, and boys, when grown, help start the baby growing. Then mothers and fathers work together to care for the baby following its birth (Lively & Lively, 1991).

Bear in mind when discussing the dual roles of parenting that it is necessary to think about the child's home situation. Many children in day care now come from single-parent homes; this has to be gently taken into account in such discussions so that the child does not feel "different" or peculiar because he has only one parent. As well, some children's families may include two mothers or two fathers. It takes a combination of sensitivity and matter-of-factness to deal with these situations successfully.

Once past the matter of simple anatomical differences, it is still the case that many adults dread questions about reproduction and because of their discomfort either evade them (just as they avoid discussing race) or give such confused or elaborate replies that the children are bewildered. Therefore it can be reassuring to learn that the kind of question most preschool children are likely to ask is, "Where did the baby come from?" "How

Ƽ   *Boys should be encouraged to use the dramatic centre.*

will it get out?" This level of questioning, common to three- to five-year-olds, is termed the "geography level" by Bernstein in a delightful book called *The Flight of the Stork* (1978). Thinking of it as a "geography" question can make it reasonably unembarrassing to explain that a baby is growing inside the mother's uterus or that it will be born through a special hole women have between their legs, near where their urine comes out but not exactly the same place.

For the slightly older youngster who wants to know how the baby gets inside to start with, it is far better to tell him or her the truth rather than to talk about animals or seeds. This is because when children see animals mating, it may look like fighting to them or they may note an expression of resigned submission on the part of the female animal—attitudes we would rather not have children associate with human intercourse. The problem with the "planting seeds" idea is that it encourages them to think too literally about this concept in terms of what they already know about gardening. I was told of one little girl who queried after such a discussion, "Well, what I want to know is, when you picked out that seed, did it have my picture on it?"

To avoid such misconceptions, I suggest that the teacher or parent explain that the mother and father start the baby growing in the mother by being very loving and close with each other and that when they are feeling this way, the father fits his penis inside the mother's vagina and a fluid passes into her that joins with the mother's egg and helps the baby start growing. I prefer this explanation because it is truthful and accurate and also because it mentions the role of warmth, caring, and mutual responsibility as being important parts of the experience.

Masturbation

Another aspect of helping children value their own sexuality has to do with dealing with masturbatory behaviour so that children are not shamed by the teacher's reprimand and do not come to feel that their sexual impulses are unclean or "bad."

Research indicates that masturbation is commonplace in adult males and females (Masters, Johnson, & Kilodny, 1994), and it is in children, too. Although the extent of such behaviour is unknown in children (Langfeldt, 1981), a Norwegian study found that 85% of the kindergarten teachers who were interviewed reported that some of the children in their classes engaged in masturbation, though only 24% of the teachers reported that such behaviour happened "often" or "very often" (Gundersen et al., 1981).

The question that confronts teachers once they admit the frequency and normality of the behaviour is what to do about it, since it is still true that masturbating is not acceptable public behaviour. It seems wisest to take the child aside and explain to her or him that you realize such behaviour feels good but that it is something people do only in private.

Meeting the Special Needs of Boys in the Preschool

Still another aspect of helping children value their own sexuality has to do with recognizing the boys' needs for role models in the children's centre. Although it is difficult to talk about this without having it misinterpreted as advocating sexist practices, experience has taught me it is necessary to remind women teachers how important it is to provide young boys with many experiences that fit their needs. LaTorre (1979), for example, cites a study that noted that the four preschool teachers who were observed paid attention to (reinforced) boys' behaviour "approximately 86 percent [of the time] when it followed involvement in feminine behaviours" (p. 91).

Boys' physical activity needs appear to differ from those of girls, at least at the present time. Research shows they tend to engage in more rough-and-tumble play than girls do (Johnson & Roopnarine, 1983) and that they are more aggressive than girls are after the age of two (Barfield, 1976; Jacklin & Baker, 1993). Some teachers tend to suppress this vigour and energy, since it is contrary to the teacher's own behaviour patterns. Although all children need opportunities for vigorous physical activity, boys *do* seem to need it especially, and we must provide for meeting that need. Their play requires large, sturdy equipment, plenty of space, and a teacher who genuinely welcomes such activity rather than regarding it as a threat to her ability to control the children.

Boys not only must be supplied with enough room to move and to let off steam but also must have the chance to form relationships with men who can serve as models for them. In an age when the divorce rate remains high and many unmarried women are electing to raise their children independently, many children in child care centres come from single-parent, mother-centered homes. The effect on the boys' developing sense of masculinity of these mother-centered, father-absent homes is at present uncertain. Herzog and Sudia (1973), after an extensive review of research, sum up their findings when they say, "The findings reviewed do not provide clear-cut and conclusive answers to . . . questions about the sturdiness of the masculine identity of fatherless boys as compared with that of boys in two-parent homes" (p. 184). However, common sense cannot help encouraging one to believe that the presence of a father facilitates sex role development (although there is also evidence that boys can develop normally without it). For this reason centres should provide boys with consistent contacts with men who care about children. Girls too benefit from such experience, since it probably helps them develop concepts of masculinity and femininity, also.

Incidentally, one of the continuing and unfortunate examples of sexism in our society is the fact that few men are employed as early childhood teachers (Meyerhoff, 1994; Nelson & Shepherd, 1992). In 1992 the national study Caring for a Living reported that out of 2383 child care workers surveyed in Canada, only 2% were male (Karyo, 1992). According to Robinson (1988), this is due in part to the perception that such work requires the nurturing qualities commonly attributed to females rather than to males, but it is also due to low pay.

These challenges mean that we will continue to need to use ingenuity in thinking of ways to include men as participants in the preschool day. High school and college men can often be employed as aides, and occasionally warmhearted fathers will volunteer to come regularly and spend time with the children. All of the contacts, though admittedly not as satisfactory as a father's continuing presence in the home, will help both boys and girls formulate their concepts of what it means to be a man or woman in our society and, ideally, will help boys and girls grow up to be sturdy, attractive men and women themselves.

Suggestions for Providing a Nonsexist Curriculum

"Are boys really better than girls at analysing problems?" "Are girls better than boys at nurturing and comforting others?" Although research indicates that the answer to these questions is no, many teachers continue to act as if these myths were true and plan their curriculum and treat children accordingly. Jacklin and Baker report there are actually only two areas in which behavioural differences between boys and girls have been reliably established. These are that "boys are found to be more aggressive than girls, whereas girls' language development and verbal abilities exceed those of boys" (1993, p. 42), but even these differences are not statistically pronounced. We may conclude, then, that there is really no prevailing *genetic* reason why both sexes cannot be equally interested in every activity offered at school. If we want this to happen, what must be changed is the culture in which attitudes toward sex roles are formed (Streitmatter, 1994).

Before embarking on approaches that may bring about changes in attitude I want to remind the reader of the difference between children's ideas of sex roles and their feelings about sexuality and gender. In our zeal to provide all children with the widest possible range of activities and developmental experiences, we must also be careful to preserve children's deep, basic valuing of their own sexuality because that positive valuing is fundamental to their feelings of identity and being worthy people.

Does this valuing mean that teachers should not seek to change former, possibly sexist curricula? Of course not. We must do all we can to widen children's horizons to the rich possibilities heretofore unavailable to many of them.

One way ideas about sex roles can be changed to be more equitable without undermining the child's pride in gender is by presenting an open curriculum that provides opportunities for both sexes to participate in all learning activities rather than restricting children to obsolete sex role expectations. Teachers should work to develop wider competence and equal privileges for both sexes. Sprafkin, Serbin, Denir, and Connor (1983) demonstrated that providing three-and-a-half to four-year-old boys *and girls* with opportunities to practise with "boy-preferred" toys such as blocks, dominoes, and building toys significantly improved the children's visual spatial ability—a skill on which boys typically score higher. This skill is fundamental to later achievements in such fields as architecture, mathematics, and engineering and so is one well worth fostering in children of both sexes.

Preschools are often the last chance children have to try out materials and activities that are contemptuously labelled in elementary school as "girl stuff" or "unfeminine." Surely activities such as woodworking and blocks should be freely available to girls, just as opportunities to enjoy dressing up or sewing should be available for boys. The chance to experience a full range of roles enriches the knowledge of each sex and, ideally, deepens understanding and empathy for the opposite sex.

Sprung and the Women's Action Alliance have produced a first-rate book (1975) replete with examples of how the preschool curriculum can be presented so that all areas, whether it be blocks or the dramatic play corner, will attract both boys and girls. *Equal Their Chances* (Shapiro, Kramer, & Hunerberg, 1981) also offers many suggestions that could either be used with younger children directly or to raise the awareness of teachers who might otherwise use such phrases as "The girls can go first because . . ." when they could easily say, "This table can go first" if they take a minute to think before they speak.

It is, of course, important not only to offer wider opportunities to girls but also to offer them to boys. For example, opportunities for additional male roles should be included in homemaking, such as scaled-to-comfortable-size men's clothing for workers of various kinds. These garments should be freely available for use by both sexes, and boys should be encouraged to join in activities such as cooking and caring for children.

Teachers may encounter a bit more resistance from boys when such cross-gender activities are first proposed than they will from girls. This is because girls are less criticized by their peers when they engage in "masculine-preferred" activities than boys are. Fagot's research (1977; 1994) indicates that even when teachers encourage boys to cook or engage in self-expressive art activity, other boys do criticize them for such behaviour, so it is well to be on the lookout for such remarks by their peers and discourage them when possible.

Greenberg (1985) presents a particularly interesting perspective on early childhood education. She points out that most of the curriculum stresses skills girls already possess but boys often lack. These include emphasis on verbal activities (large group time, for example), small muscle activities (cutting, painting, etc.), and assistance in gaining impulse control. Participation in these activities, she maintains, is virtually obligatory.

On the other hand, much of the curriculum that might remediate deficiencies in little girls' education is left to "choice and chance." Participation in such activities as block play and large muscle activities that might also aid in developing spatial awareness are a matter of self-selection (as is selection of various science activities).

Basing her recommendations on research, Greenberg suggests teachers make a special effort to provide the following activities for girls:

━━

♋ RESEARCH STUDY ♋
The Changing World of Picture Books

Research Question: Dellmann-Jenkins, Florjancic, and Swadener asked the question "Have the sex roles and cultural/ethnic themes and people included in children's picture books changed in recent years?"

Research Method: To determine the answer, the investigators analysed contemporary Caldecott Award and Honor Books and compared these results with the findings from a study done ten years earlier by Collins, Ingoldsby, and Dellmann (1984).

To make the comparison between the studies valid, the current investigators analysed their research using the same methods utilized in the 1984 study and also extended the research design to check for androgyny and cultural diversity.

The characters in the fifteen books awarded Caldecott honours during the years 1989 to 1992 were assessed according to the character's sex role and kind of participation in each story. Then ratios were calculated comparing the number of male people and/or animals in titles and illustrations with the number of female people and animals present in titles and illustrations. The ratio for nongendered animals was also calculated. The kinds of activities the characters participated in was analysed according to whether they were active/passive, and traditional/nontraditional. The androgynous quality of the characters' behaviour and their cultural diversity was also assessed.

Results: When these factors were compared with the study done ten years earlier by Collins, the researchers found that there was a slight trend toward including more females in book titles and a statistically significant trend ($p < .001$) toward including more females in illustrations. The most pronounced difference in sex roles was the increase in the number of nongendered animal illustrations. There was also a slight trend toward placing more females in central roles.

1. Activities that require spatial exploration
2. Activities for practice in large muscle coordination and development of large motor skills (increase structured gym activities)
3. Equipment that enhances investigatory activity
4. Activities that permit learning from following directions
5. Tasks that require cooperative groups of three or more children for their accomplishment
6. Tasks that encourage distance from adults
7. Opportunities for experimenting with a wide range of future career options

   Activities to be provided for boys include the following:

1. Activities that encourage listening, speaking, and conversing
2. Activities for small muscle coordination
3. Opportunities to learn from examples

Defining androgyny as being "the state of possessing the best characteristics of masculinity and femininity" (Kaplan, 1992, p. 432), the Dellman-Jenkins study found that ten of the fifteen books portrayed characters meeting this standard. They also found that seven of the fifteen books depicted people from nondominant cultures or minority groups.

Implications for Teaching: It is indeed encouraging to see that the award-winning books are becoming those that tend to be more balanced in their presentation of positive characteristics of an array of people. Whether this is happening because the results of the 1984 study and a similar study conducted in 1972 have become widely disseminated, thereby influencing the Caldecott judges to take a more gender-balanced approach to award giving, or whether it is simply the result of increased social consciousness is unknown. Whatever the reason, all of us should be thankful these high-quality, exquisitely illustrated books are available for us to share with children.

However, we cannot conclude that this study reveals a prevailing trend throughout children's literature. The Caldecott books represent the cream of the crop. One has only to read *Multiethnic Children's Literature* (Ramirez & Ramirez, 1994) or *Books Without Bias: Through Indian Eyes* (Slapin & Seale, 1992) to be reminded that severe deficiencies are still present in many children's books that portray a variety of ethnic/cultural backgrounds. Since this is the case, adults who care about the effect books have on young children must continue to rigorously review every book and apply the standards listed in Appendix D to make certain it is truly a desirable book to share.

Source: From "Sex Roles and Cultural Diversity in Recent Award Winning Picture Books for Young Children" by M. Dellman-Jenkins, L. Florjancic, & E. B. Swadener, 1993, *Journal of Research in Early Childhood Education, 7*(2), 74–82.

4. Opportunities that encourage responsibility for others and to others
5. Opportunities for nurturing activities
6. Activities for helping boys develop flexible, effective self-management skills

All teachers should take a closer look at the materials they offer for educational activities. More nonsexist, multiracial materials in the form of puzzles, lotto games, and dolls are becoming available, but these materials are rarely sufficient for the needs of the preschool. Teachers should also expect to make many of their own items; the books by Sprung (1975) and Jenkins and Macdonald (1979) listed at the end of this chapter contain directions on how to do this.

One encouraging note is the trend in children's books revealed by a series of studies of Caldecott Award winners. (The Caldecott medal is awarded to the outstanding picture book of the year.) In contrast to a study of such winners carried out in 1972 (Weitzman, Eifler, Hokada, & Ross), which found that males in central roles outnumbered females in similar roles by 3.5 to 1, a 1984 study (Collins, Ingoldsby, & Dellmann) found that books

ʕ   *Everybody needs the*
chance to try everything.

winning the award between 1972 and 1982 presented a more even balance of (approximately) 1.5 males to every female. The 1993 (Dellman-Jenkins, Florjancic, & Swadener) replication of *that* study, which is reviewed in the research study in this chapter, indicates that this trend toward better balance is continuing, albeit slowly.

Importance of Attitude and Modelling

More basic, however, than all the nonsexist curriculum in the world is the need to sensitize men and women to the negative consequences of unconsciously biased sexist teaching. What happens to the self-esteem of young boys who are criticized by female teachers for their high-energy, aggressive response to life? What effect does the constant use of such words as mail*man*, fire*man,* and police*man* have on young girls and their anticipation of future occupations?

Or, on a positive note, what do children conclude when they see their female teacher confidently using the electric drill to install a new blackboard or their male teacher matter-of-factly sewing a button on a child's shirt?

We do, indeed, have a long way to go in raising our awareness and control of the long ingrained patterns of behaviour and speech that perpetuate sexist and racist teaching, but we have come a long way, too. The danger to guard against is that complacency may permit us to become careless or to stop trying. Doing that opens the way to recapitulating the racist/sexist problem all over again.

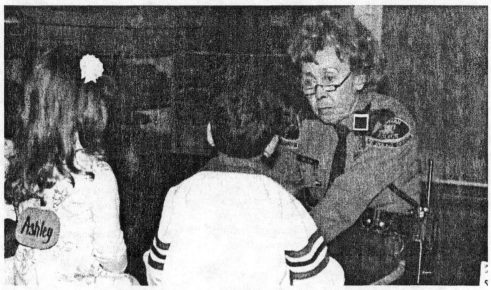

❧ *"But do you have babies and wear dresses on your mother time?" queried a skeptical Ashley.*

❧ Summary

Since children as young as age three differentiate between people of differing skin colour and gender, it is important to begin a program of cross-cultural, nonsexist education as early as possible so that they learn that *different,* be it a difference in sex or race or culture, does not mean *inferior.*

Teaching this principle of equity can be achieved in a number of ways. Fundamentally, we want to emphasize that every individual has the unique, treasurable gift of individuality to share with others. Second, no matter how unique the individual is, each person has some basic needs in common with the rest of the people in the world that can be satisfied in a variety of differing ways. And finally, every child of either sex or any colour should be encouraged to explore the full range of his or her abilities and potential competencies.

Early childhood programs that incorporate such cross-cultural, nonsexist emphases in their programs help children learn to value the differences and similarities in themselves, their friends, and their teachers as being positive strengths. It is this positive valuing that lies at the heart of equity in education.

Questions and Activities

1. Have you been with a young child when he commented on differences in skin colour or other differences related to ethnic group membership? What did he say, and what would be an effective way to reply to his comments or questions?

2. Do you feel it might be confusing or contradictory to teach children that people are alike and different at the same time?

3. It is the beginning of the year, and there are many new parents in your group whom you hope to involve in participation. List some things you plan to do that will foster this participation. Also list some policies that would subtly discourage parents from wanting to come and be part of the life of the school.

4. Do you ever wonder if perhaps you are unconsciously behaving in a prejudiced way by paying more attention to children from certain ethnic groups and less to members of other groups or favouring girls more than boys or vice versa? One way to check up on yourself is to ask a trusted colleague to keep track for various time periods of your contacts with the children over a week or more. All it takes is a list of the children's names and putting a check by each one for each contact made. If you wish to refine this strategy, plus and minus checks can be used depending on the kind of encounter, whether it is disciplinary, showing positive interest, and so on. (A word of encouragement—this behaviour is fairly easy to correct once the teacher is aware of it.)

5. Analyse the books in your centre. Are there some that present both boys and girls as effective, active people? Are there some that appear to perpetuate stereotypes of little girl and little boy behaviour? Are these necessarily undesirable?

6. *Problem:* You are working in a program that serves many single-parent families in which mothers have primary care of the children. Many of the children, therefore, have relatively little experience with men. Suggest some practical plans that would help alleviate this deficit for the children you care for.

7. Take a few minutes and make two columns headed "What I Am Good at Doing" and "What I Am Not Good at Doing" and then analyse why you are either good or not good at those particular activities. If you answer, "Well, I never learned that," identify what prevented you from learning it, whatever it was.

8. Is it really the responsibility of programs to provide information about reproduction and gender differences? If you feel it is not, how would you handle such comments as, "What happened to her wee-wee—did they cut it off?" or (from a little boy), "When I grow up, I'm gonna have six children! There won't hardly be room in my stomach I'm gonna have so many!"

Self-Check Questions for Review

Content-Related Questions

1. When incorporating multicultural and nonsexist goals into the curriculum, what are the two fundamental principles we want children to learn?

2. Are preschool children too young to notice ethnic and gender differences? Cite some examples that support the accuracy of your answer.

3. Name five things you as an individual can do to control your own prejudices.

4. Are children's books about various ethnic groups improving in quality?

5. Are children's books presenting sex roles in a more balanced manner?

6. Provide several examples of ways multicultural experiences could be consistently included in an early childhood curriculum.

7. Provide several examples of ways nonsexist experiences could be consistently included in an early childhood curriculum.

8. Why is encouraging pride in sexuality an important part of nonsexist education?

Integrative Questions

1. Can you provide examples of sexism being expressed at the college level? At the preschool level?

2. Research shows that teachers interrupt girls more frequently than they do boys. How do you think this behaviour might influence girls' concepts of their sex roles? How might the boys' sex role concepts also be influenced?

3. List some principles that cross-cultural and nonsexist education have in common.

4. There is a West African proverb that says, "A log that lies in the river a long time does not become a crocodile." Do you think this proverb applies to cross-cultural education? If so, how?

References for Further Reading

Note: Material on helping everyone overcome possible negative feelings towards individuals with special needs is covered in chapter 9, "Welcoming Children Who Have Special Educational Requirements into the Life of the Program."

Overviews of Multicultural and/or Nonsexist Education

Banks, J. A. (1994). *Multiethnic education: Theory and practice* (3rd ed.). Boston: Allyn & Bacon. Banks, a distinguished authority in this area, concludes this analysis of multicultural education by listing twenty-three guidelines curricula should follow to be truly multiethnic.

Chud G. & Fahlman, R. *Early childhood education for a multicultural society: A handbook for educators.* Vancouver: Pacific Education Press. This handbook serves as an introduction to the principles and practices of early childhood education for a multicultural society. Each chapter discusses issues, implications, and strategies relating to topics such as approaches to child rearing, orienting families to programs, and intercultural sensitivity.

Derman-Sparks, L. (1993/1994). Empowering children to create a caring culture in a world of differences. *Childhood Education, 70*(2), 66–71. This article contains a number of practical, matter-of-fact suggestions about ways to strengthen children's and teachers' defences and ability to act against prejudice. *Highly recommended.*

Derman-Sparks, L., the ABC Task Force (1989). *Anti-bias curriculum: Tools for empowering young children.* Washington, DC: National Association for the Education of Young Children. *Anti-Bias Curriculum* explains in practical terms how that approach can be integrated into the early childhood curriculum. *Highly recommended.*

Fennimore, B. S. (1994). Addressing prejudiced statements: A four-step method that works! *Childhood Education, 70*(4), 202–204. Fennimore advocates restating the speaker's prejudicial comments objectively, stating your own personal belief clearly, making a positive statement about the object of the prejudice, and then changing the subject.

Ford, C. W. (1994). *We can all get along: 50 steps you can take to help end racism.* New York: Dell. This excellent book is filled with plain talk, practical advice on combatting racism, and up-to-date references. A not-to-be-missed reference.

Gonzalez-Mena, J. (1993). *Multicultural issues in child care.* Mountain View, CA: Mayfield. This all too brief book singles out areas of concern to child care providers (separation, sleeping, discipline, etc.) and discusses how various cultures may view them differently. *Highly recommended.*

Hollins, E. R., King, J. E., & Hayman, W. C. (1994). *Teaching diverse populations: Formulating a knowledge base.* Albany, NY: State University of New York Press. Chapters cover a variety of cultures, ranging from Appalachian to Puerto Rican to American Indian. The majority of chapters have to do with teaching black children, including an interesting one on characteristics of effective black teachers. *Highly recommended.*

Murphy Kilbride, K. (1990). *Multicultural early childhood education—A resource kit.* Toronto: Ryerson University. This kit provides information to facilitate the development of a multicultural consciousness in practitioners. It includes a video and manual that address such issues as racism, culture, and migration.

Neugebauer, B. (Ed.). (1987). *Alike and different: Exploring our humanity with young children.* Redmond, WA: Exchange Press. *Alike and Different* covers usual and unusual aspects of living with differentness. Topics range from "foreign" children to giftedness to children with handicaps. Outstanding bibliography of children's books. *Highly recommended for the beginning student.*

Ontario Women's Directorate (1993). *Words that count women out/in.* Toronto: Ontario Women's Directorate. This booklet gives lists of words and discusses their effect on women.

Peck, N., & Shores, E. F. (1994). *Checklist for diversity in early childhood education and care.* Little Rock, AR: Southern Early Childhood Association. SECA provides a colourful, menu-style list of items and practices we should check in our classroom to make certain we are providing a wholesome anti-bias environment.

Saderman Hall, N., & Rhomberg, V. (1995). *The affective curriculum: Teaching the antibias approach to young children.* Scarborough, ON: Nelson Canada. This book examines the meaning of the anti-bias approach, clarifying its link to the affective development of children from infancy through the school-age years. Program plans and activities are included.

Sorti, C. (1989). *The art of crossing cultures.* Yarmouth, ME: Intercultural Press. Written by a former member of the Peace Corps, this book concentrates on adjusting to living abroad—but the lessons it teaches apply equally well to gaining understanding of people from other cultures in North America. Delightful reading.

York, S. (1991). *Roots and wings: Affirming culture in early childhood programs.* St. Paul, MN: Redleaf. This truly useful book includes discussions of what might generate prejudice, age-appropriate activities, and an exceptional chapter illustrating how cultural standards are expressed in the child's experience coupled with suggestions of ways to increase the comfort level between school and home points of view. *Highly recommended.*

Sources of Information on Ethnic and Cultural Characteristics

Brady, P. (1992). Columbus and the quincentennial myths: Another side of the story. *Young Children, 47*(6), 4–14. This article, combined with those by P. Greenberg, "Teaching about native Americans? Or teaching about people, including native Americans?" and L. Soldier, "Working with native American children," which appear in the same issue of *Young Children,* provides a valuable overview of teaching native children.

Chhim, S.H. (1989). *Introduction to Cambodian culture.* San Diego: Multifunctional Resource Centre, San Diego State University. A significant portion of recent immigration to Canada is from Asia. Thus this book and the ones on Laotian and Vietnamese culture listed later here are particularly valuable.

Feng, J. (1994). *Asian-American children: What teachers should know.* Urbana, IL: ERIC Clearinghouse on Elementary and Early Childhood Education. Feng emphasizes the diversity of this group and suggests nine ways teachers can help them. A brief bibliography is included.

Luangpraeseut, K. (1989). *Laos culturally speaking.* San Diego: Multifunctional Resource Centre, San Diego State University. This rich resource covers everything from history to culture.

Powell, G. J. (Ed.). (1983). *The psychosocial development of minority group children.* New York: Brunner/Mazel. This book is a gold-mine of information about many kinds of minorities—good reference about Hispanic youngsters.

Te, H. D. (1989). *Introduction to Vietnamese culture.* San Diego: Multifunctional Resource Centre, San Diego State University. Te includes interesting material on names and nonverbal communication as well as history and culture.

Development of Children's Racial Awareness

Katz, P. A. (1982). Development of children's racial awareness and intergroup attitudes. In L. G. Katz (Ed.), *Current topics in early childhood education* (Vol. 4). Norwood, NJ: Ablex. Katz traces the develop-

ment of race awareness through eight overlapping stages. She also presents evidence that verbal expression of those differences begins around age four, but that children do exhibit awareness of differences by age three.

Resource and Activity Books About Cross-Cultural Education

Note: There are many collections of ethnic recipes listed in the References at the end of chapter 3.

There is a real need and place for publications of activity books, but I do wish to reiterate that *providing these kinds of environmental embellishments and activities should constitute only the beginning of true multicultural education.*

Cole, A., Haas, C., Heller, E., & Weinberger, B. (1978). *Children are children are children: An activity approach to exploring Brazil, France, Iran, Japan, Nigeria, and the U.S.S.R.* Boston: Little, Brown. Although the title largely explains the contents, it should be added that each section contains recipes, information on games, holidays, suggestions for activities (some of which could be done by preschoolers), general information on the country, a few commonly used words, and a map.

Jenkins, J. K., & MacDonald, P. (1979). *Growing up equal: Activities and resources for parents and teachers of young children.* Englewood Cliffs, NJ: Prentice Hall.

Kendall, F. E. (1983). *Diversity in the classroom: A multicultural approach to the education of young children.* New York: Teachers College Press. Kendall offers a good, readily available annotated list of books for young children.

McNeill, E., Schmidt, V., & Allen, J. (1981). *Cultural awareness for young children: Asian, black, cowboy, Eskimo, Mexican, and Native American cultures.* Mount Rainier, MD: Gryphon House (Distributor). *Cultural Awareness* is distinguished by a good list of films, books, and magazines for children and adults. It divides the children's activities into family living, foods, creative activities, nature/science, language development, and special events.

Resource and Activity Books for Nonsexist Education

Northwest Regional Educational Laboratory Center for Sex Equity. (1983). *Guide to nonsexist teaching activities.* (K-12). Phoenix: Oryx Press. This is a first-rate reference that includes films, textbooks, and bibliographies.

Pogrebin, L. C. (1980). *Growing up free: Raising your child in the '80s.* New York: McGraw-Hill. A lengthy, well-written guide useful for teachers and parents in search of ideas about how to implement nonsexist attitudes in their families and themselves. Not an activity book.

Raines, B. (1991). *Creating sex-fair family day care: A guide for trainers.* Philadelphia: CHOICE, Office of Research and Improvement, U.S. Department of Education; Newton, MA: WEEA Publishing Centre (Distributor: 55 Chapel St., Newton, MA 02160). This curriculum guide was developed and field tested with family child care providers—*noteworthy in particular for its list of nonsexist children's books.*

Shapiro, J., Kramer, S., & Hunerberg, C. (1981). *Equal their chances: Children's activities for non-sexist learning.* Englewood Cliffs, NJ: Prentice Hall. Written with elementary school teachers in mind, *Equal Their Chances* takes the curriculum of the school topic by topic and provides numerous examples of how nonsexist information could and should be incorporated into those studies. Enough of the ideas could be translated to the preprimary level that the book is worth examining.

Sprung, B. (1975). *Non-sexist education for young children: A practical guide.* New York: Citation Press. This paperback contains a wealth of practical ideas for conducting a nonsexist nursery school using five curriculum topics as examples. The best reference in the field.

Material on Multiethnic and Multicultural Children's Literature

Dowd, F. S. (1992). Evaluating children's books portraying native American and Asian cultures. *Childhood Education, 68*(4), 219–224.

Harris, V. J. (1991). Research in review: Multicultural curriculum: African American children's literature. *Young Children, 46*(2), 37–44. Harris clearly defines standards of what constitutes authentic African American literature for young children and includes a list of recommended books. *Highly recommended.*

McCracken, J. B. (Ed.). (1990). *Helping children love themselves and others: A professional handbook for family day care.* Washington, DC: The Children's Foundation. A substantial portion of this worthwhile book is devoted to an annotated bibliography of children's literature that specifies sex and cultural/ethnic background of the main characters. The appropriate age for readers is included. *Highly recommended.*

National Association for the Education of Young Children. (1993). Enriching classroom diversity with books for children, in-depth discussion of them, and story-extension activities. *Young Children, 48*(3), 10–12. This very diverse list provides a broad sampling of worthwhile books for young children from a wide variety of cultures and family situations.

National Black Child Development Institute. (1992). *African American literature for young children.* Washington, DC: The Institute and the National Association for the Education of Young Children. This is an annotated bibliography of books intended to provide a "lasting connection for African American children to their history and their culture" (p. 1). Some books are out of print and must be obtained from the library but many are still available for purchase.

Ramirez, G., & Ramirez, J. L. (1994). *Multiethnic children's literature.* Albany, NY: Delmar. This valuable book provides overviews of the publishing situation of books for children from a variety of cultures and does *not* commit the sin of lumping all Asians, all native peoples, etc. together into one group. As it is, this is a helpful book, and I am hopeful it will include more books suitable for preschool children in the second edition.

Slapin, B., & Seale, D. (1992). *Books without bias: Through Indian eyes* (3rd ed.). Philadelphia: New Society. This not-to-be-missed resource book is rich in extensive book reviews (not all friendly) complete with recommendations for age appropriateness. Of particular interest is the article "How to Tell the Difference," which supplies a checklist of standards for evaluating the quality of books about native people. *Highly recommended.*

Walker-Dalhouse, D. (1993). Beginning reading and the African American child at risk. *Young Children, 49*(1), 24–28. This article features books published since 1992.

Education About Sexuality

Leight, L. (1988). *Raising sexually healthy children: A loving guide for parents, teachers and care-givers.* New York: Avon Books. In this simply written book, Leight presents a sensible discussion of developmentally appropriate approaches to sex education.

Lively, F., & Lively, E. (1991). *Sexual development of young children.* Albany, NY: Delmar. As the title implies, this book focuses on children up to age eight. It uses vignettes to introduce discussions of a wide array of sexual topics ranging from normal development to abuse and the impact of AIDS.

Sex Roles and Stereotypes

Fagot, B. I., & Kronsberg, S. J. (1982). Sex differences: Biological and social factors influencing the behaviour of young boys and girls. In S. G. Moore & C. R. Cooper (Eds.), *The young child: Reviews of research* (Vol. 3). Washington, DC: National Association for the Education of Young Children. After reviewing three major theories that attempt to account for differences in sexual behaviour, Fagot and Kronsberg trace the development of such differences through early childhood and conclude that "biological components of gender identity and sex-role behavior, while definitely of consequence, are relatively small by comparison with cultural influences" (p. 204).

Relating to Parents

Clay, J. W. (1990). Working with lesbian and gay parents and their children. *Young children, 45*(3), 31–35. Clay provides a helpful discussion and some valuable references on this subject.

Lynch, E. W., & Hanson, M. J. (1992). *Developing cross-cultural competence: A guide for working with young children and their families.* Baltimore: Paul Brookes. This book is a godsend to anyone working with young children and families who come from cultures other than the worker's own. Chapters dealing with various cultures are written by people from those cultures; each has a list of contrasting beliefs, values, and practices and another of cultural courtesies and customs. *Highly recommended.*

Wardle, F. (1989). Children of mixed parentage: How can professionals help? *Children Today, 18*(4), 10–13. Wardle points out that children from mixed marriages often experience pronounced prejudice and then offers a number of practical suggestions to remember when working with these families in order to avoid giving offence.

For the Advanced Student

Aboud, F. (1988). *Children and prejudice.* New York: Basil Blackwell. Aboud provides well-summarized research reviews concerning the emergence and possible determinants of prejudice.

Beall, A. E., & Sternberg, R. J. (Eds.). (1993). *The psychology of gender.* New York: Guilford Press. The various authors provide a review of what is known about how gender affects everyone's lives.

Child Development. The entire April 1990 issue of this distinguished research publication is devoted to research concerning minority children.

Chud G. & Fahlman, R. (1995). *Honouring diversity within child care and early education: An instructor's guide.* Victoria: British Columbia Ministry of Skills, Training and Labour. This manual represents an informed and comprehensive mass of materials for faculty of early childhood training programs who strive to integrate diversity education. There is discussion regarding the development of language, English as a second language, and bilingualism.

Fagot, B. I. (1994). Peer relations and the development of competence in boys and girls. *New Directions for Child Development, 65,* 53–65. This article summarizes research on gender roles done by this distinguished investigator during the past eighteen years. *Highly recommended.*

Greenfield, P. M., & Cocking, R. R. (Eds.). (1994). *Cross-cultural roots of minority child development.* Hillsdale, NJ: Erlbaum. This book is filled with fascinating information about how differences in culture affect the way children develop. *Highly recommended.*

Maccoby, E. E., & Jacklin, C. N. (1987). Gender segregation in childhood. In H. W. Reese (Ed.), *Advances in child development and behaviour.* New York: Academic Press. A well-written summary of research documenting that even children as young as three and four prefer to play with children of the same sex the majority of the time.

Mallory, B. L., & New, R. S. (1993). *Diversity and developmentally appropriate practices: Challenges for early childhood education.* New York: Teachers College Press. Several chapters in this book remind us there may be no single "perfect" approach to teaching that is appropriate for all children.

National Association for the Education of Young Children. (1993). Educate yourself about diverse cultural groups in our country by reading. *Young Children, 48*(3), 13–16. Puzzled about where to find additional resources about diversity, multicultural/antibias materials, or specific ethnic/cultural groups? This list provides a great starting point for any of those investigations.

Nieto, S. (1992). *Affirming diversity: The sociopolitical context of multicultural education.* New York: Longman. Nieto combines case studies with discussions intended to deepen the reader's understanding. The book is replete with examples and research. *Highly recommended.*

Streitmatter, J. (1994). *Toward gender equity in the classroom.* Albany, NY: State University of New York Press. Streitmatter contributes material garnered from observations in a preschool and more advanced classrooms in which the teachers were attempting to institute sexual equity. This thoughtful, interesting book shows how differences in philosophy are related to differences in practising that concept.

Tizard, B., & Phoenix, A. (1993). *Black, white or mixed race?: Race and racism in the lives of young people of mixed parentage.* New York: Routledge. This is an interesting account of a research study done in England that investigated older children's feelings about mixed (black and white) parentage.

Resources and Services

Annick Press, 15 Patrick Ave., Willowdale, ON M2M 1H9. This publishing house is committed to producing humorous and thought-provoking literature depicting children who respect themselves and others.

Canadian Children's Book Centre, 35 Spadina Rd., Toronto, ON M5R 2S9. This organization promotes the reading, writing, and illustrating of Canadian children's books and makes available catalogues on multicultural books for young children.

Cross Cultural Communication Centre, 2909 Dundas St. W., Toronto, ON M6P 1Z1. This community education and resource centre develops programs and materials on antiracism, multiculturalism, immigration, newcomers, and community development.

Early Childhood Multicultural Services, 1675 West 4th Ave., Ste. 201, Vancouver, BC V6J 1L8. This resource centre conducts professional development workshops and lends posters, pamphlets, books, and curriculum materials. They have provided a leadership role nationally in facilitating respect for diversity in early childhood settings.

Journals and Newsletters of Interest

Multiculturalism/Multiculturalisme. CCM/E, Suite 204, 316 Dalhousie St., Ottawa, ON K1N 7E7. This triennial publication concerns itself with issues related to intercultural education in Canada. Recent research synopses are often included.

Native Peoples Magazine. Media Concepts Group, PO Box 36820, Phoenix, AZ 85067-6820. The magazine describes itself as "dedicated to the sensitive portrayal of the arts and lifeways of native peoples of the Americas." It is published in affiliation with many museums including the Smithsonian's National Museum of the American Indian. *Highly recommended.*

Siecus Report. Sex Information and Education Council of the United States, 80 Fifth Ave., New York, NY 10011. Affiliated with the Department of Health Education of the School of Education, Health, Nursing and Arts Professions of New York University, this newsletter provides an excellent way to keep up with various publications in the area of sex education. It contains articles, book reviews, and resources for further information. Liberal in point of view.

Spectrum. Newsletter of the Multiracial Americans of Southern California (12228 Venice Blvd., #452, Los Angeles, CA 90066) is published by and about interracial families.

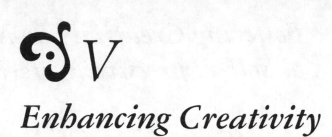

V

Enhancing Creativity

Fostering Creativity by Means of Self-Expressive Materials

15

Against the ruin of the world, there is only one defense—the creative act.

Kenneth Rexroth

Whatever an education is, it should make you a unique individual, not a conformist; it should furnish you with an original spirit with which to tackle the big challenges: it should allow you to find values which will be your road map throughout life; it should make you spiritually rich, a person who loves whatever you are doing, wherever you are, whomever you are with.

John Taylor Gatto

Have you ever wondered . . .

What to reply when a child pleads, "Draw me a horse"?

How on earth you can vary easel painting today?

How to explain to parents why your school doesn't send home pie plates with little faces glued on them?

. . . If you have, the material in the following pages will help you.

*E*arly childhood teachers have long valued creativity and sought to enhance it by fostering self-expression in the young children for whom they care. In the past we teachers have been particularly successful in presenting expressive materials and activities such as paint, clay, or dance in a manner that fosters unique personal responses from the children. But today we are coming to realize that artistic creativity represents only one facet of creative endeavour and that there are additional aspects of creativity in play and in divergence and originality of thought that should be encouraged more fully. For this reason the discussion of creativity in this book does not stop with the presentation of expressive materials but extends into two additional chapters, "Fostering Creativity in Play" (chapter 16) and "Developing Thinking and Reasoning Skills: Using the Emergent Approach to Foster Creativity in Thought" (chapter 21).

Definition of Creativity

Defining creativity where young children are concerned is rather difficult, since the commonly accepted definitions include not only the requirement that the idea or product be novel but also that it be related to reality and stand the test of being worthwhile (Tardiff & Sternberg, 1988). However, a definition by Smith (1966) suits our needs well, since it fits young children's creative abilities more aptly. He defines creativity as being the process of "sinking down taps into our past experiences and putting these selected experiences together into new patterns, new ideas or new products" (p. 43).

This "putting prior experiences together into something new" is a good description of what we hope young children will be able to do when they use self-expressive materials, play imaginatively, solve problems, and generate new ideas. It stresses originality and does not emphasize the quality of evaluation, which is less applicable to very young children, although as we shall see in chapter 21, even they can be encouraged to try out ideas, thereby going through reality testing and evaluation in an informal way.

The student should also understand that creativity is not limited to a few gifted Rembrandts and Einsteins, nor is it necessarily associated with high intelligence. The work of Getzels and Jackson (1962; 1987), Wallach and Kogan (1965), and Ward (1968) has demonstrated that high scores on creativity tests do not correlate strongly with high scores on academic tests of achievement or with high scores on standard measures of intelligence. Another finding of interest comes from a study by Margolin (1968), which indicates that teachers who deliberately foster uniqueness and originality of response in creative activities can actually increase the variety and diversity of such responses in young children.

These findings imply that we do not have to wait for that specifically gifted child to come along in order for creative behaviour to take place in our groups. The ability to generate original ideas and to produce satisfying, freshly conceived products resides in many children; and since such behaviour can be increased by appropriate responses from the teacher, it is worthwhile to learn how to do this.

Importance of Creativity

The experience of being involved in creative activity satisfies people in ways that nothing else can, and the ability to be creative appears not only to reflect but also to foster emotional health (Singer & Singer, 1990). The act of creation enhances the child's feelings of self-esteem and self-worth. (The reader can test the validity of this statement by recalling the last time she or he produced something original—perhaps something as simple as a holiday decoration or as complex as a set of bookshelves—and then recall the feeling of well-being that rose up inside when it was accomplished.) There *is* something about creating a unique product or idea that leaves people feeling good about themselves.

Creative experiences provide unparalleled opportunities for expressing emotions and, by gaining relief and understanding through such expression, for coming to terms with them (Brittain, 1979). Since they have this strong affective component, they provide a balance for the emphasis on intellectual development, which may overwhelm the rest of the program unless it is carefully managed.

While providing that balance, such activities also foster cognitive growth by providing endless opportunities for trying out ideas and putting them into practice, for seeing there are many alternative ways to solve problems, and for encouraging the use of symbols in place of "real" objects to represent ideas and feelings (Lowenfeld & Brittain, 1987; Weisberg, 1988). Incidental learning inevitably results from such experiences also. Clay changes its form when water is added; sand feels gritty between the toes; paint runs down the same way water does.

Finally, creative activities offer an excellent opportunity to individualize teaching. Materials and activities that depend on open-ended replies permit uniqueness and diversity to flourish and allow each child to be herself rather than requiring her to conform to closed system, authority-centred learning.

☙ Stages of Development

One of the peak periods for creative self-expression in our culture occurs between the ages of four and six (Schirrmacher, 1988). This stage correlates well with Erikson's developmental stage for this age, which he identifies as the stage of initiative versus guilt. Erikson's stage is characterized by reaching out, exploring, and experimenting and also reflects an increase in creative behaviour that is partially characterized by this same kind of activity.

As is true in other areas, children pass through general stages of development in the use of creative materials (Davis & Gardner, 1993; Feinberg, 1993). First, *they explore the material itself* and investigate its properties. Two- and three-year-olds, for instance, spend many satisfactory hours in what appears to be mainly manipulation and exploration of paints and brushes or in relishing the mixing of play dough, and they employ all their senses to do this. Who has not seen such a youngster meticulously painting her hands up to the elbow, or beheld another squeezing the sponge in the paint bucket, or a third looking thoughtfully into the distance as she licks the back of the play dough spoon?

Once the qualities of the material have been explored and some skill has been gained in its manipulation, the child is likely to move on to what is called the *nonrepresentational stage*. Paintings at this stage, for example, seem to have more design and intention behind them, but the content is not readily recognizable by anyone but the painter. Since painting at this stage is not always done with the intention of depicting something in particular, the teacher must beware of asking, "What is it?" lest such a question unintentionally put the child on a spot.

Ultimately the youngster reaches the pictorial or *representational stage,* in which she quite deliberately sets out to reproduce or create something. She may paint a picture of herself, or the sun in the sky, or depict a fascinating event such as the toilet overflowing or children going apple picking. As the youngsters of Reggio Emilia have so amply demonstrated, some children attain this stage of representational art in preschool, but most children develop this ability during their year in kindergarten.

Brittain (1979), in a much more detailed study, has described similar stages for the evolution of drawing from scribbling. What is particularly interesting about Brittain's work is the finding that representations of a man done by a particular child at a particular age were very similar, no matter which medium the child employed—drawing, collage, or clay.

Implications for Preprimary Teachers

One implication to be drawn from these sequential stages of development is that teachers should permit children countless opportunities to experience and explore expressive materials, because this learning is fundamental to the creative experience. The full knowledge gained through such exploration extends the ways a child may use the material, thereby enriching her creative opportunities; and the freedom to explore is also likely to keep alive her interest and openness to the medium (Amabile, 1989).

The second developmental implication is that young children, when using expressive materials, should not be expected to produce a finished product. Some four-year-olds will do this, of course; but since many will not, the expectation of some sort of recognizable result is not a reasonable creative goal to set for children in their early years.

❧ General Recommendations About Creativity

It is hoped the reader will apply to all three chapters on creativity the general comments made here about fostering the child's creativity with self-expressive materials.

Be Aware of the Value of Nonconforming Behaviour and of "Unattractive" Personality Characteristics

Torrance (1962), a long-time champion of creativity, frequently emphasized that the kind of behaviour teachers identify as desirable in children does not always coincide with characteristics associated with the creative personality. For instance, teachers who think they value uniqueness may find they do not like creative exploration as much as they thought they did when a youngster has spilled her milk because she tried holding the cup with her teeth.

Not only can this lack of conformity be inconvenient, but the teacher should also realize that some creative individuals possess character traits she may not care for. Torrance (1962) cites eighty-four characteristics that differentiate the more creative person from the less creative one. Some of the less attractive qualities include stubbornness, finding fault with things, appearing haughty and self-satisfied, and being discontented—qualities often disliked by teachers. Yet it is easy to see how stubbornness might be a valuable quality to possess when carrying through a new idea, or how finding fault and being discontented could result in questioning and analysing a situation before coming up with suggestions for improving it. In all fairness, we must admit that we do not know at present if some of these less attractive attitudes lie at the root of creativity or if some of them are only the result of squelching and mishandling by teachers, peers, and families as the child matures. On the other hand, Torrance also found that creative children possessed many likable qualities, such as determination, curiosity, intuition, a willingness to take risks, a preference for complex ideas, and a sense of humour.

The purpose of pointing out these possible problems of living with creative children is not to discourage teachers from fostering such behaviour, but to enlighten them so they will not subtly reject or discourage creative responses because they fail to recognize the positive side of such apparently undesirable behaviour. Ideally, such understanding will result in increased acceptance and valuing of creative endeavour.

Acceptance is vitally important because it will encourage children to develop these abilities further and because it will help balance the rejection and isolation to which people who dare to be different are often subjected. As long as we have creative youngsters in our care, we must help guard against rejection by recognizing and supporting originality in thought and deed.

Cultivate Three Teaching Skills in Yourself

Each creative area requires a specific teaching skill for its facilitation. The cultivation of these skills is discussed at greater length in the appropriate chapter, but they are listed here to provide the reader with a quick overview.

In fostering creativity by means of expressive materials, the teacher should make ample materials freely available and encourage children to explore and use them as their impulses and feelings require. When seeking to facilitate play, the teacher needs to be able to move with the children's imaginative ideas and respond to them by providing materials and support that keep the play ongoing and creative. When developing original thinking and attendant problem solving, the teacher must reinforce the children's production of ideas by carefully observing and listening to them, recognizing the value of what they suggest, and asking questions that encourage the further development of their ideas.

Do Your Best to Maintain an Emotionally Healthy Climate

In the chapters on emotional health, handling routines, and discipline, considerable time was spent discussing ways to keep the centre environment reasonable, consistent, and secure so that children will feel emotionally at ease. Such a stable, predictable climate is valuable for many reasons, but one of the outstanding ones is that it forms a sound base for the generation of creative activity, which in turn contributes to the development of emotional health. Children who feel secure are more likely to venture forth, try new experiences, and express themselves in creative ways than are children who are using up their energy by worrying or being frightened or anxious.

In addition, some research supports the idea that the highly structured classrooms in which preschool children are continually the focus of adult control and adult-designated activities appear to reduce the amount of creativity (Hirsch-Pasek, Hyson, & Rescorla, 1990), imaginative play (Huston-Stein, Freidrick-Cofer, & Susman, 1977), and curiosity and inventiveness (Miller & Dyer, 1975). The use of structured play materials, such as puzzles and colouring books, has also been shown to reduce divergent, creative responses to problem solving (Pepler, 1986). These findings provide yet another reason why teachers who wish to foster these creative traits should make certain there is an open structure to the program that provides many opportunities for children to think for themselves and to make choices and decisions within reasonable limits.

ঙ Use of Self-Expressive Materials to Foster the Creative Self

Expressive materials include such diverse media as painting, collage, dough and clay, woodworking, sewing, and dance. Although the materials themselves are different, some basic principles apply to all of them. (Suggested guidelines for use of specific materials are included later in the chapter.)

Value of Using Free-Form Materials

The most valuable quality that expressive materials have in common is that there is no right thing to do with them or one right way to use them; so in a real sense these materials are failure-proof for the child. As long as the child observes a few basic rules, such as keeping the sand down and seeing that the dough stays on the table and off the floor, there is no way she can make a mistake with them. For this reason alone such materials are an invaluable addition to the curriculum.

There are additional reasons why expressive materials are indispensable. Psychologists and experienced teachers agree that these experiences provide many opportunities for children to express their feelings and come to terms with them (Seefeldt, 1987). It can be fascinating to watch the development of a shy child who may begin finger- painting by using only the middle of her paper and then see her gradually come to fill her paper with rich colours and swooping strokes of joy as she gains confidence during her months at school. Since each child is free to do as she wishes, these materials also represent the ultimate in an individualized curriculum. The youngster can express who she is and what she is as something within her urges her to do; she is able to suit the material to herself in an intensely personal way.

In addition, many values associated with creative materials lie in the social, sensory, and intellectual spheres. Children who are working side by side often develop a spirit of camaraderie. As a matter of fact, research by Torrance (1988) found that five-year-olds were most willing to risk attempting difficult new tasks when working in pairs.

Using creative materials provides numerous opportunities for rich sensory input: Dough feels sticky and then firm, finger-paint feels cool, gushy, and slippery, dance makes the child aware of her body as she moves in response to the music. Finally, the amount of factual information children acquire about the substances they are using contributes to their intellectual growth: Red and yellow mixed together create orange, some woods are easier to saw than others, two smaller blocks equal one large one.

Although these social, sensory, and intellectual learnings are worthwhile, I still regard them as being like the frosting on the cake. The primary values of using expressive materials remain in the affective sphere. Expressive materials are fundamentally useful because they foster creativity, build self-esteem, and provide a safe, failure-proof experience. Most important, they can be the source of open-ended opportunities for the child to be herself and for her to express and work through her individual feelings and ideas.

Practical Ways to Encourage the Creative Aspect of Self-Expressive Materials

Interfere As Little As Possible

As I mentioned earlier, the most significant skill the teacher can cultivate in presenting self-expressive materials is the ability to let the child explore them as her impulses and feelings require, intervening only when needed. Brittain (1979), who studied various kinds of teacher interventions under such circumstances, found that the more instruction the teacher offered, the less involved the child was likely to be in the project. On the other hand, teachers who stayed entirely on the sidelines also had children stay and paint for shorter periods of time. The children who stayed longest and who were judged to be the most involved were those whose teachers "played the role of an interested adult . . . who gave support and intervened only when the child seemed hesitant about either his own powers or the next direction to take in the project" (p. 160).

This problem of when to intervene and when to abstain from interfering can be a delicate one. In recent years, as I have observed and talked with the teachers in the schools of Reggio Emilia, I have been interested to see how much more assistance they provide the children than we North American teachers do. For example, whereas I, as a North American teacher, might provide a child with a brace and bit or a formless lump of clay and encourage the child to discover on her own how to make the bit work or the clay stick together, the Reggio teacher would not hesitate to tell the child to lean hard on the bit to make it bite into the wood or show her how to dampen the edges of the clay so they will stick together. While we often hesitate to teach such specific techniques because we fear such interference will crush the children's creativity, the Italian teachers maintain that deliberately teaching specific skills empowers the children to express their ideas more fully.

So, which is the ideal approach? Where do we draw the line between support and interference? The answer to this quandary about how much is too much is that there is a great deal of difference between helping a child learn how to drill a hole and telling her where to make it and what she should do with it. This is where the Reggio teachers have something useful to share with us—they may intervene in an activity by offering instructional support, but they would never dream of interfering with the child's attempts to express her own ideas.

Of course, allowing children to explore self-expressive materials as their impulses and feelings require does not mean they should be permitted to experiment with scissors by cutting the doll's hair off or that they should be allowed to smear clay all over the school chairs to "get their feelings out." It is as true here as in other situations that the teacher does not allow children to damage property or to do things that may hurt themselves or others.

However, although inexperienced teachers occasionally allow destructive things to happen in the name of freedom, experience has taught me that the reverse circumstance is more likely to occur. Many teachers unthinkingly limit and control the use of expressive materials more than is necessary. Thus they may refuse to permit a child to use the indoor blocks on the table "because we always use them on the floor," or they may insist she use only one paintbrush at a time despite the fact that using two at once makes such interesting lines and patterns. These ideas are essentially harmless ones and should be encouraged because of their originality.

Never Provide a Model for the Children to Copy

A copy is not an original. When I was a little girl in kindergarten, the "creative" experiences offered consisted mainly of making things just the way the teacher did. I particularly recall sewing around the edges of paper plates to make letter holders and cutting out paper flowers to glue on sticks. I suppose that what was creative about these activities was that we got to pick which flowers to cut out, and as I remember, we could choose any color of yarn to sew with. Whatever educational merit such activities posses, creativity is not among them. Yet some child care centres persist in offering such experiences in the name of creativity. If the teacher really wishes to foster originality and the child's self-expression rather than his own, he will avoid models and make-alike activities and will merely set the materials out and let the children go to it themselves.

Sometimes a child will attempt to lure the teacher into drawing something for her to copy by pleading, "Draw me a house" or "Draw me a man so I can colour him." Rather than complying, the wise teacher meets this request by recognizing the child's deeper request, which is for a one-to-one relationship; so he meets this need by talking with her, meanwhile encouraging her to make the picture herself.

Understand and Respect the Child's Developmental Level

We spoke at the beginning of the chapter of the stages through which children's drawings pass as they become more mature. I am including here a developmental chart (Table 15.1) calling attention to the usual age at which children are able to copy various shapes, because some teachers do not understand that the ability to do this rests at least in part on maturation (Brittain, 1979) and so struggle endlessly to teach children at too early an age to draw squares and triangles when everyone's energies could surely be better expended teaching and learning more important things.

Understand That It Is the Process Not the Product That Matters Most to the Young Child

We live in such a work-oriented, product-centred culture that sometimes we lose sight of the simple pleasure of doing something for its own sake. For young children, however, getting there is more than half the fun. They savour the process and live for the moment. Therefore, it is important not to hurry them toward finishing something or to overstress

Table 15.1 Drawing and writing movements

Age (in years, months)	Behavior
0.1–1	Accidental and imitative scribbling.
1–1.6	Refinement of scribbles, vertical and horizontal lines, multiple line drawing, scribblings over visual stimuli.
2–3	Multiple loop drawing, spiral, crude circles. Simple diagrams evolve from scribblings by the end of the second year.
3	Figure reproduction to visually presented figures, circles, and crosses.
4	Laboriously reproduces squares, may attempt triangles but with little success.
4.6–5	Forms appear in combinations of two or more. Crude pictures appear (house, human form, sun). Can draw fair squares, crude rectangles and good circles, but has difficulty with triangles and diamonds.
6–7	Ability to draw geometric figures matures. By seven, can draw good circles, squares, rectangles, triangles, and fair diamonds.

Source: From *Perceptual-Motor Efficiency in Children: The Measurement and Improvement of Movement Attributes* (p. 85) by B. J. Cratty & M. M. Martin (1969). Philadelphia: Lea & Febiger, © 1969 by Lea & Febiger. Reprinted by permission.

the final result. They *will* love to take their creations home, of course, and all such items should be carefully labelled, at least occasionally dated, and put in their cubbies so that this is possible, but the primary emphasis should remain on doing (Edwards & Nabors, 1993).

Allow Plenty of Time and Opportunity for the Child to Use Materials So That Her Experience Is Truly Satisfying

In the discussion about sharing I made the point that it is important for each child to have enough of an experience in order to be truly satisfied before giving up the place to someone else. This is particularly true when using expressive materials. One painting or one collage is just not enough. Children need the chance to work themselves into the experience and to develop their feelings and ideas as they go along. For this reason it is important to schedule time periods that allow for many children to move in and out of the expressive experience as their needs dictate. For real satisfaction this opportunity needs to be available for an hour or an hour-and-a-half at a time.

Learn How to Make Comments That Enhance the Child's Creative Productivity

Making effective comments as the child creates will encourage her to continue and to involve herself ever more deeply in the activity. But it can be risky, as well as embarrassing, to be trapped into commenting on what the child is making either by trying to guess what it is or by asking her to name it. As mentioned previously, children often do not deliberately set out to represent anything in particular, and even if they do intend a representation, it may defy recognition by anyone else. An additional drawback to requesting that creations be labelled is that it places emphasis on the product rather than on the creative, dynamic aspect of the experience.

It is more enhancing to comment on the pleasure the child is feeling as she works or to ask her if she would like to tell you about it. "You're having such a good time doing that!" or "My goodness, you've worked on that a long time! Would you like to tell me about it?" or "Do you need some more of . . .?" These remarks show her that you are interested in and care for her, but they avoid the taint of passing judgement on the quality of what she has made or of emphasizing that the end is better than the means (Schirrmacher, 1986).

Grant the Child Who Is Dubious the Right to Refuse

Children benefit from the opportunity to stand and watch before they plunge into an activity more vigorously. Three-year-olds do a lot of this standing around, but older children who are shy or new to school may behave this way, too. This is a valid way to learn, and the teacher should respect the child who copes with new experiences in this manner. Usually after a few days she will want to try whatever it is she has been watching so intently.

A few children are extraordinarily concerned about getting painty or sticky. These youngsters are usually reassured if the teacher talks with the mother in their hearing and asks the mother to tell them that using paint and glue is all right at school. It can also help if "clean" materials, such as soap painting or snow, are offered as beginning messy activities. It should be made clear to such youngsters that there is water instantly available should they feel the need to wash their hands and that the apron will protect them and their clothes from undue contamination.

Remember to Make Self-Expressive Opportunities
Available for Children with Special Needs

One has only to peruse the majority of textbooks about early childhood special education to realize the subject of self-expressive materials is rarely touched upon, and yet these children enjoy and need them just as much as other children do. Indeed, offering them the chance to participate in these kinds of activities is of particular value to such youngsters because it provides them with the sometimes rare opportunity to take control and make independent choices about what they are doing.

Although space does not permit an extensive list of suggestions, here are a few possibilities worth considering. For children who are poorly coordinated or movement restricted it is relatively easy to include movement education activities scaled to their abilities. This might mean modifications in the height of equipment, provision of additional handholds, or inclusion of safety mats. Spodek and Saracho (1994) provide a long list of large muscle activities appropriate for children with a variety of physical challenges. Children with impaired vision will do best with art materials if the table is well lit and the materials are clearly contrasting in tone and texture. Clay and other sensorily appealing modelling materials are particularly worthwhile to offer. Children who are hearing impaired can be stimulated to try out all sorts of self-expressive materials if they are encouraged to come and see what is available for their delight. Children who are

✑   *Such a simple thing as providing a chair makes it possible for John to enjoy painting.*

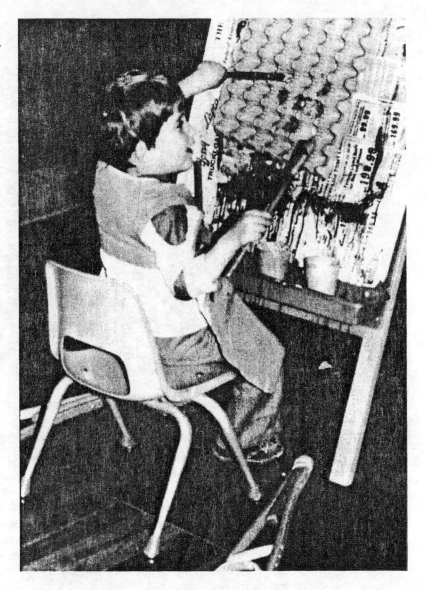

cognitively delayed will enjoy the same materials set out for the other children but at a more exploratory level. They will benefit from clear, simple instructions about whatever limits are necessary in relation to the activity.

Some Comments on the Overall Presentation and Quality of the Materials

It is important to provide enough of whatever the children are using. There is nothing sadder than children making do with skimpy little fistfuls of dough when they need large, satisfying mounds to punch and squeeze. The same thing holds true for collage materials,

ॐ   *Here's a simple solution for the perennial problem of providing a place for the children's creations to dry before going home.*

woodworking, and painting. Children need plenty of material to work with as well as the chance to make as many things as they wish.

Providing enough material for the children means that teachers must develop their scrounging and pack rat instincts to the ultimate degree. They not only must ferret out sources of free materials but also must find time and energy to pick them up regularly and produce a place to store them until they are needed. Parents can be helpful in collecting materials if the teacher takes the time to show them examples of what he needs. There are many sources of such materials in any community. (Appendix E is included to inspire the beginner.)

Variety in materials is also crucial. Creative activity should not be limited to easel painting and paper collage. The reader will find examples of variations suggested for materials, but to be quite clear, I want to remind the reader there is a difference between the use of self-expressive materials and many craft-type projects advocated for preschool children, even when these materials do not require making something just like the model.

Sometimes teachers justify such craft-type activities on the grounds that they have to do this because the parents expect it, but I have never had a parent protest the looser, freer treasures their children have borne home once they understood our goals of preserving the creative, less directive approach. Day care centres are particularly likely to be seduced by such crafts because of the need to provide variety and stimulation for the children in order to sustain their interest. Unfortunately the emphasis with these items is usually on learning to manipulate the material and on how clever the teacher was to think of doing it. The attraction for the teacher of sheer novelty tends to obscure the tendency of such crafts to be inappropriate to the age and skills of the children, to require excessive teacher direction and control, to fail to allow for adequate emotional self-expression, and to emphasize conformity rather than creativity.

It is difficult to see what real benefits children gain from string painting, for example. The string is dipped in paint and then placed between a folded piece of paper and pulled out. The results are accidental, and although the colours may be pretty, this activity is not likely to be satisfying to the child unless she manages to turn the process into finger painting—which frequent observation has proven to me to be the common outcome unless the teacher prevents it! Fortunately, there are several very good references currently available that list innumerable and appropriate ways to present basic materials that also keep in sight the fundamental values of self-expression (Bos, 1978; Cherry, 1990; Kohl, 1989; Smith et al., 1993; Wilmes & Wilmes, (n.d.)).

Finally, creative materials that will be used together should be selected with an eye to beauty. For instance, rather than simply setting out a hodgepodge, the teacher should choose collage materials that contrast interestingly and attractively in texture and colour. Pieces of orange onion bags could be offered along with bits of dark cork, white Styrofoam, beige burlap, and dry seed pods; a black or bright yellow mat would be a good choice as a collage base for these items. Finger-paint that makes a beautiful third colour should be selected. For example, magenta and yellow combine to form a gorgeous shade of orange, but purple and yellow turn out dull grey.

❧ Presentation of Specific Materials

I have selected only the more common materials for the outlines in the following pages,* but the reader can find additional suggestions in the references at the end of this chapter. I hope that these ideas will not be followed as gospel but will serve to inspire the teacher to develop and carry out his own and the children's creative ideas.

The suggestions for presentation of various materials in this and the following chapter have been written as individual, self-contained units so they may be abstracted and posted in various areas about the school should this be desired. For this reason I hope the reader will forgive a certain repetition in the descriptions of setting out and cleaning up.

Easel Painting

Easel painting is perhaps the one form of artistic endeavour offered by all children's centres, and it is an outstanding example of a creative material that is intensely satisfying to young children. In the fall, particularly with younger children and with newcomers, it is

---

*I am indebted to the staff and students of the Santa Barbara City College Children's Center for their help in formulating the following outlines.

wise to begin with the basic experience of a few colours, one size of paintbrush, and the standard, *large-sized* paper; but as the year progresses and the children's skills increase, many interesting variations and degrees of complexity can be offered that will sustain interest and enhance the experience of easel painting for the more sophisticated young artists.

When looking at paintings or other expressive products, one can be tempted to play psychologist and read various interpretations into the children's work. Although it is perfectly all right to encourage a child to tell you about what she has painted if she wishes to do so, the interpretation of children's painting should be left to experts. Correct interpretation depends on a knowledge of the order in which paintings were produced, knowledge of the availability of colours, access to the case history, and a complete record of comments made by the child while the work was in progress. In addition, young children often overpaint, restructuring paintings two or three times as they work; this increases the likelihood of misinterpretation. Since all this information is required for understanding, it is easy to see why even professional psychologists may differ considerably about interpretations of such material, and it makes sense that teachers who have only a modicum of training in such matters should be circumspect about ascribing psychological meanings to children's art.

Suggested Variations

Offer a wide variety of colours, and ask children to select those they prefer; use a different size or shape of paper or one with a different texture, such as corrugated cardboard

❧   *Easel painting is a perennial favourite of young children.*

or "oatmeal" paper. You may want the children to experiment by learning how to mix a new colour from the ones you have presented. Try using the same colour paint on the same colour paper or several shades of just one colour. Different sizes of brushes or different kinds of bristles in the same colour paint make a nice contrast. Thinner brushes encourage children to add more detail to their work. You might want to try painting to music, painting woodworking, painting the fence with water, using watercolours, having several children paint on one large sheet to make a mural, or painting on a flat surface instead of an easel. Printing and stamping, using paint and sponges, can also be an interesting although not extraordinarily successful experiment to try. Cookie cutters are really more effective to use for stamping than sponges are.

A. Preparation

1. Decide where to put the easels for the day. In summer, painting outside is a pleasure, and makes clean-up easier too.

2. Assemble the equipment. This will include easels, easel clips, aprons, paint containers, brushes, large paper, paint, and a felt marker. You will also need clothespins, drying racks or a line, a sink or a bucket, towels, and a sponge.

3. Check the paint to make sure it is rich and bright, not watery, and neither too thick nor too thin. Decide, possibly with the children's help, on what colours to offer.

B. Procedure

1. If time permits, invite one or two children to help you mix the paint. (Sometimes this is done a day in advance, but it is always good to invite a child to help: Mixing paint is interesting and educational.) Begin by shaking a generous quantity of powdered paint into the mixing container. Next, add water a little at a time, stirring constantly just as one does when making flour and water thickening for gravy. The paint should look rich and bright. It should spread easily, but not be a thin, watery looking gruel. If the paint was mixed the day before, be sure it is thoroughly stirred before pouring so that all the pigment is mixed back into the water. A dash of liquid detergent added to each container seems to help paint wash out of clothing more easily.

2. Several pieces of easel paper may be put up at one time; doing this makes getting a new sheet ready for use much faster.

3. Put just a small quantity of paint in each easel container. The paint may have to be replaced more frequently, but frequent replacement means the paint stays brighter, and small amounts mean less waste when it is spilled.

4. If necessary, invite children to come and paint, and help them put on the aprons to protect clothes. Remember to roll up sleeves firmly.

5. Write the child's name and the date on the back right-hand corner.

6. If it is windy, use additional easel clips at the bottom edges of the paper.

7. Encourage children to remember to dip brushes in the same colour paint and to do their colour mixing on the paper. Older four-year-olds can learn to rinse brushes in between times.

8. Children may use their hands in the painting as long as they keep them off other children.

9. Hang pictures on drying racks, a chain link fence, or a clothesline.

10. Children should wash hands *before* removing their aprons. Use an outdoor sink or bucket for hand washing if possible. If children must wash in the bathroom, be sure to alert a nearby teacher to keep track of what is going on. Sometimes children also enjoy sponging off their aprons. If this is the case, rejoice.

C. Clean-up

1. Encourage children to help clean up. Washing paintbrushes is usually a richly enjoyed experience. Store brushes bristle-end up to dry.

2. Put clean, unused paint back into the storage bottles and *ruthlessly discard spoiled, discoloured paint.*

3. Replace all equipment in the correct storage places.

4. Roll and store dry paintings in the children's cubbies; the paintings should go home every day. If a painting is kept for room decoration, ask the child's permission before keeping it. If such permission is refused, be sure to respect that refusal.

Finger Painting

Finger painting is one of the most tension-relieving and delicious creative experiences available. The brilliance of the colours and the general gushiness that characterizes successful participation make it both appealing and relaxing. It is particularly valuable because it is so messy, beautiful, and free, and because it is a direct sensory experience for the children. It should be offered several times a week.

Suggested Variations

Children may paint directly on the table, using a whipped soap mixture, either white or tinted with food colouring. Ivory Snow is most useful for this purpose. Remember, the children will enjoy helping beat this up. (Adding some vinegar to the wash water will make clean-up easier.) They may also finger-paint directly on the table and take prints of their painting by pressing a piece of newsprint down on it. These prints are often stunning. Shaving cream offers another attractive way to vary finger painting. Painting can be done on textured papers, or different recipes can be used for variation in texture. Using cooked laundry starch or cornstarch in place of the liquid variety is always interesting because different thicknesses can be concocted, and it is also more economical.

Cornstarch Finger Paint

Dissolve ½ cup cornstarch in 1 cup of cold water and pour mixture into 3 cups boiling water; stir constantly until shiny and translucent. Allow to cool and use as a finger-paint base, or ladle into jars and stir in tempera or food colouring.

If a thicker mixture is desired, be sure to add glycerine to reduce stickiness. Adding a little glycerine or talcum powder makes painting particularly slick. Scents such as oil of cloves may be used to add fragrance. Starch bases can be refrigerated and then offered as a contrast to warmed starch—perhaps one kind for each hand.

A. Preparation

1. Decide what kind of finger painting you will offer. There are many satisfying variations available (Hendrick, 1990).

2. Finger painting should look rich and bright. This means that plenty of paint and starch must be used.

3. Assemble all equipment before you start. Once begun, this activity is so beloved by children that the teacher will find it difficult to obtain even a moment to fetch something forgotten. Necessary equipment will include *oilcloth* or *plastic* aprons (paint soaks right through old shirts if a child leans against the table, and most of them do), finger-paint paper or a good quality butcher paper, a felt pen for names, starch, tempera paint (it is possible to buy ready-mixed finger paint, but this is likely to cost more), plastic-covered tables, something to hang the paintings on, clothespins, buckets of soapy water, sponges, and towels.

4. When weather permits, set up outside; clean-up is infinitely easier there.

B. Procedure

1. Finger-painting is more successful when children stand up. Standing enables them to use their large arm muscles more freely, reach the entire paper without straining, and really see what they are doing.

ꙮ   *Joe has a wonderful ability to let himself experience paint fully.*

2. Roll up sleeves and take off coats or sweaters. Even liberal mothers may balk at a child coated with finger-paint from head to toe. Put on aprons.

3. Allow each child to do as many paintings as she wishes, and let her return for as many as she desires.

4. Finger-paint is usually mixed right on the paper as the child works. Pour about three or four tablespoons of liquid starch on the paper. Shake powdered paint onto the starch. Ask children to tell you which colours they want, but do not let them shake it themselves; they often waste it.

5. Offer one, two, or three colours of tempera placed on different paper areas so that the children can combine them. Unless you have some special purpose in mind, pick colours that combine to make an attractive additional colour.

6. Hang up finished paintings. Offer the child a chance to make another one.

7. Show children how to rub their hands with the sponges in the bucket *before* they remove their aprons. (Many children will spend additional time squeezing the coloured soapy bucket water through the sponge—another fine sensory experience.)

8. If the day is windy or the room drafty, sponging the table lightly with water before putting the paper down will keep it from blowing away.

C. Clean-up

1. Invite some children to help clean up. (The use of soapy water and sponges will attract helpers.) Wash off table, aprons, and so forth. Be sure to wash the edges of tables.

2. Return all supplies to correct storage places.

3. Roll up dried paintings and place in cubbies.

Collage and Assemblage

Collage is particularly useful because it fosters an appreciation of the way different materials look when they are arranged together, thereby emphasizing the elements of design and composition. If collage is offered as recommended below, it also provides opportunities for deliberating over selections and making choices and provides many exposures to a wide variety of materials, which may range from cotton balls to shells and wood shavings. Also included might be bright bits of ribbon and yarn, coarse netting, sponge, tin foil, corks, and packing materials. Collage or assemblage lends itself nicely to carrying out program themes or other matters of interest to the children. Using natural materials in this kind of work adds potential beauty and interest to the activity. For example, shells, seaweed, and sand are nice to use as collage ingredients after a trip to the beach. The teacher should remember that the intent is not to have the child make a picture of where she has been or copy what the teacher has made; the intent is to encourage the appreciation of contrast in texture and colour and to foster pleasure in creating a design based on these differences.

Suggested Variations

Almost anything can be used as collage material, and it is pitiful to limit it to cutouts from magazines. This is one area in which the good scroungers are in their element. Carpet scraps, pumpkin seeds, buttons, fur, and textured papers are all attractive ingredients. *Because food is so short in the world, our centre no longer uses such items as macaroni, peas, and rice as collage materials.* The experience can be varied by using different mats and bases: Large pieces of old bark, heavy cardboard, or pieces of wood too hard to saw make interesting foundations. Food colouring can be used to tint the glue, or tempera can be added if a stronger, brighter coloured glue base is desired. The variety can be endless and the satisfaction great!

An excellent way to recycle cardboard containers involves gluing boxes and cartons together to create interesting structures. These are particularly appealing if a mixture of cylinders and square shapes are provided. The advertisements add colour and appeal, and children love painting over these once the glue has dried.

A. Preparation

1. Plan what materials to use, both background mats and collage substances. Many things may be used as a base. Cardboard, construction paper, or large pieces of bark are ideal. *Avoid using paper plates and cottage cheese lids as bases because they are too small and skimpy and do not give the children sufficient scope to work.* Select materials for contrast, variety, and beauty. Choose materials that will be aesthetically pleasing when used together.

2. Plan to use *two* tables for collage: a work table covered with newspaper and a "choosing table" from which the children will make their selections. If you set the materials out on coloured paper or in attractive containers, they will be more appealing and also easier to keep sorted and neat.

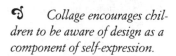

❧   *Collage encourages children to be aware of design as a component of self-expression.*

3. If the collage items are heavy, use undiluted white glue, such as Elmer's, which may be purchased by the gallon for economy. If light items such as feathers, fabrics, or paper are used, dilute the glue with starch or a *little* water.

4. Offer scissors or clippers to encourage children to modify the shape of materials to suit themselves.

5. Assemble aprons, glue brushes, white glue and containers, felt-tip pens, and collage materials.

B. Procedure

1. Give each child an apron. Roll up sleeves.

2. Encourage the child to take a collage tray and go to the choosing table. Gradually teach children to think about their choices: Would that be interesting to use? How would this feel? What would go well with what?

3. On returning to the work table, give each child a brush and glue container (with very little glue in it at a time; children need to learn that glue is not paint), or allow the child to dip each item lightly in a saucer of glue.

4. Collage takes patience and perseverance. Many younger children will spend only a little time at it, but most older children will spend fifteen or twenty minutes or longer if they are deeply interested.

5. Unless children are monitored carefully, it is easy for the choosing table to become an unsorted mess of rumpled materials. Keep it neat and good looking to facilitate judging and selection by the children.

6. Collages have to dry flat. Glue takes a long time to dry, so select a drying place that will be out of the way.

C. Clean-up

1. Children may help wash glue brushes; warm water will make this easier.

2. Return undiluted glue to the bottle and diluted glue to the thinned glue container. Remember to wipe off the neck of the bottle!

3. Wipe off furniture that has glue on it.

4. Put dried collages in cubbies.

Dough and Clay

Dough and clay are alike because they both offer opportunities to be creative while using a three-dimensional medium. They also provide particularly satisfying opportunities to release aggression harmlessly by hitting, punching, and squeezing. In addition, these materials allow the child to enjoy smearing and general messiness, activities that many psychologists value because they feel it provides a sublimated substitute for handling faeces. (Whether the reader agrees with this theory or is repelled by it, they will certainly find, if they listen, that children often do talk with relish of "pooh-pooh" while they work with this kind of material.) For all these reasons, *dough and clay should usually be presented without cookie cutters, rolling pins, or other clutter,* since these accessories detract from the more desirable virtues of thumping and whacking, as well as from making original creations.

Besides these general benefits, mixing dough helps the child learn about the transformation of materials and changes in texture. It also provides opportunities to learn facts about measuring and blending.

It is interesting to note that recent research has identified developmental stages in the use of clay just as such stages have been found in the use of other materials. Brittain (1979) comments that two-year-olds beat, pull, and mush clay, while a child of three forms it into balls and rolls it into snakes. Shotwell and colleagues (1979) identify the progression as moving from "product awareness" at twelve months to "elementary shaping" by age three.

Suggested Variations

Allow the dough or clay objects made by the children to harden, and then paint and shellac them, or dip painted clay objects in melted paraffin to give a "finish." *Occasionally* use dough and clay with accessories such as dull knives for smoothing it or cookie cutters and rolling pins to alter form. Offer chilled dough as a contrast to the room temperature variety. Cookie and bread recipes are also dough experiences. Vary the dough experience by changing the recipe. The following are two of the best.*

Basic play dough

3 cups flour, ¼ cup salt, 6 tablespoons oil, enough dry tempera to colour it, and about ¾ to 1 cup water. Encourage children to measure amounts of salt and flour and mix them together with the dry tempera. Add tempera before adding water. If using food colouring, mix a 3-ounce bottle with the water before combining it with the salt and flour. Combine oil with ¼ cup water and add to dry ingredients. Mix with fingers, adding as much water as necessary to make a workable but not sticky dough.

Many basic recipes do not include oil, but using it makes dough softer and more pliable. It also makes it slightly greasy, and this helps protect skin from the effects of the salt. Dry tempera gives the brightest colours, but food colouring may be used instead if desired. Advantages of this recipe are that it can be totally made by the children, since it requires no cooking, and it is made from ingredients usually on hand that are inexpensive. This dough stores in the refrigerator fairly well. It gets sticky, but this can be corrected by adding more flour. This is a good, standard, all-purpose, reusable dough.

The following dough is lighter and more plastic than the first one—feels lovely. It thickens as boiling water is poured in and cools rapidly so that children can finish mixing. It keeps exceptionally well in the refrigerator; oil does not settle out, and it does not become sticky—a paragon among doughs! Beautiful to use at Christmas if coloured with white tempera.

Basic play dough II

Combine 3 cups self-rising flour, 1 cup salt, 5 tablespoons alum (can be purchased at drug stores) and 1 tablespoon dry tempera. Boil 1 ¼ cups water, add ⅓ cup oil to it, and pour over flour mixture, stirring rapidly. Use.

---

*From *Total Learning: Developmental Curriculum for the Young Child* (4th ed.) by J. Hendrick, 1994, Englewood Cliffs, NJ: Merrill/Prentice-Hall.

A. Preparation

1. Cover tables with oilcloth for quick clean-up later on. Keeping a special piece of oilcloth just for clay saves work, since it can be dried, shaken off, and put away for another day without wiping. Masonite boards or plastic-topped boards can also be used handily.

2. Assemble materials: clay or dough, aprons, oilcloth, clean-up buckets, and towels. (Do not allow children to wash their hands in the sink; this is the quickest way to clog the plumbing.) If mixing dough, assemble ingredients and equipment according to the requirements of the recipe. Offer small pans of water for moistening hands only if children are using clay.

B. Procedure

1. Put on aprons and help children roll up sleeves.

2. Mixing dough:

   a. Always plan this event so the children can participate in making the dough, because this is an additional valuable learning experience and great fun.

   b. Talk about the procedure while it is going on. Ask them, "What's happening? What do you see? How does it taste? How has it changed? How does it feel?"

   c. When making dough, make at least two batches at once in two separate dishpans. This avoids overcrowding and jostling among the children.

3. Give each child a *large* lump of clay or dough. It is important to offer plenty.

4. Use the materials to foster children's imagination and creativity: Clay and dough often generate a lot of playful talk among the children. Avoid making models for them to copy. Emphasize squeezing, rolling, and patting.

5. Supervise the children's hand washing before removing their aprons.

6. Return clay or dough products to the storage container, unless items are being saved.

C. Clean-up

1. Clean-up from these activities takes quite a while, so begin early enough that the children have time to help, too.

2. Sponge off aprons and anything else that needs it.

3. Replace leftover ingredients in containers. Clay must be stored in tightly sealed containers. Make a depression in each large ball of clay with your thumb and fill with water—this is an old potter's trick that will keep clay moist until used again. Dough should be stored in the refrigerator.

4. Flush the buckets of water down the toilet to avoid clogging drains.

Woodworking

Woodworking is a challenging and satisfying experience that should be available to the children at least two or three times every week. It requires unceasing supervision from the teacher, not so much because of possible hammered fingers or minor cuts from the saw, but because an occasional child may impulsively throw a hammer and injure someone. Although rare, this can happen in the twinkling of an eye, and the teacher must be alert so that he steps in before this occurs. *Never leave a carpentry table unsupervised.* The teacher should alleviate frustration by assisting children who are having difficulty getting the nail started or the groove made for the saw.

It is essential that the school purchase good quality tools for the children to use. Tinny little hammers and toy saws are worthless. Adult tools, such as short plumbers' saws, regular hammers (not tack hammers, because their heads are too small), and braces and bits can all be used satisfactorily by boys and girls. Two real vices that can be fastened securely at either end of the woodworking table are essential to hold wood while the children saw through it. A sturdy, indestructible table is a necessity.

One of woodworking's best qualities is the opportunity it offers for doing real work. Children can assist in fixing things while using tools or can make a variety of simple items

✑   *Note the substantial table and adult-sized hammer being used. Using real tools is an important part of fostering success when offering woodworking.*

that *they have thought up.* These often include airplanes, boats, or just pieces of wood hammered together.

I particularly like offering carpentry because it is so easy to increase the challenge and difficulty of the experience as the year moves along. Children can begin with simple hammering, go on to using the saw, and finally enjoy the brace and bit. During the year they can learn many kinds of tool-related skills, and they can learn how to select the right tool for the right job. Carpentry is also an excellent way to develop eye-hand coordination. (But beware of the canny youngster who says, "Now, you hold the nail while I hit it!")

Finally, woodworking is a splendid way to harness intense energy and to sublimate anger. Hammering and sawing, in particular, are effective relievers of feelings.

Suggested Variations

Allow the children to take apart the brace and bit and the vice to find out how they work. Have a number of various-sized bits available for making different-sized holes, and purchase dowels that will fit these holes when the wood is cut into pieces. Furnish different accessories for variety: Bottle caps, film container lids, and jar lids make good wheels or decorations. String or roving cotton twisted among the nails is interesting. Unusual wood scraps that come from cabinet shops are nice. Wood gluing in place of nailing appeals to some youngsters and is a quicker form of wood construction. Many children enjoy going on to paint whatever they have made; this works well if it is done under another teacher's supervision at a separate table. Children will enjoy using a wide array of nails, ranging from flat, broad-headed roofing nails to tiny little finishing nails, which for some reason they often like to hammer in all around the edges of boards. Sandpaper is occasionally interesting, particularly if there are several grades of it available for comparison. An occasional child will also enjoy measuring and sawing to fit, although this activity is more typical of older children. Very young children will do best if soft plasterboard or even large pieces of Styrofoam packing are offered rather than wood.

A. Preparation
1. Check the wood supply in advance. You may need to visit a cabinet or frame shop or a construction site to ask for free scraps if your supply is low. Teach yourself to tell hardwoods from softwoods. Plywood and hardwoods are good for gluing but are usually frustrating for children to use in woodworking.
2. Decide whether to use any accessories, such as spools or bottle caps, for added interest.
3. Assemble wood, tools, supplies, and a pencil for labelling products.
4. Arrange tools and materials so that they are easy for children to reach. Make the arrangement attractive. Encourage children to select what they need and to replace what they do not use. Keep rearranging materials if the area becomes disorganized.

B. Procedure
1. Decide how many children you will be able to supervise at one time. For safety's sake you will probably need to limit yourself to three or four children at once. *Encourage children to work on separate sides of the table to spread them out.*
2. Help children when necessary; teach them to treat tools with respect and to use them safely.

3. Be alert to interaction between children. Self-control at this age is not highly developed: *Intervene swiftly when necessary.*

4. Be sure to encourage children who persevere in particularly difficult tasks, such as sawing through a large board or making a nail go all the way through two pieces of wood.

5. Remember to label finished products.

C. Clean-up

1. Replace tools and wood scraps in correct storage area.

2. Put finished work in cubbies.

Sewing

Sewing is not often offered in the preschool, and yet it is interesting to some children, boys as well as girls. Besides the obvious value of developing eye-hand coordination, it also offers good opportunities to experiment and to be creative. Occasionally it can be an opportunity for accomplishing meaningful work and can also provide a chance to experience the satisfaction of role playing a "motherly" activity.

Suggested Variations

You may want to try sewing on Styrofoam meat trays or sewing through plastic berry baskets; these have the advantage of being stiff and light to hold. An occasional adept four- or five-year-old will enjoy sewing top and side seams on simple doll clothes. Sometimes children enjoy sewing large buttons to material. Children may enjoy appliquéing cutouts loosely to burlap to create wall decorations for home or school. An old variation to sewing, which is fun but not really creative, is the punched cardboard sewing cards and laces enjoyed by youngsters since the turn of the century.

A. Preparation

1. Choose a loosely woven fabric as the material for sewing. Cheap dishcloths are colourful and ideal for this purpose. Thick or heavy fabric will be too difficult for the children to get the needle through.

2. Assemble the equipment: yarn or thick cotton string; fabric; large, dull embroidery needles; scissors; and embroidery hoops. Offer a choice of different colours of yarn and materials if possible. Make sure the scissors will really cut the fabric.

3. You might prethread some needles in advance. It helps to knot the thread onto the needle if it constantly slips out, provided that the material is coarse enough, or to use double threads knotted together at the ends to prevent them from being pulled out of the needle.

B. Procedure

1. Choose a fairly small group of children to work with—four or five children at a time.

2. Be prepared for stuck fingers, some frustration, and a lot of requests for help, especially the first few times. Some children are disappointed with their technique,

but do not end up sewing for them because they want it to look a certain way. Encourage them to do it their own way and be pleased with their experiments.

3. Embroidery hoops help a lot, although children tend to sew over the edges of them. Rather than constantly criticizing this tendency, you can have them snip the yarn later for an interesting fringed effect. Children will also gradually learn to sew in and out rather than up and over as they become acquainted with the material, but it takes a while to grasp this concept.

4. Safety-pin the child's name to her work.

C. Clean-up

1. Put the sewing materials away; never leave needles lying about.

2. Place finished work in cubbies.

Dance and Creative Movement

Dancing has great potential for self-expression because it stimulates the child's imagination and offers many opportunities for emotional release. Moving to music can involve the child's entire body and draw satisfying expressions of emotion and pleasure from her that other creative experiences cannot tap.

There seem to be two extremes in presenting dance experiences that are not creative. In one, the teacher conceives the dance entirely beforehand and then puts the children through the paces. Folk dances, though desirable for cultural ethnic reasons, are examples of this. This is simply providing a model for the children to copy. At the other extreme the teacher puts on some music and sits passively by while expecting the children to generate the entire experience for themselves. Children usually require more stimulation than this from the teacher to get a dance experience going. Beginning teachers often feel self-conscious about participating, but dancing with the children is essential for success. Taking a couple of modern dance classes in college frequently helps students feel more at ease with this medium.

Suggested Variations

Accessories add a great deal to dancing and are helpful materials to use to get dance started. Scarves, long streamers, and balloons help focus the child's awareness away from herself and so reduce her self-consciousness at the beginning. Ethnic dance materials offer a rich resource for dance. Folk dance records and other rhythmic songs and melodies are delightful resources on which to draw. Using percussion instruments can also vary the experience. Dancing outdoors often attracts children who shun this activity in a more enclosed setting. Remember to include dance activities that appeal to boys as well as to girls. Moving like submarines, airplanes, seals, or bears helps take the stigma out of dance for boys, who may have already decided dancing is "sissy."

A. Preparation

1. Decide what kind of music to use and familiarize yourself with its possibilities.

༒   *Following the children's suggestions encourages them to be more creative.*

    a. It is ideal to have a pianist available who can improvise as the teacher and children request, but this is by no means essential. Records or percussion instruments are also satisfactory.

    b. Familiarize yourself fully with records that are available. Choose two or three that offer a good range of rhythms and emotional expression.

    c. Do not overlook the possibilities offered by popular music. It has the virtues of being familiar and rhythmic, and it offers a wide variety of emotional moods as well.

2. Clear the largest room available of chairs, tables, and so forth.

3. Arrange to avoid interruptions. It is fatal to the experience for the teacher to answer the phone or to stop and settle a fight on the playground.

B. Procedure

1. Avoid having other activities going on in the room at the same time, although some children will need to putter around the edges watching before they join in. Accomplished teachers often feel comfortable having children drift in and out of the group, but beginners may find that a more secluded atmosphere where children may leave as they desire but where newcomers may not intrude is helpful. Do not try to have all the children in the program participate at once.

2. *The most important skill to develop in dance is the ability to be sensitive to individual responses and ideas as the children generate them and to encourage these as they come along.*

3. It is necessary for the teacher to move freely along with the children. Sometimes it helps to ask other adults to stay away while you are leading a dance activity to avoid self-consciousness. Sometimes a teacher feels more secure with another adult present.

4. It is good to have in mind a general plan that contains some ideas about ways to begin and also things to try that will vary the activity. Always have more activities in mind than you could possibly use. It is better to be safe than sorry, but remember to use the children's suggestions whenever possible. It is essential to offer relaxing experiences and to alternate vigorous activities with quieter ones to avoid overstimulation and chaos. Children enjoy showing all the ways they can think of to be kittens or the ways they can get across the floor on their tummies, or as they become more practised and at ease, ways of moving as the music makes them feel.

C. Clean-up

1. Warn the children, as the end nears, that the time is drawing to a close.

2. At the end, involve the group in some kind of quiet response to the music so that they have themselves under reasonable control as they leave the room.

3. Help them put on their shoes and socks if these have been taken off.

4. Return the room to its usual order.

Using Rhythm Instruments

There are other ways to respond to music besides dancing, and participating with rhythm instruments is one of them. This activity is both somewhat creative and somewhat an exercise in conformity, since children may respond imaginatively and individually with their instruments while doing something together at the same time. Basically, participating in a musical experience will introduce children to the pleasures and delights of sound, rhythms, and melodies. If well handled, it should also teach children to care for instruments as objects of beauty and value and should help them learn to listen to music and respond in a discriminating way.

Suggested Variations

Improvisations with musical instruments are a delight. Children can be encouraged to use them as the music makes them feel—to play soft or loud, fast or slow, together, or a few at a time. They can also make some simple instruments of their own, such as sand blocks and shakers (Hunter & Judson, 1977). Moving to music while using instruments (typically, marching) can also be a satisfying way of integrating this experience into a larger activity.

A. Preparation

1. Familiarize yourself with the music you will present. Listen to the recordings or practise on the instrument you intend to use yourself.

2. Select the instruments for the children to use.

3. Plan to start with a small group of children and a small number of instruments at first. You can always add more things later when you know how many children you can comfortably supervise.

B. Procedure

1. Instruments are not toys and must be supervised to prevent abuse when they are used. It will help if you plan in advance details such as where the children will put them when they are finished and how they will get another instrument. Decide on a reasonable procedure that will allow you to relax and not worry about the possibility of a child's stepping through a tambourine that was left on the floor.

2. Insist on these few basic guidelines: Drums and tambourines are to be hit with the hand only. (Drum heads do not stand up under steady pounding from sticks. Hit the rhythm sticks together if stick hitting is desired.) Allow one maraca to a child. Maracas crack easily when hit together.

3. Be prepared to get right into the music with the children and become involved. Your enthusiasm will communicate itself and make the experience special.

C. Clean-up

1. Warn ahead.

2. Put tapes/CDs back and return instruments to their area, arranging them so they look attractive and orderly.

❧ Summary

Early childhood teachers have always valued the creative part of the child's self and have sought to enhance its development by fostering the use of self-expressive materials. Today we also seek to foster creativity in additional ways, which include generating creative play and encouraging originality of thought.

To accomplish these goals, there are three teaching skills teachers should cultivate in themselves. When presenting self-expressive materials, they must cultivate their ability to let children explore and use them as their impulses and feelings require. When seeking to facilitate play, they must learn to move with the children's imaginative ideas and support them. When working to develop originality in thought, they must be able to recognize the value of the children's ideas and to ask questions that will encourage further development of ideas.

Creativity is particularly valuable because it increases the child's feelings of self-esteem, facilitates self-expression and the expression of emotion, provides a vital balance for the cognitive part of the program (while also promoting its growth), and helps teachers individualize their curriculum.

Teachers can foster creativity by understanding and accepting the creative child and by maintaining in their groups an environment that helps children feel secure so they become willing to risk and venture. When presenting self-expressive materials for the children's use, teachers should avoid making models for them to copy, emphasize the process rather than the product, allow plenty of time and opportunity for the child to use the material, learn to make enhancing comments, and give reluctant children the right to refuse to participate. But the most important thing to do is to make the materials freely available and let the children explore them as their impulses and interests dictate.

Questions and Activities

1. If copying a model is really inhibiting to the development of creative self-expression, why do you think so many teachers persist in having children copy projects "just the way the teacher made it"?
2. Do you think of yourself as being artistic, or are you the sort of person who "can't even hold a paintbrush right side up"? What attitudes in your previous teachers do you feel contributed to your feelings of confidence or lack of confidence in this area?
3. *Problem:* Irene is painting at the easel and gradually begins to spread paint off the paper onto the easel itself, then to paint her hands and arms up to the elbows, and then to flick drops of paint onto a neighbouring child and her painting. Should the teacher intervene and control any or all of this behaviour, or should it be allowed to continue?
4. The variations of self-expressive activities listed at the end of each section represent only a few of numerous possibilities. What other activities have people in the class witnessed that could be added to these lists?

Self-Check Questions for Review

Content-Related Questions

1. Is it true that a person must be very intelligent in order to have creative ideas?
2. Identify several values the experience of creativity offers to the growing child.
3. List and define the stages children pass through when using a material that has creative potential.
4. Self-expressive materials are one avenue open to children for creative self-expression. What are the other two? What special skill is required of the teacher in relation to each of those avenues?

5. Discuss four or more practical suggestions for encouraging the creative use of the self-expressive materials that are introduced in the chapter.
6. Select one of the self-expressive materials discussed in the chapter and pretend you are explaining to a newcomer how to present it effectively. What advice would you give him? Be sure to include some suggestions for ways he could vary the experience.
7. Explain why it is valuable for children with special needs to participate in using self-expressive materials. Provide some examples of ways materials might be adapted to make that participation more feasible.

Integrative Questions

1. A four-year-old girl has just hammered together two pieces of wood and proudly announced she has made an airplane. In addition to noting the creative value of that experience, explain how woodworking might also benefit her physical, emotional, and cognitive selves. How might the experience also be made to benefit her social self?
2. It is the policy of some schools to allow each child to make just one painting or piece of wood gluing so that all the children have a chance to do the activity every time it is presented. What are the pros and cons of this approach in relation to fostering creativity?
3. The preschool teacher in the next room has had her three-year-olds make caterpillars out of styrofoam egg cartons and pipe cleaners. Each child was allowed to decide whether to use purple or red pipe cleaners for the legs and yellow or pink ones for the antennae. Her next project is showing the children how to glue artificial flowers onto pipe cleaner stems and stick them into balls of clay for Mother's Day. Evaluate these projects in terms of their potential

creative benefit for the children. Be sure to explain why you think these projects would or would not enhance the children's creative selves.

4. Shana is a four-year-old girl in your class who is new to school and is doing easel painting for the first time. She is distressed because the paint is runny and keeps dripping down the paper as she paints with it. Explain how a Canadian preschool teacher devoted to the discovery approach might handle her predicament and compare it with the way a teacher from Reggio Emilia would be likely to handle it.

References for Further Reading

Overviews

Amabile, T. (1989). *Growing up creative: Nurturing a lifetime of creativity.* New York: Crown. This delightful book is full of sensible recommendations of ways parents and teachers can foster creativity in children. *Highly recommended.*

Belliston, L., & Belliston, M. (1982). *How to raise a more creative child.* Allen, TX: Argus Communications. This is a really good book about what to do or not to do to foster creative self-expression. The information is presented as a series of axioms, with discussion and a specific, practical list of do's for each one. *Highly recommended.*

Schirrmacher, R. (1988). *Art and creative development for young children.* Albany, NY: Delmar. Schirrmacher provides a comprehensive discussion of what creativity is. This is more than an activity book although it includes a rich resource of activities for two- and three-dimensional creative self-expressive activities.

Striker, S. (1986). *Please touch: How to stimulate your child's creative development.* New York: Simon & Schuster. Though written for parents, *Please Touch* is useful for beginning teachers, too, because of its clear discussions about, defence of, and practical suggestions for fostering various creative activities. *Highly recommended.*

Self-Expressive Materials for Children with Special Needs

Anderson, F. E. (1992). *Art for all the children: Approaches to art therapy for children with disabilities* (2nd ed.). Springfield, IL: Charles C. Thomas. Many ways to make these activities appropriate for children who are developmentally delayed, emotionally disturbed, vision impaired, etc. are included. There is an outstanding chapter on adapting art situations for children who are physically disabled. *Highly recommended.*

Hereford, N. J., & Schall, J. (Eds.). (1991). *Learning through play: Art: A practical guide for teaching young children.* New York: Scholastic. This book provides a good basic discussion coupled with many ideas for presenting specific materials. I particularly appreciate this series not only because of its practical approach but also because it invariably includes suggestions for including children with disabilities in the group.

Spodek, B., & Saracho, O. N. (1994). *Dealing with individual differences in the early childhood classroom.* New York: Longman. This is a very good book about working with children in early childhood settings who have special needs. The authors include a rare chapter on "Fostering Creative Expression" that covers movement education, music, and art.

Safety

Peltz, P. A., & Rossol, M. S. (1984). *Children's art supplies can be toxic.* New York: Center for Occupational Hazards. An unusual and useful pamphlet that identifies various dangerous materials. It also includes a lengthy list of safety-approved art materials with their trade names. Available from The Center, 5 Beekman St., New York, NY 10038.

Money Savers

Kohl, M. A. F., & Gainer, C. (1991). *Good earth art: Environmental art for kids.* Bellingham, WA: Bright Ring. Many of the creative ideas here use "trash" or recyclable materials. Each idea is coded according to appropriate age and includes variations. Activities are product oriented but could be used in freer approaches as well.

Sunderlin, S., & Grey, N. (Eds.) (1967). *Bits & pieces: Imaginative uses for children's learning.* Wheaton, MD: Association for Childhood Education International. This is such a good pamphlet that it is still in print. There are many suggestions for scroungers and pack rats here that relate to all areas of the curriculum, not just to art activities. A fine way to save money.

Aesthetics

Golumb, C. (1992). *The child's creation of a pictorial world.* Berkeley, CA: University of California Press.

Golumb includes an interesting chapter on the child as art critic.

Micklethwait, L. (1993). *A child's book of art: Great pictures with first words.* New York: Dorling Kindersly. I can't resist including this children's book because, in common with Montessori, I believe it is important to form children's taste by exposing them to examples of fine art. (My grandchildren love this book!)

Presentation of Self-Expressive Materials*

Bos, B. (1978). *Please don't move the muffin tins: A hands-off guide to art for the young child.* Carmichael, CA: the burton gallery. Nicely illustrated, *Don't Move the Muffin Tins* has many practical suggestions, including a discussion of "traps" or pitfalls to avoid when presenting basic expressive materials. It draws a nice distinction between craft and art.

Chenfeld, M. B. (1995). *Creative activities for young children.* (2nd ed.) New York: Harcourt Brace Jovanovich. This is a very good book in which Chenfeld divides activities according to such topics as bodies and people we meet. She then suggests creative activities, including art, movement, and discussion activities, that could be related to the topic. Excellent bibliographies for children and adults complete each chapter.

Cherry, C. (1990). *Creative art for the developing child: A teacher's handbook for early childhood education* (2nd ed.). Belmont, CA: Fearon. Cherry's books are always filled with practical suggestions offered by an experienced teacher, and this one on art is no exception.

Hendrick, J. (1994). *Total learning: Developmental curriculum for the young child* (4th ed.). Englewood Cliffs, NJ: Merrill/Prentice Hall. The chapter "Freeing Children to Be Creative" offers numerous recipes for doughs and finger painting.

Olshansky, B. (1990). *Portfolio of illustrated step-by-step art projects for young children.* West Nyack, NY: Center for Applied Research in Education, Simon and

---

*As I browsed through a considerable number of activity books that purported to present creative activities for children, I became increasingly depressed over the utter lack of creativity in evidence. Over and over these so-called creative activities were, in reality, tightly structured craft ideas that left almost nothing for the children to contribute in the way of their ideas or feelings. I encourage readers to look carefully at the values reflected in such activities before pawning them off on children as being creative.

Schuster. These activities are suitable for preschool-age children on up. There is great variety and activities are carefully explained—outstanding because the descriptions often show how to make the material simple or more challenging.

Painting

Smith, N. R., Fucigna, C., Kennedy, M, & Lord, L. (1993). *Teaching children to paint* (2nd ed.). New York: Teachers College Press. The title of this book is misleading since the intention is not so much teaching as *enabling* children of various ages to use paints with satisfaction.

Clay

Hagen, J., Lewis, H., & Smilansky, S. (1988). *Clay in the classroom: Helping children develop cognitive and affective skills for learning.* New York: Peter Lang. The authors describe a research project that used three methods of instruction about modelling clay. The chapter "Clay in Your Classroom" is a gold-mine of information on the practical aspects of presenting clay to young children.

Kohl, M. F. (1989). *Mudworks: Creative clay, dough, and modeling experiences.* Bellingham, WA: Bright Ring. A tremendous variety of mixtures are included together with estimates of appropriate age, palatability, and variations.

Woodworking

Skeen, P., Garner, A. P., & Cartwright, S. (1984). *Woodworking for young children.* Washington, DC: National Association for the Education of Young Children. At last, a truly practical book about woodworking for teachers and young children. This book deals with everything from how to tell softwoods from hardwoods to describing how tools should be used and how to straighten a nail. It also contains suggestions for helping children become effective young woodworkers. *Highly recommended.*

Music and Dance

Bayless, K. M., & Ramsey, M. E. (1990). *Music: A way of life for the young child* (4th ed.). Englewood Cliffs, NJ: Merrill/Prentice Hall. This is *the* outstanding book on music for young children. Replete with simple arrangements, it covers toddlers, children of nursery school age, and youngsters with special needs and also offers a rare chapter on including music for and about children from differing cultures. The resource lists are outstanding. Not to be missed.

Cherry, C. (1971). *Creative movement for the developing child: A nursery school handbook for non-musicians* (rev. ed.). Belmont, CA: Fearon. Cherry bases her approach to dance on creative movement. The material is simply presented, and all the suggested activities can be accompanied by familiar tunes and improvised words, which are included in the text.

Stinson, S. (1988). *Dance for young children: Finding the magic in movement.* Reston, VA: American Alliance for Health, Physical Education, Recreation, and Dance. This is another practical book filled with ideas for themes and the presentation of dance material. Has good resource lists.

Zukowski, G., & Dickson, A. (1990). *On the move: A handbook for exploring creative movement with young children.* Carbondale IL: Southern Illinois University Press. This helpful book is filled with simple, practical suggestions for generating dance activities. It includes a chapter on working with special needs children.

For the Advanced Student

Albert, R. S. (Ed.). (1983). *Genius and eminence: The social psychology of creativity and exceptional achievement.* Elmsford, NY: Pergamon Press. A fascinating collection of articles on genius and creativity (not always the same thing). A good book to browse through.

Davis, J., & Gardner, H. (1993). The arts and early childhood education: A cognitive developmental portrait of the young child as artist. In B. Spodek (Ed.). *Handbook of research on the education of young children.* Englewood Cliffs, NJ: Prentice Hall. This is a scholarly discussion of current cognitive theory as it is applied to understanding children's drawings.

Gardner, H. (1980). *Artful scribbles: The significance of children's drawings.* New York: Basic Books. Gardner carefully considers the relationship between drawing, development, and the other "evolving capacities" of the child. A readable, interesting, provocative book, profusely illustrated.

Golumb, C. (1992). *The child's creation of a pictorial world.* Berkeley, CA: University of California Press. Golumb bases an exhaustive analysis of how children's drawings develop on her extensive research. Included are discussions of gifted child artists and the use of art for diagnostic purposes. Fascinating reading.

Isenberg, J. P., & Jalongo, M. R. (1993). *Creative expression and play in the early childhood curriculum.* New York: Merrill/Prentice Hall. Isenberg and Jalongo present a lengthy, comprehensive discussion of the theoretical and practical aspects of creativity—the best in the field.

Rubin, J. A. (1984). *Child art therapy: Understanding and helping children grow through art* (2nd ed). New York: Van Nostrand Reinhold. The material focuses mainly on older children. Interesting reading.

Sternberg, R. J. (Ed.). (1988). *The nature of creativity: Contemporary psychological perspectives.* Cambridge: Cambridge University Press. This collection of articles presents a variety of approaches, definitions, and research studies concerned with this topic.

Fostering Creativity in Play

16

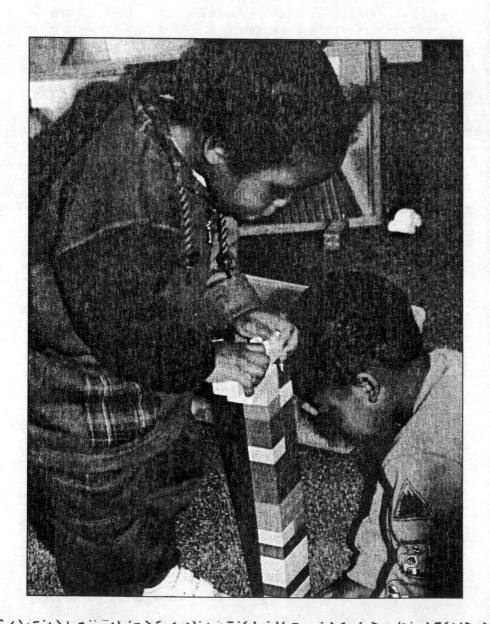

Play provides an avenue for children to express their feelings. Children who are angry or hurt can take their anger out on toys, dolls, and stuffed animals. Children who feel isolated or lonely can find solace in pretending to live in a world with lots of friends. Children who are frightened can seek safety within a game by pretending to be big and strong. In other words, children can play out their own scenarios, changing their real life situations to their own design. They can invent happy endings. They can reverse roles and become the big— instead of the small—people. They can become the aggressors rather than the victims.

Lorraine B. Wallach

 Have you ever wondered . . .

Whether play is as important as some people claim it is?

How to encourage play without dominating it?

Why some teachers think blocks are so important?

. . . If you have, the material in the following pages will help you.

When the first edition of *The Whole Child* went to press in 1975 there was only a hand-ful of citations available concerned with research and the value of play. Twenty years later it is a happy fact that citations dealing with theory, research, and practice related to chil-dren's play abound (Bergen, 1988; Frost, 1992; Isenberg & Jalongo, 1993; Klugman & Smilansky, 1990; Wasserman, 1990).

And yet, despite increasing evidence that play is the serious business of young children and that the opportunity to play freely is vital to their healthy development, early child-hood teachers find that many administrators and parents continue to misunderstand and underestimate the importance of play in the lives of children.

It is difficult to say why some adults have undervalued play to such a degree. Perhaps it is a throwback to our Puritan ethic, which is suspicious of pleasure and self-enjoyment. Unfortunately, as people advance through our educational system, they seem to conclude that any activity that generates delight must be viewed with suspicion—learning can only be gained at the expense of suffering. But play is just the opposite of this. It is a pleasur-able, absorbing activity indulged in for its own sake. The live-for-the-moment aspect of it, combined with the fact that play arises spontaneously from within the child and is not teacher determined, lends an air of frivolity to it that has led some work-oriented persons to assume it is not worthwhile.

Whatever the reason for that point of view, teachers of young children must be pre-pared all their lives to explain and defend the value of basing large parts of their curricu-lum on play. For this reason, the following pages include an extensive analysis of the many contributions that play makes to the development of the whole child.

Ꭵ Purposes of Play

Before proceeding to an analysis of play's virtues I want to point out that there is nothing wrong with providing consistent, lengthy opportunities for children to play together or by themselves simply because it is so satisfying and pleasurable to them. In a way, it is a shame we must analyse and shred play's virtues to pieces in order to defend an activity that obviously has great intrinsic value for its participants. Yet it remains a fact that preprimary teachers must be forever prepared to defend and explain the worthwhile character of play to people who continue to attack it as being a trivial waste of time, time they contend would be better spent "really learning something."

Play Fosters Physical Development

Play fulfils a wide variety of purposes in the life of the child. On a very simple level it promotes the development of sensorimotor skills (Frost, 1992; Kaplan-Sanoff, Brewster, Stillwell, & Bergen, 1988). Children spend hours perfecting such abilities and increasing the level of difficulty to make the task ever more challenging. Anyone who has lived with a one-year-old will recall the tireless persistence with which he pursues the acquisition of basic physical skills. In older children we often think of this repetitious physical activity as the central aspect of play, since it is evident on playgrounds where we see children

ॐ   *This sand play illustrates a few of the many virtues associated with play: having creative ideas (using leaves for candles), playing cooperatively together, and an older youngster helping a younger child.*

swinging, climbing, or playing ball with fervour; but actually, physical motor development represents only one purpose that play fulfils.

Play Fosters Intellectual Development

Piaget (1962) maintains that imaginative, pretend play is one of the purest forms of symbolic thought available to the young child, and its use permits the child to assimilate reality in terms of his own interests and prior knowledge of the world. Vygotsky (1978) also extols the value of such fantasy play, arguing that it is during play that children approach most closely the advanced edge of their zone of proximal development. Or, to put it another way, Vygotsky believed that it is during episodes of fantasy play, when children are free to experiment, attempt, and try out possibilities, that they are most able to reach a little above or beyond their usual level of abilities.

Thus it is evident that imaginative, symbolic play contributes strongly to the child's intellectual development. Indeed, some investigators maintain that symbolic play is a necessary precursor of the development of language (Athey, 1987; Greenfield & Smith, 1976).

Play also offers opportunities for the child to acquire information that lays the foundation for additional learning. For example, through manipulating blocks he learns the concept of equivalence (two small blocks equal one larger one) (Cartwright, 1988). Through playing with water he acquires knowledge of volume, which leads ultimately to developing the concept of reversibility.

The pioneering work of Smilansky (1968) has offered additional support for the importance of play in relation to mental development. She points out that sociodramatic play develops the child's ability to abstract essential qualities of a social role and also to generalize role concepts to a greater degree.

Saltz and Johnson (1977) found that three-year-olds who received training in either thematic fantasy play or sociodramatic play performed significantly better on some tests of intellectual functioning than did the children who only discussed fantasies (in this case, fairy tales) or who were not particularly encouraged to participate in fantasy or role playing.

Language has also been found to be stimulated when children engage in dramatic pretend play. Pellegrini (1986) found this to be particularly true in the housekeeping corner, where children tended to use more explicit, descriptive language in their play than they did when using blocks. For example, they used such phrases as "a very sick doll" or "a big, bad needle" in contrast to using "this," "that," and "those" when pointing to various blocks. (Could this be true because teachers do not teach children names for various sizes and shapes of blocks? We have no way of knowing.)

Research on the use of blocks as a means of representation (symbolization) further supports the value of play as an avenue for cognitive development. Work by Reifel (1982), Reifel and Greenfield (1982), and Reifel and Yeatman (1991) demonstrating the developmental progression of complexity in symbolic play and by Goodson (1982) in her study of how children perceive the way models of blocks could be duplicated are only two of a number of studies that show how play and thought are intertwined and the kinds of intellectual learnings that develop during children's play.

Indeed, any time children use one object to stand for or symbolize something else, whether it be blocks symbolizing a train track or a totally imaginary cup substituting for a real one, symbolic imagination is being utilized. This is a highly intellectual operation (Nourot & Van Hoorn, 1991). The extensive relationship between play and cognitive learning is well summarized by Swedlow in Figure 16.1

Play Enhances Social Development

One of the strongest benefits and satisfactions stemming from play is the way it enhances social development. Playful social interchange begins practically from the moment of birth, as the research study in this chapter demonstrates.

As children grow into toddlerhood and beyond, an even stronger social component becomes evident as more imaginative pretend play develops. Here again, the methodological analysis provided by Smilansky and Shefatya (1990) is helpful. They speak of dramatic and sociodramatic play, differentiating between the two partially on the basis of the number of children involved in the activity. Dramatic play involves imitation and may be carried out alone, but the more advanced sociodramatic play entails verbal communication and interaction with two or more people, as well as imitative role playing, make-

Figure 16.1 Children play: Children learn

If a child is to develop competencies in reading, writing, and mathematics, it is necessary to develop:

Visual memory

Auditory memory

Language acquisition

Classification

Hand-eye coordination

Body image

Spatial orientation

In order to develop these abilities, a child needs experiences with:

Configurations	Arranging objects in sequence
Figure-ground relationships	Organizing objects in ascending and descending order
Shapes	
Patterns	Classification
Spatial relationships	Verbal communication
Matching (shape, size, color)	Measurement
Whole-part relationships	Solving problems

These concepts and skills can be acquired as a child has time and space to initiate activities with such open-ended materials as:

Blocks	Dough
Cubes	Clay
Pegs	Water
Finger paint	Sand
Brush paint	Wood

Thus, the basic concepts and skills for reading, writing, and mathematics are learned as children . . .

PLAY

Source: From Swedlow, R. (1986). Chart: Children play: Children learn (p. 33). In J. S. McKee (Ed.), *Play: Working Partner of Growth* (pp. 29–34). Wheaton, MD: Reprinted by permission of R. Swedlow and the *Association for Childhood Education International,* 11141 Georgia Ave., Ste. 200, Wheaton, MD. © 1986 by the Association.

❧ **RESEARCH STUDY** ❧
Games Babies Play

Research Questions: As education coordinator for an early childhood program that was beginning a home-based parent education program for Chinese, Filipino, Mexican and American mothers of European descent, Van Hoorn wanted to find out how to strengthen cultural understandings and links between the home visitors and the families they would be serving. To further that understanding and possibly have it serve as a starting point for home visiting activities, she wanted to find answers to several questions about how mothers and babies play together. She asked the following research questions: What kinds of games do the mothers and babies play together? How do those games differ from culture to culture and what, if anything, do they have in common? How do the games reflect the culture of the family?

Research Method: The information for the study was gathered in two ways. First, the interviewer made friends with the mother and asked her to describe the games she played with her baby. Then she asked the mother to show how she played the games with her child. One-hundred-and-fifty-two interviews were conducted with mothers from four cultures: Chinese, Filipino, Mexican, and European-descent American. Assistants from the same culture as that of the mother were employed as interpreters when they were needed. Altogether, the mothers demonstrated 450 games.

Examples of Chinese games included Count the Insects (pointing to body parts), a clapping game, a swinging game, and a rowing game in which mother and child row back and forth in synchrony. Filipino games included Open/Close Them, many variations on that theme, and tickling games. Mexican games were based on clapping, tickling, and rocking or swinging accompanied by rhymed verses. The most popular American games focused on disappearance and reappearance, such as peekaboo, followed by pat-a-cake (a clapping game).

Results and Conclusions: Van Hoorn concluded that in some ways "games do appear to reflect the specific culture. The most basic way . . .

believe in regard to objects, actions, and situations, and persistence in the play over a period of time.

Sociodramatic play also helps the child learn to put himself in another's place (Rubin & Howe, 1986), thereby fostering the growth of empathy and consideration of others. It helps him define social roles: He learns by experiment what it is like to be the baby or the mother, or the doctor or nurse. And it provides countless opportunities for acquiring social skills: how to enter a group and be accepted by them, how to balance power and bargain with other children so that everyone gets satisfaction from the play, and how to work out the social give-and-take that is the key to successful group interaction.

Play Contains Rich Emotional Values

The emotional value of play has been better accepted and understood than the intellectual or social value, since therapists have long employed play as a medium for the expresis that they transmit the language" (pp. 58–59). For example, she reported that most of the Chinese games involving words mentioned family relationships; many of the Filipino games were "didactic" and played in English—a fact the mothers ascribed to the influence of American missionaries; and several of the Mexican games reflected the hardships that pervaded their lives ("Tortillitas for dad and mom who are tired," "The carpenters of San Juan, they ask for bread and they don't give them any"). Although the Americans also used language in their games, they differed from the other groups by encouraging their babies to play more independently.

Besides these interesting differences, Van Hoorn found there were many elements the games had in common no matter which culture she observed. Most of the games were traditional and had been handed down in families. These were action games based mainly on clapping, swinging, rocking, running, finger play, tickling, and appearance/disappearance. The games generally promoted the social values of mutuality, cooperation, and attachment, and mothers from various cultures signalled to babies that this was play by smiling, exaggerating their facial expressions, and emphasizing rhythmic expression.

Implications: I know of no research having to do with children that demonstrates so clearly the fact that people from a variety of cultures have some things in common and also differ in interesting ways. By identifying the elements held in common, this research holds out hope that it is possible to build bridges of understanding between people of differing backgrounds by using these commonalities as a foundation.

The study also demonstrates how valuable it is to make every effort to identify and understand what the differences are. This identification and appreciation of differences forms the rest of the foundation of understanding so indispensable when building bridges between cultures.

Source: From *Games That Babies and Mothers Play* by J. Van Hoorn. In P. Monighan-Nourot, B. Scales, J. Van Hoorn with M. Almy, (1987), *Looking At Children's Play: A Bridge Between Theory and Practice*. New York: Teachers College Press.

sion and relief of feelings (Axline, 1969; Gil, 1991). Children may be observed almost any place in the dramatic centre expressing their feelings about doctors by administering shots with relish or their jealousy of a new baby by walloping a doll, but play is not necessarily limited to the expression of negative feelings. The same doll that only a moment previously was being punished may next be seen being crooned to sleep in the rocking chair (Curry & Bergen, 1988).

Omwake cites an additional emotional value of play (Moffitt & Omwake, n. d.). She points out that play offers "relief from the pressure to behave in unchildlike ways." In our society so much is expected of children, and the emphasis on arranged learning can be so intense that play becomes indispensable as a balance to pressures to conform to adult standards that may otherwise become intolerable.

Finally, play offers the child an opportunity to achieve mastery of his environment. When he plays, he is in command. He establishes the conditions of the experience by using his imagination, and he exercises his powers of choice and decision as the play pro-

❧   *Consider the planning and social skills that were required in order for a group of four-year-olds to complete this building.*

gresses. The attendant opportunities for pretended and actual mastery foster the growth of ego strength in young children.

Play Develops the Creative Aspect of the Child's Personality

Play, which arises from within, expresses the child's personal, unique response to the environment. It is inherently a self-expressive activity that draws richly on the child's powers of imagination. Since imaginative play is also likely to contain elements of novelty, the creative aspect of this activity is readily apparent. Evidence is also accumulating that links opportunities for free play with the ability to solve problems more easily following such experiences (Sutton-Smith & Roberts, 1981).

The freedom to experiment creatively with behaviour in the low-risk situations typical of play is one of the virtues mentioned by Bruner (1974), who points out that play provides a situation in which the consequences of one's actions are minimized and there are many opportunities to try out combinations of behaviour that under other circumstances could never be attempted. In addition, Sutton-Smith (1971) points out that play increases the child's repertoire of responses. Divergent thinking is characterized by the ability to produce more than one answer, and it is evident that play provides opportunities to develop alternative ways of reacting to similar situations (Pepler, 1986). For example, when the children pretend that a fierce dog is breaking into their house, some may respond by screaming in mock terror, others by rushing to shut the door, and still others

❧   *"What was that you told me to get at the market?"*

by attacking the "dog" or throwing water on him. The work of Lieberman (1968) provides added indications that playfulness and divergent thinking are related—though which comes first remains to be determined.

Another researcher interested in "pretend" play is Garvey (1977, 1979). She points out various ways children signal to each other that they are embarking on "pretend" play or have stopped pretending. These include *negation* ("Well, you're just Jon. You can't be a monster while we eat lunch"), *enactment of a role* (crying affectedly like a baby, for example), or *stating the role or transformation that is taking place.* ("This is the operating table—lie down, baby, so I can cut you up!")

In young children creative play is expressed primarily in two ways: through the unusual use of familiar materials and equipment and through role playing and imaginative play.

No matter what value the theoretician perceives in play, the fact remains that it is common to all cultures and that it is the lifeblood of childhood. Thus Russians may offer hollow blocks while reasoning that their size promotes cooperation, whereas Canadians may offer them on the grounds that their cumbersome qualities develop feelings of mastery. But the children continue to use blocks with satisfaction regardless of adult rationalizations, just as they continue to play house on the windswept tundra of the North and in the Wendy corners of the British Infant School.

❧ Developmental Stages of Play

As is true in so many other areas, children's play progresses through a series of stages. There are two particularly well-known ways of identifying these, and a combination of the two is often used by researchers (Bergen, 1988), because they concentrate on differing aspects of the activity.

The first of these has its roots in Piaget (1962). In this theory, play is divided into stages according to the way children use play materials. Thus, play begins at the *functional* level (simple, repetitive, exploratory activity—as simple as a baby playing with her toes or a two-year-old squeezing dough through his fists). The next stage is *constructive* play (activity that has some purpose or goal, such as pouring water to fill a bucket), which develops into *dramatic play* (play involving pretend circumstances), and finally proceeds to the stage of *games with rules*.

It is the two middle levels of play, constructive and dramatic or fantasy, that are of most interest to preschool teachers. According to Butler, Gotts, and Quisenberry (1978), constructive play is most frequently seen in children aged two to four years, and it is characterized by children learning the uses of simple or manageable play materials and then employing them to satisfy their own purposes. For example, a child might learn how to string beads and then make a necklace for himself. Dramatic play increases in frequency as children mature, and the golden age of sociodramatic role playing develops between ages four and seven, although we see the beginnings of this play in much younger children. It is at this level that we see children assigning roles ranging from "teacher" to "baby" to "dog biter" to themselves and others around them (Pellegrini & Boyd, 1993).

The second commonly used system for identifying stages of play is one developed by Parten (1932, 1933), which divides play according to the kind of social interaction that is taking place between children. In this system of classification play develops from *solitary* through *parallel* play (playing beside but not with another child); to *associative* play (playing together); and, ultimately, to *cooperative* play (playing together with role assigning and planning).

This division into steps is not a mutually exclusive one, however. For example, in an analysis of just one thirty-minute observation of children at an easel, Reifel and Yeatman (1993) demonstrated that the children's play involved four levels or kinds of play (parallel, associative, cooperative, and pretend). While acknowledging that solitary play happens more frequently with younger children, research by Rubin (1977) provides evidence that there are varying levels of sophistication in solitary play. That is, while some of that kind of play takes place at the functional level, some of it, as anyone can attest who has watched a four-year-old playing alone with a dollhouse, uses a great deal of imaginative language, role assigning, and story telling at a more mature, dramatic play level. Therefore, the teacher should not assume that solitary play by older preschoolers is generally regressive and undesirable. It is particularly important to recognize the value of such individual playful preoccupation in day care centres, where children are almost relentlessly in contact with other people all day long. Children need the opportunities to think and develop their ideas through play by themselves as well as while in the company of other children, and they need opportunities for privacy too. Of course, if solitary play continues too long or is the only kind of play indulged in by a four-year-old, it should be cause for concern, but some of this less social play is to be expected and even encouraged for most children attending preschool.

Parallel play also continues to have its uses even after group play has developed, and it is often used by three-year-olds as an effective way to enter a group, the children first playing alongside and then with the group as they work their way into the stream of activities. Perhaps teachers could deliberately utilize this strategy with three-year-olds, encouraging them to play beside the other youngsters as a stepping stone to more direct social encounters.

Educational Implications

Although preschool teachers are likely to see functional, constructive, and dramatic play, they will rarely come across the final Piagetian stage—games with rules—because this kind of play is the prerogative of older children. The child care centre teacher should realize that organized, competitive games are developmentally inappropriate as well as uncreative for young children. Activities such as relay races, dodgeball, and kick the can are loved by second- and third-graders but do not belong in centres for younger children.

While hoping to foster originality and imagination in young children's play, we must realize that not every idea generated by the children will be new, no matter how supportive and encouraging the atmosphere of the school. Children's inspirations will be like flashes—touches here and there, embedded in a foundation of previously played activities. There will always be a lot of "old" mixed in with a little "new."

Finally, the teacher should be prepared for the somewhat chaotic quality of creative play, since it is impossible to organize inspiration before it happens. But this chaos can be productive, and the teacher can maintain reasonable order by picking up unused materials and returning them to their place and by seeing that the play does not deteriorate into aimless running about.

ᥫ Factors Likely to Facilitate Creative Play

Avoid Dominating the Play

As is true with self-expressive materials, teachers should do their best to avoid dominating the play experience and seek instead to foster children's abilities to express themselves in their own unique ways. Such teachers help children base their play on their own inspirations because they are convinced youngsters can be trusted to play productively without undue intervention and manipulation (Jones & Reynolds, 1992).

This freedom to generate their own ideas can be difficult for some teachers to allow, and the tension between enhancing self-expression and the temptation to use play to further adult goals is not new. As Nourot recognizes, "This paradox—balancing knowledge of the possibilities for learning inherent in play with total freedom for the child to play without adult intervention—plagued [even] the earliest early childhood educators" (1991, p. 197). Indeed, some teachers are so eager to use play as a medium for teaching that they cannot resist overmanipulating it in order to provide a "good learning experience." For example, I recently visited a teacher who had taken the children to the fire station for a visit. The next day, overwhelmed by the temptation to use play as an avenue for teaching, she set out all the hats, hoses, ladders, and pedal trucks she could muster, and as the children walked in the door, she pounced on them, announcing, "Boys and girls, I have the most wonderful idea. Remember when we went to the fire station yesterday? Well, why don't we play that here today? Chris, you can be the chief. Now, who wants to hold the hose?"

Children may learn a good deal about fire engines this way, and if this is the real purpose, very well. However, the spontaneous, creative quality of the play will be greatly reduced by the teacher's using this approach. It is generally better to wait until the children express an interest and then ask them how you can help and what they need.

On the other hand, there are other circumstances in which the teacher must assume a more direct, intervening role since, as mentioned earlier, some children come to the centre with poorly developed play skills. This approach was first investigated by Smilansky (1968) when she examined differing methods teachers might use to stimulate increased sociodramatic play among children who came from families of the poor. In her more recent work, Smilansky has continued to be a strong advocate of deliberate intervention. In *Facilitating Play* (1990) Smilansky and Shefatya cite a number of studies that indicate such intervention has produced rich dividends for these children, ranging from increased receptive and expressive language skills, higher intellectual competence, and more innovation and imaginativeness, to reduced aggression, better impulse control, and better emotional and social adjustment. Because of these benefits, sociodramatic, make-believe play should be included as a vital element in every preschool and kindergarten day, and during such play teachers should help the children gain skills rather than focusing on content or subject matter.

♍   *Teacher interest can really encourage children's satisfaction in playing together.*

Butler and associates (1978) describe this approach well when they advise that "you become an active participant in the play by making suggestions, comments, demonstrating activities or using other means relevant to the situation" (p. 68).

The problem with recommending consistent intervention in some children's play is that this can be tricky advice to give beginning teachers, since many beginners have great difficulty maintaining the subtle blend of authority and playfulness required to sustain this role. Instead, they either overmanage and overwhelm the children or reduce themselves to "being a pal"—approaches not at all what those authors had in mind. It is vital to remember that even when teaching children with special educational needs, *the purpose is not to dominate but to stimulate play*. The teacher should make interventions accordingly, stepping in only when necessary and withdrawing whenever possible. The following suggestions are intended to illustrate some effective ways of doing this.

Make a Special Point of Including Children Who Have Special Needs in the Play

It can be an unfortunate fact that children who have various disabilities are often not included in the play of other children at school. This can be due to a variety of reasons including inexperience (on both sides), being at a different developmental level than other children are, or having limited communication skills because of restricted hearing abilities or vision problems. Then, too, sometimes these children have been overly sheltered from contact with other children or have spent an unusual amount of time in special education situations in which the emphasis has been on drill and practice rather than in a more playful environment. Such youngsters in particular need the relief offered by play.

Whatever the reason for the limited participation, these children, like all other children, are entitled to and benefit from endless, rich opportunities to experience the joy of playful living. However, for this to happen may require special attention from the teacher.

A variety of specific suggestions are incorporated throughout *The Whole Child* and more thoroughly in chapter 9, but a quick reminder is included here of a basic approach that will encourage play to develop. Remember to explain in matter-of-fact terms to the other children the nature of the child's disability and to suggest some appropriate ways they could include the youngster in the activity. Be careful to always include activities in the curriculum plan at which you know the child with the handicap can be successful. (Linder's *Transdisciplinary Play-Based Intervention* (1993) and Spodek and Saracho's *Dealing with Individual Differences in the Early Childhood Classroom* (1994) are indispensable references for such activities.) Keep an attentive eye on what is happening in order to promote as much success as possible during the play experience, and be sure to commend the children in a low-key way for that success when it is appropriate to do so.

Some Practical Ways to Stimulate and Extend Play

I think about play as being like pulling taffy—the more it is stretched and extended, the better the result! To be most helpful to the children it is important to pay attention to what they are playing and to think a little ahead of what is happening so that the teacher can encourage the play to continue *before* it languishes.

One way to do this is to ask the children what will happen next. For example, if they are playing "going to the market," the teacher might ask, "Now you've got all those big bags of groceries, I wonder how you're going to get them home?" Or "I see you've bought a lot of soup and crackers—does your family have a pussycat, or an elephant? What do you suppose they'd like to eat?"

Suggesting additional roles for bystanders to fill can also extend play. Perhaps there's a child on the sidelines yearning to join the others at the airplane/rocket site. A question such as "Gee, how's that airplane going to fly without any gas?" [pause] "Perhaps Aahmed could use that hose and help you" or "I see you all have such full grocery carts—where could that check-out person be?"

It is also very important to provide enough time for play to develop (Christie & Wardle, 1992). When Johnsen and Peckover (1988) compared the kinds of play that took place among children during fifteen- and thirty-minute play intervals, they found that the amount of group play, constructive play, and dramatic play increased substantially in the later portion of the thirty-minute sessions. As they commented, it takes time for children to recruit other players, conceive and assign roles, and get the play under way. It seems to me that the play arena where this requirement of plenty of time is most apparent is the block corner, where construction requires much satisfying time before other sorts of playful interaction can begin.

And, finally, never forget the value of enriching and extending the play by use of language—putting what the children are doing into words. Doing this while the play is going on, recapitulating it in large group, and recalling yesterday's or last week's play by means of pictures or discussion at the start of the next self-select period will delight the children as well as increase their own ability to think about what they are doing or have accomplished already.

❧   *There can be more than one right way to ride a trike.*

🎜   *The children loved seeing their teacher receive her allergy shot. It sparked a lot of reminiscences as well as stimulating productive play after the nurse departed.*

Encourage Divergence of Ideas and Unusual Uses of Equipment

As in creative thought, the teacher seeks to remain open to originality of ideas in the children's play and to do everything possible to reinforce their production of imaginative ideas by giving them the satisfaction of trying out the ideas. For this reason the use of equipment is not overrestricted, and children are encouraged to use familiar equipment in original and unusual ways. Play materials are kept accessible so they are instantly available when the children require them.

Sometimes such uses can be quite ingenious. An acquaintance told me an interesting instance of such an unconventional idea. His little boy was going through the stage of flipping light switches on, something he could just manage to do by standing on tiptoe and shoving up on the switch. The trouble was that he was too short to pull the switch down again, so his father always had to walk over and turn the light off for him. This went on for several days; and finally, as he said, "I reached my limit—I'd had it. He flipped the switch, and I was just too tired to get up and turn it off. I was really mad. So I said to him, 'All right Joey, I've warned you and you did it anyway. Now *you* think up some way to turn it off, and you do it before I count to ten. No! You can't drag the chair over there; that scratches the floor.' And so," he continued, "I began to count one, two, three, four. Well, he just stood there for a minute and looked at the light and looked at me. Then he ran over to me, took my steel measuring tape out of my pocket, and hurried over to the switch. He extended the tape up to reach it, hooked the little metal lip over the switch, and pulled it down. I gotta hand it to that kid! Don't you think that was smart? After all, he's only three!"

This incident is a particularly felicitous example of using familiar equipment in an original way, but teachers can have this kind of original thinking happen at preschool too if they do not overrestrict children and equipment. Many things children want to try out are unconventional but not seriously dangerous. I have seen various children try the following things, which though unusual, were reasonably safe.

1. A child turned a dump truck upside down and pushed it along, making train noises.

2. Another one extended the slide by hooking a board to the end of it. Then, finding that it slid off and dumped her on her bottom, she talked her crony into bracing it at the end to keep it from slipping.

3. Another youngster used the half-moon plywood blocks to make a cradle for her doll.

None of these ideas worked perfectly or was earthshakingly different, but all of them had two cardinal advantages: They were original ideas that came from within the children, and they required a generous amount of imagination to make them be completely satisfactory.

And from another culture come these delightful examples collected by Spar and McAfee:

> On the Navajo reservation when I was little, I tended my grandfather's sheep. I would search out areas where I could find soft clay. I would shape figures of men and women and sheep with the clay. I would find sand and press it in my hand and shape it into a small hogan. I pushed my finger into the side to make a door and stuck a small twig in the top to make a chimney. The clay figures of the sheep went in a small twig corral near the hogan, and the people would fit into the hogan.
>
> There were many different colors of sandstone near our home. I spent hours pulverizing the sand and layering it in soft colors in an old canning jar.
>
> We made corncob dolls. The ear of corn was the doll, the silk was the hair, and the leaves were draped around the corn as clothes.
>
> We would fill the small milk-cartons our older brothers and sisters brought home from school with mud mixed with dried straw to make adobe brick. We built dollhouses with small tree twigs or branches.
>
> We played a lot with mud and water, constructing roads, ditches, rivers and canals.
>
> We molded mud-pies in empty flat cans.*

Cast Yourself in the Role of Assistant to the Child As You Help Play To Emerge

Fostering creative play demands that teachers add another skill to their repertoire: the ability to move with the child's play and support it as it develops. This does not mean that they play with the children as their peer, any more than it means they should sit on the sidelines being thankful that the children are busy and not in trouble. Rather, teachers who are skilled in generating creative play sense what will enhance the play and remain ready to offer suggestions that might sustain or extend it should this become necessary. Such teachers cast themselves in the role of supporter or facilitator of the child; they imagine themselves inside his skin and see the child's play from that point of view.

---

*From McAfee, O. (1976). "To make or buy." In M. D. Cohen & S. Hadley (Eds.), *Selecting Educational Equipment and Materials for Home and School*, p. 27. Wheaton, MD: Association for Childhood Education International. Reprinted by permission of Oralie McAfee and the Association for Childhood Education International, 11141 Georgia Ave., Ste. 200, Wheaton, MD. © 1976 by the Association.

This gives them an empathic understanding that enables them to serve his play needs well. Sometimes this insight is expressed by as simple a thing as going to the shed and getting out a variety of ropes, chains, and hooks for a construction project. Sometimes it is evident on a more subtle level as the decision is quietly made to delay snack in order that play may build to a satisfying climax.

Some of this empathic ability may go back to remembering what it was like to be a child oneself, and some of it may be related to opening oneself to sensing the child and taking time to "hear" him. It is a skill well worth cultivating because it makes possible the perception of the child's play in terms of what he intends. This enables the teacher to nurture the play by sensitively offering the right help at the right moment.

Putting the child in command of the play situation is valuable not only because it fosters his creative ability but also because it strengthens his feelings of mastery. When the teacher becomes his assistant and helper and defers to his judgement, the child is freed to determine what will happen next in his play. He exercises his ability to make choices and decisions. As mentioned previously, Erikson maintains that becoming autonomous and taking the initiative are fundamental tasks of early childhood. Creative play presents one of the best opportunities available for developing these strengths.

A Rich Background of Actual Life Experience Is Fundamental to Developing Creative Play

Children build on the foundation of real experience in their play. The more solid and rich the background of experience that children accumulate, the more varied the play will become. Field trips, holidays, and experiences with many ethnic groups, as well as things brought into the school in the way of science experiments, books, and visitors, will increase the base of experience upon which they can build their play (Woodard, 1986). There is no substitute for this background. In addition, play is thought to serve the function of clarifying and integrating such experiences (Piaget, 1962) as the child gains a greater understanding of reality through his recapitulation of it in make-believe.

Equipment Plays an Important Role in Facilitating Play

Buy Equipment That Encourages the Use of Imagination

The kinds of equipment the teacher provides have a considerable influence on the play that results. Research indicates that children younger than age three benefit from the use of realistic play props when involving themselves in pretend play (McLoyd, 1986). Then, as the children mature and as their ability to represent reality through imagination increases, it becomes more desirable to offer them less realistic items to play with (Pellegrini & Boyd, 1993). Thus a two-and-a-half-year-old may play house more freely using actual cups and saucers, whereas a four-year-old may simply pretend he is holding a cup in his hand with equal satisfaction.

Of course, I am not advocating that three- and four-year-olds should never have realistic playthings to enjoy. We all know that dolls, dress-up clothes, and little rubber animals are beloved at that age and act as powerful enhancers of play. I just mean that teachers should not go overboard on supplying every little thing. Some things are best left to the child's imagination.

Where larger pieces of equipment are concerned, however, teachers can make their money go further and enhance the potential variety of play experiences for the children by buying equipment that can be used in a variety of ways and that is not overly realistic (Chaillé & Young, 1980; Pepler, 1986). Boards, blocks, and ladders, for example, lend themselves to a hundred possibilities, but a plywood train tends to be used mostly as a plywood train. A good question to ask before investing a lot of money is, "How many ways could the children use this?" If there are three or four rather different possibilities, it is a good indication that the children will use their imaginations to think of many more.

Select a Wide Variety of Basic Kinds of Equipment

There also needs to be good range and balance to the sorts of equipment selected. This means that careful attention must be paid to all areas of the curriculum, both indoors and outdoors. For example, puzzles should be chosen not only with a varying number of pieces in mind but also in terms of different kinds of puzzles: Have they informative pictures in the frame behind the pieces? Are they printed on both sides to make them more complicated? Are they the three-dimensional kind? And outdoor, wheeled equipment should not be limited to only trikes and wagons. Instead, scooters, ride 'em toys, and a wheelbarrow should be included.

Although equipment does and should vary from school to school, it is also helpful to refer to a basic list from time to time as a source of ideas and inspirations. One of the best is *Selecting Educational Equipment and Materials for School and Home* (Moyer, 1986). This reference is particularly useful for new centres because it sets priorities for essential first-year purchases, suggests second- and third-year additions, and extends from infant through upper elementary levels.

Change Equipment Frequently

Changing accessories in the basic play areas such as the housekeeping area and the block corner will attract different children, keep life fresh and interesting for them, and encourage them to play creatively. Adding boys' clothes or an old razor (minus the blade, of course) or bringing the guinea pig for a visit might break the monotony in the housekeeping corner. Using trains, rubber animals, dollhouse furniture, or the cubical counting blocks could provide variety in the block area. Moving play equipment to a new location is another fine way to vary play and foster creativity. Boys, for example, are more likely to play house if the stove and refrigerator are out on the grass or if the house is made of hollow blocks for a change. Different locations attract different customers.

Rearrange Equipment Frequently and Recombine It in Appealing and Complex Ways

Besides moving equipment to new places, it is also valuable to consider how it can be recombined. What if we moved the mattress to the base of the low wall? Would this attract (and protect) the two-year-olds while they teeter along its edge or jump freely from it? What if the refrigerator box was moved near the climbing gym with boards, ladders, and sawhorses provided nearby? What if the pots and pans from the sandbox were included in this play? Or perhaps we might move the refrigerator carton over to the sandbox. What would happen then?

A helpful concept to understand here is the one presented by Kritchevsky and Prescott (1977) and Shipley, (1993). They point out that *simple* play units such as swings or tricycles have low absorbing power; that is, each item soaks up only one child at a time for play. When two kinds of materials or equipment are combined, such as when digging equipment is added to the sandbox, the play unit becomes *complex*. This has stronger absorptive power for children than the simple units do. Better yet are the *super play units*. These units, which combine three or more kinds of equipment and materials at once (for example, sand, digging tools, and water), do an even more effective job of drawing groups of children into cooperative play for extended periods of time. Evidently, if we wish to draw children into interactive, creative play, we should do all we can to concoct these superunits for their delight.

Of course, teachers do not have to produce all the ideas for recombining equipment and enriching play. If the children are encouraged and their ideas supported, they will contribute many fruitful ideas for such elaborations and recombinations on their own, thus providing an additional outlet for their creative ideas.

Store Equipment in Convenient, Easy-to-Reach Places

Besides purchasing equipment that will stimulate imagination and changing and recombining it to keep the play fresh and interesting, the teacher must also arrange adequate storage for these materials. This is often the place that child care centres scrimp, but good storage will keep equipment available and save the teacher's sanity as well. Storage can actually make or break a play situation, so it is well worth the time, effort, and money involved to solve this problem adequately. Material should be conveniently arranged so that it can be reached easily, and, of course, it should be returned to the same place after use to expedite locating it the next time it is needed. Labelled shelves, racks, hooks, and storage closets that are large enough all help. In addition, storage should be located close at hand so the teacher may continue to provide supervision while getting something out that the children have requested.

Keep Play Areas Safe and Attractive

The general appearance and presentation of the play areas will inspire (or discourage) children to play there. All areas should be set up at the beginning of the day in a fresh, appealing way. New touches should be added here and there to spark interest and avoid dull repetition.

Play is also better encouraged if materials are not allowed to degenerate into a shambles during playtime. No one wants to wade through a welter of costumes on the floor or build in a chaos of blocks dumped and abandoned in that corner. Attractiveness fosters attraction, and the teacher is the person who bears the primary responsibility for creating and maintaining appealing play areas.

Moreover, when things are left scattered about, they not only lose their appeal, they also become navigational hazards. Children (and sometimes teachers) rarely watch their feet as they hasten from one area to another, and loose pegs, little cars, and beads on the floor increase the likelihood that someone may fall and strike his head on the corner of a chair or table.

A Final Thought

One last reminder: Children need plenty of freedom, time, and materials if they are to become maximally involved in imaginative play. They need the freedom to move from one activity to another as their tastes dictate, they need uninterrupted time to build a play situation through to its satisfying completion, and they need enough materials to furnish a challenge and provide a feeling of sufficiency. Making these resources available is a good way to say to a child in tangible terms that there is enough of what he needs in the world and that he need not scheme and plot to get his fair share.

❦ Specific Activities to Encourage Creativity in Play*

Creative Dramatic Play—"Just Pretending"

Creative dramatic play such as dress-up and housekeeping is usually social and imaginative in nature, and its value as a vehicle for imagination cannot be overemphasized. Not only does it provide many opportunities for divergent ideas to come forth, but according to Singer and Singer (1990) such make-believe activity also has many additional benefits. Among these are that children who use more imaginative play are measurably happier, their verbalization is richer in such things as metaphors and descriptive statements, and the amount of actual physical aggression is decreased.

Pretend play always involves more than one child at a time and contains a lot of role assigning and role assuming ("Now, you be the mother and I'll be . . ."). Three-year-olds tend to play a simple version of "house," but four-year-olds love to embellish the premises with dogs, cartoon characters, naughty children, and interesting domestic catastrophes. All these activities develop the use of language, since the children will discuss and describe among themselves what is happening ("Let's get the babies and pretend they've been in that mud again."). Teachers should encourage this use of imaginative language whenever possible.

Dress-up clothes and props can enhance the play, but having unstructured materials available that may be used in many ways is even more desirable because it helps the children be inventive and use their imaginations. Thus a scarf may become a hat, an apron, a blanket, or even a child's wished-for long hair.

Suggested Variations

Some teachers enjoy assembling play kits for the children. This is all right as long as the teacher resists the tendency to supply every little thing or to offer such specific equipment that there is no room left for developing a creative use for a familiar material. It is

---

*I am indebted to the staff and students at the Santa Barbara Community College Children's Centre for their assistance in developing the outlines on the following pages.

essential to vary dress-up clothes and housekeeping accessories regularly. Using different hats and costumes, different pans, empty food packages, or a milk bottle holder and bottles can kindle new interest. Dress-up clothes for both sexes should be provided. Hats, vests, and old firefighters' jackets and boots will find favour with boys, but both sexes should be encouraged to try all kinds of garments. Ethnic costumes are a nice variation and often enhance the image of the child who lends them, but be sure these are not valuable, treasured mementos. Doctor play is always popular, partly because it represents thinly veiled concerns about sexual differences and partly because it offers invaluable chances for children to play out their fear of doctors, shots, and being hurt. The teacher should be available for interpretation and control when such play takes place. Additional variations in props that have found favour in our school include a modest amount of paraphernalia donated by a local fast food chain, obsolete typewriters and other business equipment, a birthday party box, wedding veils and bouquets, backpacks and camping gear, and, always, cowpoke accessories such as an old saddle and plenty of boots.

A. Preparation

1. Be attuned to the interests of the children. Has something happened in the life of the group that could be played through? Perhaps a child has had his tonsils out or the children went to see a car being lubricated. Have a few props available that may enhance this play if it develops. Ask the children to improvise additional items as the play develops.

2. Think back to yesterday's play: Could it be drawn over and continued with satisfaction today? Is there a little something extra that might be added to sustain interest?

3. Arrange materials attractively. If dress-up clothes are offered, hang them neatly in view, or set out play accessories in an appealing way. Make sure the clothing is clean and not torn, that buttons and fastenings are in place, and that a variety of clothing for both sexes is available.

4. Hold one or two possibilities in reserve to offer in case play begins to lag (perhaps an old piece of rope to hitch the wagon to the trike in case the children decide to lubricate a trailer truck).

B. Procedure

1. Sit nearby, or, while working in the general area, keep an eye on the role playing activity.

2. Stay alert; step in with a facilitating suggestion *before* the play deteriorates into a hassle, but be prepared for the children to refuse your idea if they wish.

3. The teacher's role is facilitation of the play, not participation as a peer. However, sometimes it is necessary to be more involved at first and then withdraw gradually.

4. Be sensitive to the children's needs as they materialize. *It is better to supply helpful equipment on the spot as requested* rather than tell the children you will "get it tomorrow; it's put away now."

5. Ask the children for ideas. For example, if they request train tickets or say they need eggs to scramble, ask them what they could use for that purpose. Encourage them to concoct solutions and produce creative problem-solving ideas.

6. Help them give direction and focus to their play by asking them occasionally what they plan to do next. "Now that your children are up from nap, I wonder what they're going to do next?"

7. Remember that too obvious an interest in the play or amused comments to other adults will make the children ill at ease and self-conscious, thereby destroying some of their pleasure in the activity.

8. Tidy up unobtrusively whenever possible in order to keep the area attractive and safe. (This advice should not be construed as advocating compulsive neatness but is intended to encourage the teacher to pick clothes up off the floor and return unused, scattered equipment to the appropriate play area.)

C. Clean-up

1. Warn the children in advance that it is almost time for the play to draw to a close.

2. Encourage them to restore order and to take satisfaction in arranging the materials for the next time. This is also a good time to chat with them about what they did and what fun they had.

3. Remove any torn, soiled, or broken materials for repair or discard them.

4. Put away accessories not intended for use during the next play period.

Blocks

Blocks, ranging from Froebel's "gifts" to the big hollow blocks designed by Hill, are one of the timeless, classic play materials that have withstood the many comings and goings of ideologies and theories of early childhood education. No matter what theory of learning is espoused by which educator, children have continued to play with blocks with concentrated devotion.

The sheer variety of kinds of blocks available for use in the preprimary school rooms attests to their appeal. These range from large hollow ones through unit blocks to the so-called cubical counting blocks (which have so many other wonderful uses besides counting!). In addition, there are a number of well-designed types of interlocking blocks available that foster the development of fine muscle abilities.

The quantity of blocks available is also an important point to consider. There is no such thing as having too many. This conclusion has been supported by Bender (1978), who found that increasing the supply of hollow blocks from twenty to seventy tripled the number of children participating, generated a great deal more conversation and role playing, reduced fighting significantly, and increased the amount of problem solving.

Unfortunately, because of their initial expense, many schools stint on this kind of equipment, but there are ways around that problem (Stephens 1991). Initially, cardboard blocks can serve as a reasonable substitute for the more expensive hollow ones, or someone with an electric saw can make an inexpensive but copious set of unit blocks from pine until the school can begin acquiring the longer lasting maple variety. Then, every year, additional blocks should be included without fail in the equipment budget.

Infants begin to stack objects (a primitive block building skill) almost as soon as they are able to sit up, and children continue to use blocks with satisfaction throughout elementary school years if they are given this opportunity. Blocks provide endless opportunities for the development of emerging perceptual-motor skills. Stacking, reaching, grasping, lifting, shoving, carrying, and balancing are only a few of the countless motor skills practiced in block play.

Possibilities for emotional satisfactions abound as well. What teacher has not seen a shy child build himself a corral and seek safety within it, or a pent-up child send blocks toppling down, or two little girls construct block houses and establish families firmly within their confines?

Blocks lend themselves readily to achieving large effects quickly, thereby building ego-expanding structures of considerable height and large dimensions, which help the child feel strong and masterful, as well as providing opportunities for him to be creative.

Blocks provide unparalleled opportunities for understanding visual-spatial relationships (Reifel, 1984). What does a structure look like when viewed from one side and then the other, or when seen from above or peered up at from underneath? They also provide opportunities for developing insight into mathematics and physics as the children struggle with cause-and-effect relationships when unbalanced towers topple down or roofs remain in place.

Blocks are also strong in their contribution to the child's learning the intellectual operations basic to Piagetian theory. They offer many opportunities for the child to grasp the principle that operations are reversible (when a tower falls, it returns to a prior form). They may be used to demonstrate conservation (four blocks can be piled into a variety of shapes and yet retain their quality of fourness), and they provide additional opportunities to demonstrate the principle of transitivity (four short blocks equal two longer ones, which in turn equal one very long one). Blocks have also been found to be very productive elicitors of language. For example, when Isbell and Raines compared the use of language in the block, housekeeping, and thematic centres, they found that the children were "more verbally fluent, used more communication units and produced more diverse vocabulary" in the block centre than in the other two locations (1991, p. 144).

Finally, blocks foster the development of creative play. By nature they are unstructured and may be used to build anything that suits the child's fancy (Cartwright, 1988, 1990). Older children enjoy planning such structures in advance, but younger ones will content themselves with the experience of stacking and balancing for its own sake and perhaps assign a useful function to the construction at a later point in the building.

Suggested Variations

Accessories that may be offered to stimulate block play are legion and can add a lot of attractiveness to the area. However, teachers should not overlook the value and delight inherent in presenting block play with blocks alone. (I make this point because, from time to time, I have seen students at the Institute become so dependent on accessories that they lose sight of the value of block construction combined with imagination and almost stifle the children with too many props.)

When accessories *are* used, the touches of colour they can lend add beauty as well as stimulation to the play. Dollhouse furniture and rug samples, small rubber animals, and miniature people are all successful accoutrements. Variations in blocks themselves, such

ᕬ   *Building this close to the source of supply is always a temptation for block builders but eventually leads to overcrowding and frustration.*

as gothic arches, flat "roofing" blocks, spools, and cubical counting blocks, add embellishment. Not all the blocks should be offered all the time; it is sound to save the arches, switches, or triangular blocks and ramps and offer them as interesting variations when the more common varieties begin to pall. The Skaneateles train is an incomparable block accessory; tracks and additional cars should be purchased every year, since it seems to be impossible to own enough of these materials. It is also fun to build pens for the rats and guinea pigs with blocks, although this requires careful supervision from the teacher for the animals' protection. Cars, trucks, derricks, boats, and airplanes are also delightful to use with block materials.

Outside, the addition of boards, sawhorses, ladders, and old bedspreads and parachutes will extend large block play in a satisfactory way. Large, sturdy boxes and cement pipes are additional accessories that make good combination units with blocks, and wagons and wheelbarrows are handy for carrying blocks about and delivering them to many locations in the yard.

It is also fascinating to combine large and small blocks indoors. Older children often enjoy using the small blocks as trimming on large-block constructions, and some creative and interesting structures can result from this merging of materials. If large blocks are moved close to where dramatic play is taking place, children will often incorporate them into the play in a way that facilitates and enlarges that activity. Moreover, Kinsman and Berk (1979) found that when these materials were combined (by simply removing a barrier that had been between them), sex-typed house and block play was reduced. Younger four- and three-year-olds in particular interacted more frequently with children of the opposite sex when this was done.

A. Preparation
   1. Make sure the blocks are well sorted and neatly arranged.
   2. Try to include accessories that are related to current curriculum interests; for example, it may stimulate play to offer some boats after a visit to the harbour.
   3. Recall what the children were interested in the previous day when they played with blocks, and be sure to have these materials (and a possible embellishment) readily available should they be called for again.
   4. Be sensitive to the expressed interests and requests of the children as they draw near the blocks; the best accessory is the one they request.
   5. Children may be attracted if the teacher builds some small, interesting structure to begin with (the old principle of the nest egg under the chicken); but this creation should be offered as a stimulus, not as a model intended for emulation.
   6. Avoid setting out every accessory the school owns. This usually results in a clutter, which ultimately discourages participation.
   7. Outdoors, a good supply of large hollow boxes should be set out at first. Children should be encouraged to get out the rest as needed. There is no point in owning a beautiful supply of outdoor blocks if they remain unused in the shed.

B. Procedure
   1. Settle yourself nearby on a low chair. *The teacher's presence is one of the best incentives to block play.*
   2. Teach the children to select blocks and carry them somewhat away from the shelves or storage shed so that everyone can easily reach more of them as building continues.
   3. Be an interested observer of the children's block play, but be ready to redirect children or offer suggestions to extend the activity according to their interests should the need arise. Avoid taking over the play; make sure it remains the children's activity.
   4. Remember that children need time to play with their block structures after they have built them. Children appreciate having the privilege of leaving such things up during nap or overnight if it is possible to arrange this.
   5. Remember to stress that block buildings belong to the children who did the work. Children may knock down their own structures but may not destroy the work of other children unless they have the owner's consent. Dumping all the blocks onto the floor and running off or throwing blocks should be prevented. Children who sweep blocks off the shelves need to stay and help pick them up.
   6. Drawing diagrams of the children's constructions from time to time or taking instant photos increases the child's interest and satisfaction in this activity. If a

copy is made, one copy can go home and the other be retained in the child's folder as part of his developmental record. Be sure to date it and note the child's companions and comments.

7. Mathematical relationships such as equality and seriated relationships should be casually drawn to the children's attention as the occasion warrants.

8. Tidy up as needed to keep the play area attractive and to make room for further building.

C. Clean-up

1. Some teachers discourage the use of blocks because they dislike picking them up, but this problem can be alleviated somewhat by encouraging the children to help, too. However, it is not desirable to enforce the rule, "You have to put away every block you got out before you leave the block corner." Because many children will not participate under these conditions, enforcement of this rule can spoil play. Teachers will obtain the best cooperation from the children if they warn far enough ahead of time that children have time to wind up their play and if they pitch in with them so everyone puts the blocks away together at the end of the morning.

2. Always categorize blocks neatly when putting them away, and shelve them with the long side in view so their size is readily apparent. *Never store blocks by dumping them into a bin or tub;* it is impossible for children to find needed sizes in such a welter, and it knocks corners off the blocks as well.

3. Return extra accessories to the block closet and arrange the remaining ones so they make attractive, colourful accents in the room.

Water Play

Water play is one of the freest, finest play opportunities we can offer children. Although inexperienced teachers often dread it because they fear the children may become too wild or overstimulated, the opposite of this behaviour is usually the case. Water play is absorbing and soothing; children will stay with it a long time and come away refreshed and relaxed if it is well presented. It is also valuable because it offers children many opportunities to work through conflicts resulting from the demands of toilet training (there is no better present for a newly trained two-year-old than a sprinkling can!), it provides relief from pressures and tensions, and it stimulates social play. Sometimes children will play companionably with others while using water, even though they remain isolated the rest of the day.

Activities such as pouring and measuring help develop eye-hand coordination. Children also acquire intellectual concepts having to do with estimating quantity (how much will the cup really hold?), with Piagetian conservation (but it looks like more in the tall bottle!), and with physical properties of water (what became of the water when we poured it on the hot sidewalk?). Crosser (1994) provides a particularly comprehensive analysis of the many things children can learn while playing with water, and chapters 20 and 21 of this book illustrate how water might be used to generate interesting curricula in depth.

❧   *Delicious!*

Water play should be offered several times a week to provide maximum satisfaction for the children. In winter a large indoor bathroom with a drain in the floor is an invaluable asset. When water play is set up in such a location, spills run off quickly. Water can be offered in deep dishpans or sinks but is best offered in larger containers, such as galvanized laundry tubs, water tables, concrete-mixing tubs made of plastic, or even wading pools. At the Institute we put the containers at floor level when possible because this keeps the children's clothes drier as they kneel and play.

Suggested Variations

Too many schools limit this kind of play to hand washing or dabbling in the sink. Although these activities are certainly better than not having water available at all, they stop far short of what children really require for this experience. Many variations can be employed for a change, although basic water play always remains a favourite. Running water from the hose is a fine thing to offer, though it is, of course, a warm weather activity. Water can be used in conjunction with a sandbox or mud pit with real pleasure. Apartments and manicured suburban gardens deprive children of the opportunity to play with such concoctions.

In addition, water can be offered to use in sinking, floating, pouring, and quantifying experiments. Unbreakable bottles and containers, as well as various sizes of sieves and funnels, can be saved for this purpose. Ice is a fascinating variation to offer, or washing activities with dolls, doll clothes, preschool furniture, cars, or tricycles can be presented. Scrubbing vegetables, watering the garden, and washing dishes should not be overlooked as additional variations, which have the added appeal of participating in meaningful work. Making a variety of pipes and joints available for assembling and using with water is fascinating to children and teaches them some valuable concepts of cause and effect. Adding sponges, soap, or a little colour will also change the appeal of the water and create additional interest.

A. Preparation

1. Decide what kind of water play you want to offer and what kind of water you wish to use (soapy, coloured, clear, hot, or cold).

2. Assemble additional equipment and accessories for play.

3. Be sure to include oilcloth or plastic aprons, deep containers for the water, sponges, and towels.

B. Procedure

1. Make any rules or guidelines clear to the children *before* they begin. Children cannot be allowed to run around in soaked shoes or clothing when it is cold. It is better to explain the temperature of the day and also the limits of the experience before someone impulsively gets drenched.

❧   *Sand and water go together like ham and eggs.*

2. The children will enjoy helping fill the tubs and setting out the equipment.

3. Put on aprons and roll sleeves up as far as possible. Remove shoes and do what you can to minimize the problem of getting wet, but be prepared for the fact that considerable dampness is the inevitable accompaniment of water play.

4. Expect some incidental splashing, but control deliberate splashing unless the weather is warm. You may give a splasher a second chance; but if a child persists, then the privilege of participating must be surrendered for a while.

5. While the children are playing, talk with them about pouring, measuring, the force of water pressure, or whatever you have planned as the focus of the activity.

6. Listen carefully to the children's comments and ideas, and change and provide equipment accordingly.

C. Clean-up

1. Children may help bail out water tubs or tip them over on the grass at the end of the play.

2. A nice let's-find-out lesson can be built around the use of a siphon when emptying the tub, and cause and effect demonstrated by simply removing the plug from the table!

3. If rags are at hand, many children like to help dry buckets and toys.

4. Replace all equipment in proper storage areas.

5. Wipe aprons and change wet clothes.

Mud and Sand

Mud and sand have wonderful, messy, unstructured qualities that make them among the most popular creative play materials in preschool (Miller, 1994). They offer rich tactile sensory experiences and provide emotional relief as well: Messing and slopping through water and sand or mud are relaxing and are thought by some psychologists to provide relief from the stringent toilet training demands of our society. These materials also facilitate a lot of social interaction. Older children play imaginatively and cooperatively with each other while digging tunnels, constructing roads, and carrying on "bake-offs"; but sand and mud are also rewarding for younger children to use, and they often settle down to this activity in a particularly absorbed and satisfied way. In short, the chance to mix, stir, pour, measure, mould, and squish sand and mud is an indispensable component of the curriculum.

Since this experience is often restricted at home, it is particularly important to offer it consistently at the centre, where it can be planned in advance and where it is relatively easy to clean up. It is good planning to locate the sandbox as far from the school door as possible, in the hope that some of the sand will shake off clothes on the way inside, and it is also sound to check pants cuffs when the play has been especially vigorous, to reduce the likelihood of dumping the whole sandbox on the carpet. The sandbox should have a wide border around it so that children may sit on it and stay warm and dry when the weather is chilly. A waterproof chest beside it will make storage of commonly used equipment easier; plastic laundry baskets also make good containers because they allow the sand to fall back into the sandbox.

Mud is different from sand, and the school should provide chances for the children to play in both these materials. A mud hole and the opportunity to dig deep pits and trudge around in mud are interesting to children, so a place in the yard should be set aside for this purpose. (If the holes are deep, it will be necessary to fence them off for safety's sake.) Children will dig astonishingly deep pits if given room, good tools, time, and opportunity, and the satisfaction of doing this work is plain to see on their faces.

Suggested Variations

It is a shame to leave the same old buckets and shovels in the sandbox day after day when there are so many interesting variations that may be employed. All kinds of baking and cooking utensils make excellent substitutes and may be readily and cheaply acquired at yard sales. Toy trucks and cars are nice to add too, particularly if they are wood or sturdy plastic, since metal ones rust and deteriorate alarmingly quickly if they are used outside. Sturdy tools of various kinds are good to use. (Remember that when digging large holes, children need real shovels or clamming shovels—often sold in surplus or sporting goods stores—just as they need real hammers and saws at the woodworking table.)

Adding water to sand and mud is the best accessory of all. It can be offered in deep galvanized washtubs or buckets or as running water from hoses (having two hoses available at once will reduce fighting and competition considerably). Many children will enjoy having temporary low tables, constructed from sawhorses and planks, added to the sandbox. Such tables are particularly helpful to provide when the weather is cold and children should not get chilled.

Substitutes for sand and water may be offered when the real thing is unavailable. Cornmeal is good for pouring and measuring and may be presented in deep tubs or a sand table indoors, but the reader should realize that cornmeal makes floors slippery and is difficult to clean up. Cleanup is easier if a small, battery-operated vacuum is kept nearby. Some schools also use rice, dried peas, or wheat as a substitute in cold weather.

Gardening is another useful variation of digging and working with mud. Since digging is the best, most involved part of gardening from the children's point of view, several weeks of this experience should be offered to the children *before* seeds are planted. The other part of gardening that young children enjoy the most is watering. Although this can be done with a hose that has a sprinkling head attached, it is easier to control if sprinkling cans and a big tub of water for filling them are provided instead. This allows the children to water to their heart's content without washing the seeds away or creating undue runoff.

A. Preparation

   1. Consider various possibilities for sand and mud play in terms of the weather and time available. If the day is warm, water is a valuable addition to this experience.

   2. Make sure the sand is at least damp so that it holds its form well when patted and moulded. It may be necessary to sprinkle it a little.

3. In hot weather, if the area is not shaded, set up beach umbrellas or large Japanese parasols to provide cool oases for the play.

4. In cold weather, encourage the children to sit on the edge of the sandbox to keep knees and seats of pants warm and dry.

5. Have some sandbox accessories set out as the children arrive, but be alert to special requests and ideas from the children. It is excellent policy to change equipment according to their expressed needs.

B. Procedure

1. Stay nearby and keep a careful eye on what is happening. Children will occasionally throw sand and will need to be controlled from time to time. Shovel users need lots of space and must learn to be careful of other people's toes and noses.

2. Think of additional ideas you might suggest to continue the play if the children's interest lags.

3. If the day is warm and water is being used freely, have the children roll up their pants and take their shoes off.

4. Encourage children to keep the sand in the box and mud in the pit so it will be there for play next time.

5. If sturdy shovels are being used for digging, make sure there is plenty of space between children and that they have shoes on so that shovel edges will not cut their feet.

6. Foster the use of imagination and language whenever possible by playfully chatting with the children about what they are doing.

C. Clean-up

1. Warn the children that it will soon be time to finish their play.

2. Solicit their help in gathering up the play equipment and putting it away.

3. If the day is warm, hose off the area to get rid of the sand and mud, or sweep up the extra sand and return it to the box.

4. Help the children brush each other off, and shake out cuffs of pants and sweaters.

5. Put away accessories that will not be used during the next play period.

℘ Summary

Play serves many valuable purposes in the life of the child. It provides occasions for intense practice of sensorimotor skills; the symbolic nature of imaginative play fosters development of the intellect and generates increased understanding of events; play facilitates role playing and develops social skills; it furnishes opportunities to work through emotional problems and to experience the relief of acting like a child instead of an adult; and it provides many occasions for children to be creative by using their imaginations and abilities to think in divergent ways. Best of all, play provides endless opportunities to experience joy and delight.

Teachers who wish to foster the creative aspects of play will seek to extend but avoid dominating it and will encourage children to try out original ways of using materials. They will purchase, plan, and arrange equipment so that creativity will be enhanced. But, above all, teachers who wish to foster creativity in play will cast themselves in the role of assistant to the children, seeking to move with and support their play as it develops and to serve their play needs to the best of the teachers' ability.

Questions and Activities

1. *Problem:* Suppose a parent comes to you, after touring the school, and says dubiously, "Well, it looks nice enough here, and I can see the children are happy; but don't they ever learn anything? Don't they ever do anything but play around here?" How would you reply?

2. Take time to make a brief record of the play of several children during the coming week. Can you find evidence in these observations that play is used symbolically by children to translate experience into a deeper understanding of events? Did you find evidence that children employ play to express emotions and work these through? Did you observe any instances in which the children generated new, divergent solutions to problems by trying them out in play?

3. What is the difference between overcontrolling play and acting in a supportive, fostering role that encourages it to develop in greater depth? Role play the same play situation, demonstrating differences between these two approaches.

4. *Problem:* In the winter, the children play outdoors at your centre, but water play cannot be offered outside for most of the year because it is too cold. Identify several ways it could be offered on a regular basis indoors.

5. Survey the play yard of your school. List the different play units around which activity occurs. Are there some that appear to generate more imaginative activities than others? Identify what properties these units possess in common. How are they alike?

6. Put all the housekeeping equipment away for a change, and offer only hollow blocks in its place and some props, such as pots and pans and dolls. Observe what happens to the children's play under these circumstances.

7. Try duplicating Bender's (1978) research by increasing the number of blocks available for the children to use (you may have to consolidate the supply of blocks from two or three rooms to accomplish this). What kinds of play did you see increase as a result of such consolidation? Did fighting increase or decrease? Do you think the results are valuable enough that it would be worthwhile to have more blocks for less time and pool the blocks permanently in this fashion?

Self-Check Questions for Review
Content-Related Questions

1. Explain how play helps each of the five selves of the child (physical, intellectual, emotional, social, and creative) develop.

2. List and describe the four developmental stages of play as identified by Butler, Rubin, and Piaget, and then list and describe the four stages of play identified by Parten. What is the difference between the two systems of classification?

3. What are three ways teachers can encourage creativity in play?

4. Describe how equipment may influence the play of children. Be sure to give several examples to illustrate your answer.

5. Pretend that you are escorting a visiting parent around your centre and compose an answer to her question, "Why do you have such a large block corner? Aren't they an awful lot of trouble to pick up all the time?" Be sure you explain the educational benefits of this material.

6. Now, explain to that same parent why you make a point of offering water, sand, and mud play to the children.

7. In regard to the Van Hoorn study about games the mothers played with their babies, give some examples of how the games differed among the four cultures studied. What points of similarity were there across the four cultures?

8. Give some examples from your own experience of how children have used equipment in new, unconventional ways. Why is it worthwhile to permit and even encourage such behaviour?

9. Is it ever appropriate for teachers to intervene in children's dramatic play? Explain why doing this is or is not a desirable approach for teachers to use.

10. Name two practical ways teachers can extend play and cause it to persist.

Integrative Questions

1. Imagine that a number of children are playing about families in the housekeeping corner. Suggest some possible ways that play could contribute to the development of each of the child's five selves.

2. A group of children playing outdoors with the tricycles have lined them all up and are playing "train." Suggest two possibilities you might propose to them that could extend their play. Be sure to put these suggestions into the sentences you would use if you were actually speaking to the children.

3. If you intended to dominate rather than extend the children's play, show how you would change your sentences to be more intrusive and overwhelming.

4. In her study of the games mothers played with their babies, Van Hoorn found there were some definite, underlying similarities about the games the mothers played, no matter which culture she observed. Identify at least one similarity and explain what you think might be the underlying reason or reasons for this similarity.

5. This is your first year teaching in a classroom of three-year-olds. You would like to add dishes to the housekeeping area, but there is no money for new ones. Propose three what-else-could-you-use-instead-of-new-ones solutions.

6. Explain how you could turn a simple play unit such as a climbing gym into a complex unit. Then explain what you might add to make it become a superunit.

7. The four-year-olds in your school have just returned from taking a bus ride.
   Possibility 1: Next day the teacher sets a number of chairs up just like the bus and has a bus driver's cap set out. She also has prepared some cut-up green paper for bus money.
   Possibility 2: Next day the teacher sets out on the children's bulletin board by the entry a number of Polaroid photos of yesterday's trip and encourages

the children to notice and comment on these as they arrive. Later on she sees a couple of children trying to fasten the wagon on to one of the trikes because they want to make a bus.

Explain which one of these situations is likely to generate more creative play by the children and provide reasons to support your answer.

References for Further Reading
Overviews

Bergen, D. (Ed.). (1988). *Play as a medium for learning and development: A handbook of theory and practice.* Portsmouth, NH: Heinemann. For a good overview of the values of play written in readable form by well-known specialists in the field, this book is hard to beat. *Highly recommended.*

Isenberg, J. P., & Jalongo, M. R. (1993). *Creative expression and play in the early childhood curriculum.* Englewood Cliffs, NJ: Merrill/Prentice Hall. This book is filled with practical suggestions about incorporating play and self-expressive materials into the classroom. *Highly recommended.*

The Teacher's Role

Jones, E., & Reynolds, G. (1992). *The play's the thing: Teachers' roles in children's play.* New York: Teachers College Press. This excellent book provides thoughtful discussions of various ways teachers can inhibit or support the play of young children—filled with examples. *Highly recommended.*

Encouraging Play by Children with Special Needs

Linder, T. W. (1993). *Transdisciplinary play-based intervention: Guidelines for developing a meaningful curriculum for young children.* Baltimore: Paul Brookes. If the reader can have only one book dealing with children who have special educational requirements, this is the one to get! In addition to many other subjects, Linder provides detailed information on play and play materials discussed in relation to developmental levels categorized according to cognitive, social-emotional, communication, and sensorimotor disabilities. *Highly recommended.*

Spodek, B., & Saracho. O. N. (1994). *Dealing with individual differences in the early childhood classroom.* New York: Longman. In a generally excellent book, the authors' chapter on "Using Educational Play" is outstanding because it provides concrete examples of ways to stimulate play for children with many differing disabilities.

Practical Advice About Generating Various Kinds of Play

Church, E. B., & Miller, K. (1990). *Learning through play: Blocks: A practical guide for teaching young children.* New York: Scholastic. Church and Miller provide many practical recommendations for presenting block play effectively—including material related to children with disabilities.

Crosser, S. (1994). Making the most of water play. *Young Children, 49*(5), 28–32. Crosser presents a detailed analysis of all the things children can learn from using this delightful substance. Also included is a list of sixteen references elaborating even further on this subject. *Highly recommended.*

Frost, J. L., & Klein, B. L. (1979). *Children's play and playgrounds.* Boston: Allyn & Bacon. A substantial book about play and how to enhance it out of doors. Profusely illustrated and practical. One of a kind.

Hirsch, E. S. (Ed.). (1984). *The block book.* Washington, DC: National Association for the Education of Young Children. *The Block Book* is the most comprehensive discussion of block play presently available. It does a satisfactory job of covering this subject in a helpful, thorough manner.

Miller, S. A. (1994). *Learning through play: Sand, water, clay & wood.* New York: Scholastic. Many activities and suggestions for presentation are included here.

Provenzo, E. F., Jr., & Brett, A. (1983). *The complete block book.* Syracuse, NY: Syracuse University Press. Lavishly illustrated, The *Complete Block Book* covers the history of blocks in the curriculum, as well as their potential uses.

Stephens, K. (1991). *Block adventures: Build creativity and concepts through block play.* Bridgeport, CT: First Teacher. A thorough description of the various kinds of learning to which blocks may contribute as well as many ideas of ways to stimulate block play are included.

For the Advanced Student

Gil, A., (1991). *The healing power of play: Working with abused children.* New York: Guilford. Gil uses descriptions of cases to explain how play therapy is used to treat children suffering from a variety of painful traumas.

Hartley, R. E., Frank, L. K., & Goldenson, R. M. (1962). *Understanding children's play.* New York: Columbia University Press. This old but invaluable book discusses the virtues of specific play materials and what each contributes to the healthy development of young children. A classic!

Monighan-Nourot, P., Scales, B., Van Hoorn, J. with Almy, M. (1987). *Looking at children's play: A bridge between theory and practice.* New York: Teachers College Press. This useful book reviews theory, recounts several examples of how real classroom teachers initiated research to find answers to their questions about play, and concludes with some more abstract philosophical discussions of the teacher's role.

Nourot, P. M., & Van Hoorn, J. L. (1991). Research in review: Symbolic play in preschool and primary settings. *Young Children, 46*(6), 40–50. For a thoroughgoing defence of play because of its contribution to cognitive intellectual growth, this article is hard to beat. *Highly recommended.*

Pettit, F. H., & Pettit, R. M. (1978). *Mexican folk toys, festival decorations and ritual objects.* New York: Hastings House. For an intriguing look at the colourful toys of another country's children, I suggest you examine this book. Full of pictures, it is fun to see the similarities and differences in play these toys imply.

Piaget, J. (1962). *Play, dreams and imitation in childhood.* New York: W. W. Norton. In his classic description, Piaget discusses how children assimilate knowledge of the world around them by means of imitation and the use of symbolic play; rather difficult but interesting reading.

Roopnarine, J. L., Johnson, J. E., & Hooper, F. H. (Eds.). (1994). *Children's play in diverse cultures.* Albany, NY: State University of New York Press. The first in a series on play in society, this book covers eight cultures ranging from Japanese to African. Generally based on research studies, the chapters often include the school's attitude toward play as well as that of the larger society. Very interesting reading.

Rubin, K. H., Fein, G. G., & Vandenberg, B. (1983). Play. In P. H. Mussen (Ed.), *Handbook of child psychology,* E. M. Hetherington (Ed.), *Volume IV: Socialization, personality, and social development.* New York: Wiley. This is a comprehensive review on the subject of play. It is an invaluable starting point for serious students of the subject.

Scales, B., Almy, M., Nicolopoulou, A., & Ervin-Tripp, S. (Eds.). (1991). *Play and the social context of development in early care and education.* New York: Teachers College Press. This unusual book approaches the discussion of play from the point of view of history and policy and then discusses its value in relation to language, literacy, and so forth.

Sigman, M., & Sena, R. (1993). Pretend play in high-risk and developmentally delayed children. *New Directions for Child Development, 59,* Spring, 29–42. The authors present careful reviews of research related to characteristics of pretend play evinced by children having a variety of disabilities ranging from autistic behaviours to Down's syndrome. A useful and rare source of information.

Other Resources of Continuing Interest

American Association for the Child's Right to Play. *IPA-USA Newsletter.* (Nancy Eletto, Play Environments, 616 Kimbark St., Longmont, CO 80501). This international association publishes various materials and conducts meetings that champion the child's right to play.

VI

Developing Language Skills and Mental Ability

17

Fostering the Development of Language Skills

18

Fostering the Emergence of Literacy

𝒮17 *Fostering the Development of Language Skills*

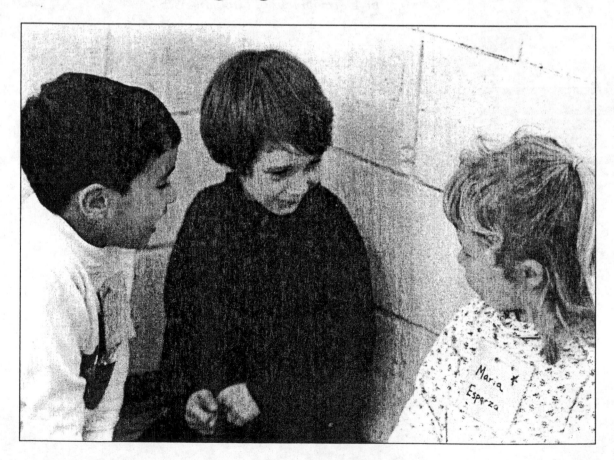

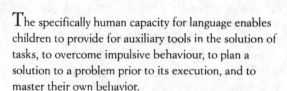

Have you ever wondered . . .

What are some practical things teachers can do to foster language development?

How to encourage children to talk with you and with other children?

Whether or not you should insist a Vietnamese child speak English at school?

. . . If you have, the material in the following pages will help you.

The specifically human capacity for language enables children to provide for auxiliary tools in the solution of tasks, to overcome impulsive behaviour, to plan a solution to a problem prior to its execution, and to master their own behavior.

Lev Vygotsky

Learning a native language is an accomplishment within the grasp of any toddler, yet discovering how children do it has eluded generations of philosophers.

Jerome Bruner

*I*n the past few years we have become increasingly aware of the value of developing language skills in early childhood, and almost without exception the newer, research-based schools have included a language component in their curriculum. This emphasis is the result of research findings that indicate that a close relationship exists between language competence and cognitive development (Bruner, 1978; Stefanakis, 1991), that differences exist between the speech of middle- and lower-class children (Bernstein, 1960; Durkin, 1982; Olson, Bayles, & Bates, 1986), and that children acquire most of their language skills, though not most of their vocabulary, by age four or five at the latest (Dyson & Genishi, 1993). As preschoolers pass the age of three, ego-enhancing boasting statements show an abrupt increase, and children begin to use more joining and collaborative statements, as well as simply talking more with their peers. Also, around age four and five, children go on to even more highly socialized speech than this—speech that takes the needs of the listener more into account. For example, four- and five-year-olds use more "because" sentences that give the listener reasons or explanations for their behaviour (Schachter, Kirshner, Klips, Friedricks, & Sanders, 1974).

Whether one sees language as being separate from thought, as did Piaget (Piaget & Inhelder, 1969), or ultimately bound together with it (Vygotsky, 1978), there is still general agreement that the development of language abilities goes hand in hand with the development of mental ability (Moshman, Glover, & Bruning, 1987). For this reason we devote considerable attention to methods of fostering language development as we study the child's intellectual self.

James (1990) has defined language as "a shared system of verbal symbols and rules that allow us to represent concepts and experiences and to communicate with others" (1990, p. 2). She points out that language is also "arbitrary, creative, and learned" (p. 2). Of course, all these things are true, but this is indeed a bare-bones definition for preschool teachers, who must come to grips with the problem of how to foster language development to maximize the child's potential for both comprehension and expression. To bring this about, teachers must understand how the ability to use language is acquired and how it develops; above all, they must determine what they can do in the children's centre to foster its growth.

The quality of the early childhood program is critical to a child's well-being and development. Children enrolled in poor quality child care programs have been found to have poorer language skills than their counterparts in good quality programs (Doherty-Derkowski, 1995).

❧ How Language Is Acquired

Knowledge about language acquisition is increasing rapidly, and it behooves preprimary teachers to know as much as possible about the process so they may apply this knowledge when teaching language skills. At the present time we have considerable information on what happens and when it happens. But since we still do not understand completely how it happens, it is necessary to employ several theories that are, at best, only partial explanations of the process.

One school of thought emphasizes the role of inborn ability, while the other theories dwell on the significance of environmental influences. Each of these theories has something to recommend it, though none of them offers a totally satisfactory explanation. The *nativist* theory, as described by Owens (1992) and originally championed by Chomsky (1968, 1981), maintains that human beings are born with an inherent, innate ability to formulate language, an ability that sets humans apart from almost all other animals. This ability or mechanism is then triggered into use by exposure to people speaking whatever language is specific to their culture. It remains difficult to either disprove or discount the existence of this unseen, intangible mechanism and also to determine whether this mechanism, if it does exist, is language specific, or whether it is a more general, cognitive ability (James, 1990; Owens, 1992).

At the other extreme is the *behaviourist* approach, which emphasizes the importance of imitation, modelling, and reinforcement as playing the most significant role in language acquisition (Brown & Bellugi, 1964; Bandura, 1977; Speidel & Nelson, 1989). Particularly in vogue during the heyday of behaviourism, this theory is currently criticized as offering insufficient explanations for how children are able to generate novel sentences they have never heard and therefore could not have learned by means of copying someone else. Still, reinforcement *does* play a significant role in language acquisition, as anyone who has lived through a child's learning to talk can cite numerous examples of mothers and babies imitating each other's speech as well as many additional later episodes of imitation.

Like the purist behaviourist approach, the third theory or model, sometimes termed the *sociolinguistic* or *social communicative* theory, also emphasizes the role environment plays in how children learn to talk. These theorists (Bruner, 1983; de Villiers & de Villiers, 1992) believe that children learn about linguistic forms and rules by interacting with the people in the environment around them. Unlike the behaviourists, who see the child as being mainly acted upon by her environment, they picture the child as being an active participant in the learning process (Vygotsky, 1962, 1978). Many proponents of this point of view also acknowledge the possible existence of an inborn predisposing mechanism for language acquisition. As Golinkoff and Hirsh-Pasek comment (1990), the current tendency appears to be that theorists are moving from more extreme positions favouring either nature or nurture toward a useful middle ground acknowledging the contributions of both.

Contributions by Adults to the Child's Acquisition of Language

The task of language acquisition faced by each child is a complex one. It may be comforting, though, to learn that adults make the child's work somewhat easier for her by using a special form or style of language when they speak to infants and very young children. Although this has been called *Motherese,* in actuality this adjustment of form is used by most adults and even older children when talking with little ones (D'Odorico & Franco, 1985). The style includes such characteristics as using a higher pitch and a wider range of pitch, speaking more slowly and distinctly, repeating words and phrases, using limited vocabulary, and coining words such as "goney-gone" and "tum-tum." Adults also tend to expand the briefer utterances of children and, most interesting of all, adjust the level of communication difficulty to the child's increasing level of understanding as the youngster matures (George & Tomasello, 1984/85).

Maternal responsiveness—that is, how much attention mothers pay to their one- and two-year-olds' attempts at talking—also makes a significant difference in the size of the youngster's vocabulary. The more responsive the mother is, the greater the child's number of words (Olson et al., 1986). Surely this implies that teachers, also, should be careful to be attentive when children want to talk with them.

Contributions of Linguistics to Understanding the Process of Language Acquisition

From the practical point of view of the early childhood teacher, the most valuable contribution of linguistics so far is the information it is providing on the order in which various grammatical structures develop in the speech of children. Although linguistic theory is too advanced and complicated a subject to be presented in detail here, two examples of the kinds of information this science is producing may help the beginning student gain an appreciation of the importance of this approach. For numerous examples of the current intricacies of linguistic research, the reader is referred to de Villiers and de Villiers (1992) and Owens (1992).

One early example of applied linguistics is the classic study by Menyuk (1963), who used the grammatical theory developed by Chomsky, a linguistic theorist in transformational grammar, to study the language of young children. Menyuk studied three- and six-year-olds and found there were few examples of restricted children's grammar at this level. Surprisingly, most of the children's speech was similar to that of adults, and the children had gained a remarkable proficiency in structuring language correctly even by age three. This is important information for the preschool teacher to possess, since it implies that we need to stress the development of language function skills earlier than age four—the point at which many children enter the school system. Obviously, if grammatical structure has been largely acquired by this time, we should be building language skills in children between eighteen months and three-and-a-half years old to be maximally effective.

In another study, Cazden (1970) also used transformational grammar to analyse the way children learn to pose questions. Briefly, she found that children first form questions by using inflection. Following that, questions become the yes-no kind, which depend on interchanging only two phrases. For example, "The boy can drive a car" would change to "Can the boy drive a car?" Next, children learn to perform a more difficult transformation, the "wh" question—"When can the boy drive a car?"—which involves two transformations. The next step involves forming negative questions: "Won't he be able to drive the car?" Finally comes the use of tag questions: "It's all right if he drives the car, isn't it?"

As more of these studies become available, it will be possible to outline sequential steps for many forms of grammatical structures. Then, following an analysis of a child's present level of ability, the teacher will be able to refer to these "maps" and know what step should be selected next for him and plan her teaching accordingly.

Contributions of Sociolinguistics to the Understanding of Language Development

Rather than focusing on how the structure of language is acquired, some researchers have become more interested in "the relation of language to social interaction" (Ervin-Tripp, 1986, p. 92), i.e., they are interested in the way children use language to

ℰ *"It's for you!"*

affect the behaviour of other people. This is now called the science of *pragmatics*. It stresses the interactional importance of the social and developmental aspects of language acquisition (Bloom, 1975; Bruner, 1975; Dore, 1986; Schiefelbusch, 1986; Snow, 1989). In this approach the *intention* of the child when speaking is accepted as being as important to consider as the form she uses while saying it. For example, a child who says "Doggie!" might mean, "I want to pet the doggie," "Pick me up, I'm scared of that doggie," or "See the doggie!"

Pragmatics is particularly interesting to teachers of preschool-age children because it provides a helpful way to learn about various aspects of children's speech that may provide clues about what teachers can do to facilitate its development. For example, studies by Ervin-Tripp (Ervin-Tripp & Gordon, 1986) reveal how children gradually progress from making simple demands based on "more," "want," and "gimme" to phrasing requests as questions at age three ("Can I have a bite?") to using hints and indirect statements by age four such as a question by one of my grandchildren, "I'm wondering if there's something in your pocket for this sweet little girl?"

One large area of study included in pragmatics centres on what rules children must learn and follow in order to carry on a conversation—which Bruner (1978) defines as being the earliest experience in learning to take turns. Besides learning such conversational rules as that one person talks at a time and that the number of people involved in a conversation can vary (Sacks, Schegloff, & Jefferson, 1974), they must also learn when and how to interrupt, how to introduce a subject into the conversation, and how to continue to talk about it over a period of time.

Another interesting area of investigation has to do with the way children change their conversational style to suit the people to whom they are talking (Cox, 1991). For example, four-year-olds have been found to use much simpler instructions when talking to two-year-olds than they use with peers or adults (Shatz & Gelman, 1973). Owens (1992) reports that children tend to be more directly demanding with their mothers than they are with other grown-ups and also to use more imperatives with children their own age than they do when speaking to adults. Sometimes this adjustment has to do with how a particular culture defines politeness and/or appropriate social roles. For example, Ervin-Tripp points out that Italian families frown on children saying "I want" unless they soften that request some way (1986). Still another kind of style or code-switching is evident in the speech of children who use a dialect or even a second language when speaking to members of their gang and quite another style when talking with their teachers at school (Smitherman, 1994).

Conclusion

And so the debate on how the miracle of language comes about continues—with, it seems, an ever widening range of things that affect its acquisition being considered. It is an exciting, fast growing area of study and research that is particularly interesting because it has attracted the attention of people from a variety of academic disciplines who, by their diversity of approaches, have greatly increased the richness of our understanding (Ingram, 1989).

One may ask at this point, "Have we reached the point where these studies offer sufficient explanations of how language is acquired?" Surely the foregoing explanations are sensible and useful as far as they go, but the fact remains that although we are in the process of acquiring linguistic maps, although we are fairly certain that imitation and reinforcement combined with an innate ability play an important role in the acquisition of these forms, and although we acknowledge that context, development, and social interaction are important influences, we still cannot explain the fundamental magic of what happens in the child's mind that enables her to substitute symbol for object and to assemble these symbols into sentences she has never heard.

❧ Developmental Milestones

In addition to understanding that grammatical structure develops according to predictable rules, teachers should become acquainted with additional developmental milestones so that they can identify children who show marked developmental lags and also so that they may have a clear idea of what is reasonable to aim for when establishing goals for language development. The teacher may find Tables 17.1 and 17.2 quite helpful, but remember that the checkpoints represent averages, and children who are developing well may often be either ahead or behind the suggested time listed. The lag should be considered serious enough to warrant concern if the child is more than a few months behind on a particular measure.

Another quick rule of thumb for checking language development is sentence length, still thought to be one of the best indicators of verbal maturity. In general, sentence length increases as the child grows older. Schachter and Strage (1982) outline a pattern for the development of language in Table 17.2.

When assessing language competence, first determine whether English or some other language is the child's dominant language and also whether he appears to possess what I term "the habit of verbalness." For whatever reason, be it temperament, age, level of

❧ *Jennifer clearly has the language situation well in hand.*

intelligence, cultural pattern, or socioeconomic status, it is evident to our centre teachers that some children use language to meet their needs more frequently than others do. We always try to note this behaviour and use the techniques described in the following section to encourage less verbally oriented children to increase their language abilities while attending the centre.

❧ Basic Ways to Foster Language Development

I. Listen to the Children

Many adults are so busy talking themselves that they drown the children out. But children learn to talk by being heard. Paying attention to what they say and listening both to the surface content and to the message underneath offer the most valuable inducements to children to continue making the effort to communicate.

Table 17.1 Milestones in the development of language ability in young children

Average Age	Question	Average Behavior
3–6 months	What does he do when you talk to him?	He awakens or quiets to the sound of his mother's voice.
	Does he react to your voice even when he cannot see you?	He typically turns eyes and head in the direction of the source of sound.
7–10 months	When he cannot see what is happening, what does he do when he hears familiar footsteps . . . the dog barking . . . the telephone ringing . . . candy paper rattling . . . someone's voice . . . his own name?	He turns his head and shoulders toward familiar sounds, even when he cannot see what is happening. Such sounds do not have to be loud to cause him to respond.
11–15 months	Can he point to or find familiar objects or people when he is asked to? *Example:* "Where is Jimmy?" "Find the ball."	He shows his understanding of some words by appropriate behavior; for example, he points to or looks at familiar objects or people, on request.
	Does he respond differently to different sounds?	He jabbers in response to a human voice, is apt to cry when there is thunder, or may frown when he is scolded.
	Does he enjoy listening to some sounds and imitating them?	Imitation indicates that he can hear the sounds and match them with his own sound production.
1½ years	Can he point to parts of his body when you ask him to? *Example:* "Show me your eyes." "Show me your nose."	Some children begin to identify parts of the body. He should be able to show his nose or eyes.
	How many understandable words does he use—words you are sure *really* mean something?	He should be using a few single words. They are not complete or pronounced perfectly but are clearly meaningful.
2 years	Can he follow simple verbal commands when you are careful not to give him any help, such as looking at the object or pointing in the right direction? *Example:* "Johnny, get your hat and give it to Daddy." "Debby, bring me your ball."	He should be able to follow a few simple commands without visual clues.
	Does he enjoy being read to? Does he point out pictures of familiar objects in a book when asked to? *Example:* "Show me the baby." "Where's the rabbit?"	Most 2-year-olds enjoy being "read to" and shown simple pictures in a book or magazine, and will point out pictures when you ask them to.
	Does he use the names of familiar people and things such as *Mommy, milk, ball,* and *hat*?	He should be using a variety of everyday words heard in his home and neighborhood.
	What does he call himself?	He refers to himself by name.

Table 17.1 Language development pattern, two to five years of age (continued)

Average Age	Question	Average Behavior
2 years (cont.)	Is he beginning to show interest in the sound of radio or TV commercials?	Many 2-year-olds do show such interest by word or action.
	Is he putting a few words together to make little "sentences"?	These "sentences" are not usually complete or grammatically correct.
	Example: "Go bye-bye car." "Milk all gone."	
2½ years	Does he know a few rhymes or songs? Does he enjoy hearing them?	Many children can say or sing short rhymes or songs and enjoy listening to records or to mother singing.
	What does he do when the ice cream man's bell rings, out of his sight, or when a car door or house door closes at a time when someone in the family usually comes home?	If a child has good hearing, and these are events that bring him pleasure, he usually reacts to the sound by running to look or telling someone what he hears.
3 years	Can he show that he understands the meaning of some words besides the names of things?	He should be able to understand and use some simple verbs, pronouns, prepositions, and adjectives, such as *go, me, in*, and *big*.
	Example: "Make the car go." "Give me your ball." "Put the block in your pocket." "Find the big doll."	
	Can he find you when you call him from another room?	He should be able to locate the source of a sound.
	Does he sometimes use complete sentences?	He should be using complete sentences some of the time.
4 years	Can he tell about events that have happened recently?	He should be able to give a connected account of some recent experiences.
	Can he carry out two directions, one after the other?	He should be able to carry out a sequence of two or three simple directions.
	Example: "Bobby, find Susie and tell her dinner's ready."	
5 years	Do neighbors and others outside the family understand most of what he says?	His speech should be intelligible, although some sounds may still be mispronounced.
	Can he carry on a conversation with other children or familiar grown-ups?	Most children of this age can carry on a conversation if the vocabulary is within their experience.
	Does he begin a sentence with "I" instead of "me," "he" instead of "him"?	He should use some pronouns correctly.
	Is his grammar almost as good as his parents'?	Most of the time, it should match the patterns of grammar used by the adults of his family and neighborhood.

Source: From *Learning to Talk: Speech, Hearing and Language Problems in the Pre-school Child* by the National Institute of Neurological Diseases and Stroke (1969). Washington, DC: U.S. Department of Health, Education, and Welfare.

Table 17.2 Development of Language

Age in Months	Characteristics of Vocalization and Language
4	Coos and chuckles.
6–9	Babbles; duplicates common sounds; produces sounds such as "ma" or "da."
12–18	A small number of words; follows simple commands and responds to no; uses expressive jargon.
18–21	Vocabulary grows from about 20 words at 18 months to about 200 words at 21; points to many more objects; comprehends simple questions; forms 2-word phrases.
24–27	Vocabulary of 300 to 400 words; has 2- or 3-word phrases; uses prepositions and pronouns.
30–33	Fastest increase in vocabulary; three- to four-word sentences are common; word order, phrase structure, and grammatical agreement approximate the language of surroundings, but many utterances are unlike anything an adult would say.
36–39	Vocabulary of 1000 words or more; well-formed sentences using complex grammatical rules, although certain rules have not yet been fully mastered; grammatical mistakes are much less frequent; about 90 percent comprehensible.

Source: From "Adults' Talk and Children's Language Development" by F. F. Schachter and A. A. Strage. In S. G. Moore and C. R. Cooper (Eds.), The *Young Child: Reviews of Research* (Vol. 3), p. 83. (Adapted from Lenneberg [1966]). Reprinted by permission. © 1982, National Association for the Education of Young Children, 1834 Connecticut Ave., NW, Washington, DC 20009.

Of course, it is not always easy to understand what they have to say. If a comment is unintelligible, it is all right to ask a child to repeat it; and if the message is still unclear, it may be necessary to admit this and say, "I'm sorry, I just can't tell what you're saying. Could you show me what you mean?" At least this is honest communication and shows children that the teacher is really interested and is trying. Occasionally another child can be prevailed on to clarify what his companion is saying.

II. Give the Children Something Real to Talk About

Children's talk should be based on solid, real, lived-through experience. Sometimes inexperienced teachers want to begin at the other end and set up group experiences wherein the children are supposed to discuss planting seeds or thinking about what will sink and float before they have been exposed to the experience itself. This means they are expected to use words that have few actual associations for them and talk about something vague and relatively meaningless. No wonder their attention wanders. It is much more satisfactory to provide the opportunity to live through the experience and to talk

❧   *Talking about a book together is a great way to encourage conversation.*

about what is happening while it is going on as well as after it has been completed. At this point the child can really associate "sink" with "things that go down" and "sprout" with the pale green tip that poked its nose out of the bean.

Note also that talk and questioning are advocated as an accompaniment to experience. In former years, some teachers of young children seemed to assume that mere exposure to interesting materials in the presence of a warm adult would automatically produce growth in language and mental ability. The work of Blank and Solomon (1968, 1969) has shown that unfocused attention in a rich environment is *not* enough. Children develop language best when they are required to use words to express concepts and thoughts about what is happening, has happened, or will happen; it is this kind of activity that produces the greatest gains.

III. Encourage Conversation between Children

As interest in the influence of social interaction on the development of speech increases, more attention is being paid to the importance of encouraging children to talk to each other. Of course, Piaget (1983) has long advocated such "discourse" and exchanges of opinion as an effective means of facilitating the acquisition of knowledge, but presently the value of conversation between children as a facilitator of language development itself is receiving attention (Garvey, 1984; McTear, 1985; Vygotsky, 1978).

Encouraging children to talk to each other has many benefits, ranging from teaching them to use words to negotiate disagreements in place of physical attacks to providing them with effective ways of entering a group. Besides these obvious advantages, as the children of Reggio Emilia consistently demonstrate, talking together can help children put ideas into words, increase their abilities to use language to explain to someone else what is happening, repeat an interesting experience, or make cheerful social contact with another youngster (Edwards, Gandini, & Forman, 1993). Most important of all, such encounters help persuade them that talking is satisfying and important—a valuable attitude to inculcate as a foundation for later interest in other language strategies related to literacy. (These strategies are discussed in more detail in chapter 18).

For these reasons, the teacher should avoid making himself the constant centre of attention, whether the situation is dramatic play or participating at the lunch table. Instead, it is important to think of oneself as seeking to increase the amount of talk *among the children whenever possible.* Such comments as "That's really interesting. Why don't you tell Blake about that?" or "Have you talked that over with Franco? He was talking about that just yesterday," provide openings for the children to relate to each other and focus attention on the relationships among them rather than keeping attention focused on the teacher.

IV. Encourage Conversation and Dialogue Between Teachers and Children

There is much more to language development than teaching the child to name colours or objects on demand, although learning the names of things has undeniable value. The skills involved in discussion and conversation are vital too, and the ability to conduct such dialogues develops rapidly throughout the preschool period (Garvey, 1984; James, 1992).

To develop these conversational interchanges, teachers must relax and stop seeing their role as one of instructor and admonisher. *Always supplying a fact or rendering an opinion in reply to a child's comment kills conversation very quickly* (Stone, 1993). Cazden (1972) quotes a perfect example of this. As she points out, the more frequent the prohibition in an adult's talk, the less the children reply.

Tape plays

Teacher: Oh, you tease, Tom, what are you telling Winston?

Tom: I tellin' him my brother Gary a bad, bad boy.

Teacher: O, now that ain't nice.

After an analysis and discussion on this tape recording, the same teacher returns to the child, and the following conversation ensues.

Teacher: Tom, what was you tellin' Winston this mornin' when you playin' with the ball?

Tom: I tole him Gary my brother.

Teacher: You like Gary?

Tom: Yeah, I lahk him, but he bad.

Teacher: Why's dat?

❧   *Genuine discussion between teachers and children fosters the generation of ideas and the language to express those ideas.*

Tom: 'Cus he walked up and set with his friend when they was singin' 'bout Jesus and the preacher was preachin'.
Teacher: Who whipped him?
Tom: Daddy—he tuk him outside and whupped him with a red belt.
Teacher: Did Gary cry?
Tom: Oh, yeah, he got tears in his eyes. Mama wiped his eyes with a rag when he come back in. Then he popped his fingers. That boy can't never be quiet.*

The example brings out another important point to remember when building conversation. *Teachers should seek to prolong the interchange whenever they can.* Tossing the conversational ball back and forth is a sound way to build fluency and also to establish the habit of being verbal.

The value of the one-to-one situation cannot be overestimated in this regard. It is not necessary to put this off and wait for a special moment; indeed, this is impossible to do if the teacher wants to talk specially with every child every day. Instead of waiting the teacher can seize many little interludes to generate friendly talk between himself and a child or between two children. One of the teachers in our centre maintains that some of her best opportunities for such chatting occur while she is helping children go to the toilet. Another capitalizes on brief moments while putting on shoes or while greeting children as they arrive at school.

---

*Adapted with permission of Macmillan Publishing Company from *The Devil Has Slippery Shoes: A Biased Biography of the Child Development Group of Mississippi* by Polly Greenberg. © 1970 by Polly Greenberg.

Teachers should monitor themselves regularly to make certain they are not talking mainly to the most verbal children, since at least one research study shows that teachers talk most to children who are the best talkers to start with (Monaghan, 1974). Some youngsters have a knack for striking up conversations with adults, whereas others do not. It is the children lacking this ability who are often overlooked and who, therefore, receive the least practice in an area in which they need it the most. If teachers make a checklist of the children's names and review it faithfully, they will be able to recall which youngsters they have talked with and which they have not and then make a particular effort to include the ones who have been passed over in conversation.

Of course, a reasonable ratio of adults to children makes it more likely there will be time for such friendly encounters, but a good ratio is not the only thing that matters. An English study found that quality of conversation between child and adult is also increased if there are not too many very young children (children under the age of three) included in the group. Stability of staff (that is, low staff turnover) also increased the quality of interaction, as did staff feelings of autonomy (when staff were supervised very closely, they tended to be more aware of needing to please the supervisor than of the value of generating meaningful conversation with the children) (Tizard, Mortimore, & Burchell, 1972). Since all these qualities stem from good management and job satisfaction of the employees, it is evident that preprimary schools that wish to foster language and its accompanying opportunity for mental development must pay close attention to solving these management problems.

Besides these one-to-one conversations, there are two classic, larger group opportunities that occur each day in the centre when it is particularly possible to generate conversation. These occur at the snack or lunch table and during group time. (Group time conversation is discussed in the following chapter.) Indeed, in a recent study Stone (1992) found that out of eighty-one narratives spontaneously produced by the preschool children he studied, the great majority occurred during lunchtime (73%). He concludes that the presence of an interested, attentive adult is crucial in developing this aspect of children's conversational ability.

Developing Conversation at Mealtimes

Gone are the days when children were expected to be seen and not heard at meals or when they had to clear their plates before they were allowed to talk. There are several practical ways the teacher can encourage conversation during meals.

Keep lunch and snack groups as small as possible. It is worthwhile to keep the mealtime group down to five or six children if possible. Anyone who has ever sat at a banquet table knows how difficult it is to get conversation going under such circumstances, and yet an occasional children's centre persists in seating twelve or fifteen children all around one table. This kills interchange, as well as making supervision difficult. Doherty-Derkowski (1995) states that large groups are associated with adults who engage in less social and language stimulation with the children.

Adults need to plan their activities so they are free to sit with the children during meals. Surprisingly often when I have visited day care centres at mealtime, I have seen staff roaming restlessly around, passing food, running back and forth to the kitchen, or leaning on counters, arms folded, simply waiting passively for the children to eat but not being part of the group at all. Good advance planning on food delivery should make it possible for staff to sit with the children, and a clearer understanding of the potential educational value of such participation should make them willing to do so. Sitting with the children fosters the feeling of family time that young children need and also encourages the relaxed chatting that makes mealtime a pleasure.

On the other hand, it is wise to avoid putting two adults together at one table. The temptation to carry on a grown-up conversation over the heads of the children can be too great when two adults eat lunch together. It is better to add more tables when more adults are present, thereby seizing this golden opportunity to reduce group size and making it more likely that individual children will join in the talk.

Think of good conservation starters. Such questions as,"Who's your favourite baby sitter?" "What would you like for your birthday?" or "Would you rather be a kitty or a dog?" will lead the children into talking about things that really interest them and that they can all share together. It is also fun to talk about brothers and sisters, new clothes, holidays, what their parents' first names are and how old they are, what they call their grandfather, or what they did over the weekend. In addition, their memories can be developed by asking them if they can remember what they had for lunch yesterday or what they saw on the way to school.

It takes tact to ensure that one ardent talker does not monopolize the conversation under these circumstances. The teacher may need to make a deliberate effort to draw all the children into the discussion lest someone be consistently drowned out. But in the space of the half hour or so that lunch requires, there is really ample opportunity for everyone to converse.

Don't let the children get by with pointing to food they wish to have passed or with saying "I want that." Conversation, as such, is highly desirable to develop at the lunch table, but mealtime also provides many opportunities to build the children's vocabulary and concepts. All too often teachers permit pointing and saying "give me" to pass for language. This is just not enough. Children need to acquire commonly used vocabulary, and mealtime is an effective place to teach this. It is easy for the teacher to make sure that the child says the real name of the food she is requesting and then give it to her promptly. There is no quicker way to teach her that talking pays off!

If the child does not know the word, the teacher can say, "This red stuff is called Jell-O. Now you can tell *me.*" When she does, he should give it to her right away and tell her, "Good for you! You said the real name." Sometimes, however, the child refuses to reply. It is best to pass over such a response lightly without making a major issue of it, perhaps saying, "Well, maybe you'll want to tell me it's Jell-O next time."

Mealtimes are also good opportunities to teach certain concepts. For example, the teacher might start by talking about the food: "What are we having today? Did any of you look in the kitchen to see what dessert is?" He might then go on to ask, "What does this meat taste like? Is it hard or soft? Hot or cold? Tough or tender? Can you think of anything else that's like that?"

❧   *When adults are interested,*
children are interested, too.

A word of warning is in order here. Mealtimes should remain basically social occasions in which verbal fluency and fun are the keynote, not opportunities for continuous dull inquisitions. Vocabulary and concept building should not be allowed to dominate the occasion, and such a delightful event as lunch should never be permitted to degenerate into a boring mechanical drill in which the talk centres on naming each food and discussing where it came from.

V. Use Questions and Answers That Generate Speech and Develop Language

Once again, the value of questions must be highlighted as we discuss effective ways of encouraging the development of language.

Ask Questions That Require More Than One-Word Answers

In chapter 21, asking questions that are open ended is advocated because doing this encourages children to see there is more than one answer to many questions. Asking these kinds of questions has an additional virtue we should think about in this chapter because they also foster language development by promoting conversation. Rogers, Perrin, and Waller (1987) conducted a series of observations of a teacher named Cathy that illustrates the value of doing this. This teacher had a particularly good relationship with the children in her care. When the researchers analysed the reasons for this, they concluded she was adept at asking the children what she termed "true questions." These were questions for which she didn't have a preconceived answer in mind. (The opposite of a "true question" is a "known answer" or fact question.)

For example, in one instance when the children had been building with bristle blocks, the following conversation took place:

> *Adam:* There's the chimney, see?
> *Cathy:* Oh-h-h. Do you have a woodstove in there? Or a fireplace?
> *Adam:* Uh-huh, a woodstove.
> *Cathy:* A woodstove.
> *Adam:* That's where the smoke comes out. Where my mom and dad live.
> *Cathy:* The what? (She leans closer to Adam.)
> *Adam:* It's our house.
> *Cathy:* Oh-h, and you built it for them, huh?
> *Adam:* Uh-huh, and we are living in it.
> *Cathy:* You're a good thing to have around. Does Nora live there, too? (Rogers et al., 1987, p. 21)

Clearly, there was no way Cathy could have known the answers in advance to the questions she asked—they reflect her genuine interest in what Adam was doing and what he had to say about it. That interest is an important element in generating true conversation.

When Replying to a Child's Questions or Statement, Elaborate

After the work of Brown and Bellugi (1964) revealed that parents spend a good deal of their time reconstructing and expanding the limited sentences used by their young children, some teachers concluded that this technique of expansion would naturally be the most effective way to teach enriched language to all young children. Thus when a child commented, "Train, bye-bye," the teacher would dutifully reply, "Yes, the train is going bye-bye." It now appears that this technique may be most effective with children about eighteen months to three years old. Cazden's work (1972) with developing vocabulary seems to indicate that expansion is not as effective as providing enriching replies when working with four-year-olds. This would mean that rather than replying "Yes, the train goes bye-bye," the teacher would respond to an older child by saying, "Yes, the engine is pulling the train out of the station. Goodbye, train. Goodbye, people." When working with older preschoolers, this kind of enrichment is superior to simple expansion in fostering language progress.

VI. When Necessary, Seek Professional Assistance Promptly

Every once in a while a teacher will come across a child who speaks rarely, if at all, or one who has a pronounced speech problem. These disabilities are discussed in more detail at the end of this chapter, but I want to emphasize here as a basic principle that it is important to seek professional help for these children promptly. Too often both teacher and parent let the year pass, hoping the child will somehow outgrow his difficulty. Although this does happen occasionally, it is generally wiser to refer such youngsters for professional help after two or three months at most. Children who have pronounced developmental lags or other speech disorders and who do not show signs of improvement by that time generally need consultation from a qualified speech therapist or psychologist, and a referral is definitely in order.

❧ *Language and Dialectical Differences*

Language and Culture in Canada

Language and culture are closely intertwined: language has been described as the primary expression of culture. In Canada, we see this relationship foremost in connection with English and French. Strong protection for the French language is seen by many as a key to the survival of the French-Canadian culture. Similarly, for other language groups, particularly First Nations, preservation of cultural autonomy and diversity is strongly linked to language retention. Nationwide, French is slipping slightly, down from 24.7% in 1981 to 23.3% in 1991. In Quebec, 83% of the population spoke French in 1991. (Tepperman & Rosenberg, 1995).

Historically, Canada's education system has failed many children and families. Many native children were robbed of their language, culture, and families through culturally insensitive school experiences. Government policies contributed to the eroding of heritage, language, and culture. These policies and resulting programs were met with resistance from the First Nations and Doukhobor communities (Chud & Fahlman, 1995).

Significant shifts in educational theory and practice, together with a strong collective voice of parents, teachers, and cultural communities, have contributed to the passing of human rights legislation and supportive government policies. Particularly over the last decade, there have been significant shifts in early childhood research, thinking, and practice that relate to diversity, language and cultural issues. Enlightened educators are learning to value children's first language by welcoming it in the classroom and reinforcing it through stories, songs, visual representation, and parental involvement.

Various specialized services are available that support language and culture. Newcomer orientation programs such as Ontario Welcome House offer supportive services to ease the transition for immigrant and refugee families. Families are offered special preschool settings that are sensitive to their situation as newcomers and that value their cultural and linguistic heritage.

Many communities offer programs with an emphasis on learning English through play-based experience. These programs provide a meaningful bridge to mainstream early education. Bilingual programs focus on supporting English as a Second Language while viewing bilingualism as an asset to children's development. (These bilingual programs are not to be confused with the sort of French immersion programs some English-speaking children have been subjected to that use vocabulary and grammar drill to inculcate a second language early. Such programs are inappropriate for young children.)

Programs designed for aboriginal families and communities provide an environment in which self-esteem and cultural continuity are central themes. The involvement of elders and other community members enriches these programs.

Which Language Should the Teacher Encourage?

In the chapter on cross-cultural education, a good deal of time was spent discussing ways to honour the cultural background the child brings with her from her home. Although there is no finer way to do this than by welcoming and encouraging her to use her native language or dialect at school, teachers are often torn between two directions on this question. On one hand, they want to make the child welcome and facilitate her learning in every possible way. This makes the use of her dominant language essential. On the other hand, the teacher cannot help looking ahead and knowing that as schools function today, each youngster will soon move on to elementary school, where she will have to speak Standard English, the dominant language of the middle-class world (Trueba, 1990).

This is quite a dilemma. Somehow the teacher who provides the first school experience for such children must stand with a foot on either side of the stream. To be maximally effective, he should be bilingual himself, as well as knowledgeable about dialectical differences that exist between himself and the children in his care. Failing this, he should at least see that the assistant teacher possesses these strengths.

The ability to switch from one form of English or even from one style of address to another is termed *code switching* (Gleason, 1981). It may turn out that the most desirable thing somehow to teach children is facility in being able to shift from one lect* to the other as the situation warrants, just as speakers of Spanish, German, or French learn to code-switch from their language to English to make themselves understood. While acquiring this skill, it is hoped that the child has the opportunity to learn Standard English in an atmosphere that values and appreciates her already present linguistic strengths rather than in one that smacks of condescension and noblesse oblige.

At present, the effects of learning two languages at approximately the same time remain difficult to assess and continue to be debated (Imhoff, 1990; Ellis, 1994). Early research studies that concluded bilingualism had a negative effect on language and possibly mental development were confounded by the presence of additional variables that affect learning and behaviour, such as poverty. When such a mixture of possible causes is present, it is next to impossible to sort the effects of one from another.

Current, more sophisticated studies suggest that when the effects of poverty are controlled, bilingualism is not a deterrent to development (Soto, 1991). As Hakuta and Garcia (1989) document, "*all other things being equal*, higher degrees of bilingualism are associated with higher levels of cognitive attainment" (p. 375). Evidently learning a second language is not hampered by possession of the first language (McLaughlin, 1987). Indeed, some research indicates that the acquisition rate for a second language is closely related to the proficiency level of the native language. The more proficient the child is in her first language, the quicker she will be able to learn the second one (Cummings, 1984).

Another continuing debate centres on when and how best to teach non-English-speaking children English (Garcia, 1990; Imhoff, 1990). Common sense argues against the folly of insisting that children try to learn important new concepts in a language they are only beginning to acquire. Imagine having to learn geometry by means of first-year French, which you are learning simultaneously—that's the stuff nightmares are made of.

---

*The word *lect* is currently the term preferred by many students in place of *dialect*.

Yet, in essence, we expect this degree of expertise from a young semi-bilingual child when we teach her "all the important things" only in her second language (Areñas, 1978; Gonzalez-Mena, 1976). Children who are coming to school for the first time are undergoing a complicated enough set of adjustments without the teacher's expecting them to function entirely in a new language at the same time.

Probably the best we can do at present, since children are expected to speak English in grade school and beyond, is to follow the bilingual model wherein young children are taught concepts first in their dominant language and then in English. This approach has been shown to be successful in a number of studies involving concept training or learning to read (Garcia & August, 1988; Macnamara, 1966; Nedler & Sebera, 1971; Orata, 1953). It has been effective with children speaking a variety of languages and ranging in cultural background from Cantonese to Irish. Moreover, it has the virtue of helping maintain the child's ability to remain bilingual rather than pushing towards proficiency only in English.

What to Do When You Do Not Speak a Child's Language

While it's all very well to discuss bilingual education on a remote level, the problem that ordinarily confronts the preschool teacher is the young child who arrives at school unable to speak any English at all. This situation is not going to go away. Increasing numbers of children in Canada are entering early childhood settings with languages other than English. Immigration to Canada is about 250 000 annually, with most newcomers settling in large urban centres such as Montreal, Toronto, and Vancouver (Citizenship and Immigration Canada, 1994). In these and other cities, children not born in Canada, or born to families who have recently immigrated, constitute a large portion of the child population. In 1994, for example, 112 844 newcomers settled in Ontario; 47 557 of them spoke neither official language; 8347 were of an age to attend child care services. Meeting the language and cultural needs of these children and their families presents a challenge to early childhood educators.

It is essential that a bridge of understanding be built between each child, his family, and the teacher. I never think about this situation without recalling the sage advice of my former head teacher, Clevonease Johnson. At that centre we had many youngsters who came to us from Vietnam and Cambodia. There they would stand, alone and bewildered, struggling not to cry as their parent and the interpreter walked out the door.

Although it wasn't possible for the teacher to acquire the child's language (at one time Clevonease would have had to have known eight languages to meet that standard), there were two phrases she said it was essential for her to know, and she never allowed the interpreter to leave without writing these down in phonetic English. The first was "Your mother will be back soon," and the second was "Do you need to go to the bathroom?" With these phrases tucked in her pocket, combined with warm smiles and many gestures, Clev felt she could handle anything!

Actually, of course, there are many additional language-related strategies that are useful to employ when working with a child who speaks another language, and several suggestions are included below. Even more valuable than these strategies, however, is the overall attitude toward cultural differences that must prevail in the centre. There is no substitute for providing the newcomer with the warm welcome and appreciation of her background advocated in chapter 14, "Providing Cross-Cultural, Nonsexist Education."

1. First of all, remember to talk to the child. Sometimes teachers give up speaking to her just because the child does not respond. However, if she isn't spoken to in English, she won't have much of a chance to learn it.

2. Encourage the child to say something right from the start if she is comfortable doing this, but remember that many children require a considerable "wait period" before they are ready to venture into an unfamiliar tongue (Ellis, 1994; Soto, 1991). This hesitancy can sometimes be overcome if other children are encouraged to talk freely to the newcomer. Children are less shy talking with each other than with the teacher.

3. When possible, pair the child with another youngster who speaks the same language. This can help her feel she has someone to turn to when feeling blocked.

4. When speaking to the child, keep your voice natural and not too loud. Talking louder does not help children understand any better, and sometimes it makes them think you are angry with them.

5. Learn the correct pronunciation of the child's name. Do not change or anglicize the name, unless the parents ask you to. Some names may be difficult to pronounce at first, but learning to pronounce them phonetically, with the family's help, contributes to a good working relationship.

6. Learn a few basic words and phrases in the child's first language (drink, Do you need to go to the toilet?, Mommy will be back soon, etc.) With the families' help, display some phrases on the bulletin board and in the program's newsletter, and incorporate them into children's songs. The Newcomer Preschool ((Dotsch & McFarlane) will give you some other good ideas.

7. Be visually expressive. Use gestures, smiles, encouraging looks, and friendliness to help the child understand and feel at ease.

8. Demonstrate what you mean as you speak. For example, ask, "Would you like to paint?" Then pick up the brush, gesture toward the paper, and repeat, "Would you like to paint?"

9. Link language to objects and real experience whenever possible. Teach nouns and verbs first; they are some of the most meaningful and useful words (except for *yes!* and *no!*).

10. Don't try to teach too many words at once, and be careful to repeat words many times until they become familiar.

11. Offer some short, easily repeated rhymes and songs each day so the child can join in with the group without being self-conscious about speaking out on her own.

12. Be careful not to overwhelm the child with attention. Too much pressure is as bad as no attention at all.

13. Encourage other children to include the newcomer in their play. Explain that she needs special help; encourage them to name things for her as they use them.

14. And, finally, be aware yourself of how limited *you* feel because you speak only one or perhaps two languages. Encourage the child's parents to help her retain the ability to be (ultimately) bilingual. In this way she will always retain the advantage of being able to communicate in two languages.

🕉 RESEARCH STUDY 🕉
How Much Culturally Sensitive Content Is Being Implemented in Child Care Centres?

Preamble

In Canada, because we live in a multicultural society, even children born into a homogeneous community are unlikely to live their lives in one. Therefore, it is important for children to develop the attitudes and skills required to live and work comfortably with people from various backgrounds. Early childhood experts have demonstrated that developmentally appropriate multicultural programming for young children has many advantages for both the children and their parents (Bredekamp, 1987). Multicultural early childhood programming acknowledges, understands, respects, and supports diversity and actively rejects prejudice or bias in regard to race, ethnicity, cultural background, religion, or language. Although children from all backgrounds deserve the full consideration of teachers, needs differ. For minority children, the affirmative atmosphere of cultural sensitivity may help them to understand and appreciate their cultural heritage and affirm a positive self-image that contributes to effective learning.

Research Question: How much of the information about incorporating multicultural content at early childhood levels is filtering down to child care centres?

Research Method: The data collected were part of a larger study using a random sample of fifty of Calgary's 170 day care centres. The programs were contacted by mail, followed by a telephone call. Forty-eight of the 50 centres contacted agreed to participate. Of these, 45 completed materials. Using the Infant-Toddler Environment Rating Scale (ITERS) (Harms, Cryer, & Clifford,

1990), the quality of the centres was evaluated. Observations were made in the toddler rooms of children between the ages of nineteen and thirty-five months. Caregivers were asked about daily routines and program policy. Directors were interviewed and left with a mail-in survey. As well as using the ITERS, researchers recorded the availability of multicultural resources, including posters, pictures, dolls, books, and role play materials. Caregivers were asked about their country of origin and race. The caregivers were rated on their caregiving skills using a revised version of the Spot-Observation Scale (Shimoni et al., 1990).

Toddler rooms were examined for the presence, appropriateness, and availability of multicultural materials. Books were inspected for positive representation of cultural diversity and/or racial minorities. Similar criteria were used for pictures and posters, dolls, and pretend-play materials.

Results: At the time of data collection, Alberta had among the lowest regulatory standards for child care centres in Canada. For example, the only required staff qualifications were that at least one person at the centre had to be eighteen years of age or older and at least one person had to have first-aid training. No other regulations were in effect regarding staff training or parental involvement.

Of the forty-five centres included in the study, thirteen (28.9%) had toddler rooms rated as good to excellent on the ITERS; another thirteen were rated as having adequate or custodial care, while the largest number of programs, nineteen (42.2%) fell into the inferior to poor range.

Only ten of the forty-five centres (10%) had from four to seven items available to the children at any given time that incorporated positive representation of cultural diversity. Seventeen centres (37.8%) had from one to three such items, while the greatest number of centres (eighteen, or 40%) had no positive multicultural materials.

A total of 106 caregivers were observed caring for the children in the toddler rooms. Of these, 25 (23.6%) were members of visible minorities, while 81 (76.4%) were Caucasian. Seventy-five (70.8%) had been born in Canada; twenty-one (19.8%) were born in the United States or England; ten (9.4%) were born in a developing country such as Jamaica, India, or Chile. Thirty-three (31.1%) of caregivers had training in early childhood education; fourteen (13.2%) had other types of training; and fifty-nine (55.7%) had only high school or less. Only one of the 106 child care workers in the study was male. There was a turnover rate approaching 50% annually.

Implication: The observations of the programs revealed several general problems that beset any effort to implement a multicultural program. As previously stated, children enrolled in poor quality programs tend to have poorer language skills. In this study, 42.2% of programs were inadequate. Staff qualifications are associated with higher rates of responsiveness, encouragement of the children's efforts, social stimulation, and the provision of developmentally appropriate activities (Doherty-Derkowski 1995). Only 31.1% of caregivers had the type of education found to benefit children.

The researchers felt that cultural programming was too often offered piecemeal. Traditional and out-of-date examples of cultural differences were often emphasized (such as showing native people living in teepees and wearing blankets), giving an inaccurate, simplistic, stereotyped view of people's way of life today. Overgeneralizations failed to recognize subgroup variations within cultures. The teachers were unfamiliar with or uncomfortable with a culturally sensitive approach.

The alarming results of this study underline the need for improved programming in child care centres. In high quality programs, the cultural and ethnic background of each child must be taken into consideration and the curriculum adjusted accordingly. It is also important that the program recognize that families differ within the same ethnic or cultural group and that not all families of a culture have exactly the same child rearing practices. There is a need for culturally sensitive curriculum development to form a part of teacher preparation programs.

In the 1991 discussion paper developed by the Canadian Child Care Federation on teacher preparation, it is recommended that ongoing and rigorous attention to program content and instructional material ensure a positive regard for multicultural issues.

The interconnections among training, early childhood, and the larger society are abundant. There is an urgent need to increase caregiver sensitivity to cultural diversity, the child rearing practices of different cultures, and their effect on the well-being of young children.

"Multiculturalism in Daycare: An Exploratory Study," B. Friesen, J. Friesen, 1992. *Multiculturalism/Multicultural-isme*, 14, Nos. 2 and 3, 1992, pp. 35-42. Reprinted with permission.

Make It Clear to the Families That You Value the Child's Native Language and Cultural Background

In the following discussion I use Spanish for the sake of brevity, but Ojibway, French, Vietnamese, or any other language could be used to make the same points.

The most important thing for children to learn about school is that it is a place where they feel welcome and comfortable. Including songs and stories in Spanish, using multi-ethnic pictures, and observing Latino customs honour the family by using the language and customs of the home at school. Asking children for the Spanish equivalents of English words will help clarify that there are different languages and, if done with respect and enthusiasm, point up the fact that the Spanish-speaking child has a special ability and skill.

It is also valuable to form close bonds of mutual concern with the parents of the children (Areñas, 1978; Bowman, 1990). Not all parents want their children to continue to learn in Spanish. This attitude varies a good deal from family to family, and teachers should discuss this subject with them, help them weigh the pros and cons, and respect their preferences in every way they can. Most families are realistic about the value of learning English and are almost too eager to have their children gain this skill. It may even be necessary to explain why Spanish is being included as a major component in the curriculum. Other families, rarer in number, will welcome the bicultural emphasis to such an extent that they may be reluctant to include English at all. The research of Bruce Friesen, described in the research study in this chapter, identifies the urgent need for caregivers to increase their cultural sensitivity in meeting the needs of young children.

Sometimes centre values in language development run counter to deep-seated cultural values in the home. For example, it may be necessary to explain to parents the positive relationship between language competence and the maximum development of intelligence. Such explanations may encourage some families to overcome their traditional view that children should be seen and not heard, and the parents may make greater efforts to encourage their children to talk more at home.

Sometimes, of course, it is the teacher rather than the family who needs to make the cultural adjustment. Some teachers, for instance, in their eagerness to promote verbalness in the children fall into the habit of allowing them to interrupt adult conversations whenever they please. This is frowned on in many homes. In such cases the teacher would do well to change his policy and encourage participation by the children while seeing to it that they continue to observe the basic good manners taught by their own culture.

When Teaching Bilingual Children, Do Not Attribute All Verbal, Expressive, and Comprehension Difficulties to Bilingualism

Many children who come to school speaking only a little English are quite fluent in their mother tongue, and for them the transition to English is not too difficult. *It is very important to distinguish between these youngsters and those who do not talk very much in either language.* These nontalkers are the ones who need all the help they can get in developing the habit of verbalness. For such youngsters the goal is to increase fluency and participa-

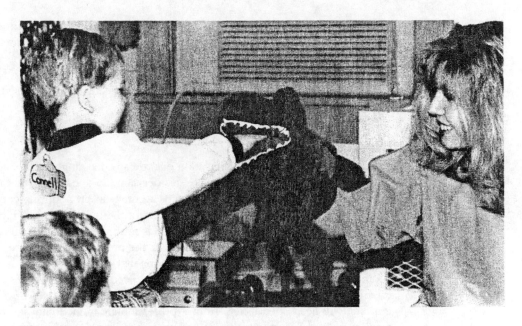

❧   *Using a simple prop often sparks participation by adding fun to the experience.*

tion in whichever language they feel more at ease; teaching English to them is of secondary importance to gaining fluency and the habit of talking.

❧ Children Who Have Special Disabilities Related to Speech and Hearing

Several kinds of speech and hearing disabilities are seen quite commonly in the preschool classroom. Indeed, the teacher may find that he is the first person to be aware that the child has a speech problem, since the parent may be too accustomed to it to notice or too inexperienced to identify it as deviating markedly from normal speech. The four problems the teacher is most likely to come across are articulation disorders, delayed speech, hearing disorders, and stuttering.

With all these conditions, if the difficulty is pronounced or continues without positive change for two or three months after the child enters the centre, the teacher should talk the problem over with the parents. Such referrals usually require both time (for the parents to become used to the idea that their child needs extra help) and tact (so that they do not feel blamed or accused of neglecting her). (For more information on how to make a successful referral, please refer to chapter 9).

There are a number of appropriate referral resources for such children. Some universities maintain speech and hearing clinics supervised by highly trained professionals. Children's hospitals usually have speech clinicians on their staffs, as do many public school boards. These people are always glad to suggest appropriate referrals for speech therapy if the youngster does not qualify for help directly from the hospital or school.

Children with Disorders of Articulation

The teacher's problem with articulation disorders is deciding which ones are serious and which should be overlooked. To make this decision, the most important thing the teacher must know is that children do not acquire accuracy in pronouncing certain sounds until they are in the first or second grade. The information included in Figure 17.1 will be helpful in determining whether a child who is mispronouncing certain sounds should be referred to a speech pathologist for help. At the preschool level, therefore, there will be many distortions, substitutions, and omissions that can be treated with a combination of auditory training and benign neglect. *However, referral is warranted when the child's speech is generally unintelligible and the child is older than three or three-and-a-half,* since it is likely that she will need special help from a professionally trained clinician to learn to speak more plainly. The only unfortunate outcome of such a referral is that the therapist might decide the child does not need special help after all. This can be mildly embarrassing to the teacher, but it is better that he take this risk if the child's speech seems seriously impaired than let her poor speech habits continue until she reaches kindergarten.

Besides knowing when to refer and when to overlook the articulation disorder, the teacher should realize that there is a lot more to correcting an articulation problem than just reminding the child, "Don't say 'wed,' say 'red'". Traditional speech therapists usually proceed by (a) using auditory discrimination games to help the child hear the error and tell it apart from other sounds, (b) eliminating the cause of the disorder if possible (for example, encouraging the parents to raise their speech standards at home so that the child no longer gets by with infantile speech patterns), (c) teaching her to make the correct sound by itself, and (d) finally incorporating it into familiar words (Hegde & Davis, 1992; Van Riper & Emerick, 1990).

The problem with this kind of isolated work is getting it to carry over into everyday speech (Gerber, 1993; Kirk & Gallagher, 1989, Manolson, 1992). To make carryover more likely, newer approaches are now coming into use (Gerber, 1993). Rather than pulling the child out of her usual environment, taking her off to a quiet place, providing isolated practice in particular skills, and then restoring her to the classroom, these therapists work right in the classroom along with the regular staff. They do their best to seize on opportunities for meaningful practice that occur as the child is involved in ongoing activities. This procedure not only means the needed language skill is integrated into the child's ordinary life, but also means that the staff has the chance to observe and learn how to provide continued practice in those skills when the therapist is no longer there (Patrick, 1993). (Please refer to chapter 9 for a more detailed discussion of how this interdisciplinary approach works.)

It is in this regard that the early childhood teacher can be the most help—not by nagging the child but by encouraging conversation. During such talk an occasional puzzled look of not understanding what the child is saying followed by pleased comprehension if she repeats the word more clearly will encourage better articulation habits. Of course, all the children will benefit from consistent auditory discrimination activities included in group time, just as they will from the many other means of developing language ability discussed earlier in this chapter.

Children with Delayed Speech

Although articulation disorders are encountered with greater frequency, the teacher is more likely to notice the child who does not talk or who talks very little. Such youngsters are often referred to nursery schools and children's centres by paediatricians and in certain cases can be helped effectively by that teacher.

Causes of Delayed Speech

Causes of delayed speech are myriad and range from the child's being hard of hearing to having a neuromuscular disorder such as cerebral palsy. Low intelligence is another common cause of delayed speech, and negativism or extreme shyness also takes its toll. Lack of sufficient environmental stimulation or low parental expectations may also mean that a child has not developed to her full verbal potential.

In such cases the teacher needs to take a keen, continuing look at the child to try and determine what lies behind the lack of speech. Making a home visit can help ascertain whether she just does not talk at school or whether her nonverbal behaviour is consistent in all situations.

It is often difficult or impossible for someone who is not specially trained to spot the cause of lags in speech development. Contrary to general opinion, children who are slow learners do not necessarily look different from their peers. I have known several instances in which mildly or even moderately delayed youngsters were denied help and appropriate teaching because the cardinal symptom of delayed speech went unquestioned by an inexperienced teacher because the child "looked normal." The services of a competent psychologist can be enlisted to identify the slow learner if the child is referred to her. Neuromuscular disorders do not always manifest themselves in obvious ways either; so when such a condition appears to be a likely possibility, a referral to the child's paediatrician is a sound approach to take.

Children who restrict themselves from talking because they are overwhelmed by the newness of school, who speak a different language, or who do not talk because they appear to have been deprived of sufficient speech stimulation at home are the ones with the brightest prognosis. In these cases the teacher can gently draw them forth and elicit more speech by responding positively to their venturings. Many of these children will make a heartening gain in fluency during the year or two they spend at the centre if the methods described in the previous section on developing language skills are applied to them.

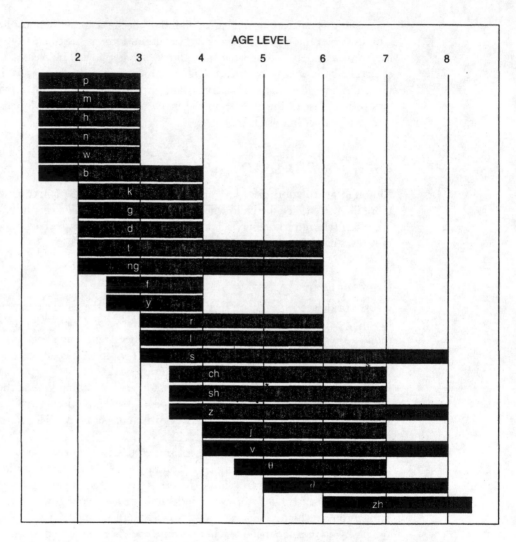

***Figure* 17.1**   Average age estimates and upper age limits of customary consonant production. The solid bar corresponding to each sound starts at the median age of customary articulation; it stops at an age level at which 90% of all children are customarily producing the sound.
Source: From "When Are Speech Sounds Learned?" by E. K. Sander, 1972, *Journal of Speech and Hearing Disorders, 37*(1), p. 62. © 1972 by the American Speech and Hearing Association. Reprinted by permission.

Children with Disorders of Hearing

Another useful way teachers can help the children in their care is to be on the lookout for those who do not hear well. This is a surprisingly common disorder, yet it often goes by unnoticed.

Studies show that as many as *one out of every three young children suffer from some form of hearing loss* (Teele, Klein, & Rosner, 1989). Ironically the most common kind of loss, a conductive hearing loss resulting from trouble in the middle ear and often due to infection, is not usually picked up in screening tests so that many youngsters who have had their hearing tested slip through the testing screen with this disability not identified. This is particularly unfortunate because middle-ear-type losses account for about 90% of all hearing losses in children and are also most amenable to cure or correction once detected. For these reasons it is important to educate parents that they should request a test for conductive hearing loss, called a *tympanometric test,* as well as a pure tone audiometer test when having their children's hearing evaluated.

Children attending centres are particularly likely to suffer from these middle-ear infections *(otitis media)* because they are exposed to more colds and upper respiratory diseases, which often lead to infections and loss of hearing acuity in the middle ear (Froom & Culpepper, 1991). If left untreated, these infections can last for months and make a real difference in how well the youngster hears what is said and, ultimately, in how clearly she speaks. Families tend to adjust to this condition without realizing the child's hearing has diminished, so it is particularly important for teachers to be alert to the sometimes rather subtle symptoms of hearing loss (Watt, Roberts, & Zeisel, 1993).

A child with the following behaviours or conditions should alert the teacher to the possibility that she may be hard of hearing. The teacher should be on the lookout for

1. The child who does not talk.

2. The child who watches you intently but often "just doesn't seem to understand."

3. The child who does not respond or turn around when the teacher speaks to her in a normal tone of voice from behind her.

4. The child who consistently pays little attention during the story hour or who always wants to sit right up in front of the teacher.

5. The child whose speech is indistinct and difficult to understand, most particularly if high frequency sounds such as *f* and *s* are missing from her speech.

6. The child who talks more softly or loudly than most of the children.

7. The child whose attention you have to catch by touching her on the shoulder.

8. The child who often asks you to repeat sentences for her or says "Huh?" a lot.

9. The child who has a perpetual cold, runny nose, frequent earaches, or who usually breathes through her mouth.

10. The child who consistently ignores you unless you get right down and look her in the eye as you talk to her.

11. Any child who has recently recovered from measles, meningitis, scarlet fever, or a severe head injury.

Such youngsters are prime candidates for audiometric testing. Of course, it is also true that children talk indistinctly, want to sit close to the teacher, or fail to pay attention for reasons other than hearing loss. But *particularly if more than one of these symptoms describe her usual behaviour,* the possibility of a hearing deficit is worth investigating. Referrals may be made to an otolaryngologist (a doctor who treats ear and throat disorders) or to the child's paediatrician, who will send her to the best place to receive help.

Hearing losses can result from many causes besides otitis media. Sometimes the loss can be remedied through surgery; but if the loss is permanent, continued professional guidance will be necessary. Although hearing aids do not alleviate all forms of deafness, they can be effective in many cases. Hearing aids combined with speech therapy and auditory training are helpful for many children suffering from loss of hearing.

Children Who Stutter

Although we do know that an easy, unselfconscious form of repetitive speech is often observed in children of preschool age, we do not yet understand why this should be the case. This first stage of repetitive speech differs markedly from the strained, emotion-laden hesitancies and repetitions of the confirmed stutterer and is more than likely liable to vanish *if teachers and family do not react to it with concern and tension.*

Teachers can play an effective role in helping parents deal with their concern over this potential problem. First, they should encourage them to relax and not to direct attention to the behaviour. This includes *not* saying to the child, "Now, just slow down; I'll wait 'till you're ready," or "Don't talk so fast," or "Your ideas just get ahead of your tongue; take it easy" (Swan, 1993). They should also reassure the family by explaining that this behaviour is common in young children who are undergoing the stress of learning to talk. The goal here is to encourage parents to relax and reduce stressful situations in the home so that the child will not become concerned about his speech.

Since stuttering increases when the child is undergoing stress, it can be helpful to avoid hurrying her when possible, to allow plenty of time for her to speak, to speak a little slowly when carrying on conversations with her, to provide her with your full but relaxed attention when she speaks to you, and to avoid putting her on the spot by asking direct questions or urging her to talk in front of others during group time (Williams, n.d.).

It is also wise to enquire of the family if something is currently making life more difficult for her at home. Do what you can to relieve that situation. Examples of stressful events could include a parent's job loss, adjusting to a new babysitter, moving, the arrival of a baby, holding the child to unreasonably high standards of behaviour, or a death or divorce in the family. Tension-relieving activities such as dramatic play, water play, and various forms of sublimated aggressive activities can be provided that may reduce some of the child's tensions and attendant stuttering.

As with other speech disorders, it is also necessary to have some rule of thumb for referral when working with a child who stutters. At the preprimary level it seems wise to refer the family for further help if they are reacting strongly to the behaviour and are unable to control their signs of concern, if they seem unable to reduce the tension-generating situations without outside help, or if the stuttering persists.

ꕶ Summary

The development of language skills in preschool children has become of cardinal interest to their teachers as evidence mounts that linguistic competence and mental ability go hand in hand.

Children appear to acquire language partially as a result of an inborn ability to do so and partially in response to environmental conditioning. Much remains to be learned in this area, and a complete explanation of how language is acquired remains one of the tantalizing mysteries of human development.

In recent years the science of pragmatics, which stresses the interactional importance of the social and developmental aspects of language acquisition, has come increasingly to the fore. In this area studies relating to the way children learn to use conversation have been of particular interest to early childhood teachers.

Teachers of young children can do many things to facilitate children's language acquisition:

1. They listen carefully to what children have to say.

2. They provide a meaningful base of experience to talk about.

3. They encourage conversation among children.

4. They talk with children themselves.

5. They use questions to generate speech and develop language.

6. When necessary, they seek professional assistance for children who require it.

In this chapter the issues of cultural sensitivity in the preschool, bilingualism, and the adjustment of newcomers to Canada were also discussed, and some suggestions were included about teaching English as a second language.

Finally, four common disorders of speech and hearing were identified: disorders of articulation, delayed speech, deficient hearing, and stuttering. Recommendations were made for classroom treatment and remediation of these disorders, and suggestions for referral were included.

Questions and Activities

1. Identify some factors in the program where you teach that encourage the development of conversation between children and adults. What are some things that discourage conversation between them?

2. List some additional conversation starters you have found useful in getting young children involved in talking with the teacher or with other children.

3. *Problem:* A mother calls and says her paediatrician has suggested that she place Silas in preschool because he has been a little slow in learning to talk. As you become acquainted with Silas, it does appear to you that his speech is slow to develop. He is three years old and still communicates mainly by grunting, nodding his head, or pointing when he wants something. List some possible reasons why his speech might be developing so slowly. How would you go about determining which cause is the most likely one? Propose a course of action that would be most appropriate for each probable cause.

4. Do you feel that teachers have the right to change something as personal to the child as her dialect or dominant language? Under what circumstances do you think doing this is warranted or unwarranted?
5. Do you advocate setting up programs that use only the child's native tongue or dialect? What would be the strong points of doing this? What might be the drawbacks?

Self-Check Questions for Review

Content-Related Questions

1. Describe three theories that attempt to explain the process by which children learn to talk.
2. On what aspects of language acquisition do people who study pragmatics concentrate?
3. About how many words should a child have at his command by the age of one? By the age of two?
4. Give some examples of what a teacher might say to encourage conversation between children.
5. List some important principles the teacher should remember for encouraging conversation between herself and the children.
7. Suppose you had a child in your room who did not speak any English. How could you help her to feel comfortable and to gradually learn a second language?
7. What are the four most common types of speech and language disorders in young children, and what might be the symptoms for each of these that the teacher should look for?
8. Should teachers and parents always be concerned when children repeat words several times when speaking?

Integrative Questions

1. Does the nativist or behaviourist theory offer more hope to a teacher who has a three-year-old child in her class who isn't talking yet? Explain why you have selected whichever theory you chose.
2. As a teacher of young children, do you think it is more valuable to understand the theories of how language is acquired or to understand the effects pragmatics has on language development? Be sure to explain why you have selected one or the other.
3. A friend has brought a female goat to visit your group of four-year-olds at school and is milking her.

Sarah Lee says, "The milk's splashing!" Give an example of what you would reply that would expand that comment. Next, give an example of a reply that would enrich and extend it.
4. Referring to the findings of the Friesen study, identify strategies to strengthen the cultural responsiveness of early childhood programs.

References for Further Reading

Overviews

Baron, N. S. (1992). *Growing up with language: How children learn to talk.* Reading, MA: Addison-Wesley. Baron provides us with an interesting, chatty book written primarily for parents but based on recent research about language development. She includes many practical suggestions about ways to facilitate its growth.

James, S. L. (1990). *Normal language acquisition.* Boston: Allyn & Bacon. This book discusses the development of language from birth through school age in clear, understandable terms. *Highly recommended.*

Lindfors, J. W. (1987). *Children's language and learning* (2nd ed.). Englewood Cliffs, NJ: Prentice Hall. This is an excellent, readable presentation of an important subject. *Highly recommended.*

Fostering Conversation

Bos, B. (1983). *Before the basics: Creating conversations with children.* Roseville, CA: Turn the Page Press. Bos's book is an utter delight! It is mostly about generating happy, wholesome relationships with children through the media of music, conversation, and movement.

McCabe, A. (1992). *Language games to play with your child: Enhancing communication from infancy through late childhood* (Rev. ed.). New York: Plenum Press. Lots of ways to develop communication skills are included that are developmentally appropriate as well as just plain fun.

Sholtys, K. C. (1989). A new language, a new life: Recommendations for teachers of non-English speaking children newly entering the program. *Young Children, 44*(3), 76–77. The title is self-explanatory.

Stone, J. (1993). Caregiver and teacher language: Responsive or restrictive? *Young Children, 48*(4), 12–18. Replete with examples, this article makes a good case for becoming more sensitive to the way the teacher's use of language affects children's responses. *Highly recommended.*

Bilingual and Multilectical Information

Dotsch, J. (1992). Newcomer preschool children: Their linguistic adaptation to childcare settings. *Multiculturalism, 14* (2–3): 24–26. The author summarizes a research study looking and three-year-old immigrant children's ability to adapt to child care settings. Issues such as settlement, cultural adaptation, and acquisition of a second language are discussed.

Soto, L. D. (1991). Research in review: Understanding bilingual/bicultural young children. *Young children, 46*(2), 30–36. Soto reviews some myths about bilingualism and then outlines research-tested, effective approaches for teaching bilingual children.

Disorders of Speech and Hearing

Allen, E., Paasche, C., Cornell, A., & Engel, M. (1994). *Exceptional children: Inclusion in early childhood programs* (1st Can. ed.). Scarborough, ON: Nelson Canada. This book includes a good chapter on facilitating language, speech, and communication. Also very useful is the chapter on bilingualism, which identifies current Canadian issues relating to learning first and second languages and lists ways teachers can support the growth of the child's home language.

Behan, B., & Fannis, J. (1990). *Signs for me: Basic sign vocabulary for children.* Berkeley, CA: Dawn Sign Press. This book presents clear illustrations based on American Sign Language signs for frequently needed words. The vocabulary is appealingly pictured— humorous when possible, and mildly multiethnic.

Manolson, I. (1992). *It takes two to talk* (2nd ed.). Toronto: Hanen Canada. This well-illustrated guidebook contains clear and practical information on how parents and caregivers can facilitate their children's language learning within everyday conversations, daily routines, and play activities.

Oyer, H. J., Crowe, B., & Haas, W. (1987). *Speech, language and hearing disorders: A guide for the teacher.* Boston: College Hill. This is a clear, quick-reading, concise book that offers practical recommendations for what the classroom teacher can do to facilitate good language habits. *Highly recommended.*

Paasche, C., Gorrill, L., Strom, B. (1990). *Children with special needs in early childhood settings: Identification, intervention, mainstreaming.* Don Mills: Addison-Wesley Canada. This book contains information on speech and language disorders and identifies resources for referral.

Patrick, S. (1993). Facilitating communication and language development. In T. W. Linder (Ed.), *Transdisciplinary play-based intervention: Guidelines for developing a meaningful curriculum for young children.* Baltimore: Paul Brookes. Patrick's lengthy chapter uses many examples and covers a variety of language difficulties, basing therapeutic suggestions on developmentally appropriate practices.

Swan, A. M. (1993). Helping children who stutter: What teachers need to know. *Childhood Education, 69*(3), 138–141. Swan provides a useful, concise article summing up what is currently known about the causes and treatment of this disorder.

Watt, M. R., Roberts, J. E., & Zeisel, S. A. (1993). Ear infections in young children: The role of the early childhood educator. *Young Children, 49*(1), 65–72. Valuable information on otitis media, its symptoms, and treatment are included in this helpful article.

For the Advanced Student

Ambert, A. N. (Ed.). (1991) *Bilingual education and English as a second language: A research handbook, 1988–1990.* New York: Garland. This valuable book reminds us by citing studies concerning Asian and French children as well as those of Hispanic origin that bilingualism is characteristic of many cultures.

Chud, G., & Fahlman, R. (1995). *Honouring diversity within child care and early education: An instructor's guide.* Victoria: B.C. Ministry of Skills, Training and Labour. This manual includes discussion of the development of language, English as a second language, and bilingualism.

Dyson, A. H., & Genishi, C. (1993). Visions of children as language users: Language and language education in early childhood. In B. Spodek (Ed.), *Handbook of research on the education of young children.* New York: Macmillan. The authors stress the role of socialization in children's language development.

Hecht, M. L., Collier, M. J., & Ribeau, S. A. (1993). *African American communication: Ethnic identity and cultural interpretation.* Newbury Park, CA: Sage. The authors provide a wide-ranging analysis of various components of African American communicative style.

Owens, R. E. (1992). *Language development: An introduction* (3rd ed.). Englewood Cliffs, NJ: Merrill/Prentice Hall. Readers who require an in-depth discussion of language acquisition and development will find this book very useful.

Additional Resources of Interest

American Speech-Language-Hearing Association. 10801 Rockville Pike, Rockville, MD 20852 (1-800-638-8255, voice or TDD). The ASHA is the professional organization for teachers to turn to when they need help finding assistance for various language disabilities.

The Hanen Program, 252 Bloor St. W., Ste. 3-390, Toronto, ON M5S 1V5. This international service is committed to helping children communicate to the best of their ability and to providing parents and teachers with the necessary knowledge and support. As well as providing direct services, they offer professional development experiences and numerous support materials. Their resources have been translated into French, Spanish, Hebrew, Dutch, Korean, Portuguese, Arabic, and Swiss German.

18 Fostering the Emergence of Literacy

What to say to parents when they suggest you teach the four-year-olds to read?

What people are talking about when they mention *emergent literacy*?

How you can get wiggly Matilda to hold still during group time?

. . . If you have, the material on the following pages will help you.

Children are provided many opportunities to see how reading and writing are useful before they are instructed in letter names, sounds, and word identification. Basic skills develop when they are meaningful to children. An abundance of these types of activities is provided to develop language and literacy through meaningful experience: listening to and reading stories and poems; taking field trips; dictating stories; seeing classroom charts and other print in use; participating in dramatic play and other experiences requiring communication; talking informally with other children and adults; and experimenting with writing by drawing, copying, and inventing their own spelling.

S. Bredekamp

A current concern of many early childhood teachers is the pressure some parents and society as a whole are putting on them to present a highly structured reading program in the preschool.

Rather than just deploring the effects such pressure would have on the children because such expectations are developmentally inappropriate, as the opening quotation makes clear, it is wiser to understand what it is parents (and, hence, society) want, and then to understand how to reassure them while protecting the children from unreasonable expectations.

Parents are not ogres; they simply want what's best for their children. They see the world as a difficult place to grow up in, they see technology advancing at a frightening pace, and they want their children to be successful, competent grown-ups who can cope with that world. They know that intellectual competence is one of the keys to effective

Children can do their part in creating a print-rich environment.

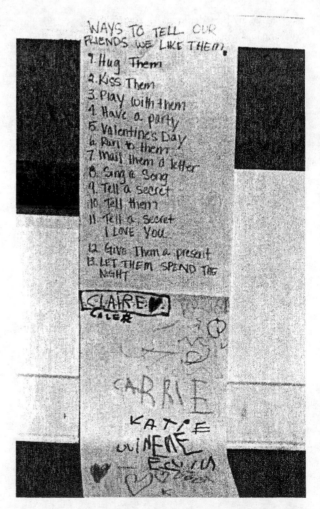

functioning in that world, and they think of the ABCs and numbers, reading and arithmetic, as being the cognitive skills that will provide their children with that competence. After all, this is what they were taught when they went to school, so it is only reasonable that they think of "real learning" as consisting of that kind of instruction.

What teachers should do is conduct a careful educational campaign with the children's parents to inform them about what the children are learning at the centre. The teachers should explain that what they are doing *is* appropriate for the children's age and developmental stage and will pave the way for learning to read more easily later on.

Part of this information will, inevitably, involve explaining how children learn from play and also explaining all the benefits children derive from being involved in such preschool activities as blocks, sand, and water. But it should also include clear-cut descriptions of the various reasoning and problem-solving skills that are incorporated into the curriculum each day, accompanied by explanations of how these abilities underlie later competence in school. These skills are discussed in detail in chapters 19, 20, and 21.

In addition to these explanations, the teacher needs to add information about all the language development activities that are part and parcel of a good preschool curriculum. She needs to emphasize that these activities construct the foundation on which reading is later built. (Please refer to chapter 17). These range from learning new words to telling a coherent story about what happened on the way to school. They include using language in conversation or using it to make the child's desires known, as well as learning that books can be a source of fascinating pleasure at group time.

Activities such as these form the foundation for later reading and writing. Parents need to understand that learning to read is a lengthy process, and much preparation and maturation must take place before it can be accomplished successfully (Fields & Spangler, 1995; Glazer & Burke, 1994). Once parents realize that the teacher knows what she is doing and that she is "really teaching the children something" that will form a solid foundation for later learning at the elementary school level, they generally stop asking about reading per se and become supportive of what is provided at the preschool level.

ॐ *Does Fostering Literacy Mean Teaching Reading?*

From one point of view, it is unnecessary to discuss implementing literacy in the preschool classroom because children have been doing it for years, anyway! Every time a child singles out his name tag and puts it on, or finds the book he has been hunting for, or supplies the phrase the gingerbread boy says as he runs from his potential captors, or counts the number of spoonfuls needed in a recipe, he is using literacy-related skills. Every time he substitutes a pretend spoon for a real one, or tells what's happening in a picture, or uses language in any form, then, too, he is engaged in emerging literacy activities because all of these activities and hundreds like them are examples of the array of skills that underlie the ultimate skills of reading and writing.

This understanding of what constitutes true literacy makes it clear that its development entails far more than learning skills such as handwriting, decoding the printed word, and spelling. As McLane and McNamee (1990) point out, "Literacy development consists of mastering a complex set of attitudes, expectations, feelings, behaviors, and skills related to the written language. This collection of attitudes and skills constitutes what has been called 'emergent literacy'" (p. 4).

And yet the idea of fostering reading and writing strategies continues to make many preschool teachers feel uncomfortable and concerned (Gibson, 1989). This resistance is not without reason. As the guardians of children's rights to be children and to learn in developmentally appropriate ways and at suitable levels, we teachers of very young children have had to resist the pressures of inappropriate expectations and methods and watered down elementary curricula for more years than we like to remember. If literacy means teaching the ABCs and phonics to three- and four-year-olds, then we must continue our resistance.

However, *emergent literacy* does not advocate such approaches. It does *not* mean that we are going to teach the children to read—far from it. Research has shown time and time again that the arts of reading and writing (for the two must go together) rely on the prior acquisition of a great many foundation concepts and strategies—strategies that teachers of young children have been encouraging children to develop for many years. Table 18.1 lists many of those activities that are basic to helping children develop literacy. Note that all of them down through scribbling in item 5 are frequently part of the preschool curriculum.

🕉 Some Fundamental Principles To Keep In Mind

The majority of the basics listed in Table 18.1 have been discussed in previous chapters, so only the most fundamental principles will be reviewed here.

Teachers Should Make It Plain They Value the Wonderful World of Books

This can be done if the teacher clearly enjoys the good book she is reading aloud as much as the children do. There is no substitute for this infectious enthusiasm.

Because children's literary and aesthetic tastes are being formed every time they come in contact with a book, it is important to select them with great care. There's really no excuse for offering children cheap and "cute" but essentially worthless books when all it takes is a trip to the library to find wonderful, beautifully illustrated ones. *Story Stretchers* and *More Story Stretchers* (Raines & Canady, 1989, 1991) are helpful resources for choosing such books. A number of additional resources are included at the end of this chapter.

The high value the teacher places on good books is also shown in more subtle ways by the care that everyone in the room takes of them. Books belong in people's laps or enjoyed in the rocking chair—not left on the floor to be trampled. Old favourites should be promptly mended and torn pages carefully taped with the children's help.

Teachers Should Emphasize How Useful the Written Word Can Be

For example, the shared experience of writing a note to the janitor asking her to leave up their block construction can make this usefulness obvious to the block builders. Empowering children by encouraging them to follow an illustrated recipe on their own provides

Table 18.1

Foundations of Literacy

Source: Let's begin reading right: Developmentally appropriate beginning literacy (3rd ed.), p. 104, by M. V. Fields and K. S. Spangler (1995). Columbus, OH: Merrill. Used by permission.

Literacy Basics

1. A print-rich environment
   adults who read for their own purposes
   adults who write for their own purposes
   frequent story time experiences
   dictation experiences
   high-quality literature
   contextualized print
   functional print
   answers to questions about print

2. A rich oral language environment
   adult language models
   adults who listen to children
   free exploration of oral language
     peer conversation
     dramatic play roles
   experiences for vocabulary enrichment
   vocabulary information as requested

3. Firsthand experiences of interest
   play
   daily living
   field trips
   nature exploration

4. Symbolic representation experiences
   dramatic play
   drawing and painting
   music and dance

5. Pressure-free experimentation with writing
   drawing
   scribbling
   nonphonetic writing
   invented spelling

6. Pressure-free exploration of reading
   reading from memory
   reading with context clues
   matching print to oral language

♂ **RESEARCH STUDY** ♂

Promoting Literacy in a Developmentally Appropriate Way

Research Questions: Morrow wanted to find out if children's voluntary literacy behaviours could be increased during play by altering the design and equipment of the dramatic play areas. She also wanted to find out what effect teacher guidance during play would have on the amount of literacy behaviour.

Research Method: The middle-class suburban sample consisted of thirteen preschool classrooms with a total of 170 children, half of each sex. The staff for each room was composed of a cooperating teacher and a student teacher. Prior to the experiment, literacy materials had not been incorporated in the dramatic play areas of any of the classrooms.

The classrooms were divided into four groups, with the three experimental groups (E1, E2, and E3) receiving the same literacy materials: various sized paper, a stapler, blank booklets, books, magazines, and writing materials such as pencils, crayons, and felt pens. The differences in the three experimental groups had to do with whether the teacher guided the play by suggesting possible literacy-based activities at the beginning of each

play period (E1 and E2) and whether a specific theme was used in the play (E2 and E3).

C1—*the control group,* in which nothing was changed

E1—*nonthematic guided play* with literacy materials placed in the housekeeping area

E2—*thematic nonguided play* with literacy materials placed in the housekeeping area

E3—*thematic guided play* with literacy materials using the theme of a veterinary office

All four groups were observed several times before the experiment began in order to establish a baseline and determine the amount of literacy activity before changes were introduced.

After that, the literacy materials were introduced into the experimental classrooms. Observations of the children's play in the control and experimental settings were made for three weeks, then, after a month's lapse, for three more weeks.

The resulting data were sorted into four categories of literacy behaviour: paper handling, attempted writing, attempted reading, and combined scores for the three behaviours.

---

the satisfaction of accomplishment for independent four-year-olds. "You didn't even have to tell me nothin'!" chortled one of the Institute youngsters the other day. "I read it all!"—and he had. Labelling containers and activity areas also helps tie together the idea that written words stand for real objects.

Opportunities that encourage children to incorporate various forms of language into their play are yet another effective way to foster emerging literacy skills. For example, Roskos and Neuman (1994) suggest that the housekeeping corner could include a phone book, cookbooks, coupons, marketing list materials, play money, and calendars, just to name a few possibilities. Office play could utilize envelopes, telephone message pads, magazines, and, of course, paper, pencils, an old typewriter or perhaps a computer,

Results: Morrow found that changing the physical design definitely did increase the amount of voluntary literacy behaviours for some of the children [the investigator notes that the use of the materials was "limited to only a few children per classroom" (p. 549)]. Children in all three of the experimental groups included more literacy behaviours during their play than did the control group. The two groups that experienced teacher guidance along with the addition of the literacy materials used the materials more than the group that did not have teacher guidance. Moreover, the introduction of the theme of the veterinarian's office produced more total literacy behaviours and more interactive play than did the nonthematic housekeeping setting. The final interesting result was that the literacy behaviour continued over a rather long period of time (three weeks of observation, a month interim, plus three more weeks of observation time).

Implications for Teaching: It is clear from this research that teachers who want their preschool children to participate in voluntary literacy activities can encourage that behaviour in a number of ways: They can add literacy materials to various dramatic play areas for the children to use as they see fit; they can provide specific play themes that encourage the use of attempted writing and read-

ing; and they can provide ideas and guidance about how these materials might be used by the children during their play.

In closing, some cautionary notes must be added as reminders. For one thing, it is evident that this activity appealed to only a handful of children in each classroom, so we should not conclude that all children will benefit from having this opportunity provided to them. On the other hand, the amount of time and satisfaction obviously present for some of the children points to the value of making such materials consistently available for those who are ready for them. The other thing to remember—which Morrow stresses—is that while the play was enhanced by the presence of the materials, provision of a theme, and teacher suggestions, the play that resulted was *voluntary* and produced by the children themselves—it was not the result of teacher domination. This is an important point to remember. When offering guidance, teachers must remain exquisitely sensitive to what is happening and stop short of the point at which play becomes manipulation by the teacher and loses its vital quality of spontaneity and delight.

Source: From "Preparing the classroom environment to promote literacy during play" by L. M. Morrow (1990). *Early Childhood Research Quarterly, 5(4),* 537-554.

---

stamps, and a stamp pad. In recent years a number of studies, exemplified by the research study in this chapter, have demonstrated how the use of such materials can positively affect children's literacy behaviour.

Even Very Young Children Can and Should Be Involved in Producing the Written Word

Perhaps the children can share with the teacher the experience of turning language into written text by dictating stories, letters, or ideas for the teacher to write down. Doing this emphasizes the relationship between reading and writing.

❧ *Providing an environment rich with possibilities for using letters and numbers during play provides many opportunities for children to practice emergent literacy activities.*

Pitcher and Prelinger (1963) studied over 300 stories told by children aged two to about six years. They found that as the children matured, their stories included an increasing utilization and mastery of space, a less clear differentiation of main characters, more happenings that affect the characters, and a significant increase in the use of fantasy and imagination. Therefore, when pursuing creative stories with preschool-aged children, the teacher should be prepared for considerable literalness in stories by younger children and a greater use of fantasy and imagination by older ones. But since the stories are personal descriptions and reflections of the children's feelings and perceptions, they may also be considered self-expressive and hence creative.

The following two examples of dictated stores are both factual and quite expressive of feelings.

The Doctor and the Nurse

Marice

When I got the cast off, we used an electric saw and I had something on my ears. The saw was very sharp and looked just like the sun.

The thing I had on my ears was round. I couldn't hear the electric saw, but the other doctors could. It played music very loud, as loud as the saw.

The doctor held my hand because he didn't think I could walk by myself. He's not a very good doctor, and I don't like him either—the first doctor I'm talking about.

The nurse clipped the cast off. She went out after that. I needed my privacy, anyways.

My House Story

Angelique

This first page will be about my dog. His name is Toulouse. Sometimes I can't play with him because he goes to dog school. At dog school, somebody makes him fetch sticks and makes him beg. Then he comes home and he shows me what he has learned. I also have a cat. His name is Goya, named after a painter. We always name our animals after painters.

Now about my grandmother and grandfather. My grandmother goes to Weight Watchers. They weigh her there without her shoes on.

Now about my grandfather. He drives a car. It's a red Datsun wagon pickup.

My house is white with a white picket fence. My grandma, grandpa, mommy, and me all live in the house.

My grandfather went to the hospital the day before yesterday. He had his operation yesterday. I don't like to have him in the hospital. He's not here to read me a bedtime story.

I miss him.

These stories mattered a lot to the children who wrote them. At that time the teachers were using little handmade books for recording the stories so that the children were free to illustrate them if they wished. This provided an additional way to work off their feelings and be creative. But it is not necessary to make story telling that elaborate an occasion. Taking the story down as the child dictates it often provides sufficient encouragement for the young storyteller. Pitcher collected her stories by waiting until a child was either sitting quietly by herself or playing alone and then by saying, "Tell me a story. What would your story be about?" This is a good way to get started. Of course, children sometimes do not want to participate. In this case the teacher just says, "Well, I expect you'll want to do it another time. I'll ask you then."

As with other creative materials, the teacher should scrupulously avoid suggesting what the story should be about or what might happen next. But it does encourage the creator to ask, "Then what happened? Then what did she do?" or "Do you want to tell me anything else?" These questions will help sweep the child along into the narrative.

Creative stories can also be stimulated by providing hand puppets (Burn, 1989) or flannel board materials, which can be set out for the children to use as they feel the need or used at group time for this purpose. Rubber dolls and toy animals offer another medium for imaginative stories and play. Creative stories can also be stimulated by providing pictures, which may be used as starting points for discussion.

Besides dictating and telling stories, children can learn to value written language by chanting along with the teacher, "I think I can, I think I can, I think I can" as she points to the words while reading the beloved *Little Engine That Could* (Piper, 1980). They can listen as the teacher reads aloud to them the note she is sending home to their family, and they can mail their letters at the post office before Valentine's Day. If attractive writing materials are assembled in a convenient spot, they can elaborate on their scribbles and use old envelopes in which to enclose the messages.

Although these literacy activities and others like them should be spread throughout the curriculum, just as *whole language* is integrated into the curriculum of many elementary schools, there is one particular experience during the day that provides an outstanding opportunity to foster emergent literacy. This is the experience of group time.

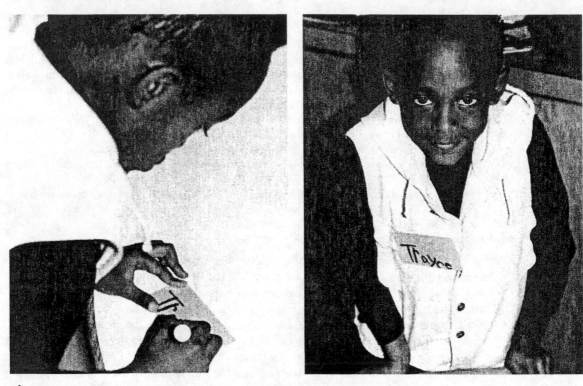

🔊   *What a wonderful beginning step Trayce is taking toward literacy.*

🔊 *Suggestions for Presenting a Language-Rich Group Time Experience*

A well-planned group time can be a high spot of the day for teachers and children, or it can become a dreaded encounter between them as the children thrash about and the teacher struggles to maintain a semblance of order.

Successful group times depend on careful advance planning by the teacher that takes into consideration such things as including enough variety, making certain the material is interesting, providing opportunities for the children to interact with the teacher, and knowing how to pace activities so they sustain the children's interest. The primary goal, of course, is to provide wonderfully enriching opportunities for the use of language and the development of emergent literacy.

Include a Variety of Activities

Unfortunately, a survey by McAfee (1985) reveals that only one out of every three teachers actually took the trouble to plan for group time at all! The same study showed that out of fourteen potential activities mentioned by teachers as being likely ingredients for group time, only a handful were actually included. Of these, the ones most frequently presented were books and music-related items.

Although books are an essential ingredient of group time, it is a pity to restrict this potentially rich language experience to only a book and a song when there are so many other interesting language-related things for the group to do together. Poetry (only mentioned three times by teachers in the McAfee study as a possibility); finger plays; auditory discrimination skills activities; and chances for discussions that involve problem solving, thinking, and reasoning skills are additional activities that merit inclusion. The inclusion of reading material that is nonsexist and multicultural is a must.

Some Specific Suggestions About Materials to Include

Do Include a Book and Poetry

The selection of a fine children's book is often the best place to begin when planning the time together, and there are many good lists of such books available (Shelton, Montgomery, & Hatcher, 1989; Sutherland, 1986). Poetry should be offered on a daily basis. (Incidentally, the only way I have ever been able to use poetry successfully has been to make a poetry file. This entails duplicating a large variety of poems from various books, mounting them on stiff cardboard to preserve them and keep them from getting lost, and then filing them according to topic. This arrangement has meant that when we suddenly need a poem about rain, all we have to do is look under that topic heading in the file and pull out a number of poems on that subject.)

Music and Finger plays Are Important, Too

Singing has its merits because it fosters language, memory, musical development, and pleasure. It takes a good deal of repetition for children to learn a new song; teachers should be prepared to sing one or two verses with them three or four times, then repeat the same song for several group times so that children can learn them well enough to sing them with verve (Wolf, 1994).

Jalongo and Collins (1985) remind us that children of different ages respond differently to songs presented by the teacher. By age two to three, children can sing an average of five different notes, join in on certain phrases of familiar songs, and show interest in records and rhythm instruments. By age three to four, children have better voice control and mastery of song lyrics. They are able to combine creative drama with singing and possess basic musical concepts such as loud-soft and fast-slow. By age four to five, children can sing an average of ten different musical notes as well as sing complete songs from memory. At that age they form the concepts of high-low and long-short tones.

Finger plays are another fine ingredient to include during groups. Again, experience has taught me that two- and three-year-olds are likely to be able to do just the actions at first and then later will add the words. But you should not be discouraged. If you persevere long enough, keep the pace slow enough, and the material brief enough, they will eventually be able to put words and actions together, which they do love to do.

Auditory Training Should Also Be Provided

A well-planned group time includes at least two additional kinds of activities besides those previously listed. The first of these is some activity that provides for auditory training and discrimination. Sometimes this can be included as part of a finger play or poem, and sometimes it needs to be a special activity. Children need work on learning to tell sounds apart and to tell when they are the same, and group time provides a fine chance to practise this skill. It is a valuable activity because it may be a helpful step toward attaining literacy, and it definitely is helpful for teaching children to discriminate among sounds so they speak more clearly.

Perhaps during a song they could sing as loud as they can and then as soft as they can; or listen to high and low notes on the autoharp, standing up when they hear a high one, and sitting down when they hear a low one; or perhaps half the children can clap their hands when they hear the sound "eee" and the other half listen for "iii."

Some other examples of activities include matching the sounds of shakers, some of which have been filled with sand, some with beans, and some with rice; everyone shutting their eyes and opening them when a particular sound is heard; listening for words left out of familiar nursery rhymes; or having the children signal when they hear sentences that do not make sense, such as "When I went to the market, I bought a camelope"—a game that appeals strongly to four-year-olds.

Many speech correction texts (Patrick, 1993) contain numerous suggestions for such activities that may be adapted for preschool children. Appendix F lists some ideas, too.

Group Time Is an Ideal Time to Provide Practice in Cognitive Skills

The second kind of activity that should be but is only rarely included in group time is one that provides practice in thinking and reasoning (such activities are described in more detail in chapters 19, 20, and 21). These include practice in the midlevel mental ability skills such as matching and temporal ordering, and also practice in the higher level skills of talking problems over and discussing how the group might solve them. Offering these activities during group time assures that all the children are receiving practice in these vital skills.

Group Time Should Provide Multiracial, Nonsexist Subject Matter

There are two additional ingredients that should also be woven into group time. Every group should contain some multiethnic or nonsexist material, or both, and conversely should not contain material that is sexist or racist. This means that the teacher will have to make a careful appraisal of the material in songs, books, and poetry before presenting them and either discard those that possess objectionable material or draw it to the children's attention and discuss it.

For example, should the teacher choose to read a book about going to the hospital, where all the doctors are white males and the nurses white females, a discussion should ensue about whether there are women doctors and male nurses and whether only white people can work at such jobs. (Please refer to chapter 14, "Providing Cross-Cultural, Nonsexist Education," for additional suggestions and for lists of multiethnic and nonsexist books).

Management Suggestions to Help Group Time Go More Smoothly

It Is Always Wise to Plan More Activities Than You Are Likely to Use

Particularly for inexperienced teachers, it is difficult to know in advance which activities will go well and which will not. It is also difficult to estimate the amount of time a particular activity will absorb. So, it is better to be safe and have extra reserves than to be caught short and run out of things to do.

Make Certain the Children Talk, Too

Include opportunities for children to respond to the teacher. During group time children should be encouraged to think, reason, and guess (hypothesize) about what is being discussed. "What would you do if you were Peter and Mr. MacGregor chased you into the potting shed?" "What *is* a potting shed, anyway?" "Do you think Peter was really sick when he got home?" "Was that the best punishment his mother could do, to put him to bed without dinner?" "What does *your* mother do when you're naughty?" and so forth. These opportunities for discussion are an invaluable part of the group experience.

Table 18.2 presents an example of one student's plan and evaluation of a group time for four-year-olds. During this time, the children were interested in "families".

Make Certain the Material Is Interesting

Part of the secret of doing this is to read the material first yourself. If you don't think it's interesting, it's a sure thing that the children won't either. It helps a lot to select books the children genuinely enjoy. Unfortunately the world abounds in dull books designed to improve children's minds but not lift their spirits. However, when books of such charm as *Mary Betty Lizzie McNutt's Birthday* (Bond, 1983), of such humour as *Gregory the Terrible Eater* (Sharmat, 1980) and *Silly Goose* (Kent, 1983), and of such sound social values as *A Chair for My Mother* (Williams, 1982), *The Goat in the Rug* (Blood & Link, 1980) *Alejandro's Gift* (Albert, 1994), and *Owl Moon* (Yolen, 1987) exist, there's really no excuse for boredom. The teacher who selects stories like these will enjoy them right along with the children, and they will arouse much comment and discussion from everyone. Remember, when a book is dull and the children are not interested, it is not necessary to read grimly through to its end; it is better to simply set it aside and go on to a more attractive choice.

Think, too, about how to present material so that it captures their attention. Using visual aids such as flannel boards helps, as does simply telling a story rather than reading it (Carter, 1994; Frelease, 1989). I have seen children absolutely enraptured by this activity; and telling stories lets the teacher look at the children all the time and be more responsive to them as they listen. Using a hand puppet also increases appeal.

Read with verve and enthusiasm. Remember, using different voices for different characters when reading *The Three Bears* (Galdone, 1985), suiting your tone of voice to the mood of the material (for example, sounding anxious and wistful when being the little bird that enquires "Are *you* my mother?") (Eastman, 1960), or building suspense during *The Three Billy Goats Gruff* (Galdone, 1981) as the children wait for the troll to appear all contribute to the fun for everyone.

Keep the Tempo of Group Time Upbeat

Pace has a lot to do with sustaining interest. Some teachers are so nervous and afraid of losing control they rush the children through the experience—ignoring children's comments and wiping out the potential richness of interchange between themselves and the children. A relaxed but definite tempo is a better pace to strive for to hold the children's attention while not making them feel harassed.

Table 18.2 Plan and evaluation of a group time for four-year-olds who were interested in families

Area	Materials	Reason for Inclusion	Was It Used?	Evaluation
Story	Radlaver, E. *Father is Big* (Bowman Publishing, 1967)	Many children today do not have a father figure. This book was not sexist; it just stated facts. Example: "His hand feels big around mine." There were actual photos that gave realistic quality.	Yes	The children seemed to enjoy the book. I got lots of comments about "my daddy." However, there seemed to be some competition as to whose daddy was biggest. This might have been bad for a child without a father. So, next time, to avoid any negative side effects, I would have used another book to read aloud (about daddies) and left this book out for individual utilization.
Poetry and finger plays	Finger play: Grandmother's Glasses	This provided a good way to include the third generation in my large group. This finger play also incorporated poetry (rhyming words) and gave the children some form of a guided activity since they were to make the actions follow the words of the finger play.	Yes	The children were familiar with this finger play and I received some advice on "how to do it." So, although I intended this activity to be teacher directed, the children felt free to give suggestions. I thought that this was good. Next time, I would probably do this finger play two times in a row—as one time went so quickly, and the children did enjoy themselves.
Auditory training	Tape recorder. Identify sound of family members on a tape recorder. Example: baby, mom, dad, child, dog, and older persons. Also could include some household sounds. Example: washing dishes, raking leaves, TV, doorbell. Ask the children, "Who is making these noises?"	It would be interesting to see if the children could identify different family members' voices. The household sounds tape could lead to good discussions of whose jobs are whose responsibilities; also, to find out if the children help at home. Would hope to encourage nonsexist ways of thinking.	No	I did not use this activity, but if I did I would try to steer the activity in a nonsexist way. Example: "Daddies can wash dishes too."

Activity	Description	Purpose	Included	Reflection
Song	"This is the Way," (sung to Mulberry Bush)	I wanted to get the children to realize all the duties that go into making a household work. I also wanted to have more movement in the large group time.	Yes	This activity did not work well. I started a verse and demonstrated the actions, but I found that some of the children just sat and watched me. So I encouraged them to get up and asked them how we would move to the next verse—raking leaves. This helped a little bit, but still not all the children had stood up before I started. Also, I might ask individual children to move to each verse, or ask them to suggest work that members of their family do around the house.
Cognitive game	Pictures of families or members of family cut from magazines. Asked the children, "What do you think is happening here?"	I wanted to hear the children's suggestions about what was going on in the pictures. I thought that this activity might give good insight into what the children's families were like. I tried to include nonsexist and multiethnic pictures.	Yes	This activity went much better than I had expected. The children seemed really interested in looking at the pictures, and I got lots of feedback. Next time, however, I would allow more time—as I feel that I quit while the children were still interested.
Discussion	See ideas for topics throughout outline.	Wanted children to realize that there are many kinds of families and all are equally good. I wanted some feedback, would mostly try to give information, new terms, etc., would hope to increase the children's positive feelings about their own families.	No	I did not include this activity because I felt it would take too much time, and I wanted to include the other areas.
Multiethnic and nonsexist area	I would probably normally end the large group session by having some "stereotyped" activities that both boys and girls could use (woodshop area, cooking area, housekeeping, etc.) and encourage everyone to use those activities.	I would use this activity in hope of encouraging the children to be involved in nonsexist type play. Also, I think that sometimes teachers "forget" to incorporate this into everyday activities.	No	Since this was not possible on this particular day, I tried to incorporate nonsexist and multiethnic material in all my other activities. Example: In a picture I showed a father cooking with his son and talked about how everyone can be a good cook.

Source: Courtesy Erika Miller, Institute of Child Development, University of Oklahoma, Norman.

✑   *Using a flannel board makes
a nice change from reading a book.*

At the same time it is important not to drag things out. This is the reason it is deadly
in a preschool group to go all around in the circle and have each child say something.
When this happens, attention lags among the other youngsters and restlessness rises like
a tide. Far better to include children spontaneously as the opportunity presents itself—a
few adding suggestions to the story, others putting figures on the flannel board, and the
entire group participating in a finger play.

Opportunities for the group to move around a bit also provide a needed change of
pace. Singing a song during which children get up and down answers the need for large
muscle activity, just as finger plays about the "eensy weensy spider" harness the energy
inherent in wiggly fingers.

Assess the difficulty of what the children will be learning and present anything that is
new or potentially difficult to understand early in group, while the children are still feeling rested. A new mental ability activity, for instance, should follow the opening songs
rather than coming at the very end of the time together.

Some Advice About Starting and Stopping

Start as soon as the children begin to gather, and quit while you're ahead. It is not necessary to wait until all the children have arrived to begin group activities. The children who
have come promptly need something to do rather than just sit and wait for stragglers. A
good action song or finger play is a fine way to begin. It catches the group's attention and
involves them immediately, and it is easy for latecomers to join in unobtrusively while this
is going on. If such late arrivals are welcomed with a quick smile rather than a reproach-
ful look, they will want to arrive more quickly next time.

❧   *When the reader enthusiastically asks for a response it sustains the children's interest and builds their discussion skills.*

Closing a group time well is equally important. Some teachers do this by ending with the same song every time to give the children a sense of finishing or completion. Others just anticipate its ending by saying something like "Well, we certainly did a lot of interesting things in group today, didn't we?" and then summarizing what was done. Still others just move smoothly into some sort of dismissal routine: "Everyone who is wearing blue jeans can go first today," (or everyone who has spotted socks, or who has freckles, or who ate oatmeal for breakfast). Children enjoy this sort of thing, and it has the advantage of not sending the entire herd off at once in a thundering way.

The most important points about finishing group time are that the children have a clear idea of what they are expected to do next and also that group time ends before the youngsters are so exhausted that the experience has degenerated into a struggle to maintain order. Finishing a group time while the children are still interested and attentive makes it more likely they will want to return because they recall group time as being a satisfying experience they enjoyed.

What to Do about Undesirable Behaviour

The McAfee (1985) survey also points out that, when teachers were asked to explain why certain group times or activities were not successful, they cited conditions that were beyond their control 75% of the time. These included such things as the children's developmental levels, their emotional or behavioural problems, home backgrounds, and classroom conditions, such as too large a group or too wide an age span. It is certainly true that all of these conditions can and do cause problems. What is distressing is that so few of the teachers saw themselves as generating some of the difficulties. Yet teachers *can* control some of the aforementioned variables.

For example, it is quite possible and valuable to suit the material to the age of the children. The younger the children, the shorter the books, poetry, and songs should be and the more opportunities should be provided for moving around. Whatever the age of the children, the teacher must remain sensitive to the group—tuned in—so she can sense when a shift of material is necessary to hold their attention. Of course, no group is completely attentive at any time. Even during a very high-interest activity, McAfee reported there were several children who were not attentive. So another thing to remember is not to expect perfection from children who are, after all, very young.

To obtain maximum benefit from such experiences, groups should be kept as small as possible. Larger groups almost always produce behaviour problems because of lack of involvement and inattention. What typically happens is that assistant teachers spend their time admonishing some children, patting others on the back, and holding still other unwilling participants on their laps. A far better solution, when a second teacher is available, is to split the group in half so that each staff member works with a smaller number of children. Under these circumstances there can be a better balance between teacher-dominated activities and conversation and discussions, and the children will pay closer attention and develop their language skills more richly.

But these recommendations do not deal with the problem of what to do about the child who is punching his neighbour, rolling over and over on the floor, or continually drifting away from the group to play in the housekeeping area.

There are a number of ways of dealing with this situation. Making certain the material is interesting is the first thing to consider. Sometimes it is effective to have the acting out youngster sit beside you as you read, turning the pages or doing other helpful things. Sometimes it is enough just to separate him from his companion. Sometimes calling the child by name and drawing his attention back to what the group is doing is helpful, although I avoid doing this as a reproach. Sometimes the behaviour can be overlooked. And, as a final resort, sometimes the child loses the privilege of staying in the group and must be sent away. The problem with this method is that an adult really has to go with him to prevent him from getting into further mischief.

Remember, almost all children who misbehave at the beginning of the year can learn to conform to the requirements of the group if they are provided with patient teaching. Hold them only to reasonable expectations. Be persistent and don't give up hope. It can be helpful to talk with the youngster privately at some time other than group time, *pointing out when he has done well,* and arranging with him in advance that he does not have to stay the entire time. Perhaps he will just try to stay for the first song and poem, or for the story, and then, *before he loses control* he can go off with the staff member and do something quiet until group time is over. The time in the group can be gradually extended as the child's ability to control his behaviour increases.

When a child has consistent difficulties enjoying group time, we should take a careful look at possible reasons within the child for this behaviour because, if most of the children are enjoying the activity, there may be some special reason that this particular child is not. Some possibilities to consider when this is the case include hearing and vision difficulties. These are common but frequently overlooked reasons for inattentiveness. The other common reason is immaturity. If the material being presented is above the child's level, he won't pay attention. Any of these conditions require sensitive discussion with the family as well as special diagnosis by an appropriate professional person. (For a discussion of how to make an effective referral, please refer to the chapters on exceptionality and parenting.)

❧ Remember That It Is Also Worthwhile to Foster Emergent Mathematical Skills

We often think of emergent literacy as referring only to language, but we preschool teachers should give ourselves credit for the many opportunities we provide for developing emergent mathematical skills as well. The trouble is that when parents ask us about what the children are learning in arithmetic, we often fail to realize all the kinds of mathematical concepts and strategies we encourage the children to employ every day.

For example, among these opportunities is the use of blocks in the curriculum—as the discussion in chapter 16 reminds us. Blocks provide numerous opportunities for children to learn such mathematical concepts as equivalency, one-to-one correspondence, and seriation—all of which are fundamental mathematical concepts. Additional concepts such as more than/less than, singular/plural, and longer/shorter also are inherent in this activity.

The wealth of picture books featuring enumeration (counting) provides evidence that counting is another form of mathematical literacy that young children relish. However, it is important to realize there is a tremendous difference between the understanding required to chant numbers from one to twenty by rote and actually understanding the concept of "ten-ness" when it is applied to how many party favours are required to add

❧   *Oh, look! This number's the same as that one.*

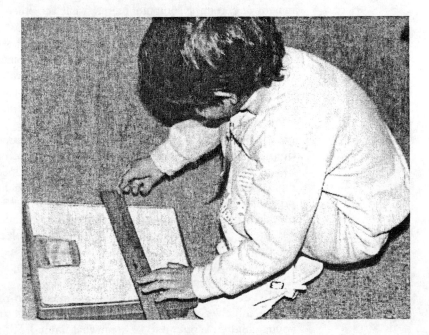

up to ten for that number of birthday guests. Measuring, weighing, and estimating quantity and size are additional examples of ways preschool teachers incorporate mathematical learning into the children's everyday lives.

In the realm of midlevel mental abilities, many of the thinking and reasoning skills advocated in chapter 20 such as grouping (class inclusion) and seriation (graduated ordering) are also fundamental to understanding set theory and number relationships. The Greenberg articles listed at the end of this chapter provide many suggestions for incorporating mathematical literacy activities in the curriculum.

❧ *Using the Computer as a Method of Preschool Instruction*

Much has been learned about the appropriate use of computers since the 1980s, when they first began to wend their way into preschool classrooms. At that time there were many well-taken objections to their use, and some of those objections and drawbacks remain today. For example, it is still estimated that only about 25% of available software is developmentally appropriate (Shade & Haugland, 1993), and much of the remainder of it is still at the "electronic workbook and drill" level. Another potential difficulty is that the majority of teaching staff are inexperienced not only in using computers themselves but also in knowing the most desirable ways to encourage their use by the children. Finally, there is the problem of expense and obsolescence. Even the most moderately priced computers remain well beyond the reach of most early childhood programs, in which increasing meagre salaries must still take priority. If only the most affluent centres can afford this equipment, might it mean that children from the more well-to-do families will have the benefit of becoming computer literate while the other youngsters are left behind? Perhaps we are indeed in danger of "replicating inequities," as Thouvenelle and her colleagues suggest (1994), when we add this equipment to some classrooms and not to others.

All of these objections, of course, can be overcome, as supporters of computers quite correctly maintain. The quality of the software is gradually improving. Staff can certainly learn to use and present computer activities in appropriate ways, and there are possibilities for money-raising schemes to purchase the equipment.

Despite objections, the tide is gradually turning in favour of including computers in preschool classrooms. In 1994 the National Association for the Education of Young Children published a book favouring their appropriate use with young children (Wright & Shade, 1994). Some of the arguments that have helped turn that tide include the following: Computers are nonjudgemental and do not scold or disapprove of "wrong" answers; programs can be suited to the level of the learner; at the preschool level, research has revealed that computers often foster cooperation and interaction among children as they use the equipment; computers can be a source of empowerment for youngsters with cerebral palsy or other physically limiting disabilities; and computers prepare children for later literacy and prevent children from becoming "computer shy" (Davidson, 1989; Kaden, 1990; Wright & Shade, 1994).

However, despite their charms, we must also remember that computers are, by nature, a highly symbolic, visually based activity. As such, their value in the education of young children is bound to be somewhat limited. We must never allow them to preempt

❧   *Gee! How come it did that?*

time best used for other activities (as television is now preempting real-life experiences at home). And yet my guess is that despite their limitations, computers will continue to make a significant place for themselves in the preschool classroom as time goes on, as more appropriate programs are written for them, and as teachers of young children become trained in how to present them effectively by linking them closely to real experience.

❧ *Summary*

The current approach to preparing children for learning the later skills of reading, writing, and doing mathematics is termed *emergent literacy*. This term includes the underlying concepts and strategies related to developing all aspects of literacy, whether written or oral.

This chapter stresses that teachers should make it plain they value good books and emphasize the usefulness of the written word by providing ways for children to use written literacy materials in their play, by writing down children's dictated stories, by encouraging the judicious use of computers, and by including carefully planned group time experiences.

Group time presents a particularly rich opportunity for fostering emergent literacy, and the chapter includes a number of practical suggestions for making that experience satisfying for both children and teachers.

Questions and Activities

1. *Problem:* The mother of a child in your group glows as she tells you her three-year-old is so smart—she knows all her ABCs and her father is drilling her every night with flash cards to help her learn to read. What, if anything, do you think you should do about this?
2. Role play a story hour in which the teacher seems to do everything possible to prevent the children from talking.
3. For the sake of variety and to extend your language building skills with the children, resolve not to use books at all during group time for a month! What will you offer instead that will enhance the language abilities of the children?
4. Make up blank paper "books" and invite the children to dictate stories to you on any relevant subject. Many youngsters will relish adding illustrations to these tales if they are encouraged to do so.

Self-Check Questions for Review

Content-Related Questions

1. Give three examples of emergent literacy activities a three-year-old might participate in with pleasure.
2. What are three fundamental principles for developing literacy that teachers should keep in mind?
3. Name three additional kinds of language activities besides songs and stories that should be regularly included in group time.
4. You have a beginning student teacher working with you in your class of three-year-olds. She reads to them in a steady monotone, never looking up and never smiling. What advice would you give her that would help her hold the children's attention?
5. Discuss some possible ways teachers could reduce misbehaviour during group time.
6. In the research by Morrow on including literacy materials in children's play, what factors did she identify as increasing the use of those materials most strongly?

Integrative Questions

1. The teacher next door who works with four-year-olds complains to you that she has a terrible time during group because the children keep interrupting her. Explain why you would or would not agree that this is undesirable behaviour on the children's part.
2. Picture in your mind's eye one of the books you most enjoy reading to children, and propose three questions based on that book that would promote discussion between you and them.
3. Then, using that book as the central idea or theme, suggest a poem, an auditory discrimination activity, and a nonsexist or multicultural idea you could use along with the book during a group time for three- or four-year-olds.
4. Morrow's research points out that the addition of teacher guidance increased the amount of literacy-related play by the children. Using "playing birthday party" as an example, describe how a teacher might manipulate the play to such an extent she takes the qualities of spontaneity and delight away from it.

References for Further Reading

Overviews

Fields, M., & Spangler, K. L. (1995). *Let's begin reading right: Developmentally appropriate beginning literacy* (3rd ed.). Englewood Cliffs, NJ: Merrill/Prentice Hall. This book discusses the underpinnings of literacy and then discusses the development of reading and writing with older youngsters. *Highly recommended.*

Glazer, S. M., & Burke, E. M. (1994). *An integrated approach to early literacy: Literature to language.* Boston: Allyn & Bacon. Glazer and Burke discuss the growth of language and literacy from birth to age eight. They include specific, practical ways to monitor caregivers' behaviours related to literacy. Well-chosen books for each age and various circumstances are a feature. *Highly recommended.*

Emergent Mathematical Literacy

Althouse, R. (1994). *Investigating mathematics with young children.* New York: Teachers College Press. Althouse shows how the curriculum standards of the National Council of Teachers of Mathematics Standards can be implemented when teaching mathematical concepts to three-, four-, and five-year-olds.

Greenberg, P. (1993). Ideas that work with young children: How and why to teach all aspects of preschool and kindergarten math naturally, democratically, and effectively (for teachers who don't believe in academic programs, who do believe in educational excellence, and who find math boring to the max) Part 1. *Young Children, 48*(4), 75–84.

Greenberg, P. (1994). Ideas that work with young children: How and why to teach all aspects of preschool and kindergarten math naturally, democratically, and effectively (for teachers who don't believe in academic programs, who do believe in educational excellence, and who find math boring to the max) Part 2. *Young Children, 49*(2), 12–18. Part 1 focuses on various aspects of counting and one-to-one correspondence. Part 2 concentrates on sets—classifying, comparing, matching, adding, and subtracting.

Stone, J. I. (1990). *Hands-on math: Manipulative math for young children.* Glenview, IL: Scott, Foresman. There are many simple activities included that help build beginning math concepts.

Strickland, D. S., & Morrow, L. M. (Eds.). (1989). *Emerging literacy: Young children learn to read and write.* Newark, DE: International Reading Association. These useful articles by well-known authorities are filled with practical suggestions.

Presenting Effective Group Times

Briggs, D. (1993). *Toddler storytime programs.* Netuchen, NJ: Scarecrow Press. This book is a godsend for teachers who want to use flannel boards with stories, poems, and music yet feel limited by their self-perceived inability to draw—there are patterns galore that accompany a large assortment of language possibilities to use with the often neglected two-year-old set.

Child Care Information Exchange. (1994). Beginnings workshop: "Storytelling." *The Exchange, 98,* 31–50. A number of practical, encouraging articles are included in this issue that should inspire us all to tell stories as well as read them. *Highly recommendedv.*

Garrity, L. (1987). *The gingerbread guide: Using folk tales with young children.* Glenview, IL: Scott, Foresman. Telling a story instead of reading one makes a delightful change of pace. It is convenient to have a number of old favourites such as "The Gingerbread Boy" and "Red Riding Hood" all in one place for quick review. This book is not illustrated, and accompanying activities are more appropriate for older children.

Jalongo, M. R. (1988). *Young children and picture books: Literature from infancy to six.* Washington, DC: National Association for the Education of Young Children. The joy of really good picture books is captured here. The author explains how to select quality books and how to present them so effectively that children will fall in love with them and with reading, too. *Highly recommended.*

Sutherland, M. (1994). Group meeting time: Making it work for everyone. *Scholastic Early Childhood Today, 8*(6), 28–35. In this concise article, Sutherland presents practical advice about group time plus a checklist for evaluating teacher behaviours that may be contributing to inattentiveness in children.

Trelease, J. (1989). *The new read-aloud handbook.* New York: Penguin Books. A sensible, easy-to-read paperback that is filled with good advice for parents and teachers on enjoying books with children. Excellent bibliography.

Wilmes, L, & Wilmes, D. (1983). *Everyday circle times.* Elgin, IL: Building Blocks. Many circle time activities divided according to such subjects as foods, self-concept, etc. are included. Suggestions include ideas for language, active games, books, finger plays, and occasional recipes.

Wolf, J. (1994). Singing with children is a cinch. *Young Children, 49*(4), 20–25. Lots of practical advice and resources are included here.

Children's Literature

Note: Please refer to chapter 14 for many references listing multicultural books.

Raines, S. C., & Canady, R. J. (1989). *Story s-t-r-e-t-c-h-e-r-s: Activities to expand children's favorite books.* Mount Rainier, MD: Gryphon House.

Raines, S. C., & Canady, R. J. (1991). *More story s-t-r-e-t-c-h-e-r-s: More activities to expand children's favorite books.* Mount Rainier, MD: Gryphon House. In these two books the authors provide a wonderful selection of really *good* books and also offer extensive ideas of ways to tie them to other activity areas. *Highly recommended.*

Raines, S., & Isbell, R. (1994). *Stories: Children's literature in early education.* Albany, NY: Delmar. This book reviews literature for children from birth to age eight and includes many examples of teachers trying different techniques. Replete with practical suggestions, it features an outstanding selection of books—multicultural books are integrated throughout the text.

Poetry and Finger Plays

Arbuthnot, M. H., & Root, S. L. (1968). *Time for poetry* (3rd ed.). Glenview, IL: Scott, Foresman. This book is a treasure. It is filled with poetry (most of which can be used at the preschool level) arranged by topic, and it also contains a valuable chapter on sharing poetry with children.

Dowell, R. I. (1987). *Move over, Mother Goose: Finger plays, action verses, & funny rhymes.* Mount Rainier, MD: Gryphon House. This nice mix of materials is divided into topics such as animals, family, and so forth.

Prelutsky, C. (Ed.). (1986). *Read aloud rhymes for the very young.* New York: Alfred A. Knopf. Delightfully illustrated, these poems are simple. They are also arranged somewhat according to subject.

Redleaf, R. (1993). *Busy fingers, growing minds: Finger-plays, verses and activities for whole language learning.* St. Paul, MN: Redleaf Press. Simple, brief, relevant verses and group time activities contributed by a very experienced teacher are included.

Computers

Sanders, J. (1987). *Do your female students say "No, thanks" to the computer?* New York: Women's Action Alliance, 370 Lexington Ave., New York, NY 10017. This brochure reminds us of the potential computer gap between the sexes and makes a good case for being careful to maintain computer equity for girls. There is also a brochure for parents entitled *Does Your Daughter Say "No Thanks" to the Computer?* (Sanders, 1989) available from the same source.

Wright, J. L., & Shade, D. D. (Eds.). *Young children: Active learners in a technological age.* Washington, DC: National Association for the Education of Young Children. This is a collection of thoughtful articles evaluating what constitutes effective and undesirable uses of computers with young children.

For the Advanced Student

Buckleitner, W. (1994). *High/Scope buyer's guide to children's software 1993.* Ypsilanti, MI: High/Scope. An up-to-date review of hundreds of software programs for children aged three to seven is presented here.

Clements, D. H., Nastasi, B. K., & Swaminathan, S. (1993). Research in review: Young children and computers: Crossroads and directions from research. *Young Children, 48*(2), 56–64. The authors present a thoughtful review of research about computers and young children that mainly cites research studies done on children beyond preschool age.

McNamme, G. D. (1990) Learning to read and write in an inner-city setting: A longitudinal study of community change. In L. C. Moll (Ed.), *Vygotsky and education: Instructional implications and applications of sociohistorical psychology.* New York: Cambridge University Press. I hope readers will not be put off by the title—actually the chapter is a delightful account of how Head Start staff and community people worked with an advisor to increase developmentally appropriate literacy activities in their centres. *Highly recommended.*

❧VII
Fostering Cognitive Development

19
Developing Thinking and Reasoning Skills: Choosing Priorities

20
Developing Thinking and Reasoning Skills: Using the Conventional Approach to Build Midlevel Mental Abilities

21
Developing Thinking and Reasoning Skills: Using the Emergent Approach to Foster Creativity in Thought

Developing Thinking and Reasoning Skills

Choosing Priorities

19

The best school, after all, for the world of childhood is not the school where children know the most answers, but the school where children ask the most questions.

John Coe

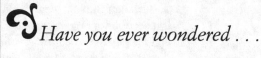

Have you ever wondered . . .

If there wasn't a better way to develop thinking skills than teaching children the names of colours and shapes?

Why working on cognitive skills always seems so boring?

How to tie children's interests and important cognitive abilities together?

. . . If you have, the material in the following pages will help you.

I have left the analytical thinking and reasoning aspect of the child's self until next to the last section for two reasons. For one thing, this kind of learning prospers best when the child is physically healthy, emotionally stable, and socially competent, so it is logical to discuss these aspects first. Creativity was discussed after that because it is so highly esteemed by early childhood teachers and, as we shall see in the following material, because it provides an indispensable avenue for developing children's abilities to generate ideas.

The second reason why I left the discussion of the cognitive-analytical self until near the end is that working with the cognitive aspect of the child's self seems to bring out the worst in some teachers. By putting these chapters near the end of the book, I hope that readers will have absorbed enough of its basic philosophy to be armed against the tendency to reduce intellectual learning to a series of isolated activities and drills or to assume that the fundamental intent in developing mental ability should be the acceleration of the child to the point of precocity.

Rather than focusing intellectual learning on academic exercises or struggling to push adequately developing children beyond their peers, the true goal of cognitive development should be to give each youngster ample opportunities to experience the satisfaction of confronting problems and proposing potential solutions to them while participating in a program that keeps children in contact with their feelings and is respectful of their ideas. It should also foster the use of language and other graphic materials to express those ideas while providing practice in certain midlevel literacy skills. Such opportunities are helpful for all children, but they are vital for children from lower economic groups, who tend to lag behind middle-class children in this area (Honig, 1982a; Meadows, 1993; Doherty-Derkowski, 1995).

ꙮ Selecting Values and Priorities in the Cognitive Realm

To help all children realize their true potential, the first thing teachers must do is get their values straight regarding what they want to emphasize in the area of cognitive development (and many preprimary teachers are very confused about this). Getting these values straight requires careful thinking about priorities—what it is most important for children to learn. Once decisions about this have been made, it also requires clear understanding of how to offer instruction that will honour these priorities and foster the development of advanced reasoning skills as well as some fundamental midlevel mental abilities.

As priorities are ranked, it is most helpful to consider them in terms of their *relative* merit. For example, is it more important that the child experience joy and verve when learning or that she learn to sit quietly and not interrupt the teacher? Is it more significant that she speak fluently and spontaneously, or that she speak Standard English? Is it more valuable that she be able to think about problems and feel confident about her ability to solve them or that she be able to pick out all the things in the room that are shaped like squares?

It is not that any of these values are reprehensible or should not receive attention: It *is* a question of deciding which goals should receive *primary* emphasis, because the teacher who elects to foster joy and verve is likely to employ a different teaching style from one who feels that quietly paying attention is vital to classroom success.

Thus we must begin by asking ourselves what are the most important things we want children to learn in the cognitive sphere and which goals should have first priority. Once these are identified, we must understand what practical, day-by-day things teachers can do to emphasize those priorities as they work with the children.

❧ What Are the Most Valuable Priorities?

Priority I: Maintain the Child's Sense of Wonder and Curiosity

As teachers of young children know, most youngsters come to school wondering about many things. They want to know where the water goes when the toilet flushes, why the dog died, and what makes their stomach gurgle. Lewis (1979) catches the essence of this when she says,

> Children in the preschool years constantly show us that they do not take our ordinary world for granted. They wonder about anything and everything, trying to figure out reasons, answers, and inner workings. A four-year-old is walking to school with his teacher one day in the autumn: "What is on the top of those trees that makes the leaves fall down?" he asks. A three-year-old produces a definition for herself: "Tomorrow is the day we sleep for." A four-year-old suddenly announces out of nowhere while he sits quietly eating at the lunch table: "There are nineteen people in this room and the nineteenth is the turtle." (p. 13)

The age of four is particularly appealing in this respect. Four-year-olds are avid gatherers of facts and are interested in everything. For this reason it is a delight to build a cognitive curriculum for them. But three-year-olds are seeking and questioning also. They

❧ *How refreshing it is that preschool children do not take the ordinary world for granted.*

are more concerned with the manipulation of materials and with finding out what everyday things and people close to them are like. This kind of investigation, although different in focus from that of the four-year-olds, may also be used to make a rich contribution to mental development.

The most obvious way to maintain children's sense of curiosity is by encouraging them to continue to ask questions and making it possible for them to find out the answers. But underlying the teacher's willingness to encourage investigation lies something deeper: the teacher's basic point of view about what children are capable of achieving. The teacher whose image of children is that they are richly endowed, strong, competent people conveys this sense of worthiness to the children. He sees his role as empowering children— enabling them *to do for themselves* rather than doing for or to them.

In this atmosphere of respect, autonomy and the willingness to venture flourishes best. It is a climate in which there is a balance of reasonableness, choice, trust, protection, spontaneity, moderate control, and challenge. Given the security of respect combined with encouragement, children sense they have a firm base from which to explore when the impulse moves them to do so.

Sometimes, rather than sustaining and encouraging curiosity, the teacher finds it necessary to reawaken it. Deci and Ryan (1982) link such uninterested, unawakened behaviour to the concept of learned helplessness (Garber & Seligman, 1980; Seligman, 1975), in which individuals have become hopeless and helpless because they feel that what they do cannot affect what happens in the environment. Therefore, one of Deci and Ryan's recommendations for generating the energy it takes to wonder and question is to encourage children to see themselves as powerful, effective people. As chapter 5 reminds us, the development of this positive sense of self is directly related to the child's sense of self-esteem (Curry & Johnson, 1990).

The teacher can also help by presenting materials that are fascinating and by modelling curiosity and wonder as well. Asking simple questions about cause and effect or wondering together what will happen next often captures children's interest and starts them observing, wondering, and thinking for themselves. Thus the teacher might discuss with the children whether the mother rabbit will do anything to get ready for her babies now that she is growing so fat and full of them, or he might ask the children whether they think it would be better to keep the ice in the sun or shade until it is time to make the ice cream and how they might find out which is better.

Given this attention from the teacher combined with a stronger concept of self, children who have not previously done so will soon begin to come alive and question and wonder for themselves. Then the teacher can encourage them and lead them on to further investigation and thinking.

Priority II: Let Cognitive Learning Be a Source of Genuine Pleasure for Children and Teacher

If we agree with the behaviourists that people tend to repeat activity that is rewarded in some way, it follows that we should do everything in our power to attach pleasure to cognitive learning. We want children to want to think and learn, and they are more likely to continue to do so if they experience pleasure while they are involved in learning. Therefore, the second most important priority that we should consider when planning a cognitive curriculum is presenting it so that it is a genuine source of pleasure. This can be accomplished in a number of ways.

Sustain Interest by Making Curriculum Content Relevant

In these days of "relevant curriculum" it has become almost a truism to say that a good curriculum for any age is based on the student's interests and that it teaches her what she wants to know. A curriculum that does not accomplish this goal breeds disinterested, dissatisfied learners, no matter how old they are (DeVries & Kohlberg, 1990). Yet even preschool teachers often lay out a year's curriculum in advance, formulated at best on knowledge of what other children in previous years have cared about. Thus a schedule will show that in September the program will be building experiences around the family, in December around holidays, and in the spring around baby animals. Although this approach has a certain value, the danger of such extremely long-range planning is that teachers may become so tied to it that they are unable to respond to the interests of the children who are now in their room, thereby deadening some of their pleasure and motivation for learning. This does not mean that the curriculum will be completely unpredictable; it does mean that the subject matter should be drawn from the current interests of the group.

Perhaps one year the children are most concerned about disasters, as were children in Alberta recently because of fires that drove many of them from their homes. Or perhaps they are particularly interested in a fantasy character from a new movie, or what to do with the baby bird that has fallen from its nest. These interests should not be ignored, but considered as possible starting points for developing a curriculum for the cognitive self and possibly for the social and emotional selves as well.

Wondering together stimulates everyone's curiosity.

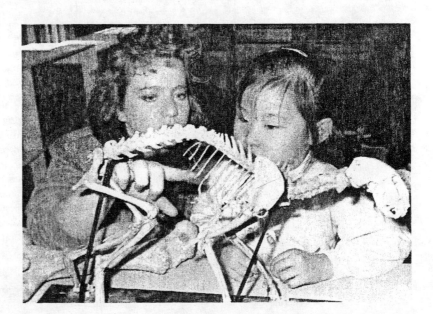

Once they have been identified, it is the teacher's responsibility to respond to the children's interests in several ways. He supplies the children with information and vocabulary about subjects that matter to them and that they cannot find out about by themselves. He employs the interest as a medium for teaching a number of basic midlevel mental ability skills such as matching and grouping that he wants them to acquire. Finally, he is constantly on the lookout for opportunities for using the children's interest to foster higher order mental abilities related to solving problems of various kinds.

Keep It Age Appropriate

Nothing is more disheartening to a youngster than being confronted with material that is too difficult. To foster pleasure in learning it is necessary to match the child's learning opportunities with her developmental level. This means that learning opportunities must be challenging but not so difficult they are beyond the child's grasp.

On the other hand, learning opportunities should be challenging enough that the bright four-year-olds in the class are not bored by too much repetition at the same ability level all year. Teachers must walk a delicate tightrope of sensitivity—not allowing themselves to be held prisoner by the concept of developmental stages, yet, at the same time, taking their knowledge of those stages into account so they expect neither too much nor too little from the youngsters.

Keep It Real

Cognitive learning should be based on actual experience and experience that makes the child an active participant (Piaget & Inhelder, 1967; Williams & Kamii, 1986; Vygotsky, 1978). DeVries and Kohlberg (1990) provide some useful criteria to apply as tests of true involvement.

Criteria of Good Physical Knowledge Activities*

The constructivist rationale and objectives emphasizing action lead to four criteria for good physical knowledge activities. These were conceptualized with activities in mind that involve the movement of objects.

1. *The child must be able to produce the phenomenon by his own action.* As stated above, the essence of physical knowledge activities is the child's action on objects and his observation of the object's reaction. The phenomenon selected must therefore be something the child can produce by his own action. The movement of a piece of Kleenex in reaction to the child's blowing or sucking on it through a straw meets this criterion. The movement of objects caused by a magnet, on the other hand, is an example of a phenomenon that is produced only indirectly by the child's action and primarily by magnetic attraction. This does not imply that magnets should be omitted from a classroom. It does imply that we should recognize the educational limitations of experimenting with magnets.

---

*From *Constructivist early education: Overview and comparison with other programs,* pp. 92–93, by R. DeVries and L. Kohlberg (1990). Washington, DC: National Association for the Education of Young Children. Used by permission.

ℰ   *Does this meet the criteria for a good physical knowledge activity?*

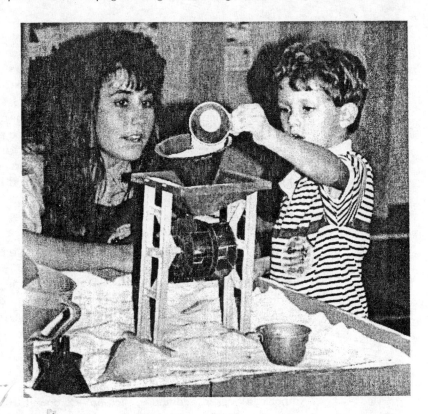

2. *The child must be able to vary his action.* When the variations in the child's action result in corresponding variations of the object's reaction, the child has the opportunity to structure these regularities. In a pool game, for example, if the child misses the target by hitting a ball too far to the left, he can adjust the next attempt accordingly. In a pinball-type game, by contrast, the child's action is limited to pulling a lever, and there is very little variation possible in how he releases the lever. The child thus cannot significantly affect the outcome. Without a direct correspondence between the variations in actions and reactions, a phenomenon offers little opportunity for structuring.

3. *The reaction of the object must be observable.* If the child cannot observe a reaction to his actions on objects, there is no content for him to structure. For example, an opaque tube in waterplay prevents observation of the water inside, and provides less material for structuring than a transparent tube.

4. *The reaction of the object must be immediate.* Correspondences are much easier to establish when the object's reaction is immediate. For example, when a child rolls a ball toward a target, she can immediately observe whether the target is hit or not, and if so, how it specifically reacts. In contrast, the reaction of a plant to water is not immediately observable, and its action on the water is only indirectly the result of the child's action. This does not imply that growing plants should be omitted from the classroom. In light of the immediacy criterion, sprouting beans on wet paper towels is a better activity to promote such understanding than watering a houseplant.

Keep Cognitive Learning Brief and Unstressful

Thinking is hard work. The episodes should be brief enough that the children do not feel strained from working too long. It is always better to stop before stress and boredom set in, since stopping at the right moment makes it more likely the child will want to return the next time.

The teacher must learn to recognize common signs of stress in children because these behaviours are an indication that it is past time to stop or that the activity needs to be modified to a more attractive and appropriate level. These signs include thumb sucking, wiggling, inattention, restlessness, hair twisting, constantly trying to change the subject, asking to leave or just departing, picking fights, and creating disturbances (Chandler, 1982; Honig, 1986a).

Enjoy the Experience with the Children

The final way to sustain children's pleasure in learning is by enjoying it with them. Cognitive learning should not be a sobersided, no-nonsense business. It is a fine time for experiences that include humour, fun, and discovery when the teacher enjoys the activity along with the children. The use of a relevant, emergent curriculum definitely enhances that pleasure. When teachers and children share learning together, everyone experiences satisfaction.

Priority III: Bind Cognitive Learning to Affective Experience Whenever Possible

Other emotions in addition to pleasure are bound to be involved in cognitive learning, since such learning does not take place in an emotional vacuum. Feelings and social experience should be a fundamental part of cognitive learning. *Good education recognizes, accepts, and deals with feelings as they arise;* it does not ignore them or push them aside until later because now it is time to learn about baby animals or study the weather. *The same principle holds true for social skills. Many opportunities for understanding and getting along with others will arise during experiences that are primarily intellectual. These moments should be capitalized on as they occur.*

The extreme importance of recognizing and including a social-emotional emphasis and guarding against the possibility of an overly academic, cognitive emphasis is being currently demonstrated by a research study taking place in Washington, D.C. This ongoing study is reviewed in the research study in this chapter.

Priority IV: Accompany Cognitive Learning with Language Whenever Possible

The word *accompany* is crucial here because language should be an integral part of, rather than a predecessor of, cognitive learning. One of the most common errors of beginning teachers seems to be that they depend too much on using language by itself when approaching cognitive development. Mere discussion about roots, petals, and stems is largely worthless for children unless they are able to tie that new vocabulary to the real experience of beans, earth, water, and sunlight.

ॐ   *It's vital that actual experience accompany language if learning is to be truly meaningful.*

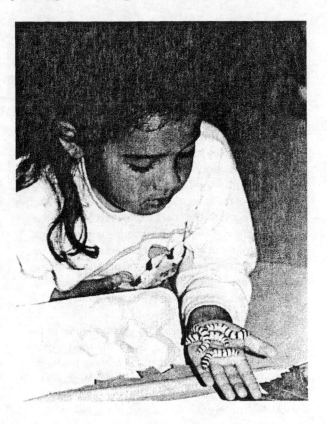

On the other hand, mere experience has also been shown to be insufficient (Blank &
Solomon, 1968, 1969). Teachers play a vital role in concept and mental development
because it is they who blend language with experience, adding a word the children cannot supply themselves or asking a thought-provoking question that leads them to think
something through more clearly. It is this deliberate interweaving that enriches the meaning of both experience and language for young children and increases the likelihood of
mental activity and development.

Spoken language should not be thought of as the only way children have of communicating ideas and feelings. Besides oral language, children also use body posture, gestures,
and expressions to communicate. As they reach the age of three-and-a-half or four, they
become increasingly adept at using a variety of graphic materials to consolidate their
ideas and explain them to other people. For example, they might use pieces of coloured
paper tinted from darkest red to palest pink to stand for (symbolize) the lowest to highest notes on a scale, or they might draw squares of various sizes to stand for those same
notes. The work of the children of Reggio Emilia is rich with a variety of materials used
to express their ideas. These include examples of dialogues, drawing and painting, and
also punched paper, cutouts, shadow plays, bent wire, and objects modelled from clay, to
name only a few of their hundred ways of making visible what they know.

❧ RESEARCH STUDY ❧
Going Down the Road to Learning—Which Path Is Best to Take?

Preamble: The research reported here is a continuation of a study begun in 1986 that was initially intended to follow a group of children from their preschool experience through the first grade. It was initiated in the District of Columbia schools because of the unacceptably high rate of retention that was occurring when the children entered the formal school system. Because the results of that study turned out to be so clear and important, the research was later extended to find out how the children were faring through grades four and five. It is that part of the research with which we are most concerned here.

In order to understand the second study, however, it is first necessary to review the results of the original one. The findings of the original research were based on studying a group of low-income children participating in three kinds of preschool models. These were characterized as being (1) academic, teacher-directed models, (2) child-initiated active learning models, or (3) middle-of-the-road models.

The results of that three-year study revealed that the children in the middle-of-the-road model did poorest of all the groups in the first grade, "scoring significantly lower in language, social, and motor development and also in overall adaptive functioning and mastery of basic skills" (Marcon, 1994a, p. 11). Evidently it is better to believe consistently in anything rather than in an inconsistent hodgepodge. But the questions remained, "Since preparation for academic success is so important in later school years, how did the children turn out who were in the academic, teacher-directed programs compared with the ones in the child-initiated active learning model?" "Did academic instruction in the preschool produce superior academic gains later on in elementary school?"

The answer is that at the first-grade level, the children from the academic programs didn't turn out so well. In fact, the youngsters in the child-initiated model "actually mastered more basic skills than did the youngsters in the academic one" (Marcon, 1994, p. 11). More ominous, still, was another trend that seemed to be appearing: Along with their lower scores in first-grade reading and math, *the social development scores of the children in the academically directed models were declining.*

When the study was repeated the following year with a second group of children, the results were the same. This provided an even stronger reason to continue to follow the children as they advanced in school.

The Follow-up Study

*Research Question:** Marcon asked, "How are the children in the academically directed and child-initiated preschool models turning out as they make the sometimes cognitively difficult transition from third to fourth and fourth to fifth grades?" "Which program has the most positive impact?"

Research Method: Information was available for 372 children who had participated in the academic or child-initiated models at the preschool level. Ninety-seven percent of the children were Black and most of them came from low-income families. Data about the children in the fourth grade were gathered from a variety of sources such as standardized tests, progress reports, and measures of social skills. The results were sorted according to whether the children had attended academic preschools or child-initiated programs. The findings from the groups were analysed and compared.

Results: Marcon (1994b, p. ix) reported that "the negative impact on achievement and social development of overly academic early childhood programs was clearly apparent by age nine. By fourth grade children who had attended academically directed pre-K programs had noticeably lower grades and were passing fewer fourth grade reading and mathematics objectives. By fourth and fifth grades, children from academic pre-K programs were developmentally behind peers and *displayed notably higher levels of maladaptive behaviour*" [italics mine] (1994b, pp. ix — x). In short, she concludes that " . . . children who attend programs that focus on academic preparation (at the expense of other aspects of development) are more likely to develop social and scholastic problems by fourth grade" (1994, p. 16).

Implications for Teaching: The findings of this study offer strong evidence of how important it is to provide child-initiated, active learning environ-ments. This is true not only because it facilitates later intellectual ability, *but also because it facilitates more positive social behaviour.* In an era when violence is rising and life seems increasingly difficult, this may ultimately be the most significant reason of all for providing child-initiated active education.

---

*Note that this study has many more facets than the material reported here can cover. Because of space limitations, only the findings related to the children attending preschool classes are summarized. Readers who desire further information should refer to Marcon, 1992, 1994a, & 1994b.

Source: From "Doing the Right Thing for Children: Linking Research and Policy Reform in the District of Columbia Public Schools" by R. A. Marcon. 1994. *Young Children, 50*(1), 8–20.

❦ *Summary*

Once we have the basic priorities of maintaining the child's sense of wonder and curiosity, keeping cognitive learning a source of genuine pleasure, binding it to affective experience whenever possible, and accompanying it with language, the next step is deciding how to go about planning for its inclusion in the life of the school.

As chapters 20 and 21 demonstrate, there are two ways to go about this. The first is the more traditional, *conventional* way that identifies certain basic midlevel mental ability skills. These skills are interwoven into themes or topics stemming from the children's interests and used by the teacher to plan ahead in order to make certain many opportunities are included for practising those skills.

The second, *emergent,* approach to cognitive learning is a more open one. It, too, draws subject matter from the interests of the children, but it unfolds gradually as curriculum opportunities emerge. Although it is certainly possible to include opportunities for midlevel mental abilities within it, the emergent approach emphasizes the development of higher order thought processes and fosters the use of creativity to achieve that goal.

Questions and Activities

1. What are some of the pros and cons of stressing intellectual development at the preschool level? Can you suggest a model for such learning that you feel would have undesirable side effects?
2. Do you agree that pleasure should be the inevitable accompaniment to learning? Can you think of occasions when this has been true of your educational experience and cases in which it has not been true? Analyse the circumstances that made the learning pleasurable or burdensome.
3. Might it be possible that early childhood teachers are depriving children of the right to learn the things that would help them succeed best in elementary school when we stress play, creativity, and mental health rather than emphasizing such skills as learning the alphabet and counting? What might be the case for placing greater emphasis on academic learning at the preschool level?
4. The text speaks of three kinds of teachers: those who do to children, those who do *for* children, and those who enable children *to do things for themselves.* Think of a teacher or mother who would generally fit each of these different categories. Support your choice by providing examples of her behaviour that substantiate your placing her in that category.

Self-Check Questions for Review

Content-Related Questions

1. What are some ingredients of an early childhood climate that are likely to encourage the growth of autonomy and the willingness to venture?
2. Describe some things teachers can do that will help cognitive learning be a source of genuine pleasure to the children.
3. Does work on cognitive learning mean that the teacher should ignore what is going on emotionally and socially among the children?
4. List the four priorities that are most important to consider when developing a curriculum for the cognitive self.

Integrative Questions

1. One of the three-year-olds in your room notices some bird tracks in the snow when the children go out to play. Suggest some spontaneous activities you could do with her that would encourage her to inter-

act with the snow herself and investigate further how the bird tracks were made. Now demonstrate that you understand the difference DeVries and Kohlberg make between active involvement and more passive interest by suggesting a couple of things you could do whereby the child did not take action herself.
2. On that same snowy day, the children are fascinated with the snow itself because it's the first snow of winter. What are some activities you could do with them that would provide some learning while remaining real fun for the children? Be sure to identify what the children would be learning and why you think they will enjoy the experiences.
3. If a teacher was "held captive by the concept of developmental stages," what might be the implications for the way he would plan the social or cognitive curriculum for the children?

References for Further Reading

Building Desirable Attitudes Toward Learning

Ashton-Warner, S. (1965). *Teacher*. New York: Bantam Books. In this classic book, Sylvia Ashton-Warner gives an exciting description of the way she approached teaching and learning and made these activities truly relevant to the lives of her young Maori students.

Bradbard, M. R., & Endsley, R. C. (1982). How can teachers develop young children's curiosity? In J. F. Brown (Ed.), *Curriculum planning for young children.* Washington, DC: National Association for the Education of Young Children. An excellent review of research is included here with implications for teachers following each portion of the review.

Development of the Brain

Brierley, J. (1987). *Give me a child until he is seven.* New York: Falmer Press. In this very good book, Brierley explains what is known about principles of brain physiology and development. The author includes discussions about the educational implications of this information for teachers of young children. *Highly recommended.*

Healey, J. M. (1987). *Your child's growing mind: A parent's guide to learning from birth to adolescence.* Garden City, NY: Doubleday. This sensible book discusses everything from how the brain develops to lateralization and learning to read.

Encouraging Children to Explore Their World

Chaillé, C., & Britain, L. (1991). *The young child as scientist: A constructivist approach to early childhood science education.* New York: Harper Collins. The emphasis on starting with the children's interests and assisting their learning by asking questions will be very helpful to readers. Two outstanding chapters are "How Can I Make It Change?" and "How Can I Make It Move?" Examples using the same topic are given for preschool and first grade. *Highly recommended.*

McIntyre, M. (1984). *Early childhood and science.* Washington, DC: National Science Teachers Association. This is a collection of brief articles about all sorts of possible science experiences and how to present them. The presentation is low key and age appropriate. *Highly recommended.*

For the Advanced Student

Deci, E. L., & Ryan, R. M. (1982). *Curiosity and self-directed learning: The role of motivation in education.* In L. G. Katz (Ed.), *Current topics in early childhood education* (Vol. 4). Norwood, NJ: Ablex. Deci and Ryan are primarily concerned with the role of intrinsic motivation. They hypothesize that children who are intrinsically motivated because of interest, rather than extrinsically motivated because of external rewards, will be more curious, self-motivated learners.

DeVries, R., & Kohlberg, L. (1990). *Constructivist early education: Overview and comparison with other programs.* Washington, DC: National Association for the Education of Young Children. The authors emphasize the importance of active learning, the value of cognitive conflict, and the virtue of figuring out (constructing) knowledge for oneself.

Meadows, S. (1993). *The child as thinker: The development and acquisition of cognition in childhood.* New York: Routledge. This valuable book covers all the significant aspects of mental ability in clearly readable style. *Highly recommended.*

Developing Thinking and Reasoning Skills

Using the Conventional Approach to Build Midlevel Mental Abilities

20

In classrooms that encourage natural, spontaneous, lively, intense curiosity in an environment of interesting and challenging materials, children will gain experiences needed for developing both linguistic and mathematical concepts. For example, by using dough, they may experience that which is alike (one dough ball is like another). In using sand, they understand things that are not alike (wet sand is not like dry sand). The environment can yield other experiences: objects that are patterned (a brick wall is patterned, children's chants are patterned): events that follow a sequence (story comes after snack); parts and wholes (cutting apples, oranges, and bananas for salad); things that have direction (a pulley lifts the pail up); objects that have size, weight, texture.

Nancy Balaban

Have you ever wondered . . .

Why studying Piaget is so important?

What specific mental abilities could be worked on at the preschool level that would build a foundation for later success in primary school?

How to include practice in these abilities and keep it fun, too?

. . . If you have, the material in the following pages will help you.

$\mathcal{T}$here is much to be said in favour of the conventional approach to a cognitive curriculum that provides opportunities for young children to practice the midlevel mental ability skills of matching, grouping, perceiving common relations, understanding the relationship between simple cause and effect, temporal and seriated ordering, and conservation of quantity. As Table 20.1 indicates, these skills help provide a foundation for the later acquisition of school-related skills. For example, matching (being able to tell whether things are the same or different) is an important prerequisite for being able to read. If one cannot tell the difference between *d* and *b*, how can one tell the difference between *dog* and *bog?* Grouping (identifying the common property of several nonidentical items) underlies the concept of class inclusion, which is necessary for understanding set theory. Grouping is also an essential element of such sciences as botany, in which classification is very important. Seriation (arranging things in regular, graduated order) gives real meaning to enumeration. Finally, common relations (the ability to identify pairs of items associated together) helps children learn to draw analogies. This fascinating ability to move from one known relationship to a second by perceiving parallels in the two sets involves transferring ideas and making such new linkages. It is surely an indispensable element in creative thought.

Each of these concepts develops over time by building on lower-level concepts. One teacher presents this explanation of progression as follows:

> Thus, grouping begins with an understanding of the concepts of same and different and the ability to match identical objects, followed by the ability to see similarities across different objects. Gradually children develop the awareness that one object may belong to several possible groups (red, round, and big) and thus can begin to understand matrices (for example, arranging objects in rows by colour and in columns by shape). Not until elementary school do they fully comprehend hierarchical classification (dogs and cats are animals; animals, people and trees are living things) and class inclusion (all dogs are animals, but not all animals are dogs).
>
> Seriation requires, first of all, an understanding of absolute size (big and small), followed by relative size concepts and the ability to compare sizes (this is bigger than that). As with grouping, children must learn that an object can have multiple size designations (bigger than some things and smaller than others). This leads to the ability to seriate, first by trial and error and with a few objects, and then without hesitation, with any number of objects. Awareness of these developmental progressions can help a teacher assess where children are in their thinking and what activities would be appropriate for them.*

Practice in these abilities entails the use of and practice in some additional mental skills that must be so generally employed that they apply to all the abilities. These are listed here rather than being repeated in Table 20.1. They include the abilities to pay attention, observe carefully, make comparisons, and use symbols (representations) in place of actual objects. The symbols might consist of models, pictures, language, or simply imaginary items as is done in play (Dyson, 1990). A base of factual knowledge is also needed.

But right from the start we must realize that practice in these skills, while worthwhile, does not provide the variety of opportunities children need if they are to develop the full array of their mental powers. In addition to midlevel reasoning skills, they also need to

---

*I wish to thank Jean Phinney of California State University at Los Angeles for contributing this explanation of developmental progressions.

Table 20.1 Links between basic mental abilities and later school-related skills

Ability	Value
Matching: Can identify which things are the same and which things are different *Basic question:* Can you find the pair that is exactly the same?	The ability to discriminate is crucial to development of other mental abilities. An important aspect of gaining literacy: discriminate between letters (such as *m* and *w*). Promotes understanding of equality. Encourages skill in figure/ground perception (separating a significant figure from the background).
Grouping: Can identify the common property that forms a group or class *Basic question:* Can you show me the things that belong to the same family?	Fosters mathematical understanding: set theory and equivalency. Children must discriminate, reason, analyse, and select in order to formulate groups. Regrouping encourages flexibility of thought. Depending on manner of presentation, may foster divergent thinking—more than one way to group items. Requires use of accommodation and assimilation. Classification is a basic aspect of life sciences: allows people to organize knowledge.
Common relations: Can identify common property or relationship between a *nonidentical pair* *Basic question:* Which thing goes most closely with what other thing?	Fosters mathematical understanding: one-to-one correspondence. Fosters diversity of understanding concepts: many kinds of pairs (opposites, cause-effect, congruent). Can teach use of analogies and riddles.
Cause and effect: Can determine what makes something else happen: a special case of common relations *Basic question:* What makes something else happen?	Basis for scientific investigations. Conveys sense of order of world. Conveys sense of individual's ability to be effective: act on his world and produce results, make things happen. Encourages use of prediction and generation of hypotheses. Introduces child to elementary understanding of the scientific method.
Seriation: Can identify what comes next in a graduated series *Basic question:* What comes next?	Fosters mathematical understanding. Relationship between quantities: counting (enumeration) with understanding, one-to-one correspondence, equivalency, estimation. If teacher presents series going from left to right, fosters basic reading skill.
Temporal ordering: Can identify logical order of events occurring in time *Basic question:* What comes next?	Fosters mathematical understanding. Conveys a sense of order and a sense of time and its effect. Relationship between things: cause-and-effect and other relationships. Prediction. Requires memory: what happened first, then what happened?
Conservation: Can understand that a substance can return to its prior state and that quantity is not affected by mere changes in appearance *Basic question:* Are they still the same quantity?	Idea of constancy (reversibility) is fundamental as a foundation for logical reasoning, basic for scientific understanding; it is also the basis for mathematical calculations involving length, volume, area, and so forth.

think up their own ideas and experience the challenge and satisfaction of solving problems. The quandary for the preschool teacher is how to provide a curriculum that
includes opportunities for both kinds of cognitive learning to take place while keeping
the material at a level that is developmentally appropriate.

Table 20.2 shows how the role of the teacher and child is quite different for each of
the approaches, but this should not imply that one role should be selected and the other
ignored. Skilful teachers use both approaches in order to present a truly balanced curriculum for the children's cognitive selves.

The main difference between the conventional and the creative-emergent approaches is
the degree of responsibility assumed by the teacher. When a teacher is using the conventional approach to work on midlevel reasoning skills, the curriculum is predetermined to a
greater extent by her. Although experienced teachers also seize spontaneous opportunities
for practising specific abilities as these arise, the majority of the learning materials are typically generated in advance and presented to the children for their pleasure and practice as a
fait accompli. For example, to provide practice in common relations the teacher might make
up a number of pairs of animals and their feet, and ask the children which feet belong to
the ducks, which to the robins, ostriches, and so on. The children are expected to apply the
concept of common relations by pairing feet and animal bodies together, thereby obtaining
practice in the emergent mathematical skill of one-to-one correspondence.

On the other hand, as we shall see in chapter 21, when one is working with the emergent, problem-solving approach, the curriculum must be more fluid since the teacher
cannot predict in advance what solutions the children may propose and what direction
the investigatory pathway may take. Of course, *planning and direction remain necessary,*
but they are done on a more ongoing basis. The result is that learning becomes less
teacher dominated and more of a mutual, collaborative experience as teacher and children share their ideas together.

For the sake of clarity, this chapter concentrates on developmentally appropriate ways
to present activities that provide practice in the midlevel reasoning skills. In days gone by
it was difficult to identify which of these skills were significant and which developmental
level fit different ages of childhood. Fortunately, in the past few years some aspects of
these problems have been resolved by the work of Jean Piaget.

✎ *Basic Concepts of Piagetian Psychology*

Although it is not within the scope of this book to attempt a comprehensive summary of
Piaget's work, any discussion of the thought processes of young children must begin with
at least a brief review of his work, since he devoted a lifetime to studying the mental
development and characteristics of young children (Piaget, 1926, 1950, 1962, 1963,
1965, 1983; Piaget & Inhelder, 1967, 1969). He was primarily interested in how people
come to know what they know—the origins of knowledge—and his work has important
implications for teachers who are interested in the cognitive development of the children
in their care.

Many of Piaget's ideas are bound to sound both familiar and comfortable to the contemporary student, since a good deal of what he said for sixty years has been practised in

Table 20.2 A comparison of learning opportunities using the conventional or the emergent creative approach

	Information Approach	Conventional Approach for Teaching Midlevel Abilities	Emergent Creative Approach for Teaching Creative Thinking and Problem Solving
Value of approach	Provides information base needed as foundation for midlevel and problem-solving skills. Widens knowledge of world.	Provides diversified practice in applying specific mental ability skills (concepts), which are valuable emergent literacy and emergent mathematical skills.	Allows children to develop full range of mental powers. Encourages application of prior knowledge to solving new problems. Empowers children to try out ideas and explain what they know to other children and adults.
Examples of kinds of mental ability skills developed by approach	Pay attention. Process information. Retain information. Recall information. Reconstruct information.	Apply specific concepts such as matching, grouping, perceiving common relations, seriated and temporal ordering, cause-and-effect relationships, and conserving to specific situations.	Generate ideas on own. Form hypotheses (reasons) why something happens and try them out. Assess and evaluate possibilities. Pursue interests in depth.
Teacher's role	Supply information to children and/or help them find information for themselves.	May use children as source to determine interest around which to build a theme. Plan ahead in order to think up and present activities and experiences for children that provide opportunities for practice and application of specific concepts.	Listen to children; follow their lead to select pathway to investigate. Plan curriculum ahead but alter and adjust plans as pathways develop direction. Encourage generation of ideas by "provoking" children to consider problems and solve them. Develop opportunities with children to try out their ideas.
Child's role	Soak up interesting information and store it in memory. Be able to recall, reconstruct, and repeat information when needed.	Participate in learning activities provided by teacher, thereby practising various mid-level mental ability skills. Acquire mental ability concepts and apply them by reasoning. Express what he knows by manipulating teacher-provided materials.	Collaborate (toss ball of ideas back and forth) with teacher to pursue interests. Think up ways to express ideas and solve problems. Try ideas out. Express ideas and what is found out through language, graphics, and child-constructed models.

early childhood centres during the same period and is similar in part to the philosophy of Dewey and Montessori (because of its emphasis on the value of experience). For a variety of reasons, however, his work passed largely unnoticed in North America until the 1960s, and it is only since then that it has been deliberately implemented in the preschool classroom by such investigators as Almy (Almy et al., 1966), DeVries (DeVries & Kohlberg, 1990), Forman and Hill (1980), Kamii (1975, 1982, 1985), Lavatelli (1970a, 1970b), Saunders and Bingham-Newman (1984), and Weikart (Hohmann, Banet, & Weikart, 1979).

Although his own realm of investigation was primarily in the cognitive area, Piaget agreed that affective, social, and cognitive components go hand in hand (Piaget, 1981; Wadsworth, 1989). Since these components are interdependent, it is evident that a school in which good mental health policies are practised and sound social learning is encouraged will also be one in which mental growth is more likely to occur.

Piagetian Categories of Knowledge

Piaget theorized that children acquire three kinds of knowledge as they grow. *Social-conventional knowledge* is the first kind. This is information that society has agreed on and that is often learned through direct social transmission. For example, English-speaking people agree that the word *table* stands for a large flat object with four legs. Rules that define what acceptable behaviour is provide another example of socially transmitted knowledge.

The second kind of knowledge is *physical knowledge*. It is information children gain by acting on objects in the real world. Information about the quality of things and what they do are examples of physical knowledge.

The third kind of knowledge is less tangible because it cannot be directly observed. It is knowledge that is developed (constructed) in the mind of the child as he thinks about objects. Piaget calls this *logico-mathematical knowledge*. The development of logico-mathematical thought, which we might also think of as being the ability to reason, ultimately enables children to develop ideas of relationships between objects. When they can grasp what it is that items in a group have in common, for instance, they are able to assign a common name to that group, thereby classifying or grouping the things together. For example, they might divide a set of pictures, sorting them into things you can wear and things you eat, and name the groups "clothing" and "food". As Kamii (1985) points out, this idea of a common property exists only in the mind. It is not inherent in the pictures themselves; it is an idea, not a physical property. It is important to remember that reasoning knowledge is closely tied to physical knowledge since reasoning usually requires a foundation of factual information, but it also differs from factual information.

It is this gradual development of logico-mathematical ability that frees children from being tied to concrete experience because it enables them to think with symbols and deal with abstractions. It takes many years for children to reach that level of maturity, however. In order to attain it, Piaget and colleagues identified a series of stages through which they must pass as they develop. These stages are outlined in Table 20.3.

Research conducted over a period of more than sixty years convinced Piaget that the order of the stages through which children progress cannot be changed, although the age

Table 20.3   Summary of the Piagetian model

Basic Stages in Developing the Ability to Think Logically	Behaviour Commonly Associated with the Stage
Sensorimotor Stage (0–2 years)* Understanding the present and real	Composed of six substages that move from reflex to intentional activity, involving cause-effect behaviour Involves direct interactions with the environment
Preoperational Stage (2–7 years) Symbolic representation of the present and real Preparation for understanding concrete operations (this is a tremendous period of transition)	Overt action is transformed into mental action. Child uses signifiers: mental images, imitation, symbolic play, drawing, and language to deal with experience. Understands verbal communication. Uses play to assimilate reality into herself. Believes what she sees; is "locked into" the perceptual world. Sees things from her own point of view, only one way at a time ("centring") and is learning to decentre. Thinking is not reversible. Intensely curious about the world. Busy laying foundations for understanding at the later concrete operations stage, which involves grasping concepts of *conservation, transitivity, classification, seriation,* and *reversibility.*
Concrete Operational Stage (7–11 years) Attainment of and organization of concrete operations Learns to apply logical thought to concrete problems	Has probably acquired the following concepts: *conservation, reversibility, transitivity, seriation,* and *classification*; that is, now believes that length, mass, weight, and number remain constant; understands relational terms such as *larger than* and *smaller than*; is able to arrange items in order from greatest amount to least amount; can group things according to more than one principle; can manipulate things in her mind, but these things are real objects. Becomes interested in following rules; games are important.
Formal Operational Stage (11–15 years) Hypothesis-making testing possible Masters logical reasoning	Age of abstract thinking; logical reasoning. Able to consider alternative possibilities and solutions. Can consider "fanciful," hypothetical possibilities as a basis for theoretical problem solving; abstract thinking, can make logical deductions and generalizations; can think about thinking.

*Note that the ages represent the *average* age of acquisition. This means that there is considerable variability in the time different children acquire the ability.

at which the stage occurs may vary. He demonstrated this convincingly in his detailed reports of investigations he conducted in which he presented problems to children and then asked them questions about their answers.

Piagetian Stages of Development

Of greatest interest to early childhood teachers is the preoperational stage that extends roughly from age two to age seven. During this stage children make the profound transition from depending on the way things appear to depending on logic and reasoning when making a decision. They become able to keep two ideas in their minds at once. In other words, children acquire the ability to think back to the original starting point and at the same time compare it in their minds with a current situation. Piaget calls this mental operation *reversibility,* and it is a good example of what is meant when we say the child is freed from concrete experience, since he performs this logico-mathematical reasoning process in his mind.

But young children who are in the preoperational stage do not possess this ability. Because they cannot consider two possibilities at once, they are unable to *conserve;* that is, they do not understand that quantity stays the same despite a change in appearance. This is because they cannot keep one idea in their minds while considering a second one.

❧   *Beginning seriation requires the understanding of size relationships.*

Thus they are likely to believe that a taller jar contains more water than a shorter jar does, even though they have previously been shown that the quantity was the same before pouring. For preoperational children, seeing is believing (Resnick, 1989).

At this stage, also, children may have difficulty shifting objects into more than one kind of category (sorting according to size and then shifting to colour, for example), taking two attributes into account at the same time, (sorting large pink circles and pink squares, small blue circles and blue squares into separate categories), or arranging a long series of graduated cylinders in regularly ascending order. Adults, however, no longer have difficulty grasping these concepts. This difference in the way children and adults think illustrates an important Piagetian principle—the thinking of children and adults differ in kind from each other. Children reason differently from the way adults do.

Additional Basic Concepts of Value

Although Piaget has been criticized on such grounds as inconsistency of theory, obscure terminology, and lack of scientific rigour, and although his work is consistently subjected to further critical evaluation and testing (Gardner, 1986; Siegel & Brainerd, 1978; Thomas, 1985), there is little doubt that despite these weaknesses he made many significant contributions to our understanding of the growth of children's mental abilities. Among these contributions is the idea that mental development is a dynamic process that results from the interaction of the child with his environment. The child acts on his own world, and by means of interaction with it he constructs his own knowledge (DeVries & Kohlberg, 1990). This is why Piaget favoured the saying that "construction is superior to instruction" (Thomas, 1992). This close observer of children maintained that they use language and play to represent reality, and for this reason he emphasized the extraordinary value of play as a basic avenue through which young children learn (1932). Finally, he stressed the importance of actual involvement of children with materials (as compared with observation and teacher explanation) and the significance of experience as a medium for learning.

At present, it appears that in addition to his general theoretical ideas, Piaget's identification of significant cognitive concepts and the steps and means by which they develop may be the most helpful contribution he has made to our understanding of the cognitive self. It is this understanding that makes it possible for teachers to generate a curriculum for stimulating the growth of cognitive abilities rather than merely teaching children an endless array of facts.

From a Piagetian Perspective, What Can Teachers Do to Help Children Develop Fully at Each Cognitive Stage?

Of course, it is neither desirable nor even possible to accelerate children markedly through the stages of cognitive development. This practice of overpressure is called *hothousing* and robs children of their childhood (Elkind, 1987; Sigel, 1987). What teachers should do instead is assist children to develop richly and fully at each stage, thereby paving the way for successful attainment of the next stage at the appropriate time.

Piaget maintained there are four factors that work together to promote cognitive growth. These are *maturation, experience, socialization,* and *equilibration.* The thinking teacher can make a helpful contribution to each of these factors as she leads children through the day.

For example, physical maturation underlies cognitive maturation, and the good health practices followed by children's centres can make a definite contribution to physical development by providing the sound nutrition, rest, and physical activity so necessary for the child's growing body to thrive.

Second, the provision of real experience with the physical world so stressed by Piaget is an essential cornerstone of early childhood education (Williams & Kamii, 1986). These experiences should include many opportunities for children to arrange things in order, to return things to their prior state, and to group them according to their common properties *as well as the chance to talk about why they have put them in particular configurations.* Opportunities for exploring other relationships such as cause and effect, as well as the basic skill of telling same from different, should also be included. (The remainder of this chapter presents many examples of ways such experiences may be integrated into the daily life of the program.)

Socialization, too, is something most early childhood teachers know a good deal about. Here, however, there is a special point that requires emphasis when discussing cognition from a Piagetian point of view. Whereas preschool teachers often think of socialization as lying in the realm of teaching children how to get along together or teaching them language (a profoundly useful social skill), Piaget thought of socialization as having another important facet. He maintained that interaction between children, particularly discussion, which he termed *argument,* is of extraordinary importance. It is through such exchanges of ideas that children test and modify what they think. And these modifications of what they think lead to the fourth factor that influences cognitive growth—equilibration.

Equilibration is the mechanism that brings maturation, experience, and social interaction into balance. It is the mechanism by which the child regulates his ideas (Wadsworth, 1989) and "puts things all together."

So if the teacher wishes to strengthen cognitive growth, in addition to providing optimum opportunities for physical maturation and real experience, she should also encourage dialogue *among* the children (as well as carrying out discussions between herself and the children). The results will be that children figure out more things for themselves. This enables them to coordinate their existing knowledge with their newly acquired knowledge by exercising the faculty of equilibration.

Thus, when the children complain that it's no fun to swing because their feet drag on the ground, instead of obligingly shortening the swing, the teacher might ask the children to propose what might be done to change that situation. Could they make their legs shorter? Could they stand up in the swing instead? Could someone push them so they could hold their legs out straight? Or . . . ? Children can think up and debate many possibilities once provided with the chance to do so. Such discussions and proposed solutions enable children to construct knowledge for themselves, construction that is so much more valuable than instruction.

❦ Some Practical Suggestions about Presenting Midlevel Thinking and Reasoning Skills in the Curriculum

Before embarking on a detailed discussion of specific reasoning abilities, I want to stress once again that the purpose of including the following material is not to foster precocity in young children. It is included because experience has taught me that hardly any preprimary teachers possess a framework that identifies significant mental abilities or explains how to go about fostering these skills in an appropriate and interesting way. Although teachers may use a few lotto games that give practice in matching or grouping, or talk from time to time about the order in which something has happened, offering these activities seems to be haphazard and fortuitous rather than part of a deliberate, coordinated plan. This may be all right for some children who seem to absorb skills through their pores, but it is unforgivable for the large group of preschool youngsters who, though possessing other strengths, apparently lack experience with these aspects of learning in their daily lives. Teachers need to get their own heads together on the subject of cognitive development so that they can systematically and regularly provide opportunities for practice of these abilities as well as the broader problem-solving skills discussed in the next chapter. (Incidentally, all the activities suggested in the following sections have been used over and over with preschool age children at the Institute of Child Development as well as by students in other preschools, so we know they are not too difficult.*) It is my hope that regular exposure to these kinds of activities will furnish all children with beginning skills that will stand them in good stead as they move on to the next stage of intellectual development.

Note that the following descriptions of activities include suggestions for children who are less advanced as well as suggestions for those who are more mature. They also stress that a diversity of experiences should be offered, *including large muscle activities.* All too often this kind of curriculum is limited to small muscle, tabletop experiences, which is most unfortunate.

Matching

Matching is the ability to perceive that two items are *identical,* and it depends on the child's grasping the concept of sameness and differentness. At our centre we have found that this is one of the easier concepts for young children to acquire. Even two- and three-year-olds will work at this occupation with interest and diligence if the materials are attractive and not too detailed.

Many commercial materials are available that may be used to provide practice in matching. These range from simple, obvious pictures with few details to quite elaborate discrimination tasks that contain a great deal of detail and subtle differences. Lotto and

---

*For a more detailed discussion of research projects dealing with teaching some of these abilities, see Hendrick (1973) or Safford (1978). The research of Meeker, Sexton, and Richardson (1970) also contains many specific examples of teaching strategies, although these focus on elementary-age children.

✑   *A simple game of animal
dominoes provides practice in
matching and the discrimination
skills that must go with that ability.*

bingo games are probably the most prevalent examples of such materials. But matching should not be limited to these kinds of activities. Younger children can grasp this concept by matching buttons (a perennial favourite), matching animal stamps or stickers, or playing simple picture dominoes. Fabric swatches and wallpaper samples are also fun to use for this purpose and can be surprisingly difficult. Incidentally, putting blocks back so that all of one kind go in the same place is a matching—*not* grouping—exercise, because the blocks are identical.

Matching experiences need not be limited to the sense of vision, of course. Children will also enjoy matching by touch (for texture and thickness), by hearing (duplicating simple sounds, rhythms, or melodies), and by taste and smell (it is interesting to cut up a variety of white fruits and vegetables, for instance, and ask the children to taste bits of them and find the ones that are the same). Imitation can also be thought of as an attempt to match actions; shadow or mirror dancing, Follow the Leader, and Simon Says may be employed for this purpose. Large muscle activities may be further incorporated by setting out two or three pictures and choosing a youngster to walk over to match one of them with the picture in his hand. (He then has the privilege of picking the next child to do this.) Children who are proficient at pumping may be asked if they can match the arc of their swings with that of the child beside them.

When asking children to complete a match, the teacher should use sentences such as "Show me the one that matches" or "Find me one that's just the same" rather than "Show me two that are just alike," since an occasional child is misled by the term *alike* and will blithely select something to show the teacher, saying, "Here, I like this one best!" Once he has acquired this verbal misconception of what the teacher means, it can be difficult to get him to change his mind; so talking about *same* rather than *alike* is the more effective choice of language.

As the child becomes more skilled, matching tasks may be increased in difficulty by making the matches more complex and difficult to analyse. This is usually accomplished by increasing the number of details that must be inspected in each picture and also by increasing the number of items to be compared. Ultimately the material shifts from depending on pictorially meaningful content to more symbolic form. This leads, finally, to using the symbols of the alphabet and numbers.

Grouping

I use the word *grouping* here in place of *classification* to remind the reader that we are discussing an elementary form of the more sophisticated skill described by Piaget (1965) wherein older children can form hierarchical classes or classify items according to a number of properties at the same time. Preschool children perform at a simpler level than classification, but four- and five-year-olds in particular are able to sort objects or pictures into categories meaningful to them. For example, I recall what happened when we were using companion animals as our focus for the week and invited the children to bring their pets to visit. When I asked Millie what kind of dog she had brought, she paused for a moment in thought and then replied, "Well, she's half collie—and half female."

Other examples of meaningful categorizing range from placing dollhouse furniture into rooms according to their function (kitchen equipment in the kitchen, for example) to sorting shells according to whether they are clams or mussels or pectens, rough or smooth, large or small. Teachers encourage categorizing every time they ask children, "Are airplanes birds? Why not?" or say "Show me all the buttons that belong together." In these instances the child is being asked to determine what it is that various items have in common—to determine the common property that defines the class—and then he is usually expected to decide whether an additional item also possesses this property and can be included.

In essence there are three ways to present such material. First, the child can be confronted with an assembled group and asked to choose things to add to it (perhaps it is pictures of clothing such as a sweater, dress, and shirt, and the additional pictures might be a doll, a pair of pants, and an ice cream cone). Second, he can be presented with an assembled group and asked to remove items that do not belong. ("Everyone who isn't wearing a plaid top, sit down.") Finally, he can be given a melange of articles or pictures and asked to sort them according to whatever criteria *he* establishes. *This third kind of presentation permits more divergent thinking* than the first two do and has the additional advantage of making regrouping according to different criteria more feasible.

Four-year-olds are rarely able to put their reasons for forming such groups into words at the beginning of the learning experience, although they can indicate by the sorting activity itself that they do perceive common properties. At our centre we have found that many of them gradually learn to explain why particular items go together as they practise, or they become able to name the class or group they have in mind (Hendrick, 1973). Thus a child who is inarticulate in the fall may by spring put a toy frog, turtle, and fish together and be able to tell us that he did this because they all like water or because "they're swimmy things."

Even though many children will at first be unable to put the reason for grouping particular things together into words, the category may be obvious to the onlooker. If a child is unable to formulate a reply after he has assembled a group, the teacher can help by saying, "Hmmmm, it looks to me as though you are putting all the red ones here and the blue ones here. Is that what you're doing?" This assists the child in translating his actions into words.

It is wise to encourage the child to determine the categories for himself whenever possible. If the teacher hands a child a box of little animals and tells him to "pick out all the red ones" or to "pick out all the ones we saw at the zoo," she has done most of the thinking for him before he goes to work. But if she says, "Show me which ones you think belong together" and follows this with, "Why do they go together?" the child must do more of the thinking for himself. This is quite different from and more valuable than expecting the child to "discover" the category the teacher has thought up.

Of course, it is not necessary to limit "grouping" activities to small muscle experiences. Every time children are asked to show how many different ways they can run or to choose what equipment they need to play house with in the sandbox, they are essentially thinking of things that fit a particular category or class just as they are determining categories when the teacher asks them, "Do you think the wheelbarrow should be kept with the wagons and scooters or with the garden equipment?" Additional practice is also provided by asking older four- and young five-year-olds to select three or four children from the group who are wearing something similar—boots, perhaps, or plaid clothing—and then have the rest of the children guess what it is they have in common.

Piaget has noted that younger children will change categories as they sort. This is a natural phenomenon and does not mean they are unintelligent. Maturation combined

ᵍ *Using a "secret" box adds lots of fun to mental ability activities.*

with opportunities to practise and talk about grouping will help the children learn to maintain consistent criteria.

Occasionally teachers become confused and attempt to teach grouping by using identical items for this purpose. Although being able to pick out things that are exactly the same and to tell them apart from those that are different is a useful literacy skill, it is not grouping; it is simple matching. *To teach grouping it is necessary to use materials that possess common properties but are not identical.*

The easiest form of grouping is sorting that requires simple responses to a prominent sensory quality such as colour (Lavatelli, 1970a, 1970b). Some children at the centre will need to begin at this level, but this is only the beginning. The task may be made more difficult by asking the children to think of a way the materials can be regrouped, by using more complex materials, by increasing the emphasis on verbalization, or by asking them to group materials according to several properties at the same time.

Perceiving Common Relations

The basic skill required in developing this concept is the ability to identify and pair items that are usually associated together but that are *not* identical. The activity of perceiving common relations is similar to grouping because it depends on the identification of a common property or bond. It differs from grouping because it involves *pairing* such items rather than working with larger numbers of them. It is useful to cultivate because it probably forms the basis for the later understanding and formulation of analogies (ring is to finger as belt is to . . . waist, buckle, or sash?). Since these combinations are usually culturally based (salt and pepper, shoes and socks, hat and head), it is important to know the home backgrounds of the children in order to be able to develop pairs likely to be familiar to them.

Opposites can also be included in this activity, since there is also a true relationship between them. Thus, hot can be contrasted with cold, up with down, and thick with thin.

We have found that three- and four-year-olds enjoy practising this conceptual task a great deal. It has the kind of appeal that riddles generally have, and the children relish pairing up an assortment of items that are either presented all together in a box or in more gamelike form in which several items are set out and their related members are drawn out of a bag one by one. There are some commercial materials on the market that are useful for this purpose, such as two-piece puzzles linking animals with their homes, or occupations with appropriate tools. (We call these *congruent relationships.*) It is also helpful to acquire many pairs of real objects or models of them that belong together and to keep a reserve of these handy to be brought out from time to time for the fun of it.

When the teacher is working with these combinations, it is usually effective for her to ask the child to pick out the thing that *goes most closely* with a selected item or that *belongs best* with it. This is language that the children understand and that is clear enough for them to be able to follow the directions.

Perceiving common relations may be made more difficult for more mature children by including less familiar combinations, by increasing the number of choices, or by setting up true analogies in which the child has to ascertain the quality common to both pairs of items.

ᔥ   *Pairing objects with pictures is a good example of a common relations activity.*

Understanding the Relationship Between Simple Cause and Effect

Although it takes children a long time to develop clear ideas of physical causality (Piaget, 1930), they can begin to acquire this concept while attending the centre. Indeed, good discipline often depends on teaching exactly this kind of relationship between action and outcome, since letting the punishment fit the crime usually results in allowing the child to experience the logical consequence of his behaviour. Thus the child who pulls all the blocks off the shelf is expected to help restack them, and the youngster who dumps his milk on the table must get the sponge and wipe it up himself.

In addition to understanding cause and effect in terms of social consequences, four-year-olds can often handle cause-related questions that are phrased as "What would happen if . . . ?" or "What do you think made something happen?" These questions are sound to use because they do not require children to apply or explain scientific principles that lie beyond their understanding but depend instead on what they can see happen with their own eyes or on what they can deduce from their own experience.

Following are some examples of successful questions:

1. What will happen if we add some sugar to the dough?
2. What will happen to your shoes if you go out in the rain without your boots on?
3. How come John dropped the hot pan so fast?
4. What made the kittens mew when mama cat got up?
5. What made the egg get hard?

Finding the answers to these questions can be accomplished by setting up simple experiments to identify the most probable cause. These experiments enable the children to try out suggested causes, compare results, and then draw conclusions about the most likely reason for something's happening, thereby introducing them to the scientific method.

For example, to determine what makes plants grow, the children might think of possibilities such as roots, water, and sunshine and then think of ways they could find out if their ideas are correct. They might think of cutting the roots off a marigold or of putting one plant in the dark and another in the sun while watering both. Or they might try growing plants with and without water. Of course, doing experiments like this may involve wasting and breaking or destroying some things, but the teacher really cannot allow a misguided idea of thrift to stand in the way of letting the children figure something out. Four-year-olds in particular enjoy carrying out this kind of investigation, although they will need help figuring out how to set up the experiment. Remember it is much more valuable for children to propose possibilities, make predictions, and try them out than for teachers to guide them to thinking of possibilities the teachers have thought up already.

Teaching about simple cause-and-effect relations presents one of the most interesting educational opportunities available to the preprimary teacher, and both natural history and physical science offer rich possibilities that can be used for this purpose. For this reason, several references on science for young children are listed at the end of this chapter.

Of course, cause-and-effect experiences need not be elaborate, full-blown experiments. Here is a partial list of simple cause-and-effect experiences identified by students in various classes: using a squirt gun, flashlight, or garlic press with dough or clay; blow-

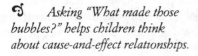

❧   *Asking "What made those bubbles?" helps children think about cause-and-effect relationships.*

ing soap bubbles; turning on a light; blowing up a balloon and pricking it with a pin; using all sorts of wind-up toys such as hopping frogs, little cars, and paddle boats; blowing a whistle; using grinders and graters; making butter; using scales (weighing heavy and light things for contrast); listening to children's hearts after they have been sitting, walking, or running; using a bank made like a doghouse (when a penny goes in the front, the dog comes out and grabs the money); turning a kaleidoscope; painting the sidewalk with water in sun and shade; striking a match; mixing paint to obtain different colours; pushing a button to make the clown move; and stretching rubber bands between various nails on a board, different tensions producing different pitched sounds.

Any of these experiences can generate good learning opportunities if the teacher encourages the children to do some predicting in advance or to explain in simple terms to each other what made the action happen.

Ordering

Ordering means arranging objects or events in logical order. The two kinds of ordering that appear to be most useful are arranging a variety of items according to a graduated scale (spatial ordering, the beginning of Piagetian seriation) and arranging events as they occur in time (temporal ordering). The basic question the child must be able to answer when dealing with either of these concepts is "What comes next?" There are many interesting activities that require a child to answer this question and to infer the logical order of either a spatial or temporal series.

Seriated Ordering

Almost any kind of item that comes in graduated sizes may be used for the purpose of teaching spatial, or seriated, ordering: various sizes of bolts and nuts, sets of measuring cups or spoons, nested mixing bowls, and empty tin cans of assorted sizes. There are also many commercial materials made for the purpose of practising seriation. Montessori cylinders are excellent for this purpose, and an examination of equipment catalogues will reveal many additional possibilities, ranging from nesting blocks to flannel board materials. Hardwood blocks, of course, present classic opportunities for becoming acquainted with the relationship between their varying lengths as well as for studying the regular relationships of equivalency that occur in block construction, since blocks may vary in length but generally are of the same width and depth.

I also favour including variations on seriation that teach gradations in quality. Grades of sandpaper can be provided so that children have opportunities to arrange them in order from rough to smooth; flavours can be provided that range from sweet to sour; tone bells can be arranged from high to low. Large muscle experiences that will draw the children's attention to graduated sizes might include having the children arrange themselves from shortest to tallest. (This can be fun to do if everyone lies down side by side and their height is marked on a big roll of paper and then the same paper is used again later in the year to measure their growth.) Or they can be given a set of four or five boxes and allowed to throw beanbags into them when they have been arranged in correct order.

The easiest kinds of seriation problems are ones in which the youngster is asked to choose which items should be added to a chain of two or three in order to continue an upward or downward trend (Siegel, 1972). Preschool children manage well using three, four, and even five and six items at a time as they become more experienced. Very young children often grasp this principle best if it is presented in terms of "This is the daddy, and this is the mother; now show me what comes next." The activity may be made more difficult by increasing the number of objects to be arranged, and even more difficult by asking the child to arrange a series and then giving him one or two items that must be inserted somewhere in the middle to make the series more complete. Finally, the challenge can be increased even more by asking the child to arrange two sets of objects in corresponding order or, more difficult yet, in contrasting order, for example, going from low to high for one set and high to low on a parallel set. This is *very* difficult! Nuts and bolts make particularly nice items to use for this purpose, as do padlocks and various sized keys and paper dolls with appropriately sized clothing.

Temporal Ordering

Recalling or anticipating the order of events as they occur in time is called *temporal ordering*. A child can be asked to recount the order in which he got up that morning: "First you got up, and then you went to the bathroom, and then . . ." Flannel board stories are another fine way to help children visualize the order in which things happen, and some social occasions also make excellent topics for discussion and pictures. Birthday parties, for example, often run quite true to form: First the guests arrive, then the birthday child opens his presents, and so forth. Recipes, also, can be set out with the ingredients arranged in the order in which they will be needed. Many of these orderly events can be played through as well as discussed—recapitulation through play is a most valuable way to rehearse the order in which events take place. Growth sequences based on human, plant, and animal development fit in here very naturally as a topic of study, as does the excellent series of sequenced puzzles generally available.

Although even two-year-olds are keenly aware of the order in which daily events occur and are sticklers for maintaining that order, as many a mother will attest, older preschoolers also need continuing practice with this concept. The level of difficulty for these more sophisticated children can be increased by adding more episodes to each event, asking the child to arrange a series of pictures and then to interpolate additional ones after the series has been formulated, asking him to arrange the events in reverse, or asking him to consider what might happen if something occurred out of order ("What if you got in the bathtub and then took your clothes off?" To which one child replied, "Nothing, as long as I don't turn the water on!") Asking children to plan an activity step by step in advance also provides practice in temporal ordering. I recall doing some serious planning with one group about how to proceed with giving my springer spaniel a bath. All went well until Lady shook herself vigorously. "We didn't plan on that!" said one four-year-old, looking with disgust at her dripping clothes.

Conserving

Perhaps no mental ability has come under more investigation than the ability to conserve quantity (Moore & Harris, 1978). When a child possesses this ability, he is able to recognize that the amount of the substance remains the same despite changes in its appear-

❧   *What mental ability is Matthew practising?*

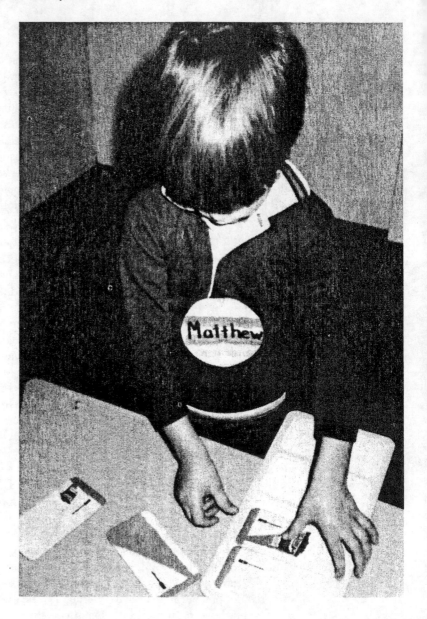

ance. When he is too young to be able to conserve (typically in our culture before age six or seven), the child is deceived by appearances into reasoning that the quantity has increased or decreased because a change in shape has made the material look like more or less. For instance, two glasses of water that have been judged equivalent will then be judged unequal when one is poured into a squat, low dish and another into a tall, thin cylinder and the two are compared again, or two balls of clay previously demonstrated to be the same amount will be judged different in quantity when one has been mashed flat or divided into many little balls.

Considerable interest has centred on the question of whether children can be taught this skill before the time they would typically acquire it, but the findings have been mixed and appear to be affected by a number of factors. For example, Inhelder (1968) reports that the amount children improve in their ability to conserve is always related to their prior level of development. Bruner (1966) reports that modifying the way materials are presented affects the children's answers to conservation problems. The age of acquisition of most conservation skills has also been shown to vary according to culture. Reporting on a survey of cross-cultural studies, Ashton (1975), for example, concluded that "acquisition of most conservation skills is delayed in non-Western cultures" (p. 481). Generally it appears that children who are on the verge of comprehending conservation may be pushed on to the next step in this process if they receive adequate instruction. The value of doing this, of course, remains open to debate.

Acceleration, however, is less important than making sure the child has ample opportunity to develop richly and fully at every level as he passes through it. This opportunity is particularly significant for children who come from lower socioeconomic levels, since evidence is mounting that such youngsters often lag behind their middle-class peers in developing such abilities (Almy et al., 1966; Golden, Bridger, & Montare, 1974; Sigel & McBane, 1967) and that additional experience and opportunities to practise may help them catch up.

Therefore, preprimary teachers should see to it that the children in their groups have many occasions to try out and experiment with the results of pouring liquids back and forth into various-shaped containers in order to learn that shape does not alter quantity. Blocks present outstanding opportunities to demonstrate conservation of mass, since it is relatively simple to see that a tower of four contains the same number of units as does a two-by-two stack. Clay and dough also lend themselves well to providing opportunities for youngsters to acquire this concept. In short, any material, whether liquid or solid, that can be divided and put together again may be used to investigate the principle of conservation.

It is also worthwhile to provide opportunities for measuring to demonstrate equality or inequality. Scales are useful in this regard, and yardsticks and measuring tapes are also valuable. Or children can create their own units of measure, using cutouts of feet or paper clips or Popsicle sticks. However, the teacher must realize that despite these aids, children who are too immature to grasp the principle of conservation will continue to insist that what their eyes tell them to be true is true.

The teacher's role in this area lies in providing many opportunities for the children to manipulate materials and experiment with changing their forms and with returning them to their prior state (reversing the reaction). In addition to supplying experiences, they should make a point of talking with the children and drawing their attention to the unchanging nature of quantity as they manipulate the materials. This is also an excellent time to build related vocabulary, such as *more than, less than,* and *equal to*. Finally, besides talking with the children themselves, teachers should foster discussion and "argument" among the children about the nature of conservation, since research (Murray, 1972; Smedslund, 1966) supports Piaget's contention (1926) that such interaction among children will help them reach correct conclusions.

ℰ   *Experiencing the relationship of quantity to the physical dimensions of the containers must be repeated innumerable times for children to acquire the concept of conservation of liquid.*

It is unlikely that children of prekindergarten age will do more than begin to grasp the principle of conservation, but it may be of interest to know how problems could be increased in difficulty should they do so. Conservation problems can be made more difficult by making the contrasts in form more extreme, that is, by making the cylinder taller and thinner or the balls of clay more numerous. (This principle is easy to remember if the reader recalls that even adults can be seduced into believing that tall, thin cereal boxes are a better buy than thick, squat ones of the same weight.) The more pronounced the apparent contrast is between the two quantities, the more likely it is that the child will be misled by appearance and forget that the quantity is actually equal.

ℰ *Provision of Opportunities for Practising Concept Formation Skills*

Develop Needed Materials

There are two ways to obtain materials to use for teaching these reasoning skills. The easiest, most expensive, and most obvious way is to rely on commercially developed tabletop activities. There are many such materials available, particularly in the areas of matching and seriation. The trouble with them is that they often are not related closely to curriculum topics, and they generally use only pictures as the medium of instruction. (Montessori materials are a welcome exception to this trend.) Their advantage is that they are readily available and convenient and can be self-selected and monitored by the children. The most significant danger to guard against is offering only commercially developed activities for concept development. This results in too narrow and dull a presentation to be fully effective.

The second way to introduce opportunities for this kind of concept development is to embed them directly in the curriculum. This is likely to be more work for the teacher, who will have to develop materials for the children's use, but it is also more satisfying because it gives her a chance to be creative and to use a much wider variety of materials and activities. Best of all, teacher-developed experiences mean that reasoning activities can be directly related to and coordinated with the topics that have interested the children. It is not difficult to generate such ideas; the plan that follows this section provides

ᴒ *This memory game gives children more sophisticated practice in matching and is fun besides.*

an example of how this can be done using the subject of water. Interested readers will also benefit from reading *Workjobs* (Baratta-Lorton, 1972), *Constructive Play* (Forman & Hill, 1980), *Piagetian Perspectives for Preschoolers* (Saunders & Bingham-Newman, 1984), *Young Children in Action* (Hohmann et al., 1979), or *The Piaget Handbook for Teachers and Parents* (Peterson & Felton-Collins, 1986).

Provide Consistent Opportunities for Practice

It is necessary to provide repeated opportunities for experience and practice (Hendrick, 1973). One or two chances to practise grouping, matching, or ordering are not sufficient. To understand these concepts fully and richly, children need to practise them consistently, using many materials and moving from simpler to more difficult activities as their skills increase.

Above All, Make Certain the Activities Are Fun

Every year the students in my college classes devise and construct a great many activities to stimulate mental development, and every year I am struck by the attractiveness of these materials. Indeed, if children happen to be passing by the door, it is all we can do to shoo them out while we are discussing what the teachers have made. Teachers seem to have a much better basic grasp of how to devise appealing materials than most manufacturers do. The teacher-made activities are so much more colourful, and they reflect a real familiarity with what young children really care about.

Pleasure is also increased for the children when the activities are at the right developmental level. The satisfaction of meeting the challenge of an activity that is just a little bit but not too much harder than what the child has already mastered is obviously gratifying. Throughout the previous discussion, suggestions have been included showing how the levels of difficulty of various abilities can be increased, so strategies will only be summarized here that might be used with any of the abilities to increase the challenge. These include adding more choices, asking if there is another way to do it, asking the children to put what they are doing into words, using a different sensory mode in place of vision (such as using only touch or only hearing), using memory, asking children to tell you something in reverse order, or using items that are less familiar. A word of caution—we have had children in our centre, usually five-year-olds, who enjoyed being challenged in all these ways; however, the key word here is *enjoyed*. The purpose is not to make things so difficult that children sweat and struggle over them. The foregoing list is included merely to provide an idea of possibilities to go on to.

Another caution I want to add is the undesirability of resorting to competition and comparison to generate "fun." Setting up activities with the aim of seeing who can do something quickest or "best" takes a lot of fun out of it for the losers. It is fairly easy to substitute something like suspense in place of competition to sustain interest. Suspense strategies can be as simple as having children pull things out of a mystery bag and then decide where they should go, or asking them to choose from one hand or the other when the teacher holds two things behind her back.

Here are some additional activities that one student developed for matching games that were fun for the children.*

Instead of choosing a cognitive game from the Centre, I decided to make an original one. The idea is based on a game my grandmother used to give me to play. She would take the buttons from her button box and ask me to "help" her by sorting them into the compartments of her sewing tray. I was always so proud that I had been able to "help."

My cognitive game is simple to make. You simply cut an egg carton in half (either plastic or cardboard). The six cups are used as the compartments, and the lid (with the cut end closed with a strip of cardboard and tape) is the tray that holds the assortment to be sorted. For my game I have chosen a kitchen assortment of shapes and sizes of macaroni and spaghetti. These objects can be dyed with a little food colouring if colour is desired. For younger children you might glue one of each thing in the bottom of each cup; for the older children this is not necessary. I have made six of these for group time. Each child receives his own individual game to work on by sorting the items into the cups.

Then to make it more fun, the teacher can use it as a group game. She can put several of each item into a "feely" box and have each child put his hand in and pick up one item and identify it in the box before he pulls it out. He can identify it by picking up a matching item from his own tray to show they are the same.

Another fun way to play this game, which the older children like especially, is to have them do the sorting with their eyes closed. Simply tell them which item they are to sort out from the others in their tray and have them do it by feel only.

Another way to use this game is to have a child choose one of the items (by turning her back) and to enclose it in her fist and pass it into the fist of the next child. That child then tries to identify it without looking (by choosing an identical item from his tray).

This cognitive game is simple to make and costs nothing. It develops the mental skill of matching as well as giving practice in haptic shape identification and can also be used for size ordering (as when the teacher asks "Which is the largest?" or "Which is the smallest macaroni?"). It can also be used to help develop receptive skills such as listening and comprehending what directions were given and following through on these, and it helps develop fine muscle control and eye-hand coordination.

❧ Sample Lesson Plan Based on the Water Unit

Some Things to Remember[†]

One of the most important things to remember about making a lesson plan is that it is only a plan. This means that it should be flexible and capable of adjusting to circumstances when something special comes along. Perhaps overnight the weather has turned cold. Then the teacher should take advantage of the skim ice on the puddles and integrate that into the curriculum. Or perhaps a youngster has brought his pet chameleon with him and the children are so fascinated that it would be a sin not to get out the lizard books and coloured cloth and forget about your carefully planned sound jar demonstration until tomorrow.

---

*Activities courtesy Mary Anderson, class of 1979, Santa Barbara City College, CA.

[†]Please refer to chapter 2, "What Makes a Good Day for Children?" as a reminder of additional ingredients of a good day.

Balance is also important to remember. This refers to a balance of quiet and active activities, a balance of interest that provides for the concerns and needs of all the children in the group, and a balance that includes educational opportunities for all five selves. The lesson plan on the following pages lists only the activities that *require special planning*. As do most teachers in their plans, *it takes for granted the inclusion of typical, basic foundation activities such as sand play, blocks, and an array of manipulative materials*.

To be effective, a curriculum needs to suit the developmental level of the children and also take their cultural backgrounds into consideration. (Please note that the lesson plan in this chapter was devised for older three- and younger four-year-olds and that there happened to be a set of Finnish twins and four Japanese youngsters in the group. The remaining children were Anglo.)

As you review the daily plan, note how the interests of the children are taken into account as the curriculum is based on something they care about, namely, water. Numerous opportunities are included for factual learning—sun melts snow, thick paint is harder to spread, and water is stored in the tank behind the toilet. Of even greater value is the inclusion of many opportunities for the children to practise the midlevel and problem-solving skills so vital for the full development of their mental powers.

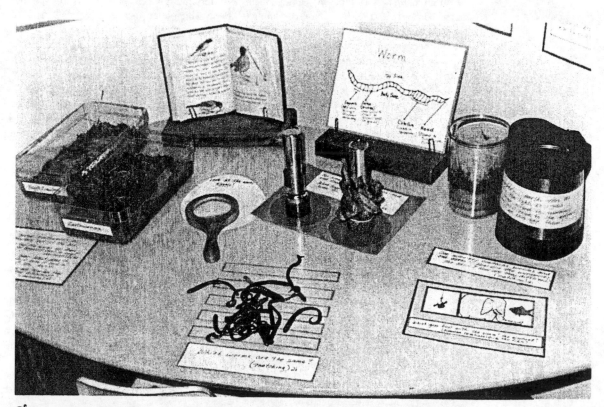

❧   *Look at all the things for children to do on this "Let's-Find-Out" table. (The worms are mostly plastic fishing lures.)*

ॐ   *"And as soon as I get these here pieces together the water will come out, and we'll have a shower!" chortles Mark.*

A Let's-Find-Out table in particular offers many opportunities for enhancing cognitive learning. These include filling a cup with crushed ice and another equally full of water and asking the children to predict if the cups will still be filled to the same level when the ice melts (matching), and, if not, how they could make them become the same level (cause-effect); using a set of teacher-made pictures of items that can be used for pouring, squirting, or just holding water and asking children to sort these according to function (grouping); arranging the sound jars from low to high tones (seriation); and encouraging children to make up a second set of jars by pouring water into additional ones, attempting to achieve the same sound (matching).

Cause-and-effect learning is added to Let's Find Out as children bring in the plant cuttings, putting some in water while leaving others dry. The water play table provides endless opportunities for children to pour and repour water into various containers, comparing how the same amount of water looks when poured into differently shaped vessels (conservation). From time to time the teacher supervising Let's Find Out and water tables will ask the children questions intended to draw their attention to what is happening and asking them to draw conclusions about their observations.

Because the lesson plan outlines just one day, a quick synopsis of some special activities of the day before and a projection for the following day are included along with the detailed lesson plan in Table 20.4. For additional ideas about using water as a topic, refer to Crosser (1994), and Hill (1977).

Table 20.4   Lesson plan: full-day program: Water and Its Uses

Time	Activities	Self	Value to Child (Highlights)
7:00–7:30	Teachers arrive and set up.		Advance set-up is invaluable for everyone's peace of mind
7:30	Children begin arriving.	Emotional Social	Teacher welcomes each child individually; helps with separation; reconfirms caring, concerned relationship with youngsters
	Self-select activities		
	Plumbing equipment available to assemble (no water)	Cognitive Physical	Recapitulates prior day's experience with pipes and joints, etc.; eye-hand coordination
	New small plastic blocks	Physical Social	Eye-hand coordination; gives some children chance to use new material before crowd arrives—takes pressure off having to share too much, too soon
	Puzzles and additional manipulative materials	Cognitive Physical	Part-whole relations; eye-hand coordination
	Housekeeping	Social-Emotional	Get along with other children; play out feelings; some creative ideas may occur.
	Dampen seeds and leave others dry.	Social Cognitive	Opportunity to help the group; part of cause-and-effect project begun the day before
8:30	*Breakfast* available for those who want it; other activities continue.	Physical Social-Emotional	Nourishment; chance for friendly, intimate time with teacher, talking and sharing
9:00–9:15	*Transition*	Social	Children learn to start and stop; conform to group; help group by tidying up
9:15–9:35	*Group time*		
	Discuss plans for afternoon field trip; how will group decide who goes to sauna and who goes to Japanese bath.	Emotional Social	Advance preparation to reduce anxiety; practice in group decision making; developing and expressing ideas

Time	Activities	Self	Value to Child (Highlights)
	Read *The Snowy Day*.	Cognitive Social	Fact and cause and effect (sun melts snow); multiethnic (all kinds of people like to make snowmen); language development
	Sing "There's a Hole in the Bucket, Dear Liza."	Cognitive Social	Temporal ordering; language; minority folk song; cultural heritage
	Introduce sound jars to be used at Let's-Find-Out table	Cognitive	Seriation; cause and effect (different amounts of water make different sounds when container is struck); teach *safe* use of glass containers
	Review Stevenson poem	Cognitive	Memory; language; cultural heritage; teaches part of water cycle
9:35 9:45	*Transition*		
9:45–11:45	*Outside: self-select activities*		
	Plumbing equipment in sandbox with running water from hose	Cognitive Social	Continue and develop yesterday's experience; cause and effect; children work together to solve problems (project may lead ultimately to bringing water over to garden)
	Large muscle equipment	Physical	Emphasize jumping, hanging, swinging, and climbing
	Tricycles	Social Physical	Cooperative play; alternating body movements
	Large hollow blocks/boards	Creative	Creative dramatic play; develop ideas through social interaction
	Cut pairs of plant pieces; take indoors to Let's-Find-Out table; put some in water, some not in water.	Cognitive	Fact: plants need water; cause-and-effect learning
	Indoors: self-select activities		
	Blocks with board accessories; small plastic blocks	Cognitive Creative	Many kinds of intellectual learning; representation of reality; creative play

Table 20.4 Lesson plan: full-day program: Water and Its Uses *continued*

Time	Activities	Self	Value to Child (Highlights)
	Easel painting using thick and thin paint	Creative Cognitive	Self-expression; cause and effect; how is paint same and different?
	Sound jars	Cognitive	Experiment with cause and effect; matching; seriation
	Dramatic play	Social	Social, interactive play; ties in with field trips in afternoon
	Bathing babies	Creative	
	Let's-Find-Out table combined with water table	Cognitive	Matching, grouping, seriation, cause/effect, conservation (see previous discussion)
11:40–12:00	*Transition:* inspect how toilet works for children who were interested in plumbing equipment	Cognitive Emotional	How things work; what becomes of urine and bowel movements; may reassure some children who fear flushing
12:00–12:35/45	*Lunch* (including fresh fruit juice sherbet)	Physical Social Cognitive	Good nutrition; social, "family" time; language development; what happens to sherbet when it melts? Can we turn it back into sherbet?
12:45–1:00	*Transition*	Physical	Toilet; get ready to care for body by resting
1:00–2:30	*Nap*	Physical Emotional Social	Relaxation-sleep; depending on skill with which nap is handled, a myriad of social and emotional learnings are possible.
2:30–3:00	*Get up, snack*—only fruit served—light snack because of bath field trip	Physical	Good nutrition combined with advanced planning for possible slight physiological stress
3:00–4:30	*Field trip* to Japanese or Finnish bath (sauna) (Parent volunteers help drive.) (Group divides in half.)	Social Cognitive Physical	Multiethnic: people meet the same need in differing ways; unisex bathing; facts about different ways people bathe; bathing and getting clean feels good.
4:30–5:30	*Children return,* play quietly with manipulative materials. *One teacher has very relaxed group time.* Some children leave early because their parents drove on the field trip.	Physical Cognitive Emotional	Chance to relax; be leisurely; talk over experience; anticipate next day's activities; look forward to more learning and fun; provides sense of completion for day

Lesson Plan

Activities the previous day. Pipes and joints were introduced; children used them outdoors and ran water through assembled pipes. Children planted seeds in pots and discussed what makes plants grow. Group decision was made to water some pots and leave others dry to see if plants would sprout without water. Discussion also took place about different ways people take baths (pictures included); upcoming field trip was discussed. Stevenson poem about river used during story time. Carpentry was offered as one of the creative activities. Dance and movement experience also included, with some raindrop music used as part of that experience.

Probable activities for the following day. Check plants for wilting and seeds for possible sprouting. Share pictures from book *Paddle to the Sea* (Holling, n.d.) (use only pictures; text too difficult) along with Stevenson poem. Children will make ice cream. Try various ways to make ice melt fast. Include discussion and sharing between groups who went to different bathing experiences. Offer baby doll bathing again, possibly with Japanese and Finnish accessories. On walk, pry open manhole cover, look at sewer pipes under the street.

❦ Summary

Piaget made many significant contributions to our understanding of cognition. Among these are his identification of various categories of knowledge and stages of intellectual development. He maintained that mental development is a dynamic process that results from the child's actions on his environment, that play is an important avenue of learning, and that children construct their own knowledge base.

The chapter concludes with detailed discussions of some basic thinking and reasoning skills that form the foundation for later, more sophisticated cognitive abilities. These include matching, grouping, perceiving common relations, temporal and seriated ordering, conservation, and understanding elementary cause-and-effect relationships. A daily schedule illustrating how these skills might be incorporated into the curriculum is found at the end of the chapter.

Questions and Activities

1. Pick up on a current interest of the children in your group and propose some thinking and reasoning activities that could be based on that interest.
2. Concoct activities that fit the various mental abilities, such as ordering and grouping, and try them out with the children. Then add variations to the activities that make them easier or more difficult in order to suit the needs of individual children in the group. Set aside some shelves in your school where these materials can be accumulated.
3. Review the activities related to mental ability in the school where you teach and identify the ones that foster literacy skills that lead to reading later on.

Self-Check Questions For Review

Content-Related Questions

1. Piaget identified three kinds of knowledge involved in children's thought. What are they?
2. List at least four important ideas Piaget contributed to cognitive education.
3. From a Piagetian point of view, explain what teachers can do to assist the cognitive development of young children.
4. This chapter discusses seven thinking and reasoning skills. Explain how these are related to later school-related skills.
5. Identify each of the reasoning skills, define them, and provide examples of how they could be included in the curriculum.

6. What is the main difference between the teaching style needed to teach the midlevel mental abilities and the teaching style needed for the problem-solving approach?

Integrative Questions

1. Cite a rule about social behaviour that would be an example of social-conventional knowledge and one that would be an example of physical knowledge.
2. Explain why *matching* and *perceiving common relations* are examples of logico-mathematical knowledge.
3. Which of the following mental abilities is most likely to foster mathematical understanding: (a) matching, (b) seriation, or (c) cause and effect? Explain why you selected the answer you did.
4. How are *common relations* and *grouping* the same? How do they differ?
5. How do *matching* and *grouping* differ?
6. What is the *scientific method*, and how is *cause-and-effect* reasoning related to it?
7. What do seriated and temporal ordering have in common—how are they alike? How do they differ?
8. Compare the two approaches to cognitive learning described in Chapter 20. What might be the strengths and weaknesses of each approach?

References for Further Reading

Overviews

Bybee, R. W., & Sund, R. B. (1990). *Piaget for educators* (2nd ed.). Prospect Heights, IL: Waveland Press. It is delightful to welcome this useful book back into print. It is filled with clear explanations of Piaget's theory combined with many examples of Piagetian tasks.

Greenberg, P. (1990). Ideas that work: Why not academic preschool? Part I. *Young Children, 45*(2), 70–80. This impassioned article vividly contrasts two points of view about the nature of education and instruction. *Highly recommended.*

Malkus, U. C., Feldman, D. H., & Gardner, H. (1988). Dimensions of mind in early childhood. In A. D. Pellegrini (Ed.), *Psychological bases for early education*. New York: Wiley. This clearly written article is a good introduction to Gardner's theory of multiple intelligences and some implications of that theory for education. *Highly recommended.*

Peterson, R., & Felton-Collins, V. C. (1986). *The Piaget handbook for teachers and parents: Children in the age of discovery, preschool–third grade*. New York: Teachers College Press. I wish I'd found this book years ago! It offers clear descriptions of some basic Piagetian principles combined with suggestions of practice activities.

Wadsworth, B. J. (1989). *Piaget's theory of cognitive and affective development* (4th ed.). New York: Longman. A good, clearly written introduction to Piaget that also deals with implications for teaching.

Curriculum Suggestions for Midlevel Thinking and Reasoning Skills

Baratta-Lorton, M. (1972). *Workjobs: Activity-centered learning for early childhood education*. Menlo Park, CA: Addison-Wesley. Photographs accompany every suggested activity, showing how a wide variety of cognitive materials can be made by the teacher. Also included are ideas for presentations of the materials and recommendations for follow-up discussions.

Crosser, S. (1994). Making the most of water play. *Young Children, 49*, (5), 28–32. Crosser presents a detailed analysis of all the things children can learn from using this delightful substance. Also included is a list of sixteen references elaborating even further on this subject. *Highly recommended.*

Graves, M. (1989). *The teacher's idea book: Daily planning around the key experiences*. Ypsilanti, MI: High/Scope. This book offers many examples of ways classification, seriation, and other mental abilities can be included on a daily basis.

Hohmann, M., Banet, B., & Weikart, D. (1979). *Young children in action: A manual for preschool educators*. Ypsilanti, MI: High/Scope Educational Research Foundation. An outgrowth of one of the early experimental programs known as the Perry Preschool Project, this book discusses the presentation of the curriculum from the Piagetian point of view.

Kostelnick, M. (Ed.). (1991). *Teaching young children using themes*. New York: Harper Collins. Twenty-four theme units ranging from self-awareness to measurement are included here. Suggested activities are numerous and include ideas for simplifying and extending them. Particularly valuable are the general information facts for the teacher included with each subject.

Saunders, R., & Bingham-Newman, A. M. (1984). *Piagetian perspectives for preschools: A thinking book for teachers*. Englewood Cliffs, NJ: Prentice Hall.

This book offers many excellent ways to implement Piagetian principles throughout the classroom.

Sparling, J., & Lewis, I. (1984). *Learning games for threes and fours.* New York: Walker. The authors break learning games into activities appropriate for four stages of development. The activities cover many mental abilities and sound like genuine fun. Developmental checklists are also included. *Highly recommended.*

Science Materials That Are Appropriate for Preschool-Age Children

Harlan, J. D. (1992). *Science experiences for the early childhood years* (5th ed.). Englewood Cliffs, NJ: Merrill/Prentice Hall. I recommend this book as being a particularly rich source of additional curriculum-related ideas, including music, finger plays, lists of children's books, creative ideas, and even some examples of "thinking games."

Lima, C. W. (1989). A to zoo: *Subject access to children's picture books* (3rd ed.). New York: Bowker. Have you ever hunted desperately for a picture book to fit a particular subject? If so, this is the answer to your prayers. It indexes everything from turtles to robots by subject, author, title, and illustrator. Available in most libraries.

National Science Teachers Association. (1992). Outstanding science books for young children in 1991. *Young Children, 47*(4), 73–75. Title is self-explanatory.

Neugebauer, B. (Ed.). (1989). *The wonder of it: Exploring how the world works.* Redmond, WA: Exchange Press. This is a delightful collection of articles about teaching science. Topics range from cooking as science to how to ask good questions and set up a science table. *Highly recommended.*

For the Advanced Student

Gardner, H. (1991). *The unschooled mind.* New York: Basic Books. Gardner, who is always delightful reading, begins with a discussion of how preschool children think and then makes recommendations of ways to improve more advanced levels of education.

Meadows, S. (1993). *The child as thinker: The development and acquisition of cognition in children.* New York: Routledge. Chapter 4 offers a thoughtful assessment of the strengths and weaknesses of Piagetian and neo-Piagetian theory.

Piaget, J. (1983). Piaget's theory. In P. H. Mussen (Ed.), *Handbook of child psychology* (4th ed.), W. Kessen (Ed.), *Vol. 1: History, theory, and methods.* New York: Wiley. This work by the master himself is a reprint from *Carmichael's Manual of Child Psychology,* 1970 edition. A classic.

Thomas, R. M. (1992). *Comparing theories of child development* (3rd ed.). Belmont, CA: Wadsworth. This invaluable book discusses a range of theories, including that of Piaget. Highly recommended for its clarity and comprehensiveness.

Developing Thinking and Reasoning Skills

Using the Emergent Approach to Foster Creativity in Thought

21

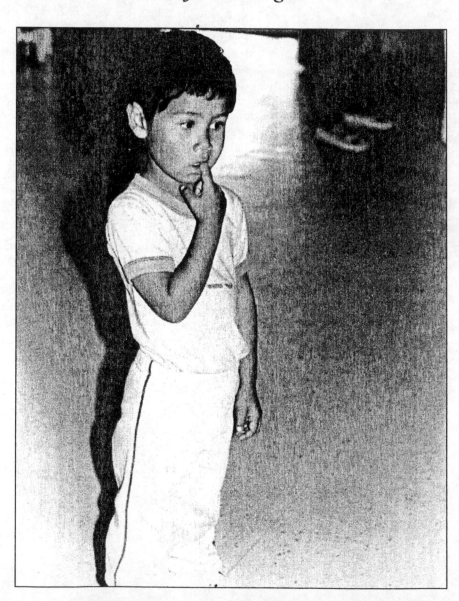

Most teachers do not distinguish questions that assess from those that assist. This results in the teacher assuming that a request for information constitutes teaching. It does not. . . . The *assistance* question . . . inquires in order to produce a mental operation that the pupil cannot or would not produce alone.

R. Gallimore and R. Tharp

Teachers of young children need to do more than give children a sweet, steady, intellectually shallow diet of things they already like. Being offered new experiences—and being supported in trying them out—provides children with a chance to develop new likes, new enthusiasms, and new areas of competence. Teachers sometimes hesitate to be too activist out of fear of pushing children. Although this fear is well founded, the other extreme is also risky.

Marion C. Hyson

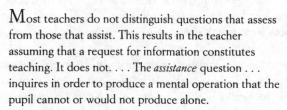

Have you ever wondered . . .

Just who this Vygotsky person is that everyone seems to be talking about?

How to help children really think up ideas for themselves?

What teachers can do to help them do so?

. . . If you have, the material in the following pages will help you.

*T*he second way to approach developing a curriculum for the child's cognitive self is to build it experience by experience, idea by idea, as a topic evolves or emerges while the teachers and children investigate it together. Hence the name, *emergent curriculum*.

Sometimes novice teachers assume the term *emergent* means that every idea must emerge from the children and that the curriculum must be entirely unplanned and spontaneous to fulfil the criteria of emerging. This is not what I have in mind when using the term. In this book *emergent* means that the direction a topic takes develops as the children and teachers investigate it together—each contributing their own ideas and possibilities as they evolve, in somewhat the same way that the children and teachers at Reggio Emilia do. The teachers do make plans in advance and have ideas for possible topics, just as the children do, but, as Rinaldi puts it so well, "these plans are viewed as a compass not a train schedule" (1994).

This image of a curriculum plan serving as a compass indicating direction and intention rather than being a predetermined schedule is particularly helpful to keep in mind when using the emergent approach. After all, if the curriculum is seen as gradually emerging it really cannot be completely scheduled in advance, but it certainly does require a sense of direction and purpose.

If we carry the image of a compass a little further, it also clarifies why I, like Loris Malaguzzi (1992), the founder and architect of the Reggio Emilia preschools, prefer to use the word *pathway* to describe the development of a topic rather than the word *project*. *Pathway* conveys the sense of a continuing journey rather than a unit that has a preplanned end or goal in mind from the start. As teachers and children venture down the pathway together, learning stems from the social interaction and collaboration that takes place along the way.

As this idea of a collaborative, learning-together approach has gained impetus, interest has also grown in the works of a Russian psychologist named Lev Vygotsky because of his emphasis on the value of the child and a more knowledgeable person working in collaboration together. Therefore, it makes sense to take a minute to consider some of his most basic ideas.

ꙮ *Some Basic Concepts of Vygotskian Psychology*

During his brief life (he died at age thirty-seven from tuberculosis) Vygotsky contributed a number of insightful ideas about cognitive development and how it takes place. He maintained that language and cognitive ability do not appear automatically as the child passes through landmark stages. Rather, they develop in part because of interaction with other people—other peers, adults, and even imaginary companions as the child grows. As the title of his book, *Mind in Society* (1978) emphasizes, the mind develops as the result of society's action upon it. Since mental development cannot be separated from the social context in which it takes place, this theory about children's mental development is often spoken of as a sociocultural or sociohistorical theory. All this means is that society (and its past development—hence historical) and the culture it generates has great influence on what the child learns and the means by which she learns it.

Perhaps the most familiar Vygotskian concept is the idea of the *zone of proximal development (ZPD)*. He defines this as "the distance between the actual development level [of the child] as determined by independent problem solving and the level of potential development as determined through problem solving under adult guidance in collaboration with more capable peers" (1978, p. 86). Vygotsky points out that with the assistance of a more knowledgeable person, the child can advance closer to the farther edge of his potential ability. Another way of saying this is that there is a difference between the current or actual level of development and the child's potential level of development. The possibility of maximum advancement depends on the assistance lent to the learner by a more knowledgeable person.

This concept of the ZPD, as it is affectionately called, has encouraged teachers striving to put the emergent curriculum into practice to see their role as first, beginning at the child's level of ability and then collaborating with her—by offering questions and cues, as well as more tangible assistance that may enable her to extend her mental abilities a bit beyond what she was previously able to do.

The peril involved in using this approach at the preschool level is that it may become so teacher dominated and developmentally inappropriate that the child becomes a puppet—manipulated into parroting ideas beyond her understanding in order to please the adult. The best protection against this happening is careful sensitivity to the child's responses. That sensitivity must be the result of continual observation not only of what the child says but also what she does. Does her physical behaviour reveal underlying stress and tension? For example, is she wiggling, twisting her feet around chair legs, grimacing, twisting her hair, gnawing on fingernails, making excuses, and not wanting to participate—just to name a few common ways of relieving tension?

The other aspect of Vygotsky's theory of particular importance to preschool teachers is his emphasis on the significance of spoken language as the mediator between the world, the child's mind, and her ability to express, understand, and explain to other people what she knows. Vygotsky theorizes that it is by using the tool of language that children are able to master themselves and gain independence of behaviour and thought. It is certainly true that many of us who work with two-year-olds have heard examples of their attempts to use language to regulate behaviour that support this contention. Who has not witnessed a child of that age say to herself, "No! No! baby!" as she reaches simultaneously for the scissors?—or dealt with a four-year-old reporting prissily on another's misdeeds in the sandbox?

Once again a peril must be noted concerning the use of language with young children: While acknowledging its indispensable value, teachers must also remember not to substitute it for real experiences—in order for language to have meaning it must be tied to the concrete world and in order for the world to acquire meaning the child must have language.

ᔐ *Getting Started*

Many teachers, particularly early childhood teachers, are very attracted to this idea of the curriculum unfolding and developing as the children's interest grows. Yet, when actually thinking about putting the approach into practice, they feel baffled and unsure about where to begin.

It is really not so difficult once the approach is analysed into its various aspects and some fundamental concepts are grasped. One of the most important of these is that it is

✑   *The basic skill the teacher needs to cultivate in herself is asking the kinds of questions likely to provoke thought.*

valuable for children to be able to generate their own ideas, figure out answers for themselves, and try out a variety of solutions until they find one that works.

In order to make this possible, the most basic skill the teacher needs to develop in himself is the ability to ask the right kind of thought-provoking questions. In order to understand how to do *that,* he must first understand what is meant by creativity and creative thinking. Once this idea is grasped it is much easier to generate questions that encourage children to think of more than one possibility as they produce ideas on their own.

✑ *How Does Creative Thinking Differ from Other Kinds of Thinking?*

Smith's definition of creativity as "the process of sinking down taps into our past experiences and putting these selected experiences together into new patterns, new ideas or new products" (1966, p. 4) applies to thought, as well as to play and the use of expressive materials. The ability to put prior experiences together to form new ideas is crucial in developing creative thinking, although building on past knowledge sometimes can produce unexpected results. I recall hearing of two young friends who were eating lunch together when the following dialogue took place.

Henry: "Well, you know, Andrew, I'm black! I'm black all over—from my head right down to inside my shoes!"

There is a pause while this information is digested in silence by his friend Andrew.

Henry continues, "But that's okay! Cuz my mother says black is beautiful!'

Andrew continues to eye Henry speculatively while Henry somewhat complacently spoons up his Jell-O. There is silence around the table.

"Well," says Andrew, putting down his spoon and looking thoughtfully at Henry, "I guess being black's okay, all right—it's okay with *me*—but you know, Henry, if you wuz green, you could hide in the trees!"

Using prior information as Andrew did to produce new possibilities is just one kind of creative thinking. Children are also thinking creatively when they produce more than one answer to a question, or conceive of new uses for familiar materials, or generate uniquely descriptive language and self-expressive stories. To do these things, they need a wealth of experience to draw upon, and they need the help and expertise of the teacher to encourage them (Leipzig, 1989).

One of the people who have helped us understand the difference between the kind of thinking processes in which only one answer is correct and the thinking processes in which many answers might be correct is Paul Guilford (1981). He has named the uncreative one-correct-answer sort of thinking *convergent* and the creative many-possible-answers kind of thinking *divergent*.

Convergent thinking is elicited by such questions as, "What colour is this?" "Can you tell me the name of this shape?" "What must we always do before we cross the street?" There is nothing wrong with this kind of mental activity; children need to have a variety of commonly known facts at their fingertips. But teaching that stops at the fact-asking information level fails to develop the creative aspect of the child's mental ability. Children who are trained like robots to produce facts when the right button is pushed are unlikely to grow up to produce the new ideas desperately needed in science, medicine, and human relationships.

Unfortunately, most teaching is still geared to convergent, one-answer learning. Zimmerman and Bergan (1971) found that even as early as first grade there was what they termed "an inordinate emphasis placed on factual knowledge questions." They reported that only about 2% of the questions asked by first-grade teachers were structured to draw forth divergent replies. Honig has also studied question-asking behaviour and reports similar discouraging findings. The children she studied averaged around twenty-seven months of age, and of the nearly 800 questions she observed being asked by caregivers, "15% were requests, 4% were reproofs, and 81% were true questions" (1982a, p. 65). This sounds encouraging until one reads that only 20% of those "true" questions were divergent and that fewer than 1% offered these children any choices!

But just because this has been true of teaching in the past does not mean it must continue. The following examples of ways to foster creativity in thought may encourage teachers to produce more divergent thinking in the children in their groups. Doing this is fun, it is interesting, and it can be exciting for both children and teachers when it is presented in the right manner. All it takes is practice.

❦ Learn to Use Questions in Ways that "Provoke" the Children Into Thinking for Themselves

Sort Out the Different Kinds of Teacher-Generated Questions: Understand the Difference Between Using Fact and Thought Questions

We have already noted that all questions are not alike because some elicit convergent and others divergent replies. This is easiest to understand if one thinks of questions related to mental development as being of three kinds: *fact questions,* which request the child to reply with one right answer, *figuring-out questions,* which require the child to apply a concept such as grouping or common relations in order to arrive at one or more right answers, and *creative questions,* which elicit an original idea (hypothesis) or solution from the youngster.

Fact questions are the simplest, and regrettably the most frequently used kind of question. They can usually be spotted because they request information ("Do you make cookies in the oven or in the broiler?" "You're right! It is a rabbit. What else do you know about rabbits?"), request labelling or naming ("Let's see, I have some things in this bag, and I wonder if you can tell me what they are?"), or request the child to recall something from memory ("How about telling us what happened when you went to the pet store? Did you buy rabbit food?"). All these questions are "closed" or convergent questions since they anticipate simple, correct-answer replies.

Figuring-out questions, which we dealt with mainly in Chapter 20, are a big step up from fact questions, but, in the final analysis, they are still going to produce right (convergent) answers. They are more advanced than fact questions because, in order to answer the question, the child must be able to apply a concept to a situation and reason out the reply. For example, to select the pictures that are the same (playing Bingo, for instance), a youngster must understand the concept of sameness and then be able to apply it by matching the pictures that are identical. Or, if she is asked how birds are not the same as butterflies, she must analyse what is the same about them and what is different. Even though there would be a number of differences to identify, and though more analysis and insight is involved than is required just to say "It's called a butterfly," the final result is the production of closed-ended, correct answers. These midlevel intellectual skills are useful because they form part of the foundation for verbal and mathematical literacy later on, but they do not provide children with opportunities to express the full range of what they know and produce unique solutions.

Creative questions, on the other hand, foster the production of original, divergent ideas and solutions. They are termed *open-ended* because the questioner does not know what the answer will turn out to be. This chapter concentrates on using these kinds of questions because these are the ones most needed when using the emergent approach.

Questions likely to draw forth such kinds of replies are phrased like this: "What could you do about it?" "How could we fix it?" "I wonder if there's another way?" "What's your opinion?" "Just suppose that. . . . Then what?" "What would happen if . . .?" or "What else . . .?"

Thinking of open-ended questions can be difficult at first since our own educations have placed so much emphasis on asking and answering fact questions, but it is possible to form the habit of doing this. In addition to learning to use the stock questions listed above, it helps to think up actual topic-related questions in advance to pose to the children such as, "What could we do for the ducklings that would make them feel happy?" "How could we get the water to their pond?" "Suppose we couldn't use a pipe; is there something else we could use instead?" These are the kinds of questions that encourage children to do creative thinking in return.

S *Learn to Handle Answers Intelligently*

Wait for Answers and Ask Only a Few Questions at a Time

One of the most important things about asking questions is learning to *wait* for an answer. This is surprisingly hard to do. Many teachers ask excellent questions but then plunge right ahead and answer them themselves. In one study of "wait time," Rowe (1974) found that teachers only waited, on the average, 1 *second* before doing this. Perhaps this is because teachers are afraid of silence or of the child's failing. But children, like adults, need time to collect their thoughts and formulate their replies. Pausing allows them to do this.

Another thing to beware of is asking too many questions. The plaintive little song by Hap Palmer puts this neatly when he enquires,

Questions, questions, askin' me endlessly
How many more must I answer today?
Questions, questions, don't drive me crazy, please,
How much more can I say?*

In our zeal to help children think we must remember that most young children are not highly verbal, and they do not enjoy long, drawn-out intellectual dialogues. To prevent questions from becoming burdensome, it is best to weave them into general discussions while the actual experience is going on, as well as to provide all possible opportunities for children to promptly put their suggestions into practice.

Encourage the Child or the Group to Produce More Than One Answer

Since more than one correct answer is possible in divergent thinking, teachers need to learn how to encourage children to propose more than one possible solution to a problem. Making sure the child's ideas are not criticized will help generate many answers, whereas the negative experience of criticism will make sensitive children clam up and refuse to take the risk of confiding a second thought (Kline, 1988). If the goal is to encourage children to mention their ideas, it makes simple good sense to welcome the suggestions and ask for more rather than to submit each one to instant critical appraisal or, worse yet, amused laughter.

The kinds of questions that often lead children to generate more ideas related to creative problem solving are sometimes called "what-else?" and "what-if?" questions (Campbell & Arnold, 1988). Questions such as "What else could you do?" or "Is there

---

*From "Feelin' Free," a record by Hap Palmer made for Educational Activities, Freeport, NY, 11520 AR 516. There are also some nice creative questions on this same record.

another way?" will stimulate many suggestions from the children. For example, Aline and Franklin, both four-year-olds, are trying to get the rat cage open to feed him. As they work, the teacher jokes with them a little and asks them, "I wonder what we'd do if the gate were really stuck and we *couldn't* get it open. How could we feed the rat then?" "We could poke it through the lines [bars]," says Franklin. "Sure we could—that's a good idea, Franklin—but let's suppose we couldn't get it through the bars; what then?" "We could teach him to reach out," says Franklin. "Yes, he likes to reach; but if he couldn't do that, what then?" There is a long silence while the children consider. "But he *can*," answers practical Franklin. "But let's imagine, just pretend for fun, that he can't. Could we feed him another way or would he just get hungry?" Suddenly Aline brightens visibly and says, "We could slide the tray out and feed him from the cellar?" (She means from underneath.) "Yes, we could," says the teacher. "My goodness, Franklin, you and Aline sure have a lot of ideas. I guess we'll be able to feed our rat after all." The children laugh with him.

This kind of elementary brainstorming can be done quite successfully with preschool children in a playful way. It encourages them to see that questions can have a number of right answers and to develop the habit of looking for more than one solution to a problem.

What-if questions encourage even freer and more creative answers than what-else questions do. Sometimes with older four- and five-year-olds this approach can be presented as a guessing game during group or lunch time. A problem can be postulated, such as "What if we didn't have any blankets at nap; how could we keep warm?" Then all kinds of possibilities can be suggested. (One of our little boys replied, "Grow fur."). Four-year-olds often delight in thinking up nonsensical solutions whose funniness adds delight to this process and exercises their sense of humour as well.

Asking the children to consider a nonsensical possibility using a variation of what-if questions provides good practice and lots of fun, too. This just-suppose approach stimulates many imaginative replies.

For example, one might ask the children to just suppose that something were true, and then consider what would happen as a result. Just suppose that bean vines never stopped growing, dogs could talk to cats, mice had wings, you were only as big as your thumb, or your wishes would come true. It is clear that some of the most interesting fairy and folktales such as "Jack and the Beanstalk," "Tom Thumb," and "Why the Sea Is Salt" are based on exactly these kinds of interesting, fantastical possibilities.

When two of our four-year-olds, Carolina and Katie, were asked what they would wish for if their wishes could come true they composed the following poem.

I wish it could be snowy every day, and I could play in it
I wish I had a long dress with a matching hat and purse
I wish I was a big person
I wish I had a house you could go out on the roof of
I wish I had a crystal star

Resist the Impulse to Always Answer the Children's Questions Yourself

Finally, when using the emergent approach to foster creative thinking, teachers must realize that learning to ask the most desirable kinds of questions is only half of what they need to know about the enquiry approach. The other half is responding most effectively to questions the children ask them. Why is it adults feel so obligated to produce answers when children ask questions? It must go back to our early training as students ourselves. How unfortunate!

Of course, many times teachers can help children make satisfying progress by supplying information they couldn't figure out for themselves, but *just as often* the children can figure things out on their own if teachers do not rush in and furnish the fact immediately. The easiest and most effective response (and yet the hardest one for many teachers to give) is just to wait a little while and see what happens next (and waiting has an additional advantage—it also provides time for the teacher to think up a question in reply that will assist the child to figure out the answer if that cue becomes necessary).

When other children can be drawn into the discussion and encouraged to add their suggestions, comments, and evaluations, even more learning will take place—providing this can be done in a friendly and not a destructive way.

✑ Special Things to Remember when Working with an Emergent Curriculum

The Number of Children's Ideas Will Be Increased If the Teacher Recognizes Their Value and Responds to Them in a Positive Way

It is easy to go on doing things the same old way or to establish a set of procedures that have become so sanctified by custom that no one considers deviating from the established formula. But an open-minded teacher who keeps on the lookout for spontaneous ideas and suggestions will find he can frequently go along with variations in approach and changes in procedure when they are suggested by the children. The teacher who is willing to let the children put their ideas into practice offers strong positive reinforcement for this behaviour, which will nourish creative talent in the children, and he will find himself blessed with ever more interesting, fresh contributions from the youngsters in his group.

For example, I remember the time we offered a cooking project that involved slicing bananas for Jell-O. The inexperienced young student in charge felt she could watch only two children working with paring knives at once and therefore sensibly limited the activity to two children at a time. A third little boy hung around and watched, badly wanting to have a chance with the bananas; but the student truthfully explained she was so new that she felt she just couldn't supervise more than two knives at once. Then he said to her, "I tell you what—I could use one of the scissors for the bananas. I know how to do that. I *never* cut myself with scissors." She immediately saw the value of his suggestion and let him snip up as many pieces as he liked.

Another independently minded two-and-a-half-year-old was going through a streak of wanting to get into the swing by herself. Since she was short and the swing was high, she struggled and wriggled, doggedly refusing assistance. Finally, she rushed away and returned with a large hollow block, which she put under the swing and used successfully as a mounting block.

Use Language Consistently along with More Tangible Ways of Trying out Ideas

Although there are perils in overintellectualizing discussions, it is important to remember that language is of genuine value in the development of ideas. Just remember that conversation must not be allowed to take the place of actual involvement with real things.

The staff at Reggio Emilia make a particular point of valuing language in such interesting ways that these warrant special discussion here. They use tape recordings as well as videotapes and photographs to capture children's comments about topics. These recordings are then transcribed so staff can review and talk them over together—searching for clues about what the children know and what turn a pathway might take next.

These transactions, though time consuming to do, have so many uses they are well worth the extra work. Besides being used for the teachers to study, some of them are also used to review events and ideas with the children—allowing the youngsters to revisit (recognize) what they have been doing and thinking about.

In addition, the transcriptions often become part of "documentation boards" assembled as the investigations continue. These boards, which combine written and pictorial documentation, are used for the children's direct benefit and also to keep the parents informed about what is going on. Ultimately, the documentation boards and transcriptions, together with other records, provide concrete evidence of accomplishment that can be very useful for assessment purposes.

Base the Curriculum on the Interests of the Children

When I dwell on the value of basing topics on the children's interests, the question of a former student always comes to mind. She asked most desperately and sincerely, "But what if the children don't have any ideas? What do I do then?"

My answer to this is that the ideas are always there if the teacher asks the right questions, waits for answers, and *listens closely enough*. Even when beginning with a potential topic generated by the teachers, note in the following example how the Reggio staff listened to the children and changed direction according to the interests of the three-year-olds.

In this particular project described by Gambetti (1993), the teachers initiated the investigation because they thought it would be interesting to find out how the three-year-olds viewed seasonal events, with late autumn as a particular focus. They began the study by talking with the children and asking them questions such as, "According to you, what is a season?" (To which one of the children replied, "Something that passes by!")

As they listened closely to what the children said it became clear to the teachers that the children were more interested in clouds and what they do than they were in seasons. So they dropped the idea of seasons and decided to follow that lead. Over a considerable period of time there ensued a variety of experiences with clouds—some suggested by the teachers and others by the children. These included looking at clouds at different times, observing frost in the morning and how the children's breath made clouds, projecting images of ice and clouds on the shadow screen, making cloud forms for screen shadows from materials suggested by the children, and drawing clouds—filled with whatever the children thought should be inside them. Finally the children decided they wanted to make "real" clouds of their own based on what they had learned about them and journeyed around the school looking for materials from which to form the clouds and materials with which to fill them. These ingredients, which were intended to represent raindrops and snowflakes, ranged from wedged paper, lace, and styrofoam to bits of mirrors and actual water. During the investigation the children were challenged (or *provoked* as they say in Reggio) to produce various hypotheses about clouds and how they work and also to solve a number of problems. For example, they hypothesized about what's inside clouds, and they solved the problem of how to represent that content and the mechanics of how to hang the clouds up in the classroom "near the sky." All required solutions (unfortunately my notes don't say what they did about the water!)

Careful recordings and pictures were made of what the children said as they worked on this project over many days. Their conclusions and explanations of what they did and why they did it were encouraged and written down, and all this information was transcribed onto documentation boards for the children, teachers, and families to review as the pathway developed.

Remember to Keep the Pathway Focused: Don't Let It Branch off in Too Many Directions

While it is all very well and good to pay attention to the children's interests, it is the teacher who must provide continuing direction to the pathway lest the group lose its way. Only the teacher has the vision to keep the entire forest in view while not losing sight of the individual trees.

Take the example of ducklings, for instance (see Table 21–1). Without consistent direction, interests might spread to barnyard animals in general, baby animals, raising a kitten, how animals swim, how people swim, what comes out of eggs, going duck hunting (remember, many children live in families in which family members hunt as a pastime), what's alive and what's dead, celebration of spring customs from other lands, and so forth.

All of these subjects will most likely provide the children with what Katz (1991) terms "smatterings" of information, i.e., mostly factual learning that is only loosely related to the children's core of interest. How much stronger it would be to focus clearly on a particular aspect of ducklings as is done in the following example and pursue the learning possibilities of that subject in more depth.

❦ An Example of How Teachers Collaborated With the Children to Develop an Emergent Pathway Using the School's Ducklings for Inspiration

Making a Map or Plan That the Investigatory Pathway Might Follow Is Essential

In Table 21.1 there are several important points for the reader to note: The original interest stemmed from the ducklings the children already cared about. The teachers, recognizing that interest, hypothesized possible investigatory directions the pathways might take. Further discussions with the children caused everyone to settle on an aspect of ducklings of interest to them all (the teachers were dying to get the ducks outside), and this in-depth concentration of ideas produced a lot of worthwhile collaborative problem solving. In addition, the process empowered the children to do something kindly and considerate for animals; it provided the possibility of including practice in midlevel

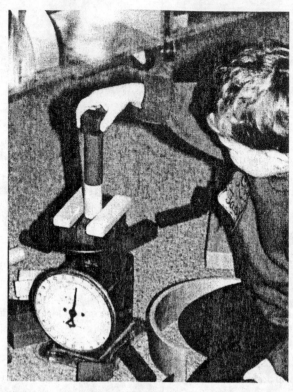

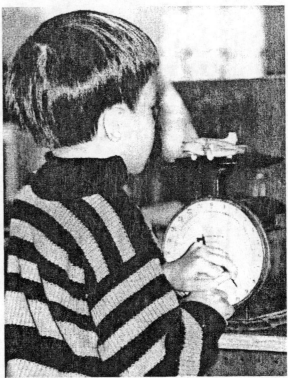

༄   *I took these pictures during one self-select period just as the children investigated what the scale could do. Just think of how many different possibilities for curriculum might stem from this hour's investigation if the teacher observed and listened closely enough to what the children were doing and saying. The use of the airplane was especially interesting—note that Wong has his hand on the needle. He actually was using the needle as a spring which, when released, shot the airplane into the air—a truly unanticipated, creative use of equipment.*

reasoning skills if the teachers thought that was advisable; and (not the least of the advantages!) it moved the ducklings, who were becoming smelly and rather large, out of the classroom.

Enable the Children to Translate Their Ideas into Concrete, Tangible Experience

The real joy and satisfaction of using the emergent approach must not be thought of as stopping at the idea stage. The real satisfaction comes from putting the proposals for solving problems into practice: trying out possible containers for water, determining what works and what lets the water soak through, seeing whether the ducks can manage the steps or really need a ramp to get in and out, and so forth.

This aspect of learning can stretch out over weeks as the children think of what could be done and put their ideas to the test of practicality. It is important to relax and allow

Table 21.1 Examples of how a pathway might emerge stemming from the children's interest in ducklings.*

Adult Visions of Possible Learning Pathways	Children's Suggestions and Ideas from Talks with Them	"Provocations": Problems to Solve When Keeping Ducks Happy	Children's Proposed Solutions	Companion Midlevel Mental Abilities that Could Be Added by Teacher
Investigate various kinds of feet (webbed, hoofs, claws, toes) and their purposes	Find out what ducks do Decide who gets to feed ducks next – who gets to care for them on weekends	Take ducklings swimming: What can we use for a pool?	Dish pan Galvanized tub Children's pool Dig hole, fill with water	*Matching* Get out Spring lotto game made of "Easter" stickers of ducks, chickens, etc.
Make more adequate housing for ducklings	Make the ducks happy: find their mothers take them swimming	How can ducks get in and out of pool?	Make them a ramp Build stairs from blocks Lift them ourselves (but we have to catch them first!)	*Grouping* Compare how ducklings and gerbils are the same and how they're different
Caring for ducklings—watching how they grow and comparing growth rate with that of baby gerbils	feed them stuff they really like talk duck talk to them let them play outside make them a shower	How can we fill the pool or tub—hose is too short	Add pipes on to end of hose Use bucket Squirt hose VERY hard Move pool	*Common Relations* Pair different pictures of feet with animals (ducks and others) they belong to
Field Trips: to farm to see other ducks to store for food to taxidermist to see stuffed ducks		Could we make a shower for them?	Hold watering can up and sprinkle ducks Tie hose to top of slide Use pipes, screw on flexible dish-rinsing hose from kitchen on pipe's end Squirt hose	*Temporal Ordering* Take pictures of ducklings as they grow and gerbils as they grow, arrange in order of development *Graduated (seriated) Ordering* Measure height of ducklings as they grow Make graph comparing growth rates with growth of gerbils
Do sinking/floating experiments				*Cause and Effect* See "Provocations"

*Form suggested by an example from Reggio Emilia

plenty of time and an unhurried pace if the children are to obtain maximum value from the experience.

Of course, creative ideas and experiments do not always work, and adults, who have a much better grasp of cause and effect, as well as more experience than children have, can often foresee problems and difficulties associated with ideas produced by young thinkers. But if the situation is reasonably safe, the children should be allowed to try their ideas out even if the adult knows they will not work. Children are entitled to the right to fail, as well as the right to succeed. The sensitive teacher will be matter-of-fact and low-key about such ineffective trials. He might say, "I'm sorry that didn't work out just right, but it was worth a try," or simply, "I can see you're really disgusted. Can I help?" or "Well, what do you want to try next?"

Children can learn as much from experiencing failures as they can from success. Sometimes they are able to modify the idea and turn it into a later triumph, sometimes not. More important than being successful is learning to accept the experience of failure as part of life while going on to try out other possible solutions.

Make Certain the Children Use Some Form of Expressive Medium to Explain to Other People What They Have Found out

The most obvious way children can communicate what they've learned is to explain it to the teacher as he writes it down for them, but there are many additional avenues for such explanations. For example, a typical Reggio approach, along with the consistent use of documentation boards, would be to have a party and show the parents the pool and the sprinkler and how much the ducks are enjoying them. Drawing pictures, no matter how unfathomable they are to the adult eye, is still another form of explanation, as is making a model of the ducks, pool, and sprinkler from clay. Or the children might make a video record, themselves, of how their ideas developed—what they tried along the way and how the completed duck pond turned out.

❧ Summary

Vygotsky's concepts of the zone of proximal development and the vital role other people play in the development of the child's mental ability, coupled with his stress on the importance of language as the mediator of social experience, have gained prominence during the past few years.

These ideas fit comfortably with the philosophy of the emergent curriculum exemplified by the preschools of Reggio Emilia. These schools, and others that foster the emergent approach, encourage the use of divergent, creative thinking by the children. In order to foster such thinking teachers should learn to use open-ended questions in ways that provoke children into thinking for themselves. They should ask only a few questions at a time, wait for answers, respond to the children's ideas in a positive way, and encourage production of more than one answer.

When following an investigatory pathway it is necessary to listen to the children and carefully observe what they are saying and doing by documenting their activity and to be willing to adjust to new directions as the investigation proceeds, while remembering to keep the subject focused. Vecchi puts it in a nutshell when she says, "Teachers provide the title, but they and the children work on the script together" (1994).

Questions and Activities

1. The next time you have to solve some sort of problem, take a few minutes and just for fun list all the ways, both silly and practical, that the problem might be solved. Try not to evaluate the merit of the ideas as you produce them, but just play around with many possibilities. Then evaluate them. Is there a fresh one included that might be a good, new, though perhaps unconventional way to solve the problem?

2. *Problem:* You have in your room a little girl about three years old who asks a lot of questions. For example, she might ask, "Why are we going in now?" When dutifully provided with the reasons, she then asks, "But why do we have to do that?" When answered, she asks, "But why?" If you were her teacher, would you think this type of enquiry should be encouraged? How would you handle it?

3. Isn't it a waste of time to let children try things out that obviously won't work? Might it not be better just to lead a discussion with them about the proposed solutions rather than going to all of the trouble of actually trying something out only to experience failure?

4. You have been reading about the emergent curriculum approach and are very eager to teach that way in your classroom of four-year-olds, but you feel a little baffled about how to begin. The teacher next door is starting the year by focusing on bears. She plans to have the children bring teddy bears from home, reward them with little bear stickers when they're good, and tell the story of Goldilocks at group time. Explain why this approach is *not* emergent and suggest some things you and the children might do concerning bears that would reflect the emergent approach more adequately.

Self-Check Questions for Review

Content-Related Questions

1. Name at least two basic concepts of Vygotskian psychological theory.

2. Explain what the difference is between *divergent* and *convergent* thinking and why each is an important aspect of thought.

3. What are three principles to remember about creative thinking?

4. There are a number of important strategies to use when asking questions and dealing with answers that encourage children to think. List several of these and explain why each is valuable.

5. Does *emergent* mean that the teacher should avoid planning the cognitive curriculum in advance? Be sure to explain your answer fully.

Integrative Questions

1. Why does Vygotsky's concept of the zone of proximal development fit so comfortably with the role of the teacher—the way the teacher is supposed to teach—when using the emergent curriculum?

2. Compare the emergent approach to cognitive development with the more conventional approach to cognitive development. Explain how they are similar and how they are different.

3. Select a learning experience based on a scientific subject (ants, for instance) and make up a list of questions on this subject that will require convergent, fact-based answers. Now modify the questions so they will be more likely to require children to do some creative thinking in order to answer them.

4. It is your first year teaching in a room of three-year-olds. You would like to add dishes to the housekeeping area, but there is no money for new ones. Propose three what-else-could-you-use-instead-of-new-ones solutions.

5. Sort the following questions into their appropriate convergent or divergent categories.

   "What did you watch on television last night?"

   After reading the book *If You Give a Mouse a Cookie* (Numeroff, 1987): "Well, according to this story, *is* it a good idea to give a mouse a cookie?"

"It looks like there are only two pieces of cheese left, but everyone wants them. What do you think we should do?"

"But what if Peter hadn't caught the wolf, what then?"

"Who remembers the name of the little monkey in this book?"

Finally, add another example of your own to each category.

6. The duckling example uses experiences with water to show how children and teachers might collaborate to develop an emergent curriculum. Think of another duck-related possibility they might pursue that would allow further opportunities for even more ideas to emerge. Suggest what some of those opportunities might be.

References For Further Readings

Overviews

Edwards, C., Gandini, L., & Forman, G. (Eds.), (1993). *The hundred languages of children: The Reggio Emilia approach to early childhood education.* Norwood, NJ: Ablex. Although the entire book is of great value, the several chapters describing actual projects may be the most helpful ones for teachers who are striving to implement the emergent approach in their own classrooms.

Kline, P. (1988). *The everyday genius: Restoring children's natural joy of learning—and yours too.* Arlington, VA: Great Ocean. This refreshing book stresses the healthy integration of learning and reminds us of the overall value of having faith in the inherent willingness and ability of children to learn.

Quick Introductions to The Reggio Emilia Approach

Gandini, L. (1993). Fundamentals of the Reggio Emilia approach to early childhood education. *Young Children, 49*(1), 4–8.

Gandini, L. (1991). Not just anywhere: Making child care centers into "particular places." *Child Care Information Exchange, 78,* 5–9.

New, R. (1990). Excellent early education: A city in Italy has it. *Young Children, 45*(6), 4–10.

Rankin, B. (1992). Inviting children's creativity: A story of Reggio Emilia, Italy. *Child Care Information Exchange, 85,* 30–35.

Moving Toward an Emergent Curriculum: Initial Steps Towards Change

Cassidy, D. J., & Lancaster, C. (1993). The grassroots curriculum: A dialogue between children and teachers. *Young Children, 48*(6), 47–51. This delightful article describes how teachers developed an emergent curriculum in a preschool class serving ten sighted and five visually impaired youngsters. *Highly recommended.*

Jones, E. with Villarino, G. (1994). What goes up on the classroom walls—and why? *Young Children, 49,* (2), 38–41. This article is a plea for thinking of bulletin boards as being more than mere decoration. It illustrates a "first step" toward documentation boards, Reggio-style.

Katz, L., & Chard, S.C. (1991). *Engaging children's minds: The project approach.* Norwood, NJ: Ablex. Katz and Chard provide practical suggestions of ways to shift from what they term *systematic instruction* to more flexible *project work.* Very helpful.

Sparling, J., & Lewis, I. (1984). *Learning games for threes and fours: A guide to adult/child play.* New York: Walker. This book provides many examples of delightful things children can learn with adult cooperation. The emphasis is on *interaction.* Activities range from simple sharing activities to ones of a more cognitive nature.

Workman, S., & Anziano, M. C. (1993). Curriculum webs: Weaving connections from children to teachers. *Young Children, 48*(2), 4–9. Examples illustrating the multitude of investigatory possibilities that could be derived from water or the self are presented here.

Asking Good Questions

Siegel, I. E., & Saunders, R. (1979). An inquiry into inquiry: Question asking as an instructional model. In L. G. Katz (Ed.), *Current topics in early childhood education* (Vol. 2). Norwood, NJ: Ablex. This chapter is *so good* it is worth seeking out at the library. It presents a list (with examples) of all sorts of questions teachers ask or *should* ask. *Highly recommended.*

For the Advanced Student

Duckworth, E. (1987). *"The having of wonderful ideas" and other essays on teaching and learning.* New York: Teachers College Press. It's good to have this essay and other stimulating ones back in print. *Highly recommended.*

Kotloff, L. J. (1993). Fostering cooperative group spirit and individuality: Examples from a Japanese preschool. *Young Children, 48(3),* 17–23. Kotloff explores the tension between teaching children to be independent and teaching them to work together for the common good. She then provides a valuable explanation of how group projects were balanced with individual opportunities for self-expression in a Japanese preschool.

Moll, L. C. (Ed.). (1990). *Vygotsky and education: Instructional implications and applications of sociohistorical psychology.* Cambridge, England: Cambridge University Press. This book really does provide discussions of theory, implications for education, and actual applications—all in one volume. An outstanding reference.

Seifert, K. (1993). Cognitive development and early childhood education. In B. Spodek (Ed.), *Handbook of research on the education of young children.* New York: Macmillan. Seifert provides clear, succinct descriptions of three theories of cognitive development: information processing theory, structural (Piagetian) theory, and sociohistorical (Vygotskian) theory. *Highly recommended.*

Suchman, J. R. (1961). Inquiry training: Building skills for autonomous discovery. *Merrill-Palmer Quarterly, 7,* 147–169. This is the article that "began it all" in the area of enquiry training. The strategies recommended are much too advanced to employ with preschool children, but the first three pages are filled with sage comments (such as "More basic than the attainment of concepts is the ability to inquire and discover these autonomously") that make searching out this article worthwhile.

Von Oech, R. (1983). *A whack on the side of the head: How to unlock your mind for innovation.* New York: Warner Books. Definitely for grown-ups, this is a helpful book that could release the reader to produce more creative ideas.

Vygotsky, L. (1978). *Mind in society.* Cambridge, MA: Harvard University Press. Vygotsky sets forth his basic theory in this very readable book.

VIII

What Lies Ahead?

22

Canadian Child Care Dilemma: Strategies for Change

Canadian Child Care Dilemma: Strategies for Change

 Have you ever . . .

Wondered what work and family issues parents face?

Wanted to improve salaries and working conditions?

Planned to share your knowledge of the benefits of quality child care?

. . . If you have, the material in the following pages will help you.

T he evidence speaks all too clearly to the fact that children are diminishing as a national priority. While it may not be a deliberate shifting of values, it is nonetheless influential in impact upon our lives and the development of our country. Despite personal sacrifices, the lack of sleep and the pain, adults require children in their lives. Without children we have no commitment to the future. We become a society without heart. It is simply too high a price to pay for temporary comfort.

Robert Couchman

O nly those who do the work of providing the care and education of young children can raise the issue of inadequate compensation from the level of a problem that should be solved one day to a problem that must be solved now.

Jim Morin

*C*hild care in Canada is a controversial and complex issue. For parents, availability, reliability, and quality care are the central concerns. For staff, the paramount issues are providing quality programs in suitable facilities and attaining professional status and wages.

᧰ *The Dilemma*

Over the last decade, research has identified the factors that make for high quality child care. The most significant relate to well-trained staff. Thus there has been a movement to increase qualifications and to try to raise wages to a level that recognizes the training and skill required. However, available funding has not kept pace with this increased demand for quality, creating a dilemma for child care providers and parents. Geographical considerations add to the complexity of child care problems. The sheer vastness and diversity of our country creates needs that are varied and diverse. Child care options that work in metropolitan cities are inappropriate for rural areas. Choices suitable in the Atlantic provinces may not be feasible or needed in the west. Needs may vary even within a province or territory. Governments must commit themselves to addressing the child care needs of Canadian families in light of unstable economic conditions, competing demand, and financial restraints.

The Need for Quality Child Care Affects Families in Many Different Ways

Regardless of all the problems faced by those who need child care, healthy gains have occurred. We are no longer arguing over the need for and use of formal and informal child care services. Our focus now is on ensuring the quality of care regardless of the mode of delivery. Although the child care debate continues, the focus of the debate has shifted and is likely to continue to do so.

Parents, professionals, researchers, decision makers, and advocates do agree on one basic tenet: quality care does make a difference in the development of young children. We know what constitutes high quality programs for young children. We are now struggling with the "hows" of providing such programs, amid the constant flux of limited funding, shifting values, economic pressures, and the unclear responsibilities and roles of parents, government, business and industry, and educational institutions. We have established that government does have a role in financing services for the care and education of young children. We must continue to devote our energies to increasing the level of government support by advocating for more spaces, alternative services, greater accessibility, and stable financial support to parents and programs. However, as stated in the opening chapter, governments will move only within the limits of perceived public opinion.

The child care needs of families are as varied as our ability to provide alternatives and to develop resources to meet these varied needs. How do we address these immediate and critical needs in the face of so many variables, impediments, and demands? Perhaps we can start by developing a problem-solving, adaptive, and flexible model. A model such as this requires us to use research well.

Agreement on developmentally appropriate practices for young children may have been the easiest step for us to make. There seems to be little or no disagreement on the importance of rich relationships among children, parents, and caregivers. Such relationships are created by supportive interaction, consistency of staff, and mutual respect. Other critical contributing factors include training qualified staff, creating safe and challenging learning environments, ratio, and group size. We know from researchers such as Howes (1990) and Doherty-Derkowski (1995) that the quality of early childhood programs has a powerful effect on children's development. This knowledge then becomes the basis for whatever environment we plan for children. We need to ensure that the components of quality care are included in the design of any early childhood program: the program must reflect the location, cultural needs, and economic confines of the families.

Financial support for services for young children does not come readily. Philosophical and financial commitments to formal and informal child care vary tremendously from province to province or territory. In any case, we must continue to explore alternative sources for funding to ensure quality programs. There are many exciting examples of cooperative arrangements and alliances within child care. Partnerships utilizing resources and expertise to meet common goals must be expanded. We must respond to challenges with innovative thinking and additional strategies to meet the emerging needs of Canadian families.

❧ *Children benefit from stable relationships with caring, educated staff.*

Problems Faced by Parents

The vignettes that follow describe some of the immediate and diversified needs of young families across Canada. Explore the problems these vignettes present. What would you advise the parent(s) in these situations? What kinds of services would you consider to meet the specific needs of these parents? How could these services be developed, funded and supported, using a range of innovative, cooperative, and flexible strategies?

Vignette 1

Danielle is a government employee in the Atlantic Region. She is a widow with a four-year-old son, Brent. Danielle's job requires her to travel on occasion. Her daily care arrangements for Brent are with a family home provider in her neighbourhood. This enables Brent to participate in neighbourhood activities after school. Danielle knows she will be out of town for three days at the end of September and has made additional arrangements for overnight care. The day before she is to leave, her supervisor informs her that there is a crisis in another part of the province that will necessitate an extension of her trip. Danielle appeals to her boss to be sensitive to her family obligations and the extraordinary child care costs that will be incurred, providing she can find suitable care at the last minute.

Of the many thoughts that flash through her mind, one of them is: Will I be forced to make a choice between my job or my child's well-being? (Would the boss's and/or employee's gender make a difference to the outcome of this vignette?)

Vignette 2

Masoumeh and Abdul decided that with the high cost of child care they would choose an in-home caregiver to look after their two children, Fatima, three-and-a-half, and Jamal, four-and-a-half. One day when Masoumeh could not come to the phone at work, Abdul received a call at his workplace from their caregiver—the third in six months! Their daughter, Fatima, had burned her hand on an iron. These parents could not help but wonder: What is happening to my child today? Is my child safe? The couple dismissed the caregiver and placed their children in a local child care centre.

Six weeks later, Abdul is driving the children to the centre. Jamal begins to whine and whimper in the back seat. Abdul asks, "What's wrong?" Jamal's response is, "Who will be my teacher today?"

In this centre the parents, supervisor, and board members are all concerned about the high turnover in staff, which they attribute to low salaries and benefits. But declines in both direct funding from government and subsidies to parents have eroded the centre's funding base, leaving barely enough to cover current expenses. A meeting is being held tonight. Masoumeh and Abdul will be there. (What do you think they will say?)

Vignette 3

Kendra and her partner are employed full time. They have two boys, Peter, three, and David, six. The boys both attend home child care three blocks from where they live. However, the caregiver's husband has been transferred and she will be moving in four weeks. Kendra feels panicked when the caregiver tells her. The quality of care her boys have received from this caregiver has been very high and Kendra is very appreciative. A coworker takes Kendra to the Human Resources Department where she works. Kendra explains her situation. She asks, "How am I going to conscientiously explore and find good care on such short notice?" An employee in the Human Resources Department immediately turns to a computerized, up-to-date listing of child care services. She makes a few phone calls for Kendra. Within fifteen minutes she has two possibilities. One nearby family home provider can take both boys within three weeks. The other, a centre close by, can take Peter immediately and will have a space for David two weeks later—unless a vacancy occurs sooner, which is quite possible. It is a large centre, considered to be well-run, that other employees are using successfully.

Kendra, her partner, and the boys arrange a visit with the potential family home provider for the next evening. The boys are disappointed about changing caregivers, but when they make their visit, the caregiver offers to read the boys a story, which they like. Afterwards a little girl in the family offers to share her toys. The children share some milk and fresh, warm cookies. They find out the caregiver looks after a friend of David's.

Vignette 4

In a province with weak child care standards, Kim and her husband Lee have been on the waiting list for their city's municipal child care centre for a year. They requested a space as soon as Kim knew she was pregnant. The couple prefer Sammy, their son, to attend the municipal centre because it is known for its high quality infant/toddler care. There are commercial centres in town with no waiting lists; however, they are known for their low quality care. Kim and Lee have been appealing to their local government to raise the standards in such centres. To their complete amazement, the government response is: fill the commerical centres first — even those with questionable standards! (Will they have to compromise their child care standards for Sammy? Will one parent have to compromise or forfeit his or her job?)

Vignette 5

Maurine lives in a small Prairie town and works in a factory. Her twin daughters, Kathy and Kellie, are three years old. They go to a nearby child care centre from 7 a.m. until 3:30 p.m., five days per week. In the middle of one night, Kathy wakes up. She has a fever and is sick to her stomach, which continues throughout the night. Around 6 a.m. she feels "a little better" and Maurine takes her with Kellie to the child care centre. The centre supervisor tells Maurine that Kathy looks tired and unwell. She takes Kathy's temperature and it is almost 39°C. She reminds Maurine of the centre's exclusion policy for sick children.

Maurine has no back-up child care arrangements. If she misses work, she doesn't get paid. She's concerned and wonders: Will Kellie come down with what Kathy has? Will I get sick too? How many days of work will I miss? How will I pay the rent?

Vignette 6

Michelle is a thirty-year-old student at a community college. She and her husband have a seven-month-old son. From the time they knew Michelle was pregnant, the couple have had their son's name on every waiting list available in every family child care agency providing infant care.

Her mother-in-law cares for her son now, but in January she leaves for Florida for the winter. Again Michelle calls many child care centres and agencies. There is no spot available for an infant. She has interviewed a list of "babysitters," but found that either she could not afford their care, or she was not satisfied with the quality.

Michelle wants and needs to graduate this year. It is not financially feasible for her to continue her Early Childhood Education studies next year. She must have subsidized "quality" care. (What will she do?)

Solutions to child care dilemmas *can* be found, especially when we think creatively and work in partnership with parents, child care centres, places of employment, government, and community resources. It is important that we, as early childhood educators, state child care needs clearly and take appropriate action to ensure quality child care.

❧ *Advocacy: For Whom Do We Advocate?*

Over the past fifteen years, the provision of child care has become a high-profile social, economic, and political issue in Canada. Every child should have access to quality child care services regardless of family income. However, this is not the case. In Canada, children's needs are going unmet in many ways.

Even though the political process affects the lives of Canadian children, they lack access to the system and are dependent upon adults to speak for them. They need us to speak out on their behalf. As early childhood educators, in partnership with parents and other concerned adults, we have the power to create change for children.

When we assume this responsibility we become advocates. We must realize that advocating on behalf of children and their families is more than just a fight for specific programs and services. Our advocacy efforts reflect assumptions about the kinds of relationships we believe should exist among families, various levels of government, and our future citizens.

Advocacy needs to become a part of our professional and ethical responsibility. If we do not assume this responsibility, parents, children and society will bear the consequences of inadequate care.

Advocacy for young children aims at maintaining, extending, or improving services to children, families, and staff. Advocacy can bring together all the significant people in the child's life to try to fulfil the child's needs through interdisciplinary teamwork.

Types of Advocacy

Caldwell (1987) identifies three types of advocacy: personal, professional, and organizational. There are many opportunities for early childhood educators to speak out on issues that affect young children and our profession.

Personal advocacy takes advantage of opportunities we have to use our expertise. It can be as straightforward as helping friends and neighbours understand what you do at your job. Help them to understand that the early years are a critically important time for learning. The goal is to communicate the implications of research findings on policies that affect young children. If you are referred to as a babysitter, gently but firmly correct that misunderstanding. Correct assumptions that child care is a custodial service with accurate information that young children thrive in stimulating learning environments. Explain how children learn through play. Assist family members to understand why quality child care costs as much as it does.

Professional advocacy attempts to challenge and reform public systems that affect children and families. This area of advocacy is generally directed toward legislative, administrative, and budgetary processes. It may involve all three levels of government. The goal is to change policies, practices, laws, and budgetary restraints to make them more responsive to children's and families' needs.

Informational advocacy refers to efforts designed to raise the general consciousness of the public about the significance of the early years and the capacity of quality early childhood programs to support optimal growth and development and to strengthen families. One target for informational advocacy is employers. A responsive employer can have a significant effect on the quality of family life and on parents' ability to respond to the demands of child rearing. You could help parents approach their employer, union, or professional association to encourage them to develop supportive personnel policies such as acceptance of the use of sick leave for a child's illness or flexible working hours to reduce the number of hours a child spends in care.

In personal, professional, and informational advocacy efforts, we go beyond the caring and educational responsibilities of our job. We reach beyond teaching and nurturing children. As early childhood advocates, we speak out and strive to improve the quality of children's lives.

Becoming Successful Advocates

The first step towards involvement in decision making is to understand how public policy affects children's lives and how we individually have the responsibility of contributing to the public debate. As early childhood educators we can contribute to advocacy by

1. being knowledgeable about child development theory,

2. sharing our professional experiences,

3. employing the skills needed to carry out the task, and

4. building consensus by joining with others.

To be effective advocates, we must develop expertise in all four areas.

1. Being knowledgeable about child development theory

Advocates must have a solid knowledge of child development, know the characteristics of safe, stimulating, healthy, and nurturing early childhood environments, be aware of a variety of child care models, and be knowledgeable about current research. A professional follows a set of principles regarding what constitutes the best practices in early childhood education. It is essential to be able to articulate those practices clearly and explain how one actually uses them. For example, a teacher of young children might say, "The work of Piaget showed that young children learn and grow best when they are actively interacting with real objects and with caring people around them. Considering this, our program provides many hands-on activities and opportunities to discuss and integrate subject areas."

✺   *To get quality services for children, we must join with others and speak out.*

It is crucial to know the results of key research studies that support the work we do. The longitudinal Perry Preschool Study demonstrated that for every dollar invested in a good preschool program for children from low-income families, more than seven dollars were returned later in reduced costs for juvenile crime, unemployment, welfare, and special education services (Schweinhart & Weikart, 1993). In a second significant study, the American National Child Care Staffing Study indicates that the adult work environment helps determine the caregiver's job satisfaction. This, in turn, affects children's well-being and development (Whitebook et al., 1990). By sharing the results of such research we are helping decision makers focus on the role policy plays in enhancing children's development.

Being able to communicate theory and research clearly and accurately through speaking and writing is crucial if we are to persuade others of children's needs.

2. Sharing Our Professional Experiences

Through our daily work with young children and their families, we become aware of the stories behind the statistics. Families experience first hand the effect of changing circumstances—the conflicts between work and family lives, the profound shortage of subsidy moneys, inadequate salaries, and poor working conditions that result in turnover of staff. As caregivers, we see these situations long before the decision makers are aware of the resulting trends. Real-life experiences help us become more persuasive; the impact of these anecdotes can stimulate policy making.

3. Employing the skills needed to carry out the task

Commitment to improving circumstances for young children and their families involves having a belief in what is essential for every child's optimal development. Advocacy is a way of thinking about what you believe and what you do. It reflects a gradual internalization of professional values and a commitment to one's role. To be more effective, advocates need to develop organizational skills, to become adept at involving others, making use of the media, and assessing the political climate. Child care advocates learn to take advantage of opportunities to speak out for children.

It is important to understand legislation, the political process, how each level of government works (municipal/regional, provincial/territorial, and federal); who has power; and who makes decisions. Advocates must educate themselves about current political issues related to the field, get involved in the passing of relevant legislation, and know what the opposition is and why it is there. Many people would like to keep early childhood educators from being more professional because they are worried that the cost of care would increase. Advocates can work together with parents to fight for more provincial/territorial and federal funds to help pay for the quality care the children deserve and the better salary caregivers merit.

Advocates need others in order to achieve their goals. They must have interpersonal communications skills that enable them to communicate effectively and sensitively with potential allies such as colleagues, parents, and the general public. The skills that they need include flexibility, cooperative problem solving, and the ability to compromise and be reflective in encouraging cooperating and fostering relationships. Strong relationships are essential to effective advocacy and it takes time to develop them. Each new relationship enlarges the network of contacts, enabling more powerful advocacy.

4. Building consensus through joining with others

Effective advocacy depends on us joining forces with others to improve practice and shape policy and public opinions. There are parents, professional organizations, coalitions, and local director networks that advocate for early childhood issues. It is important to make time to join these organizations to add a voice and help advocate for change.

Through our daily interactions with parents we can recognize our common goals and concerns for children. As parents are the primary educators of their children, it is important to involve them as much as possible, to make yourself available to them, to ask them for their opinions, and to act supportively. Parents represent a powerful consumer voice. We can help them realize their power as children's primary advocates, and by activating this power, we can dramatically expand the constituency speaking out for children. It is important that we recognize the demands on working parents and consider them when we plan strategies to involve them.

As early childhood educators, we need to establish and reinforce ties with health care professionals, educators, and other groups concerned with family, children, and issues related to poverty. Many of these professionals consider issues related to the education and care of young children important to their work. They will benefit from our expertise

---

✑ RESEARCH STUDY ✑
Canadian Advocates in Action: The Manitoba Child Care Association (MCCA)

This association has long lobbied for better salaries and working conditions for their membership. MCCA has made countless presentations to government working groups, task forces, and caucuses. This group has staged walkouts, sent bags of peanuts (to represent the pay they work for), and invoiced the provincial government for $13.3 million—the amount, in forgone wages, that early childhood educators subsidize the system for by working for low wages. The sum of $13.3 million was calculated on the basis of surveys of the membership and of data collected through the national salary survey "Caring for a Living" (Karyo, 1992). These invoices are one strategy used in MCCA's Worthy Wage Campaign, the primary goal of which is to improve the salaries and working conditions of Manitoba's caregivers. A key message is that the quality of care that children receive is directly linked to the wages, status, and working conditions of their providers. Early childhood education is as important as formal education, yet the staff earn roughly half the salary of elementary school teachers.

Resources developed by the association to support the worthy wage campaign include fact sheets for parents, regular newsletters for providers, postcards, buttons and posters, and a worthy wage day. This group is committed to bringing their message to parents, employers, politicians, the general public and, most of all, the child care community. For it is the belief of the Manitoba Child Care Association that those who provide the care and education of young children must facilitate the action necessary to solve the problem.

Source: Based on correspondence with Dorothy Dudek, Executive Director of the Manitoba Child Care Association.

---

and we will benefit by being recognized as active, interested community members. Ultimately children benefit from these alliances.

There are a number of roles you can play in these organizations. Assess your skills and the time you have available in order to decide the most effective role you can play. Each role is important, whether it be testifying at a hearing, serving on a committee, or helping to get out an important mailing. Cooperating with others and finding common ground in our advocacy efforts will allow us to make a difference for children, families, and the profession.

Join an organization that is working for quality child care in your province/territory. Every member's name adds weight to its organized efforts. An organization will help make your voice heard through coordinated campaigns for action. Organizations will also provide you with information about child care issues and options. Groups in your area likely include child care advocacy associations, early childhood education associations, women's groups, and parent resource centres.

The Canadian Child Day Care Federation publishes a bilingual Canadian directory of child care organizations (national, provincial/territorial, and local groups), child care publications, and government offices you may contact to focus your advocacy endeavours. See the end of this chapter for national organizations that provide information and leadership.

Creating change is often a slow and frustrating process. From your daily work you may feel a sense of urgency as you see the toll that inadequate services takes on children and families. It is important to recognize that progress is measured in small steps. You must keep the process in perspective and not be deterred from your commitment.

Strategies for Advocates

Speak to friends about child care issues.

Talk with employers.

Encourage parents to speak out.

Call your local politician.

Respond to legislation—put it in writing, send faxes, make phone calls.

Influence administrative decisions—budget priorities, regulations, program monitoring.

Testify at hearings.

Become involved in a political campaign.

Write a letter to the editor of your local newspaper.

Call a radio talk show.

A Real Life Strategy

Demonstraters in front of a provincial legislature held chains of paper dolls (provided by child care centres), with each doll representing a family awaiting childcare subsidy. The 7000 dolls made a graphic statement to all who saw them and increased awareness of how desperate the situation really is. (A tip from an organizer of this event—hope that it's not raining on the day of the demonstration!)

Identifying Your Issue and Focusing Your Response

Begin by choosing an area of personal interest and concern. It should be an area you want to learn more about. It is important to define your issue. If you define it in general terms, such as improving child care, it becomes too broad for specific advocacy efforts. You might choose, for example, to focus on health care practices, improving salaries and working conditions, or extended hours of care for parents.

Support for an issue depends not only on its merits, but on the timing and the focus. Focusing helps define the goal for yourself and for other advocates. It provides a consistent theme for your efforts and a way for parents, legislators, the media, and others to understand and support your issue.

It is important to assess the current political climate in your community or province/territory. Ask yourself: How can this issue be linked to current values and concerns? You will need to put this issue in the context of current social, economic, and/or political concerns and to identify what you want to happen. For example, do you want parents to be better informed about the connection between salaries and the quality of care children receive? Do you want policy makers to require additional training for child care directors? Do you want funders to be aware that the numbers on the subsidy waiting list represents actual families?

It is important to recognize that no one strategy can always work. You must be prepared to use a variety of techniques and to be persistent.

᎒᎒ *Summary*

Child care has been a public issue for three decades, but it has yet to become a public priority. An array of factors confound easy answers. Satisfactory solutions will result from the cooperative efforts of many: parents, caregivers, leaders of business and industry, government, policy makers, researchers, and you as future professionals. The child care crisis will only be solved by all of us speaking out. Collectively we can make a difference in the lives of Canada's children.

Questions and Activities

1. Complete an informal survey of five to ten friends who are not involved in early childhood education. Ask them what they think an early childhood educator does; how much money early childhood educators earn; how much they *should* earn; and how much training they should have. Discuss the responses in class and analyse the assumptions behind the different points of view. Brainstorm ways to counteract misinformation and to communicate a positive message about child care work.

2. Invite working parents to speak to the class about how the need for child care affects their work life. Focus the discussion on pressures facing parents and the incentives for employer involvement in child care.

3. Role play a dialogue between a child care teacher and a parent. The teacher is frustrated about earning a low wage and is having trouble making ends meet. The parent is frustrated about how much child care costs, wonders where all the money goes, and is upset at the prospect of a fee increase.

4. Invite a guest speaker from a local organization to discuss a current issue she or he is addressing. Identify ways the class can participate.

5. Invite several politicians to a special event at the college and ask them to join a panel discussion of current child care trends and issues.

6. Interview someone who has worked in child care while pregnant, has worked in the same program his or her own children attended, or has taught a coworker's child. Ask them to tell you about the experience.
   a) What issues or conflicts arose?
   b) How were they solved?
   c) Are there any benefits, such as reduced child care fees, to any of these situations?
   d) Does the program you work at have policies on these issues?
   e) If not, what steps could be taken?

7. A newspaper article comments that "you don't have to be a rocket scientist to change diapers'. Write a letter to the editor.

Self-Check Questions For Review
Content-Related Questions

1. List three factors contributing to the child care dilemma.

2. Name three styles of advocacy and give an example of each.

3. What are the characteristics of successful advocates?

4. What are the components of quality child care environments?

References for Further Reading
Overview

Friendly, M. (1994). *Child care policy in Canada: Putting the pieces together.* Don Mills, ON:, Addison-

Wesley. This book explores past and present child care policy in Canada as well as looking at how other countries provide child care. The author provides possibilities for a national child care program for the future. A must have for child care advocates.

National Day Care Information Centre. (1973-1994). *The status of day care in Canada..* Ottawa: Health Canada. These status reports have been published every year since 1973. They are intended to present a general overview of the rate of growth. Results are compiled according to age groups served, program sponsorship, and the number of full-time spaces compared to the number of day-care-aged children with parents in the workforce.

Statistics Canada, (1992). *Special surveys (1992). Canadian families and their child care arrangements. The Canadian National Child Care Study.* Ottawa: Supply and Services Canada. This report examines the nature of individual families, child care needs, current arrangements, factors affecting parents' choice of arrangements and their preferences and beliefs about what care arrangements would best meet their needs.

Guidelines for Quality Care For Young Children

Canadian Child Day Care Federation (1991), *National statement on quality child care.* Ottawa: CCDCF. This document was developed with feedback from many individuals from across Canada. It develops the following seven components for both group and family child care: suitability and training of care providers; child development and the learning environment; group size and ratios; adult relationships; health, safety and nutrition; and partnerships.

Doherty-Derkowski, G., (1995) *Quality matters: Excellence in early childhood programs.* Don Mills, ON: Addison-Wesley. This book summarizes numerous recent international research studies regarding the relationship between a child's well-being and the overall quality of early childhood programs. The information is essential for effective advocates.

Willer, B.A. (1990). *Reaching the full cost of quality in early childhood programs.* Washington, DC: National Association for the Education of Young Children. This book is part of the public education program of the NAEYC intended to bring additional resources to the child care system. It refers to the costs of program provision while meeting professional recommendations for high quality.

Child Advocacy

Fennimore, B. (1989). *Child care advocacy for early childhood educators.* New York: Teacher's College Press. This book contains a thorough examination of the ways in which early childhood educators can and should be advocates. It identifies strategies to advocate for children within the classroom, the family, the society at large, and the political arena.

Goffin, S.G., & Lombardi, J. (1988). *Speaking out: Early childhood advocacy.* Washington, DC: National Association for the Education of Young Children. The authors discuss practical ways to improve job satisfaction in addition to raising wages.

Morin, J. (1991). *Taking matters into your own hands: A guide to unionizing in the child care field.* Oakland, CA: Child Care Employee Project. This booklet explores issues related to unionizing, such as gains for the individual and the profession, steps to organizing, negotiations, and what is typically contained in a union contract. The author sees a unionized workforce as a necessary step towards improved wages and working conditions in the child care field.

National Organizations That Provide Information and Leadership

Canadian Child Care Federation, 120 Holland Ave., Ste. 305, Ottawa, ON K1Y 0X6 (613) 729-5289

The Child Care Advocacy Association of Canada, 323 Chapel St., Ottawa, ON K1N 7Z2 (613) 594-3196

National Action Committee on the Status of Women, 323 Chapel St., Ottawa, ON K1N 7Z2 (613) 234-7062

Canadian Association of Toy Libraries & Resource Centres, (TLRC Canada, 120 Holland Ave., Ste. 205, Ottawa, Ontario K1Y 0X6 (613) 728-3307

Appendices

Appendix A

❧ The Early Childhood Educators of British Columbia (ECEBC)

Code of Ethics

Introduction to ECEBC Code of Ethics

Early childhood educators work with one of society's most vulnerable groups — young children. The quality of the interactions between young children and their caregivers has a significant, enduring impact on the children's lives. The intimacy of the relationship and the potential that exists to do harm call for a commitment on the part of early childhood educators to the highest standards of ethical practice.

While individual children are the focus of the work done by early childhood educators, ethical practice extends beyond the child-educator relationship. Early childhood educators care for and educate young children while recognizing and supporting the nurturing and socializing responsibilities of the children's families. Early childhood educators accept their ethical obligations to the children and families they serve as both represent our society's future.

ECEBC recognizes its responsibility to promote ethical practices and attitudes on the part of early childhood educators. The following principles, explanations and standards of practice have been developed to help early childhood educators monitor their professional practice. They are intended to both guide educators and protect the children and families with whom they work. Professionalism creates additional ethical obligations to colleagues and to the profession.

This code articulates the principles and standards of practice endorsed by ECEBC. Members of ECEBC undertake as a condition of membership in the association to incorporate them into their practice. ECEBC advocates the voluntary acceptance of these principles

and standards by all early childhood educators, both members and non-members.

Structure and Derivation of the Code

Structure

Eight ethical principles are presented. These principles are intended to guide early childhood educators in deciding what conduct is right and correct. Educators may use the principles to help them make decisions when they encounter ethical problems in the course of their work. Each principle is followed by an explanation and a list of standards of practice that represent an application of the principle in an early childhood setting.

Derivation

These ethical principles were agreed upon by ECEBC after reviewing the literature on the topic of ethics, examining and evaluating the codes of ethics of various professions and consulting a number of experts in the field of professional ethics. These principles reflect the core values of early childhood education practice which are addressed in the codes of ethics of professional organizations in other jurisdictions.

When Principles Conflict

All eight principles are reflected in the ethical practice of early childhood educators. However, there will be circumstances in which the ethical principles will conflict and educators will face the dilemma of having to choose between conflicting principles. In these difficult situations it is recommended that early childhood educators carefully think through the likely consequences of giving each of the conflicting principles primacy. By evaluating the consequences it may become clear which principle ought to be given more weight.

Source: Reprinted with permission from the Early Childhood Educators of British Columbia, ©1995.

ECEBC recognizes that the resolution of ethical dilemmas can be difficult. Educators are encouraged, if time permits, to consult with colleagues and obtain different perspectives on the problem. If this consultation does not clarify the best course of action, educators are encouraged to consult the ECEBC Ethics Committee for guidance. Although the final decision will be made by the individual educator facing the ethical dilemma, consultation with others indicates a commitment to ethical practice.

The Principles of the Code

- Early childhood educators promote the health and well-being of all children.
- Early childhood educators use developmentally appropriate practices when working with all children.
- Early childhood educators demonstrate caring for all children in all aspects of their practice.
- Early childhood educators work in partnership with parents, supporting them in meeting their responsibilities to their children.
- Early childhood educators work in partnership with colleagues and other service providers in the community to support the well-being of families.
- Early childhood educators work in ways that enhance human dignity.
- Early childhood educators pursue, on an ongoing basis, the knowledge, skills and self-awareness needed to be professionally competent.
- Early childhood educators demonstrate integrity in all of their professional relationships.

Early Childhood Educators Promote the Health and Well-Being of All Children

Explanation: Early childhood educators are responsible for the children in their care. They create environments for children that are safe, secure and supportive of good health in the broadest sense. They design programs that provide children with opportunities to develop physically, socially, emotionally, morally, spiritually, cognitively and creatively. A healthy environment for children is one in which each child's self-esteem is enhanced, pay is encouraged and a warm, loving atmosphere is maintained.

Implications for Practice: In adhering to this Principle, an early childhood educator would:

- Promote each child's health and well-being.
- Create and maintain safe and healthy environments for children.
- Foster all facets of children's development.
- Enhance each child's feelings of competence, independence and self-esteem.
- Refrain from in any way degrading, endangering, frightening or harming children.
- Act as an advocate on behalf of all children for public policies, programs and services that enhance their health and well-being.

Early Childhood Educators Use Developmentally Appropriate Practices When Working with Children

Explanation: Early childhood educators understand the sequences and patterns of child development and cultural influences on those patterns. They use this knowledge to create environments and plan programs that are responsive to the children in their care. Early childhood educators implement programs and use guidance techniques that take into account the ages of the children and individual variations in their development.

Implication for Practice: In adhering to this Principle, an early childhood educator would:

- Consider cross-cultural variations in child development norms when assessing child development.
- Apply the knowledge that the stages of physical, social, emotional, moral and cognitive development within each child may be different.
- Determine where each child is on the various developmental continua and use that knowledge to create programs that allow for individual differences and preferences.
- Use developmentally appropriate methods and materials in working with children.

Early Childhood Educators Demonstrate Caring for Children in All Aspects of Their Practice

Explanation: Caring is at the core of early childhood education. Caring involves both love and labour and is reflected in the mental, emotional and physical efforts of early childhood educators in their interactions with all children. Being cared for and cared about is consistently communicated to all children.

Implications for Practice: In adhering to this Principle, an early childhood educator would:

- Respond appropriately to each child's expressions of need.
- Provide children with experiences that build trust.
- Express warmth, appropriate affection and consideration for children both verbally and nonverbally.
- Communicate to children a genuine interest in their activities, ideas, opinions and concerns.
- Support children as they experience different emotions and model acceptable ways of expressing emotions.

Early Childhood Educators Work in Partnership with Parents, Supporting Them in Meeting Their Responsibilities to Their Children

Explanation: Early childhood educators share joint interest in the children in their care while recognizing that parents have primary responsibility for childrearing and decision making on behalf of their children. Early childhood educators complement and support parents as they carry out these responsibilities. Through positive, respectful relationships with parents, early childhood educators are able to advance the well-being of children.

Implication for Practice: In adhering to this Principle, an early childhood educator would:

- Promote considerate relationships with the parents of the children in care.
- Respect the rights of parents to transmit their values, beliefs and cultural heritage to their children.
- Provide parents with knowledge, skills and support that will enhance their ability to nurture their children.
- Encourage and provide opportunities for parents to participate actively in all aspects of planning and decision making affecting their children.

Early Childhood Educators Work in Partnership with Colleagues and Other Service Providers in the Community to Support the Well-Being of Families

Explanation: Early childhood educators recognize that nurturing family environments benefit children. Early childhood educators work with other helping professionals to provide a network of support for families.

Implications for Practice: In adhering to this Principle, an early childhood educator would:

- Support and encourage families by developing programs which meet the needs of those families being served.
- Assist families in obtaining needed specialized services provided by other professionals.
- Advocate public policies and community services that are supportive of families.

Early Childhood Educators Work in Ways That Enhance Human Dignity

Explanation: Early childhood educators welcome and cherish children unconditionally. They respect the dignity of children, parents, colleagues and others with whom they interact. They demonstrate respect for diversity by valuing individuality and appreciating diverse characteristics including ideas and perspectives.

Implications for Practice: In adhering to this Principle, an early childhood educator would:

- Communicate respect by practicing and promoting anti-bias interactions.
- Support and promote the dignity of self and others by engaging in mutually enhancing relationships.
- Plan programs that communicate respect for diversity regarding ability, culture, gender, socio-economic status, sexual orientation and family composition.
- Provide opportunities for all children to participate in childhood activities.

Early Childhood Educators Pursue, on an Ongoing Basis, the Knowledge, Skills, and Self-Awareness Needed to Be Professionally Competent

Explanation: Early childhood professional practice is based on an expanding body of scholarly literature and research. Continuing education is essential. In-service skills training and self-awareness work prepare early childhood educators to fulfill their responsibilities more effectively.

Implications for Practice: In adhering to this Principle, an early childhood educator would:

- Recognize the need for continuous learning.
- Pursue professional development opportunities.

- Incorporate into practice current information from the early childhood education professional literature.
- Assess personal and professional strengths and limitations and undertake self-improvement.
- Articulate a personal philosophy of practice and justify practices on the basis of theoretical perspectives.

Early Childhood Educators Demonstrate Integrity in All of Their Professional Relationships

Explanation: Early childhood educators are truthful and trustworthy. Early childhood educators communicate honestly and openly and endeavour to be accurate and objective. Early childhood educators treat as confidential information about the children, families and colleagues with whom they work. Information may be shared with colleagues and other helping professionals as required for the care and support of children, or as required by law. Early childhood educators acknowledge real or potential conflicts of interest and act in accordance with principles of the code.

Implications for Practice: In adhering to this Principle, an early childhood educator would:

- Communicate with children, parents, colleagues and other professionals in an honest, straightforward manner.
- Conscientiously carry out professional responsibilities and duties.
- Identify personal values and beliefs and strive to be objective.
- Treat as confidential information concerning children, families and colleagues unless failure to disclose would put children at risk.
- Recognize the potential for real or perceived conflict of interest and act in accordance with the principles of the code where dual relationships with colleagues or families exist and/or develop.

Appendix B

❧ *Summary of Communicable Diseases*

Disease	Agent	Incubation	Communicable Period	Transmission	Symptoms	Remarks
Chickenpox (Herpes Zoster; Varicella; Shingles)	Virus	2–3 weeks	1–5 days before rash; no more than 6 days after first vesicles	Direct contact with vesicle fluid, soiled articles, or droplets from respiratory tract	Sudden onset; slight fever; malaise; mild constitutional symptoms, followed by eruption of lesions; followed by fluid filled blisters for 3–4 days; ending with scab	Very communicable; lesions, blisters and scabbed sores can exist at the same time; lesions are most common on covered parts of the body
Conjunctivitis (Pink Eye)	Bacteria	24–72 hours	Throughout course of infection	Contact with discharge from conjunctiva or upper respiratory tract, or objects contaminated by those discharges	Tearing and irritation of conjunctiva; lid swelling, discharge; sensitivity to light	Most common in preschoolers
Cytomegalovirus (CMV)	Virus	May be acquired during birth, but show no symptoms for up to 3 months after delivery	Virus may be excreted for 5–6 years	Direct/indirect contact with membranes or secretions; blood; urine	Usually no symptoms; may show signs of severe infection of central nervous system or liver	Most serious in early infancy; many apparently healthy children in day care have CMV in urine or saliva; *potentially serious for pregnant women*
Giardiasis	Protozoa (a cyst in the inactive form)	5–25 days	Entire period of infection	Hand to mouth transfer of cysts from stools of infected person	Chronic pale, greasy diarrhea; abdominal cramping; fatigue; weight loss	Frequently found in day care centers; carriers may be asymptomatic

Disease	Cause	Incubation	Period of Communicability	Method of Transmission	Symptoms	Comments
Hepatitis	Several viruses	Hepatitis A: 15–50 days; Hepatitis B: 45–180 days	Hepatitis A: A week before infection to one week after appearance of jaundice. Hepatitis B: From several weeks before symptoms until weeks after symptoms; may be a carrier for years	Hepatitis A: Fecal/oral route; direct contact. Hepatitis B: Contact with infected blood, saliva, and vaginal fluids, semen	Hepatitis A: sudden onset with fever, lack of appetite, nausea, abdominal pain; jaundice follows in a few days. Hepatitis B: Lack of appetite; nausea, vomiting, and later jaundice	Hepatitis A: Common in day care; severity increases with age; infections in infants may be asymptomatic. Hepatitis B: May be present but asymptomatic in young children; HB vaccine available to prevent this type of hepatitis
Measles (Hard measles; red measles)	Virus	1–2 weeks before rash to 4 days after the rash appears	Communicable from before fever to 4 days after rash	Direct contact with nasal or throat secretions or freshly contaminated objects	Fever, conjunctivitis, cough, Koplik spots; rash appears on 3rd day—usually starting on face	Easily spread; very common in preschool populations; immunization available; potentially serious for ill or young children
Meningitis (Viral)	Several viruses	Incubation varies by specific virus	Communicability varies with specific virus	Direct contact with respiratory droplets or excretions of infected person, or objects contaminated by these secretions	Symptoms vary by specific type of virus; usually sudden fever and central nervous system symptoms; may have rash	Symptoms last 10 days with residual symptoms for a year or more

Disease	Agent	Incubation	Communicable Period	Transmission	Symptoms	Remarks
Meningitis (Bacterial)	Various bacteria	2–10 days	Until organisms are not found in discharge	Direct contact with respiratory droplets or excretions of an infected person or objects contaminated by these secretions	Sudden onset of fever; severe headache; stiff neck; rash	Early detection and treatment necessary to prevent death
Mumps	Virus	2–3 weeks	6 days before until 9 days after onset of illness	Direct contact with respiratory droplets or saliva of infected person	Fever, swelling and tenderness of one or more salivary glands	Meningitis occurs frequently; Vaccine available
Pediatric AIDS	Virus	Unknown	Unknown	Contact with blood and blood contaminated fluids and objects; sexual contact with semen and vaginal fluids	Early symptoms are nonspecific: loss of appetite; chronic diarrhea; fatigue; symptoms progress to opportunistic infections and central nervous system symptoms	Use universal precautions
Pediculosis (Lice)	Lice, adult or larvae (nits)	Eggs hatch in a week; sexual maturity is reached 8–10 days after hatching	Communicable as long as eggs and lice are alive on person or clothing	Direct contact with infected person or indirect contact with contaminated objects	Itching and excoriation of infected head and body parts	Common in school children; Check with physician regarding use of over-the-counter products; some are not recommended for infants and young children

Disease	Cause	Incubation period	Communicable period	Transmission	Symptoms	Comments
Ringworm	Fungus	4–10 days	Until lesions are gone and fungus is no longer on contaminated objects	Direct or indirect contact with infected persons or contaminated objects	Lesions appear flat, spreading, and ring shaped; outer ring may be filled with pus or fluid; inside may be dry and scaly or moist and crusty	Infected children should be excluded from common swimming pools
Rubella (three-day measles)	Virus	2–3 weeks	From one week before to one week after onset of rash	Droplet spread or direct/indirect contact with objects soiled with nasal secretions, blood, urine or feces	Symptoms may range from no symptoms to cold-like symptoms such as low grade fever, malaise, and runny nose; not all infections have a rash; if it does exist, it usually starts on the face and spreads to trunk and extremities	Easily spread; high incidence in pre-school populations; immunizations available; resembles measles; *potentially serious for pregnant women*
Scabies	Mite	2–6 weeks in person with no exposure; 1–4 days after re-exposure	Until mites and eggs are killed; usually 1–2 courses of treatment, one week apart	Skin to skin contact, or contact with recently infected undergarments or bed clothes	Intense itching of head, neck, palms, soles in infants; may also involve other body creases	In persons with reduced resistance, infection will be generalized; check with physician prior to use of over-the-counter medications, because some are not recommended for infants and young children

Source: From *Preschool Children with Special Needs*, pp. 179–182, by M. T. Urbano (1992). San Diego: Singular Publishing Group. Reprinted with permission.

Appendix C

᧒ *Chart of Normal Development*

Infancy to Six Years of Age

The chart of normal development on the next few pages presents children's achievements from infancy to 6 years of age in five areas:

Motor skills (gross and fine motor)

Cognitive skills

Self-help skills

Social skills

Communication skills (understanding and speaking language)

In each skill area, the age at which each milestone is reached *on the average* is also presented. This information is useful if you have a child in your class who you suspect is seriously delayed in one or more skill areas.

However, it is important to remember that these milestones are only average. From the moment of birth, each child is a distinct individual and develops in his or her unique manner. No two children have ever reached all the same developmental milestones at the exact same ages. The examples that follow show what we mean.

By nine months of age Gi Lin had spent much of her time scooting around on her hands and tummy, making no effort to crawl. After about a week of pulling herself up on chairs and table legs, she let go and started to walk on her own. Gi Lin skipped the crawling stage entirely and scarcely said more than a few sounds until she was 15 months old. But she walked with ease and skill by 9½ months.

Marcus learned to crawl on all fours very early, and continued crawling until he was nearly 18 months old, when he started to walk. However, he said single words and used two-word phrases meaningfully before his first birthday. A talking, crawling baby is quite a sight!

Molly worried her parents by saying scarcely a word, although she managed to make her needs known with sounds and gestures. Shortly after her second birthday, Molly suddenly began talking in two- to four-word phrases and sentences. She was never again a quiet child.

All three children were healthy and normal. By the time they were three years old, there were no major differences among them in walking or talking. They had simply developed in their own ways and at their own rates. Some children seem to concentrate on one thing at a time—learning to crawl, to walk, or to talk. Other children develop across areas at a more even rate.

As you read the chart of normal development, remember that children don't read child development books. They don't know they're supposed to be able to point out Daddy when they are a year old or copy a circle in their third year. And even if they could read these baby books, they probably wouldn't follow them! Age-related developmental milestones are obtained by averaging out what many children do at various ages. No child is "average" in all areas. Each child is a unique person.

One final word of caution. As children grow, their abilities are shaped by the opportunities they have for learning. For example, although many 5-year-olds can repeat songs and rhymes, the child who has not heard songs and rhymes many times cannot be expected to repeat them. All areas of development and learning are influenced by the child's experiences as well as by the abilities they are born with.

Source: From *Mainstreaming Preschoolers: Children with Health Impairments* by A. Healy, P. McAreavey, C. S. Von-Hippel, and S. H. Jones, 1978, Washington, DC: U.S. Department of Health, Education, and Welfare, Office of Human Development Services, Administration for Children, Youth and Families, Head Start Bureau.

Table C–1 Chart of normal development

	0–12 Months	12–24 Months	24–36 Months	36–48 Months	48–60 Months	60–72 Months
MOTOR SKILLS						
Gross motor skills						
	Sits without support	Walks alone	Runs forward well	Runs around obstacles	Walks backward toe-heel	Runs lightly on toes
	Crawls	Walks backward	Jumps in place, two feet together	Walks on a line	Jumps forward 10 times, without falling	Walks on balance beam
	Pulls self to standing and stands unaided	Picks up toys from floor without falling	Stands on one foot, with aid	Balances on one foot for 5 to 10 seconds	Walks up and down stairs alone, alternating feet	Can cover 2 m (6'6") hopping
	Walks with aid	Pulls toy, pushes toy	Walks on tiptoe	Hops on one foot	Turns somersault	Skips on alternate feet
	Rolls a ball in imitation of adult	Seats self in child's chair	Kicks ball forward	Pushes, pulls, steers wheeled toys		Jumps rope
		Walks up and down stairs (hand-held)		Rides (that is, steers and pedals) tricycle		Skates
		Moves to music		Uses slide without assistance		
				Jumps over 15 cm (6") high object, landing on both feet together		
				Throws ball overhand		
				Catches ball bounced to him or her		
Fine motor skills						
	Reaches, grasps, puts object in mouth	Builds tower of three small blocks	Strings four large beads	Builds tower of nine small blocks	Cuts on line continuously	Cuts out simple shapes
	Picks things up with thumb and one finger (pincer grasp)	Puts four rings on stick	Turns pages singly	Drives nails and pegs	Copies cross	Copies triangle
	Transfers object from one hand to other hand	Places five pegs in pegboard	Snips with scissors	Copies circle	Copies square	Traces diamond
	Drops and picks up toy	Turns pages two or three at a time	Holds crayon with thumb and fingers, not fist	Imitates cross	Prints a few capital letters	Copies first name
		Scribbles	Uses one hand consistently in most activities	Manipulates clay materials (for example, rolls balls, snakes, cookies)		Prints numerals 1 to 5
		Turns knobs				Colors within lines
		Throws small ball				Has adult grasp of pencil

Paints with whole arm movement, shifts hands, makes strokes

Imitates circular, vertical, horizontal strokes

Paints with some wrist action; makes dots, lines, circular strokes

Rolls, pounds, squeezes, and pulls clay

Has handedness well established (that is, child is left- or right-handed)

Pastes and glues appropriately

Demonstrates preacademic skills

COMMUNICATION SKILLS
Understanding language

Responds to speech by looking at speaker

Responds differently to aspects of speaker's voice (for example, friendly or unfriendly, male or female)

Turns to source of sound

Responds with gesture to *hi, bye-bye,* and *up* when these words are accompanied by appropriate gesture

Stops ongoing action when told *no* (when negative is accompanied by appropriate gesture and tone)

Responds correctly when asked *where* (when question is accompanied by gesture)

Understands prepositions *on, in,* and *under*

Follows request to bring familiar object from another room

Understands simple phrases with key words (for example: *Open the door. Get the ball.*)

Follows a series of two simple but related directions

Points to pictures of common objects when they are named

Can identify objects when told their use

Understands question forms *what* and *where*

Understands negatives *no, not, can't,* and *don't*

Enjoys listening to simple storybooks and requests them again

Begins to understand sentences involving time concepts (for example, *We are going to the zoo tomorrow*)

Understands size comparatives such as *big* and *bigger*

Understands relationships expressed by *if-then* or *because* sentences

Carries out a series of two to four related directions

Understands when told *Let's pretend*

Follows three unrelated commands in proper order

Understands comparatives like *pretty, prettier,* and *prettiest*

Listens to long stories but often misinterprets the facts

Incorporates verbal directions into play activities

Understands sequencing of events when told them (for example, *First we have to go to the store, then we can make the cake and tomorrow we will eat it.*)

Spoken Language

0–12 Months	12–24 Months	24–36 Months	36–48 Months	48–60 Months	60–72 Months
Makes crying and noncrying sounds	Says first meaningful word	Joins vocabulary words together in two-word phrases	Talks in sentences of three or more words, which take the form agent-action-object (*I see the ball*) or agent-action-location (*Daddy sit on chair*)	Asks *when, how,* and *why* questions	There are few obvious differences between child's grammar and adult's grammar
Repeats some vowel and consonant sounds (babbles) when alone or spoken to	Uses single words plus a gesture to ask for objects	Gives first and last name	Tells about past experiences	Uses models like *can, will, shall, should,* and *might*	Still needs to learn such things as subject-verb agreement, and some irregular past tense verbs
Interacts with others by vocalizing after adult	Says successive single words to describe an event	Asks *what* and *where* questions	Uses *s* on nouns to indicate plurals	Joins sentences together (for example, *I like chocolate chip cookies and milk.*)	Can take appropriate turns in a conversation
Communicates meaning through intonation	Refers to self by name	Makes negative statements (for example, *Can't open it*)	Uses *ed* on verbs to indicate past tense	Talks about causality by using *because* and *so*	Gives and receives information
Attempts to imitate sounds	Uses *my* or *mine* to indicate possession	Shows frustration at not being understood	Refers to self using pronouns *I* or *me*	Tells the content of a story but may confuse facts	Communicates well with family, friends, or strangers
	Has vocabulary of about 50 words for important people, common objects, and the existence, nonexistence, and recurrence of objects and events (for example, *more* and *all gone*)		Repeats at least one nursery rhyme and can sing a song		
			Speech is understandable to strangers, but there are still some sound errors.		

COGNITIVE SKILLS

Follows moving object with eyes

Recognizes differences among people; responds to strangers by crying or staring

Responds to and imitates facial expressions of others

Responds to very simple directions (for example, raises arms when someone says *Come* and turns head when asked *Where is Daddy?*

Imitates gestures and actions (for example, shakes head no, plays peek-a-boo, waves bye-bye)

Puts small objects in and out of container with intention

Imitates actions and words of adults

Responds to words or commands with appropriate action (for example, *Stop that, Get down.*)

Is able to match two similar objects

Looks at storybook pictures with an adult, naming or pointing to familiar objects on request (for example, *What is that? Point to the baby.*)

Recognizes difference between *you* and *me*

Has very limited attention span

Accomplishes primary learning through own exploration

Responds to simple directions (for example, *Give me the ball and the block. Get your shoes and socks.*)

Selects and looks at picture books, names pictured objects, and identifies several objects within one picture

Matches and uses associated objects meaningfully (for example, given cup, saucer, and bead, puts cup and saucer together)

Stacks rings on peg in order of size

Recognizes self in mirror, saying *baby* or own name

Can talk briefly about what he or she is doing

Imitates adult actions (for example, housekeeping play)

Recognizes and matches six colors

Intentionally stacks blocks or rings in order of size

Draws somewhat recognizable picture that is meaningful to child, if not to adult; names and briefly explains picture

Asks questions for information (*why* and *how* questions requiring simple answers)

Knows own age

Knows own last name

Has short attention span

Learns through observing and imitating adults, and by adult instruction and explanation; is very easily distracted

Has increased understanding of concepts of the functions and groupings of objects (for example, can put doll house furniture in correct rooms), and part-whole (for example, can identify pictures of hand and foot as parts of body)

Begins to be aware of past and present (for example, *Yesterday we went to the park. Today we go to the library.*)

Plays with words (creates own rhyming words; says or makes up words having similar sounds)

Points to and names four to six colors

Matches pictures of familiar objects (for example, shoe, sock, foot; apple, orange, banana)

Draws a person with two to six recognizable parts, such as head, arms, legs; can name or match drawn parts to own body

Draws, names, and describes recognizable picture

Rote counts to 5, imitating adults

Knows own street and town

Retells story from picture book with reasonable accuracy

Names some letters and numerals

Rote counts to 10

Sorts objects by single characteristics (for example, by color, shape, or size if the difference is obvious)

Is beginning to use accurately time concepts of *tomorrow* and *yesterday*

Uses classroom tools (such as scissors and paints) meaningfully and purposefully

Begins to relate clock time to daily schedule

Attention span increases noticeably; learns through adult instruction; when interested, can ignore distractions.

0–12 Months	12–24 Months	24–36 Months	36–48 Months	48–60 Months	60–72 Months
COGNITIVE SKILLS, *Continued*					
		Has limited attention span; learning is through exploration and adult direction (as in reading of picture stories) Is beginning to understand functional concepts of familiar objects (for example, that a spoon is used for eating) and part-whole concepts (for example, parts of the body)		Has more extended attention span; learns through observation and listening to adults as well as through exploration; is easily distracted Has increased understanding of concepts of function, time, part-whole relationships; function or use of objects may be stated in addition to names of objects Time concepts are expanding. The child can talk about yesterday or last week (a long time ago), about today, and about what will happen tomorrow.	Concepts of function increase as well as understanding of why things happen. Time concepts are expanding into an understanding of the future in terms of major events (for example, *Christmas will come after two weekends*).

SELF-HELP SKILLS

Feeds self cracker	Uses spoon, spilling little	Uses spoon, little spilling	Pours well from small pitcher	Cuts easy foods with a knife (for example, hamburger patty, tomato slice)	Dresses self completely
Holds cup with two hands; drinks with assistance	Drinks from cup, one hand, unassisted	Gets drink from fountain or faucet unassisted	Spreads soft butter with knife	Laces shoes	Ties bow
Holds out arms and legs while being dressed	Chews food	Opens door by turning handle	Buttons and unbuttons large buttons		Brushes teeth unassisted
	Removes shoes, socks, pants, sweater	Takes off coat	Washes hands unassisted		Crosses street safely
	Unzips large zipper	Puts on coat with assistance	Blows nose when reminded		
	Indicates toilet needs	Washes and dries hands with assistance			

SOCIAL SKILLS

Smiles spontaneously	Recognizes self in mirror or picture	Plays near other children	Joins in play with other children; begins to interact	Plays and interacts with other children	Chooses own friend(s)
Responds differently to strangers than to familiar people	Refers to self by name	Watches other children, joins briefly in their play	Shares toys; takes turns with assistance	Dramatic play is closer to reality, with attention paid to detail, time, and space	Plays simple table games
Pays attention to own name	Plays by self, initiates own play	Defends own possessions	Begins dramatic play, acting out whole scenes (for example, traveling, playing house, pretending to be animals)	Plays dress-up	Plays competitive games
Responds to no	Imitates adult behaviors in play	Begins to play house		Shows interest in exploring sex differences	Engages with other children in cooperative play involving group decisions, role assignments, fair play
Copies simple actions of others	Helps put things away	Symbolically uses objects, self in play			
		Participates in simple group activity (for example, sings, claps, dances)			
		Knows gender identity			

Appendix D

∂ 10 *Quick Ways to Analyze Children's* *Books for Racism and Sexism*

Both in school and out, young children are exposed to racist and sexist attitudes. These attitudes—expressed over and over in books and in other media—gradually distort their perceptions until stereotypes and myths about minorities and women are accepted as reality. It is difficult for a librarian or teacher to convince children to question society's attitudes. But if a child can be shown how to detect racism and sexism in a book, the child can proceed to transfer the perception to wider areas. The following 10 guidelines are offered as a starting point in evaluating children's books from this perspective.

1. CHECK THE ILLUSTRATIONS

Look for stereotypes. A stereotype is an oversimplified generalization about a particular group, race, or sex, which usually carries derogatory implications. Some infamous (overt) stereotypes of Blacks are the happy-go-lucky watermelon-eating Sambo and the fat, eye-rolling "mammy"; of Chicanos, the sombrero-wearing peon or fiesta-loving, macho bandito; of Asian Americans, the inscrutable, slant-eyed "Oriental"; of Native Americans, the naked savage or "primitive" craftsman and his squaw; of Puerto Ricans, the switchblade-toting teenage gang member; of women, the completely domesticated mother, the demure, doll-loving little girl, or the wicked stepmother. While you may not always find stereotypes in the blatant forms described, look for variations which in any way demean or ridicule characters because of their race or sex.

Look for tokenism. If there are non-White characters in the illustrations, do they look just like Whites except for being tinted or colored in? Do all minority faces look stereotypically alike, or are they depicted as genuine individuals with distinctive features?

Who's doing what? Do the illustrations depict minorities in subservient and passive roles or in leadership and action roles? Are males the active "doers" and females the inactive observers?

2. Check The Story Line

The Civil Rights Movement has led publishers to weed out many insulting passages, particularly from stories with Black themes, but the attitudes still find expression in less obvious ways. The following checklist suggests some of the subtle (covert) forms of bias to watch for.

Standard for success. Does it take "White" behavior standards for a minority person to "get ahead"? Is "making it" in the dominant White society projected as the only ideal? To gain acceptance and approval, do non-White persons have to exhibit extraordinary qualities—excel in sports, get A's, etc.? In friendships between White and non-White children, is it the non-white who does most of the understanding and forgiving?

Resolution of problems. How are problems presented, conceived, and resolved in the story? Are minority people considered to be "the problem"? Are the oppressions faced by minorities and women represented as causally related to an unjust society? Are the reasons for poverty and oppression explained, or are they accepted as inevitable? Does the story line encourage passive acceptance or active resistance? Is a particular problem that is faced by a minority person resolved through the benevolent intervention of a White person?

Role of women. Are the achievements of girls and women based on their own initiative and intelligence, or are they due to their good looks or to their relationship with boys? Are sex roles incidental or critical to

Source: Reprinted with permission from the *Bulletin* of the Council on Interracial Books for Children, Inc.

characterization and plot? Could the same story be told if the sex roles were reversed?

3. Look at the Lifestyles

Are minority persons and their setting depicted in such a way that they contrast unfavorably with the unstated norm of White middle-class suburbia? If the minority group in question is depicted as "different," are negative value judgments implied? Are minorities depicted exclusively in ghettos, barrios, or migrant camps? If the illustrations and text attempt to depict another culture, do they go beyond oversimplifications and offer genuine insights into another lifestyle? Look for inaccuracy and inappropriateness in the depiction of other cultures. Watch for instances of the "quaint-natives-in-costume" syndrome (most noticeable in areas like costume and custom, but extending to behavior and personality traits as well).

4. Weigh the Relationships Between People

Do the Whites in the story possess the power, take the leadership, and make the important decisions? Do non-Whites and females function in essentially supporting roles?

How are family relationships depicted? In Black families, is the mother always dominant? In Hispanic families, are there always lots and lots of children? If the family is separated, are societal conditions—unemployment, poverty—cited among the reasons for the separation?

5. Note the Heroes and Heroines

For many years, books showed only "safe" minority heroes and heroines—those who avoided serious conflict with the White establishment of their time. Minority groups today are insisting on the right to define their own heroes and heroines based on their own concepts and struggles for justice.

When minority heroes and heroines do appear, are they admired for the same qualities that have made White heroes and heroines famous or because what they have done has benefitted White people? Ask this question: Whose interest is a particular figure really serving?

6. Consider the Effects on a Child's Self-Image

Are norms established that limit the child's aspirations and self-concepts? What effect can it have on Black children to be continuously bombarded with images of the color white as the ultimate in beauty, cleanliness, virtue, etc., and the color black as evil, dirty, menacing, etc.? Does the book counteract or reinforce this positive association with the color white and negative association with black?

What happens to a girl's self-image when she reads that boys perform all of the brave and important deeds? What about a girl's self-esteem if she is not "fair" of skin and slim of body?

In a particular story, is there one or more persons with whom a minority child can readily identify to a positive and constructive end?

7. Consider the Author's or Illustrator's Background

Analyze the biographical material on the jacket flap or the back of the book. If a story deals with a minority theme, what qualifies the author or illustrator to deal with the subject? If the author and illustrator are not members of the minority being written about, is there anything in their background that would specifically recommend them as the creators of this book?

Similarly, a book that deals with the feelings and insights of women should be more carefully examined if it is written by a man—unless the book's avowed purpose is to present a strictly male perspective.

8. Check Out the Author's Perspective

No author can be wholly objective. All authors write out of a cultural as well as a personal context. Children's books in the past have traditionally come from authors who are White and who are members of the middle class, with one result being that a single ethnocentric perspective has dominated American children's literature. With the book in question, look carefully to determine whether the direction of the author's perspective substantially weakens or strengthens the value of his/her written book. Are omissions and distortions central to the overall character or "message" of the book?

9. Watch for Loaded Words

A word is loaded when it has insulting overtones. Examples of loaded adjectives (usually racist) are savage, primitive, conniving, lazy, superstitious, treacherous, wily, crafty, inscrutable, docile, and backward.

Look for sexist language and adjectives that exclude or ridicule women. Look for use of the male pronoun to refer to both males and females. While the generic use of the word "man" was accepted in the past, its use today is outmoded. The following examples show how sexist language can be avoided: ancestors instead of forefathers; chairperson instead of chairman; community instead of brotherhood; firefighters instead of firemen; manufactured instead of manmade; the human family instead of the family of man.

10. Look at the Copyright Date

Books on minority themes—usually hastily conceived—suddenly began appearing in the mid-1960s. There followed a growing number of "minority experience" books to meet the new market demand, but most of these were still written by White authors, edited by White editors, and published by White publishers. They therefore reflected a White point of view. Only in the late 1960s and early 1970s did the children's book world begin to even remotely reflect the realities of a multi-racial society. And it has just begun to reflect feminists' concerns.

The copyright dates, therefore, can be a clue as to how likely the book is to be overtly racist or sexist, although a recent copyright date, of course, is no guarantee of a book's relevance or sensitivity. The copyright date only means the year the book was published. It usually takes a minimum of one year—and often much more than that—from the time a manuscript is submitted to the publisher to the time it is actually printed and put on the market. This time lag meant very little in the past, but in a time of rapid change and changing consciousness, when children's book publishing is attempting to be "relevant," it is becoming increasingly significant.

Appendix E

✎ A Beginning List of Free and Recyclable Materials

Material	Sources	Suggested Uses
Cardboard rolls	Gift-wrapping section of department stores for empty ribbon rolls; paper towel and toilet paper rolls	Tape two together beside each other, add string, and use as binoculars Put beans, rice, etc., inside, tape closed, and use as shakers. Use as a base for puppets, by adding decorative scraps of material. Tape several together lengthwise and use as tunnels for small vehicles. Punch holes 3 cm apart, secure wax paper over one end with a rubber band, and you have a flute.
Wood shavings and scraps	Building scrap piles, carpentry shops	
Material remnants	Interior design stores, upholsterers, clothing manufacturers	
Suede and leather scraps	Leather goods stores	
Pieces of styrofoam	Throwaways from drug stores, variety stores, radio and TV stores	Buy a supply of plastic coloured golf tees, to be hammered easily into styrofoam chunks—a perfect activity for beginning carpenters. Poke sticks, straws, etc., into styrofoam chunks to make a 3-D collage.
Computer paper used on one side, or cards	Almost anywhere computers are used	

Material	Sources	Suggested Uses
Used envelopes	Offices, schools, junk mail	Use large envelopes for safe storage of special projects. Cut the bottom corners off old envelopes and decorate each as a different finger puppet.
Small boxes	Variety stores, hearing-aid stores, department and stationery stores	Stuff with newspaper and tape shut to make building blocks. Cut ⅔ of one side of a flat box (e.g., pudding box), decorate, and fill with scrap paper cut to fit, to make an ideal notepaper holder.
Large boxes	Appliance stores, supermarkets, department stores	Decorate boxes for use as "Treasure Boxes" to store artistic creations. Tie boxes together to make a train; large boxes also can turn into houses, cars, boats, etc. Use a series of large boxes for making an obstacle course or continuous tunnel.
Plastic lids and containers	Home throwaways	Cut shapes in the lids to use as shape sorters (make shapes from other household "junk"). Use different sized containers for stacking and nesting toys. Add a wooden spoon to a large empty container, with lid, to make a perfect drum. Cut interesting shapes in lids and use as stencils for painting or colouring.
Meat trays and aluminum pie plates	Home throwaways	Use as a base for paintings and collages, Christmas ornaments, or table decorations. Put them in the bathtub or swimming pool to use as boats in water play. Equip older children with a dull needle and yarn to sew colour patterns on meat trays.
Milk cartons	Home throwaways	Cut an opening in one side, hang it up, and use as a bird feeder. Cut the top off, add a handle, and decorate with ribbon for a springtime basket.

Material	Sources	Suggested Uses
Egg cartons	Home throwaways	Sort small objects into each egg pocket by size, texture, colour, etc.
		Fill each egg pocket with earth, plant seeds (e.g., beans), and watch them grow.
		Decorate individual egg pockets and hang upside down for simple but effective bells.
		In the springtime, use separate egg pockets to house chicks made out of cotton balls painted yellow.
		Cut lengthwise and add paint and pipe cleaner legs for a cute caterpillar.
Wide-mouth jars	Home throwaways, recycling centres	Make a mini-terrarium by layering charcoal, potting soil, and humus, dampening the soil, and adding small plants; put the lid in place, but open weekly if too much moisture builds up.
		Glue a 3-D scene to the lid, fill jar with water and sparkles, put lid on, and turn upside down.
Pebbles, leaves, cones, feathers, seed pods, etc.	These natural materials abound; bird refuge for unusual feathers.	Make collages.
		Decorate other items.
Wallpaper sample books	Wallpaper stores	Decorate play areas or dollhouses.
Rug scraps	Carpet and department stores	Decorate dollhouses.
Burlap	Horse-boarding barns	Various art projects
Ticker tape and newsprint rolls and ends	Local newspaper office	
4-litre ice cream containers	Drive-ins and ice cream stores	
Art papers of various sizes and colours	Print shops	
	Local pet shops	

Source: Some materials and sources suggested by the Principles and Practices class, 1972, and The Language and Cognitive Development classes, 1973, 1976, and 1978, of Santa Barbara City College, CA; other materials and suggested uses from the resource sheet "Recycling for Fun: Creating Toys and Activities for Children from 'Beautiful Junk'" by the Canadian Child Care Federation and the Canadian Association of Toy Libraries and Parent Resource Centres.

Appendix F

❦ Activities to Develop Auditory Discrimination

Have the children put their heads down on the table. Display on a nearby shelf or table various instruments: xylophone, cymbals, tambourine, bells, and so forth. While they have their heads down, play one instrument. Children can take turns making the sounds for others to identify.

I was in the kitchen at the sink, and D. was standing at the kitchen gate. He was swinging the gate back and forth so that it would bang against the stopper. As it got louder and louder I was about to tell him to stop when I decided to use this situation for auditory discrimination. We were promptly joined by two other children. First we listened to how loud the gate could bang shut. Then I asked them if they could make it very quiet so that there was not any noise. We did these two opposites several times. Then we started very quietly and got louder and louder and louder. We tried this with our feet stamping on the floor and also clapping our hands. First we did it loud then quiet, then quiet and louder, and then as loud as we could.

Under the table I made different sounds and asked the children to identify them. I used a bell, sandpaper rubbed together, two blocks hit together, scissors opening and closing, and tearing paper. Then I asked one child to make his own sound and let the rest of the children guess what it was.

Using one sound, have the children shut their eyes while you move about the room, and ask the children to point to where you are. Then let the children be the sound makers.

Record on a tape recorder familiar sounds such as a car starting, water running, a train, a door shutting, a

refrigerator door opening or closing, or a toilet flushing (if you use this last one, do it at the end, as it tends to break up the group). Stop at each sound and have the children identify it. For older children play a series of sounds, and see how many they can remember.

I put several things in a box, one at a time, and had the children listen to the sounds: a tennis ball, toothbrush, piece of metal, and a comb. Then I put the box behind my back, put one of the objects in the box, brought it in front of me and rattled it. The children guessed what made the noise.

With my children we listened to the sounds around us when we were outside. We heard the leaves blowing, other children yelling, a car going by, and sand falling. It was fun and made the children really aware of the sounds around them.

I used a triangle with a wooden stick and a metal one. The children listened while I showed them the sticks; then I had them close their eyes and tell me which stick I had used.

Using a xylophone, strike a middle note, then play other notes and ask the children if the new note is higher or lower than the middle one. Also, for degree of loudness, strike the notes hard or lightly and ask the children if the sound is loud or soft.

Material. Cans with tops, small nails, rice, beans, salt. I made up two cans of each material. I had all the cans on the table and went around and asked the children to pick one and shake it. Then I asked them to try and find one that sounded exactly the same. Then we opened the cans to see if the cans really did contain the same ingredient. The children enjoyed playing this and wanted to have many turns.

Material. Six bottles, same size; one spoon; water. Take two bottles and put the same volume of water in them, then two other bottles with the same volume of water, and finally two more. I covered the bottles with

Source: Suggested by the Language and Cognitive Development classes, 1973, 1976, and 1978, of Santa Barbara City College.

Contact paper so the children would not see how much water each bottle held. Taking turns, the children tried to pick out sounds that matched by hitting the bottle with the spoon. If we were in doubt that the tones matched, we poured the water out and measured it.

In a small group, have one child turn his back and then have the teacher or a selected child point to someone in the group who says something. The child with his back turned guesses who has spoken; then the speaker takes his turn guessing, and the former guesser picks the next speaker.

I let each child draw out an animal picture from the "secret" box, and then they listened to me while I made various animal noises. They brought me the picture when they heard the noise that belonged to their ani-

mal. For variety, we played a tape recording of the sounds and had each child wave his card in the air when he heard "his" sound.

An activity for four-year-olds that fosters auditory discrimination is to take different flannel board pictures in which the words rhyme, for instance, *cat/hat, mouse/house, rug/bug,* and so on. Either put up a few at a time and ask children to pair the ones that rhyme, or have groups of three pictured words and ask the children to remove the one that doesn't rhyme.

For older four-year-olds, have children stand in a circle and close their eyes. One child moves around the outside of the circle several times and then stops behind one of the children, who guesses whether the child was hopping, jumping, tiptoeing, and so forth.

Appendix G

ॐ *Educational Organizations, Newsletters, and Journals Associated with Early Childhood*

Educational Organizations

ACEI
Association for Childhood Education International
11501 Georgia Ave., Suite 315
Wheaton, MD 20902

ACT
Alliance for Children and Television
344 Dupont St.
Toronto, ON M5R 1V9

Canadian Association for Young Children/L'Association
Canadienne pour les jeunes enfants
Suite 12-155, 252 Bloor St. W
Toronto, ON M5S 1V5

Canadian Child Care Federation/Fédération
Canadienne des services de garde à l'enfance
120 Holland Ave., Suite 305
Ottawa, Ontario K1Y 0X6 Canada

Canadian Children's Safety Network
c/o Canadian Injury Prevention Foundation
20 Queen St. W., Suite 200
Toronto, ON M4H 3V7

Canadian Institute of Child Health
885 Meadowlands Dr. E., Suite 512
Ottawa, ON K2C 3N2.

Children's Defense Fund
25 E St., NW
Washington, DC 20001

CWLA
Child Welfare League of America, Inc.
440 First St., NW, Suite 310
Washington, DC 20001-2085

ERIC/ECE
Educational Resources Information Center on Early
Childhood Education
805 W. Pennsylvania Ave.
Urbana, IL 61801

International Montessori Society
912 Thayer Ave.
Silver Spring, MD 20910

LDAC
Learning Disabilities Association of Canada
323 Chapel St., Suite 200
Ottawa, ON K1N 7Z2

NAEYC
National Association for the Education of Young
Children
1509 16th St., NW
Washington, DC 20036-1426

National Committee for the Prevention of Child Abuse
332 S. Michigan Ave., Suite 950
Chicago, IL 60604-4357

OMEP
Organisation Mondiale pour l'Éducation Préscolaire
School of Education
Indiana State University
Terre Haute, IN 47809

SpeciaLink:
The National Child Care Mainstream Network
186 Prince St.
Sydney, NS B1P 5K5

Newsletters

ERIC/ECE Newsletter
805 W. Pennsylvania Ave.
Urbana, IL 61801

Interaction
Canadian Child Care Federation
120 Holland Ave., Suite 305
Ottawa, Ontario K1Y 0X6

SpeciaLink
186 Prince St.
Sydney, NS B1P 5K5

Journals

American Journal of Orthopsychiatry
American Orthopsychiatric Association
19 West 44th St., Suite 1616
New York, NY 10036

Canadian Children
Child Studies Centre
University of British Columbia
Vancouver, BC V6T 1Z5

*The Canadian Journal of Research in Early Childhood
Education*
Department of Education
Concordia University
1455 rue de Maisonneuve ouest
Montréal, PQ H3G 1M8

Child Care Information Exchange
PO Box 2890
Redmond, WA 98073

Child Development
Society for Research in Child Development
University of Chicago Press
5801 Ellis Ave.
Chicago, IL 60637

Childhood Education
ACEI
11501 Georgia Ave., Suite 315
Wheaton, MD 20902

Children Today
Office of Human Development Services
Superintendent of Documents
U.S. Government Printing Office
Washington, DC 20402

Day Care and Early Education
Human Sciences Press
72 Fifth Ave.
New York, NY 10011

Developmental Psychology
American Psychological Association
1200 17th St., NW
Washington, DC 20036

Dimensions
Southern Early Childhood Association
PO Box 5403, Brady Station
Little Rock, AR 72215

Early Childhood Research Quarterly
National Association for the Education of Young
    Children
Ablex Publishing Company
355 Chestnut St.
Norwood, NJ 07648

Exceptional Children
Council for Exceptional Children
1920 Association Dr.
Reston, VA 22091

Journal of Early Intervention
Council for Exceptional Children, Division for Early
    Childhood
1920 Association Dr.
Reston VA 22091

Journal of Research in Childhood Education
Association for Childhood Education International
11141 Georgia Ave., Suite 200
Wheaton, MD 20902

multiculturalism/multiculturalisme
CCMIE
Suite 204
316 Dalhousie St.
Ottawa, ON K1Y 7E7

Nutrition Action
Center for Science in the Public Interest
1875 Connecticut Ave. NW, Suite 300
Washington, DC 20009-5728

Young Children
NAEYC
1509 16th St., NW
Washington, DC 20036-1426

References

Aboud, F. (1988). *Children and prejudice*. New York: Basil Blackwell.

Accardo, P. J., & Capute, A. M. (1991). Mental retardation. In A. J. Capute & P. J. Accardo (Eds.), *Developmental disabilities in infancy and childhood*. Baltimore, MD: Paul Brookes.

Adcock, D., & Segal, M. (1983a). *Making friends: Ways of encouraging social development in young children*. Englewood Cliffs, NJ: Prentice Hall.

Adcock, D., & Segal, M. (1983b). *Play together, grow together*. Mt. Rainier, MD: Gryphon House (distributors).

Adler, R. A., & Adler, P. (1988). The carpool: A socializing adjunct to the educational experiences. In G. Handel (Ed.), *Childhood socialization*. New York: Aldine DeGruyter.

Albert, R. E. (1994). *Alejandro's gift*. San Francisco: Chronicle Books.

Albert, R. S. (Ed.). (1983). *Genius and eminence: The social psychology of creativity and exceptional achievement*. Elmsford, NY: Pergamon.

Allen, E., Paasche, C., Cornell, A. & Engel, M. (1994). *Exceptional children: Inclusion in early childhood programs* (1st Can. ed.). Scarborough, ON: Nelson Canada.

Allen, K. E., & Marotz, L. (1990). *Developmental profiles: Birth to six*. Albany, NY: Delmar.

Allen, Lady of Hurtwood. (1968). *Planning for play*. Cambridge, MA: MIT Press.

Almy, M., Chittenden, E., & Miller, P. (1966). *Young children's thinking*. New York: Teachers College Press.

Althouse, R. (1994). *Investigating mathematics with young children*. New York: Teachers College Press.

Amabile, T. (1989). *Growing up creative: Nurturing a lifetime of creativity*. New York: Crown.

Ambert, A. N. (Ed.). (1991). *Bilingual education and English as a second language: A research handbook, 1988–1990*. New York: Garland.

American Academy of Child and Adolescent Psychiatry. (1990). *Prevention in child and adolescent psychiatry: The reduction of risk for mental disorders*. Washington, DC: The Academy.

American Public Health Association/ American Academy of Pediatrics. (1988). *Survey of selected state and municipal licensing regulations for out-of-home child care programs*. Washington, DC: Authors.

American Public Health Association/American Academy of Pediatrics. (1992). *Caring for our children: National health and safety guidelines for out-of-home child care programs*. Washington, DC: Authors.

Anderson, F. E. (1992). *Art for all the children: Approaches to art therapy for children with disabilities* (2nd ed.). Springfield, IL: Thomas.

Anderson, L., Evertson, D. M., & Brophy, J. E. (1979). An experimental study of effective teaching in first-grade reading groups. *Elementary School Journal, 79*, 193–223.

Anderson, N., & Beck, R. (1982). School books get poor marks: An analysis of children's materials about Central America. *Interracial Books for Children Bulletin, 13* (2, 3).

Anthony, E. J., & Cohler, B. J. (Eds.). (1987). *The invulnerable child*. New York: Guilford.

Antia, S. D., Kriemeyer, K. H., & Eldredge, N. (1994). Promoting social interaction between young children with hearing impairments and their peers. *Exceptional Children, 60*(3), 262–275.

Appel, M. H. (1942). Aggressive behavior of nursery school children and adult procedures in dealing with such behavior. *Journal of Experimental Education, 11*, 185–199.

Arbuthnot, M. H., & Root, S. L. (1968). *Time for poetry* (3rd ed.). Glenview, IL: Scott, Foresman.

Arenas, S. (1978). Bilingual/bicultural programs for preschool children. *Children Today, 7*(4), 2–6.

Arnheim, D. C., & Sinclair, W. A. (1979). *The clumsy child: A program of motor therapy.* St. Louis, MO: C. V. Mosby.

Arnold, L. E. (Ed.). (1990). *Childhood stress.* New York: Wiley.

Aronson, S. S. (1991). *Health and safety in child care.* New York: HarperCollins.

Aronson, S., & Smith, H. (1993). *Model child care health policies.* Washington, DC: National Association for the Education of Young Children/American Academy of Pediatrics, Pennsylvania Chapter.

Asher, S. R., Oden, S. L., & Gottman, J. M. (1977). Children's friendships in school settings. In L. G. Katz (Ed.), *Current topics in early childhood education. Vol. 1.* Norwood, NJ: Ablex.

Ashton, P. T. (1975). Cross-cultural Piagetian research: An experimental perspective. *Harvard Educational Review, 45*(4), 475–506.

Ashton-Warner, S. (1965). *Teacher.* New York: Bantam Books.

Asian American Children's Book Project. (1976). How children's books distort the Asian American image. *Interracial Books for Children Bulletin, 7*(2, 3).

Association for Early Childhood Educators, Ontario (1990). *Child abuse: A handbook for early childhood educators.* Toronto: Association for Early Childhood Educators, Ontario.

Athey, I. (1987). The relationship of play to cognitive, language and moral development. In D. Bergen (Ed.), *Play as a medium for learning and development: A handbook of theory and practice.* Portsmouth, NH: Heinemann.

Atwater, J. B., Carta, J. J., Schwartz, I. K., & McConnell, S. R. (1994). Blending developmentally appropriate practice and early childhood special education: Redefining best practice to meet the needs of all children. In B. L. Mallory and R. S. New (Eds.), *Diversity and developmentally appropriate practice: Challenges for early childhood education.* New York: Teachers College Press.

Axline, V. (1969). *Play therapy* (rev. ed.). New York: Ballantine Books.

Ayers, W. (1989). *The good preschool teacher: Six teachers reflect on their lives.* New York: Teachers College Press.

Bagley, C., Verma, G. K., Mallick, K., & Young, L. (1979). *Personality, self-esteem and prejudice.* Westmead, Farnborough, Hants, England: Saxon House.

Bailey, B. A. (1992). "Mommy don't leave me!" Helping toddlers and parents deal with separation. *Dimensions, 20*(3), 25–27, 29.

Bailey, D. B., & Wolery, M. (1992). *Teaching infants and preschoolers with disabilities* (2nd ed.). Englewood Cliffs, NJ: Merrill/Prentice Hall.

Balaban, N. (1985). *Starting school: From separation to independence.* New York: Teachers College Press.

Balaban, N. (1989). Trust: Just a matter of time. In J. S. McKee & K. M. Paciorek (Eds.), *Early Childhood: 89/90.* Guilford, CT: Dushkin Publishing Group.

Ball, D. W., Newman, J. M., & Scheuren, W. J. (1984). Teach-

ers' generalized expectations of children of divorce. *Psychological Reports, 54,* 347–353.

Bandura, A. (1977). *Social learning theory.* Englewood Cliffs, NJ: Prentice Hall.

Bandura, A. (1986). *Social learning theory: The social foundation of thought and action: A social cognitive theory.* Englewood Cliffs, NJ: Prentice Hall.

Bandura, A., & Walters, R. H. (1963). Aggression. In H. W. Stevenson (Ed.), *Child psychology* (62nd Yearbook of the National Society for the Study of Education). Chicago: University of Chicago Press.

Banks, J. A. (1994). *Multiethnic education: Theory and practice* (3rd ed.). Boston: Allyn & Bacon.

Baratta-Lorton, M. (1972). *Workjobs: Activity centered learning for early childhood education.* Menlo Park, CA: Addison-Wesley.

Baratta-Lorton, M. (1979). *Workjobs II: Number activities for early childhood.* Menlo Park, CA: Addison-Wesley.

Barbour, N. B., & Bersani, C. U. (1991). The campus child care center as a professional development school. *Early Childhood Research Quarterly, 6*(1), 43–49.

Barclay, K., & Benelli, C. (1994). Are labels determining practice? Programming for preschool gifted children. *Childhood Education, 70*(3), 133–136.

Barfield, A. (1976). Biological influences on sex differences in behavior. In M. S. Teitelbaum (Ed.), *Sex differences: Social and biological perspectives.* New York: Anchor Books.

Barnett, W. S. (1993). New wine in old bottles: Increasing the coherence of early childhood care and education policy. *Early Childhood Research Quarterly, 8*(4), 519–558.

Barnett, W. S., & Escobar, C. M. (1990). Economic costs and benefits of early intervention. In S. J. Meisels & J. P. Shonkoff, (Eds.), *Handbook of early childhood intervention*. New York: Cambridge University Press.

Baron, N. S. (1992). *Growing up with language: How children learn to talk*. Reading, MA: Addison-Wesley.

Baron, R. A., & Richardson, D. R. (1994). *Human aggression* (2nd ed.). New York: Plenum Press.

Bar-Tal, D., & Raviv, A. (1982). A cognitive-learning model of helping behavior development: Possible implications and applications. In N. Eisenberg (Ed.), *The development of prosocial behavior*. New York: Academic Press.

Barton, M. L., & Zeanah, C. H. (1990). Stress in the preschool years. In L. E. Arnold (Ed.), *Childhood stress*. New York: Wiley.

Batshaw, M. L., & Perret, Y. M. (1992). *Children with disabilities: A medical primer* (3rd ed.). Baltimore, MD: Paul Brookes.

Baugh, J. (1994). New and prevailing misconceptions of African American English for logic and mathematics. In E. R. Hollings, J. E. King, & W. C. Hayman (Eds.), *Teaching diverse populations: Formulating a knowledge base*. Albany, NY: State University of New York Press.

Baumrind, D. (1989). Rearing competent children. In W. Damon (Ed.), *Child development today and tomorrow*. San Francisco: Jossey-Bass.

Bayless, K. M., & Ramsey, M. E. (1990). *Music: A way of life for the young child* (4th ed.). Englewood Cliffs, NJ: Merrill/Prentice Hall.

Beach, B. (1986). Connecting preschoolers and the world of work. *Dimensions, 14*(3), 20–22.

Beall, A. E., & Sternberg, R. J. (Eds.). (1993). *The psychology of gender*. New York: Guilford.

Beardsley, L. (1990). *Good day bad day: The child's experience of child care*. New York: Teachers College Press.

Bearison, F. J., & Cassel, T. Z. (1975). Cognitive decentration and social codes: Communication effectiveness in young children from differing family contexts. *Developmental Psychology, 11*, 732–737.

Bednar, R. L., Well, M. G., & Peterson, S. R. (1989). *Self-esteem: Paradoxes and innovations in clinical theory and practice*. Washington, DC: American Psychological Association.

Behan, B., & Fannis, J. (1990). *Signs for me: Basic sign vocabulary for children*. Berkeley, CA: Dawn Sign Press.

Belliston, L., & Belliston, M. (1982). *How to raise a more creative child*. Allen, TX: Argus Communications.

Belsky, J., & Vondra, J. (1990). Lessons from child abuse: The determinants of parenting. In D. Cicchetti & V. Carlson (Eds.), *Child maltreatment: Theory and research on the causes and consequences of child abuse and neglect*. New York: Cambridge University Press.

Bender, J. (1978). Large hollow blocks: Relationship of quantity to block building behaviors. *Young Children, 33*(6), 17–23.

Benzwie, T. (1987). *A moving experience: Dance for lovers of children and the child within*. Tucson, AZ: Zephyr Press.

Bergen, D. (1988). *Play as a medium for learning and development: A handbook of theory and practice*. Portsmouth, NH: Heinemann.

Berger, E. H. (1991). *Parents as partners in education: The school and home working together* (3rd ed.). Englewood Cliffs, NJ: Merrill/Prentice Hall.

Berk, L. E. (1976). How well do classroom practices reflect teacher goals? *Young Children, 32*(1), 64–81.

Berkowitz, L. (1993). *Aggression: Its causes, consequences and control*. Philadelphia: Temple University Press.

Berkson, G. (1993). *Children with handicaps: A review of behavioral research*. Hillsdale, NJ: Erlbaum.

Berman, C., & Fromer, J. (1991a). *Meals without squeals*. Palo Alto, CA: Bull.

Berman, C., & Fromer, J. (1991b). *Teaching children about food: A teaching guide and activities guide*. Palo Alto, CA: Bull.

Bernal, E. M., Jr. (1978). The identification of gifted Chicano children. In A. Y. Baldwin, G. H. Gear, & L. J. Lucito (Eds.), *Educational planning for the gifted*. Reston, VA: Council for Exceptional Children.

Bernstein, A. (1978). *The flight of the stork*. New York: Delacorte Press.

Bernstein, B. (1960). Language and social class. *British Journal of Sociology, 11*, 271–276.

Bernstein, J. E., & Rudman, R. R. (1989). *Books to help children cope with separation and loss* (Vol. 3). New York: Bowker.

Berrueta-Clement, J. T., Schwein-hart, L. J., Barnett, W. S., Epstein, A. S., & Weikart, D. P. (1984). *Changed lives: The effects of the Perry Preschool Program on youths through age 19.* Ypsilanti, MI: High/Scope Educational Research Foundation.

Betz, C. (1994). Beyond time-out: Tips from a teacher. *Young Children, 49*(3), 10–14.

Beuf, A. H. (1974). Doctor, lawyer, household drudge. *Journal of Communications, 24,* 142–145.

Beuf, A. H. (1977). *Red children in white America.* Philadelphia: University of Pennsylvania Press.

Biber, B. (1981). The evolution of the developmental-interaction view. In E. K. Shapiro & E. Weber (Eds.). *Cognitive and affective growth: Developmental interaction.* Hillsdale, NJ: Erlbaum.

Biber, B. (1984). *Early education and psychological development.* New Haven, CT: Yale University Press.

Birch, L. L. (1980a). Effects of peer models' food choices and eating behaviors on preschoolers' food preferences. *Child Development, 51,* 489–496.

Birch, L. L. (1980b). Experiential determinants of children's food preferences. In L. Katz (Ed.), *Current topics in early childhood education.* Vol. III. Norwood, NJ: Ablex.

Birch, L. L., Johnson, S. L., & Fisher, J. A. (1995). Children's eating: The development of food-acceptance patterns. *Young Children, 50*(2), 71–78.

Bjorklund, G., & Burger, C. (1987). Making conferences work for parents, teachers and children. *Young Children, 42*(2), 26–31.

Blake, W. (1978). "The Little Black Boy:" Songs of Innocence. London: W. Blake, 1789. In G. E. Bentley, Jr., *William Blake's writing. Vol. I.* Oxford: Clarendon Press.

Blanchard, K., and Johnson, S. (1992). *The one minute manager.* New York: Berkley Books.

Blank, M., & Solomon, F. A. (1968). A tutorial language program to develop abstract thinking in socially disadvantaged preschool children. *Child Development, 39*(1), 379–390.

Blank, M., & Solomon, F. A. (1969). How shall the disadvantaged child be taught? *Child Development, 40*(1), 48–61.

Block, J., & Martin, B. (1955). Predicting the behavior of children under frustration. *Journal of Abnormal Social Psychology, 51,* 281–285.

Block, M. (1994). *A teacher's guide to including students with disabilities in regular physical education.* Baltimore, MD: Paul Brookes.

Blood, C. L., & Link, M. (1980). *The goat in the rug.* New York: Four Winds Press.

Bloom, B. (1964). *Stability and change in human characteristics.* New York: Wiley.

Bloom L. (1975). Language development review. In F. D. Horowitz, E. M. Hetherington, S. Scarr-Salapatek, & G. M. Siegel (Eds.). *Review of child development research* (Vol. 4). Chicago: University of Chicago Press.

Bond, F. (1983). *Mary Betty Lizzie McNutt's birthday.* New York: Thomas Y. Crowell.

Borysenko, J., with Rothstein, L. (1987). *Minding the body, mending the mind.* New York: Bantam Books.

Bos, B. (1982). *Please don't move the muffin tins: A hands-off guide to art for the young child.* Carmichael, CA: The Burton Gallery.

Bos, B. (1983). *Before the basics: Creating conversations with children.* Roseville, CA: Turn the Page Press.

Bos, B. (1990). *Together we're better: Establishing a coactive learning environment.* Roseville, CA: Turn the Page Press.

Boutte, G. S., LaPoint, S., & Davis, B. (1993). Racial issues in education: Real or imagined? *Young Children, 49*(1), 19–23.

Bower, E. M. (1981). *Early identification of emotionally handicapped children in school* (3rd ed.). Springfield, IL: Charles C Thomas.

Bowlby, J. (1973). *Attachment and loss. Vol. 1: Separation.* New York: Basic Books.

Bowlby, J. (1982). *Loss: Sadness and depression.* New York: Basic Books.

Bowman, B. T. (1990). Educating language minority children. *ERIC Digest: ERIC Clearinghouse on Elementary and Early Childhood Education.* EDO-PS-90-1.

Bradbard, M. R., & Endsley, R. C. (1982). How can teachers develop young children's curiosity? In J. F. Brown (Ed.), *Curriculum planning for young children.* Washington, DC: National Association for the Education of Young Children.

Bradburn, E. (1989). *Margaret McMillan: Portrait of a pioneer.* London: Routledge.

Brady, P. (1992). Columbus and the quincentennial myths: Another side of the story. *Young Children, 47*(6), 4–14.

Braun, S. J., & Edwards, E. P. (1972). *History and theory of early childhood education*. Worthington, OH: Charles A. Jones.

Brazelton, T. B. (1992). *Touchpoints: Your child's emotional and behavioral development*. New York: Addison-Wesley.

Bredekamp, S. (Ed.). (1987). *Developmentally appropriate practice in early childhood programs serving children from birth through age 8: Expanded edition*. Washington, DC: National Association for the Education of Young Children.

Bredekamp, S., & Rosegrant, T. (1994). Learning and teaching with technology. In J. L. Wright & D. D. Shade (Eds.), *Young children: Active learners in a technological age*. Washington, DC: National Association for the Education of Young Children.

Bressan, E. S. (1990). Movement education and the development of children's decision-making abilities. In W. J. Stinson (Ed.), *Moving and learning for the young child*. Reston, VA: American Alliance for Health, Physical Education, Recreation and Dance.

Brett, A., Moore, R. C., & Provenzo, E. B. (1993). *The complete playground book*. Syracuse, NY: Syracuse University Press.

Bricker, D., & Cripe, J. J. W. (1992). *An activity based approach to early intervention*. Baltimore, MD: Paul Brookes.

Brierly, J. (1987). *Give me a child until he is seven*. New York: The Falmer Press.

Briggs, D. (1993). *Toddler storytime programs*. Metuchen, NJ: Scarecrow Press.

Briggs, D. C. (1970). *Your child's self-esteem: The key to his life*. Garden City, NY: Doubleday.

Brittain, W. L. (1979). *Creativity, art and the young child*. Englewood Cliffs, NJ: Prentice Hall.

Bronfenbrenner, U. (1969). In H. Chauncey (Ed.), *Soviet preschool education, Vol. II: Teacher's commentary*. New York: Holt, Rinehart & Winston.

Bronfenbrenner, U. (1979). *The ecology of human development*. Cambridge, MA: Harvard University Press.

Bronstein, P., & Cowan, C. P. (Eds.). (1988). *Fatherhood today: Men's changing role in the family*. New York: Wiley.

Brown, C. C. (Ed.). (1984). *The many facets of touch: The foundation of experience: Its importance through life, with initial emphasis for infants and young children*. Skillman, NJ: Johnson & Johnson Baby Products Company.

Brown, R., & Bellugi, U. (1964). Three processes in the child's acquisition of syntax. *Harvard Educational Review, 34*, 133–151.

Brown, R. T., & Reynolds, C. R. (1986). *Psychological perspectives on childhood exceptionality: A handbook*. New York: Wiley.

Bruder, M. B. (1994). Working with members of other disciplines: Collaboration for success. In M. Wolery & J. S. Wilbers (Eds.), *Including children with special needs in early childhood programs*. Washington, DC: National Association for the Education of Young Children.

Bruner, J. (1983). *Child's talk: Learning to use language*. Oxford, England: Oxford University Press.

Bruner, J. S. (1964). The course of cognitive growth. *American Psychologist, 19*, 1–15.

Bruner, J. S. (1966). On the conservation of liquids. In J. S. Bruner, R. R. Olver, P. M. Greenfield, et al. (Eds.), *Studies in cognitive growth*. New York: Wiley.

Bruner, J. S. (1974). Nature and uses of immaturity. In K. Connolly & J. S. Bruner (Eds.), *The growth of competence*. New York: Academic Press.

Bruner, J. S. (1975) The ontogenesis of speech acts. *Journal of Child Language, 2*, 1–19.

Bruner, J. S. (1978). Learning the mother tongue. *Human Nature, 1*(9), 42–49.

Buckleitner, W. (1993a). Answers to some common questions: Kids and computers update. *Child Care Information Exchange, 93*, 75–84.

Buckleitner, W. (1993b). High/Scope buyer's guide to children's software 1993. Ypsilanti, MI: High/Scope Press.

Bullock, J. (1993). Lonely children. *Young Children, 48*(6), 53–57.

Burchinal, M., Lee, M., & Ramey, C. (1989). Type of day-care and preschool intellectual development in disadvantaged children. *Child Development, 60*(1), 128–137.

Burn, J. R. (1989). Express it with puppetry—An international language. In S. Hoffman & L. L. Lamme (Eds.), *Learning from the inside out: The expressive arts*. Wheaton, MD: Association for Childhood Education International.

Butler, A. L., Gotts, E. E., & Quisenberry, N. L. (1978). *Play as development*. Englewood Cliffs, NJ: Merrill/Prentice Hall.

Buzzelli, C. (1992). Young children's moral understanding: Learning about right and wrong. *Young Children, 47*(6), 47–83.

Bybee, R. W., & Sund, R. B. (1990). *Piaget for educators* (2nd ed.). Prospect Heights, IL: Waveland Press.

Cahan, E. D. (1989). *Past caring: A history of U.S. preschool care and education for the poor, 1820–1965.* New York: National Center for Children in Poverty, School of Public Health, Columbia University.

Campbell, K. C., & Arnold, F. D. (1988). Stimulating thinking and communicating skills. *Dimensions, 16*(2), 1, 13.

Canadian Child Care Federation (1995). *HIV/AIDS and child care: Resource kit.* Ottawa: CCCF.

Canadian Child Day Care Federation (1991). *National statement on quality child care.* Ottawa: CCDCF.

Canadian Institute of Child Health (1994). *The health of Canada's children: A CICH profile* (2nd ed.). Ottawa: CICH.

Canadian Pediatric Society (1992). *Well beings: A guide to promote the physical health, safety and emotional well-being of children in child care centres.* Toronto: Creative Premises Ltd.

Cannella, G. S. (1986). Praise and concrete rewards: Concerns for childhood education. *Childhood Education, 62*(4), 297–301.

Capute, A. J., & Accardo, P. (Eds.). (n.d.). *Developmental disabilities in infancy and childhood.* Baltimore: Paul Brookes.

Carta, J. J., Greenwood, C. R., & Atwater, J. B. (1986). *ESCAPE: Eco-behavioral system for complex assessments of preschool environments.* Unpublished coding manual for observational systems.

Kansas City, KS: Juniper Gardens Children's Project.

Carter, M. (1994). Finding our voices—The power of telling stories. *Child Care Information Exchange, 98,* 47–50.

Cartwright, S. (1988). Play can be the building blocks of learning. *Young Children, 43*(5), 44–47.

Cartwright, S. (1990). Learning with large blocks. *Young Children, 45*(3), 38–41.

Cassidy, D. J., & Lancaster, C. (1993). The grassroots curriculum: A dialogue between children and teachers. *Young Children, 48*(6), 47–51.

Cassidy, J., and Vukelich, C. (1980). Do the gifted read early? *The Reading Teacher, 33,* 578–582.

Cauley, K., & Tyler, B. (1989). The relationship of self-concept to prosocial behavior in children. *Early Childhood Research Quarterly, 4*(1), 51–60.

Cazden, C. (1970). Children's questions: Their forms, functions and roles in education. *Young Children, 25*(4), 202–220.

Cazden, C. (1972). *Child language and education.* New York: Holt, Rinehart & Winston.

CDF. (1993). Head Start moves into the 1990s. *CDF Reports14* (4).

Census Bureau of the United States. (1992). *Language spoken at home and ability to speak English for United States regions and states: 1990.* Washington, DC: Population Division, Statistical Information Office, Census Bureau. CPH-L-133.

Chaillé, C., & Britain, L. (1991). *The young child as scientist: A constructivist approach to early childhood science education.* New York: Harper Collins.

Chaillé, C., & Young, P. (1980). Some issues linking research on

children's play and education: Are they "only playing"? *International Journal of Early Childhood, 12*(2), 53–55.

Chandler, L. A. (1982). *Children under stress: Understanding emotional adjustment reactions.* Springfield, IL: Charles C. Thomas.

Chandler, P. A. (1994). *A place for me: Including children with special needs in early care and education settings.* Washington, DC: National Association for the Education of Young Children.

Chattin-McNichols, J. P. (1981). The effects of Montessori school experience. *Young Children, 36*(5), 49–66.

Chattin-McNichols, J. P.(1992). *The Montessori controversy.* Albany, NY: Delmar.

Chenfeld, M. B. (1983). *Creative activities for young children.* New York: Harcourt Brace Jovanovich.

Chenfeld, M. B. (1993). *Teaching in the key of life.* Washington, DC: National Association for the Education of Young Children.

Chenfeld, M. B. (1995). *Creative activities for young children* (2nd ed.). Fort Worth, TX: Harcourt Brace.

Cherry, C. (1971). *Creative movement for the developing child: A nursery school handbook for non-musicians* (rev. ed.). Belmont, CA: Fearon.

Cherry, C. (1981). *Think of something quiet: A guide for achieving serenity in early childhood classrooms.* Belmont, CA: Pitman Learning.

Cherry, C. (1990). *Creative art for the developing child: A teacher's handbook for early childhood education* (2nd ed.). Belmont, CA: Fearon.

Chhim, S. H. (1989). *Introduction to Cambodian culture*. San Diego, CA: Multifunctional Resource Center, San Diego State University.

Child Care Information Exchange. (1994). Beginnings workshop: "Storytelling." Redmond, WA: Author, *98*, 31–50.

Child Care Law Center. (1994a). *Caring for children with HIV or AIDS*. San Francisco: The Center.

Child Care Law Center. (1994b). *Caring for children with special needs: The Americans with Disabilities Act and child care*. San Francisco, CA: The Center.

Children Today. (1993). Important facts about pediatric emergency care. *22*(3), 3.

Children's Defense Fund. (1993). Safe Start: Key facts. *CDF Reports, 15*(8), 7.

Children's Defense Fund. (1994). *State of America's children yearbook*. Washington, DC: Author.

Children's Foundation. (1992). *Implications of the Americans with Disabilities Act of 1990 (ADA) for family day care providers*. Washington, DC: Author.

Chomsky, N. (1968). *Language and mind*. New York: Harcourt Brace.

Chomsky, N. (1981). *Lectures on government and binding*. Dordrecht, Holland: Foris.

Christie, J. F., & Wardle, F. (1992). How much time is needed for play? *Young Children, 47*(3), 28–32.

Chud, G., & Fahlman, R. (1985). *Early childhood education for a multicultural society*. Vancouver: Pacific Educational Press, University of British Columbia.

Chud, G., & Fahlman, R. (1995). *Honouring diversity within child care and early education: An instructor's guide*. Victoria: Province of British Columbia, Ministry of Skills, Training and Labour.

Church, E. B., & Miller, K. (1990). *Learning through play: Blocks: A practical guide for teaching young children*. New York: Scholastic.

Ciaranello, R. D. (1988). Autism: The prison of self. *The Stanford Magazine*, Summer, 18–21.

Cicchetti, D., & White, J. (1989). Emotional development and the affective disorders. In W. Damon (Ed.), *Child development today and tomorrow*. San Francisco: Jossey Bass.

Cicerelli, V. G., Evans, J. W., & Schiller, J. S. (1969). *The impact of Head Start on children's cognitive and affective development: Preliminary report*. Washington, DC: Office of Economic Opportunity. PB 184 328, 329.

Clark, K. B. (1963). *Prejudice and your child* (2nd ed.). Boston: Beacon Press.

Clay, J. W. (1990). Working with lesbian and gay parents and their children. *Young Children, 45*(3), 31–35.

Clements, D. H., Nastasi, B. K., & Swaminathan, S. (1993). Research in review: Young Children and computers: Crossroads and directions from research. *Young Children, 48*(2), 56–64.

Clewett, A. S. (1988). Guidance and discipline: Teaching young children appropriate behavior. *Young Children, 43*(4), 26–35.

Cochran, M. (1993). (Ed.). *International handbook of child care policies and programs*. Westport, CT: Greenwood Press.

Cohen, D. L. (1990). Early childhood educators bemoan the scarcity of males in teaching. *Education Week*, 1, 3, 12, 13.

Coie, J. C., & Kupersmidt, J. A. (1983). A behavioral analysis of emerging social status in boys' groups. *Child Development, 54*, 1400–1416.

Cole, A., Haas, C., Heller, E., & Weinberger, B. (1978). *Children are children are children: An activity approach to exploring Brazil, France, Iran, Japan, Nigeria and the U.S.S.R.* Boston: Little, Brown.

Collins, L., Ingoldsby, B., & Dellman, M. (1984). Sex-role stereotyping in children's literature: A change from the past. *Childhood Education, 60*, 278–285.

Collins, R. C. (1993). Head Start: Steps toward a two-generation program strategy. *Young Children, 48*(2), 25–33, 73.

Coner-Edwards, A. F., & Spurlock, J. (1988). *Black families in crisis: The middle-class*. New York: Brunner/Mazel.

Consumer Product Safety Commission. (1981). *A handbook for public playground safety: Vol. 1. General guidelines for new and existing playgrounds*. Washington, DC: Author.

Consumer Product Safety Commission. (1991). *Handbook for public playground safety*. Washington, DC: Author.

Conte, J. R., & Berlinger, L. (1981). Sexual abuse of children: Implications for practice. *Social Casework, 62*, 601–606.

Cook, R. E., Tessier, A., & Klein, M. D. (1992). *Adapting early childhood curricula for children with special needs* (3rd ed.). Englewood Cliffs, NJ: Merrill/Prentice Hall.

Coopersmith, S. (1967). *The antecedants of self-esteem*. San Francisco: W. H. Freeman.

Coopersmith, S. (1975). Building self-esteem in the classroom. In S. Coopersmith (Ed.), *Developing motivation in young children*. San Francisco: Albion Publishing Co.

Copage, E. V. (1991). *Kwanzaa: An African American celebration of culture and cooking*. New York: Morrow.

Corbett, W. (1993). A complicated bias. *Young Children, 48*(3), 29–31.

Corsaro, W. (1988). Children's conception and reaction to adult rules: The underlife of the nursery school. In G. Handel (Ed.), *Childhood socialization*. New York: Aldine De Gruyter.

Council for Exceptional Children. (1993). CEC policy on inclusive schools and community settings. *Teaching Exceptional Children, 25*(4), supplement.

Council on Interracial Books for Children. (1976). *Racism and sexism in children's books: Interracial Digest, # 1*. New York: NY.

Cox, B., & Jacobs, M. (1991). *Spirit of the harvest: North American Indian cooking*. New York: Stewart, Tabori & Chang.

Cox, F. N., & Campbell, D. (1968). Young children in a new situation, with and without their mothers. *Child Development, 39*, 123–131.

Cox, M. V. (1991). *The child's point of view: The development of cognition and language* (2nd ed.). New York: Guilford.

Cratty, B. J. (1986). *Perceptual and motor development in infants and children* (3rd ed.). Englewood Cliffs, NJ: Prentice Hall.

Cratty, B. J., & Martin, M. M. (1969). *Perceptual-motor efficiency in children: The measurement and improvement of move-ment attributes*. Philadelphia: Lea & Febiger.

Crocker, A. C., Cohen, H., J., & Kastner, T. A. (Eds.). (1992). *HIV infection and developmental disabilities: A resource for service providers*. Baltimore: Paul Brookes.

Crocker, B. (1993). *Betty Crocker's Mexican made easy*. Englewood Cliffs, NJ: Prentice Hall.

Crosse, S. B., Kaye, E., & Ratnofsky, A. C. (1991). *A report on the maltreatment of children with disabilities*. Washington, DC: United States Department of Health and Human Services, Administration on Children, Youth and Family, National Center on Child Abuse and Neglect.

Crosser, S. (1994). Making the most of water play. *Young Children, 49*(5), 28–32.

Cuddigan, M., & Hanson, M. B. (1988). *Growing pains*. New York: American Library Association.

Cummings, J. (1984). *Bilingualism and special education*. San Diego: College Hill Press.

Curry, N. (Ed.). (1986). *The feeling child: Affective development reconsidered*. New York: The Haworth Press.

Curry, N., & Bergen, D. (1988). The relationship of play to emotional, social and gender/sex role development. In D. Bergen (Ed.), *Play as a medium for learning and development: A handbook of theory and practice*. Portsmouth, NH: Heinemann.

Curry, N. E., & Johnson, C. N. (1990). *Beyond self-esteem: Developing a genuine sense of human value*. Washington, DC: National Association for the Education of Young Children.

Curtis, S. R. (1982). *The joy of movement*. New York: Teachers College Press.

Damon, W. (1983). *Social and personality development: Infancy through adolescence*. New York: Norton.

Damon, W. (1988). *The moral child: Nurturing children's natural moral growth*. New York: The Free Press.

Davis, C. M. (1939). Results of the self-selection of diets by young children. *Canadian Medical Association Journal, 41*, 257–261.

Davis, J., & Gardner, H. (1993). The arts and early childhood education: A cognitive developmental portrait of the young child as artist. In B. Spodek (Ed.), *Handbook of research on the education of young children*. Englewood Cliffs, NJ: Prentice Hall.

Deci, E. L., & Ryan, R. M. (1982). Curiosity and self-directed learning: The role of motivation in education. In L. G. Katz (Ed.), *Current topics in early childhood education* (Vol. IV). Norwood, NJ: Ablex.

Dellmann-Jenkins, M., Florjancic, L., & Swaener, E. B. (1993). Sex roles and cultural diversity in recent award winning picture books for young children. *Journal of Research in Childhood Education, 7*(2), 74–82.

Delpit, L. D. (1993). The silenced dialogue: Power and pedagogy in educating other people's children. In L. Weis & M. Fine (Eds.), *Beyond silenced voices: Class, race and gender in United States schools*. Albany, NY: State University of New York.

Dennis, W. (1960). Causes of retardation among institutional children: Iran. *Journal of Genetic Psychology, 96*, 47–59.

DePanfilis, D., & Salus, M. K. (1992). *A coordinated response to child abuse and neglect: A basic manual.* Washington, DC: United States Department of Health and Human Services, Administration on Children, Youth and Families, National Center on Child Abuse and Neglect.

Department of Health and Human Services (1991). *Healthy people.* Washington, DC: United States Public Health Service. 91-50212.

Derman-Sparks, L. (1993/1994). Empowering children to create a caring culture in a world of differences. *Childhood Education, 70*(2), 66–71.

Derman-Sparks, L., & the ABC Task Force. (1989). *Anti-bias curriculum: Tools for empowering young children.* Washington, DC: National Association for the Education of Young Children.

Derman-Sparks, L., Higa, C. T., & Sparks, B. (1980). Children, race, and racism: How race awareness develops. *Interracial Books for Children Bulletin, 11*(3/4), 3–9.

de Villiers, P. A., & de Villiers, J. G. (1992). Language development. In M. H. Bornstein & M. E. Lamb (Eds.), *Developmental psychology: An advanced textbook* (3rd ed.). Hillsdale, NJ: Erlbaum.

DeVries, R., & Kohlberg, L. (1990). *Constructivist early education: Overview and comparison with other programs.* Washington, DC: National Association for the Education of Young Children.

Diamond, K. E. (1993). Preschool children's concepts of disability in their peers. *Early Education and Development, 4*(2), 123–129.

Diamond, K. E., Hestenes, L. L. & O'Connor, C. E. (1994).

Research in review: Integrating young children with disabilities in preschool: Problems and promise. *Young Children, 49* (2), 68–75.

Dickinson, P. (1990). The early childhood professional. In I.M. Doxey (Ed.) *Child care and education: Canadian dimensions.* Scarborough, ON: Nelson.

Dinwiddie, S. A. (1994). The saga of Sally, Sammy, and the red pen: Facilitating children's problem solving. *Young Children, 49*(5), 13–19.

D'Odorico, L., & Franco, F. (1985). The determinants of baby talk: Relationship to context. *Journal of Child Language, 12*(5), 567–586.

Doherty-Derkowski, G. (1995). *Quality matters: Excellence in early childhood programs.* Don Mills, ON: Addison-Wesley.

Dore, J. (1986). The development of conversational competence. In R. Schiefelbusch (Ed.), *Language competence: Assessment and intervention.* San Diego: College Hill Press.

Dotsch, J. (1992). Newcomer preschool children: *Their linguistic adaptation to childcare settings.* Multiculturalism 14 (2-3).

Dotsch, J., & McFarlane J. *The newcomer preschool.* Toronto, ON: Ministry of Culture.

Dowd, F. S. (1992). Evaluating children's books portraying Native American and Asian cultures. *Childhood Education, 68*(4), 219–224.

Dowell, R. I. (1987). *Move over, Mother Goose: Finger plays, action verses, and funny rhymes.* Mount Rainier, MD: Gryphon House.

Duckworth, E. (1987). *"The having of wonderful ideas" and other*

essays on teaching and learning. New York: Teachers College Press.

Duer, J. L., & Parke, R. D. (1970). The effects of inconsistent punishment on aggression in children. *Developmental Psychology, 2,* 403–411.

Dunkle, J. L., & Edwards, M. S. (1992). *The no-leftovers child care cookbook.* St. Paul, MN: Redleaf.

Dunn, J., & Kendrick, C. (1981). The arrival of a sibling: Changes in patterns of interaction between mother and first-born child. In S. Chess & A. Thomas (Eds.), *Annual progress in child psychiatry and child development, 1981.* New York: Brunner/ Mazel.

Durkin, D. (1982). *A study of poor black children who are successful readers.* Reading Education Report No. 33. Urbana, IL: Center for the Study of Reading. ED 216 334.

Dyson, A. H. (1990). Research in review: Symbol makers, symbol weavers: How children link play, pictures and paint. *Young Children, 45*(2), 50–57.

Dyson, A. H., & Genishi, C. (1984). Nonstandard dialects in day care. *Dimensions, 13*(1), 6–9.

Dyson, A. H., & Genishi, C. (1993). Visions of children as language users: Language and language education in early childhood. In B. Spodek, (Ed.), *Handbook of research on the education of young children.* Englewood Cliffs, NJ: Prentice Hall.

Eagly, A. H., & Wood, W. (1991). Explaining sex differences in social behavior: A meta-analytic perspective. *Personality and Social Psychology Bulletin, 17,* 306–315.

Early Childhood Directors Association. (1983). *Survival kit for directors*. St. Paul, MN: Toys 'n Things Press (distributors).

Eastman, P. D. (1960). *Are you my mother?* New York: Random House.

Edelstein, S. (1992). *Nutrition and meal planning in child-care programs: A practical guide*. Chicago: American Dietetic Association.

Education Week. (1993). About 10% of youths say they have fired a gun or been shot at, new survey finds. *Education Week*, (August 4), 21.

Edwards, C. P. (1980). The comparative study of the development of moral judgment and reasoning. In R. L. Munroe, R. Munroe, & B. B. Whiting (Eds.), *Handbook of cross-cultural human development*. New York: Garland.

Edwards, C., Gandini, L., & Forman, G. (Eds.). (1993). *The hundred languages of children: The Reggio Emilia approach to early childhood education*. Norwood, NJ: Ablex.

Edwards, L. C., & Nabors, M. L. (1993). The creative arts process: What it is and what it is not. *Young Children, 48*(3), 77–81.

Eisenberg, N. (1992). *The caring child*. Cambridge, MA: Harvard University Press.

Eisenberg, N., McCreath, H., & Ahn, R. (1988). Vicarious emotional responsiveness and prosocial behavior: Their interrelations in young children. *Personality and Social Psychology Bulletin, 19*, 848–855.

Eisenberg, N., & Mussen, P. (1989/90). *The roots of prosocial behavior in children*. New York: Cambridge University Press.

Eisenberg, N., Shell, R., Pasternack, J., Lemmon, R., Beller, R., & Mathy, R. M. (1987). Prosocial development in middle childhood: A longitudinal study. *Developmental Psychology, 23*, 712–718.

Elkind, D. (1987). *Miseducation: Preschoolers at risk*. New York: Knopf.

Elliot, O., & King, J. A. (1960). *Psychological Reports, 6*, 391.

Ellis, R. (1994). *The study of second language acquisition*. New York: Oxford University Press.

Emery, R. E. (1989). Family violence. *American Psychologist, 44*(2), 321–328.

Emery, R. E., & Forehand, R. (1994). Parental divorce and children's well-being: A focus on resilience. In R. J. Haggerty, L. R. Sherrod, N. Garmezy, & M. Rutter (Eds.), *Stress, risk, and resilience in children and adolescents: Processes, mechanisms, and interventions*. New York: Cambridge University Press.

Endres, J. B., & Rockwell, R. E. (1993). *Food, nutrition and the young child* (4th ed.). Englewood Cliffs, NJ: Merrill/Prentice Hall.

Eriksen, A. (1985). *Playground design: Outdoor environments for learning and development*. New York: Van Nostrand Reinhold.

Erikson, E. (1950). *Childhood and society*. New York: Norton.

Erikson, E. (1963). *Childhood and society* (2nd ed.). New York: W. W. Norton.

Erikson, E. H. (1959). Identity and the life cycle. *Psychological Issues, 1*(1), Monograph 1.

Erikson, E. H. (1971). A healthy personality for every child. In R. H. Anderson & H. G. Shane (Eds.), *As the twig is bent: Readings in early childhood education*. New York: Houghton Mifflin.

Erikson, E. H. (1982). *The life cycle completed: A review*. New York: W. W. Norton.

Eron, L. D., & Huesmann, L. R. (1984). The control of aggressive behavior by changes in attitudes, values and the conditions of learning. In R. J. Blanchard & D. C. Blanchard (Eds.), *Advances in the study of aggression* (Vol. 1). Orlando, FL: Academic Press.

Ervin-Tripp, S., & Gordon, D. (1986). The development of requests. In R. L. Schiefelbusch (Ed.), *Language competence: Assessment and intervention*. San Diego: College Hill Press.

Essa, E. L., & Murray, C. I. (1994). Research in review: Young children's understanding and experience with death. *Young Children, 49*(4), 74–81.

Evers, W. L., & Schwarz, J. C. (1973). Modifying social withdrawal in pre-schoolers: The effects of filmed modeling and teacher praise. *Journal of Abnormal Child Psychology, 1*, 248–256.

Faber, A., & Mazlish, E. (1980). *How to talk so kids will listen, & listen so kids will talk*. New York: Avon Books.

Fadely, J. L., & Hosler, V. N. (1992). *Attentional deficit disorder in children and adolescents*. Springfield, IL: Charles C Thomas.

Fagot, B. I. (1977). Consequences of moderate cross-gender behavior in preschool children. *Child Development, 48*, 902–907.

Fagot, B. I. (1994). Peer relations and the development of competence in boys and girls. *New Directions for Child Development, 65*, 53–65.

Fagot, B. I., & Kronsberg, S. J. (1982). Sex differences: Biological and social factors influencing the behavior of young boys and girls. In S. G. Moore & C. R. Cooper (Eds.), *The young child: Reviews of research* (Vol. 3). Washington, DC: National Association for the Education of Young Children.

Farber, J. M. (1991). Autism and other communication disorders. In A. J. Capute & P. J. Accardo (Eds.), *Developmental disabilities in infancy and childhood*. Baltimore, MD: Paul Brookes.

Feinberg, S. (1993). Learning through art. *Scholastic Early Childhood Today, 8*(2), 58–61.

Feng, J. (1994). *Asian-American children: What teachers should know*. Urbana, IL: ERIC Clearinghouse on Elementary and Early Childhood Education.

Fennimore, B. (1989). *Child care advocacy for early childhood educators*. New York: Teacher's College Press.

Fennimore, B. S. (1994). Addressing prejudiced statements; A four-step method that works! *Childhood Education, 7*(4), 202–204.

Fenwick, K. (1993). Diffusing conflict with parents: A model for communication. *Child Care Information Exchange, 93*, 59–60.

Ferber, R. (1985). *Solve your child's sleep problems*. New York: Simon & Schuster.

Feshbach, N., & Feshbach, S. (1972). Children's aggression. In W. W. Hartup (Ed.), *The young child: Reviews of research*, Vol. 2. Washington, DC: National Association for the Education of Young Children.

Fields, M., & Spangler, K. L. (1995). *Let's begin reading right: Developmentally appropriate beginning literacy* (3rd ed.). Englewood Cliffs, NJ: Merrill/Prentice Hall.

Fiore, T. A., Becker, E. A., & Nero, R. C. (1993). Educational interventions for students with attention deficit disorder. *Exceptional Children, 602*, 163–173.

Flack, M. (1932). *Ask Mr. Bear*. New York: Macmillan.

Folb, E. A. (1980). *Runnin' down some lines: The language and culture of black teenagers*. Cambridge, MA: Harvard University Press.

Ford, C. W. (1994). *We can all get along: 50 steps you can take to help end racism*. New York: Dell.

Forman, G. E., & Hill, F. (1980). *Constructive play: Applying Piaget in the preschool*. Monterey, CA: Brooks/Cole.

Fox, S. S. (1985). *Good grief: Helping groups of children when a friend dies*. Boston: New England Association for the Education of Young Children.

Fraiberg, S. (1977). *Insights from the blind*. New York: Basic Books.

Frieman, B. B. (1993). Separation and divorce: Children want their teachers to know—meeting the emotional needs of preschool and primary school children. *Young Children, 48*(6), 58–63.

Friendly, M. (1954). *Child care policy in Canada: Putting the pieces together*. Don Mills, ON: Addison-Wesley.

Friesen, B., & Friesen, J. (1992). Multiculturalism in daycare: An exploratory study. *multiculturalism/multiculturalisme*, XIV (2/3), 35–42.

Froom, J., & Culpepper, L. (1991). Otitis media in day-care children. A report from the International Primary Care Network. *Journal of Family Practice, 32*(3), 289–294.

Frost, J. (1992). *Play and playscapes*. Albany, NY: Delmar.

Frost, J. L., & Klein, B. L. (1979). *Children's play and playgrounds*. Boston: Allyn & Bacon.

Fuchs, D., & Fuchs, L. S. (1994). Inclusive schools movement and the radicalization of special education reform. *Exceptional Children, 6*(4), 294–309.

Fuerst, J. S., & Fuerst, D. (1993). Chicago experience with an early childhood program: The special case of the Child Parent Center Program. *Urban Education, 28*(1), 69–96.

Furman, E. (1974). *A child's parent dies: Studies in childhood bereavement*. New Haven CT: Yale University Press.

Furman, E. (1982). Helping children cope with death. In J. M. Brown (Ed.), *Curriculum planning for young children*. Washington, DC: National Association for the Education of Young Children.

Furman, E. (1984). Children's patterns in mourning the death of a loved one. In H. Wass & C. A. Corr (Eds.), *Childhood and death*. Washington, DC: Hemisphere Publishing.

Furman, R. A. (1995). Helping children cope with stress and deal with feelings. *Young Children, 50*(2), 33–41.

Furman, W., & Masters, J. C. (1980). Affective consequences of social reinforcement, punishment, and neutral behavior. *Developmental Psychology, 16*, 100–104.

Gabbard, C. C. (1991). Early childhood physical education: The essential elements. In K. M. Paciorek & J. H. Munro (Eds.),

Early childhood education 91 / 92. Guilford, CT: Dushkin.

Gagné, R. (1968). Contributions of learning to human development. *Psychological Review, 73*(3), 177–185.

Gallimore, R., & Tharp, R. (1990). Teaching mind in society: Teaching, schooling, and literate discourse. In L. C. Moll (Ed.), *Vygotsky and education: Instructional implications and applications of sociohistorical psychology*. New York: Cambridge University Press.

Galdone, P. (1981). *Three billy goats Gruff*. New York: Ticknor & Fields.

Galdone, P. (1985). *The three bears*. New York: Ticknor & Fields.

Gallahue, D. L. (1993). *Developmental physical education for today's children*. Madison, WI: Brown & Benchmark.

Gallivan-Fenlon, A. (1994). Integrated interdisciplinary teams. *Teaching Exceptional Children, 26*(3), 16–20.

Gambetti, A. (1993a). *The Reggio Emilia approach in the United States*. Traverse City, MI: Institute on Reggio Emilia, Merrill-Palmer Institute, Wayne State University.

Gambetti, A. (1993b). *The cloud project*. Traverse City, MI: Institute on Reggio Emilia, Merrill-Palmer Institute, Wayne State University.

Gandini, L. (1991). Not just anywhere: Making child care centers into "particular places." *Child Care Information Exchange, 78*, 5–9.

Gandini, L. (1993). Fundamentals of the Reggio Emilia approach to early childhood education. *Young Children, 49*(1), 4–8.

Garbarino, J., Dubrow, N., Kostelny, K., & Pardo, C.

(1992). *Children in danger: Coping with the consequences of community violence*. San Francisco: Jossey-Bass.

Garbarino, J., & Stott, F. M. (1989). *What children can tell us: Eliciting, interpreting, and evaluating information from children*. San Francisco: Jossey-Bass.

Garber, H. L., & Heber, R. (1981). The efficacy of early intervention with family rehabilitation. In N. J. Begab, H. C. Haywood, and H. L. Garger (Eds.), *Psychosocial influences in retarded performance: Vol. II. Strategies for improving competence*. Baltimore: University Park Press.

Garber, J., & Seligman, M. E. P. (Eds.). (1980). *Human helplessness: Theory and applications*. New York: Academic Press.

Garcia, E. E. (1990). Bilingualism, cognition, and academic performance: The educational debate. *Houghton Mifflin Educator's Forum*, Fall, 6–7.

Garcia, E., & August, D. (1988). *The education of language minority students*. Chicago, Illinois: Charles C Thomas.

Gardner, H. (1980). *Artful scribbles: The significance of children's drawings*. New York: Basic Books.

Gardner, H. (1986). Notes on cognitive development: Recent trends, new directions. In S. L. Friedman, K. A. Klivington, & R. W. Peterson (Eds.), *The brain, cognition, and education*. New York: Academic Press.

Gardner, H. (1991). *The unschooled mind*. New York: Basic Books.

Garland, A. W., with Mothers & Others for a Livable Planet. (1993). *The way we grow: Good-sense solutions for protecting our families from pesticides in food*. New York: Berkley Books.

Garrity, L. (1987). *The gingerbread guide: Using folk tales with young children*. Glenview, IL: Scott, Foresman.

Gartrell, D. (1994). *A guidance approach to discipline*. Albany, NY: Delmar.

Garvey, C. (1977). *Play*. Cambridge, MA: Harvard University Press.

Garvey, C. (1979). Communicational controls in social play. In B. Sutton-Smith (Ed.), *Play and learning*. New York: Gardner Press.

Garvey, C. (1984). *Children's talk*. Cambridge, MA: Harvard University Press.

Gaston, M. (1990). *Sickle Cell Anemia*. Washington, DC: Clinical Center Communications, National Institutes of Health. #90-3058.

Gaudin, J. M. (1993). *Child neglect: a guide for intervention*. Washington, DC: United States Department of Health and Human Services, Administration on Children, Youth and Families, National Center on Child Abuse and Neglect.

George, B., & Tomasello, M. (1984 / 85). The effect of variation in sentence length on young children's attention and comprehension. *First Language, 5*, 115–128.

Geraty, R. (1983). Education and self-esteem. In J. E. Mack & S. L. Ablon (Eds.), *The development and sustenance of self-esteem in childhood*. New York: International Universities Press.

Gerber, A. (1993). *Language-related learning disabilities: Their nature and treatment*. Baltimore: Paul Brookes.

Gesell, A., Halverson, H. M., Thompson, H., & Ilg, F. (1940). *The first five years of life: A guide to the study of the preschool child*. New York: Harper & Row.

Getzels, J. W., & Jackson, P. W. (1962). *Creativity and intelligence*. New York: Wiley.

Gibson, L. (1989). *Literacy learning in the early years: Through children's eyes*. New York: Teachers College Press.

Gil, E. (1991). *The healing power of play: Working with abused children*. New York: Guilford.

Glazer, S. M., & Burke, E. M. (1994). *An integrated approach to early literacy: Literature to language*. Boston: Allyn & Bacon.

Gleason, J. B. (1981). Code switching in children's language. In M. Kaplan-Sanoff & R. Yablans-Migid (Eds.), *Exploring early childhood: Readings in theory and practice*. Englewood Cliffs, NJ: Prentice Hall.

Glueck, S., & Glueck, E. (1950). *Unraveling juvenile delinquency*. Cambridge, MA: Harvard University Press.

Godwin, L. J., Groves, M. M., & Horm-Wingerd, D. M. (1994). "Don't leave me": Separation distress in infants, toddlers, and parents. In K. M. Paciorek & J. H. Munro (Eds.), *Early childhood education 94/95* (15th ed.). Guilford, CT: Dushkin Publishing.

Goffin, S. G. (1994). *Curriculum models and early childhood education*. Englewood Cliffs, NJ: Merrill/Prentice Hall.

Goffine, S. G., & Lombardi, J. (1988). *Speaking out: Early childhood advocacy*. Washington, DC: National Association for the Education of Young Children.

Golden, M, Bridger, W. H., & Montare, A. (1974). Social class differences in the ability of young children to use verbal information to facilitate learning. *American Journal of Orthopsychiatry, 44*(1), 86–91.

Golinkoff, R. M., & Hirsch-Pasek, K. (1990). Let the mute speak: What infants tell us about language acquisition. *Merrill-Palmer Quarterly, 36*(1), 67–92.

Golumb, C. (1992). *The child's creation of a pictorial world*. Berkeley, CA: University of California Press.

Gonzalez-Mena, J. (1976). English as a second language for preschool children. *Young Children, 32*(1), 14–19.

Gonzalez-Mena, J. (1992). Taking a culturally sensitive approach in infant-toddler programs. *Young Children, 47*(2), 4–9.

Gonzalez-Mena, J. (1993). *Multicultural issues in child care*. Mt. View, CA: Mayfield.

Goodson, B. D. (1982). The development of hierarchic organization: The reproduction, planning, and perception of multiarch block structures. In G. E. Forman (Ed.), *Action and thought: From sensorimotor schemes to symbolic operations*. New York: Academic Press.

Gotts, E. E. (1989). *HOPE, preschool to graduation: Contributions to parenting and school-family relations: Theory and practice*. Charleston, WV: Appalachia Educational Laboratory. ED 3–5, 146.

Gottschall, S. (1989). Understanding and accepting separation feelings. *Young Children, 44*(6), 11–16.

Graves, M. (1989). *The teacher's idea book: Daily planning around the key experiences*. Ypsilanti, MI: High/Scope Press.

Gray, S. W., Ramsey, B. K., & Klaus, R. A. (1982). *From 3 to 20: The Early Training Project*. Baltimore: University Park Press.

Greenberg, P. (1970). *The devil has slippery shoes: A biased biography of the Child Development Group of Mississippi*. Englewood Cliffs, NJ: Prentice Hall.

Greenberg, P. (1989). Ideas that work with young children: Parents as partners in young children's development and education. A new American fad? Why does it matter? *Young Children, 44*(4), 61–75.

Greenberg, P. (1990). Ideas that work. Why not academic preschool? Part I. *Young Children, 45*(2), 70–80.

Greenberg, P. (1991). *Character development: Encouraging self-esteem and self-discipline in infants, toddlers, and two-year-olds*. Washington, DC: National Association for the Education of Young Children.

Greenberg, P. (1992a). *The devil has slippery shoes: A biased biography of the Child Development Group of Mississippi*. Washington, DC: Youth Policy Institute.

Greenberg, P. (1992b). Ideas that work with young children: How to institute some simple democratic practices pertaining to respect, rights, roots, and responsibilities in any classroom (without losing your leadership position). *Young Children, 47*(5), 10–17.

Greenberg, P. (1993). Ideas that work with young children: How and why to teach all aspects of preschool and kindergarten math naturally, democratically, and effectively (for teachers who don't believe in academic programs, who do believe in educational excellence, and who find math boring to the max)—Part 1. *Young Children, 48*(4), 75–84.

Greenberg, P. (1994). Ideas that work with young children: How and why to teach all aspects of preschool and kindergarten math naturally, democratically, and effectively (for teachers who don't believe in academic programs, who do believe in educational excellence, and who find math boring to the max)—Part 2. *Young Children, 49*(2), 12–18.

Greenberg, S. (1985). Educational equity in early education environments. In Klein, S. S. (Ed.), *Handbook for achieving sex equity through education*. Baltimore: Johns Hopkins University Press.

Greenfield, P. M., & Cocking, R. R. (Eds.). (1994). *Cross-cultural roots of minority child development*. Hillsdale, NJ: Erlbaum.

Greenfield, P. M., & Smith, J. H. (1976). *The structure of communication in early child development*. New York: Academic Press.

Greenman, J. (1988). *Caring spaces, learning places: Children's environments that work*. Redmond, WA: Exchange Press.

Greenman, J. (1993). It ain't easy being green. *Child Care Information Exchange, 91*, 36–40.

Greenspan, S. & Greenspan, N. T. (1985). *First feelings: Milestones in the emotional development of your baby and child*. New York: Viking.

Griffin, E. F. (1982). *Island of childhood: Education in the special world of nursery school*. New York: Teachers College Press.

Grollman, E. A. (1990). *Talking about death: A dialogue between parent and child* (3rd ed.). Boston: Beacon Press.

Grossman, H. J. (1983). *Classification in mental retardation*. Washington, DC: American Association on Mental Deficiency, 11.

Grusec, J. E., & Arnason, L. (1982). Consideration for others: Approaches to enhancing altruism. In S. G. Moore & C. R. Cooper (Eds.), *The young child: Reviews of research, Vol. 3*. Washington, DC: National Association for the Education of Young Children.

Grusec, J. E., & Lytton, H. (1988). *Social development. History, theory, and research*. New York: Springer-Verlag.

Grusec, J. E., & Redler, E. (1980). Attribution, reinforcement, and altruism: A developmental analysis. *Developmental Psychology, 16*, 525–534.

Guddemi, M., & Jambor, T. (1993). *A right to play: Proceedings of the American Affiliates of the International Association for the Child's Right to Play, September 17–20, 1992, Denton, Texas*. Little Rock, AK: Southern Early Childhood Association.

Guilford, J. P. (1981). Developmental characteristics: Factors that aid and hinder creativity. In J. C. Gowan, J. Khatena, & E. P. Torrance (Eds.), *Creativity: Its educational implications* (2nd ed.). Dubuque, IA: Kendall/Hunt.

Guilford, J. P. A. (1958). A system of psychomotor abilities. *American Journal of Psychology, 71*, 146–147.

Gundersen, B. H., Melas, P. S., & Skar, J. E. (1981). Sexual behavior of preschool children: Teachers' observations. In L. L. Constantine & F. M. Martinson (Eds.), *Children and sex: New findings, new perspectives*. Boston: Little Brown.

Guralnick, M. J., & Groom, J. M. (1987). The peer relations of mildly delayed and nonhandicapped preschool children in mainstream playgroups. *Child Development, 58*, 1556–1572.

Hagen, J., Lewis, H., & Smilansky, S. (1988). *Clay in the classroom: Helping children develop cognitive and affective skills for learning*. New York: Peter Lang.

Haggerty, R. J., Sherrod, L. R., Garmezy, N., & Rutter, M. (Eds.). *Stress, risk, and resilience in children and adolescents: Processes, mechanisms, and interventions*. New York: Cambridge University Press.

Hakuta, K., & Garcia, E. E. (1989). Bilingualism and education. *American Psychologist, 44*(2), 374–379.

Hale, J. (1986). *Black children: Their roots, culture, and learning style* (2nd ed.). Baltimore: Johns Hopkins University Press.

Haller, J. A. (1967). Preparing a child for his operation. In J. A. Haller (Ed.), *The hospitalized child and his family*. Baltimore: Johns Hopkins Press.

Hammet, C. T. (1992). *Movement activities for early childhood*. Champaign, IL: Human Kinetics.

Harlan, J. D. (1992). *Science experiences for the early childhood years* (5th ed.). Englewood Cliffs, NJ: Merrill/Prentice Hall.

Harms, T., & Clifford, R. M. (1980). *Early childhood environment rating scale*. New York: Teachers College Press.

Harms, T., Cryer, D., & Clifford, R. M. (1990). Infant/toddler environment rating scale. New York: Teachers College Press.

Harris, J. M. (1989). *You and your child's self-esteem. Building for the future*. New York: Carroll & Graf.

Harris, V. J. (1991). Research in review: Multicultural curriculum: African American children's literature. *Young Children, 46*(2), 37–44.

Hart, C. H., DeWolf, D. M., & Burts, D. C. (1992). Linkages among preschoolers' playground behavior, outcome expectations, and parental disciplinary strategies. *Early Education and Development, 3*(4), 265–283.

Harter, S. (1985). Competence as a dimension of self-evaluation: Toward a comprehensive model of self-worth. In R. L. Leahy (Ed.), *The development of the self*. New York: Academic Press.

Hartley, R. E., Frank, L. K., & Goldenson, R. M. (1952). *Understanding children's play*. New York: Columbia University Press.

Hartup, W. (1992). Peer relations in early and middle childhood. In V. B. Van Hasselt & M. Hersen (Eds.), *Handbook of social development: A lifespan perspective*. New York: Plenum Press.

Hartup, W. W. (1977). Peer relationships: Developmental implications and interaction in same- and mixed-age situations. *Young Children, 32*(3), 4–13.

Hartup, W. W. (1989). Social relationships and their developmental significance. *American Psychologist, 44*(2), 120–126.

Hartup, W. W. (1992). Having friends, making friends, and keeping friends: Relationships as educational contexts. *ERIC Digest*, EDO-PS-92-4.

Hartup, W. W., Glazer, J. A., & Charlesworth, R. (1967). Peer reinforcement and sociometric status. *Child Development, 38*, 1017–1024.

Hawkridge, D., Chalupsky, A., & Roberts, A. (1968). *A study of selected exemplary programs for the education of disadvantaged children*. Palo Alto, CA: American Institute for Research in the Behavioral Sciences.

Haycock, K., & Duany, L. (1991). Developing the potential of Latino students. *Principal, 70*(3), 25–27.

Healey, J. M. (1987). *Your child's growing mind: A parent's guide to learning from birth to adolescence*. Garden City, NY: Doubleday.

Heath, S. B. (1989). Oral and literate traditions among Black Americans living in poverty. *American Psychologist, 44*(2), 367–373.

Hecht, M. L., Collier, M. J., & Ribeau, S. A. (1993). *African American communication: Ethnic identity and cultural interpretation*. Newbury Park, CA: Sage.

Hegde, M. N., & Davis, D. (1992). *Clinical methods and practicum in speech-language pathology*. San Diego, CA: Singular.

Helfer, R. E., & Kempe, C. H. (1987). *The battered child* (4th ed.). Chicago: University of Chicago Press.

Hendrick, J. (1967). The pleasures of meaningful work. *Young Children, 22*(6), 373–380.

Hendrick, J. (1968). Aggression: What to do about it. *Young Children, 23*(5), 298–305.

Hendrick, J. (1990). *Total learning: Developmental curriculum for the young child* (3rd ed.). Englewood Cliffs, NJ: Merrill/Prentice Hall.

Hendrick, J. (1994). *Total learning: Developmental curriculum for the young child* (4th ed.). Englewood Cliffs, NJ: Merrill/Prentice Hall.

Hendrick, J. B. (1973). *The cognitive development of the economically disadvantaged Mexican American and Anglo American four-year-olds: Teaching the concepts of grouping, ordering, perceiving common connections, and matching by means of semantic and figural materials*. (Doctoral dissertation, University of California at Santa Barbara). Santa Barbara, CA.

Hendrick, J., & Stange, T. (1991). Do actions speak louder than words? An effect of the functional use of language on dominant sex role behavior in boys and girls. *Early Childhood Research Quarterly, 6*(4), 656–676.

Hendricks, G., & Wills, R. (1975). *The centering book: Awareness activities for children, parents and teachers*. Englewood Cliffs, NJ: Prentice Hall.

Hereford, N. J., & Schall, J. (Eds.). (1991). *Learning through play: Art: A practical guide for teaching young children*. New York: Scholastic.

Herzog, E., & Sudia, C. E. (1973). Children in fatherless homes. In B. E. Caldwell & H. N. Ricciuti (Eds.), *Review of Child Development Research* (Vol. 3). Chicago: University of Chicago Press.

Hess, E. H. (1960). In C. Uhr & J. G. Miller (Eds.), *Drugs and Behavior*. New York: Wiley.

Hetherington, E. M. (1992). Coping with marital transitions: A family systems perspective. In E. M. Hetherington & W. G. Clingempeel (Eds.), Coping with marital transitions. *Monographs of the Society for Research in Child Development, 57*(2–3), #227.

Hetherington, E. M., Stanley-Hagen, M., & Anderson, E. R. (1989). Marital transitions: A child's perspective. *American Psychologist, 44*(2), 303–312.

Hibbard, R. Z. (1988). Evaluation of the alleged sexual abuse victim: Behavioral, medical and psychological considerations. In O. C. S. Tzeng & J. J. Jacobsen (Eds.), *Sourcebook for child abuse and neglect: Intervention, treatment, and prevention through crisis programs*. Springfield, IL: Charles C Thomas.

Hilgard, E. R., & Bower, G. H. (1966). *Theories of learning* (3rd ed.). New York: Appleton-Century-Crofts.

Hill, D. M. (1977). *Mud, sand and water*. Washington, DC: National Association for the Education of Young Children.

Hill, P. S. (1992). *Kindergarten*. Wheaton, MD: Association for Childhood Education International. (Reprinted from the American Education Encyclopedia, 1942).

Hill, R. B. (Ed.). (1993). *Research on the African-American family: A holistic perspective*. Westport, CT: Auburn House.

Hills, T. W. (1992). Reaching potentials through appropriate assessment. In S. Bredekamp & T. Rosegrant (Eds.). *Reaching potentials: Appropriate curriculum and assessment for young children*. Washington, DC: National Association for the Education of Young Children.

Hirsch, E. S. (Ed.). (1984). *The block book (rev. ed.)*. Washington, DC: National Association for the Education of Young Children.

Hirsh-Pasek, Hyson, M. C., & Rescorla, L. (1990). Academic environments in preschool: Do they pressure or challenge young children? *Early Education and Development, 1*(6), 401–423.

Hodges, W. (1987). Teachers-children: Developing relationships. *Dimensions, 15*(4), 12–14.

Hoffman, M. L. (1970). Moral development. In P. H. Mussen (Ed.), *Carmichael's manual of child psychology* Vol. 2 (3rd ed.). New York: Wiley.

Hoffman, M. L. (1975). Moral internalization, parental power, and the nature of parent-child interaction. *Developmental Psychology, 11*, 228–239.

Hoffman, M. L. (1984). Empathy, its limitations and its role in a comprehensive moral theory. In W. M. Kurtines & J. L. Gewirtz (Eds.), *Morality, moral behavior and moral development*. New York: Wiley.

Hohmann, M., Banet, B., & Weikart, D. (1979). *Young children in action: A manual for preschool educators*. Ypsilanti, MI: High/Scope Press.

Hollins, E. R., King, J. E., & Hayman, W. C. (1994). *Teaching diverse populations: Formulating a knowledge base*. Albany, NY: State University of New York Press.

Hom, H. L., Jr., & Hom, S. L. (1980). Research and the child: The use of modeling, reinforcement/incentives, and punishment. In D. G. Range, J. R. Layton, and D. L. Roubinek (Eds.), *Aspects of early childhood education: Theory to research to practice*. New York: Academic Press.

Honig, A. S. (1982). Language environments for young children. *Young Children, 38*(1), 56–67.

Honig, A. S. (1985). Compliance, control, and discipline. *Young Children, 40*(2), 50–58.

Honig, A. S. (1986a). Research in review: Stress and coping in children. In J. B. McCracken (Ed.), *Reducing stress in young children's lives*. Washington, DC: National

Association for the Education of Young Children.

Honig, A. S. (1986b). Research in review: Stress and coping in children: Interpersonal relationships. *Young Children, 47*(5), 47–60.

Honig, A. S., & Lansburgh, T. (1994). The tasks of early childhood: The development of self-control—Part II. In K. M. Paciorek & J. H. Munro (Eds.), *Early childhood education 94/95*. Guilford, CT: Dushkin.

Honig, A. S., & Wittmer, D. S. (1992). *Prosocial development in children: Caring, sharing and cooperating: A bibliographic resource*. New York: Garland.

Hôpital Maisonneuve-Rosemont (1994). *Guide on the safety of children's playspaces and equipment*. Montreal: Direction de la santé publique.

Horton, J., & Zimmer, J. (1990). *Media violence and children: A guide for parents*. Washington, DC: National Association for the Education of Young Children.

Howes, C. (1988). Peer interaction of young children. *Monographs of the Society for Research in Child Development. 53*(1), #217.

Howes, C. (1990). Can the age of entry into child care and the quality of child care predict adjustment in kindergarten? *Developmental Psychology 26*(2):1–12.

Howlin, P. (1986). An overview of social behavior in autism. In E. Schopler and G. B. Mesibov (Eds.), *Social behavior in autism*. New York: Plenum Press.

Hughes, F. (1991). *Children, play, and development*. Boston: Allyn & Bacon.

Humphrey, J. H. (1988). *Teaching children to relax*. Springfield, IL: Charles C Thomas.

Hunter, I., & Judson, M. (1977). *Simple folk instruments to make and play.* New York: Simon & Schuster.

Humphrey, J. H. (1993). *Stress management for elementary schools.* Springfield, IL: Charles C Thomas.

Huston-Stein, A., Freidrich-Cofer, L., & Susman, E. J. (1977). The relation of classroom structure to social behavior, imaginative play and self-regulation of economically disadvantaged children. *Child Development, 48,* 908–916.

Hyman, I. A. (1990). *Reading, writing, and the hickory stick: The appalling story of physical and psychological abuse in American schools.* Lexington, MA: Lexington Books.

Hymel, S., Wagner, E., & Butler, L. J. (1990). Reputational bias: View from the peer group. In S. R. Asher & J. D. Coie (Eds.), *Peer rejection in childhood.* Cambridge, England: Cambridge University Press.

Hymes, J. L., Jr. (1991). *Early childhood education: Twenty years in review. A look at 1971–1990.* Washington, DC: National Association for the Education of Young Children.

Hyson, M. C. (1994). *The emotional development of young children: Building an emotion-centered curriculum.* New York: Teachers College Press.

Hyson, M. C., & Hirsh-Pasek, K. A. (1990). Some recent Spencer studies: Academic environments in early childhood: Challenge or pressure? *The Spencer Foundation Newsletter, 5*(1), 2–3.

Ianotti, R., Zahn-Waxler, C., Cummings, E. M., & Milano, M. (1987). The development of

empathy and prosocial behavior in early childhood. Paper presented at American Educational Research Association, Washington, DC, April.

Ignico, A. A. (1991). Physical education for Head Start children: A field-based study. *Early Child Development and Care, 77,* 77–92.

Imhoff, G. (Ed.). (1990). *Learning two languages: From conflict to consensus in the reorganization of the schools.* New Brunswick, NJ: Transaction Publishers.

Ingram, D. (1989). *First language acquisition: Method, description, and explanation.* Cambridge, England: Cambridge University Press.

Inhelder, B. (1968). *Recent trends in Genevan research.* Paper presented at Temple University, Fall.

Institute of Medicine. (1989). *Research on children and adolescents with mental, behavioral, and developmental disorders.* Washington, DC: National Academy Press.

Irwin, D. M., & Moore, S. G. (1971). The young child's understanding of social justice. *Developmental Psychology, 5*(3), 406–410.

Isbell, R. T., & Raines, S. C. (1991). Young children's oral language production in three types of play centers. *Journal of Research in Childhood Education, 5*(2), 140–146.

Isenberg, J. P., & Jalongo, M. R. (1993). *Creative expression and play in the early childhood curriculum.* Englewood Cliffs, NJ: Merrill/Prentice Hall.

Izard, C. (1991). *The psychology of emotions.* New York: Plenum Press.

Jacklin, C. N., & Baker, L. A. (1993). Early gender develop-

ment. In S. Oskamp & M. Costanzo (Eds.). *Gender issues in contemporary society.* Newbury Park, CA: Sage Publications.

Jackson, P. W., & Wolfson, B. J. (1968). Varieties of constraint in a nursery school. *Young Children, 23*(6), 358–368.

Jacobson, E. (1976). *You must relax* (5th ed.). New York: McGraw Hill.

Jacobson, M., & Hill, L. (1991). *Kitchen fun for kids.* Washington, DC: Center for Science in the Public Interest.

Jalongo, M. R. (1985). When young children move. *Young Children, 40*(6), 51–57.

Jalongo, M. R. (1988). *Young children and picture books: Literature from infancy to six.* Washington, DC: National Association for the Education of Young Children.

Jalongo, M. R. (1989). Career education: Reviews of research. *Childhood Education, 66*(2), 108–115.

Jalongo, M. R., & Collins, M. (1985). Singing with young children: Folk singing for nonmusicians. *Young Children, 40*(2), 17–22.

Jalongo, M. R. (1994/1995). Helping children to cope with relocation. *Childhood Education, 71*(2), 80–85.

James, S. L. (1990). *Normal language acquisition.* Boston: Allyn & Bacon.

Jenkins, J. K., & Macdonald, P. (1970). *Growing up equal: Activities and resources for parents and teachers of young children.* Englewood Cliffs, NJ: Prentice Hall.

Jennings, L. (1990, April 11). Child-abuse reports in 1989 up 10% over '88, state by state survey finds. *Education Week,* 8.

Jessee, P. O., Nagy, C., & Poteet-Johnson, D. (1993). Children with AIDS. *Childhood Education, 70*(1), 10–14.

Johansen, E. P., & Peckover, R. B. (1988). The effects of play period duration on children's play patterns. *Journal of Research in Childhood Education, 3*(2), 123–131.

Johnson, J. E., & Roopnarine, J. L. (1983). The preschool classroom and sex differences in children's play. In M. B. Liss (Ed.), *Social and cognitive skills: Sex roles and children's play.* New York: Academic Press.

Johnson, S. E. (1987). *After a child dies: Counseling bereaved families.* New York: Springer.

Jones, E., & Reynolds, G. (1992). *The play's the thing: Teachers' role in children's play.* New York: Teachers College Press.

Jones, E. with Villarino, G. (1994). What goes up on the classroom walls—and why? *Young Children, 49*(2), 38–41.

Jorde, P. (1982). *Avoiding burnout: Strategies for managing time, space, and people in early childhood education.* Washington, DC: Acropolis Books.

Kaden, M. (1990). Issues on computers and early childhood education. In C. Seefeldt (Ed.), *Continuing issues in early childhood education.* Englewood Cliffs, NJ: Merrill/Prentice Hall.

Kagan, J., & Lamb, S. (1987). *The emergence of morality in young children.* Chicago: University of Chicago Press.

Kaiser, B., & Sklar Rasminsky, J. K. (1993). Telling parents their child needs help. *Interaction, 6*(4), 13–14.

Kalter, N. (1990). *Growing up with divorce: Helping your child avoid*

immediate and later emotioanl problems. New York: Free Press.

Kamii, C. (1975). One intelligence indivisible. *Young Children, 30*(4), 228–238.

Kamii, C. (1982). *Number in preschool and kindergarten: Educational implications of Piaget's theory.* Washington, DC: National Association for the Education of Young Children.

Kamii, C. (1985). *Young children reinvent arithmetic: Implications of Piaget's theory.* New York: Teachers College Press.

Kampe, E. (1990). Children in health care: When the prescription is play. In E. Klugman & S. Smilansky (Eds.), *Children's play and learning: Perspectives and policy implications.* New York: Teachers College Press.

Kane, R. P., Wiszinckas, E., & Forquer, S. L. (1981). Prevention: Promise or premise? A training program in the primary prevention of childhood mental disorders. *Journal of Children in Contemporary Society, 14*(3), 91–100.

Kanner, L. (1944). Early infantile autism. *Journal of Pediatrics, 25,* 211–217.

Kantor, R., Elgas, R. M., & Fernie, D. E. (1993). Cultural knowledge and social competence within a preschool peer culture group. *Early Childhood Research Quarterly, 8*(2), 125–147.

Kaplan, P. (1992). *A child's odyssey* (2nd ed.). New York: West.

Kaplan-Sanoff, M., Brewster, A., Stillwell, J., & Bergen, D. (1988). The relationship of play to physical/motor development and to children with special needs. In D. Bergen (Ed.), *Play as a medium for learning and development: A handbook of theory and practice.* Portsmouth, NH: Heinemann.

Karnes, M. (1994). Outdoor play for children with special needs. *Scholastic Early Childhood Today, 8*(8), 55.

Karnes, M. B., & Johnson, L. J. (1989). Training for staff, parents, and volunteers working with gifted young children, especially those with disabilities and from low-income homes. *Young Children, 44*(3), 49–56.

Karnes, M., & Johnson, L. J. (1991). The preschool/primary gifted child. *Journal for the Education of the Gifted, 14*(3), 267–283.

Karyo Communications (1992). *Caring for a living: A study on wages and working conditions in Canadian child care.* Ottawa: Canadian Child Care Federation and the Canadian Day Care Advocacy Association.

Katz, L. (1991). Keynote address. Oklahoma City, Reggio Conference.

Katz, L., & Chard, S. C. (1991). *Engaging children's minds: The project approach.* Norwood, NJ: Ablex.

Katz, L., & McClellan, D. E. (1991). *The teacher's role in the social development of young children.* Urbana, IL: University of Illinois, ERIC Clearinghouse on Elementary and Early Childhood Education.

Katz, L. G. (1969). Children and teachers in two types of Head Start classes. *Young Children, 26*(6), 342–349.

Katz, L. G. (1993). *Distinctions between self-esteem and narcissism: Implications for practice.* Urbana, IL: ERIC Clearinghouse on Elementary and Early Childhood Education.

Katz, L. G. (1994). All about me. In K. M. Paciorek, & J. H. Munro

(Eds.). *Early childhood education, 93/94*. Sluicedock, Guilford, CT: Dushkin.

Katz, L. G., & Cesarone, B. (Eds.). (1994). *Reflections on the Reggio Emilia approach*. Urbana, IL: ERIC Clearinghouse on Elementary and Early Childhood Education.

Katz, P. A. (1982). Development of children's racial awareness and intergroup attitudes. In L. Katz (Ed.), *Current topics in early childhood education* (Vol. IV). Norwood, NJ: Ablex.

Katzen, M., & Henderson, A. (1994). *Pretend soup and other real recipes: A cookbook for preschoolers & up*. Berkeley, CA: Tricycle Press.

Kaufman, J., & Zigler, E. (1990). The intergenerational transmission of child abuse. In D. Cicchetti & V. Carlson (Eds.), *Child maltreatment: Theory and research on the causes and consequences of child abuse and negelct*. New York: Cambridge University Press.

Kempe, C. E. (1962). The battered child syndrome. *Journal of the American Medical Association, 181*(17), 17–24.

Kendall, E. C., & Moukaddem, V. E. (1992). Who's vulnerable in infant child care centers? *Young Children, 47*(5), 72–78.

Kendall, F. E. (1983). *Diversity in the classroom: A multicultural approach to the education of young children*. New York: Teachers College Press.

Kendrick, A. S., Kaufman, R., & Messenger, K. P. (Eds.). (1991). *Healthy young children: A manual for programs* (2nd ed.). Washington, DC: National Association for the Education of Young Children.

Kent, J. (1983). *Silly goose*. Englewood Cliffs, NJ: Prentice Hall.

Kersey, K. (1986). *Helping your child handle stress: The parent's guide to recognizing and solving childhood problems*. Washington, DC: Acropolis Books.

Kessler, J. W., Gridth, A., & Smith, E. (1968). Separation reactions in young mildly retarded children. Paper presented at the Annual Convention of the American Orthopsychiatric Association, Boston.

Keubli, J. (1994). Young children's understanding of everyday emotions. *Young Children, 49*(3), 36–47.

King, M. A., Oberlin, A., & Swank, T. (1993). *Creating a child-centered day care environment for two-year-olds*. Springfield, IL: Charles C Thomas.

King, N. R. (1979) Play: The kindergartener's perspective. *Elementary School Journal, 80*, 81–87.

Kinsey, A. C., Pomeroy, W. B., & Martin, C. E. (1948). *Sexual behavior in the human male*. Philadelphia: W. B. Saunders.

Kinsey, A. C., Pomeroy, W. B., Martin, C. E., & Gebhard, P. H. (1953). *Sexual behavior in the human female*. Philadelphia: W. B. Saunders.

Kinsman, C. A., & Berk, L. E. (1979). Joining the block and housekeeping areas: Changes in play and social behavior. *Young Children, 35*(1), 66–75.

Kirk, S. A. (1972). *Educating exceptional children* (2nd ed.). Boston: Houghton Mifflin.

Kirk, S. A., & Gallagher, J. J. (1989). *Educating exceptional children* (6th ed.). Boston: Houghton Mifflin.

Kliman, G. (1968). *Psychological emergencies of childhood*. New York: Grune & Stratton.

Kline, P. (1988). *The everyday genius: Restoring children's natural joy of learning—and yours too*. Arlington, VA: Great Ocean Publisher.

Klugman, E., & Smilansky, S. (Eds.). (1990). *Children's play and learning: Perspectives and policy implications*. New York: Teachers College Press.

Knowles, D., & Reeves, N. (1983). *But won't Granny need her socks? Dealing effectively with children's concerns about death and dying*. Dubuque, IA: Kendall/Hunt.

Koblinsky, S., Atkinson, J., & Davis, S. (1980). Sex education with young children. *Young Children, 36*(1), 21–31.

Kohl, H. (1984). *Growing minds: On becoming a teacher*. New York: Harper & Row.

Kohl, M. F. (1989). *Mudworks: Creative clay, dough, and modeling experiences*. Bellingham, WA: Bright Ring.

Kohl, M. F., & Gainer, C. (1991). *Good earth art: Environmental art for kids*. Bellingham, WA: Bright Ring.

Kohlberg, L. (1976). The development of children's orientations toward a moral order: Sequence in the development of moral thought. In P. B. Neubauer (Ed.), *The process of child development*. New York: Jason Aronson.

Kohlberg, L. (1985). *Essays on moral development: Vol. II: The psychology of moral development: The nature and validity of moral stages*. San Francisco: Harper & Row.

Kohn, A. (1990). *The brighter side of human nature*. New York: Basic Books.

Kohn, A. (1993). *Punished by rewards: The trouble with gold stars, incentive plans, A's, praise, and other bribes*. Boston: Houghton Mifflin.

Koralek, D. (1992). *Caregivers of young children; Preventing and responding to child maltreatment*. Washington, DC: United States Department of Health and Human Services, Administration on Children, Youth and Families, National Center on Child Abuse and Neglect.

Koralek, D. G., Colker, L. J., Dodge, D. T. (1993). *The what, why, and how of high-quality early childhood education: A guide for on-site supervision*. Washington, DC: National Association for the Education of Young Children.

Kosnik, B. (1993). Everyone is a V.I.P. in this class. *Young Children, 49*(1), 32–37.

Kostelnick, M. (Ed.). (1991). *Teaching young children using themes*. New York: HarperCollins.

Kostelnick, M. J., Stein, L. C., & Whiren, A. P. (1988). Children's self-esteem: The verbal environment. *Childhood Education, 65*(1), 28–32.

Kostelnick, M. J., Whiren, A. P., & Stein, L. C. (1986). Living with He-Man: Managing superhero fantasy play. *Young Children, 41*(4), 3–9.

Kotloff, L. J. (1993). Fostering cooperative group spirit and individuality: Examples from a Japanese preschool. *Young Children, 48*(3), 17–23.

Koulouras, K., Porter, M. L., & Senter, S. A. (1986, July). Making the most of parent conferences. *Child Care Information Exchange, 50*.

Kraizer, S., Witte, S. S., & Fryer, E. (1989). Child sexual abuse prevention programs: What makes them effective in protecting children? *Children Today, 18*(50), 23–27.

Kritchevsky, S., & Prescott, E. (1977). *Planning environments for young children: Physical space*. Washington, DC: National Association for the Education of Young Children.

Kruger, H., & Kruger, J. (1989). *The preschool teacher's guide to movement education*. Baltimore: Gerstung.

Labov, W. (1970). The logic of nonstandard English. In F. Williams (Ed.), *Language and poverty*. Chicago: Markham.

Ladd, G., & Coleman, C. C. (1993). Young children's peer relationships: Forms, features and function. In B. Spodek (Ed.), *Handbook of research on the education of young children*. Englewood Cliffs, NJ: Prentice Hall.

Lambert, W. E., & Klineberg, O. (1972). The development of children's views of foreign peoples. In M. D. Cohen (Ed.), *Learning to live as neighbors*. Washington, DC: Association for Childhood Education International.

La Torre, R. A. (1979). *Sexual identity*. Chicago: Nelson-Hall.

Lavatelli, C. S. (1970a). *Early childhood curriculum: A Piaget program*. Boston: American Science & Engineering.

Lavatelli, C. S. (1970b). *Piaget's theory applied to an early childhood curriculum*. Boston: American Science & Engineering.

Lawler, S. B. (1991). *Teacher-parent conferencing in early childhood education*. Washington, DC: National Association for the Education of Young Children.

Layman, C. (1985). *Child abuse*. Paper presented at Arkansas Association for Children Under Six, Little Rock.

Lazar, I., & Darlington, R. B. (1978). *Summary: Lasting effects after preschool: Final report to the Education Commission of the States*. Urbana, IL: ERIC/ECE.

Lazar, I., Darlington, R., Murray, H., Royce, J., & Snipper, A. (1982). Lasting effects of early education: A report from the Consortium for Longitudinal Studies. *Monographs of the Society for Research in Child Development, 47*(2–3, Serial No. 195).

Lazar, I., Hubbell, V. R., Murray, H., Rosche, M., & Royce, J. (1977). *Summary report: the persistence of preschool effects*. Washington, DC: United States Department of Health, Education, and Welfare, (OHDS) 78-30129.

Leacock, E. (1981). The influence of teacher attitudes on children's classroom performance: Case studies. In K. M. Borman (Ed.), *The social life of children in a changing society*. Hillsdale, NJ: Erlbaum.

Leavitt, T. J. (1981). Sickle cell disease. In E. E. Bleck & D. A. Nagel (Eds.), *Physically handicapped children—A medical atlas for teachers* (2nd ed.). New York: Grune & Stratton.

Lectenberg, R. (1984). *Epilepsy and the family*. Cambridge, MA: Harvard University Press.

Lee, L. C. (1973). *Social encounters of infants: The beginnings of popularity*. Paper presented at the International Society for the Study of Behavioral Development, Ann Arbor, August.

Lehrer, P. M. & Woolfolk, R. L. (Eds.). (1993). *Principles and practice of stress management* (2nd ed.). New York: Guilford Press.

Leifer, A. C., & Lesser, G. W. (1976). *The development of career awareness in young children: NIE papers on education and work (No. 1)*. Washington, DC: United States Department of Health, Education, and Welfare, National Institute of Education.

Leight, L. (1988). *Raising sexually healthy children: A loving guide for parents, teachers and caregivers*. New York: Avon.

Leipzig, J. (1989). Supporting the development of a scientific mind in infants and toddlers. In B. Neugebauer (Ed.), *The wonder of it: Exploring how the world works*. Redmond, WA: Exchange Press.

Leister, C. (1993). Working with parents of different cultures. *Dimensions of Early Childhood, 21*(2), 13–15.

Leonhard, B. (1963). Paper presented at the TAEYC Workshop, Santa Barbara.

LeRoy, C. H., Powell, T. H., & Kelker, P. H. (1994). *Teaching exceptional children, 26*(4), 37–44.

Lesser, M. & Gold, S. F. (1988). Cooperative preschools: Not just for children. *Dimensions, 16*(3), 11–13.

Levenstein, P. (1988). *Messages from home: The Mother-Child Home Program and the prevention of school disadvantage*. Athens, OH: Ohio University Press.

Lewis, C. (1979). *A big bite of the world: Children's creative writing*. Englewood Cliffs, NJ: Prentice Hall.

Lewis, M. & Louis, B. (1991). Young gifted children. In N. Colangelo & G. A. Davis (Eds.), *Handbook of gifted education*. Boston: Allyn & Bacon.

Lewko, J. H. (1987). How children and adolescents view the world of work. *New Directions for Child Development, 35* (Spring), 1–96.

Lieberman, J. N. (1968). Playfulness and divergent thinking ability: An investigation of their relationship at the kindergarten level. In M. Almy (Ed.), *Early childhood play: Selected readings related to cognition and motivation*. New York: Simon & Schuster.

Lima, C. W. (1989). *A to zoo: Subject access to children's picture books* (3rd ed.). New York: Bowker.

Linder, T. W. (1993). *Transdisciplinary play-based intervention: Guidelines for developing a meaningful curriculum for young children*. Baltimore: Paul Brookes.

Lindfors, J. W. (1987). *Children's language and learning* (2nd ed.). Englewood Cliffs, NJ: Prentice Hall.

Lin-Fu, J. S. (1978). *Sickle cell anemia: A medical review*. Rockville, Maryland: United States Department of Health, Education, and Welfare. #(HSA) 78-5123.

Lionni, L. (1987). *Swimmy*. New York: Knopf.

Lively, V., & Lively, E. (1991). *Sexual development of young children*. Albany, NY: Delmar.

Locke, D. C., & Ciechalski, J. C. (1985). *Psychological techniques for teachers*. Muncie, IN: Accelerated Development.

Loeffler, M. H. (Ed.). (1992). *Montessori in contemporary American culture*. Portsmouth, NH: Heinemann.

Lombardi, J. (n. d.). *Easing the transition from preschool to kindergarten: A guide for early childhood teachers and administrators*. Washington, DC: United States Department of Health and Human Services, Administration on Children, Youth and Families, Head Start Bureau.

Lord, C. (1982). Psychopathology in early development. In S. G. Moore & C. R. Cooper (Eds.), *The young child: Reviews of research* (Vol. 3). Washington, DC: National Association for the Education of Young Children.

Lorenz, K. (1966). *On aggression*. New York: Harcourt, Brace & World.

Lott, B., & Maluso, D. (1993). The social learning of gender. In A. W. Beall, & R. J. Sternberg (Eds.), *The psychology of gender*. New York: Guilford Press.

Love, J. M., & Logue, M. E. (1992). *Final report of the National Transition Study: Transitions to kindergarten in American schools: Executive summary*. Washington, DC.

Lowenfeld, V., & Brittain, W. L. (1987). *Creative and mental growth* (6th ed.). Englewood Cliffs, NJ: Prentice Hall.

Luangpraseut, K. (1989) *Laos culturally speaking*. San Diego: Multifunctional Resource Center, San Diego State University.

Lubeck, S. (1985). *Sandbox society: Early education in Black and White America*. Philadelphia: Falmer.

Lynch, E. W., & Hanson, M. J. (1992). *Developing cross-cultural competence: A guide for working with young children and their families*. Baltimore: Paul Brookes.

Maccoby, E. E. (1980). *Social development: Psychological growth and the parent-child relationship*. New York: Harcourt Brace Jovanovich.

Maccoby, E. E. (1990). Gender and relationships: A developmental account. *American Psychologist, 45,* 513–520.

Maccoby, E. E., & Jacklin, C. N. (1974). *The psychology of sex differences*. Stanford, CA: Stanford University Press.

Maccoby, E. E., & Jacklin, C. N. (1987). Gender segregation in childhood. In H. W. Reese (Ed.), *Advances in child development and behavior*. New York: Academic Press.

Macfarlane, J. W. (1943). Study of personality development. In R. G. Barker, J. S. Kounin, & H. F. Wright (Eds.), *Child behavior and development*. New York: McGraw-Hill.

MacFarlane, K., Waterman, J., Conerly, S., Damon, L, Durfee, M., & Long, S. (1986). *Sexual abuse of young children*. New York: Guilford Press.

Macnamara, J. (1966). *Bilingualism in primary education: A study of Irish experience*. Edinburgh: Edinburgh University Press.

Maker, C. J. (Ed.). (1989). *Critical issues in gifted education: Defensible programs for cultural and ethnic minorities*. Austin, TX: PRO-ED.

Malaguzzi, L. (1992). *A message from Loris Malaguzzi: An interview by Lella Gandini, April, 1992, La Villetta School, Reggio Emilia*. Amherst, MA: Performanetics. Produced by G. Forman & L. Gandini.

Malaguzzi, L. (1994). Tribute to Loris Malaguzzi. *Young Children, 49*(4), 55.

Malkus, U. C., Feldman, D. H., & Gardner, H. (1988). Dimensions of mind in early childhood. In A.

D. Pellegrini (Ed.), *Psychological bases for early education*. New York: Wiley.

Mallory, B. (1993). Inclusive policy, practice, and theory for young children with developmental differences. In B. L. Mallory & R. S. New (Eds.), *Diversity and developmentally appropriate practices: Challenges for early childhood education*. New York: Teachers College Press.

Mallory, B. L., & New, R. S. (Eds.). (1993). *Diversity & developmentally appropriate practices: Challenges for early childhood education*. New York: Teachers College Press.

Manolson, I. (1992). *It takes two to talk* (2nd ed.) Toronto: Hanen Canada.

Marcon, R. A. (1992). Differential effects of three preschool models on inner-city 4-year-olds. *Early Childhood Research Quarterly, 7*(4), 517–530.

Marcon, R. A. (1994a). Doing the right thing for children: Linking research and policy reform in the District of Columbia public schools. *Young Children, 50*(1), 8–20.

Marcon, R. A. (1994b). *Early learning and early identification follow-up study: Transition from the early to later childhood grades: 1990–1993*. Washington, DC: District of Columbia Public Schools.

Margolin, E. (1968). Conservation of self-expression and aesthetic sensitivity in young children. *Young Children, 23,* 155–160.

Marion, M. (1991). *Guidance of young children* (3rd ed.). Englewood Cliffs, NJ: Merrill/Prentice Hall.

Marland, S. P. (1972). *Education of the gifted and talented*. Washing-

ton, DC: United States Office of Education.

Marshall, H. H. (1989). The development of self-concept. *Young Children, 44*(5), 44–51.

Martin, H. P. (1976). *The abused child: A multidiciplinary approach to developmental issues and treatment*. Cambridge, MA: Ballinger.

Martinson, R. (1973). Children with superior cognitive abilities. In L. M. Dunn (Ed.), *Exceptional children in the schools: Special education in transition*. New York: Holt, Rinehart & Winston.

Mash, E. J., & Barkley, R. A. (Eds.). (1989). *Treatment of childhood disorders*. New York: Guilford Press.

Maslow, A. (1965). *Eupsychian management*. Homewood, IL: Dorsey Press.

Masters, W. H., Johnson, V. E., & Kilodny, R. C. (1994). *Heterosexuality*. New York: HarperCollins.

Maxim, G. (1989). *The very young* (3rd ed.). Englewood Cliffs, NJ: Merrill/Prentice Hall.

Mazur, S., & Pekor, C. (1985). Can teachers touch children anymore? *Young Children, 40*(4), 10–12.

McAfee, O. D. (1985). Circle time: Getting past "Two Little Pumpkins." *Young Children, 40*(6), 24–29.

McAfee, O. & Leong, D. (1994). *Assessing and guiding young children's development and learning*. Boston: Allyn & Bacon.

McBurnett, K., Lahey, B. B. & Pfiffner, L. J. (1993). Diagnosis of attention deficit disorders in DSM-IV: Scientific basis and implications for education. *Exceptional Children, 602,* 108–117.

McCabe, A. (1992). *Language games to play with your child: Enhancing communication from infancy through late childhood* (rev. ed.). New York: Plenum Press.

McCord, W., McCord, J., & Howard, A. (1961). Familial correlates of aggression in nondelinquent male children. *Journal of Abnormal Social Psychology, 62,* 79–93.

McCormick, P. (1994). How kids survive trauma. In K. M. Paciorek & J. H. Munro (Eds.), *Early childhood education '94–'95.* Guilford, CT: Dushkin.

McCracken, J. B. (Ed.). (1990). *Helping children love themselves and others: A professional handbook for family day care.* Washington, DC: The Children's Foundation.

McCurdy, H. G. (Ed.). (1966). *Barbara: The unconscious autobiography of a child genius.* Chapel Hill, NC: University of North Carolina Press.

McIntyre, M. (1984). *Early childhood and science.* Washington, DC: National Science Teachers Association.

McKey, R. H., Condelli, L., Ganson, H., Barrett, B. J., McConkey, C., & Plantz, M. C. (1985). *The impact of Head Start on children, families, and communities: Final report of the Head Start evaluation, synthesis, and utilization project.* Washington, DC: CSR Incorporated for the Head Start Bureau, ACYF, U.S. Department of Health and Human Services.

McLane, J. B., & McNamee, G. D. (1990). *Early literacy.* Cambridge, MA: Harvard University Press.

McLaughlin, B. (1987). *Theories of second language learning.* London: Arnold.

McLoyd, V. (1986). Scaffolds or shackles? The role of toys in preschool children's pretend play. In G. Fein & M. Rivkin (Eds.), *The young child at play: Reviews of research* (Vol. 4). Washington, DC: National Association for the Education of Young Children.

McMillan, M. (1929). *What the open-air nursery school is.* London: The Labour Party.

McNamee, G. D. (1990). Learning to read and write in an inner-city setting: A longitudinal study of community change. In L. C. Moll (Ed.), *Vygotsky and education: Instructional implications and applications of sociohistorical psychology.* New York: Cambridge University Press.

McNeill, E., Schmidt, V., & Allen, J. (1981). *Cultural awareness for young children: Asian, Black, cowboy, Eskimo, Mexican, and Native American cultures.* Mt. Rainier, MD: Gryphon House.

McTear, M. (1985). *Children's conversations.* New York: Basil Blackwell.

McWilliams, R. A., & Strain, P. S. (1993). Service delivery models. In Task Force on Recommended Practices, Division for Early Childhood, Council for Exceptional Children. *DEC recommended practices: Indicators of quality in programs for infants and young children with special needs and their families.* Pittsburgh, PA: The Council.

Meadows, S. (1993). *The child as thinker: The development and acquisition of cognition in childhood.* New York: Routledge.

Mecca, A. M., Smelser, N. J., & Vasconcellos, J. (1989). *The social importance of self-esteem.*

Berkeley, CA: University of California Press.

Medical Services Branch, Health and Welfare Canada. *Interior B.C. Native Food Guide.* Ottawa: Minister of Supply and Services Canada.

Meeker, M. N., Sexton, K., & Richardson, M. O. (1970). *SOI abilities workbook.* Los Angeles: Loyola-Marymount University.

Meisels, S. J., & Shonkoff, J. P. (1990). *Handbook of early childhood intervention.* New York: Cambridge University Press.

Meisels, S. J., Steele, D. M., & Quinn-Leering, K. (1993). Testing, tracking, and retaining young children: An analysis of research and social policy. In B. Spodek (Ed.), *Handbook of research on the education of young children.* Englewood Cliffs, NJ: Prentice Hall.

Meisels, S. J., & Wasik, B. A. (1990). Who should be served? Identifying children in need of early intervention. In S. J. Meisels & J. P. Shonkoff (Eds.), *Handbook of early childhood intervention.* New York: Cambridge University Press.

Menyuk, P. (1963). Syntactic structures in the language of children. *Child Development, 34,* 407–422.

Messer, D. (1993). *Mastery motivation in early childhood.* London: Routledge.

Meyerhoff, M. K. (1994). Of baseball and babies: Are you unconsciously discouraging father involvement in infant care? *Young Children, 49*(4), 17–19.

Michels, S., Pianta, R. C., & Reeve, L. (1993). Parent self-reports of discipline practices and child acting-out behaviors in kindergarten. *Early Education and*

Development, 4(2), 139–144.

Micklethwait, L. (1993). *A child's book of art: Great pictures with first words*. New York: Dorling Kindersly.

Midlarsky, E., & Bryan, J. H. (1967). Training charity in children. *Journal of Personality and Social Psychology, 5*, 405–415.

Miel, A., & Kiester, E. (1967). *The shortchanged children of suburbia*. New York: Institute of Human Relations Press, American Jewish Committee.

Miller, K. (1985). *Ages and stages: Developmental descriptions and activities, birth through eight years*. Marshfield, MA: Telshare.

Miller, K. (1989). *The outside play and learning book: Activities for young children*. Mt. Rainier, MD: Gryphon House.

Miller, L. B., & Dyer, J. L. (1975). Four preschool programs: Their dimensions and effects. *Monographs of the Society for Research in Child Development, 40*(5-6, Serial No. 162).

Miller, L. H., & Smith, A. D. (1993). *The stress solution: An action plan to manage the stress in your life*. New York: Pocket Books.

Miller, S. A. (1994a). *Learning through play: Sand, water, clay & wood*. New York: Scholastic.

Miller, S. A. (1994b). Sand & water around the room. *Scholastic Early Childhood Today, 8*(6), 26–45.

Milner, D. (1981). Are multicultural classroom materials effective? *Interracial Books for Children Bulletin, 12*(1).

Minister of National Health and Welfare (1995). *Canada's food guide to healthy eating: Focus on preschoolers*. Ottawa: Minister of Supply and Services.

Mirandy, J. (1976). Preschool for abused children. In H. P. Martin (Ed.), *The abused child: A multidisciplinary approach to developmental issues and treatment*. Cambridge, MA: Ballinger.

Mitchell, A. (1985). *Children in the middle: Living through divorce*. London: Tavistock.

Mitchell, G. (1982). *A very practical guide to discipline with young children*. Marshfield, MA: Telshare.

Modica, M. (1994). A positive approach to discipline in an early childhood setting. In K. M. Paciorek & J. H. Munro (Eds.), *Early childhood education 94/95*. Guilford, CT: Dushkin.

Moffitt, M., & Omwake, E. (n. d.). *The intellectual content of play*. New York: New York State Association for the Education of Young Children.

Moll, L. C. (Ed.). (1990). *Vygotsky and education: Instructional implications and applications of sociohistorical psychology*. Cambridge, England: Cambridge University Press.

Monaghan, A. C. (1971). Children's contacts: Some preliminary findings. Unpublished paper, Harvard Graduate School of Education, cited in Cazden, C. B., Paradoxes of language structure. In K. Connolly & J. Bruner (Eds.). (1974). *The growth of competence*. New York: Academic Press.

Monighan-Nourot, P., Scales, B., & Van Hoorn, J., with Almy, M. (1987). *Looking at children's play: A bridge between theory and practice*. New York: Teachers College Press.

Montagu, A. (1986). *Touching: The human significance of the skin* (3rd ed.). New York: Harper & Row.

Montessori, M. (1912). (Translated by A. E. George). *The Montessori Method: Scientific pedagogy as applied to child education in "The Children's House" with additions and revisions by the author*. New York: Frederick A. Stokes.

Montessori, M. (1967). (Translated by M. J. Costelloe). *The discovery of the child*. Notre Dame, IN: Fides.

Moor, P. (1960). What teachers are saying—about the young blind child. *Journal of Nursery Education, 15*(2).

Moore, R. C., Goltsman, S. M., & Iacofano, D. S. (1992). *Play for all guidelines: Planning, design and management of outdoor play settings for all children* (2nd ed.). Berkeley, CA: Communications.

Moore, S. B. (1982). Prosocial behavior in the early years: Parent and peer influences. In B. Spodek (Ed.), *Handbook of research in early childhood education*. New York: The Free Press.

Moore, T. E., & Harris, A. E. (1978). Language and thought in Piagetian theory. In L. S. Siegel & C. J. Brainerd (Eds.), *Alternatives to Piaget: Critical essays on the theory*. New York: Academic Press.

Morgan, E. (1989). Talking with parents when concerns come up. *Young Children, 44*(2), 52–56.

Morgan, G. G., & Shade, D. D. (1994). Moving early childhood education into the 21st century. In J. L. Wright & D. D. Shade (Eds.), *Young children: Active learners in a technological age*. Washington, DC: National Association for the Education of Young Children.

Morgan, J. (1984). Reward-induced decrements and increments in intrinsic motivation. *Review of*

Educational Research, 54(1), 5–30.

Morin, J. (1991). *Taking matters into your own hands: A guide to unionizing in the child care field.* Oakland, CA: Child Care Employee Project.

Morrison, G. (1991). *Early childhood education today* (5th ed.). Englewood Cliffs, NJ: Merrill/Prentice Hall.

Morrow, A. L., Benton, M., Reves, R. R., & Pickering, L. K. (1991). Knowledge and attitudes of day care center parents and care providers regarding children infected with human immunodeficiency virus. *Pediatrics, 87*(6), 876–883.

Morrow, R. D. (1989). What's in a name: In particular, a southeast Asian name? *Young Children, 44*(6), 20–23.

Morrow, R. D. (1991). The challenge of southeast Asian parental involvement. *Principal, 70*(3), 20–22.

Moshman, D., Glover, J. A., & Bruning, R. H. (1987). *Developmental psychology: A topical approach.* Boston: Little, Brown.

Moyer, J. (Ed.). *Selecting educational equipment and materials for school and home.* Wheaton, MD: Association for Childhood Education International.

Mrazek, P. J., & Haggerty, R. J. (1994). *Reducing risks for mental disorders: Frontiers for preventive intervention research.* Washington, DC: National Academy Press.

Murphy Kilbride, K. (1990). *Multicultural early childhood education—A resource kit.* Toronto, ON: Ryerson University.

Murray, F. B. (1972). Acquisition of conservation through social interaction. *Developmental Psychology, 6,* 1–6.

Mussen, P. H., Conger, J. J., & Kagan, J. (1969). *Child development and personality.* New York: Harper & Row.

Nachbar, R. R. (1992). What do grown-ups do all day? The world of work. *Young Children, 47*(3), 6–12.

National Association for the Education of Young Children. (1989). The National Association for the Education of Young Children code of ethical conduct. *Young Children, 1*(45), 25–29.

National Association for the Education of Young Children. (1991). *Accreditation criteria & procedures of the National Academy of Early Childhood Programs.* Washington, DC: The Association.

National Association for the Education of Young Children. (1993a). *Understanding the ADA: The Americans with Disabilities Act: Information for early childhood programs.* Washington, DC: National Association for the Education of Young Children.

National Association for the Education of Young Children. (1993b). NAEYC position statement on violence in the lives of children. *Young Children, 48*(6), 80–84.

National Association for the Education of Young Children. (1993c). Enriching classroom diversity with books for children, in-depth discussion of them, and story-extension activities. *Young Children, 48*(3), 10–12.

National Association for the Education of Young Children. (1993d). Educate yourself about diverse cultural groups in our country by reading. *Young Children, 48*(3), 13–16.

National Black Child Development Institute. (1992). *African American Literature for young children.* Washington, DC: The Institute and the National Association for the Education of Young Children.

National Center on Child Abuse and Neglect. (1975). *Child abuse and neglect: The problem and its management: Vol. II: The roles and responsibilities of professionals.* Washington, DC: United States Department of Health, Education, and Welfare, Office of Human Development, Office of Child Development, Children's Bureau/National Center on Child Abuse and Neglect. (OHD) 75:30074.

National Center on Child Abuse and Neglect. (1992). *Child abuse and neglect: A shared community concern.* Washington, DC: United States Department of Health and Human Services. Administration on Children, Youth and Families, National Center on Child Abuse and Neglect. DHHS (ACF) 92-30531.

National Center for Clinical Infant Programs. (1993). *It is no coincidence—Immunizations save lives.* Arlington, VA: Author.

National Center for Education Statistics. (1993). *Statistical analysis report. Profile of preschool children's child care and early education program participation: National Household Education Survey.* Washington, DC: United States Department of Education, Office of Educational Research and Improvement. NCES 93–133.

National Center for Health Statistics. (1993). *Advance report of final mortality statistics, 1990.*

Monthly vital statistics report. 41(7), suppl. 1–52.

National Day Care Information Centre (1973–1994). *The status of day care in Canada*. Ottawa: Minister of Supply & Services Canada.

National Head Start Bulletin. (1992). Demonstrating the use of technology for the benefit of children with disabilities in Head Start. *The Bulletin, 42*, 4–5.

National Institute for Early Childhood Professional Development. (1994). Constraints and opportunities for African American leadership in early childhood education. *Young Children, 49*(4), 32–36.

National Institute of Neurological Diseases and Stroke. (1969). *Learning to talk: Speech, hearing and language problems in the preschool child*. Washington, DC: U.S. Department of Health, Education, and Welfare.

National Institutes of Health. (1993). *Talking to children about death*. Washington, DC: United States Department of Health and Human Services.

National Pediatric HIV Resource Center. (n. d.). *Parent Information Booklets*. Newark, NJ: Children's Hospital of New Jersey.

National Science Teachers Association. (1992). Outstanding science books for young children in 1991. *Young children, 47*(4), 73–75.

Nedler, S., & Sebera, P. (1971). Intervention strategies for Spanish-speaking children. *Child Development, 42*, 259–267.

Nelson, B. G., & Sheppard, B. (Eds.). (1992). *Men in child care and early education: A handbook for administrators and educators*.

Minneapolis, MN: Men in Child Care Project.

Nemerowicz, G. M. (1979). *Children's perceptions of gender and work*. New York: Praeger.

Neugebauer, B. (Ed.). (1987). *Alike and different: Exploring our humanity with young children*. Redmond, WA: Exchange Press.

Neugebauer, B. (Ed.). (1989). *The wonder of it: Exploring how the world works*. Redmond, WA: Exchange Press.

Neugebauer, R. (1991). How's business? Status report #7 on for-profit child care. *Child Care Information Exchange, 77*, 31–34.

Neugebauer, R. (1994a). Impressive growth projected for centers into the 21st century. *Child Care Information Exchange, 95*, 80–87.

Neugebauer, R. (1994b). Recruiting and retaining men in your center. *Child Care Information Exchange, 96*, 5–11.

New, R. (1990). Excellent early education: A city in Italy has it. *Young children, 45*(6), 4–10.

Nieto, S. (1983). Children's literature on Puerto Rican themes— Part I: The messages of fiction. *Interracial Books for Children Bulletin, 14*(1/2), 6–9.

Nieto, S. (1987). Self-affirmation or self-destruction: The image of Puerto Ricans in children's literature written in English. In A. Rodriguez de Lagun (Ed.), *Images and identities: The Puerto Rican in two world contexts*. New Brunswick, NJ: Ranaction Books.

Nieto, S. (1992). *Affirming diversity: The sociopolitical context of multicultural education*. New York: Longman.

Northcutt, W. H. (1970). Candidate for integration: A hearing

impaired child in a regular nursery school. *Young Children, 25*(6), 367–380.

Northwest Regional Educational Laboratory Center for Sex Equity. (1983). *Guide to nonsexist teaching activities (K-12)*. Phoenix, AZ: Oryx Press.

Nourot, P. M. (1991). Perspectives from the field: Play and paradox. In B. Scales, M. Almy, A. Nicolopoulou, & S. Ervin-Tripp (Eds.), *Play and the social context of development in early care and education*. New York: Teachers College Press.

Nourot, P. M., & Van Hoorn, J. L. (1991). Research in review: Symbolic play in preschool and primary settings. *Young Children, 46*(6), 40–50.

Nuttall, E. V., Romero, I., & Kalesnik, J. (Eds.). (1992). *Assessing and screening preschoolers: Psychological and educational dimensions*. Boston: Allyn & Bacon.

O'Connor, R. D. (1972). Relative efficacy of modeling, shaping, and the combined procedures for modification of social withdrawal. *Journal of Abnormal Psychology, 79*, 327–334.

Odom, S. L., McConnell, S. R., & McEvoy, M. A. (Eds.). (1992). *Social competence of young children with disabilities: Issues and strategies for intervention*. Baltimore: Paul Brookes.

Office of Technology Assistance. United States Congress. (1986). *Children's mental problems and services—A background paper*. Washington, DC: Government Printing Office.

Office of Technology Assistance. United States Congress. (1991). *Adolescent health, Vol. II: Back-*

ground and the effectiveness of selected prevention and treatment services. Washington, DC: Government Printing Office.

Oklahoma Daily. (1993, November 30). National briefs: Millions with bad teeth can't afford dentist. *Oklahoma Daily*.

Oken-Wright, P. (1992). From tug of war to "Let's Make a Deal": The teacher's role. *Young Children, 48*(1), 15–20.

Oliner, S. P., & Oliner, P. M. (1988). *The altruistic personality: Rescuers of Jews in Nazi Europe*. New York: Free Press.

Olshansky, B. (1990). *Portfolio of illustrated step-by-step art projects for young children*. West Nyack, NY: Center for Applied Research in Education, Simon & Schuster.

Olson, S. L., Bayles, K., & Bates, J. E. (1986). Mother-child interaction and children's speech progress: A longitudinal study of the first two years. *Merrill-Palmer Quarterly, 32*, 1–20.

Olweus, D. (1980). Familial and temperamental determinants of aggression behavior in adolescents—A causal analysis. *Developmental Psychology, 16*, 644–660.

Ontario Women's Directorate (1993). *Words that count women out/in*. Toronto: Ontario Women's Directorate.

Orata, P. T. (1953). The Iloilo experiment in education through the vernacular. In *The Use of Vernacular Languages in Education. Monographs on Fundamental Education, VIII*. Paris: UNESCO.

Orlick, T. (1982). *The second cooperative sports and games book*. New York: Pantheon Books.

Ortiz, F. I. (1988). Hispanic-American children's experiences in classrooms: A comparison between Hispanic and non-Hispanic children. In L. Weis (Ed.), *Class, race and gender in American education*. Albany, NY: State University of New York Press.

Osborn, D. K. (1991). *Early childhood education in historical perspective* (rev. ed.). Athens, GA: Education Associates.

Osofsky, J. D., & Fenichel, E. (1994). *Caring for infants and toddlers in violent environments: Hurt, healing, and hope*. Arlington, VA: Zero to Three: National Center for Clinical Infant Programs.

Ostrosky, M. M., Skellenger, A. C., Odom, S. L., McConnell, S. R., & Peterson, C. (1994). Teachers' schedules and actual time spent in activities in preschool special education classes. *Journal of Early Intervention, 18*(1), 25–33.

Owens, R. E. (1992). *Language development: An introduction* (3rd ed.). Englewood Cliffs, NJ: Merrill/Prentice Hall.

Paasche, C., Gorrill, L., & Strom, B. (1990). *Children with special needs in early childhood settings: Indentification, intervention, mainstreaming*. Don Mills, ON: Addison-Wesley.

Pacific Oaks College. (1985). *The anti-bias curriculum*. Paper presented at the National Association for the Education of Young Children Conference, New Orleans, faculty of the college.

Paley, V. G. (1979). *White teacher*. Cambridge, MA: Harvard University Press.

Papadatou, C., & Papadatos, C. (Eds.). (1991). *Children and death*. New York: Hemisphere.

Parke, R. D. (1972). Some effects of punishment on children's behavior. In W. W. Hartup (Ed.), *The young child: Reviews of research, Vol II*. Washington, DC: National Association for the Education of Young Children.

Parke, R. D., & Duer, J. L. (1972). Schedule of punishment and inhibition of aggression. *Developmental Psychology, 7*, 266–269.

Parke, R. D., & Slaby, R. G. (1983). The development of aggression. In P. H. Mussen (Ed.), *Handbook of child psychology* (4th ed.), E. M. Hetherington (Ed.), *Vol. IV: Socialization, personality, and social development*. New York: Wiley.

Parrillo, V. N. (1985). *Strangers to these shores: Race and ethnic relations in the United States* (2nd ed.) New York: Wiley.

Parten, M. B. (1932). Social participation among preschool children. *Journal of Abnormal and Social Psychology, 27*, 243–269.

Parten, M. B. (1933). Social play among preschool children. *Journal of Abnormal and Social Psychology, 28*, 136–147.

Patrick, S. (1993). Facilitating communication and language development. In T. W. Linder (Ed.), *Transdisciplinary play-based intervention: Guidelines for developing a meaningful curriculum for young children*. Baltimore: Paul Brookes.

Patterson, C. (1977). Insights about persons: Psychological foundations of humanistic and affective education. In L. M. Berman & J. A. Roderick (Eds.), *Feeling, valuing, and the art of growing: Insights into the affective*. Washington, DC: Association for Supervision and Curriculum Development. Eugene, OR: Castalia Press.

Patterson, G. R. (1982). *Coercive family practices*. Eugene, OR: Castalia Press.

Patterson, G. R., DeBaryshe, B. D., & Ramsey, E. (1989). A developmental perspective on antisocial behavior. *American Psychologist, 44*(2), 329–335.

Patterson, G. R., Littman, R. A., & Bricker, W. (1967). Assertive behavior in children: A step toward a theory of aggression. *Monographs of the Society for Research in Child Development, 32*(5), 1–43.

Payne, V. G., & Isaacs, L. D. (1987). *Human motor development: A lifespan approach.* Mt. View, CA: Mayfield.

Peck, N., & Shores, E. F. (1994). *Checklist for diversity in early childhood education and care.* Little Rock, AK: Southern Early Childhood Association.

Pellegrini, A. D. (1986). Communicating in and about play: The effect of play centers on preschoolers' explicit language. In G. Fein & M. Rivkin (Eds.), *The young child at play: Reviews of research* (Vol. 4). Washington, DC: National Association for the Education of Young Children.

Pellegrini, A. D., & Boyd, B. (1993). The role of play in early childhood development and education: Issues in definition and function. In B. Spodek (Ed.), *Handbook of research on the education of young children.* Englewood Cliffs, NJ: Prentice Hall.

Peltz, P. A., & Rossol, M. S. (1984). *Children's art supplies can be toxic.* New York: Center for Occupational Hazards.

Pence, A. (Principal author) (1992). *Canadian child care in context: Perspectives from the provinces and territories.* Ottawa: Minister of Supply & Services Canada.

Pence, A. R. (Ed.). (1988). *Ecological research with children and families: From concepts to methodology.* New York: Teachers College Press.

Peplau, L. A., Miceli, M., & Morasch, B. (1982). Loneliness and self-evaluation. In L. A. Peplau & D. Perlman (Eds.), *Loneliness: A sourcebook of current theory, research and therapy.* New York: Wiley.

Pepler, D. (1986). Play and creativity. In G. Fein & M. Rivkin (Eds.), *The young child at play: Reviews of research* (Vol. 4). Washington, DC: National Association for the Education of Young Children.

Peterson, C., Maier, S. F., & Seligman, M. E. P. (1993). *Learned helplessness: A theory for the age of personal control.* New York: Oxford University Press.

Peterson, M. S., & Urquiza, A. J. (1993). *The role of mental health professionals in the prevention and treatment of child abuse and neglect.* Washington, DC: United States Department of Health and Human Services, Administration on Children, Youth and Families, National Center on Child Abuse and Neglect.

Peterson, R., & Felton-Collins, V. (1986). *The Piaget handbook for teachers and parents: Children in the age of discovery, preschool—third grade.* New York: Teachers College Press.

Pettit, F. H., & Pettit, R. M. (1978). *Mexican folk toys, festival decorations and ritual objects.* New York: Hasting House.

Pettit, G. S. (1992). Developmental theories. In V. B. Van Hasselt & M. Hersen (Eds.), *Handbook of social development: A lifespan perspective.* New York: Plenum Press.

Pflaum, S. W. (1986). *The development of language and literacy in young children* (3rd ed.). Englewood Cliffs, NJ: Merrill/Prentice Hall.

Phillips, D. (Ed.). (1987). *Quality in child care: What does research tell us?* Washington, DC: National Association for the Education of Young Children.

Phillips, D., & Whitebook, M. (1991). The child care provider: Pivotal player in the child's world. In L. Weis, P. G. Altbach, G. P. Kelly, & H. G. Petrie (Eds.), *Critical perspectives on early childhood education.* Albany, NY: State University of New York.

Phyfe-Perkins, E. (1981). *Effects of teacher behavior on preschool children: A review of research.* Champaign, IL: ERIC/ECE College of Education, University of Illinois, #194.

Piaget, J. (1926). *The language and thought of the child.* New York: Harcourt Brace & World.

Piaget, J. (1932). *The moral judgment of the child.* London: Routledge & Kegan Paul.

Piaget, J. (1948). *The moral judgment of the child.* Glencoe, IL: Free Press.

Piaget, J. (1950). *The psychology of intelligence.* London: Routledge & Kegan Paul.

Piaget, J. (1959). *The construction of reality in the child.* New York: Basic Books.

Piaget, J. (1962). *Play, dreams, and imitation in childhood.* New York: W. W. Norton.

Piaget, J. (1963). *The origins of intelligence in children.* New York: W. W. Norton.

Piaget, J. (1965). *The child's conception of number*. New York: W. W. Norton.

Piaget, J. (1977). *The development of thought: Equilibration of cognitive structures*. New York: Viking.

Piaget, J. (1981). *Intelligence and affectivity. Their relationship during child development*. Palo Alto, CA: Annual Reviews.

Piaget, J. (1983). Piaget's theory. In P. H. Mussen (Ed.), *Handbook of child psychology* (4th ed.). W. Kessen (Ed.), *Vol. 1: History, theory, and methods*. New York: Wiley.

Piaget, J., & Inhelder, B. (1967). *The child's conception of space*. New York: W. W. Norton.

Piaget, J., & Inhelder, B. (1969). *The psychology of the child*. Translated by H. Weaver. New York: Basic Books.

Pica, R. (1990). *Preschoolers moving and learning*. Champaign, IL: Human Kinetics.

Pimento, B., & Kernstead, D. (1995). *Healthy foundations in child care*. Don Mills, ON: Nelson Canada.

Piper, W. (1980). *The little engine that could*. New York: Putnam.

Pitcher, E. G., & Prelinger, E. (1963). *Children tell stories: An analysis of fantasy*. New York: International Universities Press.

Poest, C. A., Williams, J. R., Witt, D. A., & Atwood, M. E. (1989). Physical activity patterns of preschool children. *Early Childhood Research Quarterly, 4*, 367–376.

Pogrebin, L. C. (1980). *Growing up free: Raising your child in the '80's*. New York: McGraw-Hill.

Pollitt, E. (1990). *Malnutrition and infection in the classroom*. Paris: UNESCO.

Poresky, R. H., & Hoover, L. A. (1991). *It's what's inside that counts: Encouragement versus praise*. Paper presented at the National Conference of the National Association for the Education of Young Children: Denver, CO.

Powell, D. (1990). Home visiting in the early years: Policy and program design decisions. *Young Children, 45*(6), 65–69.

Powell, D. R. (1978) Interpersonal relationship behavior: Parents and caregivers in day care settings. *Orthopsychiatry, 48*(4), 680–689.

Powell, D. R. (1989). *Families and early childhood programs*. Washington, DC: National Association for the Education of Young Children.

Powell, D. R., & Sigal, I. E. (1991). Searches for validity in evaluating young children and early childhood programs. In B. Spodek & O. N. Saracho (Eds.), *Issues in early childhood curriculum: Yearbook in early childhood education* (Vol. 2). New York: Teachers College Press.

Powell, G. J. (1983a). Coping with adversity: The psychosocial development of Afro-American children. In G. J. Powell (Ed.), *The psychosocial development of minority group children*. New York: Brunner/Mazel.

Powell, G. J. (1983b). *The psychosocial development of minority group children*. New York: Brunner/Mazel.

Power, C., & Reimer, J. (1978). Moral atmosphere: An educational bridge between moral judgment and action. In W. Damon (Ed.), *Moral development*. San Francisco: Jossey-Bass.

Pratt, C. (1948, Reprinted 1990). *I learn from children*. New York: Harper & Row.

Prelutsky, C. (Ed.). (1986). *Read aloud rhymes for the very young*. New York: Alfred A. Knopf.

Prescott, E. (1981). Relations between physical setting and adult/child behavior in day care. In S. Kilmer (Ed.), *Advances in early education and day care: A research annual* (Vol. 2). Greenwich, CT: JAI Press.

Pressma, D., & Emery, L. J. (1991). *Serving children with HIV infection in child day care: A guide for center-based and family day care providers*. Washington, DC: Child Welfare League of America.

Provenzo, E. F., & Brett, A. (1983). *The complete block book*. Syracuse, NY: Syracuse University Press.

Radke-Yarrow, M., Zahn-Waxler, C., & Chapman, M. (1983). Prosocial disposition and behavior. In P. Mussen (Ed.), *Manual of child psychology*, E. M. Hetherington (Ed.), *Vol. 4, Socialization, personality, and social development*. New York: Wiley.

Raines, B. (1991). *Creating sex-fair family day care: A guide for trainers*. Philadelphia: CHOICE, Office of Research and Improvement, United States Department of Education.

Raines, S. C., & Canady, R. J. (1989). *Story stretchers: Activities to expand children's favorite books*. Mt. Rainier, MD: Gryphon House.

Raines, S. C., & Canady, R. J. (1991). *More story stretchers: More activities to expand children's favorite books*. Mt. Rainier, MD: Gryphon House.

Raines, S., & Isbell, R. (1994). *Stories: Children's literature in early education*. Albany, NY: Delmar.

Ramirez, G., & Ramirez, J. L. (1994). *Multiethnic children's literature*. Albany, NY: Delmar.

Ramsey, P. G. (1979). Beyond "Ten Little Indians" and turkeys: Alternative approaches to Thanksgiving. *Young Children, 34*(6), 28–52.

Ramsey, P. G. (1991). *Making friends in school: Promoting peer relationships in early childhood*. New York: Teachers College Press.

Rankin, B. (1992). Inviting children's creativity: A story of Reggio Emilia, Italy. *Child Care Information Exchange, 85,* 30–35.

Raver, S. A. (1991). *Strategies for teaching at-risk and handicapped infants and toddlers: A transdisciplinary approach*. Englewood Cliffs, NJ: Merrill/Prentice Hall.

Read, K., Gardner, P. & Mahler, B. (1993). *Early childhood programs: Human relationships and Learning* (9th ed.). Chicago: Harcourt Brace.

Redleaf, R. (1993). *Busy fingers, growing minds: Finger plays, verses and activities for whole language learning*. St. Paul, MN: Redleaf Press.

Regan, I. M., Mayfield, M. I., & Stange, B. L. (1988). Canadian alternatives in early childhood programs. *International Journal of Early Childhood Education, 20*(1), 3–11.

Reggio Children. (1994). *Historical notes; General information*. Municipality of Reggio Emilia, Italy.

Reifel, S. (1982). The structure and content of early representational play: The case of building blocks. In S. Hill & B. J. Barnes (Eds.). *Young children and their*

families: Needs of the nineties. Lexington, MA: D.C. Heath.

Reifel, S. (1984). Block construction: Children's developmental landmarks in representation of space. *Young Children, 40*(1), 61–67.

Reifel, S., & Greenfield, P. M. (1982). Structural development in a symbolic medium: The representational use of block constructions. In G. E. Forman (Ed.), *Action and thought: From sensorimotor schemes to symbolic operations*. New York: Academic Press.

Reifel, S., & Yeatman, J. (1991). Action, talk, and thought in block play. In B. Scales, M. Almy, A. Nicolopoulou, & S. Ervin-Tripp (Eds.), *Play and the social context of development in early care and education*. New York: Teachers College Press.

Reifel, S., & Yeatman, J. (1993). From category to context: Reconsidering classroom play. *Early Childhood Research Quarterly, 8*(3), 347–367.

Reis, S. M. (1989). Reflections on policy affecting the education of gifted and talented students. *American Psychologist, 44*(2), 399–408.

Reiss, D., Richters, J. E., Radke-Yarrow, M., & Scharff, D. (1993). *Children and violence*. New York: Guilford.

Research and Policy Committee of the Committee for Economic Development. (1993). *Why child care matters: Preparing young children for a more productive America*. Washington, DC: Author.

Rescorla, L., Hyson, M. C., & Hirsh-Pasek, K. (1991). Academic instruction in early childhood: Challenge or pressure? *New Directions for Child Development, 53*.

Resnick, L. B. (1989). Developing mathematical knowledge. *American Psychologist, 44*(2), 162–169.

Resnick, R., & Hergenroeder, E. (1975). Children and the emergency room. *Children Today, 4*(5), 5–9.

Rest, J. R. (1983). Morality. In P. H. Mussen (Ed.), *Handbook of child psychology* (4th ed.), J. H. Flavell & E. M. Markham (Eds.), *Vol. III: Cognitive development*. New York: Wiley.

Reynolds, M. C., & Birch, J. W. (1988). *Adaptive mainstreaming: A primer for teachers and principals*. White Plains, New York: Longman.

Rheingold, H. L. (1982). Little children's participation in the work of adults: A nascent prosocial behavior. *Child Development, 53,* 114–125.

Ricciuti, H. N. (1991). Malnutrition and cognitive development: Research-policy linkages and current research directions. In L. Okagaki and R. J. Sternberg (Eds.), *Directors of development: Influences on the development of children's thinking*. Hillsdale, NJ: Lawrence Erlbaum.

Rice, E. P., Ekdahl, M. C., & Miller, L. (1971). *Children of mentally ill parents: Problems in child care*. New York: Behavioral Publications.

Richman, N., Stevenson, J., & Graham, P. J. (1982). *Preschool to school: A behavioral study*. New York: Academic Press.

Riley, S. S. (1989). Pilgrimage to Elmwood Cemetery. *Young Children, 44*(2), 33–36.

Rinaldi, C. (1993). *The Reggio Emilia approach in the United States: Opening remarks*. Institute on Reggio Emilia, Traverse City, MI: Merrill-Palmer Institute, Wayne State University.

Rinaldi, C. (1994). *The philosophy of Reggio Emilia*. Reggio Emilia, Italy: Reggio Emilia Seminar.

Rizzo, T., Corsaro, W., & Bates, J. E. (1992). Ethnographic methods and interpretive analysis: Expanding the methodological options of psychologists. *Developmental Review, 12*, 101–123.

Robertson, J., & Robertson, J. (1989). *Separation and the very young*. London: Free Association Books.

Robinson, B. E. (1988). Vanishing breed. *Young Children, 43*(6), 54–58.

Roemer, J. as told to B. Austin. (1989). *Two to four from 9 to 5*. New York: Harper & Row.

Rogers, C. R. (1961). *On becoming a person*. Boston: Houghton Mifflin.

Rogers, C. R., & Dymond, R. F. (1954). *Psychotherapy and personality change*. Chicago: University of Chicago Press.

Rogers, C. S., & Morris, S. S. (1986). Reducing sugar in children's diets. *Young Children, 41*(5), 1–16.

Rogers, D. L., Perrin, M. S., & Waller, C. B. (1987). Enhancing the development of language and thought through conversations with young children. *Journal of Research in Childhood Education, 2*(1), 17–29.

Rogers, M. R., White, C. R., Sanders, R., Schable, C., Sell, T. E., Wasserman, R. L., Bellanti, J. A., Peter, S. M., & Wray, B. B. (1990). Lack of transmission of human immunodeficiency virus from infected children to their household contacts. *Pediatrics, 85*, 210–214.

Rohe, W., & Patterson, A. H. (1974). The effects of varied levels of resources and density on behavior in a day care center. In

D. H. Carson (Ed.), *Man-environment interaction*. Milwaukee, WI: EDRA.

Rohner, R. P. (1986). *The warmth dimension*. Beverly Hills, CA: Sage Publications.

Rojahn, J., Hammer, D., & Marshburn, E. C. (1993). Mental retardation in children. In R. T. Ammerman & M. Hersen (Eds.), *Handbook of behavior therapy with children and adults: A developmental and longitudinal perspective*. Boston: Allyn & Bacon.

Romero, M. J. (1991). Work and play in the nursery school. In L. Weis, P. G. Altbach, G. P. Kelly, & H. G. Petrie (Eds.), *Critical perspectives on early childhood education*. Albany, NY: State University of New York Press.

Roopnarine, J. L., & Carter, D. B. (1992). *Parent-child socialization in diverse cultures: Annual advances in applied developmental psychology* (Vol. 5). Norwood, NJ: Ablex.

Roopnarine, J. L., Johnson, J. E., & Hooper, F. H. (Eds.). (1994). *Children's play in diverse cultures*. Albany, NY: State University of New York Press.

Rose, D. F., & Smith, J. (1993). Public policy report: Preschool mainstreaming: Attitude barriers and strategies for addressing them. *Young Children, 48*(4), 59–62.

Rosen, S., & Granger, M. (1992). Early intervention and school programs. In A. C. Crocker, H. J. Cohen, & T. A. Kastmer (Eds.), *HIV infections and developmental disabilities: A resource for service providers*. Baltimore: Paul Brookes.

Rosenhan, D. (1972). Prosocial behavior of children. In W. W.

Hartup (Ed.), *The young child: Reviews of research* (Vol. 2). Washington, DC: National Association for the Education of Young Children.

Rosenthal, A. R. (1981). Visual disorders. In E. E. Bleck & D. A. Nagel (Eds.), *Physically handicapped children—A medical atlas for teachers* (2nd ed.). New York: Grune & Stratton.

Rosenthal, R., & Jacobson, L. (1968). *Pygmalion in the classroom: Teacher expectation and pupils' intellectual development*. New York: Holt, Rinehart & Winston.

Roskies, E. (1987). *Stress and management for the healthy Type A*. New York: Guilford Press.

Roskos, K., & Neuman, S. (1994). Play settings as literacy environments: Their effects on children's literacy behaviors. In D. F. Lancy (Ed.), *Children's emergent literacy*. Westport, CT: Praeger.

Ross, J. G., & Pate, R. R. (1987). The National Children and Youth Study II: A summary of findings. *Journal of Physical Education, Recreation and Dance, 58*(9), 51–56.

Rothman, R. (1990). Survey reveals wide latitude in reporting abuse. *Education Week, IX*(23), 1, 28.

Rotter, J. C., Robinson, E. H., & Fey, M. A. (1987). *Parent-teacher conferencing* (2nd ed.). Washington, DC: National Education Association.

Rowe, M. B. (1974). Wait-time and reward—Part one—Wait-time. *Journal of Research on Science Teaching, 11*, 81–94.

Rubin, J. A. (1984). *Child art therapy: Understanding and helping children grow through art* (2nd ed.). New York: Van Nostrand Reinhold.

Rubin, K. H. (1977). The play behaviors of young children. *Young Children, 32*(6), 16–24.

Rubin, K. H., Fein, G. G., & Vandenberg, B. (1983). Play. In P. H. Mussen (Ed.), *Handbook of child psychology*, E. M. Hetherington (Ed.), *Volume IV: Socialization, personality, and social development*. New York: Wiley.

Rubin, K. H., & Howe, N. (1986). Social play and perspective taking. In G. Fein & M. Rivkin (Eds.), *The young child at play: Reviews of research* (Vol. 4). Washington, DC: National Association for the Education of Young Children.

Rubin, Z. (1980). *Children's friendships*. Cambridge, MA: Harvard University Press.

Rutherford, E., & Mussen, P. (1968). Generosity in nursery school boys. *Child Development, 39*, 755–765.

Sacks, H., Schegloff, E., & Jefferson, G. (1974). A simplest systematics for the organization of turn taking in conversation. *Language, 50*, 696–735.

Sacks, J. J., Smith, J. D., Kaplan, K. M., Lambert, D. A., Sattin, R. W., & Sikes, R. K. (1989). The epidemiology of injuries in Atlanta day-care centers. *Journal of the American Medical Association, 262*(12), Sept. 22/29, 1641–1643.

Saderman Hall, N., & Rhomberg, V. (1995). *The affective curriculum: Teaching the anti-bias approach to young children*. Toronto: Nelson Canada.

Safford, P. (1978). *Teaching young children with special needs*. St. Louis, MO: Mosby.

Safford, P. (1989). *Integrated teaching in early childhood: Starting in the mainstream*. White Plains, NY: Longman.

Saifer, S. (1990). *Practical solutions to practically every problem: The early childhood teacher's manual*. St. Paul, MN: Toys 'n Things Press.

Saltz, E. D., & Johnson, J. (1977). Training disadvantaged preschoolers on various fantasy activities: Effects on cognitive functioning and impulse control. *Child Development, 48*, 367–380.

Samalin, N. (1992). *Love and anger: The parental dilemma*. New York: Viking.

Samalin, N., & Jablow, M. M. (1987). *Loving your child is not enough*. New York: Viking Press.

Sameroff, A. J., & Seifer, R. (1983). Familial risk and child competence. *Child Development, 54*, 1254–1268.

Sanders, J. (1987). *Do your female students say "No, Thanks" to the computer?* New York: Womens Action Alliance.

Sanders, S. W. (1992). *Designing preschool movement programs*. Champaign, IL: Human Kinetics.

Satter, E. (1987). *How to get your kid to eat . . . but not too much*. Palo Alto, CA: Bull.

Saunders, R., & Bingham-Newman, A. M. (1984). *Piagetian perspectives for preschools: A thinking book for teachers*. Englewood Cliffs, NJ: Prentice Hall.

Saylor, C. F. (Ed.). (1993). *Children and disasters*. New York: Plenum.

Scales, B., Almy, M., Nicolopoulou, A., & Ervin-Tripp, S. (Eds.). (1991). *Play and the social context of development in early care and education*. New York: Teachers College Press.

Schachter, F. F., Kirshner, K., Klips, B., Friedricks, M., & Sanders, K. (1974). Everyday preschool interpersonal speech usage: Methodological, developmental, and sociolinguistic studies. *Monographs of the Society for Research in Child Development, 156*, (39, Serial No. 3).

Schachter, F. F., & Strage, A. A. (1982). Adults' talk and children's language development. In S. G. Moore & C. R. Cooper (Eds.), *The young child: Reviews of research* (Vol. 3). Washington, DC: National Association for the Education of Young Children.

Schaefer, C. E. (1979). *Childhood encopresis and enuresis: Causes and therapy*. New York: Van Nostrand Reinhold.

Schaefer, C. E. (1984). *How to talk to children about really important things*. New York: Harper & Row.

Schaefer, C. E., & DiGeronimo, T. F. (1989). *Toilet training without tears*. New York: Signet Books (Penguin).

Schickedanz, J. A. (1994). Helping children develop self-control. *Childhood Education, 70*(5), 274–278.

Schickedanz, J. S., Hansen, K., & Forsythe, P. D. (1990). *Understanding children*. Mt. View, CA: Mayfield.

Schiefelbusch, R. (Ed.). (1986). *Language competence: Assessment and intervention*. San Diego: College Hill Press.

Schirrmacher, R. (1986). Talking with young children about their art. *Young Children, 41*(5), 3–7.

Schirrmacher, R. (1988). *Art and creative development for young children*. Albany, NY: Delmar.

Schon, I. (1994). Recent noteworthy books in Spanish for young children. *Young Children, 49*(6), 81.

Schulman, M., & Mekler, E. (1985). *Bringing up a moral child:*

A new approach for teaching your child to be kind, just, and responsible. Reading, MA: Addison-Wesley.

Schwartz, J. C., & Wynn, R. (1971). The effects of mother presence and previsits on children's emotional reaction to starting nursery school *Child Development, 42*, 871–881.

Schweinhart, L. J., Barnes, H. V., & Weikart, D. P. (1993). *Significant benefits: The High/Scope Perry Preschool Study through age 27*. Ypsilanti, MI: High/Scope Press. High/Scope Educational Research Foundation, Monograph #10.

Schweinhart, L. J., & Weikart, D. P. (1993). Public policy report: Success by empowerment: The High/Scope Perry Preschool Study through age 27. *Young Children, 49*(1), 54–58.

Schweinhart, L. J., Weikart, D. P., & Larner, M. B. (1986). Consequences of three preschool curriculum models through age 15. *Early Childhood Research Quarterly, 1*(1), 15–46.

Seefeldt, C. (1987). The visual arts. In C. Seefeldt (Ed.), *The early childhood curriculum: A review of current research*. New York: Teachers College Press.

Seibel, P. (1981). Physical handicaps and health problems. In B. P. Cartwright, C. A. Cartwright, & M. E. Wards (Eds.), *Educating special learners*. Belmont, CA: Wadsworth.

Seibert, D., Drolet, J. C., & Fetro, J. V. (1993). *Are you sad too? Helping children deal with loss and death*. Santa Cruz, CA: ETR Associates.

Seifert, K. (1993). Cognitive development and early childhood education. In B. Spodek (Ed.),

Handbook of research on the education of young children. Englewood Cliffs, NJ: Prentice Hall.

Seligman, M. E. P. (1975). *Helplessness: On depression, development, and death*. San Francisco: W. H. Freeman.

Seltzer, M. M., & Seltzer, G. B. (1983). Classification and social status. In J. L. Matson & J. A. Mulick (Eds.), *Handbook of mental retardation*. New York: Pergamon Press.

Selye, H. (1981). The stress concept today. In I. L. Kutash, L. B. Schlesinger, & Associates (Eds.), *Handbook on stress and anxiety*. San Francisco: Jossey-Bass.

Serbin, L. A., Connor, J. M., & Citron, C. C. (1978). Environmental control of independent and dependent behaviors in preschool boys and girls: A model for early independence training. *Sex Roles, 4*, 867–875.

Sexton, D., Snyder, P., Sharpton, W. R., & Stricklin, S. (1993). Infants and toddlers with special needs and their families. *Childhood Education, 69*(5), 278–286.

Shade, D. D., & Haugland, S. W. (1993). Development software awards. Paper presented at the annual conference of the National Association for the Education of Young Children, Anaheim, CA.

Shafer, M. (1982). *Life after stress*. New York: Plenum Press.

Shapiro, J., Kramer, S., & Hunerberg, C. (1981). *Equal their chances: Children's activities for non-sexist learning*. Englewood Cliffs, NJ: Prentice Hall.

Sharmat, M. (1980). *Gregory the terrible eater*. New York: Four Winds Press.

Shatz, M., & Gelman, R. (1973). The development of communi-

cation skills: Modification in the speech of young children as a function of listening. *Monographs of the Society for Research in Child Development, 38*.

Shelton, H., Montgomery, P., & Hatcher, B. (1989). *Bibliography of books for children, 1989 edition*. Wheaton, MD: Association for Childhood Education International.

Shimoni, R., MacLean, D., & MacWilliams, C. (1990). Issues in infant-toddler care: Evaluating programs. *Day care and early childhood education, 17* (3):42-46.

Shipley, C. C. (1993). *Empowering children: Play-based curriculum for lifelong learning*. Scarborough, ON: Nelson.

Shirah, S., & Brennan, L. (1990). Sickle cell anemia. Paper presented at the National Association for the Education of Young Children Conference, Washington, DC.

Sholtys, K. C. (1989). A new language, a new life: Recommendations for teachers of non-English speaking children newly entering the program. *Young Children, 44*(3), 76–77.

Shore, B. M., Cornell, D. G., Robinson, A., & Ward, V. S. (1991). *Recommended practices in gifted education: A critical analysis*. New York: Teachers College Press.

Shotwell, J. M., Wolf, D., & Gardner, H. (1979). Exploring early symbolization: Styles of achievement. In B. Sutton-Smith (Ed.), *Play and learning*. New York: Gardner Press.

Shuchter, S. R., & Zisook, S. (1993). The course of normal grief. In M. S. Stroebe, W. Stroebe, & R. O. Hansson.

Handbook of bereavement: Theory, research, and intervention. New York: Cambridge University Press.

Shweder, R. A., Mahapatra, M., & Miller, J. G. (1987). Culture and moral development. In J. Kagan & S. Lamb (Eds.), *The emergence of morality in children.* Chicago: University of Chicago Press.

Siegel, I. E., & Brainerd, C. J. (Eds.). (1978). *Alternatives to Piaget: Critical essays on the theory.* New York: Academic Press.

Siegel, L. S. (1972). Development of the concept of seriation. *Developmental Psychology, 6,* 135–137.

Siegler, R. S. (1991). *Children's thinking* (2nd ed.). Englewood Cliffs, NJ: Prentice Hall.

Sigel, I. (1987). Does hothousing rob children of their childhood? *Early Childhood Research Quarterly, 2*(3), 211–225.

Sigel, I. E., & McBane, B. (1967). Cognitive competence and level of symbolization among five-year-old children. In J. Hellmuth (Ed.), *The disadvantaged child.* Seattle: Special Child Publications.

Sigel, I. E., & Saunders, R. (1979). An inquiry into inquiry: Question asking as an instructional model. In L. G. Katz (Ed.), *Current topics in early childhood education* (Vol. II). Norwood, NJ: Ablex.

Sigman, M., & Sena, R. (1993, Spring). Pretend play in high-risk and developmentally delayed children. *New Directions for Child Development, 59,* 29–42.

Silver, A. A., & Hagin, R. A. (1990). *Disorders of learning in childhood.* New York: Wiley.

Singer, D. G., & Singer, J. L. (1990). *The house of make-believe: Children's play and the developing imagination.* Cambridge, MA: Harvard University Press.

Skeen, P., Garner, A. P., & Cartwright, S. (1984). *Woodworking for young children.* Washington, DC: National Association for the Education of Young Children.

Skinner, B. F. (1974). *About behaviorism.* New York: Alfred A. Knopf.

Slapin, B., & Seale, D. (1992). *Books without bias: Through Indian eyes* (3rd ed.). Philadelphia: New Society.

Smedslund, J. (1966). Les origines sociales de la centration. In F. Bresson & M. de Montmalier (Eds.), *Psychologie et épistémologie génétiques.* Paris: Dunod.

Smilansky, S. (1968). *The effects of sociodramatic play on disadvantaged children.* New York: Wiley.

Smilansky, S., & Shefatya, L. (1990). *Facilitating play: A medium for promoting cognitive, socio-emotional and academic development in young children.* Gaithersburg, MD: Psychosocial & Educational Publications.

Smith, A. B., Ballard, K. D., & Barham, L. J. (1989). Preschool children's perceptions of parent and teacher roles. *Early Childhood Research Quarterly, 4*(4), 523–532.

Smith, C. A. (1988). *I'm positive: Growing up with self-esteem.* Manhattan, KS: Cooperative Extension Service, Kansas State University.

Smith, J. A. (1966). *Setting conditions for creative teaching in the elementary school.* Boston: Allyn & Bacon.

Smith, N. R., Fucigna, C., Kennedy, M., & Lord, L. (1993). *Teaching children to paint* (2nd ed.). New York: Teachers College Press.

Smith, P. K., & Connolly, K. J. (1980). *The ecology of preschool behavior.* Cambridge, England: Cambridge University Press.

Smitherman, G. (1977). *Talkin and testifyin: The language of Black America.* Boston: Houghton Mifflin.

Smitherman, G. (1994). *Black talk: Words and phrases from the hood to the Amen corner.* Boston: Houghton Mifflin.

Snider, W. (November 21, 1990). Parents as partners: Adding their voices to decisions on how schools are run. *Education Week,* pp. 11–20.

Snow, C. E. (1989). Understanding social interaction and language acquisition: Sentences are not enough. In M. H. Bornstein & J. S. Bruner (Eds.), *Interaction in human development.* Hillsdale, NJ: Erlbaum.

Sobel, J. (1983). *Everybody wins.* New York: Walker.

Soderman, A. K. (1985). Dealing with difficult young children. *Young Children, 40*(5), 15–20.

Solomon, H. C., & Elardo, R. (1989). Bite injuries at a day care center. *Early Childhood Research Quarterly, 4*(1), 89–96.

Sorensen, E. S. (1993). *Children's stress and coping: A family perspective.* New York: Guilford Press.

Sorti, C. (1989). *The art of crossing cultures.* Yarmouth, ME: Intercultural Press.

Soto, L. D. (1991). Research in review: Understanding bilingual/bicultural young children. *Young Children, 46*(2), 30–36.

Sparling, J., & Lewis, I. (1984). *Learning games for threes and fours*. New York: Walker & Co.

Speidel, G. E., & Nelson, K. E. (Eds.). (1989). *The many faces of imitation in language learning*. New York: Springer-Verlag.

Spodek, B., & Brown, P. C. (1993). Curriculum alternatives in early childhood education: A historical perspective. In B. Spodek (Ed.), *Handbook of research on the education of young children*. Englewood Cliffs, NJ: Prentice Hall.

Spodek, B., & Saracho, O. N. (1994). *Dealing with individual differences in the early childhood classroom*. New York: Longman.

Sprafkin, C., Serbin, L. A., Denier, C., & Connor, J. M. (1983). Sex-differentiated play: Cognitive consequences and early interventions. In M. B. Liss (Ed.), *Social and cognitive skills*. New York: Academic Press.

Sprung, B. (1975). *Non-sexist education for young children: A practical guide*. New York: Citation Press.

Sprung, B., Froschl, M., & Campbell, P. B. (1985). *What will happen if . . . Young children and the scientific method*. New York: Educational Equity Concepts, Gryphon House (distributor).

Sroufe, L. A. (1983). Individual patterns of adaptation from infancy to preschool. In M. Perlmutter (Ed.), *Proceedings of the Minnesota Symposium on Child Psychology*. Hillsdale, NJ: Erlbaum.

Stagno, S. (1990). Cytomegalovirus. In J. S. Remington & J. O Klein (Eds.). *Infectious diseases of the fetus and newborn infant*. Philadelphia: Saunders.

Starr. R. H. (1988). Physical abuse of children. In V. B. Van Hasselt,

K. R. L. Morrison, A. S. Bellack, & M. Hersen (Eds.), *Handbook of family violence*. New York: Plenum Press.

Statistics Canada. (1992). *Special surveys (1992). Canadian families and their child care arrangements. The Canadian National Child Care Study*. Ottawa: Supply and Services Canada.

Stebbins, L. B., St. Pierre, R. G., Proper, E. C., Anderson, R. B., & Cervan, T. R. (1947). *Education as experimentation: A planned variation model. Volume IV-A, An evaluation of follow through*. Cambridge, MA: Abt Associates.

Stefanakis, E. H. (1991). Early childhood education: The effects of language on learning. In A. N. Ambert (Ed.), *Bilingual education and English as a second language: A research handbook, 1988–1990*. New York: Garland.

Stephens, K. (1991). *Block adventures: Build creativity and concepts through block play*. Bridgeport, CT: First Teacher.

Stephens, K. (1993). Making the most of outdoor play: A bounty of ideas to motivate the hesitant teacher. *Child Care Information Exchange, 91*, 49–54.

Sternberg, R. J. (Ed.), (1988). *The nature of creativity: Contemporary psychological perspectives*. Cambridge, England: Cambridge University Press.

Stevenson, J. H. (1990). The cooperative preschool model in Canada. In I. M. Doxey (Ed.), *Child care and education: Canadian dimensions*. Scarborough, ON: Nelson, Canada.

Stile, S. W., Kitano, M., Kelley, P., & Lecrone, J. (1993). Early intervention with gifted children: A national survey. *Journal of Early Intervention, 17*(1), 30–35.

Stinson, S. (1988). *Dance for young children: Finding the magic in movement*. Reston, VA: American Alliance for Health, Physical Education, Recreation, and Dance.

Stinson, W. (Ed.). (1990). *Moving and learning for the young child*. Reston, VA: American Alliance for Health, Physical Education, Recreation and Dance.

Stipek, D., Daniels, D., Galluzzo, D., & Milburn, S. (1992). Characterizing early childhood education programs for poor and middle-class children. *Early Childhood Research Quarterly, 7*(1), 21–44.

Stipek, D., Recchia, S., & McClintic, S. (1992a). Self-evaluation in young children. *Monographs of the Society for Research in Child Development. 57*(1, Serial No. 226).

Stipek, D., Recchia, S., & McClintic, S. (1992b). Study 3: The effects of winning or losing a competition with an age mate. *Monographs of the Society for Research in Child Development, 57*(1, Serial No. 226).

Stone, J. (1993). Caregiver and teacher language: Responsive or restrictive? *Young Children, 48*(4), 12–18.

Stone, J. I. (1990). *Hands-on math: Manipulative math for young children*. Glenview, IL: Scott, Foresman.

Stone, P. S. (1992). "You know what?": Conversational narratives of preschool children. *Early Childhood Research Quarterly, 7*(3), 367–382.

Stott, L. H. (1955). *The longitudinal study of individual development*. Detroit: Merrill-Palmer School.

Stott, L. H., & Ball, R. S. (1957). Consistency and change in ascendance-submission in the social interaction of children. *Child Development, 28*, 259–272.

Strayhorn, J. M. (1988). *The competent child: An approach to psychotherapy and preventive mental health*. New York: Guilford Press.

Streitmatter, J. (1994). *Toward gender equity in the classroom*. Albany, NY: State University of New York Press.

Strickland, D. S., & Morrow, L. M. (Eds.). (1989). *Emerging literacy: Young children learn to read and write*. Newark, DE: International Reading Association.

Strickland, J., & Reynolds, S. (1989). The new untouchables: Risk management for child abuse in child care. *Child Care Information Exchange, 65*, 37–39.

Striker, S. (1986). *Please touch: How to stimulate your child's creative development*. New York: Simon & Schuster.

Studer, J. R. (1993). Listen so that parents will speak. *Childhood Education, 70*(2), 74–76.

Suchman, J. R. (1961). Inquiry training: Building skills for autonomous discovery. *Merrill-Palmer Quarterly, 7*, 147–169.

Sunderlin, S., & Gray, N. (Eds.). (1967). *Bits & Pieces: Imaginative uses for children's learning*. Washington, DC: Association for Childhood Education International.

Sussman, S. W. (1984, Spring). Cooperative child care: An alternative to the high cost of campus child care. *Focus on Learning, 10*, 45–47.

Sutherland, M. (1994). Group meeting time: Making it work for everyone. *Scholastic Early Childhood Today, 8*(6), 28, 35.

Sutherland, Z. (1986). *The best in children's books: The University of Chicago guide to children's literature*. Chicago: University of Chicago Press.

Sutton-Smith, B. (1971). A syntax for play and games. In R. E. Herron & B. Sutton-Smith (Eds.), *Child's play*. New York: Wiley.

Sutton-Smith, B., & Roberts, J. M. (1981). Play, toys, games and sports. In H. C. Triandis & A. Heron (Eds.), *Handbook of developmental cross-cultural psychology* (Vol. 4). Boston: Allyn & Bacon.

Swan, A. M. (1993). Helping children who stutter: What teachers need to know. *Childhood Education, 69*(3), 138–141.

Swedlow, R. (1986). Children play, children learn. In J. S. McKee (Ed.), *Play: Working partner of growth*. Wheaton, MD: Association for Childhood Education International.

Swick, K. (1989a). Review of research: Parental efficacy and social competence in young children. *Dimensions, 17*(3), 25–26.

Swick, K. (1989b). Understanding and relating to transformed families. *Dimensions, 17*(4), 8–11.

Swick, K. J. (1991). *Teacher-parent partnerships to enhance school success in early childhood education*. Washington, DC: National Education Association & Southern Association for Children Under Six.

Talbot, J., & Frost, J. L. (1989). Magical playscapes. *Childhood Education, 66*(1), 11–19.

Tardiff, T. Z., & Steinberg, R. J. (1988). What do we know about creativity? In R. J. Sternberg (Ed.), *The nature of creativity: Contemporary psychological per-*

spectives. Cambridge, England: Cambridge University Press.

Task Force on Recommended Practices: Division for Early Childhood, Council for Exceptional Children. (1993). *DEC recommended practices: Indicators of quality in programs for infants and young children with special needs and their families*. Pittsburgh, PA: Task Force.

Tavris, C. (1982). *Anger: The misunderstood emotion*. New York: Simon & Schuster.

Taylor, H. U. (1989). *Standard English, Black English and bidialectalism: A controversy*. New York: Lang.

Taylor, K. W. (1981). *Parents and children learn together* (3rd ed.). New York: Teachers College Press.

Te, H. D. (1989). *Introduction to Vietnamese culture*. San Diego: Multifunctional Resource Center, San Diego State University.

Teele, D. W., Klein, J. O., & Rosner, B. A. (1989). Epidemiology of otitis media during the first seven years of life in children in greater Boston: A prospective cohort study. *Journal of Infectious Diseases, 160*, 83–94.

Tepperman, L. & Rosenberg, M. (1995). *Macro/micro: A brief introduction to sociology* (2nd ed.) Scarborough, ON: Prentice Hall Canada.

Terman, L. M., Baldwin, B. T., and Bronson, E. (1925). *Mental and physical traits of a thousand gifted children. Genetic studies of genius* (Vol. 1). Stanford, CA: Stanford University Press.

Thelen, E., Ulrich, D., & Jensen, J. (1989). The developmental origins of locomotion. In M. Woolacott & A. Shumway-Cook (Eds.), *A development of posture* and gait: Across the lifespan. Columbia, SC: University of South Carolina Press.

Thomas, A. (1989). Ability and achievement expectations: Implications of research for classroom practice. *Childhood Education, 65*(4), 235–238.

Thomas, R. M. (1992). *Comparing theories of child development* (3rd ed.). Belmont, CA: Wadsworth.

Thompson, G. G. (1944). The social and emotional development of preschool children under 2 types of educational programs. *Psychological Monographs, 56*(5), 1–29.

Thouvenelle, S. (1994). Do computers belong in early childhood? *Scholastic Early Childhood Today, 8*(5), 48–49.

Thouvenelle, S., Borunda, M., & McDowell, C. (1994). Replicating inequities: Are we going to do it again? In J. L. Wright & D. D. Shade (Eds.). *Young children: Active learners in a technological age.* Washington, DC: National Association for the Education of Young Children.

Thurman, S. K., & Widerstrom, A. H. (1990). *Infants and young children with special needs: A developmental and ecological approach* (2nd ed.). Baltimore, MD: Paul Brookes.

Tinsworth, D. K., & Kramer, J. T. (1990). *Playground equipment-related injuries and death.* Washington, DC: Consumer Product Safety Commission, Directorate for Epidemiology.

Tizard, B., Mortimore, J., & Burchell, B. (1983). *Involving parents in nursery and infant schools: A source book for teachers.* Ypsilanti, MI: High/Scope Press.

Tizard, B., & Phoenix, A. (1993). *Black, White or mixed race? Race and racism in the lives of young people of mixed parentage.* New York: Routledge.

Torrance, E. P. (1962). *Guiding creative talent.* Englewood Cliffs, NJ: Prentice Hall.

Torrance, E. P. (1970). Seven guides to creativity. In R. T. Sweeney, (Ed.), *Selected readings in movement education.* Reading, MA: Addison-Wesley.

Torrance, E. P. (1977). *Discovery and nurturance of giftedness in the culturally different.* Reston, VA: Council for Exceptional Children.

Torrance, E. P. (1988). The nature of creativity as manifest in testing. In R. J. Sternberg (Ed.), *The nature of creativity: Contemporary psychological perspectives.* Cambridge, England: Cambridge University Press.

Tower, C. C. (1992). *The role of educators in the prevention and treatment of child abuse and neglect.* Washington, DC: United States Department of Health and Human Services, Administration for Children and Families, Center on Child Abuse and Neglect.

Tozzo, S. G., & Golub, S. (1990). Playing nurse and playing cop: Do they change children's perceptions of sex-role stereotypes? *Journal of Research in Childhood Education, 4*(2), 123–129.

Trainer, M. (1991). *Differences in common: Straight talk on mental retardation, Down syndrome, and life.* Rockville, MD: Woodbine House.

Trawick-Smith, J., & Thompson, R. H. (1986). Preparing young children for hospitalization. In J. B. McCracken (Ed.), *Reducing stress in young children's lives.*

Washington, DC: National Association for the Education of Young Children.

Trelease, J. (1989). *The new read-aloud handbook.* New York: Penguin.

Trister Dodge, D. (1993). Places for ALL children: Building environments for differing needs. *Child Care Information Exchange, 93,* 40–44.

Truax, C. B., & Tatum, C. D. (1966). An extension from the effective psychotherapeutic model to constructive personality change in preschool children. *Childhood Education, 42,* 456–462.

Trueba, H. T. (1990). The role of culture in the acquisition of English literacy by minority school children. In G. Imhoff (Ed.), *Learning two languages: From conflict to consensus in the reorganization of schools.* New Brunswick, NJ: Transaction.

Tureen, P., & Tureen, J. (1986). Childhood speech and language disorders. In R. T. Brown & C. R. Reynolds (Eds.), *Psychological perspectives on childhood exceptionality.* New York: Wiley.

Turiel, E. (1973). Stage transition in moral development. In R. Travers (Ed.), *Second handbook on research in teaching.* Chicago: Rand McNally.

Turner, C. W., & Goldsmith, D. (1976). Effects of toy guns and airplanes on children's antisocial free play behavior. *Journal of Experimental Child Psychology, 21,* 303–315.

Tzeng, O. C. S., & Hanner, L. J. (1988). Abuse and neglect: Typologies, phenomena and impacts. In O. C. S. Tzeng & J. J. Jacobsen (Eds.), *Source book for child abuse and neglect.* Springfield, IL: Charles C Thomas.

United States Department of Education. (1991). National Center for Education Statistics. *Digest of Education Statistics 1990.* Washington, DC: Author.

Valentine, C. W. (1956). *The normal child and his abnormalities* (3rd ed.). Baltimore: Penguin Books.

Van Hasselt, V. B., & Hersen, M. (Eds.). (1992). *Handbook of social development.* New York: Plenum.

Van Hasselt, V. B., Morrison, R. L., Bellack, A. S., & Hersen, M. (Eds.). (1988). *Handbook of family violence.* New York: Plenum Press.

Van Hoorn, J. (1987). Games that babies and mothers play. In P. Monighan-Nourot, S. B. Scales, J. Van Hoorn with M. Almy. *Looking at children's play: A bridge between theory and practice.* New York: Teachers College Press.

Van Riper, C., & Emerick, L. (1990). *Speech correction: An introduction to speech pathology* (8th ed.). Englewood Cliffs, NJ: Prentice Hall.

Vanier Institute of the Family (1994). *Profiling Canada's families.* Ottawa: The Vanier Institute. of the Family. (1994). *Profiling Canada's families.* Ottawa: the Vanier Institute.

Vecchi, V. (1994). *Science or magic for making rainbows.* Washington, DC: Symposium: Multiple Intelligences and Reggio Emilia Preschools.

Von Oech, R. (1983). *A whack on the side of the head: How to unlock your mind for innovation.* New York: Warner Books.

Vygotsky, L. (1962). *Thought and language.* Cambridge, MA: MIT Press.

Vygotsky, L. C. (1978). In M. Cole, V. John-Steiner, S. Scribner, & E. Souberman, (Eds.), *Mind in society: The development of higher psychological processs.* Cambridge, MA: Harvard University Press.

Wade Houston, M. (1994). Bilingualism and second language development. In *Exceptional children: Inclusion in early childhood programs* (1st Can. ed.). Scarborough, ON: Nelson Canada.

Wadsworth, B. J. (1989). *Piaget's theory of cognitive and affective development* (4th ed.). New York: Longman.

Wakefield, H., & Underwager, R. (1988). *Accusations of child sexual abuse.* Springfield, IL: Charles C Thomas.

Walk, R. D. (1981). *Perceptual development.* Monterey, CA: Brooks/Cole.

Walker, J. E., & Shea, T. M. (1991). *Behavior management: A practical approach for educators* (5th ed.). Englewood Cliffs, NJ: Merrill/Prentice Hall.

Walker-Dalhouse, D. (1993). Beginning reading and the African American child at risk. *Young Children, 49*(1), 24–28.

Wallach, L. B. (1993). Helping children cope with violence. *Young Children, 48*(6), 4–11.

Wallach, M. A., & Kogan, N. (1965). *Modes of thinking in young children: A study of the creativity-intelligence distinction.* New York: Holt, Rinehart & Winston.

Wallerstein, J. S., & Blakeslee, S. (1989). *Second chances: Men, women, and children a decade after divorce.* New York: Ticknor & Fields.

Wallinga, C. R., & Sweaney, A. L. (1985). A sense of *real* accomplishment: Young children as productive family members. *Young Children, 41*(1), 3–7.

Wang, M. C., & Gordon, E. W. (1994). *Educational resilience in inner-city America: Challenges and prospects.* Hillsdale, NJ: Erlbaum.

Ward, W. C. (1968). Creativity in young children. *Child Development, 39,* 737–754.

Wardle, F. (1989). Children of mixed parentage: How can professionals help? *Children Today, 18*(4), 10–13.

Warren, R. M. (1977). *Caring: Supporting children's growth.* Washington, DC: National Association for the Education of Young Children.

Wass, H., & Corr, C. A. (Eds.). (1984). *Childhood and death.* Washington, DC: Hemisphere.

Wasserman, S. (1990). *Serious players in the primary classroom: Empowering children through active learning experiences.* New York: Teachers College Press.

Watkins, R. Z. (1993). Two-way communication: Sharing personal perspectives with parents. *Scholastic Early Childhood Today, 8*(1), 41.

Watson, M. W., & Peng, Y. (1992). The relation between toy gun play and children's aggressive behavior. *Early Education and Development, 3*(4), 370–389.

Watt, M. R., Roberts, J. E., & Zeisel, S. A. (1993). Ear infections in young children: The role of the early childhood educator. *Young Children, 49*(1), 65–72.

Weikart, D., & Lambie, D. (1970). Early enrichment in infants. In V. Deneberg (Ed.), *Education of the infant and young child*. New York: Academic Press.

Weikart, D. P. (1971). *Relationship of curriculum, teaching, and learning in preschool education*. Ypsilanti, MI: High/Scope Educational Research Foundation.

Weikart, D. P. (1990). *Quality preschool programs: A long-term social investment*. New York: Ford Foundation.

Weill, J. L. (1992). *Early deprivation of empathic care*. Madison, CT: International Universities Press.

Weisberg, R. W. (1988). Problem solving and creativity. In R. J. Sternberg (Ed.), *The nature of creativity: Contemporary psychological perspectives*. Cambridge, England: Cambridge University Press.

Weiss, B., & Weisz, J. R. (1986). General cognitive deficits: Mental retardation. In R. T. Brown & C. R. Reynolds (Eds.), *Psychological perspectives on childhood exceptionality*. New York: Wiley.

Weitzman, L., Eiffer, D., Hokada, E., & Ross, C. (1972). Sex-role socialization in picture books for preschool children. *American Journal of Sociology, 77*, 1125–1150.

Wenar, C. (1990). *Developmental psychopathology: From infancy to adolescence* (2nd ed.). New York: McGraw-Hill.

Wender, P. (1987). *The hyperactive child, adolescent, and adult: Attention deficit disorder through the lifespan*. New York: Oxford University Press.

Wender, P., & Wender, E. (1978). *The hyperactive child and the learning disabled child*. New York: Crown.

Wenning, J., & Wortis, S. (1984). *Made by human hands: A curriculum for teaching young children about work and working people*. Cambridge, MA: The Multicultural Project for Communication and Education.

Wenning, J., & Wortis, S. (1988). Work in the child care center: A curriculum about working people. *Day Care and Early Education, 15*(4), 20–25.

Werner, E. E. (1984). Resilient children. *Young Children, 40*(1), 69–72.

Werner, E. E., & Smith, R. S. (1982). *Vulnerable but invincible: A longitudinal study of resilient children and youth*. New York: McGraw-Hill.

Werner, E. E., & Smith, R. S. (1992). *Overcoming the odds: High risk children from birth to adulthood*. Ithaca, NY: Cornell University Press.

Werner, R. H., & Simmons, R. Q. (1990). *Homemade play equipment*. Reston, VA: American Alliance for Health, Physical Education, Recreation and Dance.

Wessel, M. A. (1983). Children, when parents die. In J. E. Schowalter, P. R. Patterson, M. Tallmer, A. H. Katscher, S. V. Gallo, & D. Peretz (Eds.), *The child and death*. New York: Columbia University Press.

Weston, J. (1980). The pathology of child abuse and neglect. In C. H. Kempe & R. E. Helfer (Eds.), *The battered child* (3rd ed.). Chicago: University of Chicago Press.

White, B. L. (1979). *The origins of human competence*. Lexington, MA: Lexington Books.

White, R. W. (1968). Motivation reconsidered: The concept of competence. In M. Almy (Ed.), *Early childhood play: Selected readings related to cognition and motivation*. New York: Simon & Schuster.

White, R. W. (1976). *The enterprise of living: A view of personal growth* (2nd ed.). New York: Holt, Rinehart and Winston.

White, S., & Buka, S. L. (1987). Early education: Programs, traditions, and policies. In E. Z. Rothkopt (Eds.), *Review of research in education* (Vol. 14). American Educational Research Association.

Whitebook, M., Howes, C., & Phillips, D. (1990). *Who cares? Child care teachers and the quality of care in America*. Final report of the National Child Care Staffing Study. Oakland, CA: Child Care Employee Project.

Whitman, W. (1871, Reprinted 1971). *The illustrated leaves of grass*. New York: Madison Square Press.

Whitmore, J. R. (Ed.). (1986). *Intellectual giftedness in young children: Recognition and development*. New York: Haworth Press.

Wichert, P. (1989). *Keeping the peace: Practicing cooperation and conflict resolution with preschoolers*. Philadelphia: New Society Publishers.

Wickens, E. (1993). Penny's question: "I will have a child in my class with two moms: What do you know about this?" *Young Children, 48*(3), 25–28.

Wickstrom, R. L. (1983). *Fundamental motor patterns* (3rd ed.). Philadelphia: Lea & Febiger.

Willer, B.A. (1990). *Reaching the full cost of quality in early childhood programs*. Washington, DC: National Association for the Education of Young Children.

Willer, B. (1992). Special research report. An overview of the demand and supply of child care in 1990. *Young Children, 47*(2), 19–22.

Williams, C. K., & Kamii, C. (1986). How do children learn by handling objects? *Young Children, 42*(1), 23–36.

Williams, D. E. (n. d.). *The child who stutters at school: Notes to the teacher.* Memphis, TN: Stuttering Foundation of America.

Williams, V. B. (1982). *A chair for my mother.* New York: Greenwillow Books.

Wilmes, L., & Wilmes, D. (1983). *Everyday circle times.* Elgin, IL: Building Blocks.

Wilmes, L., & Wilmes, D. (n. d.). *Exploring art.* Elgin, IL: Building Blocks.

Wilmes, L., & Wilmes, D. (n. d.). *Paint without brushes.* Elgin, IL: Building Blocks.

Wilson, G. L. (1980). Sticks and stones and racial slurs do hurt: The word *nigger* is what's not allowed. *Interracial Books for Children Bulletin, 11*(3/4).

Wilson, M. (1989). *The good-for-your-health all-Asian cookbook.* Washington, DC: Center for Science in the Public Interest.

Winton, P. J., Turnbull, A. P., & Blacher, J. (1984). *Selecting a preschool: A guide for parents of handicapped children.* Baltimore, MD: University Park Press.

Winzer, M. (1993). *Children with exceptionalities: A Canadian Perspective* (3rd ed.) Scarborough, ON: Prentice Hall Canada.

Witt, J. C., Elliott, S. N., & Gresham, F. M. (1988). *Handbook of behavior therapy in education.* New York: Plenum.

Wittmer, D. S., & Honig, A. S. (1994). Encouraging positive social development in young children. *Young Children, 49*(5), 4–12.

Wolery, M., Holcombe, A., Venn, M. L., Brookfield, J., Huffman, K., Schroeder, C., Martin, C. G., & Fleming, L. A. (1993). Mainstreaming in early childhood programs: Current status and relevant issues. *Young Children, 49*(1), 78–84.

Wolery, M., Strain, P. S., & Bailey, D. B. (1992). Reaching potentials of children with special needs. In S. Bredekamp & T. Rosegrant (Eds.), *Reaching potentials: Appropriate curriculum and assessment for young children* (Vol. I). Washington, DC: National Association for the Education of Young Children.

Wolery, M., Venn, M. L., Holcombe, A., Brookfield, J., Martin, C. G., Huffman, K., Schroeder, C., & Fleming, L. A. (1994). Employment of related service personnel in preschool programs: A survey of general early educators. *Exceptional Children, 61*(1), 25–29.

Wolery, M., & Wilbers, J. S. (Eds.). (1994). *Including children with special needs in early childhood programs.* Washington, DC: National Association for the Education of Young Children.

Wolf, D. P. (Ed.). (1986). *Connecting: Friendship in the lives of children.* Redmond, WA: Exchange Press.

Wolf, J. (1994). Singing with children is a cinch. *Young Children, 49*(4), 20–25.

Wolfe, D. A., Wolfe, V. V., & Best, C. L. (1988). Child victims of sexual abuse. In V. B. Van Hasselt, R. L. Morrison, A. S. Bellack, & M. Hersen (Eds.), *Handbook of family violence.* New York: Plenum Press.

Wong Fillmore, L. (1991). When learning a second language means losing the first. *Early Childhood Research Quarterly, 6*(3), 323–346.

Woodard, C. Y. (1986). Guidelines for facilitating sociodramatic play. In J. L. Frost & S. Sunderlin (Eds.), *When children play: Proceedings of the International Conference on Play and Play Environments.* Wheaton, MD: Association for Childhood Education International.

Workman, S., & Anziano, M. C. (1993). Curriculum webs: Weaving connections from children to teachers. *Young Children, 48*(2), 4–9.

Wortham, S. C. (1992). *Childhood 1892–1992.* Wheaton, MD: Association for Childhood Education International.

Wright, J. L., & Shade, D. D. (Eds.). (1994). *Young children: Active learners in a technological age.* Washington, DC: National Association for the Education of Young Children.

Wylie, J., & Wylie, D. (1983). *A fishy color story.* New York: Children's Press.

Yarrow, L. T. (1980). Emotional development. In S. Chess & A. Thomas (Eds.), *Annual progress in child psychiatry and child development.* New York: Brunner/Mazel.

Yawkey, T. D. (Ed.) (1980). *The self-concept of the young child.* Provo, UT: Brigham Young University Press.

Yawkey, T. D., & Cornelius, G. M. (1990). *The single parent family: For helping professionals and parents.* Lancaster, PA: Techtonic.

Yeates, M., McKenna, D., Warberg, C., & Chandler, K. (1994). *Administering early childhood settings:* The Canadian perspective (2nd ed.). Don Mills, ON: Maxwell Macmillan Canada.

Yolen, J. (1987). *Owl moon.* New York: Philomel.

York, S. (1991). *Roots and wings: Affirming culture in early childhood programs.* St. Paul, MN: Redleaf.

Youniss, J. (1975). Another perspective on social cognition. In A. Pick (Ed.), *Minnesota Symposia on Child Psychology* (Vol. 9). Minneapolis: University of Minnesota Press.

Zahn-Waxler, C. Z., Radke-Yarrow, M. R., & King, R. A. Child rearing and children's prosocial initiations toward victims of distress. *Child Development, 50,* 87–88.

Zahn-Waxler, C., & Smith, K. D. (1992). The development of prosocial behavior. In V. B. Van Hasselt & M. Hersen (Eds.), *Handbook of social development: A lifespan perspective.* New York: Plenum Press.

Zavitkoxsky, D. (1990). Enjoy a Docia story. *Child Care Information Exchange, 74,* 62.

Zeanah, C. (Ed.). (1993). *Handbook of infant mental health.* New York: Guilford Press.

Zion, G. (1958). *No roses for Harry.* New York: Harper & Row.

Zimbardo, P. G. (1977). *Shyness.* Menlo Park, CA: Addison-Wesley.

Zimmerman, B. J., & Bergen, J. R. (1971). Intellectual operations in teacher question asking behavior. *Merrill-Palmer Quarterly, 17*(1), 19–26.

Zukowski, G., & Dickson, A. (1990). *On the move: A handbook for exploring creative movement with young children.* Carbondale IL: Southern Illinois University Press.

♪ Acknowledgements for Chapter-Opening Quotations

1. From *Growing Minds: On Becoming a Teacher* (p. 16) by Herbert Kohl, 1984, New York:Harper & Row.

1. From *Teaching in the Key of Life* (p. 56) by Mimi Brodsky Chenfeld, 1993, Washington, DC: National Association for the Education of Young Children.

2. From *Young Man Luther* by Erik Erikson, 1958, New York: W. W. Norton.

3. From *Teaching Young Children* (p. 124) by Evelyn Beyer, © 1968 by Western Publishing Company, Inc., reprinted by permission of Bobbs-Merrill.

4. From "Making the Most of Outdoor Play: A Bounty of Ideas to Motivate the Hesitant Teacher" (p. 49) by Karen Stephens, 1993, *Child Care Information Exchange, 91.*

4. From "Resource Sheet 11" by the Canadian Child Day Care Federation, no date. Ottawa: The Federation.

5. From *Early Education and Psychological Development* (p. 5) by Barbara Biber, 1984, New Haven, CT: Yale University Press.

6. From *You and Your Child's Self-Esteem* (p. 33) by J. M. Harris, quoting John Dewey, 1989, New York: Carroll & Graf.

7. From "Parental Involvement" (p. 33) by Karen Chandler, 1995, *Interaction, 9*(2).

8. From *Last Poems*, XII, by A. E. Housman, 1922.

9. From *Honouring Diversity within Child Care and Early Education: An Instructor's Guide* Vol. 2 (p. 234) by Guida Chud and Ruth Fahlman, 1995. Victoria: Province of British Columbia, Ministry of Skills, Training and Labour.

9. From Gretchen Buchenholz, Merrycats Castle Preschool, quoted by Johnson, L. G., Rogers, C. K., Johnson, P., & McMillan, R. P. in *Overcoming Barriers Associated with the Integration of Early Childhood Settings*, 1993, National Association for the Education

of Young Children Conference, Anaheim, California.

10. From the Preface (p. 5) by Urie Bronfenbrenner in *Soviet Preschool Education* (Vol. 2: Teacher's Commentary) by H. Chauncey (Ed.), 1969, New York: Holt, Rinehart & Winston.

10. From "Having Friends, Making Friends, and Keeping Friends: Relationships as Educational Contexts," by Willard W. Hartup, 1992, Urbana, IL: *ERIC Digest*, EDO-PS-92-4.

11. From "A Positive Approach to Discipline in an Early Childhood Setting" (p. 162) by Marianne Modica, 1994, in K. M. Paciorek and J. H. Munro (Eds.), *Early Childhood Education 94/95*, Guilford, CT: Dushkin Publishing Group.

12. From *Punished by Rewards: The Trouble with Gold Stars, Incentive Plans, A's, Praise, and Other Bribes*, by Alfie Kohn, 1993, Boston: Houghton Mifflin.

13. From "Ideas That Work with Young Children: How to Institute Some Simple Democratic Practices Pertaining to Respect, Rights, Responsibilities, and Roots in Any Classroom (Without Losing Your Leadership Position)" (p. 12) by Polly Greenberg, 1992, *Young Children, 47*(5).

14. Author unknown. A particularly well-sung version of this gospel tune is available on the record *Songs of My People* with Paul Robeson. An RCA Red Seal rerelease, LM-3292.

15. From Kenneth Rexroth quoted on a calendar; from "The Motivation to Be Creative" by Teresa Amabile, 1987, in *Frontiers of Creativity Research: Beyond the Basics* by Scott G. Isaksen (Ed.), Buffalo, NY: Bearly.

15. From *Dumbing Us Down: The Hidden Curriculum of Compulsory Schooling* (p. 75) by John Taylor Gatto, 1992, Philadelphia, PA: New Society Publishers.

16. From "Helping Children Cope with Violence" (pp. 8–9) by Lorraine B. Wallach, 1993, *Young Children, 48*(4).

17. From *Mind in Society* (p. 28) by Lev Vygotsky, 1978,

Cambridge, MA: Harvard University Press.

17. From "Learning the Mother Tongue" by Jerome S. Bruner, 1978, *Human Nature, 1*(9), 42–49.

18. By permission from *Developmentally Appropriate Practice in Early Childhood Programs Serving Children from Birth Through Age 8* (p. 55) by S. Bredekamp, 1987, Washington, DC: National Association for the Education of Young Children.

19. From "Children Come First" (p. 70) by John Coe, 1987, *Childhood Education, 64*(2).

20. From "What Do Young Children Teach Themselves?" (p. 9) by Nancy Balaban, in *Early Childhood: Reconsidering the Essentials: A Collection of Papers,* 1984, New York: Bank Street College.

21. From "Teaching Mind in Society: Teaching, Schooling, and Literate Discourse" (p. 182) by R. Galimore and R. Tharp, in L. C. Moll (Ed.), *Vygotsky and Education: Instructional Implications and Applications of Sociohistorical Psychology*, 1990, New York: Cambridge University Press.

21. From *The Emotional Development of Young Children: Building an Emotion-Centered Curriculum* (p. 187) by Marion C. Hyson, 1994, New York: Teachers College Press.

22. From *Today's Family,* Robert Couchman, Scarborough, ON: Maxwell Macmillan Canada.

22. From "The Struggle for Working Wages" by Debra Mayer, 1995, *Interaction, 9*(2) 12–13.

Index